Religious Studies

Sarah K. Tyler and Gordon Reid

We would like to acknowledge the special support of Tallulah, Charly, Emily, Lily, Lin, Sophia, Danielle and Holly, Louise and Chris, and Patricia; in affectionate and grateful memory of David Anderson, love from Sarah and Gordon

91485

Philip Allan Updates
Market Place
Deddington
Oxfordshire
OX15 0SE

Tel: 01869 338652
Fax: 01869 337590
e-mail: sales@philipallan.co.uk
www.philipallan.co.uk

Design by Neil Fozzard
Printed by Raithby, Lawrence & Co Ltd, Leicester

Contents

Topic 3   God and human experience

Topic 4   God and the world

Topic 5   Human destiny

Religious Ethics

Christian Belief and Practice

The New Testament

Introduction

This textbook has been written to provide you with a resource specifically aimed at helping you in your AS and A2 work in Religious Studies. It is suitable for all boards, focusing on the most popular specification areas: Philosophy of Religion, Ethics, New Testament, and Christian Belief and Practice. It is as extensive in its coverage as any one book on such a wide range of disciplines within the subject can be, and our aim in writing has been that you should need very few other resources during your A-level course. Use the book freely, since many topics overlap, and you are bound to find material that is relevant to you in many chapters, even if it is not immediately obvious from the chapter title. Use the index at the back of the book, and not just the contents pages, as this will quickly lead you to all the sections of the book that include material related to a particular topic. For example, you will find material on God as creator in both the Philosophy and the Christian Belief sections, and material on miracles in Topics 1 and 3 in the Philosophy section.

If you choose to read widely and to research beyond the information given in these chapters, it will obviously do you no harm whatsoever, but the material that you need for a high grade at A-level is to be found between these covers. You will get more out of this book still if used in conjunction with the *Essential Word Dictionary* and *Exam Revision Notes* for Religious Studies and with the *Question and Answer Guides* in Philosophy and Ethics and in Biblical Studies, also written by Sarah Tyler and Gordon Reid and published by Philip Allan Updates.

The aims of the AS and A2 qualifications

AS qualifications consist of three modules, which may include a coursework unit. Each module examines a specific discipline within Religious Studies and all specifications allow for a considerable diversity of options. You may be studying Philosophy and/or Ethics in conjunction with Biblical Studies, Church History or World Religions, so this subject is truly multi-disciplinary. Furthermore, if you go on to A2 from the AS qualification, you will be required to demonstrate your awareness of how the different topics interlink and overlap. This will be in the form of a synoptic unit, which is intended to give you the opportunity to *draw together your knowledge and understanding of the connections between different modules from across your full Advanced GCE programme of study* (Edexcel).

AS and A2 specifications in Religious Studies are designed to encourage you to do the following:

÷ **Develop an interest in and an enthusiasm for a rigorous study of religion.**
  Your AS and A2 studies should be more than a means to an end. If you are interested in and enthusiastic about your academic studies you will do better in the exam, but you will also take away from this subject something that I don't think you

can from many others. It has real 'value-added' features, exploring aspects of human life and existence which are of perennial interest to virtually everyone who thinks about the world and our place in it. A rigorous study is one which involves being critical in the best possible sense of the word: analysing and evaluating the views of others and substantiating your own. If you are not prepared to have your own assumptions challenged in a safe and supportive environment, then Religious Studies is not for you! You may not come away from it with your views changed, but you will have had the opportunity to evaluate them against those of scholars past and present, and those of your teachers and classmates.

❖ **Treat the subject as an academic discipline by developing the knowledge and understanding appropriate to a specialist study of religion.**

This should grow out of undertaking a rigorous study of religion. In the bad old days, some people thought that RE (or Scripture) was a safety net for those who were not very academic and needed an easy option. Compulsory study of religion in the earlier years at school did not always encourage students to see it as a valuable academic discipline to be pursued in the latter stages of their school career. That has all changed! AS and A2 students will be more than aware of the academic rigour necessary to do well in this subject: knowledge of the contribution of scholars to the subject and an awareness of what enormous diversity there is in the range of views offered. The discipline is dependent on the skills developed in many other areas: language, history, philosophical debate in its wider context, and literature. The disciplined scholar relates everything to the question, alluding to narrative and text, rather than giving a blow-by-blow account in a way which may or may not be relevant, and gives responses which are ordered, structured and lead to a logical conclusion.

❖ **Use an enquiring, critical and empathetic approach to the study of religion.**

Enquiring scholars seek answers to questions of perennial importance, critically examining them before deciding which they believe to be the most convincing or effective, but not rejecting the views of others without recognising their significance. Religious and ethical views make a difference to the way in which people lead their lives and scholars must therefore understand why they are held, even if they are not in agreement with them. We need to be aware of the influence of historical, social and cultural factors on the way ideas have developed and of how the past leaves a legacy to the future. There are no 'right' answers and you will gain more credit for recognising the impossibility of definitiveness than for attempting to reach a dogmatic and unempathetic conclusion.

Assessment objectives

Assessment objectives fall into two categories:

AO1 — Knowledge and understanding
AO2 — Critical argument and justification of a point of view

More than 50% of assessment is concerned with the first objective, but you will not be able to move into the higher grade bands if you do not demonstrate your ability to fulfil the requirements of AO2. You will demonstrate that you have fulfilled the objectives by the acquisition of knowledge and the deployment of skills.

■ **You need to acquire knowledge and understanding of**:
- ⊹ key concepts within the chosen areas of study and how they are expressed in texts, writings and practices
- ⊹ the contribution of significant people, traditions and movements
- ⊹ religious language and terminology
- ⊹ major issues and questions arising
- ⊹ the relationship between the areas of study and other specified aspects of human experience

■ **You need to develop the following skills**:
- ⊹ recall, select and deploy knowledge
- ⊹ identify, investigate and analyse questions and issues arising from them
- ⊹ use appropriate and correct language and terminology
- ⊹ interpret and evaluate relevant concepts
- ⊹ communicate, using reasoned argument substantiated by evidence
- ⊹ make connections between areas of study and other aspects of experience

As you move from AS to A2 you will be expected to demonstrate a wider range and depth of knowledge and understanding and a greater maturity of thought and expression, so the weighting of the objectives shifts as you move to A2 and more marks are proportionally credited to AO2 than AO1. However, it is vital to be aware that it is impossible to obtain an A grade unless you include AO2 material in your answers. The fullest answer that demonstrates only AO1, knowledge and understanding, can obtain, at the most, a B grade.

Trigger words

The use of trigger words in questions enables you to identify the particular skills you are required to deploy. AO1 trigger words invite you to demonstrate your knowledge and understanding, whilst AO2 trigger words invite you to evaluate that knowledge.

AO1 trigger words might include: describe; examine; identify; outline; select; what; how; illustrate; for what reasons; give an account of; in what ways; analyse; clarify; compare and contrast; differentiate; distinguish between; define; examine; explain.

AO2 trigger words might include: comment on; consider; how far; to what extent; why; assess; discuss; consider critically; criticise; evaluate; interpret; justify.

You need to be aware of the difference between 'giving an account of' and 'considering critically'. To give an account you draw essentially on your knowledge, which you may then be required to evaluate through 'considering critically'. Considering critically, or assessing, or commenting on, involves drawing conclusions about the significance and value of what you have learned. There are certain words and phrases which you may find useful for this: 'This is important because'; 'The most significant is...because'; 'However'; 'On the other hand'; 'It is likely that...because'; 'Therefore'; 'Nevertheless'; 'The implications of this are'. As you work, keep asking yourself 'Why is this relevant to my answer?' and 'What are the implications of this view/issue?' Don't go onto automatic pilot, otherwise you will simply narrate facts or, worse, a story.

Approaching the course

Learning, revision and exam technique

As you prepare for your AS and A2 examinations, there are stages when your teacher will directly help you and stages when you must be prepared to work alone. In the end, teachers cannot go into the exam for you, and whilst they can give you information and guide you in the best practice for utilising that information in the exam, you have to make sure you have learned it and developed an effective examination technique.

Lessons

It is initially your teacher's responsibility to select the right information for your needs, but you should take responsibility for the way you receive it and what you do with it after the class is over. So, develop good classroom habits. Ask questions about the material. Questions can help you to clarify what you have just heard as well as clear up misunderstandings. Ask questions about the implications of the material the teacher is covering and about how it relates to other aspects of the specification. Your classes also give you the opportunity to practise the vital skill of evaluation. You will hear many views expressed which might be quite different from your own, which you can — in an empathetic (i.e. non-confrontational) way — evaluate: 'Am I right in thinking that you believe X to be right because of Y?' Be prepared in turn for your views to be evaluated by others, and to explain why you hold them: 'I think that Z is wrong because if you take Y into consideration, the conclusion cannot be X.'

Homework tasks

Because you have to write in the examination — indeed, the written word is the only vehicle you will have for assessment — you must use homework tasks as an essential tool for refining your written skills. Although past questions may take many forms, one of the most useful things you should be doing for homework is practising answering them so that you become totally comfortable with the way your board and specification requires you to use the knowledge and understanding you have gained. Your teacher can explain to you how your work is marked in accordance with the principles laid down by the exam board, so you can gain some insight into the way the system works. Every homework exercise is an opportunity to learn the topic you're working on, so don't just stick it in the back of your file when it's marked!

Independent learning and consolidation

Even the best teachers are not going to cover absolutely everything in the class time available to them, although they will use that time to provide you with virtually everything you need to do well in the exam. However, it is the time you put in outside of the classroom which will be decisive. You may read an article that no one else in your class has seen, watch a television programme, or simply go over your class notes one more time and in so doing finally understand a difficult area. There is no doubt that the top grades usually go to candidates who are prepared to do something more than attend class and do the work set.

Revision for the examination

It is never too early to start revising. From the moment the first topic has been completed in class, you should be making concise revision notes, learning quotations and making essay plans. If you leave it until the exams are looming, you will only have time to get the information into your short-term memory, and you will feel far less able to deal with the unexpected or to spend time in the exam ensuring that your written style is the best you can offer. Revision techniques do, and indeed should, vary. Everybody learns and remembers differently, so don't be led into thinking that you should be revising in exactly the same way as everybody else. Experiment with a range of strategies but make sure they are multi-sensory. This means that you should involve as many of the appropriate senses in the learning process as possible. If you are just reading through the notes in your file, you are using only one method — reading — and therefore using only one channel to receive and process that information. Reading, making fresh notes, applying them to a question, writing information out again, repeating it orally to a friend, all contribute to the cumulative process of learning and help establish the material more firmly in your memory.

As you prepare for the examination, make sure that you are absolutely certain about key issues such as the day and time of the exam! You may think this is silly, but I have marked an exam paper on which a candidate had written: 'Sorry about this, but I only just found out my exam was today'. This is not just a failure on the part of the school (if, indeed, she hadn't been told) but also a failure on her part not to make sure she did know the right day and time. Knowing dates well in advance enables you to make a revision plan, allocating specific tasks to each day as the exam approaches, so that your revision is never random or unplanned.

You must also be sure of what you will be required to do in the exam and how much time you have to do it in. This is why you must practise exam questions to time and not just under homework conditions. The best candidates can achieve a disappointing result because they haven't worked to time, writing one or two long answers, but then resorting to a plan, notes or a brief side-long answer. If you have an hour and a half to answer two questions, that means 45 minutes per question, not an hour on one and half an hour on the other.

The examination

You don't have to be fatalistic about the exam. Keep in control and even if the questions are not the ones you hoped would come up, you can think calmly and carefully and use the material you have learned to write relevant answers to the questions that are there. Don't panic and leave early, but think. Read what you have written and check it over for silly mistakes and misspellings. Ignore what everyone else is doing, even if they leave the room, faint or cry. And don't spend time in pointless post-mortems after the exam. What's done is done at this stage, and you need to have peace of mind to prepare for your next paper.

Finally...

It's not brain surgery. If you follow the instructions you are given, are conscientious, thorough, and communicate with your teacher, there is no reason why you should not do well.

It's not just down to being clever. Remember the hare and the tortoise? The hare had natural advantages but did not build on them. The tortoise was slower but he plugged away and eventually got to the winning post ahead of the hare. The fable has great relevance for students, as nothing pays off like hard work — even the cleverest students must apply themselves if they want to be certain of top grades.

People are there to help you. You need never feel alone in your quest for a good A-level grade. Every single member of staff at your school is on the same side as you, even if it doesn't always feel like it. But there are also other ways of getting help. Look out for revision courses and one-day or residential conferences, and encourage your teacher to attend exam board meetings. Everyone wants you to do well!

Tips as you approach the exam

- **What the examiner is looking for**...
  ÷ relevance
  ÷ coherence
  ÷ accuracy
  ÷ precision
  ÷ readable and presentable answers
  ÷ evidence that you have taken an AS/A-level course — i.e. academic answers, not general knowledge

- **What the examiner is *not* looking for**...
  ÷ undergraduate-level answers
  ÷ perfection
  ÷ everything you know, whether or not it is directly relevant
  ÷ more than is realistic to expect of a sixth-form student

- **How you should approach the exam**...
  ÷ with confidence
  ÷ trusting your teacher
  ÷ knowing that you have done everything you can do
  ÷ knowing what to expect on the paper
  ÷ having had lots of practice

- **How you should approach revision**...
  ÷ with a pen in your hand
  ÷ actively
  ÷ in a multi-sensory manner
  ÷ simply

÷ in your own words

÷ by getting rid of unnecessary material

■ **Revision killers**…

÷ reading through your file

÷ working with music or the television on in the background

÷ working without a schedule

÷ working without reference to past questions

Philosophy of Religion

Topic 1

Influences and philosophical principles

A The Ancient Greeks

1 Plato

Plato was born in Athens about 427 BCE, and died there about 347 BCE. In early life Plato saw war service and had political ambitions. However, he was never really sympathetic to the Athenian democracy and he could not join wholeheartedly in its government. He was a devoted follower of Socrates, whose disciple he became in 409 BCE, and Socrates's execution by the democrats in 399 BCE was a crushing blow. He left Athens, believing that until *'kings were philosophers or philosophers were kings'* things would never go well with the world. For several years he visited the Greek cities of Africa and Italy, absorbing Pythagorean notions, and then in 387 BCE he returned to Athens. There, for the second half of his long life, he devoted himself to philosophy. In the western suburbs he founded a school that might be termed the first university. Because it was on grounds that had once belonged to a legendary Greek called Academus, it came to be called the *Academy*, and this term has been used for schools ever since.

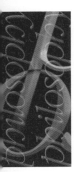

Plato's works, perhaps the most consistently popular and influential philosophic writings ever published, consist of a series of dialogues in which the discussions between Socrates and others are presented in a highly characteristic style, known as the *Socratic Method*. Most of our knowledge of Socrates is from these dialogues, and it is virtually impossible to tell which views are Socrates's and which are Plato's; Plato cautiously never introduced himself into any of the dialogues.

The works of Plato are a useful foundation for an understanding of key concepts that are of perennial concern to religious thought and philosophy. It is also interesting to see how significantly different they are in some respects, and yet remarkably similar in others. H. D. F. Kitto (1951) observed that *'It was Greek philosophy, notably Plato's conception of the absolute, eternal deity, which prepared the world for the reception of a universal religion'*. Plato's interests were wide-ranging, but those which most concern us are the nature of reality, the nature and possibility of knowledge, and the distinction between body and soul.

Plato uses his famous **allegory of the cave** to draw attention to the difference between appearances and the real world, based on his view that true knowledge is not what man has been told or shown, and which is only based on opinion, but rather what he has found out for himself after long and rigorous intellectual searching. Only what is permanent can be the source of true knowledge, not the objects of the physical world, which are always changing. The unchanging realities are those that Plato believed could only be apprehended by the mind, since those we experience through the senses are only imperfect copies. Plato was strongly influenced in his thinking by Heraclitus, who had challenged the view that reality was unchanging, with the observation that you cannot step into the same river twice, since it is in a state of flux, and thus cannot be the same river the second time. The truly unchanging, imperfect and ultimately unknowable reality should therefore be man's goal, despite the difficulties of achieving it.

In the allegory of the cave, Plato describes a group of chained prisoners who can only look ahead, although a fire behind them throws shadows on the wall. They know nothing other than their life in the cave, so they naturally believe it to be reality, and the shadows thrown onto the wall of the cave to be pictures of the real world. They do not perceive them merely as reflections of reality, or the sounds they hear to be echoes of what is going on in the real world. Plato uses this image to illustrate the mind of the unthinking man, who simply accepts what he hears, and never questions whether it is valuable, good or true. When one of the prisoners escapes from the cave, he is overwhelmed by what he finds outside and, naturally, takes some time to adjust to the daylight and what it reveals. When he finally grasps that he is now experiencing true reality, he returns to the cave to tell his former fellow prisoners. Still in the darkness, they mock him and refuse to come out of the cave themselves. Plato believed that Athenian society, which had allowed Socrates to die, resembled the prisoners in the cave, who refused to recognise their need to be enlightened, let alone the source of that enlightenment.

Plato's **theory of Forms** was highly influential in developing ideas about goodness and reality. The prisoners in the cave would always be condemned to accepting a pale copy of the truth as reality, and so would never be able to apprehend the true, absolute Form of the Good, the highest of the realities which illuminates all others. Knowledge of the Good is virtually knowledge of God, and, as Kitto (1951) observed: *'Plato, in fact, reaches a position not very far from that of the Psalmist who says, "The knowledge of God is the beginning of wisdom" — though he reaches this position by a very different road'.* The 'very different road' was mathematics, which Plato believed to be the road to understanding the spaceless, eternal entities that constituted ultimate reality — a state beyond the material, which was timelessly abstract. In a classic Christian application, Aquinas's Fourth Way, *From the Gradation of Things*, was clearly heavily influenced by Plato's theory of Forms, pointing to the need for a highest source of goodness, truth and nobility, which Aquinas identified as God.

The Forms could never be encountered in the physical world, since they were permanent and unchanging concepts — justice, truth, beauty and goodness — of which Plato believed we have an instinctive appreciation, even if we have never known a perfect example of them. He maintained that this instinctive knowledge was an indication that man has an immortal, pre-existent soul, which has encountered these forms before becoming effectively imprisoned in the physical body. At birth, the soul forgets its previous life, but through philosophy, we can be reminded of the nature of true reality and recall this lost knowledge. This process is known as **anamnesis** — literally, 'non-

'forgetting'. The soul, like the Forms, is immortal and immutable, unlike the body, which is a physical entity, and so changeable and imperfect. This is a classic dualist perspective — body and soul are two separate entities, entirely different from one another in their nature. Plato believed that people should seek to rise above the inconvenient limitations of the body and its needs and desires, and instead, seek to be identified once more with their immortal soul and united with the unchanging Forms. With death comes the final separation of body and soul, when the soul re-enters the eternal realm from which it came.

2 Aristotle

Aristotle was born at Stagira in Macedonia, northern Greece, and, together with Plato, was the most influential philosopher of the Western tradition. At age 17 he entered Plato's Academy in Athens, and left when Plato died, on the grounds that he disapproved of the Academy's growing emphasis on mathematics. Eventually he was to become by far the most renowned of all the pupils of Plato, who called him 'the intelligence of the school'. Aristotle then accepted the invitation of Hermias to reside at Assos before moving on to Mytilene on the island of Lesbos. Between *c.* 343 and 340 BCE he acted as tutor to the young Alexander the Great.

Aristotle founded a school of his own, the *Lyceum*, so called because Aristotle lectured in a hall near the temple of Apollo Lykaios (Apollo, the Wolf-God). It was also called the *Peripatetic school* because Aristotle, at least on occasion, lectured to students while walking in the school's garden. He built up a collection of manuscripts too — a very early example of a university library. The school continued quite successfully under Aristotle's directorship, emphasising natural philosophy. In 323 BCE, however, news arrived of the death of Alexander the Great in Babylon. As it was well known that Aristotle had been Alexander's tutor, he feared that an anti-Macedonian reaction in Athens might lead to trouble. When the accusation of 'impiety' was raised, Aristotle feared he might suffer the fate of Socrates. Saying he would not allow Athens to 'sin twice against philosophy', he retired to Chalcis, his mother's hometown, and died there the next year.

Aristotle was an empiricist philosopher, who was devoted to deepening his understanding of experience. As Magee (1997) writes, he was *'working always from inside experience, never trying to impose abstract explanations on it from the outside'*. Aristotle's work was significant in that he not only looked for scientific explanations, but he asked important questions about the nature of scientific explanation and organised two thousand years' worth of logic. For hundreds of years his work constituted the largest systematic body of knowledge in existence, and even in the seventeenth century, when modern science was emerging, it was against the Aristotelian paradigm that it had to struggle before establishing itself. However, none of the works that Aristotle prepared for publication survived, and all we know of his thought is that which was written up from his lecture notes.

Although Aristotle was devoted to Plato, he did not agree with his theory of Forms, since, as an empiricist, he did not believe that true reality could not be encountered in the real world. On the contrary, he maintained that the only real knowledge we have is of the empirical world, and the only reliable information is that which can be gained

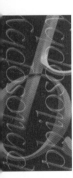

from it. One of the key questions that Aristotle sought to answer was what it means for something to exist. Unlike Plato, he did not understand Forms to be abstract, but rather believed they consisted of matter and could be perceived by the senses. God was an exception to this, as he could be a Form, yet not have matter. Aristotle identified four causes culminating in a complete explanation of what causes something to exist:

÷ The **material cause** of something answers the question 'What does it consist of?'
÷ The **efficient cause** answers the question 'How did it happen?'
÷ The **formal cause** answers the question 'What are its characteristics?'
÷ The **final cause** answers the question 'Why is it here?' or 'What is its purpose?'

Once all four causes have been established, the complete explanation for the existence of an item has been found. The most important of these causes is the final cause, which is **teleological** — that is, concerned with ultimate end or function — since this is what gives an item its ultimate goodness. Aristotle maintained that everything has a final cause, even if it isn't immediately apparent, and this way of thinking was echoed down the centuries in the various forms of the **Teleological Argument** for the existence of God.

Aristotle was also interested in tracing all movements back to a first mover, and it is clear that the first of Aquinas's Five Ways, an important part of the **Cosmological Argument** for the existence of God, is directly dependent on the thought of Aristotle. Aristotle concluded that a chain of movers has to begin with an unmoved or prime mover, something which is not itself moved, but which could cause other things to move. He called this prime mover God, a final cause in itself, and which causes things to be, not simply through physical or mechanical momentum but through an act of love. Because all things want to be in the image of God's perfection, they are drawn towards him, the necessary being who is eternally good and on whom all other things depend. God himself is engaged in no other activity but a purely intellectual contemplation of himself, which, rather oddly, Aristotle suggested was the activity that causes movement in all other things, and is eternal, transcendent and immutable.

Like Plato, Aristotle was interested in the relationship between soul and body, which he saw as a psycho-physical unity of soul and body. The human soul is essentially the body and its organisation. But Aristotle did identify another quality that it possesses — reason, the means by which humans can develop intellectually and morally. However, Aristotle was no dualist, and insisted that body and soul are as inseparable from each other as *'the wax and the shape given to it by the stamp'.* The only exception he made was that reason somehow lives on after the body dies, without conveying in that idea any concept of the post-mortem survival of personal identity.

Summary and key terms

■ **Plato** was an Athenian and a follower of Socrates, and believed that government should lie in the hands of the philosopher ruler. His works feature Socrates as the key figure.

■ **Allegory of the cave** — true reality and knowledge of what is true belong outside the realm of the physical and empirical, and can only be apprehended by the mind. Despite the difficulties inherent in so doing, we should attempt the intellectual quest to find true reality.

- **The theory of Forms** — the absolute Form of the Good is the ultimate, perfect reality, and all else is a pale reflection of it. However, because we instinctively recognise the Form of the Good, our souls must be pre-existent and will be reunited with the Form after death.
- **Aristotle** — pupil of Plato who rejected Platonic dualism. A strong empiricist, he believed that knowledge is only obtainable through experience and the senses. The Form of something is physical, not abstract. He traced four causes for a thing or being: material, efficient, formal and final. The final cause is most important, as it is teleological, and identifies the purpose and function of a thing or being. A first, unmoved mover is the final cause, which Aristotle identified as God, moving all things out of love. He saw body and soul as a psycho-physical unity, although the soul has a distinct quality — reason — which lives on after the death of the body.

Exam watch

This topic is unique to one examination board in terms of specific questions on the exam paper, but it is clear that the issues that concerned Plato and Aristotle are absolutely central to the debates between religious philosophers which have continued to the present day. This material is vital background to arguments for the existence of God, discussions about life after death and the relationship between soul and body, and to the nature of the Good, even if you won't have to answer a question on Plato's or Aristotle's thought per se.

Review questions

1 Outline Plato's theory of Forms and the allegory of the cave.
2 Examine and evaluate the effectiveness of these theories.
3 What did Aristotle understand by the 'final cause'?
4 Evaluate Aristotle's view that everything has a purpose.

B Judaeo-Christian influences

1 God as creator

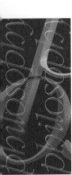

For all the interest that the Ancient Greek thinkers displayed in the question of the origins of the universe, the solutions that they reached were essentially impersonal. They looked for explanations that were logical and coherent, but those explanations had no direct relationship with human beings, still less a personal interest in them. The biblical writers portray God very differently, and although he is a transcendent, sovereign creator, on whom all things depend, his creation of humanity and the universe is for a purpose. From a Christian perspective, Claus Westermann (1987) observes that the creation narratives — indeed the whole primal history (Genesis 1–11) — is vital in setting the scene for the whole '*history of the relationship between God and humanity, begun in the creation of the human race and leading to Christ and his work*'. The creation narratives, therefore, are best understood as the introduction to the relationship between God and humanity, which is explored in the rest of the Bible and which will have its culmination in an eschatological future that lies beyond the immediate scope (despite attempts to predict its nature and timing) even of the biblical writers.

Commentators have spilt much ink over the interpretation of Genesis 1–3 — the narratives of creation and the fall, which contain the essential germ of the biblical view of God as creator. Essentially, the narratives have either been interpreted literally and fundamentalistically, or been seen to contain truth that is not literal or scientific, but which offers an insight into the relationship between God and the world. Of course, these two views are not necessarily mutually exclusive, since a fundamentalist will still hold that the narratives contain more than simple literal facts. (See pp. 91–99 for more discussion on religious and scientific explanations of the universe.) In any case, the key theme is the complete dependence that the created order, including human beings, has on God. The biblical writers never debate the existence of God, or use the narratives to engage in dialogue with those who may hold different views about the origin of the universe. It is utterly taken for granted that creation is the result of the direct and omnipotent act of God and, consequently, that the universe has no independent or necessary existence, and depends on God for its continuation.

Nevertheless, it is evident that the biblical writers were not working in a vacuum. The narratives of Genesis 1–2 share remarkable similarities to the creation myths that emerged in the Babylonian traditions, especially the epic *Euma elish*, which recounted the God Marduk's defeat of the sea monster Tiamat and his subsequent creation of heaven and earth. There are also allusions to Baal's defeat of the sea monster Leviathan in the Canaanite texts from Ugarit, which may have influenced the Genesis account. However, although these narratives may have indirectly influenced the biblical writers, the Genesis accounts contain none of the polytheistic and more outlandish mythological features of the Babylonian accounts. Nevertheless, Westermann comments that because the principal themes of the whole primal history are to be found in the early traditions of so many cultures, they clearly express something which is common to all human history.

Interestingly, there are two distinct accounts of creation in Genesis 1 and 2. The first account, from the Priestly tradition, has a formulaic style, characterised by repeated phrases: '*And God said "Let there be…"*'; '*And there was…*'; '*And God saw that it was good*'. The act of creation takes place over a structured period of six days, followed by a day of divine rest. The narrative does not make explicit whether God created **ex nihilo** (out of nothing) or whether he ordered pre-existing matter that was '*without form and void*' (1:2). Traditionally, creation *ex nihilo* has been held to be the case, with God creating matter when before there was none. Augustine further suggested that time itself was created by God in this same act.

The second account, possibly older, is more narrative in style, more naïve, and describes God's creative activity anthropomorphically. It is linked directly with the events of the fall in Genesis 3 and it begins to address some of the questions that were left unanswered at the end of Genesis 1, most specifically why, if God had created a perfect universe (1:31), there are clearly things and situations in the world which we consider to be imperfect. Common to both accounts, however, is the fact that the human race is the goal of God's creative work; the universe is **anthropocentric**. Whether humans are created last (1:27) or first (2:7), they are the climax and purpose.

They are distinguished from the rest of creation, being in the image of God (1:26) and given life by the direct and personal action of God's spirit (2:7); they are given authority over the animals (2:19), the opportunity to participate in God's creative work (2:15), and everything necessary for their survival is in the garden in which God places them (2:9).

The events of the fall clearly explain why creation is not perfect. God's creation of individuals as morally free agents leads inevitably to their falling away from the perfection of their relationship with God, with each other, and with the created order. It is certainly not a complete explanation, however, since it arguably raises more questions than it answers. What was the serpent — *'more crafty than any other creature God had made'* (3:1) — doing in the garden? Did God know that humanity would disobey him and intend that sin and its consequences should come into the world? If so, does this suggest a malevolent God? These questions continue to puzzle religious thinkers and there are no universally satisfactory answers to them. (See pp. 68–78 on the Problem of Evil for some suggestions of how they may be resolved.) However, the narratives attempt to explain puzzling, or otherwise inexplicable, phenomena: why clothing is worn (3:21); why we struggle to make a living from the earth (3:17–19); why women suffer in childbirth; and why there is inequality between the sexes (3:16). Westermann (1987) again claims that the narrative needs to be understood in the context of the whole vision of the Bible, Old and New Testaments: *'What is said here holds for the entire human race, for God is the creator of all of humanity. It is this universality that most clearly links the narrative of the human race and its trans-gression with the account of the life and passion of Christ in the New Testament'*. He also observes how the creation narrative has its antithesis in the flood story (Genesis 6–8), after which God promises that he will preserve his creation, despite its faults, to the end of time.

The creation narratives are only the tip of the iceberg as far as the biblical writers' presentation of God as creator is concerned, for the theme runs throughout the Old Testament, and is expressed vividly in the Psalms and the Wisdom literature. When Job questions God's plans and purposes, God rhetorically replies, *'Where were you when I laid the foundations of the earth?'* (Job 38:4), and the Psalmist testifies to God's continued sustaining of the created order: *'Who by thy strength has established the mountains…who stills the roaring of the seas?'* (Psalm 65:6–7). Above all, Isaiah expresses the utter sovereignty of God, who cannot be challenged by humanity or by the false gods which humanity, in its ignorance, carves and worships: *'I am the Lord, and there is no other. I form light and create darkness, I make weal and create woe, I am the Lord, who does all these things'* (Isaiah 45:6–7).

2 God's goodness

The biblical portrait of God also differs sharply from the Greek conception of the eternal Forms, in that God is no more an objective model of perfection than he is an impersonal creator. The goodness of God is not a remote quality or attribute, but is expressed through his direct activity in the lives of his people — both through the standards he sets and through his responses to his people in their attempts to live up to those standards. Although God himself is more than a model of goodness, he is held to be

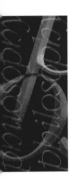

perfectly good, and the nature of his goodness is to be understood analogically — God's goodness is not the same as human goodness. If this is so, then nothing can lead to describing any of God's actions as cruel, vindictive or vengeful. J. S. Mill argued that a good God should not act differently to a good person, so we cannot justify apparently evil acts of God on the grounds that he is divine. Nevertheless, the existence of evil and suffering are classically seen to present a huge problem for religious believers: if God is both omnipotent and benevolent (good and loving), then why does he permit evil? (This issue is fully discussed on pp. 68–78.)

One of the central questions in religious moral philosophy is that which concerns the relationship between God and goodness. Does God create moral standards that he issues as commands, or does he command that which he already knows as good? This is known as the **Euthyphro Dilemma**. (For a fuller discussion of this, see pp. 152–154.) This dilemma is difficult to solve, since religious believers tend to use God's commands as a point of reference when deciding what is good, but are aware that sometimes their relationship with God might call them to do something which they know rationally would be considered wrong. Peter Vardy (1998) writes:

Reason and morality normally go together but, just occasionally, it is possible for a love relationship with God to cause someone to do something which goes against society's accepted norms. It may call one of us to leave mother and father, brothers and sisters for a higher love... In the Christian life, lived as part of a love relationship with God, it is just possible that this relationship might call an individual to act against what appears to be rational, reasonable and understandable.

The goodness of God, therefore, cannot be measured by human standards of goodness, but is to be experienced within a relationship which is based in faith, not reason. The classic example of someone who was called to do something that society would condemn as wrong is Abraham's call to sacrifice Isaac. Vardy observes that because Abraham trusted his relationship with God, he was able to hold to two contradictory facts: God's promise to him that he would have many descendants through Isaac, *and* that he would sacrifice Isaac, as God had commanded him to do. The fact that he ultimately was not required to do so is not the point; Abraham responded in faith assuming that he would be so required.

God's goodness therefore does not depend on circumstances or on him acting in an entirely predictable manner. If it did, then the believer would only be able to love and worship God when he was experiencing God's goodness in a consistent, unchanging way. The experience of many biblical characters shows that not to be the case: Job, Ezekiel, David, Paul, Stephen and Jesus himself, to name but a few. Despite their experiences, these characters, and others like them, accepted that God's goodness is ultimately incomprehensible, but is utterly reliable.

For the Israelites, God's goodness was experienced through his covenant relationship with them, first revealed in the giving of the Law, including the Ten Commandments (the Decalogue) at Sinai. The commandments set out standards of behaviour towards God and towards others, and are sometimes called the *ethical decalogue* to distinguish them from the *ritual decalogue* of 34:17ff. They are certainly not a law code, for they are not comprehensive enough for that, dealing in the most general terms with moral

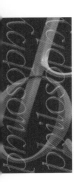

behaviour and attitudes. However, acceptance of them indicated the willingness of the people of Israel to enter into a covenant relationship with God that separated them from all other nations. It was a free response to a free act of grace by God, but it did bring certain obligations upon the people, who were expected to represent God and his goodness to the other nations. It is for this reason that the highest standards of behaviour were required of them, and they could not expect to be immune from God's judgment if they violated his standards of goodness: *'You only have I known of all the families of the earth; therefore I will punish you for all your iniquities'* (Amos 3:2).

Nevertheless, God's goodness is not inflexible. Although he is angry when his people violate his standards, and because he is just he must judge, he does not do so hard-heartedly. The book of Hosea balances God's divine wrath (which Israel's conduct deserved) against God's desire for them to repent and return to him: *'I will not execute my fierce wrath against them, I will not return to destroy Ephraim: for I am God and not man; the Holy one in your midst'* (Hosea 9:11). Philip Yancey (1997) uses the book as an example of God's grace — his undeserved favour shown to sinful man:

In a manner of speaking, grace solves a dilemma for God… On the one hand, God loves us; on the other hand, our behaviour repulses him. God yearns to see in people something of his own image reflected; at best he sees shattered fragments of that image. Still, God cannot — or will not — give up.

The God who created the heavens and the earth, and who is perfectly good, is eager to forgive, and since '"*my thoughts are not your thoughts, neither are your ways my ways*", *declares the Lord'* (Isaiah 55:9), he can do what he likes, and go to whatever lengths he chooses to be reconciled with his people. Hosea was told to marry a cultic prostitute to learn the lesson of God's unfailing love, even when his goodness was deeply offended by human sin. Yancey writes:

Absurdly, against all odds, the irresistible power of love won out… Hosea welcomed his wife back home… I marvel at a God who allows himself to endure such humiliation only to come back for more.

God's goodness is not only displayed in the life of the nation Israel but in the personal experiences of believers. The Psalmist frequently writes of his experience of God's goodness underpinning his own life, especially when he is in situations of peril. Psalm 69 starts with the cry *'Save me, O God! For the waters have come up to my neck…'* (69:1), and ends with the exclamation, *'I am afflicted and in pain; let thy salvation, O God, set me on high! I will praise the name of God with a song; I will magnify him with thanksgiving'* (69:29–30). The biblical characters knew God personally and trusted in his goodness, whatever was going on around them.

For the New Testament writers, the ultimate demonstration of God's goodness is, of course, the sending of Jesus. God takes the initiative to overcome the natural inclination to sin which is in all men, and provides the means of redemption in the new covenant promises in Jeremiah 31:31f — the covenant that will be written on human hearts, not on tablets of stone. John 3:16 expresses it perfectly: *'For God so loved the world that he gave his only Son, so that all who believe in him should not perish but have eternal life.'* God's willingness to sacrifice his son is the model of goodness. It is the saving act to which humanity is called upon, by the New Testament writers, to make a life-changing response, freeing ourselves forever from the impossible task of measuring up to the perfect, unchangeable, God.

3 God at work in the world

Crucial to the biblical writers' portrait of God is the view that he intervenes in the world and engages with it, and with his people. They maintained that God acted in this way on numerous occasions with the specific aim of furthering his purposes for the whole of creation, for his people, Israel, and in the lives of individuals. Interestingly, however, this runs counter to the equally important view that God is **transcendent**. This term means that God stands above or beyond the world, and in the realms that are beyond the limits of any human experience. Arguably, God transcended even himself in the creation of the world. The term is contrary to **immanence**, which holds that God, or the divine, is within human experience or within the world.

In the earliest religious traditions, the deities were those powers on which nature and society were utterly dependent and they were understood to be immanent rather than transcendent. Hence, the gods of Greece and Rome were depicted anthropomorphically, and personified as aspects of nature and society. However, Plato's idea of the perfect Form of the good and the absolute expressed the principle of transcendence; the divine belongs to a realm beyond direct human experience, although ultimately attainable by the individual who is prepared to leave behind the limitations of the physical world. The Judaeo-Christian picture is something of a paradox: *'The God of the Bible stands above the world as its sovereign Lord, its Creator and its Saviour; but he appears in the world to set men tasks to do, speaking to men in demand, in promise, in healing and fulfilment'* (Halverson and Cohen (eds.), 1960).

The biblical view is that God may be known through creation, which God himself declared to be good, but it is not the supreme reality and is not *perfectly* good. Thus, to worship creation would be idolatry; rather, the creator himself must be worshipped. In the Christian tradition, God comes decisively into the world in the figure of the incarnate Jesus, a unique and unprecedented revelation of the transcendent God.

Christian thinkers have variously emphasised these two aspects of God's relationship with the world. Late twentieth-century Protestant thought tended to stress his immanence in an attempt to harmonise religion with modern understandings of science and human nature — for example, that God works in the world through the process of evolution. On the other hand, the thinking of scholars such as Karl Barth and Reinhold Niebuhr stressed that God stands above the world as sovereign judge, and humanity can only experience his grace once he has experienced his judgment. Through his grace, God draws near to humanity, and the transcendent becomes immanent in the lives of those who have faith.

Throughout the Bible, God's action in the world is consistently illustrated by accounts of miraculous events in which God suspends the laws of nature to accomplish his purpose and guide the course of history. The biblical writers had no concept of natural law that determined how the universe operates and so when God intervenes in the course of events, it is never portrayed as a violation of natural laws. This certainly avoids the problem of why God would break his own rules when performing a miracle, since there are no rules to break or laws to violate:

Belief in miracles exists where nature is regarded only as an object of arbitrariness...which nature uses only as an instrument of its own will and pleasure. Water divides or rolls itself together like a firm mass...the sun now stands still, now goes backward. And all these contradictions of nature happen for the welfare of Israel, purely at the command of Jehovah, who troubles himself about nothing but Israel.

(Feuerbach (ed.), 1957)

The Old Testament uses three Hebrew words to describe God's action in the world:

- ⁙ **Oth** — an act of God that sends a message to his people or to pagan rules, for example the events that led to the Exodus, which reveal that God has a special plan which he works to fulfil.
- ⁙ **Mopeth** — an extraordinary event which God performs on behalf of his people, such as Aaron's rod turning into a serpent.
- ⁙ **Pele** — God's sovereignty in performing actions on behalf of his people, used when recalling what God has done in the past.

The account of God's miraculous intervention in the Israelites' war against the Amorites in Joshua 10:1–15 is a classic example of God's work in the course of history and in the natural order to bring about his purposes for his people. Three events take place during the battle which demonstrate that God is in control, each more amazing:

(i) He throws the enemy into confusion: *'Indeed most of the conflicts in the settlement of Israel in Palestine are represented as being settled by this psychological factor rather than by bitter hand-to-hand fighting'* (Gray, 1986).
(ii) He sends hailstones as divine weapons: *'More died because of the hailstones than the men of Israel killed with the sword'* (Joshua 10:11).
(iii) *'The sun stayed in the midst of heaven and did not hasten to go down for about a whole day'* (Joshua 10:13).

The Deuteronomistic Historian presents all three factors as being the responsibility of an interventionist God to ensure the Israelites' victory over the Amorites in their quest to occupy the land, although there are obviously important issues of interpretation. Gray suggests that in the oldest source on which the Deuteronomist drew, the Book of Jashar, a national epic devoted to warlike exploits (10:13), no miracle was implied, but rather *'an atmospheric obscuration which masked the advance of the Israelites'*. The *Pickering Bible Commentary* (1979) observes: *'The one thing clear is that the Lord helped his people to exploit their victory; neither we, nor the inspired writer, can fully explain how this was accomplished'*. Whatever the interpretation, the narrative displays the characteristic feature of biblical accounts to attribute all events — natural and supernatural — to divine providence, based on a firm conviction that a transcendent God frequently acted immanently in order to accomplish the purpose he had declared for his people and for the whole of creation. (For a full discussion of the philosophical problems of miracles, see pp. 78–84.)

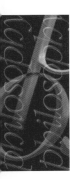

Summary

- God is a **personal creator**, involved in the sustainment and continuance of the created order. The creation narrative introduced the whole biblical story. Whether literal or symbolic, the writers took for granted the existence of God and the utter dependence of creation upon him. But remarkable similarities with Babylonian creation myths show they were dealing with universal themes. Two accounts of creation are both **anthropocentric** — creation is for the benefit of humanity. The fall of man explains puzzling questions about creation and humanity and our relationship with God. As creator, God is sovereign, and his people, who are limited, cannot question his actions.

- God's **goodness** is also personal and expressed in his direct activity in his people's lives — although the problem of evil raises key challenges to this. Commitment to God may involve commitment to actions which, from a human perspective, are not good, e.g. God's command to Abraham that he sacrifice Isaac. God's goodness does not depend on circumstances, and biblical figures experience his goodness in a range of contradictory situations. The covenant relationship reveals God's goodness to the people of Israel, and their commitment to it is expressed in their acceptance of his Law. High standards of goodness are expected, so judgment will be inevitable — but God's love can transcend his anger. His personal goodness meets individuals in crisis and, in the incarnation and death of Jesus (the new covenant), meets all men who respond in faith.

- The **transcendent** God is above or beyond the world, but the **immanent** God engages with it in continuing activity. The biblical picture holds these two positions in tension, and the transcendent God ultimately becomes immanent in the incarnation.

- **Miracles** — examples of God's action in the world, although biblical writers had no concept of the violation of natural law. In Joshua 10:1–15, for example, God prevented the sun from setting in order to ensure victory for Israel. Whatever the explanation, it demonstrates the biblical view attributing all events to divine providence.

Key terms

Anthropocentric — centred around the needs and interests of man.

Euthyphro Dilemma — the problem of whether something is good because God commands it, or whether God commands that which is good.

Ex nihilo — 'out of nothing'. Used to refer to God's activity in creation.

Immanent — God known in his activity within the world.

Transcendent — 'being beyond'. In the context of God, it is used to describe his being beyond and outside the world.

Exam watch

 These are quite sophisticated ideas to grapple with and you need to be able to make reference to philosophical principles and biblical concepts — they are not to be thought of as contradictory, but as complementary in these topics. Remember that you will need to evaluate these issues, and must be ready with some thoughtful comments about how the divine attributes can be reconciled with evidence in the world — evil, suffering, scientific discoveries and explanations.

Review questions

1 What do religious believers mean when they speak of God as creator? Does this involve a literal interpretation of the creation narratives?

2 *'God's goodness is impossible to express or experience. It can only be known through obedience to his commands.'* Examine and evaluate this claim.

3 Explain what religious believers mean by a miracle. How far might the notion of God's action in the world be vital for religious belief?

4 How does the problem of evil pose a serious challenge to the nature of God?

C The principles of proof

1 Types of proof

Arguments for the existence of God should always be thought of in terms of proofs. A proof is: *'An argument which starts from one or more premises, which are propositions taken for granted for the purpose of the argument, and argues to a conclusion'* (Swinburne, 1979). Thus, a proof can be represented in the following way:

Premise + Premise = Conclusion

or

P + P = C

Note that there need not be more than one premise, however, so a proof may simply be:

P = C

Alternatively, a proof may consist of more than two premises (see p. 51 for an example of a proof that consists of six premises).

A proof is a statement which *cannot be false*: e.g. 4 + 4 = 8. Such a proof is therefore logically necessary — it would be absurd to suggest alternative solutions; a logically necessary statement consists of a set of premises and a conclusion that cannot be disputed. These may include mathematical statements (as above) or tautologies, e.g. 'A circle is round'; 'The Queen of England is female.'

Other proofs, however, are only proofs in so far as they lead to conclusions that are possible or probable. Evidence points towards a certain conclusion, perhaps based on prior experience, or on similar instances, but it is still possible for there to be a different conclusion than that reached on previous occasions, for example:

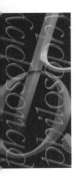

Premise One: The sun is shining today.
Premise Two: The sun shone yesterday.
Conclusion: The sun will shine tomorrow.

It is possible, even likely, that the sun will shine tomorrow, but there is still the chance that it may not. Forecasts may prove inaccurate, and hence, it would be a probable conclusion, not a logically necessary one. This is the problem of induction: past experience guides judgements about the future, but it cannot be necessarily true.

Proofs of this kind often work from a general assertion to a more specific conclusion, for example:

Premise One:	Huw sings well.
Premise Two:	Huw is Welsh.
Conclusion:	All Welsh men sing well.

Just as the one instance of Huw's fine singing voice would not be sufficient to justify saying that all Welsh men sing well, neither would the general assertion that all Welsh men sing well be sufficient to assume that Huw, by virtue of being Welsh, must, of necessity, sing well. If you come across an increasing number of good Welsh singers, this may indeed increase the probability of an inherent singing ability in Welsh men, but it is not conclusive; nor is it necessarily true that because Huw is Welsh he sings well, because 'singing well' and 'Welsh' are a not a tautology. In other words, 'Welsh' does not mean 'sings well' in the way that 'circle' means 'round'.

Probability measures the relative frequency or likelihood of an event taking place, or of circumstances unfolding in a particular way. It demands that we make judgments. If A and B are the case, how likely is it that C will follow? We consider the evidence available to us, and judge, or evaluate, whether the evidence points to a particular conclusion. All the evidence has to be taken into consideration if we want to be as certain as it is possible to be that in such a case our conclusion is the most likely, because the connection or association between events points to it. Hence, proofs may be *either*:

(a) *a posteriori*, synthetic and inductive, *or*
(b) *a priori*, analytic and deductive

A *posteriori*, synthetic and **inductive** proofs are based on premises argued or drawn from experience, which do not contain the conclusion but which argue to a conclusion that is not logically necessary. The more evidence-stating factors we employ, the greater the likelihood may be of the conclusion being correct, but it can always be disproved. We cannot conclusively prove it to be the case but can only establish degrees of probability. For example:

P1:	The sun shines in July.
P2:	The sun is shining today.
C:	It is July.

Just as it was impossible to claim that the conclusion 'The sun will shine tomorrow' is logically necessary, so it would be impossible to make this claim with a high degree of confidence. It may be more likely that it is July rather than November or February, but there is no logically necessary reason why it should not be June or August or any of the other months of the year. The sun *may be more likely* to shine in the summer months than the winter months, but that is all we can say.

P1:	Mr Brown had the opportunity to murder Mr Green.
P2:	Mr Brown had the motive to murder Mr Green.
C:	Mr Brown murdered Mr Green.

This is a classic inductive argument that may lead to the right conclusion, but just because the evidence *appears* to point to Mr Brown as the most likely suspect, it may be quite circumstantial, and the true culprit might be someone quite different. Hence, if the evidence is interpreted differently the conclusion might be altogether different.

A priori, **analytic** and **deductive** proofs are based on premises that are not drawn from, or dependent upon, experience, but which contain a logically necessary conclusion. We learn no more from the conclusion than we already knew from the premises, and the use of analytic terms means we are using terms that cannot be misinterpreted. They have a clear and distinct meaning. For example:

P1: Jane is a spinster.
P2: A spinster is an unmarried female.
C: Jane is an unmarried female.

This typical deductive proof demonstrates the ***de dicto*** principles of *a priori* arguments. The word 'spinster' has a specific and accepted meaning that it would be foolish to question or redefine. Hence, once we have established that Jane is a spinster, we have necessarily established that she is both female and unmarried, since that is what spinster means. It does not mean anything else — that she is happy, sad, clever, witty, dull, an electrician or an actress — but it does logically establish *by definition* that she is an unmarried female.

P1: All female monarchs are queens.
P2: Elizabeth is a female monarch.
C: Elizabeth is a queen.

Although, colloquially, the word 'queen' may have other meanings, the most accepted meaning is female monarch, and to claim that Elizabeth is a female monarch but not a queen would be logically impossible. These examples would illustrate the same principles if masculinised — 'bachelor' and 'king' work in the same way.

2 Proving God's existence

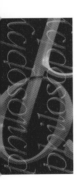

Arguments for the existence of God effectively proceed in the same way — from premises to conclusion, using inductive or deductive reasoning — and it is essential to understand the different ways in which these kinds of proof work if we are effectively to evaluate the arguments for the existence of God. Criticisms made of the classic proofs are very often specific to the argument, as later chapters will illustrate, but initially we need to assess whether an argument has an inherent weakness based on the *kind* of proof it is. It is important to be clear whether the proponents of the argument in question are arguing that God's existence is logically necessary and that he cannot *not* exist, or whether they are suggesting that God's existence is highly probable, and in fact may be the best explanation for certain phenomena. Criticisms of the arguments will be essentially different: if an *a priori* argument fails to provide a convincing reason why God cannot *not* exist, or if an *a posteriori* argument leads to a more convincing conclusion than God, then the arguments have failed to prove their case, although for fundamentally different reasons.

Proving God deductively

P1: God is that than which nothing greater can be conceived.

P2: That than which nothing greater can be conceived must exist.

C: God must exist.

This is known as the Ontological Proof. The Ontological Proof demands that if we accept the definition of God as '*that than which nothing greater can be conceived*', then we must accept that he possesses, analytically, existence, since that than which nothing greater can be conceived must necessarily possess all perfections, and existence, according to the Ontological Proof, is a perfection. The definition of God as '*that than which...*' works in this case in the same way as we saw spinster, bachelor, king or queen working.

Proving God inductively

P1: All events require a cause.

P2: The universe is an event.

C: God is the cause of the universe.

This proof will also become familiar; it is the basis of the Cosmological Argument. The proof leads only to a probable conclusion because there is no analytic, logically necessary, *a priori* reason why God should be the cause of the universe and not anything else. Neither are the premises themselves logically necessary — there is no compelling reason to agree conclusively that 'all events require a cause'. It is only on the basis of our regular experience that we assert that all events have a cause, and experience can be:

÷ deceptive

÷ limited

÷ open to many interpretations

Three other important arguments for the existence of God also work inductively. These are:

÷ the Design (or Teleological) Argument

÷ the Moral Argument

÷ the Argument from Religious Experience

All three arguments work from the basis of human experience, whether it is of the natural world or more individual and subjective experiences. We might criticise the Design Argument on the basis that it draws conclusions about the nature of certain phenomena in the universe which go beyond the evidence, or the Argument from Religious Experience because we question the value of the testimony on which it is based, but in both cases we are questioning whether the conclusion is the right one to draw on the basis of the evidence provided. Both types of reasoning have distinctive strengths and weaknesses.

Inductive reasoning is strong because:

÷ it relies on experience that may be universal, or at least may be testable

÷ it is flexible — there is more than one possible conclusion

÷ it does not demand that we accept definitions as fixed

But it may be weak because:

+ it relies on accepting the nature of the evidence
+ it demands overwhelmingly good reasons for accepting that the conclusion is the most likely
+ alternative conclusions may be just as convincing

Deductive reasoning is strong because:

+ it does not depend on variable or misunderstood experience
+ it accepts that words and definitions have fixed and agreed meanings
+ there are no alternative conclusions

But it may be weak because:

+ it leads to apparently logically necessary conclusions
+ it depends on whether one accepts that the premises are analytically true
+ it can only say that if certain phenomena are the case, we might be able to make certain claims about them

Arguments for the existence of God are therefore strong or weak in terms of their form, even before you consider their content. For example, if you consider that an inductive argument is relatively stronger than a deductive argument, because it is based on evidence, then it may be thought to be more secure, even before the content of the proof is evaluated.

Why have scholars offered proofs for the existence of God?

Proofs have been offered as an explanation for certain phenomena within the universe that are not self-explanatory and require an external explanation.

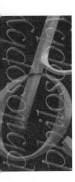

+ They appeal to reason and logic. It may be possible to show that the non-existence of God is logically impossible — that is, that it is impossible to conceive of his non-existence. This could be claimed from an examination of the term 'God', which Anselm claimed contained everything that was necessary to know about God, including the indisputable fact of his existence.
+ They provide a means of interpreting evidence in terms of God rather than something else. Since the universe is religiously ambiguous, it can be interpreted in religious or non-religious ways. Arguments for the existence of God seek to demonstrate that the most satisfactory way of interpreting the universe is by reference to God.
+ Arguments for the existence of God serve to complement faith. It is hardly likely that the proponents of the classical arguments came to believe in God as the basis of their proofs. They already believed in God's existence, but proofs serve to substantiate the reason to believe, and those reasons can support faith when it undergoes times of trial.

Problems with proofs

+ The experience we access to reach conclusions about God is limited and the reasoning powers we employ are limited because they are human. The evidence of our senses may not lead us towards a conclusive proof, and relying on the testimony of others demands that we are convinced that their interpretation of the evidence is correct.

∻ Atheists may argue that since believers do not allow anything to count against their belief in God, then all arguments are flawed because the criticisms raised against them will not be allowed to carry any real weight. They may claim that their conclusions are just as likely as those of theists, and there is no way of verifying or falsifying either position.

Is there a solution?

John Hick argued that eschatological verification could be the solution to establishing whether the atheist's or the theist's claims were valid. This means verification at the end of time, and he draws an analogy between two travellers who are heading down the same road. Neither knows where it leads but one believes that it leads to the Celestial City. He will be proved right or wrong when he gets to the end of the journey but in the meantime he has to live by faith:

During the course of the journey...they entertain different expectations...about its ultimate destination. And yet when they do turn the last corner, it will become apparent that one of them has been right all the time, and the other wrong... their opposed interpretations of the road constituted genuinely rival assertions...whose status has the peculiar characteristic of being guaranteed retrospectively by a future crux.

(Hick, 1966)

Summary and key terms

- A **philosophical proof** will be either *a posteriori* or *a priori*. The difference lies in whether its premises are based on experience or reason.
- *A priori* proofs offer a **deductive**, **analytic** method of proving something to be **logically necessary**. To prove a case *a priori*, the premises on which the argument is based must be logically necessary. In such a case the conclusion is contained within the premises. However, if the premises are not logically sound, the conclusion cannot be logically necessary and the argument has failed or will lead to absurd conclusions. The **Ontological Argument** for the existence of God is typically *a priori*.
- *A posteriori* proofs are inductive and synthetic, and demonstrate the probability of something being the case. To prove a case *a posteriori*, evidence must be accepted as reliable and subject to one universal interpretation. In all other cases, an *a posteriori* proof will offer one of a number of possible conclusions and it is necessary to show that there is overwhelming evidence why one conclusion rather than another should be the correct one. Typically, the **Design (Teleological)** and **Cosmological Arguments** are *a posteriori*.
- Arguments for the existence of God attempt to resolve the difficulty of proving the existence of a God who is not subject to empirical testing but who may offer the simplest explanation for certain phenomena within the universe. They may fail because they still require believers to draw upon their everyday experience of the world and to use limited, human language in order to make claims about the existence of a deity which is believed to be transcendent and ineffable. Ultimately,

arguments or proofs for the existence of God will only be **eschatologically verifiable** — proved true or false — at the end of time.

Exam watch

You may not be asked specifically about proof in this way in your exam, but it will certainly be expected that you can write an essay about the arguments for the existence of God with an underlying understanding of these principles. They should be the foundation for your evaluation of the classic arguments and for any discussion of why attempts to prove the existence of God may succeed or fail. If you are not able to include a discussion of these principles, you will have to fall back entirely on considering whether the proofs are strong or weak simply in and of themselves, and you will run into the danger of just listing what various scholars have said about them, rather than demonstrating your greater philosophical awareness.

Review questions

1 Using examples, consider:
   (a) What is an *a priori* argument?
   (b) What is an *a posteriori* argument?
   (c) Which may be considered more successful as a proof of the existence of God, and why?
2 What are the purposes of arguments for the existence of God?
3 Can an atheist use argument and proof any more successfully than a theist?
4 '*An analysis of arguments for the existence of God will result in valid philosophical reasons to believe in God.*' Discuss this claim with reference to any two arguments for the existence of God.

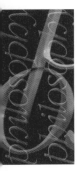

D Faith and reason

Hick's illustration used at the end of the previous section suggests that during this life believers simply have to walk a road of faith, believing that the road they follow will lead to a destination which eschatologically proves that God exists and that their faith has been meaningful. Such faith may be criticised as being anti-intellectual, and believers criticised as having failed to weigh and balance evidence in a rational way. However, for believers, faith should arguably demand that a process of testing, assessing and evaluating the evidence has taken place, otherwise their faith claims are merely unsubstantiated opinion. Drawing conclusions about empirical matters also involves a process of testing evidence, and the same skills are used in matters of faith.

We need, therefore, to be very clear about what we think faith *is* and in what ways it differs from reason. The first point to bear in mind is that there can be no single definition of faith. There are many thousands of religious believers, and whilst perhaps there may not be many thousands of definitions and understandings of what faith is and what it entails, there is certainly more than one. Ludwig Wittgenstein's concept of 'language games' helps here: just as there are many activities which we might justifiably categorise as 'games' which are not identical to each other, so there are different types of faith which resemble one another yet retain their own individual characteristics. We will look at some of these in the course of this section.

However, we need a starting point, and let us consider, therefore, that faith is distinct from that which we call knowledge. When we know something, we suggest that there is no question of it being false, but faith can be mistaken. Nevertheless, those who have religious faith do not live in a permanent state of doubt about that in which they have faith (at least, most do not). They hold their beliefs in the existence of God, his goodness, the existence of an afterlife, or whatever, as strongly as the scientist believes that the earth is round and they have reasons for believing what they hold to be true.

Nevertheless, believers are not exempt from being required to justify their beliefs, and philosophers have approached this in different ways. Some — Descartes, for example — argued that reason can provide a firm foundation for faith; Anselm maintained that the Ontological Proof would enable him to know the existence of God through the use of reason even if his faith failed him. On the other hand, Kierkegaard maintained that reason contradicts religious faith, whilst Aquinas claimed that it supplements it.

1 What is faith?

Religious faith can be divided into two types:

÷ **Propositional faith** — the belief that there is an objective reality to which we ascribe the term God, and that we can make claims about him which are objectively true.
÷ **Non-propositional faith** — a trust in God which may be held even when evidence or experience would seem to point against it. This kind of faith must be based in some personal knowledge of God, and not simply in the acceptance of facts about him.

Propositional faith has certain similarities to our knowledge of things in the world. Our belief that there is a God who is omnipotent and who created the world, for example, might in some ways be similar to our belief that there is a president of the United States, in so far as most of us have not met him and yet believe in his existence from media reports, or have not visited China, and yet believe that it is where the atlas suggests it is. However, non-propositional faith is something different again — it requires us to take a step further from saying that God exists in some objectively real way (which many nominally religious people might feel perfectly comfortable saying) to believing that we have a personal relationship with that same God, which makes a difference to the way we look at the world and live our lives.

Basil Mitchell uses the **parable of the partisan and the stranger** to illustrate the nature of non-propositional faith. In a time of war, a partisan meets a stranger who claims to be the leader of the resistance. The stranger urges the partisan to have faith in him whatever the circumstances, even if he sees the stranger acting in ways which appear to contradict this claim. The partisan is committed to his belief in the stranger's integrity, even when his friends think he is a fool to believe in him. When the stranger appears to be withholding help, or even acting contrary to the partisan's interests, he still believes that the stranger is on his side, and has overwhelming reasons for maintaining his faith. His original encounter with the stranger gave him sufficient confidence to hold on to his faith in him, even when the evidence weighed against it.

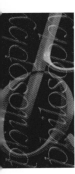

This kind of faith does not allow anything to count decisively against its claims, and the word 'decisively' is important, since the partisan does not deny that sometimes the stranger acts in a way which is contrary to the claims that the stranger made about being 'on his side'. However, the relationship that he established with the stranger at their first meeting has had vital implications for his continued belief in the stranger's integrity.

Kierkegaard's **Postponement Argument** also maintains that religious faith depends on a commitment that requires religious believers not to abandon their faith, even when it is being seriously challenged. This is not because they hold fast to a set of meaningless trivia, to which experience makes no difference, but rather because they have taken a leap of faith that enables them to hold fast to their faith, even when rational arguments to support it fail, or when experience poses serious challenges to it (e.g. suffering and evil). Perhaps Kierkegaard's position is vulnerable in this respect, however, in that religious believers should be able to confront the challenge of both experience and argument. But as Mitchell's parable demonstrated, believers who have entered into a significant faith commitment do recognise the challenges posed, but do not allow them to count decisively against their faith.

Kierkegaard's argument may also be understood as a suspension of judgment. Since in this world and this life the existence of God cannot be decisively proved, we are forced to live as if God does not exist if we are to wait until such proof can be adequately demonstrated. However, this means that we would never be able to make a decision about the personal implications of God's existence, which could have disastrous eschatological consequences. Hence, the believer has to take a step of faith, even when evidence is sparse. Hick's principle of **eschatological verification**, already discussed, works along similar lines. Believers know that their faith will not be confirmed or denied until they reach the end of the road, but they live in the expectation that it will be confirmed, and this gives meaning to their lives and the choices they make.

Kierkegaard proposed a further argument — the **Passion Argument** — to demonstrate that reason is not an appropriate foundation for faith. He argues that religious faith is not about being objectively certain, but about having an intense passion, and the more risk and sacrifice involved, the greater that passionate faith is. If there were a stronger probability of God's existence, the strength of that faith would inevitably weaken, and it would be less valuable. Certainty is therefore not desirable for a life of true faith.

Arguably, Kierkegaard's approach could lead to absurd consequences if we argue that it is valuable to believe passionately in the existence of something for which we have no objective reason or proof. At some stage in our life we may believe in the existence of elves, the tooth fairy, or Santa Claus, but we would be hard-pressed to insist on the value of continuing to believe in them when evidence pointed against it:

Many American children are caused to believe in Santa Claus. But they would not be justified in clinging to this belief after they discovered their parents filling their stockings late Christmas Eve. They would in such a case have a reason for believing that Santa Claus is only a myth.

(Sire, 1994)

2 Bliks

If we did insist on believing in the existence of Santa Claus long after our childhood had passed, allowing nothing to count against it, and finding in every piece of contrary evidence something that would somehow support our continuing belief, we would have what R. M. Hare termed a **blik**. A blik is best understood as a way of looking at the world which is neither verifiable nor falsifiable, but which is not meaningless because it influences the way we interpret the world and the way in which we live. In a debate with Anthony Flew, Hare maintained that religious faith was a blik, although bliks are not confined to religious beliefs. He used the parable of the lunatic and the dons to illustrate his theory:

A certain lunatic is convinced that all the dons want to murder him. His friends introduce him to all the mildest and most respectable dons that they can find, and after each of them has retired, they say 'You see, he doesn't really want to murder you; he spoke to you in a most cordial manner; surely you are convinced now?' But the lunatic replies, 'Yes, but that was only his diabolical cunning; he's really plotting against me the whole time, like the rest of them; I know it, I can tell you.' However many kindly dons are produced, the reaction is still the same.

(Cited in Mitchell (ed.), 1971)

Nothing will count against his belief, and in the same way, Hare argues, nothing will count against that of the religious believer. If asked why he believes, he will simply say, 'Because I do', and since that is the very nature of a blik, that's all he can say. Hare suggests that we all have bliks, not just about murderous dons or the existence of God; whenever Hare gets in his car and turns on the ignition he is operating on the basis of a blik — that the steering will not fail. James Sire (1994) describes it thus:

Suddenly someone asks us why we are doing it and we are at a loss. 'I do believe' we say to ourselves. I believe lots of things. From the simple matter of believing that my computer will work when I turn it on, to the much more questionable belief that my broker is honest or that my fiancée loves me in ways she loves no one else, everything I do is predicated on belief. Sometimes I question my beliefs — especially the complex ones, the ones involving people, life goals, politics and religion. But I always have them. Belief is automatic.

Wittgenstein argues that faith is a process of 'seeing as', or 'experiencing as', which is akin to a blik. Just as we might see a pattern on a page and perceive it or experience it as something quite different to the next person (Wittgenstein's famous example was of the 'duck-rabbit', an image which could equally be 'seen' as a duck or a rabbit), so too we perceive the world differently. Because the world is religiously ambiguous, it can equally be perceived as having religious significance or not — the religious believer interprets the data of the world religiously, the non-believer does so non-religiously; and the ambiguity will only be resolved eschatologically. Neither atheist nor theist will be able to convince each other that their interpretation of the evidence is more reasonable, since they will interpret the 'evidence' quite differently.

3 Anti-realism

So far we have been considering the nature of religious faith as related to an objective reality, and the problems which accompany an attempt to prove the existence of that reality. This is a **realist** approach, working on the assumption that *'a statement is true because it corresponds to the state of affairs that it attempts to describe'* (Peter Vardy's definition). However, anti-realism does not attempt to make statements cohere with an objective reality, but claims that *'Truth depends on what is agreed within the community which depends on the rules of the language game, not on dispassionate enquiry'* (Vardy, 1999). Faith looks like something completely different if we understand it in anti-realist terms. Religious claims belong to their own language game, and to submit them to scientific testing would represent a misunderstanding of how those claims are used and of their context. All language games are self-contained and claims made within them require no justification; hence, when atheists say 'God does not exist' they are not contradicting the theists who say 'God exists', although each are saying that they do not share the 'form of life' to which the other subscribes. It is not, however, a question of who is speaking the truth and who is not.

Although this approach does away with the problems of conflicting truth claims, it does not recognise the fact that most believers when they make a claim about God's existence or his nature *are* saying something which they believe to be objectively true and to cohere with reality. (For more about bliks and anti-realist language, see pp. 115–126.)

4 Non-foundationalism

We have established that if religious faith is a blik, and hence cannot be verified or falsified, we are claiming that religious faith is not dependent upon philosophical justification. This is the principle of **non-foundationalism**, which contradicts **foundationalism** — the view that religious beliefs must be justified by reference to other beliefs. If so, religious beliefs are properly basic beliefs; those which, in Alvin Plantinga's terms, *'don't get their warrant by way of warrant transfer from other beliefs'*.

Plantinga rejected foundationalism on the grounds that if all beliefs need to be justified by reference to other beliefs, then many statements (not just religious ones) would be rendered false since there is nothing that can give them their 'warrant', and like Logical Positivism (see p. 116), it could not meet its own demands — that is, foundationalism itself cannot be justified by reference to other beliefs. Religious belief is therefore a basic belief which itself provides the foundation for other beliefs, but which does not itself need to be proven or demonstrable. In *Are Christian Beliefs Properly Basic?*, Keith DeRose explains:

A properly basic belief, then, is best construed as a sufficiently warranted belief warranted by virtue of its immediate warrant, i.e. independent of any transferred warrant it may enjoy. Thus, a properly basic belief may have some transferred warrant, so long as it doesn't depend on this transferred warrant to be sufficiently warranted.

(http://pantheon.yale.edu/~kd47/basic.htm)

Whilst Plantinga's proposal that religious beliefs need no transferred warrant relieves believers from the burden of finding justification for them, it is worth bearing in mind that theists do attempt to provide rational justification for what they believe — the arguments for the existence of God being a case in point. Either, then, religious

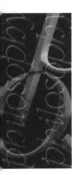

belief is not properly basic, or believers fail to realise that it is, and — perhaps under pressure from atheists — unnecessarily attempt to justify it.

However, Dave Hunt (1996) argues that faith does require a firm foundation of evidence and reasoning because it concerns matters of eschatological importance: '*One may be willing to allow some uncertainty in earthly matters, but only a fool would be comfortable with even the smallest degree of doubt in things which affect him eternally*'. He suggests that the biblical writers do not maintain that religious beliefs should be beyond justification, but that true faith should be founded upon fact, not feelings, intuition or emotion. However, appearances can be deceptive, and our perception of things is quite different from what we actually see — for example, when we read, we do not 'see' the pages and print, but rather an impression made on our brain cells carried by light waves into the eyes and along nerve connections to the brain. We also believe things that we cannot see — the existence of China, for example, if we have never been there. In such a case, we rely on the experience of others and their reports.

In the case of God, Hunt argues, if seeing were believing, no one would believe in his existence, since '*He dwells in the light which no man can approach, who no man has seen, nor can see…*' (1 Timothy 6:16). Faith makes contact with that which is beyond sight, as the writer to the Hebrews makes clear: '*Faith is…the evidence of things not seen*' (Hebrews 11:1). Furthermore, the things in which we place most value are frequently those that are beyond empirical proof — love, joy, peace, truth and goodness, for example. Plato, of course, had perceived this long before the New Testament writers, and we have already examined how his theory of the Forms proposed that the world which is outside our empirical experience is more real than that which we experience through the senses. Real knowledge, he believed, lay beyond the physical (see pp. 3–4). Similarly, Hunt argues that '*Faith must stand on the basis of evidence which is independent of physical sight and scientific verification, but which is irrefutable*'. What this involves therefore is trust, which is only possible through personal knowledge of God, not human religious leaders or allegedly authoritative texts, doctrines or claims.

Hunt conjoined reason, evidence and faith in a vital relationship: '*Reason and evidence may legitimately point the direction for faith to go — and must do so. Indeed, faith must not violate evidence and reason or it would be irrational. Faith takes a step beyond reason, but only in the direction which reason and evidence have pointed*'. He rejects the 'leap of faith' school as promoting an irrational response to nothing more than feelings, intuition and unsubstantiated personal preference, which could apparently justify belief in Star Wars as much as God. Hunt claims, '*Eventually, that belief will prove a delusion and the bubble of euphoria will burst, leaving the person worse off than before*'.

What is good evidence for faith?

Both Hume and Kant rejected reason as the foundation for any secure knowledge of the way things are. In *An Enquiry Concerning Human Understanding*, Hume wrote: '*All inferences from experience, therefore, are effects of custom, not of reasoning*', whilst Kant, in *Prolegomena to Any Future Metaphysics*, claimed that: '*Reason by all its a priori principles never teaches us anything more than objects of possible experience, and even of these nothing more than can be cognized in experience… Reason does not teach us anything concerning the thing itself.*'

Reason is:

÷ **fallible** — we may be mistaken in the conclusions we draw
÷ **limited** — by our experience and the information currently available to us
÷ the basis on which to interpret evidence, but which needs to be illuminated by imagination if man's ideas are to develop
÷ a **rational** means of checking our beliefs or demonstrating their logical possibility

If reason, therefore, cannot confirm to us the existence of God, what counts as good evidence for religious belief? Is it the kind of experience to which we turn to support scientific beliefs? When it is said that religious belief is non-rational, very often it means that it is non-scientific, and hence its claims cannot be verified by the kind of repeatable testing of hypotheses that we would observe in the laboratory. Scientific claims too are open to revision if experience tells against them, however good the evidence for them may have appeared in the first place. Religious beliefs are less open to change — some would say they are immutable, although it is clear that there are considerable problems if we fail to recognise the needs to make them accessible and understandable in a world which is very different from the one in which they first emerged.

5 The will to believe

The evidence on which religious beliefs are based is essentially relational. It is the relationship with God into which believers have entered which provides the evidence — non-tangible and unverifiable — that they require to continue to believe. Remember how Mitchell's partisan had established a relationship with the stranger at their first meeting which was sufficient for him to stand firm in his belief in the stranger, even when events could have counted decisively against it. In a personal relationship, the critical, rational approach taken by the scientist is often inappropriate, and can serve to kill the relationship rather than enhance it. The man who endlessly telephones his partner to establish her whereabouts, questioning every detail — the noise in the background, her previous and subsequent movements, her possible companions — is not using reason to confirm or deny what he cannot see. Rather, he is beyond reason. So, too, believers who continually demand that God prove himself will never be satisfied unless ultimately they are prepared to allow the relationship that they have with God to speak for itself.

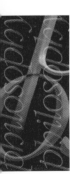

William James adopted a similar approach which he termed '*the will to believe*'. Whilst scientific methodology requires objectivity and neutrality, we do not apply this to every aspect of our lives and there are times when we allow what we hope and fear to influence what we choose to believe rather than insisting upon rigorous testing of our beliefs. James argued that this is particularly true of religious beliefs which are both *forced* (unavoidable whether we believe or don't believe) and *momentous* (they make a significant difference to our lives).

Pascal's Wager

No discussion of the nature of faith would be complete without reference to Pascal's Wager. The French mathematician and philosopher maintained that atheism (non-belief in God) was an irrational stance, since reason — seasoned with a fair pinch of prudence

— should determine that we choose to believe. Pascal observed that there were two possible choices and four possible outcomes:

Choices	Outcomes	
	If correct	**If wrong**
Believe that God exists	Eternal bliss – all gain	Extinction – no gain; no loss
Do not believe that God exists	Extinction – no gain; no loss	Eternal punishment – all loss

Pascal maintained that the rational person will choose to believe since if correct, it is the choice which will guarantee heavenly bliss, and if wrong, no loss has been suffered. Although making this choice may involve some sacrifices during earthly life — obedience to moral rules, for example — Pascal maintained that it was a small price worth paying when the potential rewards were so great. However, to risk the terrible possibility of eternal punishment by betting on God's non-existence was a gamble only a fool would take. Hence, theism is the safe bet, the only option that the rational person should take.

Pascal's theory is simple and not without its attractions for that very reason, but he makes some fundamental errors. First, few religious believers would be prepared to accept that true belief is nothing more than the result of a gamble, and that God would be prepared to reward someone with eternal life if that was the only reason they had chosen to believe. It is tantamount to thinking we can fool God into believing that we have faith when we are only operating on the basis of self-interested calculation.

Second, Pascal seems to think that we can choose to believe that God exists in the same way that we can choose to believe that circles are round or that there are giraffes in Africa. To assume that God exists and to act as if he does, demands more than just an intellectual assent to a safe option. Our deepest beliefs are influenced by many personal factors and if our background and upbringing lead us to believe that God does not exist, we cannot just override them on the basis of a wager.

Finally, if Pascal is wrong about God being the one who will provide rewards and deal out punishments in the afterlife, then the gamble is pointless. The most he can say is that this is what God might do if he exists. Furthermore, he seems to reduce religious belief not only to a gamble, but to nothing more than a way of determining our eschatological fate. He has nothing to say about the benefits of religious belief before death, and implies that a deathbed conversion is all that is required to be saved from the perils of hell.

Summary

- Does religious belief involve blind faith or the rational processes of scientific testing?
- **What is faith?** There are many types, but with shared features and characterised by reasons why a believer holds to be true that which they believe.
- **What is good evidence for faith?** Kant and Hume argued that it must be *a posteriori* and not *a priori*. It is not scientific — rather it is relational. Knowing God provides the grounds for a relationship of trust and faith which does not demand endless questioning. We choose to believe (James), rather than insisting upon rigorous testing of our beliefs.

- **Dave Hunt** — faith without evidence is irrational, but believing is not the same as seeing. Evidence points in the direction which faith must go.
- **Pascal's Wager** — faith is a gamble on the likely outcome of belief or non-belief.

Key terms

Anti-realism — if religious beliefs are not related to an objective reality, they cannot conflict with other beliefs about that which is objectively true.

Bliks — religious beliefs cannot be verified or falsified. We believe because we cannot do otherwise and our interaction with the world is influenced by our beliefs.

Non-foundationalism — religious belief is 'properly basic', needing no 'warrant transfer'.

Non-propositional faith — a trust in God which may be held even when evidence or experience would seem to point against it (parable of the partisan and the stranger). This kind of faith must be based on some personal knowledge of God, and not simply on accepting facts about him.

Passion Argument (Kierkegaard) — faith involves risk.

Postponement Argument (Kierkegaard) — faith is dependent on believing, despite challenges to belief.

Properly basic belief — beliefs which *'don't get their warrant by way of warrant transfer from other beliefs'* (Plantinga).

Propositional faith — the belief that there is an objective reality to which we ascribe the term God, and that we can make claims about him which are objectively true.

Realism — *'A statement is true because it corresponds to the state of affairs that it attempts to describe'* (Vardy).

Suspension of judgment — we have to make decisions now, although they will only be eschatologically verified.

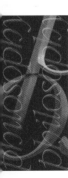

Exam watch

Not all the major examination boards specifically examine this topic, although it may form part of a coursework essay or a synoptic task. However, whether you deal with it in the exam or by other means of assessment, this is a difficult subject. It requires an accurate and relevant handling of specialist language and key terms, and sophisticated philosophical skills. It is not for the fainthearted, but those who enjoy grappling with more conceptual elements should use it to shine, since it is likely to be avoided by the less confident candidates.

Review questions

1 Examine and evaluate at least two different ways of understanding the nature of religious faith.

2 Are faith and reason mutually exclusive?

3 Does faith in God involve more than commitment to the proposition that he exists and possesses certain attributes?

4 Do you find Plantinga's suggestion that religious faith requires no justification convincing?

Topic 2

Arguments for the existence of God

A The Cosmological Argument

1 The need for an explanation

The Cosmological Argument in all its forms responds to the instinctive human aware-ness that the existence of the universe is not explicable without reference to causes and factors outside itself. It cannot be self-causing since it is contingent and only the existence of a first, necessary cause and mover explains the origin of an otherwise 'brute fact'. The argument assumes that the universe has not always been in existence, and for it to come into being, an external agent is necessary. That agent is given the name God. The Cosmological Argument, therefore, and its sister, the Teleological Argument, are concerned with finding an explanation for the universe. Both arguments look to the universe and find that it is not self-explanatory, and it demands that we ask questions about its origin, nature and purpose. Such questions might include:

÷ Why is there something rather than nothing?
÷ Why does the universe possess the form it does, and not some other form?
÷ How can the series of events which culminate in the universe be explained?
÷ Must a chain of movers have a first cause, or is an infinite regress of causes a sufficient explanation?
÷ What kind of cause or agency is necessary for the universe to come into being?
÷ How can the features (i.e. regularity and purpose) of the universe be explained?

The success of the Cosmological Argument will depend entirely on our willingness to ask these questions and to seek an answer to them, and we should not take for granted that everyone is inclined to do so. It was this question that F. C. Copleston and Bertrand Russell famously debated in 1947, Russell doubting whether it was even meaningful, let alone important, to argue the case for a cause of the universe, and having established that for him it was 'a question that has no meaning', declared to Copleston, 'What do you say — shall we pass on to some other issue?' For Copleston this was an unsatisfactory response, and he later wrote:

If one does not wish to embark on the path which leads to the affirmation of a transcendent being, however the latter may be described...one has to deny the reality of the problem, assert that things 'just are'; and that the existential problem is a pseudo-problem. And if one refuses even to sit down at the chessboard and make a move, one cannot, of course, be checkmated...

(Copleston, 1961)

The Cosmological Argument is not satisfied with finding partial explanations for the universe either, but seeks a complete explanation, or what Leibniz called a 'sufficient reason'. It is over this need for a complete explanation that supporters and opponents of the argument are crucially divided:

Russell: But when is an explanation adequate? Suppose I am about to make a flame with a match. You may say that the adequate explanation of that is that I rub it on the box.

Copleston: Well, for practical purposes — but theoretically, that is only a partial explanation. An adequate explanation must ultimately be a total explanation, to which nothing further can be added.

(Cited in Hick (ed.), 1964)

The Cosmological Argument reaches the conclusion that God is the ultimate, complete and adequate explanation for the universe, and possesses in himself all the necessary characteristics to be that complete explanation. In this way, although the argument is essentially *a posteriori*, it does depend on the Ontological Argument having proven that God is analytically a necessary being. But more of that later.

Richard Swinburne is a great contemporary supporter of the quest for explanation reflected in the Cosmological Argument. He writes:

The human quest for explanation inevitably and rightly seeks for the ultimate explanation of everything observable — that object or objects on which everything else depends for its existence and properties... A may be explained by B, and B by C, but in the end there will be some one object on whom all other objects depend. We will have to acknowledge something as ultimate — the great metaphysical issue is what that is.

(Swinburne, 1996)

For Swinburne, as for Aquinas before him, God is the simplest explanation:

Theism claims that every other object which exists is caused to exist and kept in existence by just one substance, God... There could in this respect be no simpler explanation than one which postulated only one cause. Theism is simpler than polytheism. And theism postulates for its one cause, a person, infinite degrees of those properties which are essential to persons...infinite power...infinite knowledge... and infinite freedom...

(ibid.)

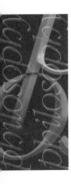

(*Note:* The principle that the simplest explanation is the most satisfactory, and the most likely, is known as *Ockham's Razor*, sometimes expressed by the recommendation 'Do not multiply entities unnecessarily'. In other words, if a simple, single, self-sufficient explanation can be found, there is nothing to be gained philosophically or intellectually in pursuing other explanations.)

The Cosmological Argument is not just a Christian attempt to prove the existence of the classical theistic deity. Plato and Aristotle postulated the need for a craftsman and a cause of all things, and the Islamic form of the argument, known as the Kalam Argument, which goes back to al-Kindi (*c.* 870) and al-Ghazali (1058–1111), proposes a

Cosmological Argument as follows:

P1: Whatever comes into being must have a cause.
P2: The universe came into being.
C: The universe must have a cause.

The difficulty inherent in the argument is that it postulates a cause which comes into existence without having a cause itself, but, arguably, there is no reason why there may not be such a cause, only that science has not yet discovered it. The principle is that if something does not contain its own reason for existing, then it must have been caused by something else, and that by something else again. Only when we arrive at a self-causing, necessary being can we say we have reached the end of the chain of causes and effects.

Remember that the Cosmological Argument is ***a posteriori***, **synthetic** and **inductive**. (The terms are explained on pp. 15–16.) This has important implications for the success or failure of the argument since the conclusion it reaches is not contained within the premises, so we need to establish overwhelming reasons to argue that God is a better conclusion than any other to which the evidence may point.

2 Aquinas and the Five Ways

The most famous Christian application of the argument was offered by Thomas Aquinas (1225–1274) in the *Summa Theologica*. He proposed 'Five Ways' which proved the existence of God, of which the first three are Cosmological Arguments, whilst the fourth is a form of an Ontological Argument, and the fifth, a Teleological Argument.

The First Way — from motion

It is certain, and evident to our senses, that in the world some things are in motion. Now whatever is moved is moved by another... It is therefore impossible that in the same respect and in the same way a thing should be both mover and moved... If that by which it is moved be itself moved, then this also must needs be moved by another... But this cannot go on to infinity, because then there would be no first mover, and, subsequently, no other mover... Therefore it is necessary to arrive at a first mover, moved by no other; and this everyone understands to be God.

(Thomas Aquinas, *Summa Theologica*, Third Article, 'Whether God exists',
cited in Hick (ed.), 1964)

We can set this argument out in the form of premises and a conclusion:

P1: Nothing can move itself, since nothing can be both mover and moved, yet things are evidently in motion.
P2: An infinite chain of movers that has no beginning can have no successive or ultimate movers.
C: There must therefore be a first mover that causes motion in all things, and this we call God.

Aquinas called motion 'the reduction of something from potentiality to actuality'. For example, fire, which is actually hot, changes wood, which is potentially hot, to a state of being actually hot. Motion, therefore, is a change of state, and not just movement in time and space from one place to another. However, that motion requires an explanation since we know that nothing can be in both potentiality and actuality in the same respect — in other words, nothing can be simultaneously hot and cold. Something is required to bring about the change from hot to cold and vice versa and it must be something upon which that which is changed is dependent. Aquinas argues that God is the initiator of change and motion in all things.

The Second Way — from cause

The Second Way is from the nature of efficient cause. In the world of sensible things we find there is an order of efficient causes. There is no case known (neither is it, indeed, possible) in which a thing is found to be the efficient cause of itself; for so it would be prior to itself, which is impossible… Therefore it is necessary to admit to a first efficient cause, to which everyone gives the name of God.

(ibid.)

This follows the same lines of reasoning as the first way:

÷ All things are caused and since nothing can be its own cause (a logical impossibility)…
÷ there must be a first cause (God) on which all other causes depend.
÷ An infinite chain of causes is rejected since in an infinite chain there can be no first cause.
÷ God is therefore the first cause of all that exists.

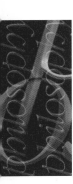

In this first way, Aquinas observes that there is something different about God. Whilst all other beings are caused, God is not. Furthermore, God is not just the first cause in a chain of causes which are otherwise just like him, he is one on whom all subsequent causes and effects are dependent. In the Second Way, as with the first, Aquinas rejects an infinite chain of causes but insists that without a first cause there could be no subsequent causes and so in effect, without a first cause, there would be nothing at all.

We could set out Aquinas's arguments so far as follows:

P1: The universe exists and is in a constant state of flux.
P2: Everything in existence has a cause and that which is in a state of motion must be moved.
P3: Causes come before their effects; that which is moved cannot move itself.
P4: A chain of causes and effects, movers and moved cannot regress to infinity.
P5: There must therefore be a first cause and first mover which is not in itself an effect.
P6: This first cause/mover is dependent on nothing else to come into existence.
P7: This first, self-causing cause, self-moving mover, is God.
C: God exists.

The Third Way — from necessity and contingency

The Third Way is taken from possibility and necessity… We find in nature things that are possible to be and not to be, since they are found to be generated, and to be corrupted, and consequently, it is possible for them to be and not to be… Therefore if everything can not-be then at one time there was nothing in existence…(and) it would have been impossible for anything to

*have begun to exist and thus even now nothing would be in existence, which is absurd...
Therefore we cannot but admit the existence of some being having of itself its own necessity,
and not receiving it from another, but rather causing in others their necessity. This all men speak
of as God.*

(ibid.)

Hence:

- ÷ Everything we can point to is dependent upon factors beyond itself and thus is contingent.
- ÷ The presence of each thing can only be explained by reference to those factors which themselves depend on other factors.
- ÷ These factors demand an ultimate explanation in the form of a necessary being (God), dependent on nothing outside himself.
- ÷ God's necessary existence is established ***de re***. The very nature of things in the universe demands that God exists necessarily and not contingently. Copleston defines such a being as one that must and cannot *not* exist.

The third is perhaps the most interesting of the ways. Since beings and items in the universe are capable of existing or not existing (i.e. are contingent), it is impossible that *all* beings should be capable of existing or not existing, or else where would the impetus for the existence of anything come from? Copleston (1961) maintained that if we do not postulate the existence of a necessary being, '*we do not explain the presence here and now of beings capable of existing or not existing. Therefore we must affirm the existence of a being which is absolutely necessary and completely independent.*'

3 Other approaches to the argument

In *Theodicy*, Gottfried Leibniz explained the Cosmological Argument in the form of the principle of sufficient reason:

Suppose the book of the elements of geometry to have been eternal, one copy having been written down from an earlier one. It is evident that even though a reason can be given for the present book out of a past one, we should never come to a full reason. What is true of the books is also true of the states of the world. If you suppose the world eternal, you will suppose nothing but a succession of states, and will not find in any of them a sufficient reason.

Liebniz's argument is that even if the universe had always been in existence, it would still require an explanation, or a sufficient reason for its existence, since we need to establish why there is something rather than nothing. By going backwards in time forever we will never arrive at such a complete explanation. Leibniz identified that even if we are sure that the universe has always existed, there is nothing within the universe to show *why* it exists — it is not self-explanatory, so the reason for its existence must lie outside of it. At the heart of the argument is the premise that there must be a cause for the whole which explains the whole, and unless this is accepted as a meaningful and purposeful exercise, the argument will fail.

Another key feature of Aquinas's form of the Cosmological Argument is the rejection of infinite regress. After all, if we were satisfied with the explanation that all effects and causes, movements and mover, could be traced back infinitely in time without ever needing, factually or logically, to arrive at a first cause, then there is no purpose to the argument. J. L. Mackie illustrates Aquinas's rejection of infinite regress with a modern analogy: we would not expect a railway train consisting of an infinite number of carriages, the last pulled along by the second last, the second last by the third last, and so on, to move anywhere without an engine. This analogy demonstrates the principle of dependency in the argument; in an infinite series of causes and effects there is nothing to support them. God is like an engine — not just another truck, but a machine that has the power to move without requiring something else to act upon it.

Copleston supported Aquinas's rejection of infinite regress on the grounds that an infinite chain of **contingent beings** could only ever consist of contingent beings, which would never be able to bring itself into existence. The most an eternal series of contingent beings can do is maintain an eternal presence of contingent beings; it cannot explain how they came into being in the first place:

You see, I don't believe that the infinity of the series of the events — I mean a horizontal series, so to speak — if such an infinity could be proved, would be in the slightest degree relevant to the situation. If you add up chocolates, you get chocolates after all and not a sheep. If you add up chocolates to infinity, you presumably get an infinite number of chocolates. So if you add up contingent beings to infinity, you still get contingent beings, not a necessary being. An infinite series of contingent beings will be, to my way of thinking, as unable to cause itself as one contingent being.

(Cited in Hick (ed.), 1964)

Richard Swinburne (1996) argues that the real need for an explanation lies in the fact that it is more likely that there be nothing rather than something:

It is extraordinary that there should exist anything at all. Surely the most natural state of affairs is simply nothing: no universe, no God, nothing. But there is something. And so many things. Maybe chance could have thrown up the odd electron. But so many particles! Not everything will have an explanation. But...the whole progress of science and all other intellectual enquiry demands that we postulate the smallest number of brute facts. If we can explain the many bits of the universe by one simple being which keeps them in existence, we should do so — even if inevitably we cannot explain the existence of that simple being.

The supposition that the universe had a beginning, which is the cornerstone of the Cosmological Argument, is surprisingly supported in many ways by the findings of modern science (see pp. 91–99). The Big Bang theory, although typically seen as offering a challenge to religious interpretations of the universe, proposes a finite history of the universe — a beginning point, not an infinite regress of events. Furthermore, if the universe has an infinite history, then an infinite number of years must have already passed to arrive at the present, which is nonsense.

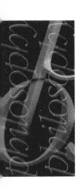

Key terms

Aseity — a necessary being possesses the quality of aseity.

Contingent beings — beings that are dependent upon other beings or events. A contingent being may also be called a possible being.

Necessary being — a being that is not dependent on other beings, but is self-causing and self-sustaining.

4 Criticisms of the argument

David Hume proposed the classic criticisms of the Cosmological Argument in *Dialogues Concerning Natural Religion*. More recent scholars have taken up his criticisms, and they essentially revolve around three issues:

1 Why presume the need for a cause?
2 Why look for an explanation for the whole?
3 Is the concept of a necessary being meaningful?

Hume, like Russell after him, argued that the notion of a necessary being is an inconsistent one since there is no being the non-existence of which is inconceivable. Even if there was such a being, why should it be God? He stated:

Any particle of matter, it is said, may be conceived to be annihilated, and any form may be conceived to be altered. Such an annihilation or alteration is not therefore impossible. But it seems a great partiality not to perceive that the same argument extends equally to the Deity, so far as we have any conception of him...

(Cited in Hick (ed.), 1964)

Even if it were reasonable to postulate a first mover/cause, why should it be the God of classical theism? Aquinas is guilty of an inductive leap of logic in moving from the need for a first mover to identifying it as God when nothing in the premises of the argument leads logically to that conclusion. Obviously, proponents of the argument believe that they have overwhelmingly good reasons why it should be God rather than anything else, but Hume argued:

Why may not the material universe be the necessarily existent being, according to this pretended explication of necessity? We dare not affirm that we know all the qualities of matter; and for aught we can determine, it may contain some qualities which, were they known, would make its non-existence appear as great a contradiction as that twice two is five.

(ibid.)

Hume is playing Devil's advocate here — he knows that the nature of the universe is such that it would be virtually impossible to claim that it possessed some essential necessity, but his point is this: why should we be able to say that God — unknowable and inconceivable — possesses qualities which make his non-existence logically impossible? Furthermore, any perceived truth of the claim that there is a God cannot be assumed in order to establish the verisimilitude of an argument which is supposed to prove his existence.

Hume observes that the argument begins with a concept familiar to us — the universe — but claims to be able to reach conclusions about things that are outside our experience. This criticism applies to all arguments from natural theology or which attempt to argue from some facet of human experience to God, and yet proponents of the argument claim that there is sufficient evidence in the natural world to point irrefutably to the existence of God.

To the question of why, if we can explain each item in the chain, we need to find a cause for the whole chain, Hume wrote:

Did I show you the particular causes of each individual in a collection of twenty particles of matter, I should think it very unreasonable should you afterwards ask me what was the cause of the whole twenty. This is sufficiently explained in explaining the cause of the parts. (ibid.)

Hume's criticism is effectively arguing that partial explanations should be quite sufficient and that it is somehow gratuitous to seek an explanation for the whole if we are able to explain the parts. The linking together of individual causes and effects into a whole is merely arbitrary, Hume maintained, and makes no difference to the nature of things.

Even if specific instances of things in the universe require an explanation, why should this be the case for the universe as a whole? It does not work to move from the specific to the general. This is a well-worn criticism that Russell famously exploited in his dialogue with F. C. Copleston using a **reductio ad absurdum**:

Every man who exists has a mother, and it seems to me your argument is that therefore the human race must have a mother, but obviously the human race hasn't a mother — that's a different logical sphere. (ibid.)

In the dialogue, Russell claimed that some things are 'just there' and require no explanation, and that the universe was such a case. It is a 'brute fact'. Interestingly, Russell did not dismiss the quest for an explanation per se. He maintained that it was a fallacy to assume that you would arrive at one: *A man may look for gold without assuming that there's gold everywhere; if he finds gold, good luck, if he doesn't, he's had bad luck* (ibid.).

Finally, the Cosmological Argument could be criticised for presuming a principle of shared essences. We say whatever is moved is moved by something already moving, and what is caused is caused by that which is already caused, but is this necessarily the case? After all, as has been variously suggested, a king does not need to be crowned by a monarch, dead men don't commit murders, a surgeon who amputates limbs need not be limbless, and a farmer who fattens his livestock need not himself be fat!

5 The perennial value of the argument

Despite the many criticisms that have been raised against the argument, its strength as an *a posteriori* argument, which draws on evidence that is universally available and which in itself cannot be challenged, gives lasting appeal.

Whilst John Hick maintained that *'The atheistic option that the universe is "just there" is the more economical option'*, Richard Swinburne disagrees, arguing that *'God is simpler than anything we can imagine and gives a simple explanation for the system'*. According to Herbert McCabe (1980): *'The question is: is there an unanswered question about the existence of the world? Can we be puzzled by the existence of the world instead of nothing? I can be and am; and this is to be puzzled about God'*.

However, although it is perfectly reasonable and legitimate to propose as a hypothesis that there is a God who created the universe, the argument will only work if it reduces the number of unanswered questions. Ultimately, the argument cannot explain God, only postulate God as an explanation, and if we are not satisfied with the idea of God as a being who himself requires no explanation, the argument will fail.

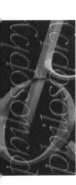

Summary

- **The Cosmological Argument** — seeks to satisfy the need to find an explanation for the universe and to answer questions about origins and existence. It stands or falls on whether those questions are perceived to be meaningful and necessary, and whether a complete, sufficient explanation is somehow better than partial explanations. Swinburne argues that since it is more reasonable that there is nothing rather than something, then the existence of something needs to be explained.
- **The Islamic Kalam Argument** — pre-dates Aquinas's model, arguing that nothing comes into being with being caused. Three of Aquinas's Five Ways — motion, causation, and necessity and contingency (possibility) — point out that there cannot be an infinite chain of movers, causes or necessary beings, and all need a first, ultimate and complete explanation. A relationship of dependency exists between causes and effects, movements and movers.
- **Leibniz** — sought not just to show that something exists but why it does. Infinite regress will provide no answers because it does not offer the possibility of something possessing a different agency which can bring a chain into being. Mackie used the analogy of an infinite chain of railway carriages going nowhere without an engine; Copleston — an infinity of chocolates cannot lead to a sheep.
- **David Hume** — argued that necessary existence is an incoherent concept, and that the Design Argument does not prove the God of classical theism — rather, it moves from what we know to what we don't know. He asked, why seek a cause for the whole? Why does anything need an explanation at all?
- However, *a posteriori* arguments have **perennial value**. God is the simplest explanation. We will always be asking questions about the nature and origin of the universe.

Exam watch

The same words of warning are applicable to all the arguments for the existence of God. First, it is vital that you have grasped the material on proof and probability before you look at the Cosmological Argument. The questions asked at A2 will demand that candidates can look at arguments in the context of the philosophical concept of proof and you will cut yourself off from valuable marks if you can only offer an outline and basic critique of the argument. In many cases too a ceiling mark will be set for students who offer a competent, even good, summary of the argument, but who then fail to address the question set. Even at AS you should be able to use the appropriate terminology and go beyond what is effectively a narrative of the argument. To this end, try to avoid thinking of the argument simply in terms of Aquinas, Hume, the Kalam Argument, or any other formulation of the argument or its criticisms, but think of it in terms of what it is seeking to *do*. This means understanding pp. 29–31, which are about the need to find explanations for the universe and items within it. Only then will you be in a position to understand the implications of the argument and its weaknesses.

Review questions

1. (a) Examine the key features of the Cosmological Argument for the existence of God.
   (b) For what reasons have some thinkers rejected the Cosmological Argument? How far is it possible to regard the Cosmological Argument as strong?

2 How far does the Cosmological Argument serve to provide a coherent explanation of the universe?

3 *'It is possible for there to be a consistently religious and a consistently atheistic interpretation of the universe.'* How far does the Cosmological Argument serve to support a consistently religious interpretation of the universe?

B The Teleological Argument

1 Explaining order and purpose

In our study of the Cosmological Argument we saw how its proponents place considerable emphasis on the need to find an explanation for why the universe exists when it could so easily not exist. The universe itself is neither factually nor logically necessary, so its very existence is something which demands an explanation. The Teleological Argument (from the Greek, **telos**, meaning end or purpose) is in effect a special application of the Cosmological Argument in that it too, through an *a posteriori*, inductive, synthetic argument, attempts to propose an explanation for a particular feature of the universe.

In short, the Teleological (or Design) Argument claims that certain phenomena within the universe appear to display features of design, in so far as they are perfectly adapted to fulfil their function. Such design cannot come about by chance and can only be explained with reference to an intelligent, personal designer. It is possible to draw an analogy between the works of human design and the works of nature, and to conclude that there are sufficient similarities to infer design of a similar nature. Since the works of nature are far greater than the works of man, an infinitely greater designer must be postulated, which points towards the existence of God as the one who possesses the necessary attributes.

Like the Cosmological Argument, the Design Argument is an ancient one, significantly predating Christianity. The raw material on which the argument is based is again the universe — immediately and universally accessible to humans — and the notions arising from a close examination of that universe are not exclusively Christian, or even theistic. Order, or at least the appearance of it, is hard, though not impossible, to deny. The question therefore is how we explain the order evident in the universe. There are certainly explanations which do not lead to the God of classical theism, or indeed to any personal explanation at all — in that a personal explanation involves a being (or beings) who operates on something at least approaching the principles of intelligence, involved in the planning and ordering of the human race. However, proponents of the Design Argument maintain that a non-theistic explanation for the orderliness of the universe is not a complete explanation. Theists need not be committed to rejecting scientific explanations of the universe and its features, but they will not be satisfied that these explanations are the whole story. Richard Swinburne (1996) writes:

So there is our universe. It is characterised by vast, all persuasive temporal order, the conformity of nature to formula, recorded in the scientific laws formulated by humans. It started off in such

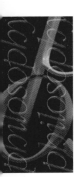

a way...as to lead to the evolution of animals and humans. These phenomena are clearly things too big for science to explain... Note that I am not postulating a 'God of the gaps', a god merely to explain the things which science has not yet explained. I am postulating a God to explain what science explains; I do not deny that science explains, but I postulate God to explain why science explains.

Just as the Cosmological Argument aimed to explain a range of phenomena within the overall question of why the universe exists, so too does the Teleological Argument consider a variety of features which are all raised by a contemplation of the question, 'Why is the universe is as it is?' Broadly speaking, those features are:

- ÷ **Order** — regularities in the behaviour of objects and laws in the universe which seem to hold good almost all the time.
- ÷ **Benefit** — the universe is more than an orderly structure, providing all that is necessary for life and more. The presence of beauty, for example, appears to be beneficial without being technically necessary.
- ÷ **Purpose** — objects within the universe appear to be working towards an end or purpose. Humans are goal-orientated, and it appears that the universe consists of goal-orientated beings or items. Conceivably, the universe as a whole may be working towards an ultimate purpose.
- ÷ **Suitability for human life** — the order exhibited by the universe provides the ideal environment for human life to exist and to flourish.

In seeking to explain these features, proponents of the Design Argument are committed to rejecting an apparently easy explanation: chance. The features of order and purpose, suitability for human life, even the providential nature of the universe, could all be explained as the result of one huge coincidence, akin to taking a million six-sided dice and with a single throw turning up a six on every one of them. The Teleological Argument seeks to demonstrate that the delicate balance of the universe is such that the probability of it coming about by chance is far too remote to be even a partial, let alone complete, explanation.

There are many ways in which this has been expressed, but the following parable offered by Dave Hunt (1996) is a useful starting point:

Suppose two survivors of a shipwreck have drifted for days in a life raft across the South Pacific and at last are washed ashore on an island. Their great hope, of course, is that the island is inhabited so they can find food, medical attention and a means of returning to their distant homes. Pushing their way into the jungle, they suddenly come upon an automated factory operating full tilt. Though no persona is visible, products are being manufactured, packaged and labeled for shipping. One of the parties exclaims 'Praise God! The island is inhabited! Someone must have made and oversees this factory!' 'You're crazy,' replies his companion. 'There's absolutely no reason to believe that this thing was designed and put together by some intelligent being. It just happened by chance over who knows how many billions of years.' The first man looks down at his feet and sees a watch with a broken wristband lying in the dirt. Again he exclaims, 'Look! A watch! This proves the island's inhabited!' 'You've got to be kidding,' retorts his companion. 'That thing is just a conglomeration of atoms that happened to come together in that form by chance plus billions of years of random selection.'

The two characters in this parable represent sharply opposing positions — one believes that the evidence he sees leads to the only possible explanation that the island is inhabited by intelligent and purposeful beings, whilst his friend maintains that such an explanation goes way beyond the evidence, and is satisfied to say that it has come about by chance. Of course, the division need not be so sharp, as Swinburne observed. It is possible to recognise the claims of science with regard to evolution and modern cosmology, but still to find the need for God to explain those explanations. However, the burden of proof seems to rest with the theist to demonstrate that the universe demands in some way the existence of an intelligent, designing mind, which created and planned the universe for the benefit of the beings — and not just human beings — that inhabit it.

2 Classic approaches to the argument

Thomas Aquinas included a form of the Teleological Argument as the fifth of his Five Ways, which he termed 'From the Governance of the World':

We see that things which lack knowledge, such as natural bodies, act for an end, and this is evident from their acting always, or nearly always, in the same way, so as to obtain the best result. Hence it is plain that they achieve their end not fortuitously, but designedly. Now whatever lacks knowledge cannot move towards an end, unless it be directed by some being endowed with knowledge and intelligence...and this being we call God.

(Cited in Hick (ed.), 1964)

In the first three ways we saw how Aquinas rejected the possibility of an infinite regress of movers and causes to explain the existence of contingent, mutable beings, and concluded that a first mover and first cause, to which he gave the name God, was a necessary requisite of the universe. In the Fifth Way, he observes that non-rational beings nevertheless act in a way which leads to the best result — he might have given as an example the annual migration of vast pods of grey whales from their sub-arctic feeding grounds off the Alaskan coast to their Mexican breeding grounds, a journey of some 20,000 km, taking up to three months. Aquinas maintained that since such behaviour patterns rarely change, and their end result is beneficial, there must be a purpose to them, and if non-rational beings can work towards such a goal, something must be directing them to do so.

Although Kant did not subscribe to the Teleological Argument in particular, he did comment in *Critique of Pure Reason*: '*This proof always deserves to be mentioned with respect. It is the oldest, the clearest and the most accordant with the common reason of mankind*'. It is the *a posteriori* and empirical nature of the argument which accords it such favour. Reason tells us that the behaviour of the universe and its inhabitants is not satisfactorily explained by the universe itself, and an intelligent authority, external to the universe, seems to be the simplest solution.

William Paley and the watch

William Paley (1743–1805) is often criticised for offering a version of the Teleological Argument 30 years after David Hume had soundly denounced the argument for resting on the insecure foundations of an unsound analogy — that drawn between humanly manufactured machines and the world. However, given that the argument continues to be strongly supported in the twenty-first century, this seems to be an unnecessarily

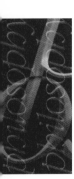

harsh criticism. Indeed, Richard Swinburne (1996) claims: *'The analogy of animals to complex machines seems to me correct, and its conclusion justified'*.

Paley's analogy of the watch and the watchmaker is a classic of its genre:

In crossing a heath, suppose I pitched my foot against a stone, and were asked how the stone came to be there, I might possibly answer that, for anything I knew to the contrary, it had lain there for ever; nor would it, perhaps, be very easy to show the absurdity of this answer. But suppose I found a watch upon the ground, and it should be inquired how the watch happened to be in that place, I should hardly think of the answer which I had before given — that, for anything I knew, the watch might always have been there. Yet why should not this answer serve for the watch as well as for the stone? Why is it not as admissible in the second case as in the first? For this reason...that when we come to inspect the watch we perceive...that its several parts are framed and put together for a purpose...

(Cited in Hick (ed.), 1964)

Just as the discovery of a watch on a heath could not be satisfactorily explained by saying it had 'always been there' the order evident in the universe demands an explanation. The watch serves as an analogy for the world: it demonstrates purpose, design and **telos** (an end or ultimate function). All parts of the watch unite to fulfil that function and this unity cannot be explained by chance.

Paley anticipates several criticisms against his argument, some of which had been addressed by Hume, and argues that they do not destroy the essential aim of the argument — to demonstrate that the watch (world) is the product of a designer. He does not intend to draw any conclusions about the character of the designer, or even of the design, in terms of its perfection, infinity or rarity. Rather, he claims, even if the watch goes wrong or shows evidence of bad design (e.g. the problem of evil), or if we have never seen a watch before, we could still deduce that it had been designed, and if we cannot work out the function that individual parts contribute to the whole, it does not disprove that it has been designed.

Paley is highly critical of the suggestions that the watch might have taken on the form it has by chance or by some impersonal operating agency, such as a principle of order or the laws of metallic nature, or even that the appearance of design was in some way a trick to persuade people that it had been designed. Above all he objects to the criticism that it is impossible to come to conclusions about design on the basis of the limited information available:

He knows enough for his argument; he knows the utility of the end: he knows the subserviency and adaptation of the means to the end. These points being known, his ignorance of other points, his doubts concerning other points, affect not the certainty of his reasoning. The consciousness of knowing little need not beget a distrust of that which he does know.

(ibid.)

Paley goes on in his argument to show the intricacy of animals and humans, leading to the conclusion that God must have been their maker. He famously used the example of the eye that appears to have design and clearly has a purpose. In keeping with scientists and naturalists of the eighteenth century, he was struck forcibly by the intricacy of human bodies and their component parts. The invention of the microscope probably did much to increase an awareness of this complexity.

3 Other applications of the argument

The argument from probability

Richard Swinburne approaches the argument from the angle of probability, suggesting that since theism itself is highly probable, the evidence of design and order in the universe increases this probability. He makes a number of key observations about the universe: its fittingness for human life and its scope, allowing human beings to share in God's creative activity and to make significant choices. These features, he believes, are to be expected within a theistic system:

The simple hypothesis of theism leads us to expect all the phenomena that I have been describing with some reasonable degree of probability. God being omnipotent is able to produce a world orderly in these respects. And he has a good reason to choose to do so: a world containing human persons is a good thing... God being perfectly good, is generous. He wants to share.

(Swinburne, 1996)

A providential universe

Swinburne argues that theism is the best explanation for the design that is apparently evident in the universe, and points not only to the order and purpose it displays but to the **providential** nature of the universe — it contains within it everything that is necessary for survival. He maintains that it is a universe in which humans are designed to occupy the highest position, and that natural laws function within the universe, making it a place where humans can meaningfully contribute to its development and maintenance. This kind of universe is, he argues, the kind of universe that God would have reason to create, and not just for human beings but for animals too. The higher animals can reason and plan, observes Swinburne, and are enabled to do so by the predictability of the most obvious aspects of the natural world. This aspect of the argument also implies that God had a choice about the kind of universe he could create and, as a result, the universe cannot be the product of chance.

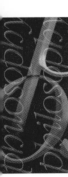

The Aesthetic Argument

The universe is more than simply orderly; it possesses a natural beauty beyond that which is necessary to live. Some of that beauty is part of order — the beautiful patterns of the stars, for example, or the changing colours of the seasons. Our appreciation of it reflects not only our attraction to that which is aesthetically pleasing, but also our dislike of chaos. Chaos is ugly and we seek to impose order upon it if it does not occur naturally.

However, we also find beauty in things which are not part of the natural world and have no part to play in the survival of the species. Art, music, literature and culture all contribute to the way we perceive the world as a beneficial, appealing and attractive place, although we would be able to live without them. F. R. Tennant observes:

Nature is not just beautiful in places; it is saturated with beauty — on the telescopic and microscopic scale. Our scientific knowledge brings us no nearer to understanding the beauty of music. From an intelligibility point of view, beauty seems to be superfluous and to have little survival value.

(Cited in Cole, 1999)

This aspect of the universe has long appealed to a wider audience than educated philosophers, inspiring religious writers and thinkers. The nineteenth-century Jesuit poet Gerard Manley Hopkins wrote of how the beauty of the universe is besmirched by man, and yet rises up again to reveal God's glory:

The world is charged with the grandeur of God,
It will flame out, like shining from shook foil...
And all is seared with trade, bleared, smeared with toil...
And for all this, nature is never spent;
There lives the dearest freshness, deep down things...

More prosaically, Mrs C. F. Alexander is well known for writing:

All things bright and beautiful,
All creatures great and small,
All things wise and wonderful,
The Lord God made them all.

Design and evolution — the anthropic principle

Contrary to what might be suggested, the Teleological Argument need not reject the principles of evolution in order to postulate a designing God. However, theistic supporters of evolution argue that scientific principles alone are not sufficient to explain how evolution led to the perfectly balanced natural order that prevails. Again, F. R. Tennant writes:

The fitness of the world to be the home of living beings depends on certain primary conditions — astronomical, thermal, chemical, and so on, and on the coincidence of qualities, apparently not causally connected to each other. The unique assembly of unique properties on so vast a scale makes the organic world comparable to a single organism... The world is compatible with a single throw of the dice and common sense is not foolish in suspecting the dice to have been loaded.

(Cited in Vardy, 1999)

This is known as the **anthropic principle**, which proposes that the reason and purpose of the universe's existence is the support of human life:

As we look out into the Universe and identify the many accidents of physics and astronomy that have worked together to our benefit, it almost seems as if the Universe must in some sense have known that we were coming.

(Freeman Dyson, cited in Barrow and Tipler, 1986)

According to this perspective, scientific explanations of the universe are compatible with the Teleological Argument since evolution or a cosmic explosion can be seen to be the means that the designer has employed. Furthermore, it could be claimed that the order of the universe is beyond chance — in other words, the odds on it coming about by chance are so remote as to render it virtually impossible. Evolution could then be part of God's plan for the world. Although many Victorian Christians found their faith seriously challenged by Darwin, in the late nineteenth century Archbishop Temple claimed: *'The doctrine of evolution leaves the argument for an intelligent Creator and Governor of the earth stronger than it was before'* (cited in Cole, 1999). Indeed, it is possible to argue that the laws which govern natural selection were brought about by God because, through them, human beings and animals would evolve. Richard Swinburne (1996) maintains: *'The very success of science in showing us how deeply orderly the natural world is, provides strong grounds for believing that there is an even deeper cause of that order'.*

(For more on the relationship between religious and scientific interpretations of the universe, see pp. 91–99.)

Order and probability

It is possible to criticise this view, however, with the observation that unless the universe did contain exactly the right conditions for life and if there were no natural laws, there would be no humans or animals, and we would not be here to comment upon how improbable it all is! In other words, of course we perceive order in the universe — there could be nothing else, or we would not be here to perceive it. Order is not improbable, and we should not approach it as if it were extraordinary. Akin to this idea is that of A. J. Ayer, who claimed that to speak of a designed universe is meaningless, since unless we could say what the world would be like without design we cannot reach the conclusion that this world is designed.

However, the *amount* of order in the universe still needs an explanation, since it would appear to be far more than is necessary for human survival. Furthermore, Swinburne observes that we don't simply perceive order rather than disorder but are amazed by the fact that there is order rather than disorder. Just because we are there to observe it doesn't make it less improbable. He illustrates this with a parable:

Suppose that a madman kidnaps a victim and shuts him in a room with a card-shuffling machine. The machine shuffles ten packs of cards simultaneously and then draws a card from each pack and exhibits simultaneously the ten cards. The kidnapper tells the victim that he will shortly set the machine to work and it will exhibit its first draw, but that unless the draw consists of an ace of hearts from each pack, the machine will simultaneously set off an explosion which will kill the victim, in consequence of which he will not see which cards the machine drew. The machine is set to work, and to the amazement and relief of the victim the machine exhibits an ace of hearts drawn from each pack.

(Swinburne, 1996)

Swinburne claims that it would not be adequate for the victim to claim that there is *no explanation* required as to why the ten aces appeared, since if they hadn't he would not be there. It is not legitimate to say that the cards came up as they did because the victim survived!

True, every draw, every arrangement of matter, is equally improbable a priori — that is, if chance alone dictates what is drawn. But if a person is arranging things, he has reason to produce some arrangements rather than others.

(ibid.)

4 Criticisms of the argument

David Hume argued that to draw an analogy between the universe and human works is highly dangerous to the theist since it leads inevitably to *anthropomorphism*. In

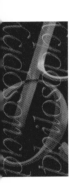

order to make the analogy work, God's qualities and characteristics have to be closely identified with those of human beings, removing from God the divine distinctiveness that the believer surely wants to preserve. If God is to be compared with a human designer, then it serves only to emphasise his limitations, changeability and fallibility, and in no way serves to support the view that a single deity of infinite capacity designed and created the universe with a benevolent interest in his creatures.

The implications of this criticism are important, since comparison with a human agent would surely imply that God is non-moral, limited and fallible, and that his creation is conceivably *'only the first rude essay of some infant deity, who afterward abandoned it, ashamed of his lame performance…it is the production of old age in some superannuated deity, and ever since his death has run on from the first impulse and active force which he gave it'* (cited in Hick (ed.), 1964).

In fact, the presence of order could be explained in many ways without reference to God. Since the universe is religiously ambiguous, it cannot be assumed that God is the only explanation for its features. Whilst there may be grounds for saying that the designer was very powerful and highly intelligent, it is a significant step further to say that the designer is all-powerful and morally perfect.

Whether the argument succeeds or fails depends entirely on how each individual judges the evidence. Some may maintain that there is insufficient evidence for claiming that there is design in the universe at all, still less that it can only be explained with reference to God. Just as Hick's travellers on the road to the Celestial City interpret the evidence they encounter in different ways, so too can the evidence proposed by supporters of the Teleological Argument be variously and legitimately interpreted.

The problems of evil and suffering

Evil and suffering could be said to deal a significant blow to the argument and we can legitimately question the idea that the universe is a particularly harmonious and beautiful place. J. S. Mill wrote: *'Next to the greatness of these cosmic forces, the quality which most forcibly strikes everyone who does not avert his eyes from it is their perfect and absolute recklessness. They go straight to their end, without regarding what or whom they crush on their road'* (cited in Hick (ed.), 1964). Mill argued that the most we can claim is that the designer of the universe might be benevolent, but must be seriously limited in power to allow such suffering.

Product of chance

It is said that in any quantum interaction, all possible states are actualised in some universe or other, with universes constantly diversifying. The resulting parallel universes have no contact with each other, and each observer observes only one universe. However, all universes are equally real. Given the possible combinations, it is not surprising that at least one produces intelligent life, but this is the product of chance rather than design. This is akin to the argument that if an infinite number of monkeys were all put together in a room, each with a typewriter, one of them would produce the works of Shakespeare!

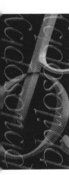

Intelligent design

Natural selection cannot be interpreted as the way in which an intelligent designer plans and directs his creation. Richard Dawkins (1986) expresses it thus:

A true watchmaker has foresight; he designs his cogs and springs, and plans their inter-connections, with a future purpose in his mind's eye. Natural selection, the blind, unconscious, automatic process which Darwin discovered, and which we now know is the explanation for the existence and apparently purposeful form of all life, has no purpose in mind. It has no mind and no mind's eye. It does not plan for the future. It has no vision, no foresight, no sight at all. If it can be said to play the role of the watchmaker in nature, it is the blind watchmaker.

Lack of experience

The analogy on which Paley's form of the argument depends is unsound, since it argues from that which we know to that of which we are ignorant. How can we legitimately draw an analogy between that which we know to be limited and imperfect to that which we claim is unlimited and perfect? Furthermore, it is not clear whether the analogy is intended to refer to parts of the universe or the universe as a whole. Whilst we might agree that parts of the universe appear to have a purpose, it is difficult to argue the case for the universe as a whole having such purpose — if so, what is it and how do we discern it?

Like causes and effects

Like effects do not infer like causes. Hume identified the problem of induction in this respect. We infer a designer when we see design because custom has taught us that this is a legitimate connection to make. In most, if not all, cases where there is design there is a designer, but the problem of induction demands that we ask why, rationally, we infer this association. Like effects may infer like causes in 99 out of 100 cases, but not necessarily in 100 out of 100 cases.

Summary

- **Teleological (Design) Argument** — seeks to explain order, rejecting chance as too improbable to lead to the type of universe we live in. A non-theistic explanation is not complete; science goes some way to explaining it, but not all the way. Four features need explaining: order, benefit, purpose, and suitability for human life. But the evidence of the universe is ambiguous and so it is up to the theist to demonstrate why God is the most likely cause of order.
- **Aquinas** — believed that non-rational beings aim towards a beneficial goal which could only be explained by reference to a designer.
- **Paley** — the world, like a watch, has features of design that demand an explanation. A designer is still likely, despite our ignorance of the world and despite features of 'bad' design.
- **Swinburne** — God is the best explanation for a universe which contains all the features of our world. God has a reason to create a world in which human beings can plan and make predictions, based on a degree of regularity.

- **Aesthetic argument** — beauty goes beyond what is needed for human survival; it gives pleasure and reflects God's glory.
- **Anthropic principle** — the reason and purpose of the universe is to support human life.
- The **improbability** of design needs explaining. Just because we are there to observe it does not make it less improbable.
- **Criticisms** — anthropomorphism; other explanations just as likely; the existence of evil and suffering needs to be explained if there is an omnipotent designer; we should not reject chance since if there are many worlds, one will have the appearance of design; order is the result of natural selection by a 'blind watchmaker'; we cannot always infer like effects from like causes.

Key terms

Aesthetic Argument — beauty in the universe requires an explanation.

Analogy — making a comparison between two objects or situations in order to emphasise the similarities between them.

Anthropic principle — the reason and purpose of the universe is to support human life.

Anthropomorphism — speaking of a non-human in human terms or as having human attributes.

Providential — a universe in which God foresees and controls future events in order to care for his creation.

Telos — end or purpose.

Exam watch

This is an enormously popular topic and it is highly likely that you will not only see it on your exam paper, but will choose to write an essay on it. It is essential, then, that you are in a position to use technical terminology in relation to this argument — for example, to identify it as an inductive, *a posteriori* argument. Named philosophers are unavoidable here but should not be onerous to learn since their views are linked with the argument and critiques of the argument from the outset. Whilst there may be a great temptation to find an exhaustive range of philosophers who have contributed to the Design Argument, remember that you only have a limited amount of time in the exam. You can gain credit from demonstrating a clear and analytical understanding of the traditional presentations of the arguments.

Review questions

1 Consider how far the creation of the world is analogous to the human invention of the computer.

2 Evaluate the view that the Design Argument is essentially difficult to destroy.

3 *The Design Argument is a more likely explanation for the existence and characteristics of the universe than any non-theistic explanation.* Examine and discuss this claim.

4 (a) Examine the Design Argument for the existence of God.

(b) What are the strengths of the Design Argument? Comment on some of the criticisms raised against this argument.

C The Ontological Argument

1 Anselm's *Proslogion*

The form of the Ontological Argument

Unlike the Cosmological and Teleological Arguments, the Ontological Argument is *a priori*. You will recall that an *a priori* argument is one which does not rely on the evidence of the senses, or the world around us, for either its premises or its conclusion, but rather it moves by logical stages to a conclusion which is self-evidently true or logically necessary. The Ontological Argument is also deductive and analytic. The premises of a deductive argument contain the conclusion that it reaches, and the argument is structured in such a way as to make the conclusion the only possible one that could be deduced from its premises. Because it is analytic, it is true by definition alone. Hence, the Ontological Argument reaches conclusions about the existence of God that are based on the definition of God used in the premises. This argument has come under considerable criticism over the centuries; Aquinas and Kant emerged as two of its most vociferous opponents. However, the Ontological Argument has also appealed to many important thinkers: Descartes, Spinoza and Liebniz among them. The most famous proponent, however, was Anselm, and in modern times his argument has been supported by Malcolm and Plantinga.

Reductio ad absurdum

In 1078 Anselm, then Archbishop of Canterbury, proposed in the *Proslogion* that the existence of God, held by him to be true by virtue of faith, was true by logical necessity. The process of his reasoning led him to the conclusion: '*Thanks be to thee good Lord, thanks be to thee, because I now understand by thy light what I formerly believed by thy gift*'. Effectively, Anselm attempted to prove the existence of God by way of **reductio ad absurdum**. This method of reasoning aims to demonstrate the truth of something by reducing to absurdity the very opposite of what you are aiming to prove. In Anselm's case, the opposite of his conclusion would be that God does not exist, which he aims to show to be absurd by means of an argument which demonstrates that the existence of God is logically necessary (i.e. he cannot *not* exist).

The content of the argument

The argument can be broken down into three stages:

1 The definition of God as *that than which nothing greater can be conceived* and its implications.
2 Why the non-existence of God is logically impossible.
3 Why 'the fool' believes that which is impossible to be true.

Anselm based the argument on the word 'God' and what is meant when the word is used. He made an assumption which is crucial for the argument to work, and that is that 'God' is effectively shorthand for 'that than which nothing greater can be conceived' or 'the being than which nothing greater can be thought'. His argument is that when

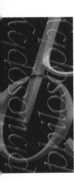

believers (and non-believers, for that matter) speak of God, they intuitively understand what is meant by the concept of God — that he is 'greater' than all other beings, not spatially, of course, but in the sense that he is supremely perfect. 'That than which nothing greater can be conceived' *must* possess all perfections in order to be so described and when we speak of God we speak of such a being.

Perfection and existence

Furthermore, Anselm argues that if such a being does indeed possess all perfections, then it must exist. This apparently radical assumption is based on the principle that existence is a perfection — something which can be possessed or lacked by a being or thing, and which contributes to our understanding of the nature of that thing. Anselm places existence in the same category as he would place goodness, love, wisdom or justice, for example, and by so doing he treats it as a predicate — a defining characteristic.

This step is important to the argument because it establishes that existence may be possessed or lacked, and that to possess existence is necessarily greater than to lack it. Existence may be *in re* (in reality) or merely *in intellectu* (in the mind). That which exists in the mind may hypothetically possess all other great-making qualities, but that which exists in reality is undeniably greater. Anselm writes:

Now we believe that thou art a being than which none greater can be thought...clearly that than which a greater cannot be thought cannot exist in the understanding alone. For if it is actually in the understanding alone, it can be thought of as existing in reality, and this is greater. Therefore, if that than which a greater cannot be thought is in the understanding alone, it can be thought of as existing also in reality, and this is greater... Without doubt, therefore, there exists, both in the understanding and in reality, something than which a greater cannot be thought.

(Cited in Hick (ed.), 1964)

Anselm attempts to clarify his thinking by use of an analogy. When a painter considers his next work it is already in his mind and he has a clear idea of it. However, it cannot be said to exist until he has painted it — when it exists in reality and not just in the mind. Such existence, Anselm maintains, is undeniably greater than existence *in intellectu*, and since God is that than which nothing greater can be conceived, God must possess the perfection of existence both in reality and in the mind. If this was not the case, then something other than God that did exist in reality would be greater than God, and this is impossible.

Thinking through the argument

Like all the arguments for the existence of God, the Ontological Argument can be set out in a series of premises and a conclusion, aiding our understanding of how its logical processes appear to work. Study these examples:

1 God exists or does not exist.
2 If God does not exist, then a greater being can be conceived, but this is impossible (a *reductio ad absurdum*).
3 Therefore, to say God *does not* exist is a logical impossibility.
4 Therefore, God exists.

1 God exists either in the understanding alone or in the understanding and in reality.
2 That which exists in reality is greater than that which exists in the understanding alone.
3 God is that than which nothing greater can be conceived.
4 If God is that than which nothing greater can be conceived, he must possess all perfections including real existence.
5 If God did not possess real existence, something else, which did possess real existence, would be greater than God.
6 This is a logical impossibility, given the definition of God (3).
7 Therefore God exists in reality.

1 God is that than which nothing greater can be thought.
2 The concept of God exists in the understanding.
3 God is a possible being (i.e. he may exist in reality).
4 If God only exists in the mind and is *only* a possible being, he may have been greater than he is if he also existed in reality.
5 If this is so, then God is a being than which a greater *can* be thought.
6 This is impossible, for God is a being than which *none* greater can be thought.
7 Therefore God exists in reality as well as in the mind.

Necessary existence

In all this, Anselm makes clear that his understanding of God is of a being possessing necessary existence. This concept was also integral to the Cosmological Argument, but applies differently to the Ontological Argument. In this case, God's necessary existence is *de dicto* necessary — by definition. Because the definition of God requires that he should exist, to deny his existence would be absurd. When this is fully understood, it is impossible to deny the existence of God, as Anselm explains:

For something can be thought of as existing which cannot be thought of as not existing, and this is greater than that which can be thought of as not existing... So, then, there truly is a being than which a greater cannot be thought — so truly that it cannot even be thought of as not existing... He therefore who understands that God thus exists cannot think of him as non-existent.

(ibid.)

The fool

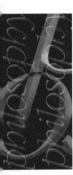

Nevertheless, Anselm is, of course, aware that the existence of God can, and is, denied by the atheist. In response to this, he cites Psalm 53 — '*the fool has said in his heart there is no God*'. The psalmist's fool is the atheist who, Anselm observes, says what is impossible to say since it cannot possibly be true: that God does not exist. Nevertheless, the atheist does say this and Anselm explains that this is because the atheist has failed to understand the full implications of the concept of God. Had the atheist grasped the real meaning of God as that than which nothing greater can be conceived, it would be impossible for him to deny his existence. Since, for him to deny the existence of God, the atheist at least has a concept of God in his understanding, it should be a short step for him to recognise the impossibility of denying the existence of such a being:

Can it be that there is no such being since, 'The fool hath said in his heart "There is no God"'?... But when this same fool hears what I am saying — "A being than which none greater can be thought" — he understands what he hears... even if he does not understand that it exists... Even the fool, then, must be convinced that a being than which none greater can be thought exists at least in his understanding.

(ibid.)

2 Descartes and the perfect being

René Descartes (1598–1650), the influential French thinker, reformulated the Ontological Proof specifically in terms of necessary existence. It appealed to him as a rationalist philosopher who sought to prove the existence of God by reason alone, rejecting as untrustworthy information that came from the senses alone. Doubting all his knowledge, he realised that the very act of doubting proved his own existence, inspiring the famous saying '*Cogito, ergo sum*' (I think, therefore I am).

As Descartes could conceive of his own existence, he could also conceive of the existence of a perfect being:

1 I exist.
2 In my mind I have the concept of a perfect being.
3 As an imperfect being, I could not have conjured up the concept of a perfect being.
4 The concept of a perfect being must therefore have originated from the perfect being itself.
5 A perfect being must exist in order to be perfect.
6 Therefore a perfect being exists.

OR

1 The idea of God is the idea of a supremely perfect being.
2 A supremely perfect being has all perfections.
3 Existence is a perfection.
4 A supremely perfect being has the perfection of existence.
5 It is impossible to think of God as not existing.
6 God exists.

Descartes maintained existence belonged analytically to God as three angles were analytically predicated of a triangle, or, less convincingly, as a valley was a necessary predicate of a mountain. However, whilst we may agree both, that our own existence is something of which we can be certain, and that the necessary essence of a triangle is triangularity, Descartes might have a notion of a perfect being, but this is not to say that everyone shares such a notion. Descartes suggests that the notion of a perfect being is in some way innate, but this seems to be something of a simplification. Furthermore, he claims that an imperfect being cannot think up the concept of a perfect being. We can surely conceive of as many perfect things, people or beings as we please, and allowing for the fact that no two people are likely to share exactly the same concept of what constitutes a perfect being, the only question that remains is whether such a being then therefore exists in reality or not.

3 Gaunilo and Kant

Gaunilo and the perfect island

Anselm's argument was refuted in his own life time by Gaunilo, who demonstrated in a *reductio ad absurdum* of his own that if the logic of the argument were applied to things other than God it led to invalid conclusions. Replacing the word 'God' with 'the greatest island' led to an argument which had the same form as Anselm's, with true premises, and yet which leads to a false conclusion:

1 I can conceive of an island than which no greater island can be thought.
2 Such an island must possess all perfections.
3 Existence is a perfection.
4 Therefore the island exists.

Even if 'the greatest island' were substituted for 'the greatest *possible* island', the argument would still yield an invalid conclusion since, quite clearly, to conceive of an island in all of its perfections does not guarantee its existence or bring it into existence. Thus, Gaunilo's criticism strikes at the heart of the ontological proof which depends on accepting that (i) perfection necessarily entails existence and (ii) that which is perfect must, of necessity, exist.

Kant: existence is not a predicate

Whatever, therefore, and however much our concept of an object may contain, we must go outside it if we are to ascribe existence to the object.

Fundamental to both Anselm's and Descartes's form of the Ontological Argument is that existence is a predicate, an attribute, or a quality that can be possessed or lacked. Such qualities may be size, shape, colour, temperature, personality traits, or intelligence, for example. These may or may not belong to a thing or being, and their presence or absence is part of our understanding and apprehension of it. However, Kant observed that existence is not associated with the definition of something, since it did not add to our understanding of that thing. We must establish the existence of something before we can say what it is like, not the other way around, and so if there is a perfect being then he must exist, just as if there is a triangle, then it must have three sides, but we cannot ascribe existence *a priori* to our definition of a perfect being, which is tantamount to saying 'An existing God exists.'

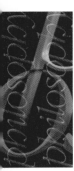

Aquinas had already questioned this important aspect of the Ontological Argument, claiming that Anselm was guilty of making a 'transitional error' — that is, moving from the definition of God to the existence of God. Furthermore, Aquinas observed that Anselm was guilty of making an assumption about the definition of God that was not necessarily shared by all believers. Understanding the meaning of the term 'God' means only that God exists in the understanding, not in reality. God's existence in reality must be demonstrated *a posteriori*, as Aquinas's Cosmological Argument attempts to show. Kant similarly maintained that empirical data are the only reliable means of knowing anything about the universe and hence a move from definition to reality is a false manoeuvre.

4 Evaluating the argument

Support for Kant

The twentieth-century philosopher G. E. Moore demonstrated further the strength of Kant's principle that existence could not be grammatically used as a predicate because the word does not function as other predicates do. He proposed taking the following statements:

A: Some tame tigers do not growl.
B: Some tame tigers do not exist.

Statement A is perfectly meaningful, implying that there are beings that answer to the description 'tame tiger' and that a characteristic of some of them is that they do not growl. However, statement B, which uses 'do not exist' in the same way that 'do not growl' was used in statement A, is not meaningful in the same way. We learn nothing about tame tigers in this statement apart from the fact that they do not exist, which presumably means there is nothing to learn about them anyway!

Bertrand Russell also furthered Kant's observations. He proposed that 'existence' was not a predicate but rather a term used to indicate the instance of something in the spatio-temporal world. Therefore, 'Some tame tigers exist' does not tell us anything about their nature but it does indicate that there is an instance of such beings in the world. 'Cows are brown' and 'Cows are brown and exist' effectively tell us only one thing: 'Cows are brown'. 'And exist' indicates that they occupy a place in the world, but it is a tautology since by saying that they are brown we are presumably referring to existent cows rather than imaginary ones.

David Hume

David Hume considered the argument a failure because it made a false assumption about existence — that necessary existence was a coherent concept. He argued that existence could only ever be contingent (dependent and limited) and that all statements about existence could be denied without contradiction. All things which could be said to exist could also be said not to exist. Thus, Hume did not agree that any form of existence could be analytically true. It is simply a matter of fact.

*Both Hume and Kant showed that it is not possible to move from the **de dicto** necessity of a proposition to the **de re** necessity of God... They also challenged the very idea of anything being necessary, maintaining that the only things that are necessary are linguistic statements where truth represents convention (for instance, **de dicto** necessary statements such as 'all triangles have three angles').*

(Vardy, 1999b)

Support for the argument

Despite the work of these influential critics, the argument has also been supported by leading thinkers. Amongst them was Leibniz, who argued that since it is impossible to think of God as lacking any perfection — '*a simple quality which is positive and absolute, and expresses without limitation whatever it does*' — he must exist, since to possess all perfections but not to exist would be meaningless.

Norman Malcolm proposed a form of the argument in support of necessary existence, working on the presumption that if God *could* exist, he *does* exist, since he cannot *not* exist. The argument can be framed thus:

1 God is that than which nothing greater can be thought.
2 Necessary existence is a perfection.
3 If God possesses all perfections, he must possess necessary existence.
4 A necessary being cannot *not* exist.
5 If God *could* exist, then he would exist necessarily.
6 It is contradictory to say that a necessary being does not exist.
7 God must exist.

Furthermore, Malcolm argues that God's existence is either necessary or impossible, but he cannot possess contingent existence. Hence, God must have necessary existence. Malcolm observes that God is a special case — unlike contingent beings, for whom existence is merely possible. However, as we have already seen, if we adopt Hume's view, necessary existence may be an incoherent concept and so Malcolm's form of the argument will fail.

Alvin Plantinga suggested that since we are able to imagine any number of alternative worlds in which things may be quite different — for example, a world in which Luciano Pavarotti did not choose to become an operatic tenor, but was a house painter instead — there must be any number of possible worlds, including our own. However, if God's existence is necessary, he must exist in them all and have all the characteristics of God in them all. This is because, Plantinga argued, God is both maximally great and maximally excellent. He proposed that:

A: There exists a world in which there is a being of maximal greatness.
B: A being of maximal excellence is omnipotent, omniscient and omnibenevolent in all worlds.

Bear in mind, however, that if there is a world of maximal greatness and a being of maximal excellence, there is no reason why there should not also be a being of maximal evil occupying all possible worlds. Plantinga's form of the argument does not therefore prove the exclusiveness of the omnipotent God.

Anti-realism

It is arguable that the Ontological Argument is successful if we accept that the statements made are not objectively but subjectively true statements, which *'cohere with other true statements made within a particular form of life'* (Vardy, 1999b). Proponents of the Ontological Argument are already committed to certain claims, most especially that God is that than which nothing greater can be conceived, and all that this entails. Anselm maintained that the existence of God was necessary and self-evident, and on this assumption the Ontological Argument cannot fail. However, 'God necessarily exists' is a claim that may be rejected by realists as meaningless, unverifiable and unfalsifiable, because it does not correspond to the state of affairs which it describes. The anti-realist approach does not demand absolute truth, but rather that something be true within its peculiar context. Hence, for Anselm and his supporters the claim that God

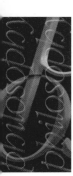

is, **de dicto**, necessarily existent, is true within their particular 'form of life', as are other claims made within the religious system to which a believer subscribes.

Despite the criticisms outlined by its opponents, the Ontological Argument could therefore be considered to succeed if it is understood as an expression of what the believer already holds to be true, rather than a proof that an objective reality to which the term 'God' is ascribed exists objectively in the objective universe.

Deductive reasoning

The success of the Ontological Argument also depends on how successfully it works as a deductive proof. Without the evidence and experience of the universe on which to draw, the argument must be analytically sound. In this respect, it may be successful if the first premise is universally accepted. However, whilst 'God is that than which nothing greater can be conceived' may be true for *some* believers, it is not necessarily the case for all. If believers can understand God in other terms or describe him in other ways, or if there are good reasons for rejecting Anselm's definition, then the argument fails. Only if true premises lead to valid conclusions can a deductive argument be said to have fully succeeded. This cannot be said of the Ontological Argument, and as such it is flawed.

Summary

- **Form of the argument** — *a priori,* deductive and analytic. Conclusion is contained in the premises and so theoretically it is a strong — even undefeatable — argument. However, the argument may only support an anti-realist view of God — that his existence is true and necessary within the 'form of life' of the religious believer — and a deductive argument is only as strong as its first premise. There may be good reasons for raising doubts about the validity of the premises of the Ontological Argument.
- **Anselm** — proposed a **reductio ad absurdum** that aimed to demonstrate the impossibility of denying God's existence. Based on the definition of God as *that than which nothing greater can be conceived,* it sought to prove that God exists **de dicto** necessarily — by virtue of his very definition. Simple outline: (1) God is that than which nothing greater can be conceived; (2) That than which nothing greater can be conceived possesses all perfections; (3) Existence is a perfection; (4) God must exist.
- **The fool** — atheists, unaware of the implications of the definition of 'God', are able to say the impossible — that God does not exist. But if they truly understood what 'God' meant, they would realise this is absurd.
- **Descartes** — God is a perfect being and so must exist since existence is necessary for perfection, in the same way that three angles are necessary to a triangle.
- **Criticisms of the argument** — (1) Anselm's argument attempts to define God into existence, by claiming that that which is the 'greatest conceivable' must exist in reality (Gaunilo). (2) Anselm is guilty of making a 'transitional error', moving from existence **in intellectu** to existence **in re** (Aquinas). (3) Anselm and Descartes use 'exist' as a predicate (a defining characteristic), which is grammatically unsound since it adds nothing to the description of a being or thing, hence the argument fails (Kant). (4) 'Exists' serves only to indicate the instance of something within the spatio-

temporal world (Russell). (5) Necessary existence is an incoherent concept (Hume). (6) 'Exists' acts differently from other predicates (G. E. Moore).

- **Modern support for the argument** — (1) As a necessary being God cannot not exist, and since God is either necessary or impossible, he must exist (Malcolm). (2) God must exist as a being of maximal excellence and greatness in all possible worlds (Plantinga). (3) If the proof is understood as an anti-realist expression of the significance of God to the believer, then it may be considered to have a useful function to play within the religious language game.

Key terms

De dicto — of words.
De re — in the nature of things.
In intellectu — in the mind.
In re — in reality.
Necessarily existent — cannot *not* exist.
Ontological — concerned with being.
Predicate — an attribute or characteristics belonging to the description of a thing.
Reductio ad absurdum — to reduce to an absurdity.

Exam watch

All arguments for the existence of God are popular topics for candidates in exams, and the Ontological Argument seems to be one of the most user-friendly. It does not lend itself to trite observations about the beauty of the world or oversimplistic accounts of the origin of the universe, either religious or scientific. However, the form of the argument is not simple. You need to ensure that you are absolutely confident about the way in which a deductive argument is intended to work so that you can thoroughly evaluate the argument for both its strengths and its weaknesses. Work carefully through different ways of setting out the argument in both premises and conclusions until you are sure you understand why and how it works. There are many philosophers and writers who have contributed to this argument. Do not attempt to learn everything about all of them but, similarly, try to move beyond Anselm, Descartes and Kant. The majority of sound candidates can discuss these three, so gain yourself more marks by being able to say something accurate and thoughtful about some of the other contributors. This topic is a good one for demonstrating that you understand and can use philosophical terms accurately and in context. If you get them wrong, it will look particularly silly, so take this as an opportunity to display your philosophical know-how rather than make foolish mistakes.

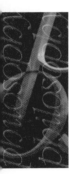

Review questions

1 Compare and contrast the Ontological Argument with any *a posteriori* argument for the existence of God.

2 (a) Outline the main features of the Ontological Argument for the existence of God.
   (b) In what ways and for what reasons have scholars criticised the argument?
   (c) Does the argument remain strong despite these criticisms?

3 '*An examination of arguments for the existence of God will yield convincing reasons to believe in God.*' Discuss and assess this claim with reference to the Ontological Argument *and* one other argument for the existence of God.

D The Argument from Religious Experience

1 The value of the argument

This argument is *a posteriori* by its very definition, since it is concerned with whether direct experience of God can provide any proof of his existence. The Cosmological and Teleological (Design) Arguments aim to prove that experience of the universe can lead to conclusions about God's existence, but these work by indirect methods; here we are working from God to God. If God manifests himself in direct ways, is it possible to deny that he exists? Davies (1982) writes:

The claim is that without appealing to anything other than a direct contact with God, one can have reasonable grounds for asserting that there is a God. Just as I can reasonably say that there is a bed in my room because I have encountered it, so I can reasonably say that there is a God because I have directly encountered him.

The first modern evaluation of religious experience was made by Schleiermacher in the early nineteenth century, in his book *On Religion: Discourses to its Cultural Despisers*. He defined religious experience as one which yielded a sense of the ultimate, an aware-ness of wholeness, a consciousness of infiniteness and finiteness, an absolute depend-ence, and a sharp sense of contingency. These criteria have dominated the evaluation of religious experience well into the twentieth century. At a time when David Hume's work had offered overwhelming arguments against the rationality of Christianity, Schleiermacher's vital contribution was his claim that the central feature of faith did not lie in doctrine, but in a fundamental human experience. He observed that each world religion presented a different facet in the whole kaleidoscope of religious experi-ence: for Judaism, it was to be found in obedience to the Torah; for Islam, in the majesty of Allah; for Christianity, in the experience of the infinite within the finite, through the incarnation. In 1917, Rudolf Otto drew attention to religious experience in a specific way, coining the term 'numinous', from the Latin **numen** (divinity). He created a phenomenology of the sacred, offering descriptions of specific religious experiences which placed evidence on the 'wholly other' nature of God to which the experient is drawn.

However, as psychology developed in the late nineteenth century, study of religious experience became empirically rooted, and William James's work is still regarded as a classic of this type. He took typical examples of religious experience from literature and arranged them into characteristic types, ranging from those that had no apparent religious significance to those which were more intensely religious. He identified exemplars of particular varieties of religious experience, such as Paul's conversion, which was held at the time to be the model of the conversion experience. William James observed that religious experience draws on the common store of emotions — happiness, fear, wonder — but is directed at something divine. The result of such an experience will be reverence, a joyful desire to belong to God, a renewed approach to life. Such symptoms will be testimony to the reality of the experience, even if other physiological symptoms are present. James observed that even pathological elements should not detract from it, if positive fruits are borne from the experience; the results of religious experience are the only reliable basis for judging whether it is a genuine experience of the divine.

Although in the first half of the twentieth century, philosophers and psychologists, influenced by the claims of logical positivism, lost interest in the study of religious experience, in the last fifty years the empirical approach has been reasserted and surveys have shown that as many as 50% of individuals believe they have had, at some time in their lives, an experience which could be classified as religious. In 1969 the Religious Experience Research Unit in Oxford (now named after Alastair Hardy, one of the original researchers) advertised in newspapers inviting respondents to describe mystical experiences, especially in childhood. They avoided using the term 'religious experience', but asked a single question: 'Have you at any time in your life had an experience of something completely different from your normal life, whether or not you would describe it as God?' One of the most interesting factors to emerge from the study was that for many of the respondents it was the first time they had told anyone of their experience and yet it was often described by them as the most important moment of their life. In the light of this, John Hull, of Birmingham University, suggests that *'A major educational task remains to encourage people not to repress such significant experiences'*.

2 Religious experience as proof of the existence of God

On the evidence gleaned from studies of this kind, and if sheer weight of testimony to religious experience alone were sufficient to prove the existence of God, then our debate would surely end here. However, if we are to argue convincingly for religious experience as a direct proof of God, then we must be clear as to why God should reveal himself, if indeed he does, and why we should believe accounts of such experiences.

Richard Swinburne (1996) argues forcibly for the case that *'An omnipotent and perfectly good creator will seek to interact with his creatures and, in particular, with human persons capable of knowing him'*. He suggests that God has reason to make himself known through authentic revelation, to enable humanity to bring about the good, and to intervene personally (not necessarily miraculously) in the lives of individuals out of his love for them. Hence, Swinburne's subsequent evaluation of religious experience as offering grounds for the existence of God is influenced by the fact that he believes that God, omnipotent and all-loving, has good reason to make himself known through religious experience.

The principles of credulity and testimony

Furthermore, Swinburne alludes to the findings of David Hay (1990) and draws the conclusion that since it has been the case that many millions of people have had an experience of what *seems to them* to be God, then it is a basic principle of rationality that we should believe them. This is what Swinburne calls the **principle of credulity** — unless we have overwhelming evidence to the contrary, we should believe that things are as they seem to be. Swinburne (1979) describes it thus: *'How things seem to be is a good guide to how things are. If it seems…to a subject that X is present, then probably X is present'*. This is an important notion for religious experience, since it draws not on empirical evidence that we interpret through the five senses, but on non-empirical

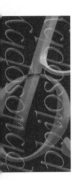

evidence that must be interpreted through the use of our religious sense. We are aware that sometimes we have an experience of something which seems to be the case — seeing someone who *seems to be* a friend but, as they turn, we realise that our experience was mistaken and that it is a stranger. However, these mistaken interpretations of our experience do not prejudice us against all future experiences. We do not doubt every future occasion when we see a friend, assuming that because we were mistaken once, we will be mistaken every time. We continue to trust that our senses are dependable enough to be relied on to interpret our experiences correctly. Hence, even if two people differ over the nature of a religious experience, it does not immediately render the experience suspect, just as we would not doubt that everyone who saw green as green was wrong just because one colour-blind person declared it to be blue.

Essentially, if we are told that someone has had experience X, then we should believe that experience X has taken place, even if someone else has had experience Y instead, or no experience at all. If we wait until we have uniform testimony and common interpretation of every experience, let alone just religious ones, we will end up doubting all our experiences and those of others, which is absurd. Davies (1982) writes: *'We certainly do make mistakes about reality because we fail to interpret our experience correctly; but if we do not work on the assumption that what seems to be so is sometimes so, then it is hard to see how we can establish anything at all…'.*

We can illustrate this with the analogy of explorers in the jungle. A group of explorers travels into the depths of the jungle and there discovers an entirely unknown creature. Excited by this discovery, a second group travels to the jungle and carries out its own investigation. This group discovers no such creature. Does this give it reasonable grounds for asserting that the initial group was wrong and that the creature does not exist? Of course not. The experience of the first group has not been falsified by the experience of the second — it was simply a different experience, which does not render the first invalid.

Swinburne offers a second testimony which should encourage us to consider religious experience to be good grounds for proving the existence of God: **the principle of testimony**. He describes it thus: *'In the absence of special considerations the experiences of others are (probably) as they report them'* (Swinburne, 1979). We cannot work on the basis that we constantly doubt people's accounts of religious experiences any more than we doubt basic facts about the world that we have not directly experienced ourselves. Swinburne identifies three types of evidence that may well give us grounds for saying that a person's experience is not as they report it:

÷ The circumstances surrounding the experience render the resultant perceptions unreliable — e.g. hallucinatory drugs.
÷ We have particular evidence that things are not as they are reported — e.g. we know that the person was not in the place that he or she claimed to be during the experience.
÷ There is evidence that the experience was not caused by God — e.g. the person who 'experienced' God had been fasting or had a fever.

However, Swinburne dismisses all these factors. Most religious experiences do not take place under the influence of drugs; evidence that things are not as they reported would have to be decisive, not merely ambiguous; and the fact that fasting or fever may contribute to the experience does not mean it is a complete explanation for it. Davies (1982) observes: *'The truth of a belief is not affected by the factors that bring the belief about'*. So, even if Mr Z were habitually having hunger-induced hallucinations on which he based his belief in God, it does not mean that his reports were always unreliable.

These observations highlight the problem of induction and how it affects our interpretation of experience. We make generalisations on the basis of our regular experience, and work on the assumption that what has proved to be the case in the past will turn out to be the case in the future. However, we are sometimes mistaken, since inductive knowledge is not certain but based on information which *may* be changeable even if it is not constantly changing. John may frequently be drunk, and his accounts of experience subsequently unreliable, but we do not have grounds to assume that he will therefore never be able to give a reliable account.

3 Arguments against the case for religious experience

However convincing these arguments may appear, religious experiences are significantly different to other human experiences because they are fundamentally not subject to objective testing — we cannot carry out a scientific experiment to determine whether they have, in fact, revealed God. They are therefore ambiguous and can be interpreted variously. Ludwig Wittgenstein employed the notion of **seeing-as:** a random series of dots and lines could be perceived as representing a particular form, but each person perceives it differently; some may perceive beauty, others ugliness. Experiencing-as, or seeing-as, may also be unreliable because we can mistake what we experience. R. M. Hare describes the lunatic university lecturer who believes that all his colleagues want to kill him and interprets all their actions, however benign, as evidence for his belief. His interpretation of experience is clearly mistaken, but he continues to hold on to it. This is what Hare calls a **blik** — an unverifiable and unfalsifiable way of looking at the world. Strong arguments, therefore, are offered against the validity of religious experience:

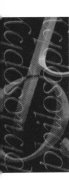

1 Fundamentally, of course, if God does not exist, there can be no experience of him, and all seeming religious experiences must be interpreted in some other way. It is equally likely that any religious experience may be open to a non-religious interpretation and if, as the logical positivists claimed, the notion of God is an impossible, meaningless notion, then he cannot be experienced.
2 If everyday experiences are deceptive, experiences of the divine are even more so. There are too many reasons for doubting when a person claims to have experienced God that he or she has, in fact, done so, and there are no agreed tests for verifying that the experience has been one of God.
3 The testimony of religious believers is especially questionable and cannot be counted as reliable evidence. Those who claim to have experienced God have some pre-existing religious belief, so their evidence is not unbiased.
4 Religious experiences are the manifestation of psychological needs. Once those needs are identified they can be satisfied without reference to religion, which is nothing more than an illusion created by people to enable them to cope with

the haunting fear of death and alienation. Similarly, the emotions and sensations that accompany religious experience can be explained by biological or neurological factors.

Are these criticisms decisive?

We have already examined some strong arguments offered by both Swinburne and Davies which deal with certain criticisms, but there are other factors we can consider further:

1 If claims of religious experience are essentially invalid because the notion of God is a meaningless one, there must be evidence that counts decisively against the existence of God. However, Swinburne (1996) argues that *'In so far as other evidence is ambiguous or counts against but not strongly against the existence of God, our experience (our own or that of many others) ought to tip the balance in favour of God'*. For the theist, the existence of God is a simpler explanation for many phenomena than those proposed by science or atheistic rationality, and the claims of logical positivism have long since been dismissed by thinkers as offering a practical way of evaluating the meaningfulness of assertions. Furthermore, if religious experiences have a decisive effect on the life of those who experience them, then they cannot be considered to be ultimately meaningless.

2 Claims of religious experience are certainly made and withdrawn on a regular basis, but this does not mean that they can never be valid, or even that they are frequently invalid. Furthermore, if it is possible to have a mistaken experience of X or Y, it must be possible to have a valid experience of X or Y. In other words, if it is possible to have any kind of experience of God, then it must be reasonable to assume that some experiences of God actually are experiences of him. The fact that we cannot establish agreed tests for religious experience need not discourage us. Wittgenstein famously asserted, *'Doesn't testing come to an end?'* Some things just have to be accepted without question, rather like basic beliefs (as discussed in Topic 1, pp. 24–25).

  It is possible too that there are tests for the validity of religious experience: the effects that it has on the experient and his or her life; the emotions and feelings associated with the experience — awe and wonder, for example, rather than unhappiness and fear; the content of the experience itself — we would not, for example, be inclined to trust an account of an experience which involved God giving an instruction to rape and murder. However, in reality few claimants to religious experience would testify to such a thing.

3 What are the grounds for claiming that the testimony of religious believers is any less reliable than that of non-believers? It is possible that religious believers would like their claims of having experienced God to be verified, but it is equally possible that non-believers would seek to ensure that they are falsified. Why is the onus on believers to defend their accounts rather than on sceptics to disprove them? Furthermore, we should not be surprised that religious experiences are more likely to be experienced by religious believers. After all, they know what to look for and are more likely to recognise the experience when it arrives! Not all religious experiences occur to

believers anyway, and the story of the young Samuel in the temple (in 1 Samuel 3) is a good example of an experience of God coming to someone completely unprepared for it and without the tools to interpret it. However, once Eli explains it to him, Samuel is able to respond appropriately.

4 It is true that religious belief may satisfy many deep psychological, emotional and physical needs, but it does not follow as a corollary from this that all religious experiences and behaviour can therefore *only* be explained in naturalistic terms. Furthermore, the Bible makes clear that God deliberately seeks to meet human needs and will make himself available to people in their time of despair, as Elijah's experience at Mount Horeb (1 Kings 19) suggests. If religious experiences meet psychological and emotional needs, they are further authenticated as experiences of God who, as Swinburne (1996) suggests, *'will love each of us as individual creatures, and so has reason to intervene... simply to show himself to individuals, and to tell them things individual to themselves.'*

In conclusion:

The only way to defeat the claims of religious experience will be to show that the strong balance of evidence is that there is no God. In the absence of that strong balance, religious experience provides significant further evidence that there is a God... I suggest that the overwhelming testimony of so many millions of people to occasional experiences of God must, in the absence of counter-evidence, be taken as tipping the balance of evidence decisively in favour of the existence of God.

(ibid.)

Summary and key terms

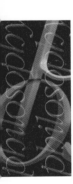

- Religious experience offers **direct experience** of God, not indirect, as the classical arguments do. Therefore, if it can be verified, it is potentially very powerful evidence for the existence of God. Close examination over the last two centuries of types of religious experience has established anthropological, psychological and empirical methods of researching them. There is overwhelming evidence that a significant proportion of the population have had a religious experience of some kind.

- The incidence of religious experience is compatible with what we would expect of a loving, involved God.

- The **principle of credulity** — how things seem to be is a good guide to how they are. If people claim religious experience, then it is reasonable to assume this is what has occurred.

- The **principle of testimony** — the experiences of others are as they report them. Why assume people are lying about religious experience?

- Do we have good reason to doubt people's claims? Not in all cases. The **problem of induction** tells us that although experience may often be reliable, it is not always so. Hence, just because someone is often mistaken about their experience doesn't mean that they are always so mistaken.

- Experiences are ambiguous, and there are no agreed tests for verifying religious experience. Believers may be unreliable in their reporting and experiences may fulfil psychological needs.

- However, we do need *decisive* evidence against the existence of God, and experiences may be verified by their results. There is no reason why believers should be more unreliable than non-believers, or why an experience which meets psychological needs should therefore be unreliable.

Exam watch

After the weighty analysis of the previous three arguments, this may come as light relief. Religious experience as a proof for the existence of God is particularly attractive as you can contribute to discussion here even if you felt rather left behind in the debates over the more conceptually complex arguments. However, keep your mind firmly on the issue of whether religious experience is a good basis on which to argue for the existence of God; do not stray into peripheral matters. It is a mistake to think that this topic is an easy one because it is more immediately accessible: it is essential that you apply philosophical skills of analysis to it just as you would to the Ontological Argument. Do not write about this topic because you think you can just express strong religious beliefs or non-beliefs and get credit for it.

Review questions

1 Analyse these statements:
 If God exists we should be able to experience him.
 It is possible to experience God, therefore he exists.
2 Examine and evaluate the Argument from Religious Experience.
3 *Using the evidence of religious experiences to prove the existence of God is unreliable and fraught with difficulties.* Examine and discuss this claim.

E The Moral Argument

1 Aquinas and the Fourth Way

The association between religion and morality is a complex one, although it is nevertheless one which is, to a considerable extent, taken for granted. However, there are many aspects to the relationship which philosophers and theologians have grappled with. Amongst them, we might consider:

- Is it possible to be religious but not moral?
- Is it possible to be moral but not religious?
- What is the relationship between God and goodness?
- Does the existence of a moral law presuppose the existence of a supreme moral law-giver?
- If God does not exist, then is everything permissible?

Above all, the question that we are concerned with in this section is whether morality in some way demands the existence of God. The gist of the moral argument is whether the existence of morality leads to proof of the existence of God. Note, of course, that it is therefore important to establish first whether there is a moral law, or anything that can be considered to be 'good'. Nevertheless, the existence of an objective moral law seems to be taken for granted by those who support the moral argument, although it is arguable that moral commands are anything but objective. (See pp. 128–133 for discussions on the problems of defining morality and pp. 152–154 for more on the relationship between God and morality.) However, although these questions are important, our concern in this chapter is to examine the work of those philosophers who have argued that the existence of a moral law and of moral goodness is meaningful only if we postulate the existence of God.

In the *Summa Theologica*, Aquinas argued that the gradation to be found in things pointed irrefutably to the existence of God:

Among beings there are some more and some less good, true, noble and the like. But more and less are predicated of different things according as they resemble in their different ways something which is the maximum…so that there is something which is truest, something best, something noblest… Therefore there must also be something which is to all beings the cause of their being, goodness, and every other perfection, and this we call God.

(Cited in Hick (ed.), 1964)

Aquinas's arguments were based on Plato's eternal Forms, or archetypes, which claimed that the contingent realities of which the human mind is aware are merely pale copies of a greater, unseen reality, which is eternal. In this case, the goodness, virtue or truth found in human beings and in the contingent world is a reflection of the supreme or perfect goodness of God, to whom contingent beings owe their lesser goodness. Furthermore, God, being perfect in goodness, is also perfect in his very being, or existence — hence the Fourth Way is a form of an Ontological Argument as well as a Moral Argument. God's moral perfection and authority were evidence for his existence, and all lesser forms or reflections of goodness were striving towards the ultimate good which is their cause, and participate in some way in that ultimate reality.

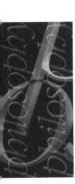

Interestingly, the twentieth-century philosopher F. C. Copleston, in discussion with Bertrand Russell, claimed: *'I do think that all goodness reflects God in some way and proceeds from him, so that in a sense the man who loves what is truly good, loves God even if he doesn't advert to God'* (ibid.). However, Aquinas's Fourth Way does not suggest how good can be defined. All we know is that God is the supreme source of it and it is his very essence to be perfectly good. Obviously, too, it is possible to question whether good can only be measured by reference to the divine. Copleston maintained that it was necessary to refer to God in order to be able to distinguish between good and evil, whilst Russell argued: *'I love the things that I think are good, and I hate the things that I think are bad. I don't say that these things are good because they participate in the Divine goodness'* (ibid.).

2 Kant: morality alone proves the existence of God

In *Critique of Pure Reason*, Kant argued that only one fact is indisputable, and that is the existence of a moral law, which cannot fulfil its goal unless God exists. He maintained that everyone can discern a moral law evident in the universe and they have a duty to seek the highest form of the good, which he coined the **summum bonum** (the state of pure virtue crowned with perfect happiness). This duty is a **categorical imperative**, which must be pursued for its own sake, and not for any **hypothetical imperatives**, which put preferences ahead of that which is inherently good. Good actions should be universalisable and free. Nevertheless, Kant observed that since the moral law would never be satisfied in this life, and since people would never be capable of achieving the *summum bonum*, then the existence of God is necessary, if the goal of morality is to be realised.

Kant's argument was based on the principle that we find it rationally satisfactory that true virtue should be rewarded by happiness, since virtue is not — although, arguably, it should be — its own reward. The achievement of the *summum bonum* is therefore an obligation — and this is the key term for understanding Kant's argument. An obligation — something which *ought* to be accomplished — must logically be something which is possible to accomplish. However, since human beings are so evidently unable to accomplish this perfect state of affairs, Kant maintained that:

Accordingly, the existence of a cause of all nature, distinct from nature itself and containing the principle of this connection, namely of the exact harmony of happiness with morality, is also postulated... It follows that the postulate of the possibility of the highest derived good (the best world) is likewise the postulate of the reality of a highest original good, that is to say, of the existence of God.

(ibid.)

Kant's proof for the existence of God led on to a proof of the absolute necessity of an after-life, a post-mortem existence, in which the achievement of the *summum bonum* would ultimately be accomplished. Kant observed how the moral law, whilst requiring happiness to be satisfied, does not itself guarantee that end; neither can human beings themselves ensure that virtue is rewarded and evil punished. However:

Christian morality supplies this defect...by presenting a world wherein reasonable beings single-mindedly devote themselves to the moral law; this is the Kingdom of God, in which nature and morality come into a harmony which is foreign to each as such, through a holy Author of the world who makes possible the highest good.

(ibid.)

Kant maintained that morality and the postulate of a divine being who satisfied the moral law is known *a priori*. In other words, it is not our experience of the world which points to the existence of God, but we know by reason that morality demands his existence. Moral behaviour per se is not invalid if God does not exist, but Kant maintained that if the goal of morality is to be achieved, then God is demanded to bring it about.

Weaknesses of this approach

Kant's crucial weakness is a logical one; he argues that *ought* implies *can*, and yet states that whilst human beings ought to bring about the **summum bonum**, they are not able to do so. Having said this, he then assumes, *a priori*, that God can do so, and moreover, is the only agency or being capable of doing so. Perhaps people see the value of the **summum bonum**, and desire it, and perhaps God may be, according to classical theism, the most likely agency for its accomplishment, but this cannot be proven in isolation from other considerations. Furthermore, Kant maintains that virtue must be rewarded, and yet in his own theory of duty and ethics (see pp. 142–144), he claims that a moral action is one that is performed independently of any anticipated reward or goal.

3 Objective moral laws

John Henry Newman famously argued that objective moral laws had their origin in a personal lawgiver: *'If, as is the case, we feel responsibility, are ashamed, are frightened at transgressing the voice of conscience, this implies that there is One to whom we are responsible, before whom we are ashamed, whose claim on us we fear'* (cited in Davies, 1982).

Newman makes a link between the existence of a moral law, which imposes certain demands upon us, and the existence of a God who fixes that law and to whom we are obliged for its upkeep. Essentially, he is arguing that our experience of morality is such that it leads us to conclude the existence of a lawgiver; otherwise our moral experience has no foundation and makes no sense. H. P. Owen argued similarly: *'It is impossible to think of a command without a commander… Either we take moral claims to be self-explanatory modes of impersonal existence, or we explain them in terms of a personal God'* (ibid.). In other words, unless there is something more than that which we know through natural science, our notions of morality have no objective foundation and they rest on nothing more than illusion.

But does this prove the existence of God? Morality might prove the existence of God if we were able to prove that the only conceivable source of moral authority is God. If the source of authority lies elsewhere, however, then it will not succeed as a proof. Considerations of probability are inherent here: is it more or less likely that God is the source of morality? Is he the simplest explanation for moral law? Is it necessary, as Owen suggests, to argue for a *personal* source of morality or is it satisfactorily explained in terms of impersonal forces, such as society, rationality, evolution or education?

To argue convincingly that the existence of God is a prerequisite of objective moral laws demands too that we believe that morality rests on obedience to objective commands. If we interpret morality as subjective, or non-cognitive, then such arguments will lead nowhere. If moral commands are merely emotive expressions of approval or disapproval with no basis in objective fact, or if they are relative to our culture, then they cannot prove the existence of an objective lawgiver, and we must look to other arguments for the existence of God.

Summary

- Does the relationship between religion and morality provide convincing grounds to prove the existence of God? Does morality presuppose the existence of God, or can it be explained in other terms?
- **Aquinas's Fourth Way** — that which is good, true and noble owes its being to that which is supremely good, true and noble, and participates in its essence.
- **Kant** argued that the moral law could not fulfil its goal unless God existed to bring about the **summum bonum**. The human race was obliged to bring this about, but was not able to do so, so the responsibility lay with God, who would bring it about in a post-mortem existence.
- The existence of objective moral laws demands the existence of an objective moral lawgiver, or such laws can be explained only in terms of '*self-explanatory modes of impersonal existence*' (H. P. Owen).
- However, it is possible to identify what is good without acknowledging the existence of God or that goodness shares in the divine essence.

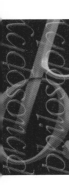

- It is a logical contradiction to say that human beings are obliged to bring about the *summum bonum* and yet are incapable of doing so. Why should God be the only being so capable?
- It is questionable whether moral laws are objective, or whether they are better understood as subjective expressions of personal preference, cultural norms or social evolution.
- Are moral commands even linguistically meaningful? The Logical Positivist School argued that both moral claims and religious language claims were meaningless and can therefore provide no valid grounds for making statements about objective reality.

Key terms

Categorical imperative — an action performed for its own sake, out of duty, and not for any other motive or outcome, e.g. 'Be kind.'

Hypothetical imperative — an action performed in order to bring about a specific or general goal, e.g. 'If you want to be liked, be kind to your friends.'

Objective moral laws — codes of morality which have an empirical or factual basis.

Summum bonum — the perfect state of affairs; virtue crowned with happiness.

Exam watch

Although the forms of the moral argument outlined here are very well known, rarely do students' answers on this topic seem to live up to the information available. The three forms of the argument discussed — God as the source of good; God as the postulate of pure reason; God as the objective lawgiver — should provide you with a clear structure for answering a range of questions on the moral argument. The topic lacks favour with students, who much prefer to write about the other classical arguments for the existence of God. However, there are no traps here, and it is worth your while practising essays on this topic to give you further choice in the exam.

Review questions

1 *'The argument from morality increases the likelihood that God exists.'* Discuss.

2 If one believes that God exists, does it follow that one is morally compelled to obey him?

3 *'There is no need to explain morality in terms of a personal God. Morality is satisfactorily explained in terms of society and upbringing.'* How far does this view challenge the Moral Argument for the existence of God?

Topic 3

God and human experience

A The problem of evil

'Either God cannot abolish evil or he will not: if he cannot then he is not all-powerful; if he will not, then he is not all good.' (St Augustine)

1 Types of evil

Broadly speaking, there are two types of evil:

- **Natural evil** is the apparent malfunctioning of the natural world, which produces diseases, earthquakes, famines and so on: *'Natural evil is the evil that originates independently of human actions, in disease, in bacilli, in earthquakes, storms, droughts, tornadoes, etc.'* (Hick, 1968).
- **Moral evil** is the result of human actions which are morally wrong, such as murder, war and cruelty: *'Moral evil I understand as including all evil caused deliberately by humans doing what they ought not to do, or allowed to occur by humans negligently failing to do what they ought to do, and also the evil constituted by such deliberate actions or negligent failure'* (Swinburne, 1996).

The *consequence* of evil is **suffering**, which can involve physical pain and mental anguish. In addition to the pain it produces, suffering often appears to be unjust and the innocent are sometimes seen to suffer most. Evil may be further categorised and some scholars are concerned with the peculiar nature of animal suffering; psychological, emotional and mental suffering; the evil of contingency (that things corrupt and die); and the question of whether death itself is an evil which itself demands an explanation.

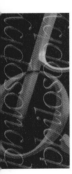

2 Analysing the problem

This classic problem of evil presents four distinctive problems of its own:

- A theological problem — it challenges the nature of God.
- A philosophical problem — it compels the believer to accept conflicting claims that are logically impossible to reconcile.
- A diverse problem — evil manifests itself in many ways that demand different explanations.
- A challenging problem — it is a problem that will not simply go away. The existence of evil and suffering is an objective reality which it is hard, if not impossible, to deny.

Hence, Richard Swinburne (1996) claims: *'There is a problem about why God allows evil, and if the theist does not have (in a cool moment) a satisfactory answer to it, then his belief in God is less than rational, and there is no reason why the atheist should share it'.*

The problem of evil is a real challenge for those who uphold the notion of the all-loving, all-powerful God of classical theism; the monotheistic God of Judaism, Christianity and Islam. For such believers, there is only one God and he is the all-powerful creator of the universe — which leads to a powerful dilemma:

÷ God has created the universe out of nothing and is totally responsible for it. If he is all-powerful, then he can do anything that is logically possible. This means he could create a world that is free from evil and suffering.

÷ God is omniscient and knows everything in the universe; he must, therefore, know how to stop evil and suffering.

÷ He is omnibenevolent and, in his love, would wish to end all evil and suffering.

÷ No all-loving God would choose that his creation suffer for no reason.

÷ Yet evil and suffering do exist, so either God is not omnipotent or omnibenevolent *or* he does not exist.

St Thomas Aquinas recognised the power of such arguments in his *Summa Theologica*, when he suggested that the existence of God and the existence of evil did seem logically impossible: *'But the name of God means that He is infinite goodness. If, therefore, God existed, there would be no evil discoverable; but there is evil in the world. Therefore God does not exist'* (cited in Hick (ed.), 1964).

2.1 The inconsistent triad

The problem can be viewed as an **inconsistent triad**. For the theist, God is (a) omnipotent and (b) all-loving. These qualities make God a being worthy of worship. However, (c) evil exists. This means that either (a) or (b) must be logically inconsistent and therefore untrue.

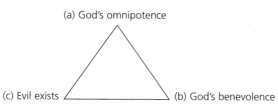

(a) God's omnipotence

(c) Evil exists   (b) God's benevolence

The atheist David Hume, in his book *Dialogues Concerning Natural Religion*, supported this view, suggesting that the qualities of omnipotence, omnibenevolence and evil cannot all exist. At best only two of them can. Thus, either:

1 God is not omnipotent, *or*
2 God is not omnibenevolent, *or*
3 Evil does not exist.

Hume concluded that since evil does exist, then the loving God of classical theism does not.

2.2 Qualification and theodicy

Now it often seems to people who are not religious as if there was no conceivable event…the occurrence of which would be admitted by sophisticated religious people to be a sufficient reason for conceding…'God does not really love us.'

(Flew, 1955)

Flew argues that the biggest challenge that the believer faces is allowing that the existence of suffering (or other reasons to deny the existence of God) are real challenges that demand an answer. It is not enough to say 'Oh well, we don't really understand how God works', and to carry on believing in the same way. If we say 'God's love is not like human love, so we can't expect him to intervene where there is suffering', this is simply *qualifying* God's love rather than demanding that we find good reasons why he should not intervene. In his **parable of the partisan and the stranger**, Basil Mitchell observed that theists should '*face the full force of the conflict*' — that is, not avoid the problem of suffering, but confront it, without allowing it to count decisively against their belief, but avoid uttering '*vacuous formulae*' such as 'It's God's will', which are neither explanations nor justifications.

However, as Aquinas recognised, logical argument only works if we think of God's goodness as being of the same nature as human goodness, whilst in fact it can be argued that God's goodness is a very different concept from human goodness. It is conceivable that God allows evil to exist as part of his greater plan of love. In such a case, there is no logical contradiction in God still being regarded as all-loving and all-powerful, since he has a reason for evil to exist. Such an approach has led to religious thinkers evolving theodicies to explain what God's reason is. A **theodicy** (literally 'righteous God') is an argument that suggests God is right to allow the existence of evil and suffering because, in some way or another, they are necessary and essential.

3 Solving the problem

3.1 Augustinian theodicy

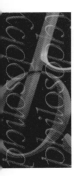

In his works *Confessions* and *De Genesi ad Litteram*, St Augustine (354–430 CE) argued that the Bible shows that God is wholly good and that, in Genesis 1, he is described as creating a world that was perfectly good and free from defect. There was no evil and suffering: '*God saw all that he had made, and it was very good*' (Genesis 1:31). Evil itself is not a thing or a substance and therefore God did not create it. Evil is really the going-wrong of something that is good — for instance, blindness is not a state in and of itself, but an absence of sight. Hence, Augustine termed evil a '**privation** of good', which came not from God, but from those entities that had free will — angels and human beings. These turned their back on God, the supreme good, and settled for lesser goods. He used the story of Adam and Eve to highlight the disobedience of the human race: '*Did God not say, "You must not eat fruit from the tree that is in the middle of the garden, and you must not touch it, or you will die"? "You will not surely die," the serpent said to the woman. "For God knows that when you eat of it your eyes will be opened and you will be like God, knowing good and evil"'* (Genesis 3:3–5).

As a consequence, the state of perfection was ruined by human sin and the delicate balance of the world was destroyed. Natural evil came through the loss of order in nature, and moral evil from the knowledge of good and evil, which human beings had discovered through their disobedience. As a result, they could no longer remain in paradise, a state which was now forbidden to them: *'So the Lord God banished him from the Garden of Eden to work the ground from which he had been taken'* (Genesis 3:23). Augustine said that both forms of evil were a punishment and that human beings have brought suffering upon themselves because they are all 'in the loins of Adam' (seminally present). Christians refer to this as **original sin**. For Augustine, the human race is as guilty and deserving of punishment as Adam.

Furthermore, God is right not to intervene to put a stop to suffering, since the punishment is 'justice' for human sin and God is a just God. However, Augustine concludes that if God were simply just, then everyone would receive his or her full and rightful punishment in hell. However, in his infinite love and grace, he sent his son, Jesus Christ, to die so that those who believed and accepted him could be saved and go to heaven. In this respect, the theodicy is *soul-deciding*: humanity's fate is decided on the basis of Adam's sin and the individual's response to God's offer of salvation.

Criticisms of the Augustinian theodicy

One of the principal critics of Augustine has been Schliermacher (1768–1834). In his book *The Christian Faith*, he suggested that Augustinian theodicy was logically flawed. Schliermacher argued that it was a logical contradiction to say that a perfectly created world had gone wrong, since this would mean that evil had created itself out of nothing, which is logically impossible. Either the world was not perfect to start with, or God made it go wrong. If this is the case, claimed Schliermacher, then it is God, and not humanity, who is to blame. A further criticism is that, if the world was perfect and there was no knowledge of good and evil, how could there be the freedom to obey or disobey God, since good and evil are unknown? If humans chose to disobey God, then knowledge of good and evil must have already existed.

The Augustinian theodicy can also be criticised on a scientific level. Augustine's view that the world was made perfect and damaged by humans is contrary to the theory of evolution, which asserts that the universe began as chaos and has been developing, not diminishing, continually. Moreover, suffering is essential to survival — things must die in order that others might eat and live. God must bear the responsibility for this, and yet to call it evil calls into question the whole natural order, implying that God should have created the world quite differently. Moreover, Augustine's view that every human was seminally present in Adam is not biologically accurate and all of humanity is not guilty of Adam's sin. This means that God is unjust in allowing humans to be punished for someone else's sin. Essentially, to use the Genesis narrative as a means of providing a theodicy is perhaps due to a misunderstanding of what the purpose of the narrative is. Read as a myth, it may seek to explain certain puzzling phenomena within the world, but to assume it does so in an objectively true way is not necessarily justified.

Finally, the existence of hell as a place of eternal punishment seems to contradict the existence of an all-loving God. If hell was part of the design of the universe, and God knew that the world would go wrong anyway, why did he still allow it to happen? This suggests a capricious, even malicious God — quite the contrary of what a theodicy sets out to defend.

3.2 Irenaean theodicy

In his work *Against Heresies*, St Irenaeus (130–202 CE) also suggested that evil could be traced back to human free will. However, he differed from Augustine by saying that God did not make a perfect world in the first place and that evil has a valuable part to play in God's plans for humanity.

Irenaeus thought that God was partly responsible for evil, in the sense that God created humans imperfectly, in order that they could develop into perfection. Irenaeus believed that God created humans in his own image (Genesis 1:26), but with the intention of allowing them to develop into his 'likeness' or perfection of character later. For Irenaeus, being in God's image meant having intelligence, morality and personality, but perfection would only be accomplished as humanity was changed into God's likeness, developing over time. Irenaeus explained that God could not have created humans in complete perfection, because attaining the likeness of God needed the willing co-operation of human individuals. In other words, absolute goodness and perfection had to be developed by humans themselves, through willing co-operation with God. This meant God had to give them free will, the only means by which they can willingly co-operate or act without coercion. Moreover, freedom requires the possibility of choosing good instead of evil, and therefore God had to permit evil and suffering to occur. Irenaeus claimed: *'How, if we had no knowledge of the contrary, could we have instruction in that which is good?'*

Irenaeus went on to explain that, according to the Bible, humans chose evil and rejected God's way. God had to permit this, because he gave humans free will. Had he intervened, Irenaeus observed, humans would have lost their freedom and their essential character: *'If anyone do shun the knowledge of both kinds of things...he unaware divests himself of the character of a human being.'* God created the natural order to include the possibility of good as well as evil and suffering. He then stood back to allow humans to use their free will for good or evil and he will not intervene, or else that freedom is lost. Irenaeus concluded by suggesting that, eventually, evil and suffering will be overcome and the human race will develop into God's perfect likeness and will live in Heaven, where all suffering will end forever and God's plan will be complete: *'He will wipe every tear from their eyes. There will be no more death or mourning or crying or pain, for the old order of things has passed away'* (Revelation 21:4).

Modern scholars have developed Irenaeus's ideas still further. John Hick highlighted the importance of God allowing humans to develop for themselves. He suggested that if God had made us perfect, then we would have had the 'goodness' of robots, which would automatically love God without thought or question. He said that such love would be valueless and that, if God wanted humans to be genuinely loving, then he was right to let them have the freedom to develop this love for themselves. Hick said that, to achieve this, God had to created humans at an **epistemic distance** from himself. This is a distance in dimension or knowledge. It means that God must not be so close that humans would be overwhelmed by him. If they were, they would have no choice but to believe and obey; but in keeping a distance, God allows humans to choose freely.

Moreover, the world has to be imperfect. If it were a paradise in which there was no evil and suffering, then humans would not be free to choose, since only good could actually occur. Similarly, without the existence of evil and suffering, humans would not

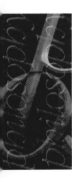

be able to develop positive and admirable qualities such as love, honour or courage, and would thus lose the opportunity to develop into God's likeness. If God constantly interfered, making everything good, then humans simply could not develop. This is known as the **counter-factual hypothesis**. In *Philosophy of Religion*, Hick (1973) said that while the world is not '*...designed for the maximisation of human pleasure and the minimisation of human pain, it may nevertheless be rather well adapted to the quite different purpose of "soul making"'*.

Hick is suggesting that the world is a place of soul-making — that is, a world where humans have to strive to meet challenges in order to gain perfection. And, of course, to do this, evil and suffering must necessarily occur. This is not inconsistent with Christian beliefs about the value of suffering, as St Paul observed: '*We rejoice in our sufferings because we know that suffering produces perseverance, perseverance, character, and character, hope*' (Romans 5:3).

Criticisms of the Irenaean theodicy

The Irenaean theodicy allows room for the concept of evolution and avoids some of the problems associated with Augustine, particularly the notion that evil seemed to have come from nowhere. However, it still has a number of weaknesses.

÷ Irenaeus suggested that everyone would go to heaven. This does not seem fair and just; it contradicts religious texts of many faiths and makes being good pointless — if everyone goes to heaven, what is the point of going out of your way to do good?
÷ The challenges of the world do not always result in genuine human development, and often seem to produce nothing but great misery and suffering, e.g. the Holocaust. Does the world really need such extremes of suffering to produce good?
÷ D. Z. Phillips (1976) argued in *The Concept of Prayer* that love can never be expressed by allowing suffering to happen: '*What are we to say of the child dying from cancer? If this has been "done" to anyone that is bad enough, but to be done for a purpose planned from eternity — that is the deepest evil. If God is this kind of agent, He cannot justify His actions and His evil nature is revealed.*'

Against these criticisms remains the view of Irenaeus that heaven is there for everyone because:

÷ If life simply ended in death, God's purpose would never be fulfilled.
÷ Only a supremely good future in heaven can justify the magnitude of suffering.
÷ Many 'evil' people are mentally disturbed and cannot be held totally responsible for their actions, and they cannot be punished for eternity.

3.3 Process theodicy

Process theodicy is a far more modern idea, stemming from the views of A. N. Whitehead (1861–1947) and developed by David Griffin (1976) in his book *God, Power and Evil: A Process Theodicy*. It is a radical theodicy in that, unlike the others, it actually suggests that God is not, in fact, omnipotent at all. He did not create the universe because the universe is an uncreated process of which God is himself a part. In other words, God is part of the world and the universe and is bound by natural laws. God's role in creation was to start off the evolutionary process, which, eventually, led to the development of humans. But God does not have total control and humans are free to ignore him.

Humans have very limited knowledge of God and his will. Moreover, God too suffers when evil happens since, like everything else, he is part of the universe. Whitehead described God as the *'fellow sufferer who understands'*.

God cannot stop evil since he lacks the power to change the natural process. Yet he bears some responsibility for it, since he started off the evolutionary process knowing that he would not be able to control it. Griffin (1976) claimed: *'God is responsible for evil in the sense of having urged the creation forward to those states in which discordant feelings could be felt with greater intensity'*. God's actions are justified on the grounds that the universe has produced sufficient good to outweigh evil — in other words, this universe is better than no universe at all.

This theodicy has several advantages:

÷ It removes the problem of why God does not put an end to evil and suffering — he simply lacks the power to do so.
÷ The fact that God suffers too means that he can identify with the suffering of humanity.
÷ Believers are encouraged to fight alongside God against evil.

Criticisms of process theodicy
However, there is something disquieting about the theodicy. In fact, some philosophers have doubted if it is a theodicy at all, since it actually denies that God is all-powerful in the first place and as such it fails to fulfil one of the essential characteristics of a theodicy — that it does not qualify the nature of God in order to justify or explain the existence of evil. In doing so, it brings into question whether such a limited God is actually a being worthy of worship. Moreover, if God cannot guarantee victory over evil, then what is the point of human efforts?

Finally, whilst it may be the case that the good has outweighed the evil, this is not much comfort to those who have actually suffered and, since there is no promise of heaven, there is no certainty that the innocent will be rewarded.

3.4 The freewill defence
Modern philosophers have begun to look more closely at the notion of 'free will', which underlined the work of both Irenaeus and Augustine, and have developed it into a theodicy in its own right called the 'freewill defence'. The defence is as follows: this world is the logically necessary environment for humans to develop as humans, since it provides freedom in the form of real choices which produce both good and evil. Without such choices, we would not be free and not be human. This does pose difficult questions, such as why does God permit such severity of suffering? However, supporters of the defence, such as Richard Swinburne, have suggested that God cannot intervene because to do so would compromise human freedom and take away the need for humans to be responsible, thus preventing human development: *'The less he allows men to bring about large-scale horrors, the less freedom and responsibility he gives them'* (Swinburne, 1979).

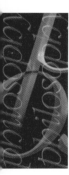

In *The Existence of God*, Swinburne used death as an example. If humans were immortal, they would have infinite chances to get things right. Although death is suffering of sorts, it means that life is limited, but a limited lifespan means that humans must take their responsibilities seriously — there may be no second chance: *'If there is always another chance there is no risk.'* In other words, the world needs to contain natural laws that can cause death, however much suffering this may cause: *'If men are to have knowledge of the evil which will result from their actions or negligence, laws of nature must operate regularly: and that means that there will be victims of the system.'*

Similarly, if we argue that certain evils are simply too great, then we have to suggest how much evil is acceptable. John Hick suggested that the problem with this is that if we deem certain evils as being too great, then we begin to go down the scale of evils until even the slightest suffering becomes too much. For instance, if we say that cancer is too severe, then what about heart disease, a cold or a headache? He suggests that we must either demand a world with no evil and suffering in it at all, or accept what we have now; there can be no middle ground.

Criticisms of the freewill defence

One of the problems that the freewill defence fails to answer is the criticism levelled at the other theodicies, namely the issue that divine love cannot be expressed through suffering. Furthermore, many people still reject God. Could not God have created people who would always freely choose him? *In Evil and Omnipotence*, J. L. Mackie (1955) wrote:

God was not, then, faced with a choice between making innocent automata and making beings who, in acting freely, would sometimes go wrong: there was open to him the obviously better possibility of making beings who would act freely but always go right. Clearly, his failure to avail himself of this possibility is inconsistent with his being both omnipotent and wholly good.

However, John Hick argued that, in such a case, humans would not be truly free, since God would always know they would choose good — their actions would have been decided before they were actually made, even if we were under the illusion that we were acting freely.

3.5 Monism

Monism is not a theodicy, but it is a challenge to the concept of evil itself. Monists claim that the universe is a single, harmonious unity that is good. Everything is good, and evil is a mere illusion in our minds. It causes a *feeling* of suffering only because we cannot see the whole picture, but if we could, we would realise the illusion.

Spinoza (1632–77) argued that we tend to assess things wrongly — we assess things in terms of how useful they are to us (and hence we may miss their true value) and we assume that there are norms to which humans, animals and natural objects conform, and hence we regard a shrivelled tree to be defective. Spinoza said that, if we looked at the universe objectively, without putting us first, we would see that everything has a unique value: *'All things are necessarily what they are, and in Nature, there is no good and evil.'*

In his work *Theodicy*, Leibniz said that this world was the *'best of all possible worlds'* because God, in his infinite wisdom and goodness, could not have made it any other way. Thus evil must be an illusion — it cannot have any reality in such a world. Mary Baker Eddy, the founder of the Christian Science Movement, argued that evil is in the mind. She suggested that evil had no reality and that when sufferers realise that there is no reality to their pain, they can do nothing other than stop suffering.

Criticisms of Monism

Monism is not very widely supported; it seems to contradict our own experience of the world in which there is, plainly, evil and suffering, and as such is counter-intuitive. Moreover, it does not really explain why a loving God would allow humanity to suffer from an illusion. Most important of all, it trivialises evil and suffering — if evil is only an illusion, why should we try to be good and avoid evil? And how would we know if we were doing evil anyway, since it is an illusion?

Conclusion

The problem of evil and suffering is a major argument against the existence of God. And for those who do not believe in God to begin with, the problem of evil effectively strengthens their point of view. Religious believers find it difficult to explain — some use the rather unsatisfactory argument that we, as humans, cannot understand the ways of God and that God has a purpose that we cannot comprehend. In doing so they fall into the trap of qualification that Anthony Flew so despises.

The problem raises all sorts of issues about the nature of life and death and whether the struggle of life is worthwhile. It challenges the power of God, by asking whether he can prevent evil, intervene and work miracles. There are no easy answers but the issue is well summed up by Swinburne (1996):

A generous God will seek to give us great responsibility for ourselves, each other, and the world, and thus a share in his own creative activity of determining what sort of world it is to be. And he will seek to make our lives valuable, of great use to ourselves and to each other. The problem is that God cannot give us these goods in full measure without allowing much evil on the way.

Summary

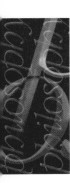

- **Nature of the problem** — if God is all-good, all-powerful and all-knowing, then why does he allow evil and suffering to continue in a world over which he is, presumably, in control?
- **Types of evil**: natural evil — malfunctioning of the natural order *or* the way in which we perceive natural phenomena that cause us harm; moral evil — the wrongdoing of humanity towards each other or in causing damage to the natural order.
- **Solving the problem** — not by **qualification**, arbitrarily changing the nature of God to suit difficult circumstances — rather by **theodicy,** a rational justification for the existence of evil.
- **Augustinian theodicy** — based on Genesis 1–3. A conservative, traditional theodicy that explains the corruption of a perfect creation because of human disobedience. Allows for free will (a benefit) to have negatively influenced the perfect environment

in which humans were placed. Evil, however, is a privation, not a substance, since a perfect deity cannot have created it. Those who are destined to be saved will be able to overcome the effects of the fall, but others will go to hell.

- **Irenaean theodicy** — a more liberal, forward-looking theodicy, which allows for an evolutionary view of the world, and gives to evil a positive, or **teleological**, function. Through making the right free choices, humans can grow towards perfection, although they were not created perfect. Evil and suffering are necessary stimulants towards their making the right choices. God remains at an **epistemic distance**, so as not to be overwhelmingly obvious to humans and unduly influence their choices.

- **Process theodicy** — a modern theodicy which argues that God is *not* omnipotent, but, like humans, strives within the universe to bring about the best result. He will not always succeed.

- **The freewill defence** — incorporated into both Augustinian and Irenaean theodicies. The creation of human free will was the best choice God could have made, since it allows humans to grow in power, freedom and knowledge. It is logically impossible that humans should be both free and yet always make the good choice, so evil is an inevitable part of the created order.

- **Monism** — a tenuous theory, suggesting that evil has no reality and is an illusion. The world consists of one substance only, which is good.

Key terms

Epistemic distance — a distance of knowledge, dimension or awareness.

Privation — an absence or lack.

Qualification — redefining the nature of God in order to avoid the implications of the problem of evil.

The inconsistent triad — the philosophical problem of evil posed as a logical impossibility. Evil cannot exist if God is both all-powerful and all-good.

Theodicy — a defence of God that offers reasons why God should permit evil to exist whilst not qualifying his nature.

Exam watch

I'm sure your heart lifts when you reach this topic! It is universally popular and in most cases produces a candidate's most successful response in the exam. Nevertheless, there is scope to answer more critically and in more depth than most students realise. You can pick up marks for a clear understanding of material you have evidently not found difficult to absorb, but more marks can be gained by demonstrating a strong philosophical awareness of the concepts involved. Explore the topic beyond Augustine and Irenaeus, to consider the ways in which these classical theodicies have been taken up by important twentieth-century contributors to the debate. Use technical vocabulary accurately and relevantly; play around with the nature of the problem and not just its solutions, and you have the ideal material for a very strong answer.

Review questions

1 '*The existence of evil is an insurmountable problem for religious believers.*' How far do you agree with this statement?

2 (a) What do religious believers understand to be the problem of suffering?
 (b) Outline two solutions to the problem.
 (c) Consider the success or otherwise of these solutions.
3 (a) For what reasons does the existence of suffering cause philosophical problems for a religious believer?
 (b) Outline two solutions to these problems and comment on their success.

B Miracles

1 The concept of miracle

A miracle occurs when the world is not left to itself, when something distinct from the natural order as a whole intrudes into it.

(Mackie, 1982)

There seems to be broad agreement amongst scholars that a miracle must have the following three essential characteristics:

1 It must break the laws of nature.
2 It must have purpose and significance.
3 It must have the possibility of a religious interpretation.

Although it is possible to use the term 'miracle' in other ways too — to describe a scene of great natural beauty, for example, or to speak of some particularly fortuitous event or a change for the better in someone's personality — for our purposes we will consider that a miracle is most accurately defined as an event which includes these three essential criteria.

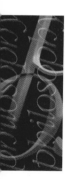

Miracles are a type of religious experience, in that they are attributed to the supernatural power of God, and claims of miraculous events have been examined in great depth over the centuries. Miracles have always had the power to convert people and to confirm religious belief, and there are thousands of testimonies given down the ages of people who claimed to have experienced miracles. Nevertheless, the problem of how to define a miracle is a weighty one and must be resolved at least to some extent before it is possible to consider whether they are conceivable, logically possible, or whether accounts of miracles should be considered reliable. Scholars throughout the centuries have been divided in their views on the nature of miracles.

For St Thomas Aquinas, there were three kinds of miracles:

1 Events done by God, which nature could never do, e.g. stopping the sun (Joshua 10:13). Such an event might arguably be deemed logically impossible, or less strictly, a physical or natural impossibility.
2 Events done by God, which nature could do, but not in that order, e.g. the healing of paralysis and exorcisms (Mark 1:31). These events would not be inconceivable, but certainly highly unexpected.
3 Events done by God, which nature can do, but God does without the use of natural laws, e.g. healing by forgiving sins (Mark 2:5). Such an event would take place in the

natural order of things, but the means by which God brings it about characterises it as a miracle.

For Aquinas, miracles in all these cases could be defined as: *'Those things…which are done by divine power apart from the order generally followed in things.'*

This is not without its difficulties, however. What Aquinas is suggesting is an **interventionist** God, who only acts on certain, almost random occasions, a God who is, in effect, little more than a spectator of human affairs. We could illustrate this view with the picture of a father standing on the sidelines watching his son play hockey. When his child is knocked to the ground and appears to be injured, the father rushes onto the pitch to give aid, but whilst all is going well, he just stands and watches. However, there is no compulsion upon him to hurry onto the pitch even at the moment of crisis. He may refrain from doing so for any number of reasons, not least because his son might be deeply embarrassed! This is contrary to the classical theistic view, which says that God, as a loving father, constantly interacts with his creation, not just occasionally or when he feels he has no other option.

The problem of natural laws

Moreover, Aquinas's argument is based on the idea that God breaks natural laws. The problem here is that we may not actually know all natural laws, nor how they operate. We might not, therefore, be able to tell if a natural law has been broken or not. John Hick suggests that natural laws may, in fact, be no more than *'…generalisations formulated retrospectively to cover what has, in fact, happened'*. Similarly, if a natural law is 'broken', this may be no more than saying that something happened that we did not understand or expect. Yet scientists argue that, within nature, a certain number of unexpected or random actions may occur. Indeed, in his work *Philosophy of Religion*, Mel Thompson (1996) argues that *'The idea of a miraculous event introduces a sense of arbitrariness and unpredictability into an understanding of the world.'* Thompson appears to be suggesting that we can allow for 'arbitrariness and unpredictability' without introducing the complicating factor of miracles.

In response, Richard Swinburne says that the laws of nature are reasonably predictable and that if an apparently 'impossible' event happens, then it is fair to call it a miracle. He gives examples of such events in the Bible:

…the resurrection from the dead in full health of a man whose heart has not been beating for twenty four hours and who was dead also by other currently used criteria; water turning into wine without the assistance of chemical apparatus or catalysts; a man getting better from polio in a minute.

(Swinburne (ed.), 1989)

Swinburne suggests that people do recover from illness, are resuscitated from death, and water can be turned into wine with the aid of chemicals, but what determines whether we call it a miracle is the way and the time scale in which these things occur — outside the normal conditions in which such changes usually happen. Hence, such events are not logical impossibilities — akin to a circle being squared — but are remarkable for the way in which they occur, their timing or the circumstances involved, and they fulfil Aquinas's second and third categories of miracle.

2 The purpose of miracles

Just to say that a miracle is *defined* as God intervening in natural laws is not enough — there must, surely, be a reason for God's actions. Swinburne, in *The Concept of Miracle*, suggests that a miracle must also have a deeper religious significance: *'If a god intervened in the natural order to make a feather land here rather than there for no deep, ultimate purpose, or to upset a child's box of toys just for spite, these events would not naturally be described as miracles'.*

The fact that some miracles appear to be almost as arbitrary and purposeless as these examples raises serious criticisms of miracles on moral grounds, and many testimonies do little to redress this problem. For example, in St Clare's Basilica in Naples, the people regularly gather to see the 'miracle' of St Gennaro's blood liquifying before their eyes. Peter Vardy (1999a), in *The Puzzle of God*, questions such miracles on moral grounds: *'A God who intervenes at Lourdes to cure an old man of cancer but does not act to save starving millions in Ethiopia — such a God needs, at least, to face some hard moral questioning'.*

Other modern philosophers agree. For example, Maurice Wiles (1986) writes: *'It seems strange that no miraculous intervention prevented Auschwitz or Hiroshima. The purposes apparently forwarded for some of the miracles acclaimed in the Christian tradition seem trivial by comparison'.*

This leads on to the criticism that the actual occurrence of certain miracles seems to be incompatible with the notion of the love and justice of God. God appears to help some people through miracles, but not others — if he is indeed all-loving and just, he should treat everyone equally — for example, within Judaism, he saved the Jews in the Exodus, yet he did not save the millions of Jews who died in the Holocaust.

This may not be altogether accurate, however, since Jesus is recorded as claiming that the purpose of his miracles was to bring people to believe in him. He did not cure everyone he met — his miracles were for this broader purpose, although that is not to say that individuals did not also benefit specifically: *'Just believe it — that I am in the Father and the Father is in me. Or else believe it because of the mighty works you have seen me do'* (John 14:11).

Christian believers might also argue that humans do not understand God or the way in which he acts, and that it is impossible to make definite statements about God's work, one way or the other. If we claim that God should or shouldn't have intervened in a particular way or in particular circumstances, we are claiming that somehow we know how God should act, and if this were the case, we would presumably have the mind of God ourselves.

3 The interpretation of miracles

Miracles as coincidence

In *Religion and Understanding*, R. F. Holland suggested that a miracle is nothing more than an extraordinary coincidence that is seen in a religious way (an example of 'seeing as'). He uses the example of a small boy who is stuck on a railway line. The driver of the express train, who cannot see the boy, unexpectedly faints and falls onto the brake lever, bringing the train to a halt, and saving the boy. His mother claims that a miracle

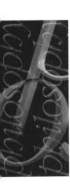

has taken place even after she has been told what led up to the event. According to Holland: *'A coincidence can be taken religiously as a sign and called a miracle.'* If the mother has reason to believe that a miracle has taken place and has some pre-existing belief that God acts miraculously in the world, then however the event is explained to her, she will continue to interpret it in this way. However, Holland's interpretation makes a miracle dependent on personal interpretation, which is of necessity subjective, and which will vary from person to person: one person says an action is a miracle, the other says it is not; how are we to judge?

Are miracles symbolic?

Those who subscribe to the **realist** point of view have suggested that miracles are purely for the faithful and that, if there is a God, he would indeed make them happen, to increase the faith of his people. Anti-realists, however, say that 'coincidences' and similar events are not miracles because God plays no part in them. They suggest that miracles are events that help believers to understand the nature of God — they may be symbolic rather than objectively real events, and are only properly understood by the religious believer — such as the signs in John's Gospel.

Along similar lines, in the nineteenth century D. F. Strauss, in *The Life of Jesus Critically Examined*, adopted the term 'myth' to cover all the miraculous elements in the gospels. He shifted the focus from the 'story of a *miraculous occurrence*' to '*the story* of a miraculous occurrence'. Controversially for his time, he argued that the miracle stories were not helpful proofs of Jesus's messiahship, but rather problematic parts of the biblical narrative, since history and science were concerned with an observable train of cause and effect, and not the intervention of forces outside the scope of empirically verifiable events.

In the 1940s, Rudolph Bultmann wrote: *'It is impossible to use electric light and the wireless, and to avail ourselves of modern medical and surgical discoveries, and at the same time to believe in the New Testament world of spirits and demons.'* He claimed that the modern reader must **demythologise** the biblical text to extract the meaning that its writers intended to convey, but which, to the modern mind, was obscured by concerns about 'what really happened'. The miracle stories were effective vehicles for conveying deeply spiritual truths, but the modern mind has lost the key for interpreting them. Removing the miraculous elements of the story would, Bultmann argued, make it possible to re-experience the Gospel in a more relevant way.

4 Do miracles actually happen?

The views of David Hume

David Hume defined a miracle as *'A transgression of a law of nature by a particular volition of the Deity'* and claimed that *'Nothing is esteemed a miracle, if it ever happens in the common course of nature'.* In his classic work, *An Enquiry Concerning Human Understanding*, Hume argued that it will always be impossible to prove that a miracle has happened. He took the view that all questions of truth had to be answered by the evidence of experience, and that the evidence we have is unreliable: *'No testimony is sufficient to establish a miracle unless it is such that the falsehood would be more miraculous'*.

He proposed four grounds for disbelieving the evidence we have for miracles:

+ *'There is not to be found in all history, any miracle attested by a sufficient number of men, of such unquestioned good sense, education and learning, as to secure us against all delusion.'*
+ *'The passion of surprise and wonder, arising from miracles...gives a tendency towards belief of those events... A religionist may be an enthusiast and imagines he sees what has no reality.'*
+ *'It forms a strong presumption against all supernatural and miraculous relations that they are observed chiefly to abound amongst ignorant and barbarous nations.'*
+ *'In matters of religion, whatever is different is contrary...every miracle, therefore, pretended to have been wrought in any of these religions...destroys the credit of those miracles.'*

What Hume is suggesting is that there has never been a miracle which has been witnessed by a sufficiently large number of reliable, objective witnesses and that, in fact, those who see miracles tend to be religious believers anyway, people who are essentially 'looking' for miracles. Moreover, miracles are not seen in 'civilised' countries, but in primitive ones. Finally, he says that all the different religions cannot each be true — yet they all claim that miracles are performed by their deities. Hume suggests that these testimonies cancel each other out, making all testimony unreliable.

Problems with Hume's view

The major criticism of Hume's four points is that they are really far too general to be regarded as convincing evidence:

+ Hume does not say what would constitute a sufficient number, or what 'unquestioned good sense, education and learning' actually means. Do the witnesses have to have a university education, for instance? Equally, he only refers to 'men' — are women therefore unreliable witnesses?
+ Do only religious people see miracles? Moreover, are religious people unreliable anyway?
+ Hume says that miracles are chiefly observed in 'ignorant and barbarous' nations — yet even in Hume's time the countries that reported the most miracles were France and Italy. Did he consider them 'ignorant and barbarous'?
+ Finally, is it not possible for God to work miracles for all people, not just Christians? Swinburne (1971) writes: *'Evidence for a miracle wrought in one religion is only evidence against the occurrence of a miracle wrought in another religion if the two miracles, if they happen, should be incompatible with each other'.*

Modern philosophers, such as Swinburne, have been prepared to consider the possibility that the best explanation for an event is indeed that it is a miracle. They claim that the evidence in favour of a miracle must be considered properly, not simply dismissed because it may not be scientific. It is wrong simply to assume that miracles cannot occur. The principle of **Ockham's Razor** could be applied here — this principle argues that the simplest explanation for an unusual event is generally the most philosophically viable explanation. There is no reason why, when all other issues have been considered, the explanation for an unexpected event should not be that it is, in fact, a miracle. Moreover, Swinburne (1996) argues in his work *Is There a God?* that, as a **principle of credulity**, we should normally accept what people tell us to be the truth: *'We ought to believe things as they seem, unless we have good evidence that we are mistaken'*. Furthermore, Swinburne (1979) claims: *'If there is a God, one might well expect him to make his presence known to man, not merely through the over-all pattern of the universe in which he placed them, but by dealing more intimately and personally with them'*.

To conclude…

There is no certain answer as to whether or not miracles actually occur and, given their unverifiability, there is no decisive reason why it may not even be possible that miracles are the work of unseen beings or aliens, or are the result of undiscovered powers within the human mind. In the light of this, then, perhaps the most that can be said is that a miracle is an event that is interpreted within the context of religious belief and faith as an act of God. This definition of miracle is sufficiently inclusive to cover events that are not violations of a natural law but understood by believers to have religious significance and to be, in some way, the result of God's direct, personal and interventionist action in the world, or in the lives of believers.

Summary

- **Definition of miracle** — religious interpretations of miracle usually amount to a breach of a natural law, brought about by God, for a beneficial purpose, and which reveals his will and purposes in some way.
- **Aquinas** — three miraculous ways in which God can work within the natural order which may or may not involve a violation of natural law.
- **Hume** — whilst rejecting the occurrence of miracles, he maintains that should one occur, it would constitute a violation of natural law. But if natural laws cannot be broken, then no miracle can occur. What, therefore, is the status of natural law? Are natural laws fixed or flexible? Can God break his own laws?
- **Miracles as coincidences** — no violation of natural law is needed here, but rather an event given a religious interpretation. This is highly subjective.
- **Miracles as symbolic events** — not literally true events that defy natural law, but symbolic stories that convey religious messages. The miraculous element of the story may need to be removed to make the story meaningful to a modern age.
- **Why should God perform miracles?** Do they suggest a malevolent or arbitrary God who does not intervene in every situation where his power is needed, but only where he randomly chooses to act? Do they close the epistemic distance between God and human beings? Are they his response to humanity's 'special pleading' (Swinburne)? Do they reveal his glory, power and eschatological purposes? Is God obliged to intervene in the natural order?
- **Hume's critique of miracles** — the unreliability of people's testimony, their love of wonder, the dubious origin of accounts of miracles, and the low probability of them occurring should lead us to reject all accounts of miracles. Swinburne, however, argues that we should be inclined to believe people's accounts rather than be sceptical unless we have very good reason to think they are lying.

Key terms

Anti-realist — subjectively true.

Demythologise — remove the miraculous or mythological elements from narratives.

Interventionist — an act which intervenes in the regular or expected pattern of things.

Natural law — that which happens regularly within nature.

Ockham's Razor — the principle that the simplest explanation is the most likely.

Principle of credulity — we should believe what people say unless compelled to do otherwise.

Principle of testimony — that people generally tell the truth.

Realist — objectively true.

Exam watch

Questions on miracles generally ask you to consider definitions of a miracle, to give reasons why miracles might support or undermine religious belief, or critically to evaluate Hume's critique of miracles. In all these cases it is important to remember that this is a philosophy exam, and that extended accounts of miracles, whether biblical or contemporary, will gain few marks. Don't just write about Hume either, except where you are particularly asked to do so. There are plenty of other scholars with much more up-to-date things to say about miracles, although Hume's contribution is a classic of its type. Whatever your opinion on miracles, you must not fall back on vague statements such as 'God loves us so he will perform miracles' and fail to support them using the opinions of scholars. It is easy to preach or to launch into an atheistic diatribe when writing about this topic, so remember that the examiner is not actually interested in your personal opinion.

Review questions

1 (a) What problems are there in defining miracles?
 (b) For what reasons may an account of a miracle be considered unreliable?
 (c) In what ways might the occurrence of a miracle support religious belief?
2 (a) Identify the way in which one philosopher understands the term 'miracle'.
 (b) Consider the arguments that may be used to discredit belief in miracles and the ways in which belief in miracles might nevertheless still be strong.

C Religious experience

1 The nature of religious experience

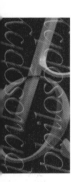

Human beings constantly enjoy a succession of experiences of a wide variety: physical and empirical experiences of objective reality (which some would claim are the only reliable experiences available to us); psychological and emotional experiences, which are rooted in human feeling and responses to stimuli; intellectual and aesthetic experiences; experiences that are private and individual, and those which are shared and corporate, although still open to a range of interpretations. All of these experiences are usually consistent with other previous experiences of the same or a similar kind and their interpretation consistent with previous interpretations. Religious experiences are beyond ordinary, worldly, empirical explanation and are most usually likely to take place within a context of religious expectancy and hope. Even if they occur suddenly, it may well be the final outcome of a long and drawn-out period of searching and struggling with questions about spiritual and ultimate realities. Religious experiences, like any other experiences, may be individual — where an individual is made aware of a transcendent reality — or corporate — where a gathering of people, usually already focused on the divine, appear to be influenced by powers beyond normal control and understanding.

All types of religious experience, and the peculiar nature of it, are found in biblical literature, which provides a useful source of case studies for a comparison of religious experiences and an examination of their nature and purpose. Some biblical experiences have become textbook cases: Moses sees a burning bush and hears a voice calling him to a particular mission (Exodus 3); Elijah experiences a great storm, followed by a 'still small voice' and a command to continue his prophetic activity (1 Kings 19); Isaiah sees the Lord lifted up high in the temple and hears a voice telling him to take God's message to his people (Isaiah 6). In all these cases the protagonist sees and hears outward phenomena that acquire a special, symbolic significance, and at the same time believes that he is called to a special task — usually involvement in a situation of conflict on an international scale.

In the New Testament, the high point of Jesus's disciples' experience during his ministry is the Transfiguration (Mark 9.2ff & //s), although it seems to have only had a temporary impact on them, and it wasn't until after the resurrection that they became fully conscious of the implications of their experiences. On the road to Emmaus after Jesus's death, two disciples meet Jesus but fail to recognise him until they experience him breaking bread, a moment of revelation which causes them to interpret their walk on the road with him as a religious experience — their hearts were 'strangely warmed' (Luke 24:13ff). As with the Old Testament experiences, visual and verbal symbols are given a special interpretation and demand a response from the experient.

What unites all these events is that they are experienced by those who are actively called to be part of God's ongoing purposes. They are not self-contained experiences, which separate the experients from the world, but engage them with it, sometimes in great conflicts such as those that Elijah was forced to confront. One of the crucial tests of the integrity of a religious experience is its results, and the response that the individual makes to the experience is crucial here. Despite his fear, Elijah returns to continue the fight against Baalism in Israel; despite their despondency, the disciples on the Emmaus Road are encouraged to believe in the power of the Resurrection.

Paul Tillich identified a feeling of 'ultimate concern' as being characteristic of religious experience, which was a subjective, but not trivial, sentiment, since it demanded a decisive decision from the experient. However, he observed that it was possible for some people to be part of a religious community, sharing its life and rituals, and yet never making a decisive commitment of their lives as a result of experience either by sharing the life of the religious community and being governed by its 'ultimate concern' or by suddenly grasping as critical a concern that had previously been regarded as unimportant or illusory.

Religious experiences need not simply be thought of in terms of a specific event, since for religious believers whose lives are lived in a state of 'God consciousness', all things have the potential to be a religious experience: the beauty of the natural order, their daily experiences, and the way they believe that they fit into the plans and purposes of God.

2 Conversion experiences

The word 'conversion' comes from the Greek term *metanoia*, which means to 'turn again' or to 'return'. It is also often translated as 'repentance', although the Greek term does not carry any intrinsic religious significance. It is used in the New Testament to refer specifically to the 'conversion' of both Jews and Gentiles to the Gospel. Conversion need not involve a religious experience in the common sense of the word, but could be a gradual process that culminates in a sense of certainty, assurance and conviction, possibly after years of spiritual searching. Conversion may be from one major religion to another — Christianity to Buddhism, for example — or from one denomination to another within one religious tradition — for example, Anglicanism to Catholicism. In an age when there is an increasing interest on the part of Christians to witness to the 'unchurched' there are many testimonies of conversions from a life in which belief in God and religious commitment had no place whatsoever, to making a profound spiritual commitment. David Wilkerson (1978), in his book *The Cross and the Switchblade*, describes his experiences as an independent missionary pastor in New York, ministering to violent street gangs. He witnessed many conversions of this kind among hardened, atheist gang members, whose lives were utterly transformed by their decision. Nicky Cruz, the feared leader of the Mau Maus, describes the experience in his own book, *Run Baby Run*:

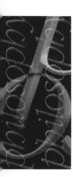

I opened my mouth but the words that came out were not mine. 'O God, if you love me, come into my life. I'm tired of running. Come into my life and change me. Please change me.' That's all it was. But I felt myself being picked up and swept heavenward… I was literally baptised with love… For the first time in my life it made sense. I had become new. I was Nicky and yet I was not Nicky. The old way of life had disappeared. It was as though I had died to the old way — and yet I was alive in a new kind of way… All my fear was gone. All my anxieties were gone. All my hatred was gone. I was in love with God…with Jesus Christ…and with all those around me. I even loved myself.

(Cruz, 1968)

Paul's conversion, which is described on three separate occasions in Acts, is often considered a classic of the type. On the road as he travelled to Damascus to persecute the church there, he saw a light and heard the voice of Jesus calling him to ministry. Three days of blindness were ended after a visit from Ananias, who had had his own religious experience when he was called to disciple Paul, and his life was changed forever. Interestingly, however, John Hull questions whether conversion is the correct way of describing Paul's experience. He observes that Paul had no distinct concept of Christianity, but rather that his interpretation of Judaism was refocused by the experience. He still saw himself as a Jew, but the experience became a lens through which his understanding of his Judaism was interpreted.

John Wesley's experience fits a fourth type of conversion experience — that which leads a believer into a deepening commitment and a new appreciation of their faith, typically of the personal dimension that belief in God may involve. Wesley was conscious of the missing personal dimension of his Christianity. But one day in May 1738 he had a vivid experience that enlivened his faith. He wrote: *'I felt my heart strangely warmed, I felt I did trust Christ, Christ alone, for salvation; and an assurance was given me, that he had taken away my sins…'* (cited in Cole, 1999).

3 Mysticism

A mystical experience is one in which the subject becomes overwhelmingly aware of the presence of the ultimate and experiences feelings of being utterly swept up in the presence of God. Blaise Pascal described the experience as: *'Fire, God of Abraham, God of Isaac, God of Jacob, not of the philosophers and the scientists. God of Jesus Christ. Joy, joy, joy, tears of joy.'* Mystical experiences are enormously wide-ranging, but there appear to be several common features:

❖ A profound sense of union and unity with the divine.
❖ A transcending of time.
❖ A 'noetic' experience (William James) or a 'showing' (Mother Julian of Norwich) — in other words, not just a subjective experience, but something is clearly revealed to the experient.
❖ A sense of joy and well-being.

The mystical experience is often associated with religious revival. Douglas V. Steere observes that *'as long as it flourishes, it constitutes a continual challenge to what William James calls "a premature closing of accounts with reality" in terms of an exclusively ethical, institutional, theological or intellectual presentation of religion'* (Halverston and Cohen (eds), 1960). It is vital, then, to the continuing life of the religious community, and gives a glimpse of another world beyond empirical and earthly realms.

For the earliest Christians, it seems that mystical experience in the form of direct experience of the Holy Spirit was available to all (e.g. Acts 2, 1 Corinthians 12, 14) until it was taken over by ascetic specialists and the experience became narrowed down to a spiritual elite. The association of mysticism with special acts of preparation has encouraged the view that mysticism is a special discipline, available only to a spiritual few. Three steps of preparation have been identified:

❖ **Purgation** — ridding the soul of tendencies that prevent it from paying attention.
❖ **Illumination** — preliminary disclosures which focus attention.
❖ **Contemplation** — the stage in which the presence of the divine penetrates the believer.

Scholars have made many attempts to divine what goes on in a mystical experience. Paul Tillich described two stages: an objective event or encounter, followed by a special understanding of that event as the result of ecstasy — a special way of looking at the event which reveals its religious significance. Rudolph Otto famously coined the term '**numinous**' to describe the event, though it is not exclusive to mystical religious experiences. He traced it back to the ***mysterium tremendem et fascinans***, which he said was the origin of religion. In mystical experiences, the individual was both attracted and repelled by a sense of awe and wonder. Simon Peter's words to Jesus after the miraculous catch of fish express this paradox well: *'Depart from me, for I am a sinful* man, O Lord' (Luke 5:8); as do Isaiah's in the temple: *'Woe is me! For I am lost; for I am a man of unclean lips, and I dwell in the midst of a people of unclean lips; for my eyes have seen the King, the Lord of hosts'* (Isaiah 6:5). Both men felt a fascination despite their initial reaction to draw back in fear. They sensed mystery, awe and wonder at being in touch with that which they knew to be beyond themselves (transcendent) and yet which they were encountering within their own objective world — in Peter's case, by the lake, and in Isaiah's, in the temple.

Furthermore, there appear to be two types of mysticism: **introvertive** — in which the mystic looks inwards on his own experience and perceives his own oneness with the divine; and **objective** — where the experience of the mystic is like that of the poet, contemplating outward circumstances. The poetry of Gerard Manley Hopkins is akin to mystic contemplation:

> *Lovely the woods, waters, meadows, combes, vales,*
> *All the air things wear that build this world of Wales.*
> *Only the inmate does not correspond:*
> *God, lover of souls, swaying considerate scales.*
> *Complete thy creature dear O where it fails,*
> *Being mighty a master, being a father and fond.*

Those opposed to mysticism as a legitimate part of Christian experience might be so for a number of reasons, but primarily because it supposes a kind of spiritual elitism that suggests salvation comes through attaining a mystical goal and not through Jesus's work on the cross. This has echoes of **gnosticism**, which was spurned in the early church for teaching that special knowledge and revelation was the way to salvation, rather than it being a gift of divine grace. Other criticisms of the mystical approach are that it is opposed to the institutions of the church and the sacraments as the media of that divine grace, and that it has no link with ethics. Rudolph Otto suggested that the numinous was isolated from morality, as it was concerned with nothing other than a pure sense of the holy. Furthermore, because mystics encounter the otherworldly in their experiences, some critics claim that mysticism is opposed to traditional doctrines of eschatology.

However, Douglas V. Steere writes in support of mysticism: *'The mystic's witness to the accessibility of the living presence…in the hearts of contemporary men and women has been an enormous encouragement to the religious yearnings of men'* (Halverston and Cohen (eds), 1960).

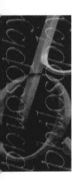

4 Corporate experiences

Although many religious experiences, such as those described above, have a deeply personal significance, many are reported as happening within a corporate gathering. In Acts 2:1–4, Luke describes one of the most important corporate religious experiences in the Christian tradition:

When the day of Pentecost had come, they were all together in one place. And suddenly a sound came from heaven like the rush of a mighty wind, and it filled all the house where they were sitting. And there appeared to them tongues as of fire, distributed and resting on each one of them. And they were all filled with the Holy Spirit and began to speak in other tongues as the Spirit gave them utterance.

This kind of charismatic experience is familiar to many Christians who meet in congregations that regularly experience such phenomena. The church at Corinth clearly did, as Paul writes to them with specific guidance as to how their meetings were to be conducted to allow corporate, charismatic experiences to be truly beneficial to the edification of the whole church (1 Corinthians 12–14). In the early 1990s many churches reported a wave of corporate, charismatic experiences that left many Christians divided about their origin and purpose. In *The 'Toronto' Blessing*, Dave Roberts (1994) writes about the experience of the pastor of the Elim Pentecostal Church in Loughborough:

He went to the normal 9.15am service. At the 11.15 service things suddenly became different. There was a tremendous awe, and sense of the presence of God. After some time Roy asked people forward for prayer and immediately people began to fall down under the power of God. Whole groups of the congregation fell without anyone being near them. There was a lot of crying and a lot of heart-searching. God was obviously present.

Corporate experiences of this kind have an enormously powerful effect on those present, though not all by any means. Many Christians remain sceptical about the validity of such experiences, whilst not denying that God seeks to interact directly with his people, individually and as a body. In a crowd of like-minded individuals, it is arguably easy to be swept along in a tide of emotion and to feel compelled to be sharing the same experience as fellow worshippers. Researchers have recreated in the laboratory the conditions which often prevail at large religious gatherings — music, lighting, repetition of words and phrases, repeated patterns of behaviour — and it has been conjectured that the techniques used and the atmosphere generated in services and meetings stimulates physical and psychological reactions which can be misinterpreted as an experience of the divine. However, such findings cannot be decisive, and in *Introduction to the Philosophy of Religion* Davies (1982) observes significantly that '*The truth of a belief is not affected by the factors that bring the belief about*'.

(See pp. 57–64 for a discussion on the value of religious experience as an argument for the existence of God.)

Summary

- Religious experience is experience that is beyond ordinary explanation and empirical phenomena. There are many biblical examples: Isaiah 6; Exodus 3; Acts 2; I Kings 19; Mark 9; Luke 24. All involve a calling to God's purposes and challenge the experient with difficult circumstances. The effect on the life of the experient is crucial.
- **Paul Tillich** — religious experience is identified by a feeling of '**ultimate concern**'.
- **Conversion experiences** — may be a vivid experience of transformed life, or a gradual process; may be from one religious tradition to another, or from one denomination, or from no belief at all. Examples of Paul (Acts 9), Nicky Cruz, John Wesley.
- **Mysticism** — the experient becomes overwhelmingly aware of the ultimate and is swept into the presence of God. May involve preparation and contemplation. Keeps

alive the ongoing spiritual dimension of religious belief and practice. A **numinous** experience that repels and attracts.

- **Corporate experiences** — may involve charismatic phenomena and shared expression of belief and the emotions which it generates.

Key terms

Conversion — an experience which brings about a change.

Corporate — experience that is shared by a group, usually those who share a common religious belief.

Mysticism — an experience in which the ultimate reality is vividly encountered.

Numinous — an experience of that which is wholly other.

Exam watch

Most questions on religious experience ask how well it may serve as a proof for the existence of God, but you also need to be able to consider types of religious experience and the problems of interpretation that they raise. The issue is always one of interpretation, since the phenomena of religious experience are those that can be interpreted in non-religious ways. However, you need to be careful not simply to dismiss religious experience as automatically better interpreted naturalistically or psychologically. Have some case studies ready to use and analyse them intelligently.

Review questions

1 What are the distinctive characteristics of religious experience?
2 Explain the concept of mysticism. Is mysticism an integral part of religious belief?
3 Is it ever possible to verify whether or not a religious experience has taken place?

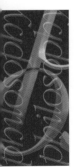

Topic 4

God and the world

A Interpreting the universe

1 Religious and scientific interpretations of the universe and human origins

There are so many different ways in which both religious believers and scientists go about attempting to explain the creation of the universe and human origins that it would be foolish to assume that the debate between them is a simple one. Consider this wide range of views which may be adopted:

- **Evolutionary creationism** — God created the universe through the process of evolution.
- **Evolutionary mysticism** — there is some mystic meaning behind the evolutionary process.
- **Evolutionary materialism** — only matter exists and evolution is nothing but the working-out of its laws.
- **Evolutionary progressivism** — a metaphysical meaning can be found in evolutionary progress.
- **Age-day flat creationism** — creation of organic life involved miraculous intervention by God but in separate acts over a long time span.
- **Gap-theory creationism** — creation was a re-creation after a disaster, involving miraculous intervention by God.
- **Young-earth creationism** — creation involved miraculous intervention by God over a period of 144 hours some 6–8,000 years ago.

All these views of world origins include some understanding of God's involvement, but each suggests a different way in which God's activity took place, or is continuing to take place. The range of views is influenced by the variety of approaches that religious believers may take to the Bible:

- **Fundamentalists** — believe in the literal truth of scripture and its propositions, e.g. that God created the universe *ex nihilo* (out of nothing).
- **Liberalists** — believe that the Bible was not written directly by God but by people who used their own religious experience to communicate their beliefs using different literary styles and adapting material to their culture and traditions, e.g. that the creation narratives are mythological narratives which explained unknowable phenomena.

+ **Traditionalists** — believe that although the Bible is full of truth, some parts of it have to be reinterpreted, although they are not necessarily in agreement as to which parts these are.

For our purposes, scientific interpretations of the origins of the cosmos and of human development come into conflict with religious interpretations in two key areas: the theory of evolution by natural selection, and big bang cosmology.

Darwin's **theory of evolution** by natural selection claims the following:

+ Because of competition for food, the young of any species compete for survival.
+ Those young that survive to produce the next generation tend to be characterised by favourable natural variations that are passed on by heredity (natural selection).
+ Each generation may improve adaptively over the succeeding generations, and this gradual and continual process is the source of evolution of the species.
+ All related organisms are descended from common ancestors.
+ The earth itself is not static, but evolving.

The Big Bang theory claims the following:

+ Some 15 million years ago, a tremendous explosion started the expansion of the universe.
+ At the time of this event all of the matter and energy of space was contained at one point. What existed before is completely unknown and is a matter of pure speculation.
+ It was not a conventional explosion, but rather an event filling all of space as all the particles of the embryonic universe rushed away from each other. It consisted of an explosion of space within itself, unlike an explosion of a bomb, when fragments are thrown outwards.
+ The big bang lay the foundations of the universe.

2 The problem of religious ambiguity and scientific certainty

It is commonly assumed that science and religion represent such opposing disciplines that they cannot, under any circumstances, be reconciled. This debate reaches a climax in debates about the origin of the universe: if the universe is the product of processes which can be explained, if not in their entirety then at least to a significant extent by scientific research and its findings, is there any need for God? Is the role of a divine, personal creator made redundant if we can explain the universe and human origins in terms of big bang cosmology, natural selection and evolution? Before we are in a position to attempt to answer these questions, we need to investigate why scientific and religious explanations of the universe and its phenomena are perceived by many as incompatible.

What is the problem?

+ Is it a problem of interpretation?
   Science and religion are faced with the same data — e.g. fossils, variety of species, the structure of human bodies, DNA — but their significance may be interpreted differently.

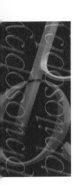

+ A problem of language and genre?
Religious discourse frequently makes use of myth, metaphor, symbol or allegory; scientific debate depends on objective assertions that can be either verified or falsified. Science deals with literal fact; religion is like poetry.

+ A problem of how versus why?
Is science concerned with the mechanics of the universe and religion with the meaning of it?

+ A problem of purpose versus meaninglessness?
Does the religious believer seek a meaning, purpose and goal to the universe whilst the scientist perceives it as ultimately meaningless?

+ A problem of the nature of human significance?
Is the religious believer committed to finding a special significance for human beings whilst the scientist sees them as nothing more than the species at the top of the evolutionary chain?

+ Does science deal with questions that can be definitely decided while religion is a matter of personal choice?

What are the solutions?
There are broadly three possible solutions to this dilemma:

+ Scientific explanations are wrong; religious explanations are right. For example, scientific 'evidence' is a trick, an illusion, the work of Satan or a misinterpretation of empirical data.

+ Religious explanations are wrong; scientific explanations are right. For example, religious explanations belong to the 'pre-scientific' age before a scientific paradigm had been widely accepted. Even belief itself can be scientifically explained: *'What a person believes is a function of the structure, the neural structure of the brain, particularly as it has been determined by the summation of his experience. To give a reason is to attempt to justify the particular brain structure one has...'* (Sire, 1994). According to this view, there is no rational reason for belief, or for why a person should believe one thing rather than another, and no room for seeking meaning or significance in what is merely a biological mechanism for survival.

+ Both are correct within their particular **form of life**:
Scientific realism — science provides us with a true picture of an independently existing reality.
Non-realism — the truth of our assertions about the world is not independent of our relation to the world, and whether our claims are true or false is connected with how we establish whether they are true or false. This view represents an **anti-realist** interpretation of religious discourse in that it does not attempt to make objectively true statements that cohere to reality, but argues that the claims made by religious believers are part of a language game which represents a particular form of life, in this case the life of the religious community. According to this view, we should not be asking questions about the truth of religious claims but about how they are being used: *'Don't ask for the meaning, look for the use'* (Wittgenstein). Scientific claims belong to their form of life and are used correctly or incorrectly within their language game,

so neither believer nor scientist is in a position to criticise the other, since they are not playing the same game by the same rules.

3 How does science work?

The science/religion debate has become prominent over the last 200 years because science as a discipline has developed so rapidly and significantly during that period. Why is this so?

True assumptions

The success of science...is obvious; modern science rests on true assumptions, and what went before rested on false assumptions. So long as you believe that...the sun moves around the earth, you won't make much progress. But when you start to work with correct assumptions, your researches set off on the right track and progress is more or less inevitable.

(Horner and Westacott, 2000)

The view expressed above depends, of course, on accepting that the assumptions claimed as true by scientists *are* true. In fact the process of getting new assumptions accepted as true is often fraught with difficulties.

The right method

A scientific approach is characterised by claims which have to be supported by evidence, using a methodology which distinguishes between science and non-science. A creationist view, for example, is not based on evidence which has been collected, but on the authority of scripture which is accepted by **faith**. The theory of evolution, on the other hand, is based on observations of fossil records, species, mutations and extinctions. If new evidence came to light that explained these phenomena better than the explanation of evolution, the old theory would be cancelled out by the new.

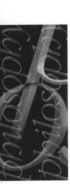

Modern scientific methodology is based on experience, which is itself dependent on experimentation (hypothesis testing) and observation. Scientists make predictions based on their experience, and work on the principle that what has happened in the past is a reliable predictor of what will happen in the future. However, what is the justification, or rationalisation, for this? This raises the **problem of induction**. Induction involves examining our past experience, comparing it with present experience, identifying any new or unusual circumstances, and calculating how likely it is that future experience is likely to lead to the same conclusions that we have reached in the past. For example:

Observation 1: Every cup of hot chocolate I have drunk so far has not proved fatal to me.

Observation 2: No unusual circumstances are present today to give me reason to suspect that drinking this cup of hot chocolate may be fatal.

Conclusion: Drinking hot chocolate today will have the same consequences as it has had on all previous occasions.

This conclusion is not reached by applying reason; in other words, it is not an *a priori* or deductive conclusion. Nevertheless, even though it does not *logically follow* that the chocolate will not prove fatal, I feel confident in drinking it because I make certain assumptions:

÷ Nature operates in a uniform manner.
÷ I have had experience of a sufficient number of previous, similar circumstances to make the generalisation that future events will bring similar results, and not yield unexpected ones.

However, do we simply *assume* what we are trying to prove? This process is not deductive, but can it be justified according to **probability**? The probability of drinking the chocolate proving fatal is low; the probability of it being non-fatal is high. There is an element of risk, but because we accept the risk as being so low we are not deterred from drinking the chocolate. As Dean L. Overman states in 'A case against accident and self-organisation' (cited in *Evolution on Trial*):

An objective, reasonable person who follows mathematical and other logical thought processes and the principles of the scientific method will not favour a proposition which has a very low probability over a proposition which has an extremely high probability.

(http://www.accuracyingenesis.com/words.html)

Essentially, we believe that we can make a connection between observed (past) and unobserved (future) cases, and the basis on which we do this is because we are informed by custom. David Hume observed that *'All inferences from experience, therefore, are effects of custom, not of reasoning'* but noted that it is questionable whether this is a rational basis upon which to operate. As Ravi Zackarias (1999) explains:

The principle of causality, then, according to Hume, is nothing but an associate of successive impressions. Through habit and custom we expect that the succession will take place; in reality there is no necessary connection. In short, nothing authorises even science to formulate universal and necessary laws.

So, does science deal with questions that can definitely be decided after all? Everyday science (e.g. making computers) may deal with definite questions, but not when we are confronted with a **paradigm shift**. Furthermore, not all sciences deal with 'hard' facts; human sciences such as psychology or sociology use scientific methods (research, experimentation, observation) and put forward scientific arguments (e.g. that girls do better in single-sex schools than in co-educational ones), but they cannot offer any decisive proofs. A debate of this kind can lead to very emotional disputes as the two parties try to push forward their viewpoint, and usually the best conclusion is that there is truth on both sides and although there might not be any empirical or mathematical way of resolving the matter, it is within the realms of reasonable judgment.

T. S. Kuhn and paradigm shifts

In his book *The Structure of Scientific Revolutions*, T. S. Kuhn (1970) made a distinction between **normal science** and **revolutionary science**. Normal science works on a set of basic assumptions about which there is no dispute and within the limits of the prevailing paradigm in a given field. Revolutionary science, however, occurs when there is a struggle between the prevailing paradigm and one that threatens to supersede it, leading to what Kuhn termed a 'paradigm shift'. Kuhn cites as examples of such shifts the transition from Aristotelian to Galilean thinking, and from Newtonian to Einsteinian thinking. As a paradigm shifts, it is inevitably accompanied by dispute and uncertainty as opposing schools of thought are pitched against one another. A new paradigm will face opposition until a sufficient body of evidence and experience vindicates it, but when paradigms conflict it is because they rest on incompatible assumptions. Darwin's theory of natural selection faced precisely this situation, which he acknowledged:

A crowd of difficulties will have occurred to the reader. Some of them are so grave that to this day I can never reflect on them without being staggered, but, to the best of my judgment, the greater number are only apparent; and those that are real are not, I think, fatal to my theory.

(Cited in Banner, 1990)

The duck-rabbit

Paradigm shifts are analogous to the shift of perception illustrated by Wittgenstein's duck-rabbit (see p. 23), known as a **Gestalt** switch. Such a shift does not change the character of the world, or the objects in it, but changes take place in the way the data are interpreted. Hence, if the theory of evolution is correct, it has been correct for all time. It did not come into being because Darwin discovered it, although the evidence which he perceived as pointing to natural selection was then perceived differently, and led to a change in the interpretation of that data and everything which followed from it.

However, because different paradigms typically characterise different historical periods, it appears to be possible for a statement such as 'God created the world *ex nihilo*' to be true in one historical period and false in another — a form of relativism inevitably operates. Kuhn suggested that truth in science was evolutionary since, if science progresses, later theories must somehow be closer to the truth than earlier ones. But is this an appropriate model when comparing religious and scientific truths? If a creationist view of the universe was 'true' until Darwinism, and modern cosmology brought about a paradigm shift, does this make the later paradigms more truthful than the biblically based perception of the world and its origins? Or are we trying to force an evolutionary relationship between two entirely different types of truth?

Change, dispute and uncertainty in science

The concept of the paradigm shift reveals scope for change in science, and with change there is inevitably dispute. As Michael J. Behe explains in 'Darwin's Black Box: the biochemical challenge to evolution' (cited in *Evolution on Trial*):

Since no one knows molecular evolution by direct experience, and since there is no authority on which to base claims of knowledge, it can truly be said that the assertion of Darwinian molecular evolution is merely bluster.

(http://www.accuracyingenesis.com/words.html)

When we go beyond the realms of normal science, we enter into unknown and insecure territory which demands belief as much as the acceptance of religious doctrines. As Mark A. Ludwig observes, in 'Computer viruses, artificial life and evolution' (cited in *Evolution on Trial*):

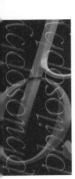

The philosophical commitments of Darwinism seem to be poisoning it from within. Darwin's hypothesis is undeniably linked to the idea that atomistic materialism is absolute truth, because it posits that materialism is not in the laboratory but in history. Therefore, Darwinism demands a degree of philosophical commitment which ordinary science does not. That makes Darwin's hypothesis philosophically fragile. It requires belief. Despite the fragility of this idea, it has become the scientist's paradigm, and he is rarely ready to admit that it is fragile and charged with philosophy.

(http://www.accuracyingenesis.com/words.html)

In his book *In Defense of the Faith*, Dave Hunt (1996) quotes the eminent British astronomer Fred Hoyle, who sharply observed that scientists are frequently as compelled as religious believers to hold fast to a teaching rather than risk excommunication from the scientific community: *'Most scientists still cling to Darwinism because of its grip on the educational system… You either have to believe the concepts or you will be branded a heretic'.*

4 Could science prove the need for an intelligent, purposeful creator?

Even if the whole universe consisted of organic soup, the chance of producing the basic enzymes of life by random processes without intelligent direction would be approximately one in 10 with 40,000 zeros after it… Darwinian evolution is most unlikely to get even one polypeptide right, let alone the thousands on which living cells depend for survival.

(Hunt, 1996)

It is not only scientists with a religious faith that have observed in recent decades that science cannot provide all the answers about the creation and development of the universe and its species. It may be able to guide us towards some answers, but many scientists have claimed that what science has discovered itself needs an explanation, which science cannot provide. This accounts, in some measure, for the continued appeal of the Cosmological and Teleological Arguments, based on quasi-scientific observations which it would appear cannot be fully explained by science. Josh McDowall (1999) observes: *'Oddly enough, of all the worlds in collision today, it is the scientific world that is increasingly giving the greatest and most shocking evidence in favour of God's existence'.*

McDowell cites a range of phenomena which he and others argue point to a creation directed by a purposeful mind:

÷ The structure of DNA is analogous to written messages.
÷ Science can now demonstrate the need for intelligent causes.
÷ Modern cosmologists are amazed at the narrow margin which is allowed for cosmic evolution.

Significantly, he quotes Stephen Hawking (1987):

This means that the initial state of the universe must have been very carefully chosen indeed if the hot big bang model was correct right back to the beginning of time. It would be very difficult to explain why the universe should have begun in just this way, except as an act of God who intended to create beings like us.

Essentially, Hawking is suggesting that it is possible that whilst science might provide an explanation, it may not provide a *complete* explanation and that it might be necessary to look beyond the findings of science for something that explains what science has discovered. As we saw in our discussion of the Cosmological Argument (pp. 29–38), for the religious believer, God is the best and simplest explanation.

Summary

- Religious and scientific interpretations of the universe are *diverse* — there is not just one scientific and one religious interpretation. Many religious interpretations attempt to *combine* a scientific perspective with God's intervention and continuing involvement in creation. Religious interpretations of the universe are influenced by varying interpretations of scripture.
- Why do science and religion conflict? Is it a question of language, interpretation of data, meaning and purpose, significance, mechanics?
- What are the solutions? Is one right and the other wrong, or are there ways of seeing them as compatible? Are they both 'true' within certain criteria of truth?
- Scientific methodology has led to the rapid development of science — evidence and experimentation leading to correct assumptions. But the **problem of induction** poses the question, why do we believe that the past is a reliable guide to the future? Is this a rational way of proceeding?
- Revolutionary science does not work on the principle that science offers set answers. **Paradigm shifts** force a shift in thinking, leading to periods of change and uncertainty in science. There is no reason to assume that today's paradigm — e.g. evolution — will not be proven wrong by new evidence tomorrow.
- But could science prove that there is intelligent, purposeful design in the universe? If scientific explanations are not complete in themselves, then a further explanation may still be required. Is God then the simplest explanation?

Key terms

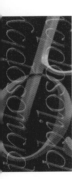

Big Bang cosmology — the theory that an enormous explosion started the universe around 15 billion years ago.

Evolution by natural selection — the scientific theory that the individuals within a species that are best adapted to their environment will survive to produce offspring, passing on favourable hereditary characteristics. All organisms share common ancestors and the universe as a whole is evolving.

Induction — the method of reasoning which leads us to draw conclusions about the future on the basis of what we know of the past.

Paradigm — the prevailing way of interpreting the world.

Probability — the relative frequency or likelihood of an event taking place, or of circumstances unfolding in a particular way.

Religious ambiguity — the view that the universe does not provide overwhelming evidence of God's direct involvement, so it can be interpreted religiously or non-religiously.

Scientific realism — science provides us with a true picture of an independently existing reality.

Exam watch

The best answers on this topic don't get bogged down in lengthy descriptions of the different possible ways of interpreting or explaining the universe, which are invariably too simplistic or inaccurate. Avoid tedious narratives of Genesis 1–2 as they add very little to your answer. Gather your marks through careful evaluation of whether it is reasonable to argue that either science or religion has the answer, not both, or whether some kind of compatibility can be found. There are no right answers as far as the examiner is concerned — just well or badly constructed essays.

Review questions

1 (a) Outline the key differences that may exist between a scientific and a religious account of the origins of the universe.

  (b) How may these two types of account be compatible with each other?

2 Consider the challenge to religious belief presented by modern cosmology in relation to the teaching offered in Genesis 1.

3 In what ways do the approaches of science and religion differ? Are differences between them made comprehensible by understanding them as representing two distinct 'forms of life'?

B Critiques of religious belief

1 Atheism and agnosticism

Atheism

Atheism means, literally, 'without/no God'. However, there are many reasons *why* people may hold an atheistic position and it should not be assumed that all atheists have rejected belief in God for the same reason. It is also important to note that there is a difference between strong and weak atheist positions. 'Weak atheism' is simple scepticism — disbelief in the existence of God. 'Strong atheism' is an explicitly held belief that God does not exist.

The word 'atheism', however, has in this contention to be construed unusually. Whereas nowadays the usual meaning of 'atheist' in English is 'someone who asserts there is no such being as God', I want the word to be understood not positively but negatively. I want the originally Greek prefix 'a' to be read in the same way in 'atheist' as it customarily is read in such other Greco-English words as 'amoral', 'atypical', and 'asymmetrical'. In this interpretation an atheist becomes: someone who is simply not a theist. Let us, for future ready reference, introduce the labels 'positive atheist' for the former and 'negative atheist' for the latter.

(Flew, 1984)

Consider the following reasons why atheists may adopt their position:

÷ There is no such being to whom the description 'God' can be given. The Logical Positivists, for example, held that since 'God' is a metaphysical term, it is meaningless even to ask questions about the existence of God, let alone believe in it.

÷ So-called experiences of the divine can be accounted for without reference to God.

Samuel Butler wrote: *'Theist and atheist — the fight between them is as to whether God shall be called God or have some other name'* (Pepper (ed.) 1991). For example, an atheist may claim that the visions of a mystic can be explained in terms of feverish hallucination, whilst the theist may claim that they are direct experiences of the divine.

÷ Apparently contradictory states of affairs in the world — evil and suffering, for example — count decisively against the existence of God: *'The existence of a world without a God seems to me less absurd than the presence of a God, existing in all his perfections, creating an imperfect man to make him run the risk of Hell'* (Armand Salacrou, ibid.).

÷ Believers in God are deluded or have been deluded by religious leaders for their own unscrupulous purposes.

÷ A dislike and distrust of organised religion may lead to rejection of belief in God. Religious systems can be satisfactorily explained in terms of social, psychological or political factors.

÷ A hatred of religious beliefs and believers: *'The sort of atheist who does not so much disbelieve in God as personally dislike him'* (George Orwell, ibid.).

÷ Belief in God serves only to support those who are emotionally, intellectually or psychologically weak.

Agnosticism

An **agnostic** holds that it is not possible to know whether God exists, or to know his nature. The term was coined in the nineteenth century by Thomas Huxley, as the opposite of 'gnostic', the Greek term used in the early church to describe those who professed to have special revelatory knowledge of the divine. Agnostics may well claim to be open to the possibility of knowledge leading to belief rather than non-belief, but may not be able to say what it would take for them to believe. Hence, it is possible to say that agnosticism is merely another form of atheism.

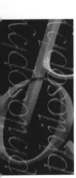

Agnosticism is essentially concerned with the problem of what we can genuinely know. The critical philosophy of David Hume brought into question the status and character of positive knowledge. He pointed out that it was only knowledge of regular sequences and connections that we could observe and it did not imply knowledge of causes, powers, natures, essences or purposes. This began the disassociation of science from metaphysics. With the steady progress of the sciences and the analytical attention of philosophers to what scientists were doing, it became abundantly clear that science was capable of dealing only with questions that arose in the course of research that could be tested. Loose questions, general questions, questions about causes and origins, and other traditional metaphysical questions, were not the kind with which science was, or would ever be, competent to deal. By the time that T. H. Huxley invented the word 'agnosticism', the onus was on believers to justify their belief, to show why they should be taken seriously:

Positively the principle may be expressed: In matters of the intellect, follow your reason as far as it will take you, without regard to any other consideration. And negatively: In matters of the intellect, do not pretend that conclusions are certain which are not demonstrated or demonstrable. That I take to be the agnostic faith, which if a man keep whole and undefiled, he shall not be ashamed to look the universe in the face, whatever the future may have in store for him.

(T. H. Huxley, *Agnosticism*)

2 Sociological approaches

Sociologists may perceive religion as more than belief in God or the supernatural, but as a system which attempts to provide an ultimate solution to explaining human existence or which serves a function within society as a whole.

Émile Durkheim

Durkheim's functionalist theory of religion argues that religion serves to unite and preserve the community. He defined religion as: *'A unified system of beliefs and practices relative to sacred things...beliefs and practices which unite into one single moral community called a church, all who adhere to them'* (Durkheim, 1954).

Durkheim was not concerned with the variety of religious experience of individuals but rather with the communal activity and the communal bonds to which participation in religious activities lead. He likens a religious community to a primitive clan that worships a totem, symbolising God and the unity of the clan. The clan and God are one and the same, hence there is no separate entity called God, and thus God does not exist. What does exist is a unified social system which believes that it owes its being to God. This belief is expressed in shared rituals, values and identity, it discourages change, and explains phenomena that make little sense.

Religion, he argued, is not only a social creation, but it is in fact society divinised. Durkheim stated that the deities that people worship together are only projections of the power of society. Religion is essentially social, occurring in a social context, and when people celebrate sacred things, they unwittingly celebrate the power of their society, to which they give sacred significance. Durkheim argued that in the modern world, people needed to recognise that they had become dependent on a society to which they had given religious significance, and must *'discover the rational substitutes for these religious notions that for a long time have served as the vehicle for the most essential moral ideas'* (Durkheim, 1961).

Criticisms of Durkheim's view

÷ Religious believers distinguish between membership of their religious community and belief in God. Their loyalty is to God, not to the community.

÷ The theory does not explain how religious believers — for example, Old Testament prophets, or radical reformers such as Martin Luther King — are sometimes prepared to go against society and even to reject it.

÷ Durkheim's thesis was modelled on primitive aboriginal societies, and is therefore not a true reflection of modern religious belief and practice.

÷ Society constantly changes; beliefs about the nature of God are timeless and unchanging.

Karl Marx

Marx argued that God was an invention of the human mind in order to satisfy emotional needs, declaring that *'The first requisite for the happiness of the people is the abolition of religion'* (Pepper (ed.), 1991). The ruling classes used religion to dominate and oppress their subjects, offering them an illusion of escape — *'It eased pain even as it created fantasies.'* He was convinced that *'religion is so fully determined by economics that it is pointless to consider any of its doctrines or beliefs on their own merits'.*

Marx observed that people created God, not vice versa, and religion was an alienating force, ascribing to God powers that were in fact possessed by the people. People had therefore lost control of their destiny through their belief in God. He maintained that when a revolution overthrew the ruling class, and religion was abolished, the oppressed masses could be liberated. Only by loving one another rather than God could people regain their humanity.

Ironically, according to Marx religion had originated in revolutionary movements, but once detached from its roots, it had been used by the ruling classes to dominate and oppress. Inequality was legitimised in the name of religion, discouraging the subject classes from recognising their real situation and seeking to rise above it. Although religion offered a release from distress, it was a false release, and thus, claimed Marx, was *'the opium of the people'*.

Marx imagined primitive communist societies in which the members of the community owned all resources jointly. People would have duties and roles, but their work would be an extension of their personality and would be inherently fulfilling to them, while at the same time contributing to the good of the entire community. In such a system, goods would be shared throughout the group, so each person had what they needed to live (food, clothing, shelter) and to be productive (raw materials), but no more. In such a society, religion would no longer be needed to fulfil the function that a capitalist society forced upon it.

Criticisms of Marx's view

÷ In most societies, the separation between church and state is far greater than Marx assumed.

÷ **Liberation theology**, in countries where there is considerable poverty such as South America, has blended Marxism and Christianity in an attempt to change the nature of society for the oppressed without rejecting belief in God.

÷ Religion is a force that is open to interpretation, and so it can be an influence for both change and stagnation. The internal philosophies of some religions may appear to discourage change, whilst other more radical branches encourage it. The biblical picture of God is of a deity who transforms situations and lifts up the oppressed.

÷ Weber (1904) suggested that religion promotes social change and that capitalism had developed in Europe due to the Protestant ethic of hard work and self-denial.

3 Psychological approaches

Sigmund Freud

Freud argued that religion is a projective system, a *'universal neurosis'* or illusion, which, he claimed, people should *'disregard in its relation to reality'*. God, therefore, has no reality, but is a creation of the human mind. Like Durkheim, Freud saw the origins of religious belief as lying with primitive tribes. The tension between the dominant male and the subordinate males (sons) culminates in the overthrow of the father (a manifestation of

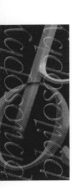

the Oedipus Complex), but the subsequent guilt of the sons leads them to elevate his memory and to worship him. The **super-ego** then takes the place of the father as a source of internalised authority, which is derived from the family, education and the church. It represses anti-social impulses such as killing and, by inducing fear and guilt, it is crucial for civilisation. It is this we call the conscience, and God is not only a father substitute, but also a projection of the super-ego. Freud maintained that an individual was dependent upon religion to *'make his helplessness tolerable'*, and that whilst individuals maintained this unhealthy dependency they would never be truly happy.

Criticisms of Freud's view

- Freud attributed all religious behaviour to the projection of psycho-sexual drives and claimed that people's attachment to God depended on their relationship with their father. However, Nelson and Jones found that the concept of God correlated more highly with a person's relationship with their mother than with their father.
- Kate Lowenthal distinguished between **projective religion**, which is immature, and **intrinsic religion**, which is serious and reflective. Freud assumed that all aspects of belief in God were immature, and he neglected the diversity and development of religious beliefs.
- Arthur Guirdham argued that Freud overplayed the connection between belief in God and the psycho-pathological tendencies of much organised religion, and between the feeling of security in the womb (the **oceanic feeling**) and religious belief. He observed that Freud's anti-religious stance may be thought just as neurotic as the religious preoccupations of others.
- Freud strove to be objective, although by current standards the methods he used probably allowed his biases to influence his data. His influence in psychology has declined over the years, and his theories of the primal horde have been rejected as mere conjecture.

Carl Jung

Jung was Freud's pupil, but left Freud's following when they disagreed over the importance of sexuality and spirituality to one's psychological development — Freud emphasised sexuality over spirituality; Jung disagreed. Jung was concerned with the interplay between conscious and unconscious forces. He proposed two kinds of unconscious: personal and collective. Personal unconscious (shadow) includes those things about ourselves that we would like to forget. The collective unconscious refers to events that we all share, by virtue of having a common heritage (humanity). For example, the image (archetype) of a mythic hero is something that is present in all cultures, and they are often viewed as gods. Jung was fascinated with non-Western religious perspectives, and sought to find some common ground between East and West. In doing so, Jung had a very broad view of what it means to be empirical. Suppose, for example, that I hear a voice that I think to be God's, but you (sitting beside me) do not. To Jung, this would constitute an empirical observation. To most contemporary scientists, however, it would not be considered an empirical observation, and because this is a decisive area of disagreement, far less research has been done on Jungian approaches to religion than on the Freudian perspective.

4 Arguing for the non-existence of God

÷ The problem of evil could be seen to be the strongest atheistic argument. (For a full discussion of this topic, see pp. 68–78.)

÷ Science and rationalism have made a significant contribution to atheistic belief since the Enlightenment. It is possible to explain the world religiously and non-religiously, as we saw in our discussions of the Cosmological and Design Arguments, and therefore the existence of God cannot be decisively proved by referring to the evidence provided by the natural world. (See pp. 29–47 for these topics, and pp. 91–99 for a discussion of religious and non-religious interpretations of the world.)

÷ Modernism rejects the literal use of terms such as 'heaven', 'hell' or 'demons', claiming that they are merely representations of outdated mythological concepts. (See pp. 124–125 for more on this.)

÷ Advances in biblical criticism and analysis, which discouraged a literal interpretation of the text and revealed the writers' use of sources and the way in which they had been influenced by their cultural environment, could give grounds for arguing that the Bible cannot contribute in any way to proving the existence of God.

Can God be disproved?

If it is not possible to prove decisively the existence of God, it must also be impossible to disprove it. It is questionable whether the atheist really is on any stronger ground than the theist, bearing in mind that the same rules of proof and probability must apply to an atheistic argument as to a theistic one (see pp. 14–20). The biblical writers did not countenance the possibility of atheism or suggest that it may have any intellectual or philosophical credibility: it is *'the fool'* who has *'said in his heart there is no God'* (Psalm 10:4; 53:1). However, theists may argue that even within theistic belief there remains an element of agnosticism, since the transcendent God is ultimately unknowable and cannot be presumed to be known fully.

Summary and key terms

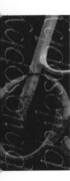

■ **Atheism** — a disbelief in the existence of God *or* an explicitly held belief that God does not exist. Reasons for holding such a view will vary widely and may be based on philosophical, logical, sociological, psychological or scientific justifications.

■ **Agnosticism** — the view that it is not possible to know whether God exists or to know his nature. Essentially concerned with the universal problem of what we are able to know.

■ **Sociological approaches** — Durkheim adopted a functionalist view of religion: that it serves a socialising and controlling function in society. Society is worshipping itself in the guise of God, which unites them in a common bond and discourages revolutionary change. Marx saw this as a tool for the ruling classes to prevent the working classes from recognising their true position. A revolution would enable them to realise the function that religion plays in their lives and to overthrow it, along with the ruling classes.

■ **Psychological approaches** — Freud traced religion back to its primitive roots in the primal horde. Belief in God as the father figure substitute is a **universal neurosis** that prevents people from facing up to the reality of their mortality. Jung identified the use of archetypes or models deep in the collective human unconscious which become 'gods'.

- **Other atheistic arguments** — problem of evil; scientific explanations of the universe; modernism.
- **Problem of atheistic arguments** — it is ultimately no easier to falsify the existence of God than to verify it. The atheist's position is not philosophically stronger.

Exam watch

Make sure you distinguish very clearly between an atheistic argument — i.e. one that argues against the existence of God for any one of a number of reasons — and a critique of religion, which offers reasons why religious systems have developed and are maintained other than worship of an objectively real deity. You can fit these critiques into a question on atheism, but make sure that their purpose is clearly identified. A critique of religion need not necessarily be atheist, however, since it is possible for a theist to believe in the existence of God but to reject organised religion as a human-made phenomenon that serves other purposes. Don't fall into the trap, either, of assuming that the atheist's argument is stronger than the theist's. Both are attempting to make claims about a transcendent being who is, strictly speaking, no more falsifiable than verifiable. You could argue that the atheist is in a stronger position since a God who cannot be empirically proven is more likely not to exist than to exist. This depends, however, on assuming that empirical evidence is the only evidence which would count in favour of God's existence.

Review questions

1 (a) What is meant by atheism?
  (b) What is meant by agnosticism?
  (c) Outline and evaluate two arguments for the non-existence of God.
2 For what reasons may atheism be considered to be philosophically a stronger position than theism? Is this the case?
3 'It is possible for there to be a coherent theistic explanation of the universe and a coherent atheistic explanation.' Examine and evaluate this claim.

Topic 5

Human destiny

A Body, soul and post-mortem existence

1 The relationship between body and soul

The principal problem in the question of life after death is what survives — the body, the mind/soul, or both? To an extent, it depends on what we mean by being human. Human beings are characterised by the physical (body) and the mental/spiritual (mind/soul). The physical body can be seen and identified as a matter of fact, but the mind/soul cannot be analysed in the same way. In *God and the Mind Machine*, John Puddeford suggests that the characteristics of the mind include **qualia** (sensory experiences such as taste) and **intentionality** or **aboutness**, i.e. I don't just *think*, I think *about something*. The problem is therefore whether mind and body are of one and the same nature (**monistic**) or have two natures (**dualistic**).

Dualism is the notion that humans have composite natures — part of them is material (physical body) and part is non-material (mind/soul). René Descartes said that the body is spatial but not conscious, whilst the mind is non-spatial and conscious, with feelings, thoughts and all those things that cannot be located physically. Descartes believed that the body and mind were separate but that they interact — and that the state of the body will affect the mind and vice versa. He identified the point of interaction as the brain.

This is not very easy to comprehend — if we have two natures, then do they both end when we die? Or do we have the odd situation of one of them surviving? Descartes himself believed that when people die, their soul is able to continue with God after death, as the same individual which existed in physical form on earth. In *Discourse on the Method* he wrote: '*Our soul is of a nature entirely independent of the body, and consequently...it is not bound to die with it. And since we cannot see any other causes that destroy the soul, we are naturally led to conclude that it is immortal.*'

There are problems with dualism. For instance, if we have two natures, then do they both end when we die, or does one survive? Moreover, there does seem to be a link between the mind and the body — we know, for instance, that there are things we do to the body which can affect the mind, such as taking drugs or alcohol. Similarly, science seems to be revealing links between the mind and the physical brain — surgeons can, apparently, split the brain and create 'two minds', indicating the dependence of the mind on the brain. Finally, our physical characteristics give us an identity and the way in which others respond to our physical selves has an effect on our minds.

2 Ryle and the ghost in the machine

An alternative to dualism is materialism or behaviourism, which is the view that so-called mental events are really physical events occurring to physical objects — that when we feel emotion, for instance, this is just the interacting of chemicals in our physical body. Gilbert Ryle (1949), in *The Concept of Mind*, dismissed dualism as a theory about a 'ghost in a machine', that is, the 'ghost' of the mind in the 'machine' of the body. He rejected the notion that body and mind are separate entities, calling it a 'category mistake'. Ryle famously supported this view by using the example of the university. He proposes the case of the overseas visitor who is shown around a collegiate university town, and sees the college, libraries, playing fields, and the like, only to ask 'But where's the university?', failing to appreciate that the university is not something separate from its constituent parts. Ryle advocated philosophical behaviourism — all mental events are really physical events interpreted in a mental way. Thus, our mind is not a separate entity, but just a term meaning what we do with our physical bodies. Bryan Magee (1997) writes: *'The human body is a single entity, one subject of behaviour and experience with a single history. We are not two entities mysteriously laced together. We have made what Ryle calls a category mistake'.*

However, critics suggest that this does not explain all mental behaviour — if we are, for example, wishing, this does not mean we are physically behaving in a particular way. This had led some scholars to favour the **identity theory**, which suggests that mental and physical events are one and the same thing and that 'mind' really means 'brain' — thus, if I say 'I have a pain' or 'I feel happy', what I am really saying is 'I have such and such a neural process'. However, such a view falls foul of Leibniz's **Law of Identity**, which says that if things are identical then they must share identical properties. Having a wicked thought (mind) is not the same as having a wicked body state (brain).

3 Personal identity

The heart of the problem lies in the issue of what constitutes our personal identity, and hence what constitutes a person. Obviously, on the level of observation, the body is the means by which we can know the identity of a person, but what if the body fails and enters a comatose state? Clearly, we still regard that individual as a person, or we would not be faced with such overwhelming moral dilemmas when deciding whether to end life support when a patient appears to be in an irreversible coma. On the other hand, is a person's identity to be limited to the body? When we think, for example, of great writers or scholars such as Shakespeare, it is not their bodies which define them, but their minds.

Essentially, the question is what survives after death: is it really *us* who survive the death process? If, as the dualists suggest, only the mind/soul survives, then our physical attributes and experiences are of no consequence. Where does the soul come from, anyway? Is it meaningful to speak of God *creating* a soul — a non-empirical, unverifiable entity? Alternatively, if we survive as body and mind, then in what state is the body — are we old, young, fat, thin? Do we age? Do we eat and drink? Are we 'recreated' in the form in which we died, or as we were at some optimum stage in our lives?

We have no answers. Indeed, Anthony Flew in *New Essays in Philosophical Theology* summed up the dilemma well when he questioned whether or not it was even meaningful to talk about life after death — after all, if there is life after death, then, in a sense, there is no death at all. Flew considers that it is therefore not meaningful even to *talk* about life after death, still less to consider what form it might take, since death and life are two mutually exclusive categories. In a plane crash there are those who survive and those who die, but there is no one who 'survives death'. He also argues that pronouns and proper nouns — I, me, you, father, brother, Sarah, Gordon — refer to real, living human beings, and not to souls or to dead persons or to immortal beings, to whom you cannot ascribe personal identity.

Proponents of language game theory can resolve this by claiming that talk of post-mortem existence is part of a religious language game and has meaning for those who participate in it. Furthermore, language becomes stretched and, applied to new situations, is meaningful, even if it was not previously communicable. If the phrase 'surviving death' is meaningful and not misleading to those who hear it, then it is a legitimate way of speaking.

B The nature of the afterlife

1 Desirability of life after death

Despite these considerations, one of the certainties of life is that one day our earthly life in our current physical form will end. Human beings consistently return to the question of whether life ever really ends or whether it continues in some other form, time and place? This is one of the great mysteries, and it is not just a religious issue, since many who would not consider themselves to be religious believers find the prospect of a post-mortem (after death) experience highly desirable. Why? There are many reasons:

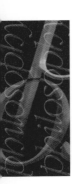

- ÷ Death has a powerful effect on us. It can make us sad, angry and frightened. Our feelings for others and ourselves are often truly expressed in the way we deal with their death.
- ÷ We find it hard to accept that this life is all that there is. We feel that there ought to be something beyond our earthly existence, which gives meaning to it.
- ÷ The moral law needs to be balanced, with good rewarded and evil punished. Since this seems not to be done in this life, then an afterlife, overseen by a moral commander, is necessary.
- ÷ Our earthly life is short and restricted. The afterlife would be the place where human potential could ultimately be fulfilled.
- ÷ We place high value on human life, as illustrated by the vast range of ethical dilemmas which centre on the question of the sanctity and quality of life, when life begins and when it ends. It is hard to conceive of something of such high value ending, even if its continuation demands that we postulate some alternative mode of existence.
- ÷ The Bible talks of an afterlife — for example the resurrection of Jesus. The afterlife is seen as a gift from God:

Following as a corollary from faith in a good and loving God...that which has been begun by God during man's life on earth, the creation of sons fit for full fellowship with him, will be continued and completed by God, in his own time and in his own ways, beyond the confines of earthly life.

(Robert McAfee Brown, *A Handbook of Christian Theology*)

÷ In Eastern religions, there is strong support for the concept of reincarnation — the belief that the soul migrates after death to another body, until it is finally released into a higher form.

If life after death is such a desirable prospect, we need to be certain that what continues after is truly us. In a post-mortem existence, we require our personal identities to be intact. But this raises problems — will we survive death as we are, or will we be given a new mode of being with which to continue our existence? The most common areas for consideration that may help in finding answers to such questions are:

÷ reincarnation/rebirth/transmigration of the soul
÷ near-death experiences
÷ parapsychology
÷ immortality of the soul
÷ resurrection of the body

2 Reincarnation/rebirth/transmigration of the soul

In the Hindu and Buddhist traditions the view is held that we have lived many lives before and that, on death, we will be reborn again. The conditions of our present lives are believed to be a direct consequence of our previous lives.

According to the **Vedic tradition**, there is an ultimate reality — **Brahman**. Everything else is **maya** — a temporary and finite illusion. Within maya there are a limitless number of souls who all seek union with Brahman. (In fact, all souls are Brahman — their individuality is itself an illusion.) The theory of **karma** and rebirth is concerned with the soul's journey from illusion to reality (**Nirvana**). The soul continues from life to life, being reincarnated until it finds the eternal truth; after this the soul is not reborn any more and is united with Brahman. Thus, when an individual dies, their mental, or non-bodily, aspects live on and the next birth is determined by how good or bad their karma was in the last life:

Just as a person casts off worn-out garments and puts on others that are new, even so does the disembodied soul cast off worn-out bodies and take on others that are new.

Bhagavad Gita

Evidence frequently cited for this is the fact that many people seem to be able to remember fragments of previous lives, perhaps under 'hypnotic regression' (discussed more fully under 'Near-death experiences' below).

Philosophically, however, there are problems. Human beings seem to require three things to make up their individuality — body, memory and psychological pattern (personal identity). If we apply these to reincarnation, when we are reborn bodily, continuity is lost. If we cannot remember our previous lives, then memory is lost. With only psychological pattern remaining, it would be impossible to determine if one person is the rebirth of another since, unless they displayed identical characteristics, all we could say is that reincarnated people are 'similar' to those who went before.

3 Near-death experiences

Dr Raymond Moody, in his work *The Light Beyond*, studied many cases of people who had, to all intents and purposes, died (during a surgical operation) and subsequently been resuscitated. Many claimed similar experiences — floating out of their bodies, travelling down a tunnel and emerging in a world of light where they met either Jesus, another religious figure consistent with their own religious or cultural tradition, or a dead relative.

Despite the apparent frequency of such experiences (not just amongst religious believers), such accounts present problems: experients could be dreaming, or remembering some lost subconscious memory (*cryptomnesia*) or a hallucination caused by a lack of oxygen to the brain. Similar problems are encountered in cases of **hypnotic regression**, where a person, under hypnosis, appears to relive an episode of a former life — a life which occurred before their present one. The person's voice may change, even their language, and they are able to recall dates, events and people. The problem is one of verification — the person may simply be recalling a lost memory of something they had read or heard many years before and forgotten at a conscious level. The true source of the information is often discovered when the person is re-hypnotised.

4 Parapsychology

The Spiritualist Movement claims that there is a spirit world where people go after death and that the dead can be reached and communicated with by **mediums**. There is some biblical evidence for this when the Witch of Endor raises the spirit of the prophet Samuel (1 Samuel 28:13). However, the Law of Moses forbade the consulting of mediums and ordered their death: *'A man or woman who is a spiritualist or medium among you must be put to death'* (Leviticus 20:27).

The philosophical problems are twofold. On the one hand, the Spiritualist Movement has suffered at the hands of hoaxers; on the other hand, if the spirit world is real then what is the point of it? Do we just continue living as we did on earth? Nevertheless, John Hick (1964) observes that *'Even if we discount the entire range of psychical phenomena, it remains true that the best cases of trance utterance are impressive and puzzling and, taken at face value are indicative of survival and communication after death'.* Indeed, if the evidence of occult activity and parapsychology were considered reliable, they could provide the best grounds for verifying the reality of an afterlife, although it is debatable whether such verification would be acceptable to religious believers.

5 Immortality of the soul

As we have already established, some thinkers take what is known as a dualist view of the body and mind, and argue that the body is an outer shell for the real self, which is non-bodily, mental and spiritual. The body is contingent and mutable and will therefore one day decay and die, but the mind is a separate entity and, being non-contingent, is immortal and immutable. Thus, when the body dies, the soul leaves its fleshly prison and continues to survive after the death of the physical body.

In *Phaedo*, Plato suggested that the body belongs to the physical world and, like all physical things, it will one day turn to dust. However, the soul belongs to a higher realm where eternal truths, such as justice, love and goodness, are imperishable and endure forever. For Plato, the aim of the soul is to break free from the chains of physical matter

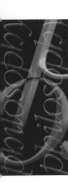

and fly to the realm of ideas — the spiritual realm of true reality, where it will be able to spend eternity in contemplation of the true, the beautiful and the good. Hence, Plato claimed: *'Ordinary people seem not to realise that those who really apply themselves in the proper way to philosophy are directly and of their own accord preparing themselves for death and dying'* (*Phaedo*, 63e–64a). In other words, the soul which has spent its earthly existence contemplating and pursuing these ideal forms will be ready to enter into the afterlife without regret. In *Phaedo*, Socrates tries to reassure his friends that he is in exactly this position: *'…when I have drunk the poison, I shall leave you and go to the joys of the blessed'*. He is able, therefore, to face death with equanimity, even whilst his less enlightened friends are asking trivial questions about how he should be buried. (Refer to pp. 3–4 for information on Plato's view of the mind–body relationship and its implications for life after death.)

Kant believed that the purpose of existence is to achieve the ***summum bonum*** or complete good, and human beings cannot achieve this in the space of one short lifetime. Kant suggested that there is therefore a moral obligation on God to help human beings to achieve the complete good by granting them eternal life. Otherwise, he said, morality would be pointless. Thus the 'summum bonum *is only possible on the presupposition of the immortality of the soul.'*

More recently, John Hick (1985), in *Death and Eternal Life*, suggested: *'If the human potential is to be fulfilled in the lives of individuals, these lives must be prolonged far beyond the limits of our present bodily existence.'* Nevertheless, the philosophical problems revolve around whether or not a disembodied soul is really *us*. What do we look like? Do we retain our distinguishing characteristics if our personal identity is distinct from our body?

Many Christian theologians suggest that personal identity is strongly linked to the physical body. Aquinas believed that the soul animates the body and gives it life. He called the soul the ***anima***, that which animates the body. In *Summa Theologica* he said: *'Now that the soul is what makes our body live; so the soul is the primary source of all these activities that differentiate levels of life: growth, sensation, movement, understanding, mind or soul, it is the form of our body.'* According to Aquinas, the soul operates independently of the body, but it is through its link with a particular human body that the soul becomes individual and therefore needs the body: *'Elements that are by nature destined for union naturally desire to be united with each other; for any being seeks what is suited to it by nature. Since, therefore, the natural condition of the soul is to be united to the body…it has a natural desire for union with the body, hence the will cannot be perfectly at rest until the soul is again joined to a body. When this takes place, man rises from the dead.'*

In *Summa Theologica*, Aquinas looked at the question of where souls go when we die. He suggested three alternatives:

+ Hell — a place of eternal punishment, where the worst sinners go. Time passes.
+ Purgatory — a place where lapsed Christians undergo purification and punishment to purge their souls from sin. Time passes.
+ Beatific vision — the highest joy; the unchanging vision of God, for faithful Christians and those who have completed Purgatory. Time does not pass.

Indeed, for many, the whole concept of life after death is bound up not so much in philosophical questions of personal identity and the mind–body question, but rather with the prospect of an eternal heavenly dwelling place, or with eternal punishment in hell. These concepts raise many interesting questions:

÷ Would a loving God consign anyone to hell, or would he ensure that all would enjoy heaven?
÷ If there is a life after death, should it be available universally or only to those who believe in God?
÷ Are heaven and hell real places or are they just metaphors or symbols?
÷ Is the prospect of a heavenly afterlife the ultimate theodicy?

6 Resurrection of the body

The doctrine of bodily resurrection suggests that resurrection and eternal life depend on an act of God's divine love. Bodily resurrection is nothing to do with resuscitating corpses (as in the raising of Lazarus, for example). It is the re-creation by God of the human individual, not as a physical being who has died, but as a spiritual being. We know little of what this means but, using the evidence of the resurrection of Jesus, we note that he appeared before his disciples with a body, he talked and ate with them, they touched him and they saw his scars. Yet he is different — he appears and disappears — he is beyond death: *'Look at my hands and my feet…touch me and see; a ghost does not have flesh and bones as you see I have'* (Luke 24:39). There is further support for the view that mind and body must be united in the resurrection in Job 19:25: *'After my skin has been destroyed, then in my flesh shall I see God.'*

St Paul explains that the resurrected body is spiritual and therefore can last forever: *'For the trumpet will sound, the dead will be raised imperishable, and we shall be changed. For the perishable must clothe itself with the imperishable, and the mortal with immortality'* (1 Corinthians 15:52). Paul appears to be envisaging an entity that is identifiably bodily but, because of its spiritual nature, is crucially different from the physical body, which has died.

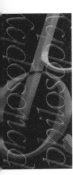

The philosophical problems here again concern the question of whether or not the resurrected person is really *us* — if death is extinction, then the resurrected person must be a copy of you, since you have died forever. But if a copy, then can it be said truly to be the same person? After all, a copy of a painting by Monet would not be considered to be *the same* as the original, but rather something of far less value. What about the appearance of the resurrected body? Jesus looked the same, but if this is to be so for us then it raises dilemmas — does the body look as it did on the point of death? On the other hand, even those closest to Jesus did not recognise him when they first saw him after his resurrection, but it is not made clear what it was that prevented them from making an immediate identification. And what of physical defects? Are they cured, or are the blind, for instance, blind for eternity? What about our mental and emotional problems? Do these all remain, or are we healed and made perfect? And if we are made perfect, then is that really us?

A possible answer to these problems is offered by John Hick's **replica theory**, where he suggests that if someone dies and appears in a new world, with the same memories and physical features, then it is meaningful to call this replica the same person. For instance, Hick says that if a man in London died and the next instant appeared in New

York and had the same memories and bodily features, then we would be conscious of him being the same person as the one who died in London, even though we would not understand how he resurrected in New York. It would, says Hick, be reasonable to call the replica the same person as the one who died.

Hick argues further that since God is all-powerful, it would be perfectly possible for him to create a replica body of a dead person, complete with all the individual's memories and characteristics, and to do so in a place inhabited by resurrected persons:

Mr X then dies. A Mr X replica, complete with the set of memory traces which Mr X had at the last moment before his death, comes into existence. It is composed of other material than physical matter, and is located in a resurrection world which does not stand in a spatial relationship with the physical world.

(Hick, 1966)

In *Philosophy of Religion*, Hick adds that God would re-create us: '*...as a resurrection replica in a different world altogether, a resurrection world inhabited only by resurrected persons.*' Such a view supports the visions described in Revelation: '*Then I saw a new heaven and a new earth, for the first heaven and the first earth had passed away... I saw the Holy City, the new Jerusalem, coming down out of heaven from God...*' (Revelation 21:1–2).

Ultimately, however, we are still left with the problem of whether any kind of post-mortem existence can be verified. John Hick resolves this with the principle of **eschatological verification**. He envisages two travellers walking down a road, one of whom believes it leads to the Celestial City, and one who believes that there is no final destination. Which one of them is right will not be verified until they reach the end of the road, although their particular positions will have a vital influence on the way they experience and interpret what happens to them on the way.

Summary

- **Relationship between mind and body** — crucial issue for developing any kind of debate on life after death. Two main positions need to be considered: the **dualist** perspective — that mind and body are separate entities and that after the death of the physical body the soul is freed to enter into a post-mortem existence, unconfined by the body; and the **materialist** perspective — that body and soul are a psychophysical unity which are united after death as they are before it.
- **Personal identity** — determined by the nature of the relationship between mind and body. We need to establish whether we believe that identity is rooted in mind or body, since we presumably anticipate that any post-mortem existence involves continuity of identity.
- **Key thinkers** — Plato and Descartes (dualism); Aquinas, Gilbert Ryle and John Hick (materialism). What contribution do sacred texts make to this debate?
- **Desirability of life after death** — assumed in this debate, but why? It is necessary to consider why we might consider post-mortem existence to be a more attractive option than extinction of body and personal identity.
- Further to this is the question of whether it is meaningful to speak of life after death or whether it is a contradiction or logical impossibility.

- Is life after death therefore in any way **verifiable**? What contribution is made by parapsychology, near-death experiences, or remembered lives? Ultimately, **eschatological verification** is the only means of verifying life after death.
- **Form of post-mortem existence** — disembodied spirit or resurrected body? Is either option more conceivable than the other? Is **reincarnation** any more conceivable than the prospect of personal identity continuing without a body, or in bodily form in a place inhabited by resurrected bodies?

Key terms

Dualism — the belief that mind and body are separate entities.

Eschatological — concerned with the end of time.

Immortality of the soul — the belief that the soul belongs to the realm of the eternal and can therefore exist after the death of the contingent body.

Materialism — the belief that mind and body cannot be separated and that each influences the other.

Post-mortem existence — a continued life after the death of the physical body.

Reincarnation — the soul (or essence of personal identity) is literally re-clothed in flesh to live again in a new body or outward form.

Resurrection — the recreation of the physical body.

Exam watch

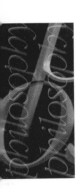

This is frequently a favourite topic for students, yet it rarely leads to full and fruitful answers. Candidates tend to grasp the basic material about disembodied existence compared with bodily resurrection, but often get side-tracked and fail to answer the question directly and relevantly. The question of personal identity tends to get rather lost, and issues about verification of the afterlife or the reasons for belief in a post-mortem existence confuse many candidates. With all this in mind, approach questions on this topic thoughtfully. What are you actually being asked about? If the question asks first about the relationship between mind and body, don't leap straight into talking about life after death. You need to build your answer gradually and relevantly. You will invariably be given a choice in what you write about too, so you don't need to feel that you have to cover everything. If you are studying Hinduism or Buddhism for one of your options, then you will probably feel more confident talking about reincarnation than if you are studying the New Testament, so don't bluff or waste time making random comments. Concentrate on those issues you have studied properly. Similarly, make sure you understand a few scholarly contributions fully, and use them wisely. Hick's replica theory or Ryle's category error can be easily misunderstood and gain you only the odd mark, but think them through carefully and practise using them in essays and you will gain significant credit.

Review questions

1. (a) Analyse the differences between belief in survival of the disembodied soul and belief in resurrection.

   (b) Consider which of these two beliefs might provide the stronger philosophical basis for a belief in life after death.

2. Examine and assess the claim that life after death is ultimately unverifiable.

3. 'To think of body and soul as two separate entities is to make a category mistake.' Evaluate the strengths and weaknesses of this claim.

Topic 6

Religious language

1 The problem of religious language

Religious language is language that deals with God and other theological matters, including religious worship, practice, behaviour and doctrine. It includes terms which we ascribe only to God in their primary context (e.g. omnipotent) and words which are about distinctively religious beliefs (e.g. the Last Judgment). However, even when we speak of religious issues we invariably have to use language that is drawn from our common linguistic and lexical store, and this raises problems of a particular kind. How can we use everyday language to speak of the supreme deity? Surely God is above and beyond all human experience and notions, and the language which we use to speak of him should reflect that distinctiveness in some way. The primary problem of religious language is just this: we have very little language which is reserved exclusively for talk of God and religious belief, so we are compelled to find ways of making human language work effectively when applied to God. This is a notoriously difficult task and has led to considerable philosophical and theological disputes. Furthermore, that language which we do reserve specially to apply to the deity and to talk distinctively of religious belief or activity is often criticised for its obscurity. Can we therefore begin to talk meaningfully about God at all? Consider how common language is used to talk of God and his activity in the world and in salvation. There are peculiar problems inherent in speaking of God 'doing' something in the world — creating, sustaining, or intervening, for example — as well as speaking of how God demonstrates qualities such as mercy, justice or love.

Religious language — like all language — falls broadly into two categories: cognitive and non-cognitive language. **Cognitive** or **realist** language makes factual assertions that can be proved true or false — e.g. statements that are believed by those who use them to contain meaningful, objective, factual content: 'God exists'; 'God loves us'; 'God will execute a final judgment'. These are not *Crypto-commands, expressions of wishes, disguised ejaculations, concealed ethics, or anything else but assertions'* (Flew, 1955). Cognitive claims assume a **correspondence theory of truth** between the language used and the concepts or objects to which that language refers.

Non-cognitive or **anti-realist** language is used to make claims that can be interpreted in some other way, perhaps as symbols, metaphors, ethical commands or other non-literal modes of expression. It is language that serves some other function than that of expressing factually, objectively true claims; it expresses the meaning that religious discourse has for an individual and the community to which he or she belongs. Such language — which includes the use of symbol and myth — assumes a **coherence theory of truth**; truth or falsity is related to the other statements with which it is associated, rather than to objectively real situations. Truth acquires a relative status.

One of the primary debates in this topic is whether religious language is meaningful. Some thinkers argue that it is not because it does not deal with factually verifiable assertions. Others argue that it is meaningful because it can be verified, at least to the believer's satisfaction, if not that of the non-believer, but also because not all religious language is intended to function cognitively. The verification and falsification debates pivot around this key issue and it is to these we shall turn first.

2 Verification and falsification

The verification principle

In the 1920s a famous group of philosophers, the Logical Positivists (also known as the Vienna Circle), influenced by Ludwig Wittgenstein's **picture theory of language** (a statement is meaningful if it can be defined, or pictured, in the real world) and following in the footsteps of the sceptic David Hume, derived a radical new theory of language which was termed the 'verification principle'. They claimed that only assertions that were, in principle, verifiable by observation or experience could convey factual information (i.e. that the means by which they could be tested were known, even if they could not be tested in practice). Assertions that there could be no imaginable way of verifying must either be analytic (self-explanatory) or meaningless.

According to their criteria, meaningful assertions fall into one of three categories:

÷ **Analytic statements** — which are true by definition (e.g. a circle is round) or tautologous (e.g. all dogs are dogs). An analytic statement cannot be false, and contains the germ of its own verification. Such a statement is a logical proposition and is necessarily true; for example, 'A bachelor is an unmarried man' is necessarily true.
÷ **Mathematical statements** — $2 + 2 = 4$.
÷ **Synthetic statements** — which can be verified or falsified by subjecting them to testing. Statements of this kind are **empirical propositions**, which can be known only through observation and are contingently true or false. Empirical propositions include all facts about the world, since, conceivably, any fact about the world could have been otherwise — there is no logically necessary reason why they should be as they are. Hence, the assertion 'Elephants are pink and have green toenails' is a meaningful statement since, although it is not true, it can be tested by observation. 'All wicked people will come to a bad end' is not meaningful since it is impossible to test, so the question of whether it is true, false or a matter of opinion is not even an issue. Truth and meaning are therefore considered to be distinct concepts.

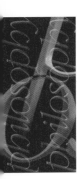

Hence, the verification principle demands that an empirical proposition has meaning only if there is a situation in which observations verify it as true. In this way, the Logical Positivists applied the principles of science and mathematics to all language statements, declaring that, like knowledge, language has to be based on experience. However, if a statement can theoretically be verified, then it passes the criteria of meaningfulness as laid down by the Logical Positivists. For example, 'There are mountains on the dark side of the moon' was not verifiable in 1936 when A. J. Ayer wrote *Language, Truth and Logic*, but it was theoretically possible to construct a means of verifying it.

Implications for religious language

Since statements about God are neither analytically true nor open to verification by observation, they are therefore rendered meaningless. According to the Logical Positivists, claims to have experienced God are subjective, not universal, and there are no reliable grounds for testing them. Hence they cannot be the basis for empirical propositions about God.

The question 'Does a transcendent God exist?' is rejected, since although it seems to be cognitive (asking a question about an objective reality), our experience of the world does not admit of transcendent things.

However, the verification principle has wider implications for language.

- All statements that express unverifiable opinions or emotions are rendered invalid, as are ethical statements. (See pp. 131–132 for more about emotivism in relation to ethical statements.)
- General laws of science, which are accepted as true, cannot be verified, since there is no way that they can be *absolutely* verified. For example, to say that 'All water boils at 100 degrees centigrade' is untestable and, hence, meaningless.
- Historical statements such as 'The Battle of Hastings took place in 1066' cannot be verified by sense experience (in this case because there is no one alive who could claim to have experienced it).
- A. J. Ayer proposed a weak form of the verification principle to avoid some of these more obvious problems, arguing that if it is possible to know what would, in principle, verify a statement, then it is meaningful. Religious language statements, of course, still do not fit into this category, however, since they ultimately refer to a transcendent being which is not even verifiable in principle.

The verification principle is clearly not without its weaknesses, and although it was a popular philosophical tool in the academic world prior to the Second World War, it soon became apparent that it was fatally flawed and '*People began to realise that this glittering new scalpel was, in one operation after another, killing the patient*' (Magee, 1997). Interestingly, some time later, A. J. Ayer admitted himself that his weak form of the principle allowed for any statement to be, in principle, verifiable. Key problems included the decisive question of what was the status of the verification principle itself. What observations could be made to verify or falsify it? It seemed that the verification principle failed its own test. Furthermore, was it consistent with modern science, as it intended to be? Many scientific statements concern matters that are not meaningful, according to the rigorous criteria laid out — statements such as 'atoms exist' or 'forces exist', for example. Scientific language is not entirely free from metaphor, using models and analogies to describe concepts that are beyond the naked eye, so it became clear that many forms of language that the positivists wanted to protect would have become suspect if their own criteria were applied. As far as religious language claims are concerned, Keith Ward observed that God's existence *can* be verified in principle, since God himself can verify it, and John Hick argued that eschatological verification would verify beliefs about the afterlife. Significantly, too, many religious language claims are also historical in nature, and if other historical statements were allowed by virtue of being verifiable in principle, then statements such as 'Jesus rose from the dead' would also have to be permitted as meaningful.

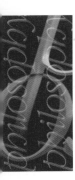

The falsification principle

The failure of the verification principle led to a new challenge: *'What would have to occur or to have occurred to constitute for you a disproof of the love of, or the existence of, God?'* (Flew, cited in Hick (ed.), 1964). Rather than demand that an assertion be verifiable, the falsification principle demands that the speaker must be able to say what would count, at least in principle, in its falsification. Hence: *'In order to say something which may possibly be true, we must say something which may possibly be false'* (Hick, 1966).

Flew was influenced by the work of Karl Popper, the philosopher of science who claimed that science is more concerned with falsification of hypotheses than with their verification. Anthony Flew used Wisdom's parable of the gardener to illustrate how believers are guilty of not allowing evidence that fails to prove the existence or love of God to actually count against their theological statements. If believers are reduced to saying 'God's love for us is incomprehensible' because they cannot explain why God is apparently allowing a child to die of an inoperable illness, then Flew maintains they are simply allowing their definition of God to *'die the death of a thousand qualifications'* (ibid.) Believers must be able to say what would cause them to question, and conceivably to withdraw, their claims about God, even if they are considering them only as hypothetical possibilities. To say 'God exists' must include the possibility that he might not exist or that he might not exist in the way that the believer maintains. However, Flew argues: *'Now it often seems to people who are not religious as if there was no conceivable event…the occurrence of which would be admitted by sophisticated religious people to be a sufficient reason for conceding…"God does not really love us then" (ibid.).'* In other words, Flew maintained that if believers' statements about God can be made to fit into any circumstances, however potentially challenging, then they have no meaningful content and cannot be considered to have any empirical (real world) implications.

Flew argued that such dogged reluctance by believers to see their assertions challenged sounded the death knell to religious language claims, but other scholars felt that their integrity could be salvaged. R. M. Hare proposed that believers' statements are **bliks**: *'Ways of regarding the world which are in principle neither verifiable nor falsifiable — but modes of cognition to which the terms "veridical" or "illusory" properly apply'* (ibid.). Just as in the case of the man who thinks all his colleagues want to kill him, and cannot be dissuaded from this despite evidence which is apparently to the contrary, so too believers will not be dissuaded from their belief in God; they will not allow it to be falsified. However, because this belief makes a significant difference to their lives, it is not meaningless. It matters. (See p. 23 for an outline of Hare's analogy.)

Basil Mitchell offered the parable of the partisan and the stranger (see p. 21) to demonstrate that believers do recognise challenges to faith without allowing them to be conclusively falsified. Mitchell observed that there are three ways in which believers can react when their assertions are challenged. They can treat them as:

÷ provisional hypotheses to be discarded if experience tells against them
÷ vacuous formulae, to which experience makes no difference and which make no difference to life
÷ significant articles of faith

Since believers' claims about God fall into the third category, believers will neither abandon them (the first category) nor, as Flew maintains, qualify them (the second). Rather, believers recognise these claims as being open to serious conflict and challenge, but will not allow experience to count decisively against them. As such, the claims are unfalsifiable.

Richard Swinburne argued that many statements cannot be falsified, and yet they still have meaning:

...there are plenty of examples of statements which some people judge to be factual which are not apparently confirmable or disconfirmable through observation. For example, some of the toys which to all appearances stay in the toy cupboard while people are asleep and no one is watching actually get up and dance in the middle of the night and then go back to the cupboard, leaving no traces of their activity.

(Cited in Davies (ed.), 2000)

3 Language game theory

Jettisoning his picture theory of language, Ludwig Wittgenstein later proposed that religious language is anti-realist, expressing a form of life without making statements which are true or false. Language can be correctly or incorrectly used within the rules of the game, but its primary purpose is not to make factual statements. Thus, it is non-cognitive. All forms of life have their own language and hence stand alone from each other. Perhaps the greatest strength of language games is the fact that the player of one language game cannot criticise the player of another, or enter into the game without first learning the rules and conventions of the language, since language games have their own **criteria of coherence**. Wittgenstein was concerned only with the *use* of language, rather than the meaning of it, since it was the context which defined its function. Just as in a game of cricket certain terminology is applied in a way that is appropriate to that game and not to another, so too can religious language be used appropriately or inappropriately, reflecting the way the speaker understands the world.

Wittgenstein illustrated the principle thus:

Suppose someone were a believer and said, 'I believe in a Last Judgement,' and I said, 'Well, I'm not so sure. Possibly,' you would say that there was an enormous gulf between us. If he said, 'There is a German aeroplane overhead,' and I said, 'Possibly, I'm not so sure,' you'd say we were fairly near... Suppose someone is ill and he says, 'This is a punishment,' and I say, 'If I'm ill, I don't think of punishment at all.' If you say, 'Don't you believe the opposite?' — you can call it believing the opposite, but it is entirely different from what we would normally call believing the opposite. I think differently, in a different way. I say different things to myself. I have a different picture.

(Cited in Mitchell (ed.), 1971)

The two understandings of illness described in this conversation — one essentially religious, and one not — reflect different forms of life, neither necessarily right nor wrong. They use language in different ways and need to be understood in that context. If we misunderstand the way religious language claims are made, then we will respond in the wrong way, like the scientist who rushes off to the laboratory to test the contents of the chalice, having heard it described in the Eucharist service as 'The blood of Christ'.

Wittgenstein said of this kind of misunderstanding: *'For a blunder, that's too big'* (ibid.). The concept of category mistake is helpful in understanding this way of understanding language: to speak of a 'soul' and to try to see it as a physical object would lead to the kind of problems inherent in using religious language inappropriately.

The way in which we decide what is appropriate use of language is, effectively, by convention, since meaning grows out of the context in which terms are used and the activity which surrounds that context rather than out of relating the terms to particular objectively real objects. Participating in the game will enable players to learn the rules of context and when to apply them, and when errors occur it is because language has 'gone on holiday' — i.e. has been used in the wrong context.

Advantages of language game theory

- It recognises the distinctive and non-cognitive nature of religious language and distinguishes it from other uses of language.
- Language games unite believers in a common bond and provide boundaries for the correct use of language.
- Believers can be initiated into the rules of language.
- Language games defend language against criticism from other 'forms of life'.

Weaknesses of language game theory

- Language games do not allow for believers' claims to be objectively true.
- Because religious language is distinct from all other language, it alienates those outside the game.
- Who makes the rules? How can we be sure they are correctly interpreted? Can they be changed? By whom?

4   The *via negativa*

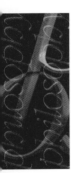

The **via negativa**, which Pseudo-Dionysius used in the *Mystical Theology*, insists on speaking negatively about God, ruling out that which the divine mystery is not as a way of speaking indirectly of what the divine mystery is. Thought of as an aspect of mystical practice, the *via negativa* begins by negating the least appropriate characterisations of God and then proceeds to negate even the most honourable and lofty names for God that we can imagine. The problem of speaking meaningfully about God could arguably be resolved by resorting to the principle of **negation**. Since it is impossible for humans to use human language of God and of humans without confusion, then to speak of God in terms of what he is not may avoid some of the more obvious pitfalls. Peter Cole (1999) notes that *'...by denying all descriptions of God, you get insight and experience of God rather than unbelief and scepticism'*.

This approach denies the possibility of describing God in concrete terms, especially since such terms seem to reduce the divine to the level of human understanding rather than elevating the soul to a transcendent understanding of the divine. Hence, rather than saying that God is love, for example, one would say that he is *not-love*, because he is ultimately so much more than what this term can convey that it would be better to say that he is not that term at all. But how, exactly, does one focus on negative content? Since the concept of God as *not-love* is not rational, it requires the power of another faculty, higher than reason, so it is not a particularly straightforward method of speaking of God after all!

A central tenet of Don Cupitt's early theology was the *via negativa*: *'I try to show the restless iconoclastic character of belief in God, which continually strives after intelligible content, and yet must by its own inner dialect always negate any proposed specific content.'* However, used on its own, the *via negativa* cannot distinguish theism from atheism, since to say that God can only be spoken of in negatives effectively denies God altogether. (Remember the sceptic in the parable of the gardener who pointed out that an invisible, inaudible, intangible gardener was essentially no gardener at all.) Surely believers want to say something positive about God and would ultimately question whether speaking of him in terms of negation says anything meaningful about him at all. Nevertheless, negation does emphasise the unknowability of God, and Aquinas observed that an affirmative statement has to have a subject, and God, who is above all things and existentially different from them, cannot be a subject.

5 Analogy

'Analogies are proportional similarities which also acknowledge dissimilar features' (D. Burrell, cited in Richardson and Bowden (eds), 1989). The principle of analogy follows from the observation that to use language either equivocally or univocally of God creates peculiar difficulties for the believer. **Univocal** language employs a term in exactly the same sense, so to speak of God's love and John's love would be to speak of the same type of love in both cases. David Hume observed: *'Wisdom, thought, design, knowledge — these we justly ascribe to him because those words are honourable among men, and we have no other language by which we can express our adoration of him.'* This method certainly makes God accessible and understandable, since to know the nature of God's love we only need to know what humanly it means to love. However, a different problem arises, of course. If God's love and human love are exactly the same, then God is not differentiated from God and we fall into the trap, again, of anthropomorphism. Aquinas wrote in the ***Summa Theologica***:

But no name belongs to God in the same sense that it belongs to creatures; for instance, wisdom in creatures is a quality, but not in God. Now a different genus changes an essence, since the genus is part of the definition; and the same applies to other things. Therefore whatever is said of God and of creatures is predicated equivocally.

Equivocal language is used when applying the same word to two entirely different things, and thus employing two entirely different meanings. If we apply the words 'love', 'just', or 'good' to God, we can also apply them to human beings, but it is accepted that we mean them in quite different ways; God's love is not of the same nature and quality as John's love, for example. The advantage of using language in this way is that we stress the distinctiveness of God's qualities and avoid the perils of anthropomorphism. However, we do run the risk of making God so different from humans as to render understanding of him impossible. If we were asked to clarify the nature of God's love, all we could say is that it is entirely different from human love. Aquinas wrote in the ***Summa Theologica***:

Neither, on the other hand, are names applied to God and creatures in a purely equivocal sense, as some have said. Because if that were so, it follows that from creatures nothing could be known or demonstrated about God at all; for the reasoning would always be exposed to the fallacy of equivocation.

By way of compromise, Aquinas argued that the gradation to be found in things pointed irrefutably to the existence of God, but also showed that all good and worthy things in humans belong first to God and so are **analogously** related to him:

Among beings there are some more and some less good, true, noble and the like. But more and less are predicated of different things according as they resemble in their different ways something which is the maximum...so that there is something which is truest, something best, something noblest... Therefore there must also be something which is to all beings the cause of their being, goodness, and every other perfection, and this we call God.

(ibid.)

For example, because God is the cause of good things in humans, we can use the description 'good' of both God and humans but, as the cause of human goodness, God's goodness is greater. However, the effects resemble their cause, and thus their goodness is related, but different:

Hence from the knowledge of sensible things the whole power of God cannot be known; nor therefore can His essence be seen. But because they are His effects and depend on their cause, we can be led from them so far as to know of God whether He exists, and on to know of Him what must necessarily belong to Him, as the first cause of all things, exceeding all things caused by Him.

(ibid.)

Analogy therefore enables us to speak meaningfully about the transcendent God by virtue of the comparable relationship between him and contingent beings. Although different from humans, God makes himself known to us through experience, so we are able to find **points of correspondence** that enable him to overcome the distance between the human and the divine, and make discourse possible.

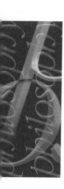

The mechanics of analogy

÷ Everything that is said of humans belongs to God in a greater and more perfect way, although we know of human qualities first and from them learn of God's. Hence, we know and understand what human wisdom entails from our direct experience of it, and this provides us with the basic information we need to postulate the greater wisdom of God.

÷ If we remove all creaturely concepts from a word and project what is left onto God, then we learn that God is without limit. This is known as the principle of **remotion and excellence**.

÷ Ian Ramsey proposed **models and qualifiers** — we take a human attribute (the model) and ascribe it to God, qualifying it to make clear that it is infinitely enhanced when applied to God, and leading us to an understanding of the infinite nature of God. Note that this is a positive act of qualification, rather than the negative approach as criticised by Anthony Flew.

+ **Analogy of proportion** — all good qualities belong proportionately to God and to humans, and thus we know that proportionately they must exist pre-eminently in God, but in a lesser way in humans. Although we still cannot fully know God's nature, by analogy we can reach some understanding of it.

+ **Analogy of attribution** — God is the cause of all good things in humans and other beings and thus attributes to them what belongs to him first in a greater and higher sense. Such analogies can be downwards or upwards: we can conceive of God's faithfulness because we know first what human faithfulness is and we project it upwards to reflect God's greater faithfulness.

6 Symbols

Symbolic language, including metaphors, similes, signs and myths, is a form of non-cognitive language. Erika Dinker-von Schubert defines a symbol as: *'A pattern or object which points to an invisible metaphysical reality and participates in it'* (Halverson and Cohen (eds), 1960). Symbols **identify** — point to the concept they are conveying — and **participate** — share in some way in the meaning of that concept. Symbols may be pictorial, abstract, verbal or active (a symbolic action, such as Eucharist or baptism). Many are common across religious traditions, particularly those which have a naturalistic basis — light and darkness, for instance. Others have a special significance for one religion. So, for example, the cross (a central symbol in the Christian tradition) immediately identifies for believers the death of Jesus, but it does more than simply point to it in a factual way. It participates in it by bringing to the believer's consciousness what Jesus's death signifies:

+ salvation from sin
+ sacrifice and atonement
+ victory over death
+ the defeat of satan
+ God's love for the world
+ Christian hope of eternal life

Paul Tillich used the example of a national flag as a symbol which conveys nationalism, patriotism and national identity. It is more than a sign that simply provides information or instructions, such as a traffic light or street sign. Symbols express what the believer feels about what that symbol conveys. They transcend facts and should therefore not be interpreted literally, as this leads only to misunderstanding. Symbols are subtle modes of communication which belong to high-level discourse. Whilst symbols do not belong exclusively to religious language, they are of particular value to discourse which deals with issues that are beyond the factual and objective:

The development of symbolism in religious language is not a process of the encrustation of an original, simple idea with distracting and extraneous illustration or ornament. Like all other serious human discourse, religious language requires a symbolic foundation.

(Rowan Williams, cited in Richardson and Bowden (eds), 1989)

Tillich was attracted to symbolic language as a means of expressing the nature of God as *'the ground of our being'* or *'that which concerns us ultimately'*. Note that this is a non-cognitive way of describing God, avoiding speaking of him as an objectively real, anthropomorphic-type figure, who may or may not have real existence. In more recent times, Don Cupitt adopted a similar view, that religious language should not be about trying to express the transcendent in language, which is ill-equipped for this purpose, but about expressing inner feelings. This anti-realist approach was supported by the neo-Wittgensteinian D. Z. Phillips, who claimed that the term 'eternal life' should not be understood as meaning literally living forever, but as expressing a quality of life available in the present (not unlike realised eschatology).

Whilst symbols are useful ways to communicate truths which go beyond the factual world, their interpretation can pose difficulties:

÷ They can become the focus of worship in themselves and the object of veneration.
÷ They can be trivialised and their original meaning lost.
÷ They can become outdated, like myths. For example, Sallie McFague in *Models of God in Religious Language* claims that many religious symbols are anachronistic because of their patriarchal roots, suggesting that symbols such as Father and Son should be adapted to Mother and Friend.
÷ Paul Tillich, who was particularly concerned to establish a way in which Christianity could be meaningful to a modern audience, wrote of this: '*It is necessary to rediscover the questions to which the Christian symbols are the answers in a way which is understandable to our time'*.

7 Myth

Myth is a symbolic, approximate expression of truth which the human mind cannot perceive sharply and completely, but can only glimpse vaguely, and therefore cannot adequately or accurately express.

(Burrows, 1946)

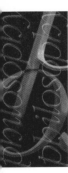

Myths embody and express claims that cannot be expressed in any other way, frequently making use of symbol, metaphor and imagery in a narrative context. Myths are not to be thought of as conveying information that is *not true*, but rather conveying concepts that go beyond basic **true–false descriptors** to express that which is otherworldly. In so doing, they allow humans to gain an insight into cosmological and existential questions that are difficult to express in cognitive terms.

Mythological language was used extensively by the biblical writers. The well-known myths of creation, the fall and the flood, attempt to explain the mystery of human origins and human nature. Mythological language is used to describe apocalyptic events, eschatological expectations and the phenomena which will accompany them. For example, Paul described the anticipated second coming of Jesus thus: '*For the Lord himself will descend from heaven with a cry of command, with the archangels' call and with the sound of the trumpet of God...and men, both alive and dead, will rise to meet the Lord in the air'* (1 Thessalonians 4:16).

Even more than symbol, myth faces the fundamental criticism that it is outdated and deals in anachronistic concepts. In the nineteenth century, D. F. Strauss suggested that the way to deal with this was to shift the focus of myth from 'the story of a *miraculous occurrence* to the *story* of a miraculous occurrence.' Do you see the difference here? In the first case it is being assumed that an objectively true narrative about a miracle is being communicated; in the second, that a religious truth embodied is being conveyed in story form, which is not necessarily objectively true. Rudolph Bultmann famously claimed: *'It is impossible to use electric light and the wireless, and to avail ourselves of modern medical and surgical discoveries, and, at the same time, to believe in the New Testament world of demons and spirits.'* He argued that it was necessary to access the **kerygma**, or the abiding truth of the revelatory, authoritative word, which was the real tool in kindling faith, and to do this religious language must be demythologised. However, for many, all Bultmann did was to secularise the New Testament.

Bultmann's claim was that myth made it harder for the twentieth-century mind to grasp the truth of the biblical message. However:

- Mythological language is so deeply engrained in theological discourse it may be impossible to dispense with it.
- If religious language is anti-realist — that is, not concerned with making true or false statements about objective reality — then it need not be a burden to communication.
- Myths are part of a religious language game and it is important to understand how they should be interpreted rather than being concerned with trying to establish what 'really happened'.
- *'Because myths have their birth not in logic but in intuitions of transcendence, they are of value to traditions that seek to describe the action of the other worldly in the present world. However, the term "myth" must be a servant and not a master'* (J. W. Rogerson, cited in Coggins and Houlden (eds), 1990).

Summary

- **Problem of religious language** — essential difficulty of speaking of the transcendent in limited, human language. How can it therefore be meaningful?
- **Verification principle** — an assertion is meaningful if it can be verified by sense experience or is an analytic statement. Hence, religious language statements are meaningless. However, they are verifiable in principle or eschatologically. The verification principle fails its own criteria, so it is undermined as a tool for linguistic analysis.
- **Falsification principle** — a statement is meaningful if what would count against it can be said. Parable of the gardener: religious claims *'die the death of a thousand qualifications'* (Flew). Lunatic and the dons: religious claims are **bliks** (Hare). The partisan and the stranger: religious claims are not decisively falsifiable (Mitchell).
- **Language game theory** — language belongs to its **form of life** and can only be understood in that context. Its significance depends on use, not meaning. Hence, religious language cannot be criticised if it is not being used in its correct context.
- *Via negativa* — speaking of God in terms of negation (saying what he is *not*) avoids the problem of anthropomorphism, and of trying to express the difference between God's positive qualities and those of humans.
- **Analogy** — rejects equivocal and univocal claims about God, but uses comparison to express similarity and difference between God and humans.

- **Symbolism** — non-cognitive language that *participates* in what it aims to convey. Expresses more than cognitive claims, giving the meaning too of the terms of actions. Avoids objectifying God, who is *'the ground of our Being'* (Tillich).
- **Myth** — symbols sustained in narrative, expressing cosmological and existential truths. Bultmann proposed **demythologisation** as a means of releasing these truths to make them meaningful to a contemporary audience.

Key terms

Analogy — analogies are proportional similarities which also acknowledge dissimilar features.

Bliks — unverifiable, unfalsifiable ways of looking at the world.

Cognitive (realist) language — assertions that make factual claims about an objective reality.

Equivocal — same word used with different meanings.

Myth — a symbolic, approximate expression of truth.

Non-cognitive (anti-realist) language — language which serves another function and which is made meaningful by its context.

Symbol — a pattern or object which points to an invisible metaphysical reality and participates in it.

Univocal — same word used with the same meaning.

Via negativa — assertions which emphasise what God is not rather than making positive claims about him.

Exam watch

Once you commit yourself to answering a question on religious language in the exam, you really need to explore the many different topics in this long chapter, which all interconnect — although you could do a little judicious selection. Verification, falsification and language game theory can all be used to answer questions on whether religious language is meaningless, whilst symbol and myth are at the heart of questions about non-cognitive language. You may be asked to choose to write about two or three out of analogy, myth, symbol and language games, so there is some scope for selective revision. The *via negativa* needs to be included in an essay on analogy as one of the ways of speaking about God that is rejected in favour of analogous statements.

Review questions

1 *'Religious language can only be understood in the context of religious belief.'* Examine and discuss the significance of this claim.

2 *'All religious language claims are meaningless.'* For what reasons might this assertion be made?

3 With reference to either myth *or* symbol, evaluate its effectiveness in facilitating talk of God.

4 How far does the doctrine of analogy solve the problem of talking meaningfully about God?

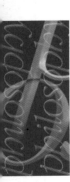

Religious Ethics

Topic 1

Ethical theory and ethical decision-making

A Ethical language

1 Defining morality

Before we can begin to establish what constitutes good or bad moral or ethical behaviour we need to consider whether we can define what morality *is*. The branch of moral philosophy that is concerned with this issue is **meta-ethics**, which examines the issue of what we mean when we say that a thing or an action is good, bad, right, wrong, moral or immoral. A primary consideration is whether ethical language can be said to have any meaning. If we are unclear as to the meaning of basic ethical terms such as these, then how can we begin to make authoritative, or at least convincing, claims about the morality of particular actions? The statement 'Killing is wrong' is complicated enough, since we are immediately faced with a vast range of different situations in which not everyone would agree that killing was wrong, but if we are not even sure about what we mean by 'wrong' then ethical debate will be fraught with difficulties.

The word 'good' has many meanings and most of them are not used in a moral context. I may say that my computer is 'good' because it fulfils the task that it was purchased to fulfil, and because I get enormous enjoyment from using it, but I am not ascribing moral status to it, because a computer is not a moral agent. Similarly, we use the word 'ought' in different contexts: 'Teachers ought to be kind to their students' carries quite different implications from 'You ought to take an umbrella with you'. The first statement is prescribing a particular mode of behaviour which is based on our opinion of how teachers ought to behave and so is a moral statement, whilst the second recommends a course of action on the basis of certain objective facts.

A key factor in all this is whether ethical dilemmas are **subjective** or **objective**, that is whether they are based on personal preference or on external facts. If a moral opinion is independent of external facts, then it is essentially internal and is to do with how we feel about an ethical issue, and therefore subjective. An objective fact, however, is related to how things actually are in the real world. We deal with such facts constantly: the chair is red; the sun is shining; London is the capital city of England. These facts would be the case irrespective of how I feel, or even whether I exist at all, and so they are true for everyone, not just me or my friends. If moral values are objective, then they are similarly true for everyone. Whether morality deals in facts or opinions is a crucial issue for ethical debate and the key to this is whether we can place goodness in an objective category, since it is clearly open to so many different interpretations.

If morality is objective, then it is **cognitive**. Cognitive language deals with making propositions about things that can be known and so can be held to be true or false. If it is subjective, then it is **non-cognitive** — it deals with matters that are not simply resolved by establishing if they are true or false. This is a non-propositional view, which understands language as serving some other function than that of making true/false claims. For example, if I witness a boy smashing car windscreens, and report it to the police, then I am reporting a fact, but if I tell them that I thought the boy was wrong to be doing so, I would be reporting my feelings about it, and this would not be a fact. The boy doing the smashing may not consider his actions to be wrong, so it is a subjective and not an objective matter, even if most people share my opinion.

Furthermore, there is arguably a difference between an ethical issue and a moral issue. The distinction is hard to define, but a way of understanding it may be by thinking of a moral issue as one which is concerned with relationships, life and death — for example sex, marriage, homosexuality, euthanasia, murder, stealing, fraud, abortion, or transplantation of organs. All these issues have implications for human relationships, although some are clearly more direct than others. An ethical issue, however, is one that deals more with our perception of what is acceptable in a social sense. Sometimes these categories may overlap, but a good example of something that was an ethical issue rather than a moral dilemma was whether the BBC news reporters should have worn black ties to announce the death of the Queen Mother in April 2002. Allegedly the royal family was 'furious' because Peter Sissons, a BBC news reporter, wore a burgundy tie rather than a black one. Issues of respect, decency and honour were possibly at stake, and people would have had their own opinion as to whether it was right or wrong, but no lives were at risk or fundamental principles of universal human conduct in jeopardy.

2 The naturalistic fallacy

A key problem in attempting to reach a definition of morality is commonly referred to as the **is–ought gap**, or the naturalistic fallacy. Naturalistic theories of ethics (discussed in the section 'Tools for ethical decision-making', pp. 139–151) attempt to define good in terms of something that can be identified in the world or in human nature — for example, claiming that what is natural, or what makes us happy, fit or healthy, is good. If we adopt this approach, we are effectively turning an *is* into an *ought*. G. E. Moore argued that it is not acceptable to identify morality with any other concept, such as happiness, because any attempt to do so will not be able to accommodate the full measure of the concept and so will always be inadequate. Most importantly, if we say that something *is* the case, we are making a descriptive statement of how things actually are. It describes facts about the world and items in it: 'Oranges are a good source of vitamin C.' A normative or prescriptive statement says that something *ought* to be desired or done: 'You ought to eat oranges.' David Hume observed that there is nothing in a descriptive statement that allows us to proceed from what people *actually* do (a factual statement) to making a rule about what people *ought* to do (a value judgment). For example, it would be unfair to move from a statement of fact that women are better parents (if, say, an experiment produced that result) to saying that therefore men ought not to be single parents.

All attempts to move from an *ought* to an *is* face the same problem — they attempt to describe a situation that logically dictates what an individual is then obliged to do. However, there is no reason why we should not ask why we ought to do this. If I ask why I ought to eat oranges, the reply might be that they are a good source of vitamin C, but this is not sufficient in itself. I can further ask why I should care that they are a good source of vitamin C and be given the answer that they are good for my health. But even this is not enough, because I might not be concerned about looking after my health, and certainly not consider that there is any moral obligation upon me to do so.

In ethical terms, to say that something is good, and therefore prescribe it as a moral action that we are obliged to perform, is unconvincing to many. Why should we seek the happiness of the greatest number, do our duty, or pursue the virtues? These may be good in some circumstances, or even most, but that alone is not sufficient to make them a matter of moral obligation. John Searle argued, however, that it is possible to derive an *ought* from an *is* in the case of promising. If I say that 'I promise to…' then I take on the obligation of fulfilling that promise, so the fact of speaking the words leads me to carrying out my obligation to do so.

3 Intuitionism

Proponents of intuitionism argue that ethical terms cannot be defined, since the properties ascribed to them, such as 'good' or 'ought', can also be defined in non-ethical terms. G. E. Moore (who developed the concept of the naturalistic fallacy in his book *Principia Ethica*) is famous for arguing that 'good' can be defined no more successfully than 'yellow'. If we are asked to define yellow, or indeed any colour, we can only define it in terms of something else which possesses what we consider to be the quality or characteristics of yellow. We give examples of yellow and yellow things, but we do not define yellow itself. In the same way, ethical values cannot therefore be defined, but are self-evident and can be known only directly by intuition. Certain things are perceived to be good, such as compassion, but this is not because humans reason it to be so with reference to natural or empirical observation. Good is not a matter of opinion, but something that we can all ascertain through reason. Moore argued that goodness resists definition because people have different moral opinions without logical contradiction, and yet there is a remarkable similarity in the way in which people reach moral conclusions and even in the conclusions they draw. An inner sense directs humans to know what is right or wrong, but, as Moore argued, '*If I am asked "What is good?", my answer is that "good is good", and that is the end of the matter.*'

Problems with intuitionism

÷ People who intuit and those who use reason may reach different conclusions and there is no obvious way to resolve their differences.

÷ How can we be sure that our intuitions are correct? Is it a gut feeling? Is it God's direction? How reliable is experience as a guide?

÷ Intuition may be considered to be a meaningless concept since it is non-verifiable.

✤ In the eighteenth century, David Hume argued that we have a motivation for acting in certain ways, although intuitionists may respond to this with the suggestion that if we feel motivated towards a particular action it is because we have an innate desire to do it that goes beyond reason.

4 Emotivism

Often referred to as the 'Hurrah!–Boo!' theory, the emotive theory of ethics stems from the work of the Logical Positivists, who sought to do away with all metaphysical language, which they deemed to be beyond empirical verification and thereby meaningless. Thus, at its extreme, emotivism argues that if we make a claim such as 'Abortion is wrong', this is not to make a value judgment based on an objective point of reference, but rather we are simply saying 'I don't like abortion' or, more colloquially, 'Abortion — boo!' A. J. Ayer (1936) reduced all moral talk to an expression of the speaker's feelings and maintained that to say, for example, 'Abortion (or murder) is wrong' is making a kind of primitive noise. Ethical claims are not designed to make factual claims but to invoke certain emotional responses in the hearer, and so what they mean is less important than what they accomplish. They cannot be rationally justified, although they do serve in some way as an instruction. 'Abortion is wrong' is more than an arbitrary expression of opinion. It is a recommendation to others not to abort a foetus: 'Abortion is wrong' equals 'Do not have an abortion'. Nevertheless, no matter how many reasons I may give for why I think abortion is wrong (or right), it is still fundamentally an expression of my opinion.

Rudolph Carnap took a similar view, although he considered ethical claims to be commands, not ejaculations. If we maintain that ethical claims are commands from God, then we are effectively adopting this view, whilst suggesting a rational reason for calling them commands. Bertrand Russell claimed that moral judgments express a wish, and R. B. Braithwaite maintained that they serve to bind the community together. This is a **non-cognitive**, or **anti-realist**, view of language, which takes the stance that language does not make factually true claims, but serves some other function.

C. L. Stevenson argued that ethical judgments express the speaker's attitude and seek to evoke a similar attitude in the audience, but he does allow that our attitudes are based on beliefs that provide reasonable grounds for holding them. We may know that a certain course of action will bring about particular results and thus argue in its favour. Nevertheless, he does allow that even our most fundamental attitudes may not be rooted in any particular beliefs, in which case we cannot reason about them.

Problems with emotivism

✤ Ethical statements are not usually judged according to the response of the listener but on the claims themselves. 'Abortion is wrong' makes a claim that can be discussed and evaluated. Its power does not simply lie in how others respond to it.

✤ If ethical claims were contingent on emotions, then they would change as emotions changed. Neither could they be universal claims, since the emotions of different speakers would vary.

✤ Even when moral statements are carried by a weight of public emotion, that does not make them the reason that they are adopted and it does not make them right.

÷ Emotivism effectively prescribes complete freedom of action on the basis that everyone's opinion is equally valid, and hence everyone is free to do what they choose irrespective of the opinion of others.

÷ How can we judge between two people's moral opinions? What criteria are there — if any — for judging the relative merits of a moral viewpoint?

÷ Emotions can unite people in a common moral bond, but they can also isolate individuals and groups.

÷ The emotional force with which a moral view is expressed is no recommendation of its value.

÷ As part of the linguistic philosophy of the Logical Positivists, Ayer's approach to ethical language may be largely discredited since it proposed a method of analysing the meaningfulness of language which it was itself unable to satisfy.

Summary

■ **Meta-ethics** is the branch of moral philosophy concerned with ethical language — what morality *is* and whether ethical talk is meaningful. Ethical terms — good, ought — have many contexts. Are ethical statements **cognitive** or **non-cognitive**, **subjective** or **objective**? Do they make claims that are universally shared or are they meaningful only to the speaker?

■ **The naturalistic fallacy** — defining good leads to problems of the *is–ought* gap: can statements of fact lead justifiably to statements of value and dictate what an individual should do?

■ **Intuitionism** — non-naturalistic approach that aims to resolve these problems. Ethical terms cannot be defined any more successfully than colours. Their meaning is self-evident and can only be known by intuition. Good is ascertained through reason and is not a matter of opinion. This theory is supported by the remarkable amount of common ground that exists between individuals on ethical matters.

■ **Emotivism** — ethical statements have no cognitive meaning but are expressions of emotion and personal preference. They are designed to generate similar feelings in the hearer and to instruct them to adopt certain behaviour patterns. Some emotivist thinkers do suggest, however, that we still have reasons for holding the ethical views we have. There are considerable problems with emotivism, not least that it renders all ethical debate valueless.

Key terms

Cognitive language — claims that refer to matters of factual, objective truth.
Non-cognitive language — non-factual claims.
Objective — claims that refer to external facts or values.
Subjective — claims that are based on personal preference.

Exam watch

This is a good topic to get to grips with in the exam, as it lends itself less to rambling 'all I know' answers than some questions on ethical theories such as utilitarianism or deontology. Keep your response precise and to the point, use clear examples to illustrate the observations you make about the use of ethical language, and include relevant scholars' names to give your answer a firm structure.

Review questions

1 (a) Explain what scholars mean when they say that ethical statements are merely expressions of opinion.

  (b) How far do you consider such views to be justifiable?

2 (a) What is the problem of the *is–ought* gap?

  (b) In what ways have scholars sought to overcome the problems posed for ethical language by the naturalistic fallacy?

B Ways of understanding ethical decision-making

1 Virtue ethics

The great Greek philosopher Aristotle was influenced in his thinking by his conviction that all things and all human beings have a purpose or function — a **telos**. A complete explanation of anything would include its final cause or purpose, which is, ultimately, to realise its potential and to fulfil its goal. For human beings, Aristotle maintained that the ultimate goal is human flourishing and developing those characteristics best suited to the realisation of a virtuous human being. His emphasis was not on what people *do*, but on what kind of person they *are*, although *being* a kind person, for example, is essentially accomplished by practising acts of kindness until the habit of being kind is firmly established in a person's character.

Aristotle maintained that the virtues are those qualities that lead to a good life — qualities such as courage, compassion, honesty or justice. The person who aims to cultivate these qualities is maximising their potential for a happy life — a quality of happiness described as *eudaimonia*, which involves being happy and living well. It is of intrinsic value, not a means to an end, and should be desired for its own sake, not only for individuals but also for the society of which they are members. Individuals who develop the virtues will be able to act in an integrated way, deriving satisfaction from doing the right thing *because* it is the right thing, and not for any external reasons or goals. They will not act in a particular way either because they *ought* to do so or because they *want* to do so, but simply because they have identified the *right* way to act.

For Aristotle, the right way to act is to follow the **golden mean**. This is a perfect balance between two extremes, such as cowardice and foolhardiness, which are both vices; in this example the golden mean is, of course, courage — a virtue which human beings are not born with but which they should cultivate in the way that they might cultivate good health or fitness. People should learn from good role models, train and exercise this virtue, until it becomes an automatic way of living and behaving and part of their character, which they can exercise without conscious effort or will. In this way they will become courageous people. It may involve performing courageous acts but, more importantly, their character will acquire the virtue of courage and their actions will be motivated by courage.

Virtue ethics underwent something of a revival in the later twentieth century. Elizabeth Anscombe observed that ethical codes which lay stress on moral absolutes and laws are anachronistic in a society which has effectively abandoned God, and she urged a return to a morality which is based on human flourishing. Similarly, Richard Taylor rejected a system of morality which is based on divine commands and which discourages people from achieving their potential. Interestingly, he argued that the emphasis Christianity places on human equality does not encourage individuals to strive to be great but rather advocates a self-negating humility. Philippa Foot argued that although the virtues cannot guarantee happiness, they can go some way to achieving it, whilst Alastair MacIntyre noted that in moral dilemmas, naturalistic theories of ethics are of little value as they are time-consuming and overly complex. A virtue-based approach to ethics is more realistic and applicable to people's everyday situations.

Virtue ethics has appeal because it can be accommodated by both religious and secular morality. Despite Taylor's observations, Jesus can be held up as a model of the virtuous person, in whom weakness becomes strength and death is transformed into life. It is a simple system based on universal well-being for the individual and the community, and in holding up models of virtuous people it does not set unrealistic goals. It is accessible by reference to the real world, since if I describe a person as courageous, the description immediately generates a picture of someone who lives in a particular way and whose way of life recommends itself to the observer. Its greatest strength, perhaps, is that it attempts to link theoretical and practical approaches to ethics and maintains that theories of moral behaviour have objective value as part of developing a good life.

Weaknesses of virtue ethics

÷ How do we decide which virtues are those to be cultivated the most? Why should we prefer certain ideals to others? Virtues have relative value in different cultures and whilst physical courage is considered highly valuable in some societies, intellectual prowess is rated more highly in others. A value judgment still has to be made as to which virtues are most desirable, and it is possible that even the most self-evidently virtuous person might not be considered by everyone to be a desirable role model. Susan Wolf writes: *I don't know whether there are moral saints. But if there are, I am glad that neither I nor those about whom I care most are among them*' (cited in Ahluwalia, 2001). In other words, not everyone wants to cultivate the virtues or maintains that they are intrinsically good.

÷ Aristotle's principle of the golden mean is not easy to apply to all virtues. Whilst courage does appear to be a mean between cowardice and foolhardiness, is there a mean virtue of compassion or loyalty? Is it possible to take compassion to an extreme whereupon it becomes a vice? Even where there is a mean, how do we identify where it lies? When does courage become foolhardiness?

÷ Aristotle gives no guidance in situations where virtues conflict and where we need rules to guide our actions. Because the emphasis of the approach is on being rather than doing, it can also be seen as a rather selfish theory, which places greater emphasis on personal development than the effect our actions have on others.

÷ The virtues valued by Aristotle are essentially masculine ones, frequently associated with the battlefield, such as bravery and honour. Conceivably, therefore, the approach could be seen as chauvinistic, giving little credit to more feminine virtues such as humility and empathy.

2 Teleological ethics

Some years ago, newspapers reported an accident... A family had gone away...and had left their keys with their neighbour... A few hours before they were due to arrive home...the neighbour thought he would do them a favour and make sure they would come home to a nice toasty house. He went in and turned on the furnace... The house burned down and the family came home to a burned-out lot... Suppose it had been reported by a classical utilitarian. Then the article might have ended up like this: 'This neighbour will have to answer for the consequences of this terrible deed.'

(Rosenstand, 2000)

This may appear to be a facetious example, but it illustrates the nature of a society in which only the consequences of our actions matter — one in which all actions are judged according to teleological criteria. How would we begin to calculate the rights and wrongs of any given situation? Would it be simple or complex? Would it work practically? Above all, would it enable us to make reliable moral decisions?

Like the Teleological Argument for the existence of God, a teleological ethical theory concerns purpose. The basis for judging the morality of an action is the results it is likely to yield — its consequences. Hence, teleological theories are **consequentialist**, and whether an action is good/bad, right/wrong depends on the outcome. There are several immediate implications of this:

- There can be no moral absolutes (i.e. things that are always right or wrong whatever the circumstances).
- Nothing is **inherently** right or wrong.
- Actions have only **instrumental** value (i.e. help us get something else that we want) rather than **intrinsic** value (i.e. valued purely for their own sake). Some things have both values, for example education, which is good in itself but also instrumental, since it helps people gain employment.
- Motives are neither good nor bad, but are morally neutral.
- What constitutes a good, moral consequence? This is a problem for a number of reasons:
  - The moral value of a consequence depends on the individual's personal preference.
  - How can a group of individuals reach a consensus on what is a good consequence?
  - How far-reaching should consequences be? Are we concerned with immediate or ultimate consequences?
  - How can we judge the moral value of a consequence when there are so many conflicting factors?

Teleological ethical theories tend to rely on a **principle of utility**. This is the measure of the usefulness, or fittingness for purpose, that an action may have. We can propose any principle of utility we like. If we believe that the best or most moral action we can perform is one which will enable consequence X or Y to come about, then we must assess, using a principle of utility, how likely or effective action A or B will be in contributing to that consequence. Both utilitarianism and situation ethics establish a principle of utility for judging the morality of an action. For utilitarianism the principle of utility is 'the greatest happiness of the greatest number'; for situation ethics, it is *agape* (Greek word for 'love'). Both these principles have some underlying weaknesses:

- Happiness and love are relative concepts. We have different expectations of each which vary considerably under a huge range of circumstances.
- Does happiness or love always justify the suffering of others?
- Are some types of happiness or love better than others?
- Happiness and love are surely abstract qualities. If so, how do we measure them?
- Are we certain that happiness or love are the best possible qualities by which we can judge the *moral* value of an action? Are they not possibly motivated by selfish goals?

However, if happiness and love are not the best criteria for judging the moral value of an action, then what are better? Happiness and love are universally valued; they are individually and corporately upbuilding and satisfying and are desirable in themselves, but they can be open to abuse — perhaps at the expense of justice. Would justice, prudence or duty be better criteria for determining the morality of an action? Maybe so, if we don't want to take the risks involved in placing excessive value on emotive concepts such as happiness or love. But we need to consider the implications of a society based on qualities such as justice — a society based on desert, not on generosity or compassion. Love motivates our actions far more than inflexible rules based on justice and desert, and it is surely in the nature of humanity to show compassion and to give more than is deserved.

How workable are teleological theories?

Consequences have real effects. To say that 'the thought counts' may be a truism, but consequences are what we have to live with. We are forward-looking creatures, who tend to ask 'What would happen if…?' We feel compelled to act or are restrained from acting, depending on what we envisage to be likely consequences. Our richest dreams for the future often remain unfulfilled because we cannot face the consequences of fulfilling them. We weigh the various likely outcomes and discard some actions because the happiness or well-being of some may suffer, even if that of others may be increased. But because we do not know what all the consequences of our actions will be, we have to act on information that is:

- limited
- based on precedent
- predictive
- fallible and changeable

How can we avoid making judgments about the future without being influenced by the past? Can we really be truly situational? We may reach different conclusions as to whether Mother A — a 15-year-old school girl who has run away from home — or Mother B — a 35-year-old married barrister — is morally justified to have an abortion, but do we really reach these conclusions free from the baggage of all previous situations?

Can we operate independently of all moral absolutes, laws or norms? However far we try to make moral judgments situationally, we cannot entirely avoid an inherent sense of right and wrong. In any case, are utilitarianism and situation ethics completely free of absolutes? Happiness and love may simply *appear* not to be absolutes because they replace less flexible, compassionate absolutes such as duty.

3 Absolutism

For those thinkers who are uncomfortable with the flexibility of the teleological approach, absolutism may be a better way to resolve ethical dilemmas. Absolutism is commonly associated with **deontology**, a term which comes from the Greek ***deontos*** meaning 'duty'. Deontological ethical theories are concerned with examining the motivation for an act, not its consequences, and upon that basis establishing whether it is a morally right action. Deontological ethicists take the view that moral principles can be established ***a priori*** — that is, without experience. They are independent of experience because they are **inherently right**, irrespective of the outcome. A deontologist will maintain that there exists an **absolute moral law** or code which can be discerned without reference to any hypothetical consequences, but which is always and intrinsically right. If something is absolute, then it is right in all circumstances and for all people, irrespective of the likely outcome. Hence, if killing is absolutely wrong, it is wrong in all situations, and if preserving life is absolutely right, it is right in all situations. This is clearly quite different from a teleological approach to ethics, which adopts a more (although not exclusively) relativist approach and is concerned with *ends* rather than *means*.

Moral absolutism can also be known as **hard universalism**, which holds that there is one universal moral code and does not acknowledge even the possibility of there being more than one set of morals. It is at the opposite end of the spectrum to **moral nihilism**, which claims that there are no moral truths. Although absolutists might claim that they are right because they are right, more frequently they will attempt to demonstrate through reasoning and evidence the legitimacy of their position. This may be by making reference to the moral law evident in nature, or through the inherent truth of certain claims which can be universalised.

Taking an absolutist approach makes it possible to evaluate moral actions in a critical way, since if an individual or group is not conforming to the recognised absolute standard or law, they can justifiably be condemned for it. However, this depends entirely on societies and individuals coming to an agreement as to what constitutes absolute morality. An absolutist approach attempts to ensure fairness in decision-making, since we cannot work on the principle that one rule is right for one and one for another; but, again, this depends on being confident that it is not appropriate to treat people differently in different situations.

4 Relativism

Moral relativism argues that moral values are grounded in social custom. Plato was a relativist, claiming that 'Man is the measure of all things.' The principle holds that there are no absolute universal standards but that whether or not it is right for individuals to act in a certain way depends on, or is relative to, the society to which they belong. Moral judgments are therefore true or false relative to the particular moral framework of the speaker's community. Moral diversity is explained by the fact that moral beliefs are the product of different ways of life and are matters of opinion that vary from culture to culture (**cultural relativism**) or from person to person and in different situations (**moral relativism**). Furthermore, our conceptions of morality should be based on how people actually behave (**de facto values**) rather than an ideal standard of how people should behave (**ideal values**), because there is no one right or wrong way of behaving. No individual or culture can claim to be morally superior in its values, beliefs and practices, and it is not possible or acceptable to judge the views or practices of any culture because there is no overriding standard against which it can be judged. A relativist approach too would reject the discrimination of individuals or groups for their religious beliefs, even if they were representative of a very small minority of the population, and hold that in a country where religious beliefs different to our own are held, we should respect their conventions — for example, women visiting an Islamic country should dress appropriately, even if they do not adopt that mode of dress at home.

The implications of this position

÷ There is no point in moral debate since opposing moral claims can be simultaneously true, relative to the culture from which they emerge.

÷ However, moral relativism would allow us to establish right and wrong simply by consulting the community; if society does not progress, neither does morality. There is no room for social reform since reformers would be seen to be challenging the norms of society.

÷ If you want to propose a particular moral viewpoint — e.g. 'It is right to rape teenage girls' — all you need to do is form a community of like-minded moralists! This would not generally be considered an acceptable justification of an immoral action and underlines the impracticality of relativism.

÷ Moral relativism considers the views of other cultures to be true for them, and therefore not worthy of debate.

÷ J. L. Mackie observed that the morality of individuals tends to be shaped by their society, not the other way round. He rejected the view that there is an absolute standard of good, but argued that although individuals are inclined to *think* that there is an objective standard of goodness, this reflects nothing more than a psychological need to find such a standard.

÷ Moral relativism may not be clear on whether the application of moral rules differs between cultures or groups or whether the rules are themselves entirely different.

÷ Moral subjectivism is sometimes considered a sub-category of moral relativism. However, moral subjectivism does not claim that each *culture* is right in its own way but rather that *people* are right in their own way. This is exceptionally tolerant but cannot solve moral conflicts since there is never any common denominator to which to refer and any individual moral stance is considered equally valid.

÷ Relativists do, however, adopt an absolute principle: 'Be tolerant of everyone's different moral codes.'

÷ Arguably, relativists fail to recognise the similarities between the morality of different cultures, and place too much emphasis on the variations. Furthermore, societies are complex — there can be no one culturally agreed morality.

Summary and key terms

- **Virtue ethics** — the purpose of every human being is to *flourish* — to develop those characteristics most suited to a virtuous human character, which are of benefit to society and which maximise the potential for **eudaimonia**. People should aim for the **golden mean** until it becomes an automatic way of living and an intrinsic part of their character. The theory is accessible and apparently universal, placing emphasis on qualities considered to be desirable in all human beings. Problems: How do we decide which virtues are most desirable? Where does the golden mean lie? How do we deal with conflicting virtues?

- **Teleological ethics** — the basis for judging the morality of an action is consequence, not motivation. Nothing is inherently wrong and actions have instrumental value. A **principle of utility** should be applied to measure the moral worth of an action in terms of how effective it is in bringing about the desired outcome. Teleological ethics recognises the moral implications of the consequences of our actions, *but* depends on being able to make reliable predictions.
- **Absolutism** — there are fixed moral laws which apply in all situations. Moral principles are *a priori*, inherently true, and universalisable. People are treated the same in the same circumstances.
- **Relativism** — there are no absolute standards, but 'right' is relative to society or the individual, and moral judgments are relative to the moral framework of the speaker's community. No individual or culture can claim that their value judgments are better than others, only different. *But* moral debate is impossible and similarities between the moralities of different cultures are not recognised.

Exam watch

Make sure that you have grasped the principles behind all these ways of understanding ethical decision-making — they essentially revolve around whether we believe that morality is inherent and intrinsic, or whether we need to judge it according to situations, circumstances or outcomes. You will need to be in full command of these issues when you come to write essays on major ethical theories such as utilitarianism or Kantian deontology.

Review questions

1 (a) Outline what moral philosophers understand by relativism.
  (b) Is it true to say that some things are always wrong or always right?
2 (a) Examine the key features of virtue ethics.
  (b) Are the virtues inherently desirable?
3 Assess the value of judging the moral value of an action by its consequences.
4 Assess the key features of a deontological approach to ethics.

C Tools for ethical decision-making

1 Natural moral law

True law is right reason in agreement with nature. It is applied universally and is unchanging and everlasting...one eternal and unchangeable law will be valid for all nations and all times, and there will be one master and rule, that is God.

(Cicero)

The thinking of Aristotle heavily influenced Thomas Aquinas, the great Christian proponent of natural moral law, and in particular the view that all things have a purpose to which they work. That purpose can be understood through an examination of the natural world and through the Bible, which reveals the purpose for which God created man. Natural law is available to all, since everyone with some reasoning capacity is able to see that the universe works according to certain patterns and rules that do not change. In *Summa Theologica*, Aquinas maintains that there is a moral code towards which human beings naturally incline, and this he calls **natural moral law**. Natural law is:

÷ accessible through the natural order
÷ universal
÷ unchanging
÷ for all time
÷ relevant to all circumstances
÷ given by God
÷ perceived by all human beings, although only believers in God acknowledge that it has implications for them beyond the grave

Natural law draws its inspiration from the Bible as well as from the common reason of mankind. Paul in Romans 1–3 argues that the moral law of God is evident from the nature of humans and the world: '*Ever since the creation of the world, his invisible nature, namely his eternal power and deity, has been clearly perceived in the things that have been made*' (Romans 1:20). Paul maintains that since natural moral law is so clearly evident in the universe, sinful humans have no excuse for wrongdoing. In Matthew 19:3–9 Jesus observes that the divorce law in the Torah is a concession to the sinful nature of humans and not what God had originally intended in the order of creation: '*For your hardness of heart Moses allowed you to divorce your wives, but from the beginning it was not so*' (Matthew 19:8). Hence, natural moral knowledge should make it clear that divorce is wrong.

The principle of natural law depends on establishing the purpose of human life. Aquinas maintained that it is to live, reproduce, learn, worship God, and order society. All things must operate in accordance with these principles to which humans are naturally inclined. God gives humans the power of reason to accomplish these purposes, whether they believe in him or not, and everything is created to a particular design and for a particular purpose; fulfilling that purpose is the 'good' towards which everything aims. However, although the natural law, instituted by God, gives people the opportunity to work towards the good in all things, Paul recognised that this is not always possible, '*since all have sinned and fallen short of the glory of God*' (Romans 3:23). Humans will fall short of God's best for them because this is a fallen world and humans violated the perfect relationship with God and the natural order that was instituted at creation (Genesis 2 and 3). Nevertheless, rational people will desire communication with God and will act to accomplish it, despite human limitation. Any action which brings humans closer to this goal is good, and any action which takes them further away is wrong. Aquinas maintained that all individuals also have a purpose specific to themselves that fulfil the skills and talents given to them by God.

Whilst the goal of a relationship with God is open to all, other goals are only open to some. This is potentially controversial, since if some individuals are more naturally endowed with talents than others, does this suggest that God has been fair and equitable in his distribution of them? Do some people have no special talents? The parable of the talents in Luke 19:11–27 is overlaid with a multitude of meanings, but one may conceivably be about God-given skills and abilities and how he expects them to be utilised.

Aquinas identified four kinds of law: **eternal law** — God's will and wisdom, which is revealed in **divine law**, given in scripture and through the church, made known in **natural law**, from which **human law** is derived. Human law, exercised through the state and government, is therefore seen to be an extension of natural and divine law. Paul again writes in Romans 13:1: '*Let every person be subject to the governing authorities. For there is no authority except from God, and those that exist have been instituted by God.*'

The strengths of natural law

Natural moral law is a simple, universal guide for judging the moral value of human actions, and the purposes which Aquinas proposes for human existence are common to all human beings. Moral law is made accessible by our reason, and it makes God's reason accessible to a believer because humans and God share the same rationality. Upholders of naturalism would argue that the law ought to reflect the universal set of morals that all humans can discern from the universe in this way.

Natural law appeals to the sense we have that morality is more than just a matter of what people's personal preferences and inclinations may be. Even though different cultures and individuals may reach different conclusions on the rightness or wrongness of a moral action, there is a prevailing sense that some things are of intrinsic value. However:

÷ Aquinas assumes that all men seek to worship God; many would see this as artificial, not natural. Furthermore, he assumes that God created the universe and the moral law within it. These assumptions are not natural ones for the atheist to make.

÷ By giving pride of place to reproduction as one of the common, universal aims of humankind, Aquinas opens up thorny issues for homosexuals (what if homosexuality is genetically explained and therefore 'natural'?) and for those who are biologically incapable of having children, let alone those who, for personal reasons, choose not to do so.

÷ Aquinas thinks of every individual and every part of every individual as having a particular function to fulfil. This goes against the 'portfolio' thinking of modern times, by which we recognise the variety of functions that people can fulfil.

÷ There is no room for situationism, relativism, consequentialism or individualism.

÷ Aquinas commits the *naturalistic fallacy*: he maintains that moral law comes from God (a matter of fact in his thinking) and therefore that we ought to obey it (a value judgment).

÷ He makes no room for evolutionary change, but suggests that human beings and human nature have remained the same since creation. This does not even allow room for the divine redemption of human beings through Christ.

÷ Aquinas's understanding of human purpose is limited. If he claims that it is the purpose of humanity to reproduce, how would he explain his own decision to be a celibate priest? He gets around this by saying that there is room for some individuals to fulfil a different purpose as long as humanity as a whole works towards the general purposes. Nevertheless, he still does not seem fully to allow for the fact that the fulfilling of individual and exclusive purposes is an integral part of a person's personal relationship with God. Surely the Apostles had a purpose which was quite different to that fulfilled by other followers of Jesus, for example?

2 Kantian deontology

Immanuel Kant espoused a deontological, or absolutist, approach to ethics, judging morality by examining the nature of actions and the will of the agents rather than the goals they achieved. A primary reason for adopting this approach is that we cannot control consequences because we cannot control the future, however hard we may try. Whilst Kant was not unconcerned about the outcome, since he effectively argued a form of the golden rule — *'Do to others what you would have them do to you'* (Matthew 7:12) — he insisted that the moral evaluation of actions cannot take consequences into consideration. Furthermore, he believed that since all men possess reason and a conscience, it is possible for all people to arrive at an understanding of moral truths independent of experience. Morality is *a priori*, not *a posteriori*, and because reason is universal, then moral reasoning leads to the same results over and over again.

Kant argued that the universe is essentially just and that the moral law would be satisfied (the good rewarded and the bad punished) in a post-mortem existence. To this end, he claimed, the existence of God is a necessary requirement of a just universe and for the moral law to be balanced. Kant attempted to discover the rational principle that would stand as a **categorical imperative**, grounding all other ethical judgments. The imperative would have to be categorical rather than **hypothetical**, since true morality should not depend on individual likes and dislikes or on abilities, opportunities or other external circumstances. Kant's distinction between these two imperatives is vital for his approach. Kant believed that moral commands are not hypothetical imperatives, which are commands that tell us how to achieve a particular end. For example, if someone asks me how to get to Catford Bridge, I tell them: 'Take the Hayes train from Charing Cross'. If they follow this command they will achieve their end, which is to get to Catford Bridge. Moral commands, however, do not tell us how to achieve an end but are ends in themselves. They express our absolute and unconditional duty to act in a certain way, and Kant considered them to be of supreme importance.

Kant maintained that *'it is impossible to conceive of anything at all in the world, or even out of it, which can be taken as good without qualification, except a good will'.* A good will could be cultivated by use of reason and by working to be rid of those tendencies which make rational decision-making impossible. Personal preferences lead to hypothetical imperatives, or commands that have a reason behind them: *'If you want to be well liked, be generous to others'.* This does not espouse generosity as an *a priori* principle, but offers a reason why one should be generous. Kant argued that whilst personal preferences and inclinations are not necessarily wrong, they cannot be trusted as a reliable guide to what is morally right. Essentially, Kant argued that if we act according to our duty in any given circumstance, we will act rightly. Duty supersedes personal inclinations and unworthy motives. He was concerned to find *the* categorical imperative which would provide the fundamental moral groundwork for all actions and he found this in the **principle of universalisability**. He formulated this in his **formula of the law of nature**, which demands that human beings *'act in such a way that their actions might become a universal law'*. If the rule or maxim governing our actions cannot be universalised, then it is not morally acceptable, and if you cannot will that everyone follow the same rule, then it is not a moral rule.

Universalisable principles are those which apply not just in specific cases but to everyone. 'Don't run so fast!' applies just to the person who is running, but 'Be kind!' can be applied to everyone, without logical contradiction. Similarly, 'Be fair to your customers so they will come back to your shop' is not a universalisable principle, as it seeks to achieve an end — continued custom — whereas 'Be fair to your customers' is a principle which could be applied to every shopkeeper irrespective of circumstances. Kant used the example of the institution of promising to illustrate his maxim. If, having promised to repay a loan, I see something I want to buy, but to do so would mean spending the money I should be repaying, I would not be acting on the universalisable principle 'Keep your promises' but would presumably be advocating another principle — 'Keep your promises unless doing so would deprive you of something you want'. This latter principle is clearly not universalisable, or the whole institution of promising would break down. Kant's **formula of kingdom of ends** laid down the principle that every action should be undertaken as if the individual is *'a law making member of a kingdom of ends'*. This is to ensure that every individual appreciates how significant a part he or she plays in establishing moral guidelines and rules.

Kant clearly placed great faith in human beings as being able to work rationally to such a conclusion and to act freely according to principles. He also placed great value on respect for persons, who, unlike things, are never merely of instrumental value, but of intrinsic value. This means that although people may be useful, they should not be considered to be means to achieve an end, but to be ends in themselves. Deontology acknowledges human rights and justice as inviolable, something which utilitarianism overlooks.

Strengths of the theory

+ Motivation is valued over consequences, which are beyond our control. An immoral motive cannot be justified by unforeseen good consequences, but a good motive is, in itself, worthy of value.
+ It is a humanitarian principle in which all people are considered to be of equal value and worthy of protection.
+ Justice is always an absolute, even if the majority does not benefit.
+ It recognises the value of moral absolutes that do not change with time or culture. There must surely be some things which are beyond fad or fashion.
+ It provides objective guidelines for making moral decisions, without the need for lengthy calculation of possible outcomes.

Weaknesses of the theory

+ *'There is more to the moral point of view than being willing to universalise one's rules. Kant and his followers fail to see this fact, although they are right in thinking such a willingness is part of it'* (Frankena, 1973).

+ Moral obligations appear arbitrary or inexplicable except by reference to duty. In reality our decision-making is influenced by many more factors than these, and it is indeed questionable whether duty is as good a motive as Kant suggested.

+ If we are to act according to our duty, then how do we deal with conflicting duties? (For example, in time of war 'telling the truth' might conflict with 'saving life'.) W. D. Ross argued that we have ***prima facie*** duties that automatically override others — duty to family and loved ones before strangers, for example.

+ How far can a good will or motive mitigate a disastrous outcome? Furthermore, are we really only concerned to know the *form* of moral behaviour (e.g. duty) or do we want to know more about its *content*? Are we satisfied with being told 'Do your duty' without understanding why?

+ When taken to its logical extreme, the principle of universalisability is absurd. Anything could technically be universalised, but this does not make it a moral command. Hence the principle is exposed by a *reductio ad absurdum*. 'All men called Joe who are unemployed should rob a bank on Tuesday' is in theory universalisable, but clearly fails Kant's test in all other ways.

+ Kant argues that what is good to do is what we ought to do and that what is inherently good and intrinsically right is the way in which we ought to behave for the mutual good of all, irrespective of consequences. In this respect, critics of Kant have accused him of committing the *naturalistic fallacy* — of 'turning an *is* into an *ought'*.

+ Whilst Kant's approach avoids the problems of emotivism — that all moral behaviour is the outcome of our personal preferences — it may go too far in the other direction since he makes no allowances for compassion or sympathy in motivating our actions.

3 Utilitarianism

What then could be more plausible than that the right is to promote the general good — that our actions and our rules, if we must have rules, are to be decided upon by determining which of them produces or may be expected to produce the greatest general balance of good over evil?

(Frankena, 1973)

Utilitarianism is a nineteenth-century ethical theory, most often attributed to Jeremy Bentham, John Stuart Mill and Henry Sidgwick, who adopted the principle that right actions are those that produce the greatest total pleasure for everyone affected by their consequences, and wrong actions those that do not. Bentham discovered the phrase *'greatest good of the greatest number'* which was coined originally by Frances Hutcheson in Joseph Priestly's *Essay on Government*. Bentham was motivated by the desire to establish a universal theory which could be applied to all ethical situations, and his influence on nineteenth-century society and beyond was considerable, as he sought a theory of ethics which would iron out the deep inequalities of his time. Later, in the mid-twentieth century, 'ideal utilitarians' such as G. E. Moore agreed in principle with the philosophy of nineteenth-century utilitarians, but held that some things other than pleasurable experiences were intrinsically good.

The principle of utilitarianism claims that in a moral dilemma we should choose the action most likely to bring about the greatest happiness of the greatest number, or to express it negatively, that action which would lead to the **least pain for the least number**. Thus, in one set of circumstances, action A may be the most appropriate, whilst under other circumstances, action B might bring more happiness for more people. No action, therefore, is judged solely on its own merits, but must be judged in terms of its usefulness in any one particular set of circumstances. The theory is thus one of **universal ethical hedonism**: if an action brings or increases pleasure, then it is right. Bentham proposed the **hedonic calculus** to calculate the most pleasurable action. Seven elements are taken into consideration:

- intensity
- duration
- certainty
- propinquity (remoteness)
- fecundity (chance of there being further pleasures)
- purity (not followed by pain)
- extent

Bentham attempted to provide a means to *quantify* happiness. This would potentially give us an objective means of calculating which action was more likely to produce happiness by reaching a happiness score. It would therefore theoretically be possible to calculate whom it was morally right to rescue first from a fire: a child, a pregnant woman, an old man, or a scientist who possessed the formula for the ultimate cure for cancer. Peter Vardy and Paul Grosch (1994) cite the case of a young married woman who is planning a skiing trip but finds herself to be pregnant. She can use a hedonic calculus to work out what to do: if she chooses to abort the pregnancy in order to ski, the pleasure will be minor and temporary; if she chooses to abandon the holiday, the long lasting and intense pleasure of having the child will outweigh her initial disappointment.

John Stuart Mill developed the principle by referring to *qualitative* rather than *quantitative* pleasure, recognising some of the problem inherent in Bentham's formulation. He argued that pleasures of the mind should take precedence over physical pleasures and that once basic human requirements for survival were fulfilled, a human being's primary moral concerns should be for the higher-order goods. He claimed that '*It is better to be a human being dissatisfied than a pig satisfied; better to be Socrates dissatisfied than a fool satisfied*'. The danger of Bentham's hedonic principle is that demonstrably lower pleasures such as sadism could be justified if they were being carried out by the majority on the minority. Mill believed that it should be possible to educate people to seek higher pleasures — the Covent Garden flower seller, who enjoys her weekly bottle of gin, should be educated to find greater pleasure in going to the opera along with the well-to-do classes which buy her flowers. Bentham, on the other hand, had maintained that it is a matter for each individual to decide what is good or bad and, as such, his principle was an egalitarian one.

Mill also contributed the **harm principle** to utilitarianism in answer to the question of how much pressure the majority was allowed to exert on the minority. He wrote:

That principle is, that the sole end for which mankind are warranted, individually or collectively, in interfering with the liberty of action of any of their number, is self-protection. That the only purpose for which power can be rightfully exercised over any member of a civilised community, against his will, is to prevent harm to others.

(Cited in Rosenstand, 2000)

Nina Rosenstand observes that the harm principle is at the foundation of the principle of civil liberties — that citizens have within their right to privacy to do whatever they wish as long as it does no harm. She asks, however, how we would evaluate the case of a suicidal teenager. Would society have no right to interfere because she is harming no one but herself? Mill would argue that she is causing harm to others, not least her grieving family and to other teenagers, who might be encouraged to follow her example. This latter is indirect harm, however, and Mill did not allow for the majority to interfere on the grounds that other adults might imitate the actions of others.

Strengths of utilitarianism

+ The evaluation of moral choices is influenced only by personal preferences, which may be unreliable, if there is no consideration of consequences.
+ Utilitarian theories hold with the general consensus that human well-being is intrinsically good and actions should be judged according to their effect on this well-being.
+ Jesus preached an ethic of love, requiring men to work for the well-being of others: '*Do to others as you would have them do to you*' (Matthew 7:12).
+ Motives may be good or bad, but only consequences have a real effect on human well-being. Arguably, we have little interest in people's intentions, however well-meant, if the outcome has a negative effect on us.
+ The principle encourages a democratic approach to decision-making. The majority's interest is always considered, and a dangerous minority is not allowed to dominate.
+ Present circumstances can be judged without reference to precedents. Just because it would be wrong for woman A to have an abortion, it does not necessarily follow that in woman B's completely different circumstances it would be wrong for her.
+ It is an approach which asks that we consider no more than the greatest good of the greatest number, and it does not rest on any controversial or unverifiable theological or metaphysical claims or principles. Interestingly, the theory could be adapted to suit either a religious or non-religious perspective on the world, but its greatest appeal may be to a secular thinker.

Weaknesses of the theory

+ Its practical application requires the ability to predict long-term consequences of an action, and to predict those consequences with unfailing accuracy. Past experience can, to some extent, guide future experience, but we know that there is no guarantee that circumstances will turn out exactly the same. People may suffer at second or third hand, even if the immediate consequences of an action fulfil the conditions of the principle.

- The theory gives no credit to motivation. Not every action done out of good will is going to result in good consequences, but the attitude with which it is performed should be worthy of some credit.

- The theory cannot be used to determine what is really universally good. Under Bentham's theory it would be possible to justify acts of sadism or torture if the majority, no matter how perverted their pleasure, carried them out. Mill's qualitative principle does go some way to addressing this weakness, however.

- Even in less extreme circumstances, we cannot assume that the majority is always right. There should be room for both the majority and the minority views to be accommodated.

- The theory relies on a single principle. This is too simplistic. We cannot solve every dilemma by reference to one ethical theory, because every ethical dilemma is multi-faceted and unique in some way.

- Values such as justice can have no place, since the majority may not support that which is just. Similarly, the rights of an individual or group can be ignored if it is not in the interests of the majority to respect them, and Bentham was known to remark that all talk of rights was '*nonsense on stilts*'.

- Those who are religious believe that the responsibility for bringing about the best outcome belongs to God and not to humans.

- It makes no allowance for personal relationships: if a man's wife is dying in a fire, reason would not tell him first to rescue an eminent politician who was also in danger even if, arguably, greater happiness was to be gained. We have *prima facie* duties to those whom we love which will always be more important to us than duties to a society of unknown individuals.

- Happiness may be seen to be a rather dubious benefit to some religious believers — quite different to joy, peace, loving kindness, patience and charity, which are the gifts of the Spirit. Many religious believers have been motivated to endure pain and humiliation for a cause they believe to be true, and have not shirked it for an easier road to happiness:

> *Imagine the case of Joan of Arc. It seems unlikely that her campaign to rid France of the English was motivated entirely or even mainly by the search for pleasure. It is hardly credible that she was experiencing pleasure as she stood at the stake and the flames began to rise around her body… It seems more plausible that she…was experiencing pain for the sake of something she valued more highly than pleasure.*
>
> (Horner and Westacott, 2000)

The biblical writers did not suggest that happiness should be the motivating factor behind all human actions. They did not *expect* happiness. Paul wrote: '*Who shall separate us from the love of God? Shall tribulation, or distress, or persecution, or famine, or nakedness, or peril, or sword? As it is written, "For thy sake we are being killed all the day long". No in all these things we are more than conquerors through him who loved us*' (Romans 8:35–36).

- In general, happiness is a very unspecific term which can cover a range of satisfaction that a person might get from a particular activity. If it is not specifically locatable or identifiable, it becomes a rather fragile tool for the utilitarian.

Rule utilitarianism

In response to some of these criticisms of **act utilitarianism,** rule utilitarianism was developed as a more sophisticated application of the theory. Rather than claiming that we should always perform that action which promotes the greatest happiness, rule utilitarians suggest that our actions should be guided by rules which, if everyone followed them, would lead to the greatest overall happiness. Human experience has shown us that there are certain rules that tend to promote happiness — such as the keeping of promises, and refraining from stealing, killing and lying. We know, for example, that it is better not to imprison the innocent since, ultimately, this undermines respect for the law. Rule utilitarianism proposes that we consider the practical consequences of an action before carrying it out, not to assess each situation as if it were new, but to follow rules that have been established according to the principle of utility. The rules might not always be inherently and absolutely true, but they are useful tools for evaluating actions — they have instrumental value in themselves.

This approach is subdivided into **strong** and **weak** rule utilitarianism. The former claims that certain rules which we agree have instrumental value should always be kept, whilst the latter acknowledges that there will be circumstances in which it would be better to allow for exceptions.

4 Situation ethics

Joseph Fletcher, an American Episcopalian moralist, coined the phrase 'situation ethics' in his 1966 book of the same title. In the spirit of the decade, he was responding to what he felt were the failures of legalism inherent in ethical systems that propose rules to govern human behaviour, whilst at the same time rejecting **antinomianism** — a total abandonment of rules and principles. His was a subjective approach to ethics which was influenced in part by existentialism, which maintains that we can only know truth via our own personal experience. Situationists take the example of Jesus in dialogue with the Pharisees as the model for their moral code. Whilst the Pharisees elaborated the Torah to accommodate every possible situation, Jesus went back to first principles. When asked about divorce law, Jesus referred them back to creation (Mark 10:1&//s), rather than the Law of Moses, which was designed to accommodate sinful human nature. The story of the woman caught in adultery shows Jesus adopting a classic situationist approach (John 8:2–11), demonstrating love, compassion and integrity, and revealing the weakness of using absolute laws as a means of judging individual moral cases. Fletcher maintained that there was a middle way between legalism and antinomianism and this lay in the application of ***agape***, the love which Jesus commanded: *'You shall love the Lord your God with all your heart, and with all your soul, and with all your strength and with all your mind; and your neighbour as yourself'* (Luke 10:27); *'Greater love has no man than this, that a man lay down his life for his friends'* (John 15:13); *'And this is his commandment, that we should believe in the name of his Son Jesus Christ and love one another, just as he has commanded us'* (1 John 3:23).

Like utilitarianism, situation ethics is based on a single principle which enables humans to enter every situation armed with the experience and precedents of past situations, but willing to lay them aside if the principle of love (*agape*) is better served by so doing and will enable us better to bring about the greatest good. Fletcher carefully defined love:

+ It was always good, and the only norm.
+ Love and justice are the same, for love is justice distributed.
+ It is not necessarily liking, and only the end of love justifies the means.
+ It makes a decision there and then in each individual situation.

Fletcher proposed four presumptions of situation ethics:

+ **Pragmatism** demands that a proposed course of action should work, and that its success or failure should be judged according to the principle.
+ **Relativism** rejects such absolutes as 'never' or 'always'.
+ **Positivism** recognises that love is the most important criterion of all.
+ **Personalism** demands that people should be put first.

John A. T. Robinson seized upon Fletcher's work in his famous book *Honest to God*. He argues that if humans operate within the spirit of love, they will be prevented from performing immoral acts. No rules are necessary, because love will decide then and there in the situation the best course of action. Robinson (1963) wrote: '*Dr Fletcher's approach is the only ethic for "man come of age". To resist his approach in the name of religion will not stop it, it will only ensure the form it takes will be anti-Christian.*'

A situationist approach is also associated with the work of Karl Barth, who argued that it is a misunderstanding of divine revelation to encase it in a straitjacket of rules and orthodoxy. He argued that God's will for human beings should not be limited by human reasoning, church teaching or society.

Strengths of situationism

+ Individual cases are judged on their own merits, irrespective of what has been done in similar situations in the past.
+ Individuals are not subject to rules which bind them. Nothing is intrinsically wrong or right, except the principle of love.
+ Love seeks the well-being of others, even if the course of action is not one of preference.
+ It is modelled on the teaching of Jesus, and so could be considered a truly Christian ethic.

Weaknesses of situationism

+ The theory was greeted with considerable scepticism by some leading Christian thinkers. Professor Graham Dunstan wrote of Fletcher's theory: '*It is possible, though not easy, to forgive Professor Fletcher for writing this book, for he is a generous and love-able man. It is harder to forgive the SCM Press for publishing it*'. In *The Honest to God Debate*, Glyn Simon wrote: '*A false spirituality of this kind has always haunted the thinking of clever men…*' (cited in Howatch, 1990).
+ Despite Fletcher's attempt to be anti-legalistic, the application of one principle only makes it a legalistic approach. To say no rules apply, and yet to also say the only rule is love, is something of a contradiction.
+ Most ethical dilemmas offer an obvious course of action without resorting to situationism, but Fletcher illustrated the theory with extreme moral dilemmas:

A man with stomach cancer will die in six months without treatment that will cost $40 every three days. He must give up work, and borrow on his life insurance to survive for three years *if he follows this course of action. However, if he refuses treatment, he will die with his life insurance valid, providing his family with $100,000 after his death. If he refuses treatment, it is tantamount to suicide, but if he accepts it, his family will be heavily in debt after his death. What should he do? What is the loving thing in terms of his intention and the consequences for others?*

When the Americans were attempting to decide whether to drop the atomic bomb on Hiroshima and Nagasaki the committee responsible for advising President Truman was divided. Some were totally opposed. Others felt that the Japanese should be warned about the bomb's potential by dropping it first on an uninhabited part of the country. Others still felt that the dropping of the bomb was the only way to ensure the end of the war. In the event, the bomb was dropped on civilian and military targets. Was this right?

(Fletcher, 1966)

✧ The theory is teleological, dependent on the calculation of consequences. It is impossible to be unfailingly accurate in making such a calculation. Like utilitarianism, too, it reduces normative ethics to a single principle and one way of evaluating moral action. Fletcher acknowledged that his approach was very similar to utilitarianism and, this being the case, the theory is open to many of the same criticisms that are levelled at utilitarianism.

✧ The theory justifies adultery, murder and even genocide in the interests of love. Surely Fletcher is guilty of calling good what is in reality evil?

✧ Fletcher is overly optimistic about the capacity of human beings to make morally correct choices, and not to be influenced by personal preferences. Human beings need the guidelines offered by rules to avoid moral chaos.

✧ Law and love are seen as mutually exclusive, yet Paul writes that love is the fulfilling of the law (Romans 13:10).

✧ How can we arbitrate a case in which two people reach different conclusions about an action, yet both claim to be acting in the interests of love? Furthermore, are our actions as independent and flexible as Fletcher assumes? If we act in discrete ways in apparently similar circumstances, our actions tend to appear to be unfair rather than moral.

Summary and key terms

- **Natural moral law** — described by **Aquinas**, who said that all things in nature fulfil a specific purpose and this is the case for humans too. The ultimate goal for humans is to worship God, but also to survive and reproduce. Moral reasoning can be drawn from the natural world, which provides all the necessary information for humans to make reasoned moral decisions. This moral law is eternal and unchanging, and enables humans to fulfil their purpose and their natural inclination towards the good. It is instituted by God, is absolute, and cannot be substituted by the whims of fashion or personal preference.

- **Kantian deontology** — argues that morality is absolute and is accessible through reason. It is essentially based on motivation and a **categorical imperative** that all actions should be universalisable. Categorical imperatives are the only legitimate moral command as they are intrinsic and not instrumental or based on personal preferences or ends. A **universalisable action** is one which can apply in all situations and takes into consideration the need for all people to be given **intrinsic value**.

- **Utilitarianism** — a consequentialist approach to ethics based on a **principle of utility** which promotes the greatest happiness/pleasure for the greatest number (GHGN), or least pain. Bentham's **hedonic calculus** aims to provide a score that calculates and thereby quantifies happiness. Mill adopted a qualitative approach — higher pleasures are of greater value. According to the **harm principle**, the majority can only exert pressure on the minority to conform if there is danger of causing harm. Utilitarianism advocates a **relativist, situationalist** approach to ethical dilemmas. There are no **absolutes** or **intrinsic moral commands**, though **rule utilitarianism** recognises that some rules which lead to the greatest happiness of the greatest number should be kept.

- **Situation ethics** — term coined by Joseph Fletcher, whose principle of utility was love. No absolutes, but a situationalist approach, which identifies the needs of individuals' particular circumstances. It was modelled on Jesus's ministry and debates with Pharisees, which put people first and love as the only norm. Fletcher responded to the spirit of the late twentieth century which sought to move away from law to a relativist approach to moral dilemmas, and to bring Christian thinking in line with the experiences of those in the modern world.

Exam watch

 Many candidates are keen to answer questions on these ethical theories and you should be able to score good marks for doing so. Thorough learning is essential, as is an ability to use proper terminology accurately. The main skill that will ensure your answers are of the highest quality, however, is that of evaluation. You must be able to think carefully through the strengths and weaknesses of these approaches to ethical decision-making and evaluate whether, ultimately, they are workable, practical and rational ways of resolving dilemmas.

Review questions

1. (a) Outline the main features of utilitarianism.
   (b) Examine critically criticisms that have been raised against utilitarianism.
2. (a) Examine what is meant by natural law with reference to morality.
   (b) Analyse and evaluate the strengths and weaknesses of natural law as an ethical theory.
3. Is Kant's theory practical in the real world?
4. How far might situation ethics provide a useful tool for the resolution of universal moral dilemmas?

Topic 2

Ethical perspectives

1 God and morality

Then tell me, what do you say the holy is? And what is the unholy? For consider, is the holy loved by the gods because it is holy? Or is it holy because it is loved by the gods?

(Plato, *Euthyphro*, fourth century BCE)

The nature of the relationship between God and morality — if there is one at all — is a vital one for religious believers to resolve. If at least part of what it means to believe in God is to live in obedience to his will and his law, then the way in which God makes moral commands is crucial to understanding how humans should respond to them. R. B. Braithwaite claims that to be religious and to make religious claims is to be committed to a set of moral values. He uses the instance of religious conversion, which includes a reorientation of the will, to illustrate this point. Religious language is the language of morality and religious believers have committed themselves to particular ways of behaving. This includes refraining from some actions and fulfilling others. However, how do we know what believers are committed to?

For a religious believer, even if you get away with the most outrageous crimes on earth, you will be punished by God in the hereafter (when those who have resisted the temptation to do wrong will be rewarded), so even if you think that you can escape earthly punishment it is not in your eschatological interest to do so! On the other hand, if there is no God to support the demands of the moral law, then there is no threat of punishment or promise of reward, and so morality is meaningless. This is an existentialist view; if God does not exist, then everything is permitted.

Of course, it is not necessarily the case that God, even if he exists, should be the sole arbiter of morality. The classic problem was concisely expressed by Plato in the **Euthyphro Dilemma**:

Is something good because God commands it?

or

Does God command that which is good?

The first position assumes that a moral action is one that is willed by God; he is the source of morality and humans act morally when they fulfil God's will obediently. This view effectively argues that a moral law is made right by virtue of **divine command**. The God who makes the command is an omnipotent creator of moral standards and without him there would be no moral right and wrong. This has the advantage of placing God clearly above morality — it is not an independent yardstick that exists separately of him, but is under his control.

However, there are clear problems. If God commands something, is this sufficient

grounds to say that it is moral? It has the effect of making the moral law *arbitrary*, since it depends on God's whims. If he commanded someone to kill all people with red hair, would that make it morally right to do so? According to this position it would be, but would humans be correctly interpreting what they believed God was commanding? If we say no, because we *know* that God in his wisdom would not command such a thing, then we are saying that killing people with red hair (or indeed anyone) is wrong in itself, and so God would not make that command. In his wisdom he knows it to be wrong, but this means that God is not all-powerful after all because he recognises and is subject to a natural law of reason which human beings also share. God's power is therefore limited by reason, and although this may not be sufficient to lead to atheism, it does lead to a limited deity. Other problems also emerge:

+ How do we deal with situations in which God does not expressly give a command? How do we establish his will in these situations? Religious believers may argue that we do so by extrapolating from the information we do have. For example, the Bible might not say anything specific about euthanasia, but it does provide sufficient information on the general principle of killing for us to use it for moral guidance.

+ Does it mean that anything that God commands becomes a moral law? Many of God's commands appear not to be in themselves moral. For example, the Book of the Covenant in Exodus 23ff includes many commands concerning religious ceremonial and food laws which arguably have no moral status — e.g. 'Do not boil a kid in its mother's milk.' Similarly, does God forbidding what's wrong *make* it wrong? If this is the case, then God could forbid anything and it would be morally wrong — putting your left shoe on before your right shoe, for example. This would be plain silly, and would utterly trivialise God's lawmaking authority.

+ Furthermore, if something is good because God commands it, then what is the nature of God's goodness? Is he good because he obeys his own laws or because he is the creator of them and hence possesses a greater degree of goodness applicable only to him? Surely we should be able to judge God's goodness against some independent standard if we believe that his moral commands bind humanity to obedience to him?

+ There are many people who don't believe in God and still make judgments concerning right and wrong which they believe to be reliable. A non-believer must surely, therefore, be able to be moral, at least in the socially accepted sense, without consciously deriving moral standards from God.

+ If moral behaviour is motivated by fear of God's punishment, this seems to be a rather questionable basis for morality. If it is linked with God at all, surely it is better if his people obey him out of love rather than fear. This view also demands that there is an afterlife in which rewards and punishments are given out, and this in itself is impossible to verify.

The second position — that God commands that which is good — also assumes a link between morality and God, but suggests that moral values are not established by God's will. Rather, he operates according to moral laws already in place in the universe. The problem of this view is that God is limited by laws of morality to which he responds, rather than laws which he sets, but also that we must wait for God to reveal what is moral by commanding it. He is the channel through which moral values are passed down to human beings.

The range of problems identified here may lead us to the conclusion that morality is actually *opposed to* religion. If belief in God requires human beings to accept and fulfil his will obediently, then human freedom is fundamentally violated, whatever the relationship between God and morality. If humans are not free to make their own moral choices, then they cannot be truly moral, since a genuinely moral action cannot be coerced. Furthermore, a God who demands that humans surrender their freedom in this way cannot be worthy of worship. Others may argue that since many atrocities have been carried out in the name of religion, it is not possible to claim that morality either supports or is included in religion. Kierkegaard argued that we should not confuse ethics or morality with doing the will of God. He used the example of God's command to Abraham to sacrifice Isaac (Genesis 22), where God clearly commanded something which was not, according to usual human standards, moral. In this case, however, Abraham was being called to obedience which went beyond human understanding of morality, and being bound to the moral law of society would have been a hindrance to fulfilling God's will.

Ultimately, we need to ask whether the fact that something is perceived to be 'God's will' is sufficient grounds for obeying a command, or refraining from a prohibition. Jean Porter (1995) exposes this problem:

> *If the only good argument against suicide consists in the claim that it usurps the authority of God, it follows that someone who is terminally ill and subject to extreme and untreatable suffering must be told to continue to endure her suffering for an indefinite future, **only** because it would usurp the authority of God for her to end her life. Suffering is part of life and we should be prepared to endure what we must... Yet there is something deeply disturbing about the argument that people ought to be prepared to accept suffering...which could be alleviated...for **no other reason** than that God has not given us the authority to act in the appropriate ways. Is the God of love so easily offended or is God's authority so precarious?*

2 Conscience

Conscience may be defined as *'the inner aspect of the life of the individual where a sense of what is right and wrong is developed'* (Atkinson and Field (eds), 1995) or as the way in which people judge their own moral actions. Joseph Butler wrote in the eighteenth century, *'There is a principle of reflection in men, by which they distinguish between and disapprove their own actions'*, and in *Gaudium et Spes*, a document of Vatican Two, the council wrote: *'Deep within his conscience man discovers a law which he has not laid upon himself but he must obey'.* Kant maintained that the conscience was the arena in which humans turned an *is* into an *ought*. The role of conscience in making moral decisions and acting upon them is thus universally recognised as being highly significant, to the extent that 'conscientious objections' are respected as having, to some extent, a greater force than laws and rules which generally govern society. For example, although abortions can be obtained legally, no doctor would be compelled to carry out an abortion if his or her conscience dictates that abortions are morally wrong.

But what is the conscience? Even before Paul wrote of the role of the conscience as the judge, under God, of our behaviour, which acts to control and interpret our actions, Greek and Roman philosophy had already developed a strong view of it. Horace wrote '...*have nothing on your conscience, no guilt to make you turn pale*', and Cicero claimed that '*If conscience goes, then everything collapses around us*'. The New Testament view of conscience is as a guardian of believers' moral health, prompting them to respond to their moral code by stimulating feelings of guilt or well-being. Christians would, in principle, claim that:

÷ Conscience is universal whether man believes in God or not, and is God given (Romans 2:12ff).
÷ It has been affected by the fall and thus is corrupted and imperfect (Genesis 3).
÷ It can be redeemed by Jesus Christ, whose death cleanses man's unhealthy conscience, and enables man to retune his conscience with the divine will (Romans 3:21–22).

However, conscience needs to be instructed and trained; it is not entirely innate, if at all. The more right choices human beings make, the more they will be naturally inclined to make the right choice every time, without this imposing on their free will. Aquinas maintained that the conscience was '*the mind of man making moral judgments*' and the realm in which humans exercised their reason in working out what was right. It would eventually lead them to an acknowledgement of God's moral law and that which was in accordance with their conscience, but it would involve using logical powers of reasoning and making judgments based on previous experience and what has been revealed in scripture. For the believer, it must involve a continuous attempt to discern God's will, or the 'mind of Christ', to act in the best interests of the community of believers, and to build up spiritually the church and the individual.

In the New Testament, conscience is understood as the faculty which reminds us when we are doing wrong, by stimulating feelings of guilt and shame. Since it is a faculty that can be trained and developed by society, then it is especially important for the Christian to remain within the society of the church and not the world if their conscience is to be developed in a Godly direction. Aquinas associated conscience with natural law, as the means that enables us to recognise rationally what behaviour befits true human nature and calling. The New Testament writers associate the Holy Spirit in some way with these promptings, and as the means by which God spoke directly to Apostles, evangelists and prophets. The Holy Spirit is the operative force within the church, so the two combine as a decisive guide to moral and spiritual behaviour.

Modern views of conscience tend to emphasise the negative role it plays, since it stimulates feelings of guilt and shame and is in constant need of social education. For the Christian, this is a useful function if such feelings are aroused by objective, not imagined, guiltiness, and if the prickings of conscience lead to a changed lifestyle. However, conscience is not an infallible guide, but a relative measuring tool. J. V. Langmead Casserly writes: '*Nevertheless, a well trained conscience remains a factor of the utmost importance in the moral life*' (Halverson and Cohen (eds), 1960).

If conscience is essentially that feeling within us which drives us to evaluate our moral actions, then Thomas Nagel (1987) argues that it is crucial to morality:

You've probably heard it said that the only reason anybody ever does anything is that it makes him feel good, or that not doing it will make him feel bad. If we are really motivated only by our own comfort, it is hopeless for morality to try to appeal to a concern for others. On this view, even apparently moral conduct in which one person seems to sacrifice his own interests for the sake of others is really motivated by his concern for himself: he wants to avoid the guilt he'll feel if he doesn't do the 'right' thing, or to experience the warm glow of self-congratulation he'll get if he does. But those who don't have these feelings have no motive to be 'moral'.

However, this does not necessitate that conscience owes its origin to God, or that it is universal in its direction. Conflicts between society and the individual and between societies in general occur over matters of conscience. Individuals have the right to conscientiously object to taking up arms in defence of their country, but for others this would be thought a despicable and cowardly choice, not a matter to be respected as the workings of conscience. The World Trade Center attack on 11 September 2001 stimulated many discussions about conscience: some claim that the terrorists who planned and executed the attack were acting legitimately on the promptings of their conscience, and as such should be exempt from sanctions. Since it is ultimately subject to human interpretation, conscience must err at times, but who can be a reliable judge of this and who can correct it when it does err?

There can be no guarantee either that the voice of conscience comes from God. Freud understood the conscience as a moral policeman, the internalised super-ego, which controls and socialises people but is capable of doing great damage to their mental health, particularly when it is confused with religion. He believed that the Christian conscience frustrates the development of sound mental health by imposing rules and taboos on the individual that have their basis not in reality but in a *'universal neurosis'*. Sociologists propose the view that the conscience is the product of upbringing, education, socialisation and circumstances, and it is therefore not inherent in human beings, and does not owe its origin to God. Decisions made on the basis of conscience must therefore be understood as relative and situational, and cannot be universalised.

3 Freedom and determinism

It is certainly the case that our concept of morality would have no point or application, and therefore no meaning outside of the context of a community of persons, who are normally and normatively capable of rational, autonomous action.

(Porter, 1995)

The relationship between human freedom — or the lack of it — and moral behaviour is a crucial one, since it is generally accepted that our freedom to perform a morally good action or to refrain from a bad one is a vital part of the way we evaluate that action. If we believe that every action is *determined* — that is, that the totality of a person's experience, knowledge, genes, circumstances, pre-existing relationships, *and* the fact that there are laws of nature which govern everything in the world, have a part to play in their decision-making — then we cannot reasonably blame an individual for acting wrongly or praise them for doing something good. Not everyone agrees on this point. Some would argue that even if our actions are inevitable, it does not stop them being morally good or bad and so it is still appropriate to praise or blame. However, if we think that morally bad actions are determined in advance, our approach towards people who perpetrate them may be more like that of someone encouraging a dog not to chew the furniture. We don't hold them morally responsible, but we will still try to persuade them against this behaviour so they act differently in the future. But we would not reason with them about it. It is the fact that we think that we can reason with other human beings about their moral choices that leads us to believe that human moral behaviour is, to some extent at least, free, and that we can make significant choices about the way in which we behave. We also believe that this freedom is in itself important and that our freedom and that of other human beings should not be violated by intruding on our capacity to make reasoned choices about things which are of direct concern to us. Jean Porter (ibid.) argues that '*So long as...respect for rationality or autonomy is taken to be the foundational moral commitment, it is necessary either to deny that we have moral obligation to any of these sorts of creatures, or else,...to contrive a notion of rationality or autonomy that will somehow fit the situations of at least some of them*'.

Reinhold Niebuhr observes that the distinguishing mark of history is that human beings impose their desires and goals upon nature and have freedom to do this because they are able to understand the way in which single events belong to a general pattern. Humans can remember past events and use that memory to affect what happens in the future. Although they are driven by natural hungers, they are not limited by them. And, since many motives and causes may exist in any given situation, history cannot be the basis for making an accurate prediction of what humans will do. Interestingly, Niebuhr argues that since every event, once having taken place, can be interpreted as an inevitable and determined consequence of a series of events, there is a temptation to be more deterministic in our view of human behaviour than may be appropriate. He cites the 'endless variety and unpredictability of the historical drama' as proof of the reality of human freedom, and notes that although the Bible assumes a divine providence over all human destiny, it does not violate human freedom, but rather gives meaning to it. God is not an arbitrary despot, but a sovereign who respects and honours the freedom of his subjects.

But perhaps we should not assume that we are free. What, then, are the alternatives? The most extreme is **fatalism**, which in its most general form argues that future events cannot be altered, and that all our actions and desires are pointless because they are themselves part of an unalterable pattern. Fatalism does not explain why this pattern of events exists; it just states that it does.

Determinism, however, claims that everything is determined by prior causes, and that everything requires a **sufficient reason** to occur as it does. This is a basic assumption of modern science, that with enough information we could predict with complete accuracy what would happen in the universe at any given future moment. **Hard determinists** claim that all freedom is illusory, although this is a difficult position to maintain with conviction. Whether we think of freedom primarily as **practical freedom** (freedom to do what one wishes) or **metaphysical freedom** (being responsible for one's choices), we can appeal to reason and counter the determinist's argument with the claim that we *feel* free. Furthermore, if we take hard determinism to its logical extreme, we are forced to acknowledge that even holding a deterministic view is itself determined.

Soft determinists hold that there is still a clear difference between free and unfree actions, since I am free to perform an action as long as I am not coerced into doing it or prevented from doing it. There may be factors which influence my actions — for example, if I am on a diet, I may choose a yoghurt rather than a piece of cheesecake, but I *could* have chosen to have the cheesecake, and it remained an open possibility right up to the moment of choice. In a sense I determined the choice by doing it, but I could have done the opposite, and it didn't just happen out of the blue, because there was an explanation for my making the choice I did.

Other, more subtle, factors also limit our freedom to make moral choices. However much we may want to make a particular choice or perform a particular action, our freedom to do so will be limited, to some extent at least, by our nature. This is known as **liberty of spontaneity**. An individual who is shy and retiring by nature will find it hard to make certain moral choices that would come more easily to a gregarious and fearless character. **Liberty of indifference** describes the freedom we have when, free from all constraints including those of our background, beliefs, culture and other relationships, we can make an unfettered choice.

Ultimately, the argument that we are essentially free in our actions and choices seems to be the most universally accepted, even if we also accept that a vast range of factors influence our freedom. If we do adopt this view, then we must also accept the fact that we are in some way responsible for our actions, and this is the crucial issue for morality. Responsibility rests ultimately in the fact that what I do follows largely, if not entirely, as a consequence of elements of my character for which I am responsible, and that we do this not just at the most crucial points in our lives when we make decisions which have ultimate consequences, but all the time.

Jean-Paul Sartre argued that the fact that we are free is the fundamental truth about being human, and the heart of human experience is the experience of being free. He claimed that we are always self-consciously aware that at any time we could be making choices to be acting or thinking in different ways and that we can act upon that freedom at will. Every conscious moment is therefore a moment of choice. For Sartre, however, this was a burden, not a privilege. He argued that in human beings '*existence precedes essence*', meaning that we have no fixed nature that determines what we will do or a specific purpose to fulfil. We make our choices without the guidance or security of metaphysical or religious doctrines or any objective reason to believe that the basis upon which we make a choice is better than any other. We are '*condemned to be free*' and make our choices in '*anguish, abandonment and despair*'.

Summary

- **God and morality** — is God the ultimate arbiter of morality? Does he command that which is good, or is something good because God commands it? If God created moral laws, then is his law sufficient to say something is moral? How do we know what God commands and what do we do when no express command is made? Is it possible for a non-believer to be moral? Is it sufficient to say that something is 'God's will' to justify it on moral grounds, irrespective of personal situations and concerns?
- **Conscience** — what is it and what guides it? How is it trained? Is it innate? The Christian view is that conscience has been corrupted by the fall and needs to be

retrained within the society of the church. **Aquinas** believed that reason informs the conscience. The modern view is more negative — conscience stimulates feelings of guilt and shame, but it is a relative, not infallible, guide. How do we judge the reliability of conscience and evaluate its conflicting dictates? **Freud** said that conscience is the super-ego, which controls people's actions, but it has become overlaid by religious rules and taboos. It is not inherent and does not owe its origin to God.

- **Freedom** — essential to making moral judgments, since a determined action cannot be worthy of praise or blame; neither should we impose on the freedom of others to make reasoned choices. **Niebuhr** argued that history is distinguished by the human ability to identify a chain of causes and effects. We are not limited by natural hungers and, although the Bible speaks of divine providence, God does not violate human freedom but gives meaning to it. If not free, are we determined? How far are our choices the result of factors which are ultimately beyond our control? Even if we are largely free, we accept that a vast range of factors have a decisive effect on our freedom although we are also responsible for our actions. **Sartre** considers this responsibility to be a negative factor, leading to *'anguish, abandonment and despair'.*

Key terms

Conscience — *'the inner aspect of the life of the individual where a sense of what is right and wrong is developed.'*

Euthyphro Dilemma — Is something good because God commands it *or* does God command that which is good?

Hard determinism — the view that all freedom is illusory.

Metaphysical freedom — being responsible for one's choices.

Practical freedom — freedom to do what one wishes.

Soft determinism — the view that I am free to perform an action as long as I am not coerced into doing it or prevented from doing it.

Exam watch

Questions on the relationship between God and morality are common, and you should also be aware of the material on the Moral Argument (on pp. 63–67) for this topic. There are a range of arguments and positions on this view and you should cover them freely. Make sure you don't fall into the trap of preaching here — 'We should be moral because God tells us to' is not an A-level response. Ensure that you have some scholarship to back up your responses. Freedom and determinism is a very difficult area and needs to be approached with caution. Demonstrate to the examiner that you are fully aware of the different types of freedom and determinism and how they relate to issues of morality and religious belief — otherwise your answer could become very general.

Review questions

1 (a) Outline the reasons why it may be claimed that morality and religion are linked.

  (b) Examine and comment on the reasons given for suggesting that they are not linked in this way.

2 *'Limits are placed on the extent to which an individual can be punished if there is doubt as to their moral freedom through mental illness, coercion or other restrictions on their liberty.'* Examine and discuss this claim.

3 (a) What do scholars understand by 'conscience'?

 (b) How convincing is the claim that conscience is the voice of God?

4 Examine and evaluate the following claims: *'God commands that which is good'; 'Good is that which God commands.'*

Topic 3

Practical ethics and
the individual

A Applying ethical theory to moral dilemmas

Ethical theories develop because we face ethical or moral dilemmas: it is because we
find ourselves torn between a reluctance to lay aside all moral absolutes, and a paradoxical fear and attraction of the consequences of our actions, that moral dilemmas are
just that — dilemmas. If we knew for certain what to do every time we were faced
with a moral dilemma, there would be no need for debates about ethical theories.
Debates and theories grow out of the need to find answers to questions and dilemmas
which are not immediately self-evident. But the ethical dilemmas that confront us
on a daily basis are rarely of the magnitude of those which occur in professional,
medical or therapeutic environments. The ethical dilemmas we face are usually so
minor that we barely recognise them as such. Whether to give money to a young
man and his dog sitting mournfully outside a railway station, or whether to help a
friend with a piece of examined coursework, are moral dilemmas with which we
might easily identify. Do we utilise ethical theories to help us reach the right conclusion? Almost invariably, no; they are too time-consuming and would require us to
obtain too much background information in order to reach an appropriate decision.
Instead, we tend to act instinctively, not after the long and drawn-out processes that
teleological theories effectively demand.

The problem

*'Moral argument tries to appeal to a capacity for impartial motivation which is supposed to be
present in all of us.'*

(Nagel, 1987)

Nagel exposes the precise problem of applying ethical theory to moral dilemmas: ethical
theories involve rational processes, reasoning and analysing the situations we are in,
in order to reach a rational conclusion. Moral dilemmas are personal, subjective and
emotive, and to apply reason to their resolution is not a natural step for us. To apply
to a moral dilemma the processes prescribed by a given ethical theory we need to
remain emotionally removed from the dilemma itself, which takes a considerable effort
of will.

We need to be aware from the start that the way in which ethical theory may help
resolve moral dilemmas is limited. When faced with resolving the abortion dilemma

in practice, or even attempting to reach a theoretical position on homosexuality, it is hardly likely that an individual, unless they can remain emotionally removed from the personal implications of their dilemma, will resort to an ethical theory to resolve it.

Analysing the problem

Let's look at how the characters in two modern novels express these difficulties very well. The first example is from *Madison's Song* by Kay Plowman (2001). The novel is about a successful but vulnerable woman, Madison, who falls in love with a colleague, and has to make very challenging decisions about the complex and difficult relationships on which her life is based. At this point in the narrative she has split up from her lover (Gerry), because she thinks that by doing so she can save her husband (Andy) from professional catastrophe.

> *'You're committing the naturalistic fallacy, Annie.'*
>
> *'What's that when it's at home?'*
>
> *'Inferring an ought from an is. Gerry is seeing other women again, therefore I ought to do something about it.'*
>
> *Annie looked puzzled.*
>
> *'We do it all the time,' I told her. 'Gerry is the love of my life; therefore I ought to do whatever is necessary to be with him. Gerry is unprepared to make a commitment to me, and Andy is in need of my help, therefore I ought to drop Gerry and stick by Andy. And does ought mean the same as right? So I left Gerry and stayed with Andy because that's what I felt I ought to do, but was it right? If it was right for Andy, does that make it right for me? Or Gerry? Does the fact that Gerry so obviously doesn't give a damn mean it was right, wrong, or morally neutral? What was important? My motives? Duty to Andy, perhaps? Or the consequences? Andy's back at the Dragon, but I'm miserable. Do they cancel one another out, or does Andy's happiness (if indeed he is happy) outweigh my unhappiness? Let's do a Hedonic Calculus to work it all out.'*
>
> *Annie was staring at me in bewilderment.*
>
> *'Get a grip, Madsy, you can't turn it all into some academic debate. If you're really unhappy without Gerry then go and see him. Tell him you still love him and you want to be with him and see what happens from there. But if you're not going to do that, then just accept the decision you made and go forward, but don't try to analyse it all to death.'* (Plowman, 2001)

Apart from demonstrating a remarkable amount of philosophical knowledge for two characters in a modern romance, Madison and Annie express exactly the point about relating real-life dilemmas to ethical theory. Let's look at the problems they identify:

÷ **The naturalistic fallacy.** Ethical theories frequently attempt to define what is good or right — e.g. happiness, love or duty. This enables the utilitarian, for example, to ask: 'Does this action generate the greatest happiness for the greatest number? If so, you *ought* to do it. This *is* a good action so we *ought* to carry it out.' However, the characters in the narrative expose the impossibility of 'inferring an ought from an is' in daily life. Whilst many situations may lead us to feel that we ought to do something in response, there are big difficulties with that 'ought'.

÷ **Ought implies can.** Ought equals obligation, as Kant argued, but to be obliged to do something we *cannot* do is nonsense. Whatever reasons prevent us from doing something, be they physical, practical, emotional or psychological, the fact remains that we only ought to do what we are capable of doing and are genuinely free to do. Even without knowing precisely what hinders Madison from doing what Annie suggests, we can see that she cannot resolve her moral dilemma by 'inferring an ought from an is'.

÷ **Does ought mean the same as right?** We are often taught that it is our duty to act in a particular way rather than another, but we need to decide what a right action really is. Duty infers putting others before ourselves and we are often brought up to see this as a moral absolute:

The basis of morality is a belief that good and harm to particular people (or animals) is good or bad not just from their point of view, but from a more general point of view, which every thinking person can understand. That means that each person has a reason to consider not only his own interests but the interests of others in deciding what to do.

(Nagel, 1987)

Madison appears to be questioning whether *ought* is enough to make some-thing *right*. Who is it right for? If her action has been at the expense of her own personal happiness, but has brought happiness to others, is it therefore right? Is it even better if she has brought happiness to others by denying it to herself? Does the fact that she doesn't seem sure that others have been made happy by it make any difference?

÷ **What is the real value of the consequences of our actions?** Three consequences seem to have been derived from her action: (1) she is unhappy; (2) Andy is 'back at the Dragon', which appears to be a positive consequence; and (3) Gerry 'doesn't give a damn' — a sort of non-consequence, perhaps. So, one person is definitely unhappy, one person may be happy, and one person has no feelings about it what-soever. As a utilitarian, what would you say about whatever moral choice she has made? Not much, I think! Would a hedonic calculus help? It would leave all the char-acters involved scoring pretty low on a happiness scale, and Madison's sarcastic remark about using the calculus illustrates the fact that it would be a totally inap-propriate tool in such an emotionally charged situation.

÷ **The value of intuition.** Finally, Annie, who seems to have no stake in the decision her friend has made, comments: '…you can't turn it all into some academic debate'. Annie suggests that Madison should act *intuitively* — how she *feels* is what should motivate her actions, not what she thinks or attempts to reason. Annie appears to see the dilemma very simply, implicitly questioning whether ethical argument has any value at all.

Later in the narrative, Madison seems to come down on this side of the academic and moral fence — her situation cannot be resolved by applying a theoretical approach.

Whilst there could never be any moral justification for what I was doing to Andy, everything in me cried out that I was doing the only thing that offered me any hope of happiness in the future. All my philosophical training balked at such a hedonistic principle. Maybe it was essentially utilitarian; perhaps the greatest happiness of the greatest number was served if Gerry and I, Ben and Josh, were made happy by the consequences of my actions. Numerically, we outweighed

Andy, yet such a method of moral calculus served only to underscore why Mill had called Bentham's theory fit for swine. And would we be happy anyway? What guarantee could either of us offer the other? I was certain that no self-respecting deontologist could find the faintest justification in my actions, no categorical imperative, no principle of universalisability, could be established on the basis of my selfish choice.

(Plowman, 2001)

The second example is from *Scandalous Risks* by Susan Howatch (1990). In this novel Howatch describes an ecclesiastical community in 1963, the year J. A. T. Robinson wrote *Honest to God*. Robinson advocated bringing Christianity and Christian morality up to date, making it fitting for 'man come of age', a phrase he adopted from Bonhoeffer. He advocated Fletcher's situation ethics as the only way in which the modern Christian can find morality meaningful in the late-twentieth century. Howatch puts her characters in a moral dilemma which they attempt to examine from the position of situation ethics:

'Well, you see it's like this... I seem to have got myself into rather a peculiar situation with a clergyman...'

'Oh, I'm very used to clergymen in peculiar situations,' said Father Darrow.

'We're madly in love, but it's all very confusing.'

'There's a wife, I daresay, in the background,' suggested Father Darrow helpfully.

'Yes, but we've both accepted that there can be no divorce... The real problem is what sort of relationship we can have. You see, he believes — and he's terribly modern in his outlook — he believes there are no hard and fast rules any more when it comes to dealing with ethical situations; all you have to do is act with love... The catch is that you have to act with the very best kind of love, pure and noble. So if a man loves a girl and says to himself: "Do I take her to bed?" the answer's not yes, it's no, because if he really loves her he won't want to use her to satisfy himself in that way.'

'This sounds like the New Morality outlined by Bishop Robinson in Honest to God.*'*

'So you know all about that... What do you think of it?'

'The important question is what you think of it.'

'I just don't know any more, I'm so confused. My clergyman, following the New Morality, says that even though he's married, we're allowed a romantic friendship so long as we truly love each other, because...we'll be high-minded enough to abstain from anything...that would hurt either us or other people... Well, that's fine...but the deeper I get into this relationship the less sense that seems to make... I mean, if you love someone you do want to go to bed with them...'

'You're saying that the gap between Dr Robinson's idealism and your experience of reality has now become intolerably wide...'

(Howatch, 1990)

So what's going on in this scene? The girl (Venetia) has sought Father Darrow's help to understand the way in which her romantic friend rationalises and conducts their relationship along the lines of situation ethics. He will not fully consummate their relationship because in refraining from so doing he is showing true *agape*, but neither does he recognise any moral absolutes which would forbid him, as a married clergyman, to engage in *any* sort of intimate relationship with her.

÷ Venetia makes clear that attempting to conduct this relationship within the parameters of situation ethics has led to unhappiness. Her objection is that it is *counter-intuitive* — the concept of love espoused by New Morality does not appear to bear any relation to reality, but only to theory.

÷ Situation ethics rejects hard and fast rules. However, these characters expose a problem of doing away with rules: confusion. Venetia implies that she would feel less confused about her relationship with her clergyman if he simply said, 'I can't go to bed with you because I am a married clergyman and it would be wrong.' Instead, he muddies the waters. Arguably, there is a moral absolute still at work — 'show pure, noble love' — but Venetia and Father Darrow seem to conclude that all that is going on is a lot of self-deception.

÷ Ethical theories are *idealistic*; moral dilemmas are *realistic*. Rarely do our real-life situations conform to the neat solutions that would apparently be available to us if we applied the principles of ethical theory.

÷ *'It remains true...that a man must in the moment of decision do what he thinks is right. He cannot do otherwise. This does not mean that what he does will be right or even that he will not be worthy of blame or punishment. He simply has no choice, for he cannot at that moment see any discrepancy between what is right and what he thinks is right'* (Frankena, 1973).

Exam watch

Despite these problems, you are still going to have to be able to relate an ethical theory to moral dilemmas in your exam, so here's some advice…

1 Keep the dilemma simple, e.g. 'An ethical dilemma which may be analysed by the principles of utilitarianism/situation ethics is the production and distribution of pornography.'

2 Outline simply the ways in which, in principle, the theory might help, e.g. 'A utilitarian might argue that since in any moral dilemma we need to be sure of the greatest happiness of the greatest number, we must investigate how many people are being brought happiness from pornography and how many people are suffering. They may take into account the profit made by the manufacturers, the income earned by the models or actors, the pleasure derived from those who purchase it. On the other hand, they may consider the possibility that both makers and consumers are being exploited and that pornography does not contribute to the edification of society or the individual. Taking into account Mill's distinction between higher and lower pleasures, they may decide that pornography is indisputably a lower pleasure which should therefore be jettisoned in favour of listening to Mozart.'

3 Then make clear, using the principles we have identified in the analysis of these narratives, that there is no way in which an ethical theory can take into account all the elements involved in a moral dilemma, and offer a universal, realistic, perennially applicable judgment.

Review questions

1 With reference to one moral dilemma in sexual ethics, consider how far utilitarianism may help to reduce the problems raised?

2 Can any one ethical theory serve to solve all moral dilemmas?

3 Consider the contribution of any *two* ethical theories to the solution of at least one moral dilemma.

B Medical ethics

I will maintain the utmost respect for human life from its beginning, even under threat, and I will not use my medical knowledge contrary to the laws of humanity.

(The Declaration of Geneva (September 1948) —
the modern version of the Hippocratic Oath)

1 The sanctity of life

The principle of the sanctity of life is based on the teaching of Genesis 2:7: '*Then the Lord God formed man of dust from the ground, and breathed into his nostrils the breath of life, and man became a living being.*' Psalm 139:13ff also supports the view that God is responsible for the existence of all human life: '*For thou didst form my inward parts, thou didst knit me together in my mother's womb. I praise thee, for I am fearfully and wonderfully made.*' The prophet Jeremiah was told by God: '*Before I formed you in the womb I knew you, and before you were born I consecrated you*' (Jeremiah 1: 5). The New Testament continues to support the principle; for example in Acts 17:25, Paul declares: '*He himself gives to all men life and breath and everything.*'

It is possible to hold to the sanctity of life principle without reference to religious principles, since it works on the premise that life is of intrinsic value, a view that many, if not most, human beings are likely to uphold. Nevertheless, if life is sacred (set apart for God's purposes) and created by him, then by definition he must be the one who has control over its end as well as its beginning. Once God has set a life in motion, he can only end it. Thus, an illness that ends in natural death represents a complete life, brought to an end by God within his own timing and purpose, whilst euthanasia represents a challenge to God's divine will. The principle maintains that outside certain circumstances (in themselves arguable) innocent human beings have the right not to be deliberately killed (i.e. involuntary euthanasia), nor should they seek to end their life (i.e. voluntary euthanasia). Life is precious to God and whilst it is not necessary to preserve it at all costs (e.g. with the use of prohibitively expensive and ultimately futile medical care), it must not be disposable for utilitarian reasons — to save money, or to avoid inconvenience to others.

In 1997 the Royal College of Paediatrics and Child Health in Britain published guidelines on withholding or withdrawing life-sustaining treatment in children. It proposed five cases in which this might be considered: brain death; PVS; severe disease where treatment only delays death; where survival would leave the child with severe impairment and unable to make future choices; where further treatment is more than the child or family can bear. However, those who hold an extreme sanctity of life position would argue that continuing aggressive treatment, even under such circumstances, is appropriate in the treatment of children. D. Gareth Jones comments:

In my view, the use of treatment under such circumstances is akin to worshipping "life"… The hallmark of a Christian approach is love for one's neighbour, which translates into the care and protection of the dying infant; there is no room for exploitation, even with the best of intentions.

(Jones, 1999)

Personhood

Life is not the same as **personhood**, for life can belong to any living being — a vegetable has life, as does a fish, a reptile or any kind of mammal. Personhood, however, belongs to human beings, and represents a part of them that is separate and distinct from biological life. It is personhood which makes us different from animals and which leads us to make important legislation about human beings and to place special value on them. Mary Anne Warren argues that a person is characterised by having:

÷ consciousness and ability to feel pain
÷ a developed capacity for reasoning
÷ self-motivated activity
÷ capacity to communicate a variety of messages
÷ self-awareness

Interestingly, newborn babies as well as foetuses do not possess all these criteria, and neither may some adults who are sick or suffer from dementia or other forms of mental illness. However, all foetuses can be said to have the *potential* to fulfil these characteristics. A foetus is a potential person in the way that a student in a class is a potential graduate of that class. By way of analogy, I remember when I was studying Theology at university that a fellow undergraduate objected to the custom of referring to us as 'Theologians' on the grounds that we were Theologians in training — potential Theologians — but not yet actually Theologians. The foetus is a potential person, and as such should be granted the respect due to persons, but it will not be necessary or appropriate to grant to it all the rights and purposes that it will have when it becomes an actual, fully developed, person.

The concept of personhood can also therefore be linked to the fact that we have human rights which cannot be granted to other species — freedom of speech, for example. Because we are persons in interaction (i.e. we interact with other human beings in a meaningful way), we consider issues about life and death as they relate to human beings very differently from how they relate to animals. Not all agree that this is a fair distinction, of course, but broadly speaking, whilst we do not consider there to be serious moral issues arising from a veterinarian putting a terminally sick animal to sleep, we do consider that there are serious moral issues regarding euthanasia. Abortion raises the same kind of questions.

2 The embryo and the foetus

Experimentation with embryos has enormous potential for eventually eliminating a huge range of inherited diseases and for identifying genetic traits that render an individual susceptible to particular illnesses, such as heart disease or cancer (**negative eugenics**). Nevertheless, there are important moral issues to consider. In theory, certain desirable characteristics could be fostered in an embryo before implantation (**positive eugenics**) — intelligence, physical attractiveness, or a preferred gender, for example. This is against the spirit of Psalm 139:13ff, which maintains that God determines every feature and characteristic of an individual even before conception. (This might lead to the interesting question of how a Christian might feel about cosmetic surgery.) Whilst characteristics can be screened out (conceivably a good use of God-given technology), characteristics perceived as positive (i.e. attractive physical features) might be substituted. In either case, it may be argued that human beings are meddling in matters that only belong to God. Cloning of human beings is now more than a theoretical possibility, and the furore over GM foods indicates that it is not just Christians who are concerned about the potential of science to create and transform all manner of life.

Eggs and sperm are fused in the laboratory to create embryos for implantation after being fertilised *in vitro*. However, many more embryos are created than are needed and the discarding of unused embryos is a serious moral issue for some Christians. The issue is one of when life begins. If it is thought that an embryo has life from the moment of fertilisation, then the following syllogism will apply:

P1: It is wrong to destroy human life.
P2: Embryos have human life.
C: It is wrong to destroy embryos.

The use of aborted foetuses for experimentation is also a matter of concern. On the one hand, it may be seen as a means of bringing some good out of the termination; on the other, does it rather condone the practice of abortion? Furthermore, the spectre of designer babies is often raised when considering the moral implications of genetic engineering. Technology may mean that embryos can be screened for congenital disorders, eradicating inherited conditions from the family tree. Is this against the principles of natural law or is it using God-given technology to bring hope and healing to those who would otherwise suffer?

The status of the foetus

The religious question in all this is 'what is the theological significance of the foetus or of prenatal life?' The Bible offers a number of clues but provides no overwhelming evidence upon which to reach generalisations:

÷ The biblical writers include prenatal life within the human community and they recognise that there is continuity between the foetus and the adult it will become. For example, in Genesis 25:23, the struggle between Esau and Jacob in the womb is seen to prefigure the struggle they will have as adults.
÷ God's knowledge and care extends to the foetus. The Psalmist observes: *'Surely I have been a sinner from birth, sinful from the time my mother conceived me'* (Psalm 51:4).
÷ The beginning of life in the womb is seen to be a gift from God which is the result of God's plan and blessing and human activity. At creation God commanded that humans *'Be fruitful and multiply'* and he continues to bless humanity with the potential to fulfil that command.

It is clear, then, that God protects his people before birth and as they develop in their mother's womb, but is it possible to use these references as the basis for a detailed understanding of how God views all foetuses? D. Gareth Jones observes:

One of the striking features of the biblical writings is that they leave a great deal unsaid that would have been of interest to us today... They do not address the question of whether a very early embryo is a person with the rights of a person. The writers did not think like this, and were not interested in questions such as these. They are our problems, and it is our responsibility to decide what response is appropriate for those seeking to be faithful to God.

(Jones, 1999)

Nevertheless, religious believers will continue to maintain that there is no doubt that care of the foetus and compassionate concern for the unborn is important, not least because they represent the weak and disadvantaged for whom God has special concern.

Embryo research

These theoretical concerns have real practical implications in the laboratory. Should research be carried out on human embryos, or does it mark the limits of where the religious believer maintains that it is reasonable for science to go? Embryo research may occur under four main categories:

* Research on human embryos that have been spontaneously aborted. Consent has been given by the mother, and the cause of the foetus's death is accidental and unavoidable.
* Research on embryos that have been produced as part of a fertility programme but that are surplus to requirements. The couples in the programme have donated them in the hope that the research will provide information on fertility.
* Research on embryos produced specifically for the purposes of research.
* Research on specific embryos which will hopefully be returned to the mother after they have received gene therapy to replace defective genes.

These cases raise different ethical problems, but it is important to appreciate that without *any* research on embryos we would have no knowledge of foetal development at all and this would have considerable implications for antenatal care. The question at stake, then, is under what conditions embryo experimentation should take place.

For many religious believers the first scenario poses no moral dilemmas, since the foetus is already dead and its death has not been brought about for the purpose of experimentation.

In the second category, the potential of the embryos to develop is brought to an end, but this would be the case anyway, since they are no longer required as part of the fertility programme. As part of an experimentation programme they are now, at least, being used for a constructive purpose.

The third case is perhaps the most controversial — life is generated in the laboratory for no other purpose than experimentation. For many this comes closest to 'playing God', and allows scientific research to take precedence over the value of human life.

The fourth case is complex and raises a different debate. What right do humans have to replace defective genes? Who decides what is defective or not? Is a (possibly hypothetical) 'homosexuality gene' a defective gene? Is it wholly good that genetic treatment can lead to the elimination, in part at least, of genetic diseases such as Huntington's, cystic fibrosis and certain forms of cancer? Positive eugenics is viewed as possibly less controversial, but it still raises fears about its potential to manipulate human nature and, ultimately, the whole community. The information that can be provided by genetic screening, not only in embryos but in adults too, can be used to control the lives of individuals in many ways. Some of these may be good — they provide individuals with vital information about their genetic makeup which can guide them in making choices concerning healthcare. However, if employers are able to obtain genetic information about employees, the potential for discrimination and stigmatisation is considerable. Motivation is the important factor here. It may be argued that the positive use of genetic technologies is a legitimate part of fulfilling God's command to be stewards of creation, but what may be at fault are the motives of those who make use of that technology. Careful supervision and legislation of the work of genetic scientists might be seen to be the key to ensuring that their work glorifies God rather than replaces him.

3 Abortion

Definitions and legalities

- ❖ **Therapeutic**, **procured** or **surgical abortion** is a moral issue; **spontaneous abortion** or **miscarriage** is not. Therapeutic abortion may arguably include contraceptive devices such as the IUD or the 'morning-after pill' since these act as abortifacients, which prevent implantation, but it is more usually carried out by surgical or medical means after the foetus has implanted in the womb. Abortion is not illegal but, like many other medical procedures, must be subject to certain legal guidelines.
- ❖ **Timescale** — in the UK, the Abortion Act of 1967 limits abortions to the first 24 weeks of pregnancy. Applications are regularly made to reduce this time limit.
- ❖ **Circumstances** — abortion may be permitted if the woman, her existing children or the child itself will suffer physically or mentally. This includes taking into consideration whether the child is in danger of being born handicapped or suffering from a congenital illness, or if the woman's life or psychological health are at risk.
- ❖ **Recommendation** — two doctors must independently recommend that abortion is appropriate. This does not technically allow for abortion on demand, since any doctor may refuse to recommend a termination for any reason, including grounds of conscience. However, pro-life advocates (opponents of abortion) argue that the law effectively provides for it and makes it possible for any woman to be granted a termination on demand.

Abortion and the beginning of life

Consider this set of premises and conclusion:

P1: It is wrong to take a human life.
P2: A foetus is a human life.
C: Abortion is wrong.

On these grounds, if a foetus possesses human life and it is wrong to take human life, then abortion is morally wrong. However, if a foetus, for whatever reason, does not possess human life, then we may reach a different conclusion:

P1: It is wrong to take a human life.
P2: A foetus does not possess human life.
C: Abortion is not morally wrong.

The abortion debate frequently revolves around this issue, influenced by the Catholic view that the foetus is a person from conception, a view which was established as late as the latter part of the seventeenth century, when early microscopes first revealed that a foetus seemed to have the appearance of a tiny, but fully formed person. Augustine, however, had stated that terminating a pregnancy before the foetus is able to feel anything is not murder, because the soul is not yet present — a time he established as before 40 days for male foetuses and before 90 days for females.

Our discussions earlier in this chapter revealed that the issue of when life begins, or what constitutes personhood, is a complex one, but it is crucial for many issues within medical ethics that are concerned with the beginning of life. Adopting one of the following five points in the development of the foetus at which life might be said to begin may help clarify the issue:

❖ **Fertilisation** — sperm and egg unite and the full potential of the foetus is established. At this point over 40% of eggs are lost naturally, but abortion would be forbidden at any point in the pregnancy on the grounds that life has already begun. This is the extreme conservative view.

❖ **Implantation** — the fertilised egg is implanted into the wall of the womb. Even though this occurs before a woman is aware that she is pregnant, again abortion would not be permitted by conservatives.

❖ **Quickening** — the moment when the foetus moves in the womb, traditionally associated with the Augustinian concept of ensoulment. Very early abortion is acceptable.

❖ **Viability** — the point at which the foetus can be considered to be independent of the mother for the purposes of medical care. Late abortions are acceptable for a range of permitted reasons.

❖ **Birth** — the extreme liberal view. Genuine independent existence can only be established with the first breath. Abortion is permitted, in principle, until birth.

Whose rights anyway?

Another significant issue in the abortion debate is that of rights. When a woman seeks an abortion she is asserting her right to make a choice that has implications for her, for the foetus and, indirectly, for all those who have a role to play in her life and in that of her potential child. Pro-abortionists, or pro-choice advocates, argue that the woman has significant rights:

❖ over her body
❖ over her life — including the next nine months, eighteen years or fifty years
❖ over the choices that she makes about her future
❖ over the effect that her choices will have on others with whom she is already in a relationship
❖ over the choices she makes about the future of a foetus which will become a dependent child

Judith Thomson (1971) argues the case of the famous violinist in her article 'A defence of abortion'. If a woman were to wake to find that a famous violinist whose kidneys had failed had been plugged into her blood supply and would continue to be so for nine months, she would be under no moral obligation to agree to continue the procedure. If she did agree, it would not be out of moral compulsion, but out of compassion. Thomson argues that pregnancy is an analogous situation, and the woman should be able to choose whether or not to carry the child to full term without the moral obligation to do so. The only provisos she makes are that the woman should have taken reasonable precautions to prevent it happening, and if continuing the pregnancy meant only a minor inconvenience to her, then she should do so.

Pro-choice advocates also appeal to compassion, citing cases in which the mother and conceivably the rest of her family are likely to suffer unbearable strain if the pregnancy were to continue. Anti-abortionists (or pro-life advocates) also appeal to justice (rights) and compassion, but on behalf of the foetus. They argue that the foetus may have the right:

÷ to fulfil the potential it has to life
÷ to the life it already possesses
÷ not to be killed
÷ to be fairly represented by an impartial third party (i.e. not the mother or father)
÷ for its life — whatever its physical condition — to be considered valuable

This last point is particularly important when a pregnant woman is offered an abortion on the grounds that her child is likely to be born with severe handicaps. The argument here is one of 'quality of life' and there is often an assumption that a severely handicapped person is unlikely to enjoy good quality of life. John Stott asks, '*Who can presume this?*', and cites Alison Davis, a speaker at the Hyde Park Rally in 1983, who described herself as a '*happy spina bifida adult*'. She is reported as saying: '*I can think of few concepts more terrifying than saying that certain people are better off dead, and may therefore be killed **for their own good**… Most handicapped people are quite contented with the quality of their life*' (Stott, 1999). However, it is possible to argue that the foetus also has the right:

÷ to a life free of pain
÷ to a 'minimum quality' of life
÷ to be a wanted child

This position would assert the case for the foetus's right to be aborted if it were likely that these conditions could not be met. Others might also claim that even though the foetus may be a person, the rights of the mother take precedence as long as the foetus is not able to survive outside the mother's womb.

The doctrine of double effect

If the mother's life is considered to be of greater value than that of the foetus, then she clearly must have considerable rights. She may exercise her right to continue that life without danger to her physical or mental health, but if she, or others who are in a position to influence a decision regarding a termination, are opposed in principle to abortion, then the **doctrine of double effect** may come into play. If an abortion is necessary to save the life of a pregnant woman — say, for example, she has cancer of the uterus and needs an urgent hysterectomy — an abortion may be justified since it would be a secondary, albeit inevitable, consequence of a primary action. In other words, if the uterus is removed the foetus will die, but this was not the *primary intention* of the operation, which was to save the mother's life.

The abortion debate can be viewed from both a utilitarian and a deontological perspective. The utilitarian will focus on *consequences*. An anti-abortion utilitarian may cite the cases of many thousands of foetuses that have died, whilst a pro-abortion utilitarian may cite the deaths of many women in illegal abortions which would be the consequence of outlawing abortion. An anti-abortion deontologist will focus on *rights and duties* and may argue that the foetus, as a person, has inalienable rights which are intrinsically valuable, whilst the pro-abortion deontologist will argue that the mother's right to life is more inherently valuable than that of the foetus, at least until it can survive outside the womb.

4 Childlessness and the right to have a child

Infertility brings great emotional pain to couples who genuinely desire to have children. Whilst some might be able to redirect their parental skills and needs into other work or to accept that it is 'God's will' that they are childless, for others the only answer they seek is to be able to have a child. Even whilst some religious believers may consider it to be wrong and against the principles of natural law to use medical technology to increase fertility, others may recognise that those who suffer from infertility experience great psychological pain and need to be ministered to as much as those who have suffered the death of a child. Infertility treatment might be a blessing to them, and it should not be disregarded. In *Valuing People*, D. Gareth Jones (1999) argues that the use of fertility therapy, up to and including IVF, does not constitute an '*abrogation of the marriage bond*' and although '*artificial means can be pursued for unworthy motives or in a grossly excessive manner, neither is inevitable…*'.

If we can accept that there is nothing immoral about making use of fertility treatments, then what is the potential moral problem? Arguably, it is the problem of 'doomed embryos'. In the course of fertility treatment a number of successfully fertilised embryos may be discarded, or lost in miscarriage. In the latter case there can surely be no question of moral wrongdoing, and it is likely that the woman would not even have known that she had been pregnant. As a high percentage of spontaneous abortions occur even when conception has been entirely unassisted, it would be unfair to place the loss of an embryo that has been fertilised **in vitro** in a different moral category. The same surely applies with embryos that are lost following multiple implantations. If four eggs are implanted to maximise the chances of carrying one to term, three are lost, and one successfully develops, is there a moral problem concerning the lost three? Were they irresponsibly and immorally fertilised and implanted, in the full knowledge that they were likely to be lost? Surely, as long as care is taken to minimise factors that may increase the likelihood of embryos being lost in future (e.g. maternal lifestyle or chemical imbalances), the risk is one which is justifiable and is not a violation of the sanctity of life?

A further case is when multiple embryos are produced, some implanted and others frozen for possible use in the future. If they are not used, they will be destroyed. This is a scenario that has been publicly raised and many Catholics especially have expressed strong views on the implications it has for the sanctity of life and the value of the embryo. However, although the loss of the embryo in this case is not accidental, the doctrine of double effect may help. The frozen and unused embryos are destroyed, but their destruction was not the purpose of their creation. They were not fertilised *in order* to be destroyed at some future date, and the loss of some embryos is an *'unintended end result of a life-affirming process'* (Jones, 1999). It may be questionable, though, whether the over-stimulation of the ovaries to produce, say, fifty eggs, in the hope of one being successfully fertilised and implanted is morally acceptable. If we view the embryo as having the equivalent moral status of an adult and the destruction of one as murder, then quite clearly there is an enormous problem. However, the area is notoriously grey and whilst the Bible has nothing specific to say on the issue of embryos, we cannot *'extrapolate ethical guidelines from biblical silence to solve dilemmas at the frontiers of contemporary scientific debate'* (ibid).

Surrogacy brings with it the potential for enormous emotional trauma. Even if the child is not conceived through an act of sexual intercourse, the father forms a bond with the surrogate that could be seen as that of a second partner, breaking the 'one flesh' principle which is fundamental to a religious understanding of marriage. The unfaithfulness is implied rather than actual, but the potential for damage to the father's relationship with his wife is enormous. Furthermore, what about rights? Whose rights are paramount? The surrogate's? The 'client' parents'? The child's? Nevertheless, where all other attempts at having a child have failed, surrogacy may seem to be a lifeline to infertile couples, and women who are prepared to bear a surrogate child could be seen to be making an enormously altruistic gesture.

A Christian attitude to surrogacy is likely to be cautious. Interestingly, the case of Abraham, Sarah and Hagar (Genesis 16) provides something of a cautionary tale. Acting within what was culturally acceptable for the time, Sarah suggests to Abraham that he have a child with her maid Hagar, since she was apparently unable to conceive, despite God's promise to Abraham that he would have an heir. Once Ishmael is born, however, the tension between Sarah and Hagar escalates, and Sarah sends her away from the household although Hagar is told by God to return. When Sarah herself gives birth to Isaac, the tension rises again. Sarah is unable to watch Isaac and Ishmael playing together without fear that Ishmael will inherit what was rightfully Isaac's, and she tells Abraham to get rid of Hagar and Ishmael for good.

Whilst surrogacy, legally monitored, may seem to be an ideal solution to the problem of childlessness for many couples, the risks are high. All parties concerned need to be certain that the conditions under which the surrogacy is contracted are those which can realistically be adhered to once the child is born, and that the implications it has for the relationships between parents, child and surrogate have been clearly thought out. John Stott (1999) writes: *'In surrogacy, even if both sperm and ovum are contributed by the married couple, a physical and emotional bonding takes place between the "mother" and the child she is carrying, which may later be hard to break'*.

In recent years the value of surrogacy to enable homosexual men to have a child using their sperm, artificially inseminated into the surrogate, has opened up new avenues of debate. Lesbian couples are also increasingly exercising a choice to have a child, carried by one partner who has been artificially inseminated, often using the sperm of a close friend. The implications here are different again. If the God-given method of conception is through heterosexual intercourse, is it legitimate to circumvent this means in order to have a child? But if a married couple are permitted to avail themselves of fertility treatment, including AIH (artificial insemination by husband), is there any logical reason why a lesbian woman or an unpartnered woman should not be able to do so as well? The issue is, of course, a moral one rather than a logical one, although it may be invidious to suggest that a lesbian, a gay man, or an unpartnered man or woman could not be as effective a parent as a heterosexual member of a couple.

Contraception

Whilst many couples pursue their 'right' to conceive even whilst nature may be dictating otherwise, many more pursue their 'right' not to conceive. For most people in the twenty-first century, conception is a choice and not a foregone conclusion. The Catholic Church has traditionally held a hard conservative line on contraception, only recently open to some possible flexibility, since according to natural law, every act of sexual inter-course must, in principle, be open to the possibility of conception. Indeed, Augustine maintained that contraception introduced moral corruption into the marital relation-ship. However, not all Christians maintain such a hard line and for many Christian couples today, responsible family planning, in its literal sense, is seen as entirely appro-priate. Nevertheless, some methods of contraception may be considered to be more viable than others: the IUD and the drug RU468 (the 'morning-after pill') may not be considered 'Christian' options, since they act after the event rather than before — they are not methods of contraception per se.

The 'morning-after pill' is the subject of a document issued by the Society for the Protection of the Unborn Child in January 2002, which lays out medical and ethical reasons why this form of 'emergency contraception' is both dangerous and unethical. SPUC argues that '*when a human sperm fuses with a human egg to form an embryo, a human life begins*' and that the complete DNA structure that dictates genetic charac-teristics is determined at conception. A device or substance which acts after concep-tion ends the life of the embryo and is therefore an abortifacient, not a contraceptive. The 'morning-after pill' changes the character of the lining of the womb so that an embryo cannot implant in it and the embryo dies. SPUC claims that despite an increase in prescriptions for the drug, abortion rates have continued to rise, and that the govern-ment's campaign to increase its availability over the pharmacy counter is dangerous. Pharmacists cannot check the medical history of women who take the drug, and the effect on the body of such high dosages of hormones is unnatural and, in many cases, unnecessary.

Today, many Christians maintain that contraception is not an evil, but feel that in most cases Christian couples should, at some point in their marriage, be open to the possibility of bearing children. For some, the deliberate refusal to conceive children has important implications and could even be interpreted as an act of sinful rebellion or, at least, a rejection of God's gift of life. This position follows from the view that the primary purpose of marriage is procreation. However, even the most committed

Christian couples are unlikely to approach procreation purely in biological terms and have as many children as they are physically capable of.

5 Medical care and resources

We live in an age where there are more medical resources and easier access to universal health care than ever, and, in principle, this is surely a good thing. Most members of society can look forward to a long, healthy life, and in the absence of unusual circumstances or unfortunate occurrences, this is not an unreasonable expectation. Our life span is increasing as our life styles become healthier and less dangerous, and the boundaries between life and death are pushed increasingly outwards. Nevertheless, the availability of medical care and the increase in the life span of the general population bring with them new problems. How do medical practitioners make decisions about life and death that would have been unnecessary a hundred, or even fifty, years ago? When an 80-year-old Alzheimer's patient, with no prospect of returning to the lifestyle she had previously enjoyed, suffers from stomach cancer, do surgeons rush to operate with the same alacrity as they do to treat the 32-year-old mother whose husband and two young children wait anxiously in the relatives' room? If the answer is no, then we are entitled to ask why not.

In another scenario, John Doe is a 50-year-old with a 30-a-day smoking habit. He suffers a heart attack and consultants recommend a quadruple heart bypass. If he continues to smoke it is likely that the beneficial effects of surgery will be outweighed by the negative effects of smoking. He is not prepared to give up his habit, and on this basis the consultant refuses to put him forward for the operation, believing that public money can be better spent on a patient who will accept a strict regime to maximise the chance of the operation being a success. John Doe has a fatal heart attack one year later. Was the consultant justified in making this decision, or was it his obligation to provide life-saving surgery, irrespective of John Doe's irresponsibility? After all, surely John Doe has the right to do what he wants with his life?

D. Gareth Jones observes that three major factors legitimately come into play when considering the allocation and distribution of medical resources: complexity of procedures, competition for resources, and the age of patients. He argues that it is reasonable, where there are high levels of competition for resources, that the needs of younger patients should come first. Interestingly, he claims that this is in keeping with a Christian perspective on life and death in enabling us to come to terms with mortality and accepting aging as part of life rather than an obstacle to be overcome: *'Society has an obligation to help people from youth to old age, but by the same token it does not have an unlimited obligation to continue the extension of life in old age'* (Jones, 1999).

As far as the second scenario is concerned — the case of John Doe — we need to consider whether it is ever right to let someone die, albeit indirectly. From a Christian perspective, physical life is not all there is. It is a gift from God, but not the only gift, and it is a gift which may be given back to him when the time is right to do so. However, Jones writes: *'Whenever we are confronted by the question of letting someone die, we are confronted by an actual person and not by life in general. We cannot, therefore, escape from the question of whether the life before us is a personal life, or whether it has a future as a personal life'*. I would argue, therefore, that John Doe's consultant is not entitled

to refuse him the operation he needs. John Doe is alive and has a future as one who has a personal life. There is no absolute certainty that stopping smoking will render the operation totally successful, or that continuing to smoke will lead inevitably to its failure. Furthermore, John Doe may tell his consultant today that he will not give up smoking, but tomorrow decide that he will, after all, abandon the habit. He has the freedom to make a range of choices today and in the future, and this, crucially, identifies him as having a future personal life.

6 Euthanasia

Euthanasia is the intentional killing by act or omission, of one whose life is deemed not worth living.

(Atkinson and Field (eds), 1995)

The term 'euthanasia', based on the Greek terms *eu-thanatos* meaning 'easy death', is defined in the *Oxford English Dictionary* as referring to a 'gentle' death, and in its current sense it is used to refer to the deliberate bringing about of such a death, often described as 'mercy killing'. It is seen to be a key issue in modern medical ethics, although the practice of euthanasia and infanticide was endemic in the ancient world and in primitive cultures. In recent years sympathy towards euthanasia has risen, especially in the Netherlands, described as *'one of the most striking evidences of the development of the post-Christian society in contemporary Europe'* (ibid.).

Most discussion revolves around the issue of **voluntary euthanasia** ('mercy killing') carried out at the express wish of the patient, but there are four other types of euthanasia:

❖ *Active euthanasia* — the result of positive action (e.g. lethal injection) on the part of a carer.

❖ *Passive euthanasia* — the omission or termination of treatment that is prolonging the patient's life. This is already carried out in the case of severely damaged neonates, and may also apply to withdrawal of life support from comatose patients.

❖ *Involuntary euthanasia* — carried out without the express permission of the patient, which may or may not be because he or she is incapable of expressing a view.

❖ *Assisted suicide* — the provision of means and/or opportunity whereby a patient may terminate his or her life.

Support for euthanasia

❖ Pain-free death — the assumption or expectation that death will be preceded by serious pain that can only be controlled to a limited extent by drugs gives rise to considerable support for euthanasia.

❖ Death with dignity — many fear a prolonged death, drawn out by the application of medical technology with the express purpose of delaying death as long as possible. During this time, the patient may become increasingly dependent on others, and unable to control bodily and mental functions. An earlier death is frequently considered more desirable.

❖ Social fears and pressures — the breakdown of traditional family structures which provide care for the elderly and ill has led to an increasing fear of the old and sick being abandoned to a faceless and ill-equipped health service, or left alone to die. Medical advances too may encourage a philosophy in favour of euthanasia, as expensive, glamorous life-saving treatments are promoted above palliative care, even though these may ultimately prove futile. Where there is a desperate need for organs for transplantation, death may be desirable at a time when the body's organs are still relatively healthy and transplantable. A fear of dementia and the effects of Alzheimer's disease may also encourage thoughts of euthanasia in patients and the elderly.

Implications of euthanasia

❖ Even patients in a persistent vegetative state have been known to recover. Recovery from brain injury takes place at different rates and it is only after a period of twelve months that it is diagnosed as persistent, i.e. permanent. However, there are well-documented cases of recovery after this time, although as every month goes by the likelihood of recovery is diminished.

❖ Not all illnesses diagnosed as terminal will necessarily end in death. Cases where patients have been given a terminal prognosis, only to live significantly longer than anticipated or to recover entirely, are by no means rare. For the religious believer there is always the possibility of God's divine intervention, either through the channels of medicine or through a miraculous healing. The believer will be confident to leave their healing, or otherwise, in God's hands.

❖ The development of effective palliative care means that terminal patients will not necessarily face a painful, undignified death. The hospice movement aims to care for terminal patients and to educate the public and the medical profession in alternatives to a painful death or euthanasia. However, at present, access to hospice care is limited and expensive, and palliative care does not attract significant numbers of health-care professionals.

❖ Death is not necessarily an evil. We live in an age when we are so protected from the reality of death that we come to see it as an outrage. In response we tend to have a paradoxical relationship with death — we pursue treatment as far as medical care can allow, and yet we seek to avoid a drawn-out dying process. If we were able to feel more comfortable about death and dying, seeing each life as complete and perfect in God's sight, then the conflict between those who support euthanasia and those who oppose it might be resolved.

❖ Living wills, or advance directives — instructions made by individuals in times of health regarding future health care — may be intended to guard against the resuscitation of a patient who will be seriously brain damaged or otherwise incapacitated. However, such documents rarely have legal status. At the time when they are applied, the patient may hold different views but be unable to express them. Medical practitioners may also fear that, in this litigious age, if advance directives were to acquire legal status, more time would be spent playing 'hunt the living will' when patients are admitted for emergency treatment than spent tending to their needs.

❖ Why not legalise euthanasia? In 1993 the House of Lords unanimously rejected any change in the law to permit euthanasia, arguing that '*It would be next to impossible to ensure that all acts of euthanasia were truly voluntary and that any liberalisation of the law was not abused.'*

÷ Views on euthanasia are influenced by the different perspectives people hold on death. Ultimately, Christians believe that this life is lived from the perspective of the next, and decisions made about it should be made in the context of our relationship with God. The influential evangelical Joni Ereckson Tada, herself a quadriplegic, writes:

God knows you're heading for a hereafter. For those who, apart from Him, prematurely end their lives hoping to find relief there will only be a hereafter of vast and utter disappointment. For those who believe in Jesus, the dying process becomes the most significant passage of their lives.

(Tada, 1992)

A completely different view, however, was expressed by Friedrich Nietzsche:

In a certain state it is indecent to live longer. To go on vegetating in cowardly dependence on physicians and machinations, after the meaning of life, the right to life, has been lost, that ought to prompt a profound contempt in society... I want to die proudly when it is no longer possible to live proudly.

(Cited by Wyatt, 1998)

John Wyatt observes:

Human life span is limited, not just as a curse, but out of God's grace... Even though human death is an evil to be fought against, and a reality which can never be sought intentionally, it may also at times be accepted, even welcomed, as a sign of God's mercy.

(ibid.)

Richard Swinburne (1996) argues that death is not an evil:

God does not in general have any obligation to create. That is why death is not itself an evil, death is just the end of a good state, life (and, in any case, one of which God may choose to give us more, by giving us a life after death). Death may be an evil if it comes prematurely or causes great grief to others, but in itself is not an evil.

Thomas Nagel (1987) writes:

The fear of death is very puzzling... How can the prospect of your own nonexistence be alarming in a positive way? If we really cease to exist at death, there's nothing to look forward to, so how can there be anything to be afraid of?

The views we hold about life and death thus inform our attitudes to euthanasia, and for the religious ethicist there is an ongoing tension between valuing life as God's gift and recognising when life naturally and legitimately ends.

Summary and key terms

■ The **principle of the sanctity of life** — underlies all issues that are of concern in medical ethics, and revolves primarily around when life begins and ends, and what constitutes personhood, or being identifiably a human person. The Bible asserts a strong doctrine of the sanctity of life, created and sustained by God, and that each person has unique identity as a personal and distinct part of his creation.

- **Personhood** — may include a range of factors including the ability to make conscious decisions and to interact with others. The point at which life begins may be linked with personhood, or may be distinct from it. The Bible supports the view that life and personal identity begin at conception, but does not provide sufficient evidence to establish a 'theology of the embryo' since this was not an issue of relevance to the biblical writers.
- The **status of the embryo** — has implications for embryo experimentation, fertility treatments, genetic engineering and abortion. The **abortion** debate revolves around these key issues, and that of the **rights** of mother and foetus. The issue becomes one of choice, and whether the mother is free to make choices which have implications for the foetus but which are made on the tacit understanding that her rights take precedence over those of the foetus.
- **Conception** and **contraception** — the right to have a child and the contrary right not to conceive. How far might measures to conceive or to prevent conception violate biblical principles concerning procreation, the life of the foetus and the 'one flesh' bond between marriage partners?
- **Medical treatment** and **euthanasia** — the ethicist may be concerned to establish how far medical treatment should be used to prolong the life of patients, taking into account their age and health, and, ultimately, what role the doctor, patient and moral philosopher should play in deciding when it is right to die, particularly in a climate where there is increasing pressure on the courts to legalise voluntary euthanasia, even if only on a case-by-case basis.

Exam watch

It is essential that you do not go down the route of anecdote and generalisations in essays on medical ethics. This is a very popular subject area and it serves many candidates faithfully as a topic for coursework essays, but it is easy to fall flat on your face if you do not underpin everything you say with knowledgeable explanation of the principles that are at stake, rather than the generalities. Use plenty of scholarship and philosophical terminology, and develop a clear argument as you work through your essays, and you'll stand out from those students who are still relying on their GCSE material because they haven't appreciated that these are far more complex and conceptual issues than they may at first appear.

Review questions

1 State the arguments for and against the existence of moral absolutes — the view that some actions are always intrinsically wrong — with reference to experiments on human embryos.
2 *'Made in the image of God.'* How far should humans be able to manipulate the means of life to create beings made in their image?
3 *'Every pregnant woman has the absolute right to choose to have an abortion.'* Critically analyse this claim.
4 *'The case for euthanasia has no theological, philosophical or social justification.'* Discuss.
5 Critically consider the dilemmas which confront a general medical practitioner.

C Sex and relationships

1 Marriage and divorce

Marriage is a total troth communion which can be broken by any kind of prolonged infidelity, whether through the squandering of monies, unwillingness to share of self, breaking of confidences or other betrayals of trust.

(Atkinson and Field (eds), 1995)

Genesis 2:24 advocates the legitimacy of marriage over and above all other sexual partnerships. The **one flesh principle** assumes that a sexual relationship is an integral part of marriage, although it is not the only important characteristic. Both Old and New Testament writers used the analogy of marriage to describe the relationship between Israel and Yahweh and between Jesus and the church, emphasising the need for exclusive commitment of one to the other. In principle, all other sexual relationships are seen as wrong in the eyes of God and undermine or exclude the trust and protection that marriage offers to both partners.

Sex and morality

Even a cursory glance at the contribution made by the biblical writers on the subject of marriage clearly indicates that it has long been an issue of concern for religious believers. That concern is still relevant in the twenty-first century and has resulted in widely differing attitudes to the issues of marriage and divorce, not just amongst religious believers but also in the media, parliament, law and in academic debate. The law combines the legal and moral issues of marital relationships in a distinctive way. Adultery may be considered immoral, and it may be legitimate grounds for a legal divorce, but it is not a crime. Sex with many heterosexual partners may be thought to constitute an immoral lifestyle, but some thinkers argue that sexual activities that take place between consenting adults, married or unmarried, heterosexual or homosexual, are not a matter of morality. Rape *is* both immoral and illegal because it involves the violent assault of one person upon another without the other's consent. Professor H. L. A. Hart (1986) draws an important distinction between what is moral and immoral: '*Sexual intercourse between husband and wife is not immoral, but if it takes place in public it is an affront to human decency*'. He argues that a private sexual act could not harm anyone except '*a few neurotic…persons who are literally "made ill" by the thought of it*'.

Religious perspectives

For religious believers, the issues are fairly clear-cut. The biblical view of marriage is that it is ordained by God, and that one man and one woman make a commitment to an exclusive and binding relationship (Genesis 2:24) that will last until the death of one of the partners. Within that relationship there is a natural hierarchy (Ephesians 5:22–3) in which the husband is the head, over the wife. He is bound to love and honour her, as she is bound to respect and honour him. The New Testament writers are in agreement that that breakdown of this divinely ordained relationship through divorce is not desired by God, although sometimes inevitable, and that the relationship should be preserved as a holy one (Matthew 19:3–9). In Islam too, divorce is not forbidden (not **haram**) but is considered to be *'of all permitted things, the one most hated by Allah'*.

The major Christian denominations all accept the New Testament pronouncements on marriage, but whilst agreeing that the relationship should ideally be lifelong, denominations are divided as to how strictly they interpret the biblical teaching on divorce. Even within denominations, Christians will vary in how rigorously they apply biblical teaching. Decisions about whether to allow divorced Christians to marry again in church, or even whether to condone the marriage of a Christian to a non-Christian, will often be matters of conscience. An individual minister may not be troubled by the prospect of conducting the marriage service of a divorced person, but, aware that others in the church would be challenged by it, may refuse to allow the service to take place.

Jesus appears to have taught that a man or woman is bound not to separate from his or her spouse (Mark 10:11–12) and that the Jewish law provided for divorce only as a concession to humanity's hardness of heart. However, both Matthew and Paul suggest reasons for permitting separation. Matthew differs from Mark, even though they appear to be working from the same source. He adds what is known as the **exceptive clause**: *'And I say to you; whosoever divorces his wife, **except for unchastity**, and marries another, commits adultery'* (Matthew 19:9). Mark had not made this provision for unchastity, and although Matthew may have included it only to satisfy his Jewish-Christian readers, who would have been horrified at the prospect of staying married to an unfaithful partner (cf. Matthew 1:19), some modern-day Christians accept this as biblically permissible grounds for divorce. Paul's provision may seem rather more rarefied in a time when Christian commitment is often nominal, but he allows a Christian person to separate from a non-Christian spouse who refuses to stay with him or her: *'In such a case the believer is not bound'* (I Corinthians 7:15). This was an important provision at a time when conversion to Christianity often meant total abandonment of a traditional way of life.

Whilst it is likely that both Christians and non-Christians would still argue that adultery violates beyond repair the bond of exclusive commitment, it is also possible to maintain that the Christian principle of forgiveness should be allowed to take precedence over the exceptive clause which is, itself, a concession. It provides permissible grounds for divorce if a divorce is sought, but it does not command it. Selwyn Hughes (1983) argues that adultery need not be the inevitable end to marriage, but rather that the Christian is under a much stronger imperative than the non-Christian to seek reconciliation.

If it is the sexual tie that characterises marriage and if its breach is the only permissible grounds for divorce, then a Christian who seeks a divorce for any other reason, including cruelty, could be said to be acting immorally. Secular ethicists would be unlikely to take this position, but readily recognise that there are many ways in which the mutual bond of trust and commitment can be broken, and that it is an unreasonable imposition on the emotional and physical well-being of the individual to refuse to allow other grounds for separation. The Christian may well agree that in cases of severe physical violence, a woman is entitled to seek protection for herself and her children, but may well also claim that she and her husband should then attempt to overcome these problems through prayer and counselling.

The nature of the marriage relationship

The preponderance of attitudes towards the marriage bond and the permissibility of divorce suggest that religious and ethical views on marriage will inevitably be diverse, and there is another area still to be considered. In Ephesians 5:22ff and 1 Peter 3:1ff, the writers suggest that the marriage relationship is hierarchical, modelled on the hierarchy of God and humans. In a marriage relationship, the man is the head of the wife as Christ is the head of the church. As such, she is called to love and respect him. His task is to love her '*as Christ loved the church and gave himself up for her*' (Ephesians 5:25). These passages have aroused much debate amongst Christian thinkers and much derision amongst non-Christians. If the woman is to respect her husband (Ephesians 5:33) and indeed to be submissive to him (1 Peter 3:1), it must say little for the equality of women and men in the eyes of God. One Christian viewpoint is that the concept of headship is a theological, not a sociological, one, because the model is Christ's headship over the church which is rooted in love and sacrifice, not domination and power. Such love involves the man in ensuring that the needs of his spouse are met even if it is to his personal detriment, because in loving his wife he loves his own body (Ephesians 5:29). In turn the wife is reminded to show respect for her husband not because she is inferior to him but because it is characteristic of a man to need to receive respect. It is argued that the biblical writers have provided a blueprint for a divinely ordained marriage that supernaturally anticipates the needs of each partner, and is not a culturally anachronistic model for female subjugation.

Marriage, divorce and 'the new morality' of situation ethics

A useful analysis of the ethics of marriage and divorce was outlined by John A. T. Robinson (1963), in his controversial book *Honest to God*, in which, influenced by the situation ethics of Joseph Fletcher, he offers an approach to the moral problems of marriage and divorce in the later twentieth century. (See pp. 148–150 and pp. 164–165 for more discussion of situation ethics and its application to the moral dilemmas of marriage and adultery.)

Robinson maintained that there had been a 'wind of change' in morality which Christian thinkers had to recognise or else they faced the downfall of Christian morality altogether. Christianity was still associated with old, traditional morality which had served it well in the past, but which '*would be calamitous if we allowed Christianity to be dismissed with it*'. Traditional morality, Robinson claimed, assumed that morals were based on laws handed down by God that were eternally valid for human behaviour. Certain things were always wrong (sins) or always right, and provided the basis for whether society judged them to be crimes. He identified traditional thinking on marriage and divorce to be a particular arena in which this kind of thinking prevailed: '*There is, for instance, a deep division on the interpretation of the "indissolubility" of marriage. There are those who say that "indissoluble" means "ought not to be dissolved", ought **never** to be dissolved. There are others who take it to mean "cannot be dissolved".*' These views were grounded, Robinson claimed, in the opinion that marriage is a metaphysical reality which survives independently of the actual physical relationship and which cannot be affected by any objective facts or legal manoeuvres: '*It is not a question of "Those whom God has joined together let no man put asunder": no man could if he tried*'.

Furthermore, Robinson exposed the view that marriage is based on the absolute command of God and that Jesus interpreted the Old Testament teaching on marriage in the same legalistic way. He argued that this view was, in fact, what people expect the church to stand for, and are shocked when it is questioned, but that in reality '*it is a position that men honour much more in the breach than the observance*'. Instead, Robinson proposed, the moral teachings of Jesus were not intended to be '*...understood legalistically, as prescribing what all Christians must do, whatever the circumstances... they are illustrations of what love may at any moment require of anyone*'. Jesus's teaching on marriage, therefore, was not a new law which stated '*that divorce is always and in every case the greater of two evils... it is saying that utterly unconditional love admits of no accommodation; you cannot define in advance situations in which it can be satisfied with less than complete and unreserved self-giving*'.

Robinson argued that it was impossible to begin from a position of saying 'sex relations before marriage' or 'divorce' are inherently wrong or sinful, because the only intrinsically wrong thing is a lack of love. He cites Joseph Fletcher: '"*If the emotional and spiritual welfare of both parents and children in a particular family can be served best by divorce, wrong and cheapjack as divorce commonly is, then love requires it*"... *And this is the criterion for every form of behaviour, inside marriage or out of it, in sexual ethics or in any other field. For nothing else makes a thing right or wrong.*'

2 Homosexuality

Christians are often divided over the contentious issue of homosexuality — the term coined at the end of the nineteenth century which describes the sexual attraction to a person of the same sex. Whilst for some it is the ultimate taboo, and homosexuals should not be welcomed into Christian fellowship, still less into the ministry, for others it is the natural way that some individuals have been created by God. Arguments are often biblically based but are also strongly influenced by personal opinion, experience, prejudice and the way in which society has viewed homosexuality over the centuries.

The causes of homosexuality

Much scientific research has gone into attempts to understand the origin and causes of homosexuality. It was not removed from the American list of psychiatric disorders until as recently as 1973 and attempts are still being made to establish that there is a fundamental medical cause — a hormonal imbalance or a genetic predisposition. Attempts have also been made to identify a 'homosexual gene' which would establish in some way that homosexuality was a natural predisposition for some. Nina Rosenstand (2000) argues that should this be established, then traditional objections to homosexuality — that it is a moral choice that goes against nature, and (in relation to male homosexuality) places adolescent boys in danger of seduction — would no longer be valid. She observes that there would be no reason to discriminate against homosexuals on the belief that it was an immoral choice, but suggests that it may open up new doors for discrimination: parents may seek 'screening' of their children for homosexuality, in the hope of finding a 'cure' if they tested positive.

Psychiatrist Anthony Storr (1964) writes that homosexuals '*have a vested interest in*

affirming that their condition is an inborn abnormality rather than the result of circumstances; for any other explanation is bound to imply a criticism of themselves or their families and usually of both…'. Freud claimed that male homosexuality was a personality disorder which was the result of failing to develop fully into adulthood, and he traced the causes of homosexuality back to the relationship between a child and his parents. Elizabeth Moberly (1983) supports this view: *'A homosexual orientation does not depend on a genetic predisposition, hormonal imbalance or abnormal learning processes, but on difficulties in the parent–child relationships, especially in the earlier years of life'*. However, the jury is still out on the origins of homosexual orientation, and little research at all has been carried out on bisexuality.

Christianity and homosexuality

Whatever the origins of homosexual orientation, religious believers are deeply divided over how to deal with it in the world and in the religious community. The Lesbian and Gay Christian Movement maintains that *'human sexuality in all its richness is a gift from God gladly to be accepted, enjoyed and honoured…'* whilst the Roman Catholic Church states in the *Declaration on Sexual Ethics* that *'In sacred scripture homosexual acts are condemned as a serious depravity and presented as a sad consequence of rejecting God'*. On the other hand, the Methodist Church declared: *'For homosexual men and women, permanent relationships characterised by love can be an appropriate and Christian way of expressing their sexuality.'* A diversity of views therefore exists, and the 1998 Lambeth Conference of the Church of England Bishops established that four perspectives on homosexuality were held, ranging from conservative to liberal:

÷ Homosexuality is a disorder from which the Christian can seek deliverance.
÷ Homosexual relationships should be celibate.
÷ Whilst exclusive homosexual relationships fall short of God's best for man, they are to be preferred over promiscuous ones.
÷ The Church should fully accept homosexual partnerships and welcome homosexuals into the priesthood.

The Bible and homosexuality

For Bible-believing Christians, a biblical argument against homosexuality seems to be a convincing one. The biblical concept of marriage suggests that the only divinely ordained, legitimate sexual relationship is one between heterosexual partners who voluntarily give up all other potential sexual partners to 'cleave' (Genesis 2:24) to their spouse. The creation narrative describes woman as being created specifically and specially for man — *'a helper fit for him'* (Genesis 2:18) — and, by implication, this suggests that another of exactly the same kind, a man, would not fulfil this requirement. The 'one flesh' principle indicates that the primary characteristic of the marriage bond is the sexual relationship between partners, and with it goes the creation ordinance, *'Be fruitful and multiply'* (Genesis 1:28, 9:1). Clearly, a homosexual partnership does not have this potential, and could thus be said to be 'unnatural' according to the principles of natural law.

The biblical writers understood that marriage is more than procreative, however. The use of the marriage analogy to describe the relationship between Yahweh and

Israel (Hosea 2:16) and between Jesus and the church (Revelation 21:2) affirms the unique and exclusive nature of the marriage bond. Israel and the church are both described as female figures — a wife and a bride — not male, and the relationship they share with God is to be monogamous and free from the perversions that characterised pagan worship of the Canaanite gods. The exclusive commitment which Israel and Yahweh share singles the relationship out from all others, and is appropriate only, Christians claim, to the bond of trust that can be established by marriage.

Not only is the biblical view of the pair bond exclusively heterosexual, the biblical writers are also swift to condemn homosexual practices. In Leviticus 20:13 the Israelites are warned that homosexuality carries with it the death penalty, and the story of Lot and the angelic visitors suggests that it was an even more serious sin than heterosexual rape (Genesis 19). All who participate in homosexual acts are condemned, including Canaan who appeared to have taken sexual advantage of his father, Noah, whilst he was asleep (Genesis 9:25). His descendants, the Canaanites, are cursed for following the same practices, and any Israelite who *'lies with a man as with a woman'* (Leviticus 18:22) will be *'vomited out of the land'*. D. S. Bailey (1986) wrote of these passages: *'It is hardly open to doubt, that both the laws in Leviticus relate to ordinary homosexual acts between men and not to ritual or other acts performed in the name of religion'*. Homosexuality was seen as being violent as well as perverse, as in the case of Sodom — *'Then they pressed hard against the man Lot, and came near the door to break it down'* (Genesis 19:9). In Judges 19:22–30 an attempted homosexual rape leads to the gruesome murder of a concubine, who ironically becomes a victim in order to avoid the worse sin — *'This vile thing'* — of homosexual rape.

Certainly, the people of Israel had good reason to avoid the homosexuality that characterised the Canaanite cults and the land they were setting out to conquer. Participation in their practices was a gross violation of the covenant relationship with Yahweh and did not increase the fruitfulness of the people, which was essential if they were to dominate the land. However, the theme is continued in the New Testament, especially by Paul, who included homosexuality in the list of moral evils that jeopardise a man's salvation: *'Do not be deceived; neither the immoral, nor idolaters, nor adulterers, nor sexual perverts…will inherit the Kingdom of God'* (1 Corinthians 6:9–10). The most specific teaching against homosexuality is found in Romans, in which Paul suggests that it was a result of the fall after which *'Men…gave up natural relations with women, and were consumed with passion for one another, men committing shameless acts with men'* (Romans 1:27). Despite the fact that Jesus is not recorded as addressing the problem himself (probably because he preached in a predominantly Jewish culture, whilst Paul ministered in a Greek society where homosexuality was more commonly practised), it is clear that there is a strong biblical argument against homosexuality. This is sufficient for many Christians to argue (controversially) that it is sinful and can only be dealt with through repentance, forgiveness, prayer and healing.

Countering biblical arguments

D. S. Bailey offered a re-evaluation of these traditional arguments against homosexuality, drawing attention to the use of language and the culture from which biblical teachings emerged. First, the sin of Sodom, which seems to lay the foundations for

condemnation of homosexual practices, is ambiguous. Although it is possible that the Hebrew verb **yada** ('to know') may allude to sexual knowledge, it could simply mean 'to become acquainted'. If this is the case, then the sin of Sodom was not homosexuality, but lack of hospitality, as Ezekiel 16:49 suggests. Isaiah 1:10 suggests it was hypocrisy and social injustice, whilst Jeremiah 23:14 cites deceit and general wickedness. Furthermore, condemnation of homosexual acts in the Bible often appears to relate to pagan practices, and many of the passages seem to be condemning idolatry (1 Kings 14:24, Deuteronomy 23:17). Paul says of this own teaching on marriage that he has '*No command of the Lord, but I give my opinion as one who by the Lord's mercy is trustworthy*' (1 Corinthians 7:25), so it is conceivable that with no corroborating account in the gospels, Paul may have been speaking entirely from his own perspective. Since it is clear that some of his teaching no longer has cultural relevance — the instruction to women to cover their heads in church, for example — it is possible that his teaching on homosexuality may also be culturally relative.

Other arguments defending homosexuality are rather more tenuous, however — the suggestion that David and Jonathan shared a homosexual relationship (1 Samuel 18:1), or even that Paul's ready acceptance of the celibate life was because he was himself homosexual.

Homosexuality and morality

Even if homosexuality is an important issue for religious believers, is it an issue of moral concern? John Harris (1984) claimed that sexual activities of any kind should not be seen in a moral context but rather as an issue of manners and etiquette. His view is not unlike the harm principle of J. S. Mill, who claimed that the only right that society had to interfere with the lives of individuals was to prevent them causing harm to others. Harris maintains that whilst homosexuality does not cause harm to society as a whole, the individual's sexual relationships should be private and free from moral judgments. It is debatable, however, whether it is an exclusively private matter. It was evidently not so for the biblical writers who were concerned with the impact that homosexuality could have on a community, whether it be in Israel or in Corinth.

The principle of natural law is strongly opposed to homosexuality on the grounds that the purpose and goal of a sexual relationship should be procreation, although Paul himself seems not to support that view: '*Do not deprive each other except by mutual consent and for a time*' (1 Corinthians 7:5) appears to suggest that sex serves other purposes of love and intimacy.

For many religious believers, the issue is not so much one of sexual orientation but of sexual activity; the former may not be a matter of choice, but the latter is. Mark Bonnington and Bob Fyall (1996) propose that the solution lies in loving, but non-genital, same-sex relationships:

An important contribution can be made through the rehabilitation of friendships between persons of the same sex. Warm companionship without any sexual element is not something that should be regarded as odd by the Christian community. Rather, it is to be welcomed as a valuable way of developing affectionate bonds within the church and providing the human support and comfort that most of us find we need.

In an article in *The Times* ('Church must defend gay rights', 21 June 1994), Canon Anthony Harvey claimed that *'Christian teaching should be revised in this area as it has been in other areas such as the acceptance of slavery and the subordination of women to men'*, and whilst the Church of England does not recommend physical expression of homosexual orientation, it acknowledges that the church must respect those who *'are conscientiously convinced that they have more hope of growing in love for God and neighbour with the help of a loving and faithful homophile partnership, in intention lifelong, where mutual self-giving includes the expression of their attachment'* (*What the Churches Say*).

3 Pornography

Religious believers are, in general, opposed to the production and use of pornographic material for a range of reasons:

- Pornography is associated with violence.
- It violates the status of human beings as made in the image of God.
- It involves and encourages addiction and generates millions of pounds for those who produce it.
- It encourages the subordination of women.
- It demeans the nature of a loving sexual relationship between husband and wife.
- The Christian call to holiness is undermined. Pornography encourages Christians to adopt worldly views and conform to worldly standards.
- Although Christians are free from the constraints of the law, they must be wise and sensitive to what is upbuilding and positive. Pornography does nothing to further the Kingdom of God or humanity's relationship with God.

In *Laid Bare: A Path Through the Pornography Maze*, Claire Wilson-Thomas and Nigel Williams (1996) reported that in Great Britain alone, the annual expenditure on pornography was estimated at the time at £60 million, whilst the third richest man in Britain was Paul Raymond, the publisher of a string of pornographic magazines and the owner of the Raymond Revue Bar in Soho, an entertainment venue devoted to sexually explicit entertainment. Pornography therefore represents big money and there is little commercial or political incentive to limit the activities of those who produce and promote it. Furthermore, in 1979 the Williams Committee concluded that there should be no restrictions on the written word because of *'its importance in conveying ideas'*. All books, therefore, irrespective of their content, are VAT-exempt because they are considered educational.

Pornographic material is universally and easily accessible, in books, magazines, videos, the Internet and telephone lines. Much of it is not illegal, although the places where it can be purchased and advertised are controlled — not always successfully, especially in the realms of Internet porn — in the interests of protecting minors. The easy availability of pornography is not just a concern for religious believers. Sociologists have long been aware of the connections between pornography and violent crime. Ted Bundy, the American serial killer executed in 1989, was clear that pornography had played a decisive role in his life and his crimes. In his final interview with James Dobson (*Fatal Addiction*, Focus on the Family videos), he claimed: *'I have lived in prison for a long time. And I've met a lot of men who were motivated to commit violence just like me. And without exception, every one of them was deeply involved in pornography'*. Obviously, it cannot only be Christians who are concerned about this, but there are distinctive elements in the Christian response to the problems raised by pornography which make them a particularly strong pressure group in the fight against it.

Human worth

Christians believe that humans were made in the image and likeness of God (Genesis 1:27) and as such are set apart for God's purposes and called into a relationship in which they share in God's creative work and exercise dominion over the created order. The distinctiveness of the way in which God created humans sets them apart from the rest of the creation, calling them into a life which reflects the uniqueness of their relationship with God. Since all humans are called into that relationship and are equal in value in the sight of the creator, then all are entitled to be treated with respect and dignity, and must respect each other. Whether humans accept that God has a claim on their lives or not, Christians believe that they have nevertheless been created for that special relationship and have been sanctified by it. There are special responsibilities, therefore, which humanity is called to exercise within the created order: primary among them is an acknowledgement of others as called into a relationship of dignity, equality and holiness.

The implications of this are obvious: humans are not to subject their fellow humans to any acts which degrade their special status and do not glorify their creator. Acts of violence, humiliation and exploitation, which are characteristic of pornography, are thus inappropriate. Christians do not argue that it is women alone who are degraded and exploited by pornography. Pornography has a serious effect on those who have access to it — they too are victims of a multi-million pound business which has little incentive to lose custom. If pornography is addictive, which some people believe it to be, it is not easy to avoid becoming involved in increasingly aggressive forms. Wilson-Thomas and Williams (1996) describe the experience of Mike, who was introduced to pornography by school friends:

It did not take him long to be heavily involved with pornography: all he wanted was more porn. Soon that did not satisfy and he went to Soho to find some prostitutes so that he could experience for himself all the perversions he had been reading about… Mike is now able to look back…realising 'how close I came to committing rape'.

This may sound polemical, but if pornography has such an escalating effect, then it is right for religious believers to be concerned. It has, they argue, the effect of putting human beings under bondage to spiritual forces that are not of God, the aim of which is to separate them entirely from God and lead them into destruction.

The status of women

Women and men who are involved in the production of pornography are also frequently exploited. Very often, those who become part of the pornography business do so out of financial need. Homelessness, poverty and loneliness can make men and women desperate, and involvement in the pornography industry can appear to be a lucrative and glamorous solution to their problems. The particular role of women in the pornography trade is also of concern. In the Bible, women are not downtrodden and subject to the power of men, as many interpretations of biblical literature would try to claim; rather, they are seen as the glory of man, and worthy of deep respect. The woman of Proverbs 31 seems to be the biblical model for the ideal woman, and she knows exactly how to look after herself: *'A good wife, who can find? She is far more precious than jewels. The heart of her husband trusts in her, and he will have no lack of gain... Give her the fruit of her hand, and let her works praise her in the gates'* (Proverbs 31:10–11, 13). In the Song of Songs, the bride is deeply respected and revered by her husband: *'How fair and pleasant you are, O loved one, delectable maiden! You are a stately palm tree and your breasts are like its clusters. I say I will climb that palm tree now and lay hold of its branches'* (Song of Songs 7:6–8). Even though the language used is sensual, the woman is honoured for her beauty, not exploited for it. Not all religious believers, however, nor even all church leaders, share this view. Gretchen Gaebelein Hull (1987) writes:

I was traveling home from a church-related conference and found myself with extra time in the airport. In the stationery store I noticed a minister I had met at breakfast, and I went into the store to ask if he would like to discuss the conference over a cup of coffee. As I came up behind him I saw that he was preoccupied with a pornographic magazine featuring naked women in provocative poses; disillusioned, I just walked out again. The message was finally getting through to me: to all too many Christian men, women were not even second-class citizens. Women were objects.

This theme is continued in the New Testament. Paul writes: *'Even so husbands should love their wives as their own bodies... For no man ever hates his own flesh, but nourishes and cherishes it as Christ does his church'* (Ephesians 5:28–29). Pornography does not reflect this kind of love and respect for women who work in the industry, or the partners of those who use it. Christian (and other religious) beliefs about marriage are not just concerned with issues of divorce, but with the nature of the marriage bond itself. In Genesis 2:24, man and woman are called into an exclusive relationship which is characterised by 'leaving and cleaving' and by the 'one flesh' principle. Both are violated by the use of pornography as the man's wife ceases to be the one to whom he 'cleaves' alone. A silent but powerful image takes her place in the marriage pair-bond. This process is described by Wilson-Thomas and Williams (1996):

Sally had been happily married for ten years...when her husband started getting heavily involved with pornography... He was beginning to use violence to make her submit to his wishes. She felt less and less a person of worth and more and more a possession for sex... For Sally, pornography had ruined her marriage and her life.

The call to holiness

Finally, the Christian call to holiness is threatened and offended by pornography. Christians believe that not only are humans as a species set aside for a special relationship with God, but those who have acknowledged that relationship and the call it has on their lives are required to live lives of holiness which honour and reflect the nature of God. Paul writes in Romans 12:1–2:

I appeal to you therefore, brethren, by the mercies of God, to present your bodies as a living sacrifice, holy and acceptable to God, which is your spiritual worship. Do not be conformed to this world, but be transformed by the renewal of your mind, that you may prove what is the will of God, what is good and acceptable and perfect.

It is obvious that involvement in pornography cannot possibly characterise the life of a Christian who is committed to presenting himself or herself as holy and acceptable to God. Paul and Jesus were aware that the world was a place in which Christians live, work, worship God, and bear witness to others, and they must be in it in order to be salt and light to the world (Matthew 5:13–16). However, this should not include conforming to the ways of the world — Christians must be in it but not of it (John 17:13–16). Paul had to face the reality of this problem in Corinth, where the new church still lived side by side with the pagan world. Their attitude to sexual matters was far more liberal than he had known under Judaism and could not co-exist with the Gospel. He reminds the Corinthians that the blood of Jesus has brought them freedom, but that freedom must be to seek what is beneficial in building up Christians in their faith: *"'All things are lawful to me', but not all things are helpful… Shun immorality… Do you not know that your body is a temple of the Holy Spirit within you, which you have from God? You are not your own; you were bought with a price. So glorify God in your body'* (1 Corinthians 6:12, 18–20).

Summary

- **Marriage and divorce** — the biblical basis for heterosexual marriage lies in the 'one flesh' principle and the unique pairing of man and woman. But is it a moral issue or are sexual relationships, including marriage, a matter of private concern? The biblical writers consider them to be central to how a believer relates to God and society. Divorce is permissible in the Old and New Testaments, though not recommended, but believers are divided over whether it is always or sometimes permissible, on what grounds it might be allowed, and the implications it has for remarriage. Biblical teaching influences views about the status of men and women within marriage and may need to be reinterpreted for a new era. **John Robinson** argued that biblical morality was no longer appropriate for the modern era and claimed that Jesus's teachings were not intended to imprison humanity by absolute, unbreakable rules. Divorce therefore may, in certain circumstances, be the most loving outcome for a family.
- **Homosexuality** — divided views over cause and explanation for homosexuality, and many consider it crucial to establish whether it is 'natural'. Religious views vary from liberal (homosexual partnerships as valid as heterosexual ones) to strict (homosexuality as a disorder). Biblical condemnation seems to be universal, although it may be culturally relative. Is homosexuality a moral issue, or is it a matter of private sexual conduct which should only be condemned if it causes harm to others? Arguments against homosexuality should be understood in the light of the possibility that it may be in some way a legitimate expression of human love.
- **Pornography** — most ethical and all religious systems would find it difficult to argue for the moral acceptability of pornography. Associated with exploitation and violence,

it diminishes human worth and the status of women, and may be addictive. The sanctity of the 'one flesh' principle in marriage is violated by it and it challenges the Christian call to be holy in a corrupt world.

Exam watch

These are interesting and personal issues, and for that reason you do need to give yourself some academic distance from them if you are going to write a balanced essay that will gain you credit. It is easy to get bogged down in your own opinions, and this will not impress the examiner. There are more than two sides to every issue discussed in this chapter, and you must show that you are aware of this in a sensible and articulate way. Sweeping generalisations and judgments just won't do — back up everything you say with a biblical reference, a scholarly quotation or an ethical theory.

Review questions

1 Discuss the problems that an acceptance of homosexuality poses for Christians.

2 (a) Outline and suggest reasons for the major differences in ethical and religious views concerning marriage.

 (b) To what extent may the differences outlined reflect changes in social and cultural practices?

3 Can there ever be an ethical and religious justification for pornography?

Topic 4

Practical ethics and society

A War and peace

1 The biblical view of war

One of the oldest and most fundamental functions of the state is to accomplish and preserve security for the individual and for the nation. For the people of Ancient Israel, deliverance from their enemies was one of the most important promises they could expect as a result of faithfulness to their covenant relationship with Yahweh, and the value of peace and security for the individual citizen, particularly for those with no political or military power themselves, is described in Micah 4:4: *'They shall dwell every man under his own vine and his own fig tree and none shall make them afraid.'* In early Israel, conflict was the natural means to establish the land and maintain its security as the people took Yahweh's promise by the horns and settled in the already populated land of Canaan. God is presented as a God of action and his activity is frequently seen in his engagement in conflict with those who oppose him and his will for his covenant people. But his ultimate goal is not destruction or power for its own sake, but to bring about a redeemed people who can carry out his purposes. Enemy nations serve their own function as instruments of judgment on God's people, but then will face God's judgment themselves: *'When the Lord has finished all his work on Mount Zion and on Jerusalem he will punish the arrogant boasting of the King of Assyria and his haughty pride...'* (Isaiah 10:12).

The Old Testament writers too are aware of the limits of what military strength can achieve and the dangers of engaging in international intrigue unless it is guided and directed by Yahweh: *'Ephraim is like a dove, silly and without sense, calling to Egypt, going to Assyria. As they go I will spread over them my net; I will bring them down like birds of the air'* (Hosea 6:11–12). Jeremiah's warning to Zedekiah not to deceive himself about the interests of the Babylonians is ignored at his peril (Jeremiah 37) and the necessity of justice as the only reliable basis for peace is expressed in Isaiah 32:16ff: *'Then justice will dwell in the wilderness...and the effect of righteousness will be peace...and my people will abide in peaceful habitation, in secure dwellings and in quiet resting places.'*

The biblical writers are aware that unless war is conducted under the guidance of Yahweh — when it can be remarkably bloody and vindictive, as the command to Saul to slaughter all the Amalekites indicates (1 Samuel 15) — it is rooted in human selfishness and greed. Rivalry over land and wealth, international and individual pride and status are more likely to result in war than conflicts emerging out of a genuine desire to fight evil with good. Nevertheless, the struggle between the people of God and their enemies is seen as a precursor of the great final, cosmic, spiritual battle which will come at the end of time, and will be led by the Messiah and his heavenly armies. The outcome of this battle is already determined:

And when the thousand years are ended, Satan will be loosed from his prison and will come out to deceive the nations which are at the four corners of the earth… And they marched up over the broad earth and surrounded the camp of the saints and the beloved city, but fire came down from heaven and consumed them, and the devil who had deceived them was thrown into the lake of fire and sulphur where the beast and the false prophet were, and they will be tormented day and night for ever and ever.

(Revelation 20:7–10)

This is the greatest and most legitimate battle to be fought, and the biblical writers urge God's people to engage in it in the confidence that victory is already on their side, even when it may appear to the contrary.

Even whilst he engaged in hand-to-hand conflict with Satan, Jesus refused to take the way of military power to achieve his goal, and challenged his disciples when they attempted to do so themselves: *'Put your sword back into its place; for all who take the sword will perish by the sword. Do you think that I cannot appeal to my Father and he will at once send me more than twelve legions of angels? But how then should the scriptures be fulfilled?'* (Matthew 26:52–54). Rather, Jesus told the disciples to expect to suffer personal injury and humiliation without resistance or resentment, even whilst he — and they — would engage in direct conflict, not only against the forces of Satan in the spiritual world but against the opposition of the Jewish religious leaders and, at times, the might of the Roman empire. Jesus exemplifies Kingdom ideals of righteousness and peace, to love enemies and resist revenge. Jesus's opposition to violence, however, is not against the prevention of wrong or the protection of those in need, but against personal insult and threat. When motivated by love for others, opposition and persuasion may necessitate force. Millar Burrows (1946) writes:

Both Old and New Testaments offer ground for assurance that any people or nation, however sinful, may by repentance and reformation find mercy and redemption, and any nation may be brought to destruction by corruption and injustice… The destruction of the world's peace, or of civilisation itself by nations which are ruled by hatred or greed, and do not desire peace or justice, must be prevented.

Burrows argues that like the people of the Old Testament, all nations must consider themselves to be responsible, not self-aggrandising, instruments of God, but must guard against the growth of international distrust and suspicion, relying on the Christian principle of love to work out the appropriate forms and methods for doing so. John Stott (1999) observes the following:

…the quest for peace is much more costly than appeasement. We admire the loyalty, self-sacrifice and courage of serving soldiers. Yet we must not glamorise or glorify war in itself…in some circumstances it may be defended as the lesser of two evils, but it could never be regarded by the Christian mind as more than a painful necessity in a fallen world.

2 The implications of modern warfare

However, the biblical concept of war against evil and the legitimacy of fighting in defence of right, even when tempered by a rejection of violent retaliation, could not take into consideration the extent to which human power to destroy the human race and the world would grow. Whilst in conventional warfare there was a real possibility of controls and limits and it was essentially (although since the First World War, not exclusively) an engagement between armies, modern warfare has changed the parameters considerably. War now involves whole civilisations and the whole planet, which can be destroyed many times over by the weaponry available to almost all governments and military powers. Between 1945 and 1985 there were 80 wars, including civil and guerrilla wars, and even after the end of the Cold War — when it was estimated that the superpowers possessed a combined total of 50,000 nuclear warheads — the nations of the world still possess vast amounts of nuclear weaponry. The devastation caused by the attacks on Hiroshima and Nagasaki was the result of two relatively small explosions, and the short- and long-term effects of a large attack are beyond calculation. But the nuclear threat, serious though it is, is not the only worrying implication of modern warfare and our attitude to war. Arms expenditure is astronomically high and the effects of landmines, especially on the already poor and destitute, have been given wide publicity before and after the death of Princess Diana.

Nevertheless, since the Second World War there has perhaps been something of a change in the public consciousness concerning war. Nina Rosenstand (2000) observes that wartime stories with moral lessons were very common in the past, in a time when to die for one's country was a heroic and valuable sacrifice. However, we now belong to an age in which marching off to war is no longer seen as glamorous, and it is important to distinguish between the glory of war per se, and honourable wartime conduct. Rosenstand argues that even though the concept of war as the fulfilment of manly values vanished with the end of the First World War, the concept of honour in war is still important:

Although war is, for most people, the last moral option for dealing with conflict (and no moral option at all for pacifists), we can still talk about the moral conduct of the soldier… Even in stories with an anti-war message, the honour, decency and heroism of the characters are emphasised by being contrasted with the meaninglessness of war.

3 Just war theories

For all its talk of war and the appropriate response to violence, threat and evil, the Bible still does not settle the central question of whether a religious believer should participate in warfare. Whilst the church's view has been that it may be a proper duty for a Christian to fight for justice, pacifism has been a significant enough minority view for it to be taken seriously, and the right to conscientious objection is recognised by many nations. The problem is not just theoretical. The early church adopted the principle of non-retaliation and absolute or total pacifism, based on the teaching of Jesus: *'Do not resist one who is evil. But if anyone strikes you on the right cheek, turn to him the other also…'* (Matthew 5:39). However, a hundred years after Christianity had become the official religion of Rome, the empire believed that the reluctance of Christians to fight was weakening their defences. Augustine responded with the just war theory, which consists of nine principles, six concerning the beginning of war (***jus ad bellum***) and three, its conduct (***jus in bello***). The theory recognises that whilst life is sacred, it may, at times, be taken in order to protect or defend the lives of others, and that the divine cause of justice may be related to political concerns which, without glorifying it, nevertheless necessitate war.

Resort to war: *jus ad bellum*

+ War must be fought for a **just cause** — to save life or protect human rights; to secure justice, remedy injustice; it must be defensive, not aggressive. The principle of the theory, however, is not to justify all wars and it should be recognised that there are times when the potential cost of war, in terms of lives lost and the long- and short-term effects on the community, may require that some injustices be left unremedied. Discretion still remains the better part of valour. The concept of defensive war as just is problematic, however, since it can lead to the assumption that the defender is always right and that the aggressor always wrong, and raises the question of when intervention in an unjust situation (e.g. Saddam Hussein's regime in Iraq) would be considered technically aggressive, and yet justifiable.
+ War must be declared by a **competent authority**. In most cases, the government would be the legitimate authority to declare war, although in the Islamic concept of *jihad*, the legitimate authority is that of a religious leader.
+ There must be **comparison of justice** on both sides. This is, of course, difficult to achieve, since both sides will inevitably maintain that they are fighting a just cause.
+ There must be **right intention**, which must be as just as its cause, i.e. not with the deliberate intention of assassinating a country's leader and not undertaken in a spirit of hatred or revenge.
+ It must be a **last resort**, after all negotiation, arbitration and non-military sanctions have failed.
+ There should be a **reasonable likelihood of success**, so that its outcome results in a better state of affairs than would otherwise prevail.

Conduct in war: *jus in bello*

+ There should be a **reasonable proportion** between the **injustice being fought** and the **suffering inflicted** by war. The cause of justice must not be upheld by unjust means, which would include inflicting suffering on those the war was intending to protect.
+ **Proportionality** must be exercised, i.e. the use of armaments must be proportional to the threat and only minimum force should be used.
+ Warfare must be **discriminate** — that is, civilians must be protected as far as possible, and should not be direct targets. This is, of course, impossible to preserve entirely, but the principle is that the intentional killing of civilians be prohibited. Furthermore, it is difficult to make a precise distinction between combatants and non-combatants, since many civilians work directly in support of the war effort, even while they may not be engaged in conflict. The use of nuclear weapons renders discrimination impossible.

Clearly then, the principles of the just war theory have come under considerable criticism, not least from those who maintain that it is an impractical approach to warfare in the modern age. The theory is just that — a theory — and does not guarantee that it will be appropriately applied or that it will necessarily be applicable to all circumstances. Furthermore, the theory can be applied to any war to make it *appear* to be just, since both sides will apply it in such a way that their claim to justice is legitimate, and yet both claims cannot surely be equally valid.

As discussed above, the reality of nuclear war brings an entirely new dimension to the ethics of warfare, and the existence and use of nuclear arms go way beyond the conditions of warfare that were envisaged by Augustine. Modern weapons are capable of destroying the whole of human civilisation, and attempts to refine attacks to hit only military targets are open to human error. In a nuclear age, therefore, religious believers may feel that they have no option but to revert to pacifism rather than risk the escalation of a war that originally appeared to be containable. For those who hold that the principle of the sanctity of life demands that all deliberate acts of killing — including those in war — are forbidden, the just war theory can never legitimise military action, which is nothing more than state-approved and state-sponsored murder.

3 Pacifism

Pacifists maintain that early Christian pacifists perceived war to be incompatible with their Christian obedience; the requirement to love our enemy is absolute and the authority and function of the state is incompatible with this. **Absolute** or **total pacifism** therefore allows them no engagement in military activity, even if it is allegedly just. Although it is not the official stance of many denominations, notable exceptions include Quakers, Mennonites and Amish, the 'Peace Churches' who adopted the position held by the 'Radical Reformers' and Anabaptists of the sixteenth century.

The key to pacifism is commonly rooted in the Sermon on the Mount (Matthew 5:38–48), which is considered normative for all people and governments. Disciples are not to resist evil people, but to turn the other cheek, love their enemies, pray for their persecutors, and give up their right to *lex talionis* — justifiable and limited retribution for injustice. Jesus is presented as the model of this stance, resisting neither betrayal nor arrest, trial nor crucifixion, and forbidding his disciples to fight on his behalf. He was the innocent martyr, *'led like the lamb to the slaughter, and as a sheep before her shearers is silent, so he did not open his mouth'* (Isaiah 53:7). On the cross he prayed for those who crucified him and brought a criminal into the kingdom of heaven. He refused to rebel against the occupying Roman power, and did not advocate tax avoidance or civil disobedience. In Romans 13, Paul teaches that the state should be respected as the legitimate bearer of God's authority to rule, and that rebellion against the state is disobedience to God. He proposed that in dealings in general with the world, Christians should meet their enemies not with violence but with kindness, and so *'heap burning coals upon their heads'*, whilst respecting the legitimacy of the ruling authority to punish evil-doers.

The principles of absolute pacifism have been at the heart of the Peace Churches since the 1500s. Conrad Grebel, a leader of the Swiss Brethren, said in 1524: *'True Christians use neither worldly sword nor engage in war, since among them taking human life has*

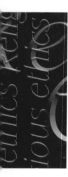

ceased entirely, for we are no longer under the Old Covenant... The Gospel and those who accept it are not to be protected with the sword, neither should they thus protect themselves.' George Fox, the founder of Quakerism, alluding to James 4:1ff, claimed in the mid-seventeenth century that *'I lived in the virtue of that life and power that took away the occasion of all wars and I knew from whence all wars did rise, from the lust, according to James's doctrine'.* The Peace Churches covenanted to settle disputes by practising the principles laid out in Matthew 18:15–19 — non-violent resolution of disagreements through peaceful confrontation and negotiation.

Reinhold Niebuhr criticised the naivety of the absolute pacifist stance as neglecting the equally important biblical principles of justice and the wrath of God whilst over-emphasising peace and reconciliation. He argued that pacifists essentially shirk their responsibility for striving for justice and are sometimes guilty, therefore, of accepting tyranny and oppression rather than fighting against evil.

Those who take the view that violent struggle for justice is sometimes legitimate, but maintain that the sanctions which applied to past wars can no longer be applicable in modern warfare, adopt **relative**, **selective** or **nuclear pacifism**. The biblical principle at stake is that of the *'shedding of innocent blood'* (Genesis 9:4, Leviticus 17:11). This distinction was made abundantly clear throughout the Old Testament, and both Judas and Pilate in Matthew's Passion Narrative echo the abhorrence of being guilty of shedding innocent blood. The message is that the authority that God has given to the legitimate rulers of the state is limited and must only be used to protect civilians and to bring about a just end by just means. Discrimination and proportionality are key concerns for the relative pacifist. The Second Vatican Council recognised that it was necessary to take a fresh appraisal of the just war theory in a nuclear age, since conventional approaches to war were not compatible with modern weapons of warfare, and declared: *'Any act of war aimed indiscriminately at the destruction of entire cities or of extensive areas along with their population is a crime against God and man himself.'* In a similar vein, the Church of England's unofficial report, *The Church and the Bomb*, concluded: *'...the use of nuclear weapons cannot be justified. Such weapons cannot be used without harming non-combatants, and could never be proportionate to the just cause and aim of war... In our view the cause of right cannot be upheld by fighting a nuclear war'* (cited by Stott, 1999).

In the Sermon on the Mount, Jesus is attributed as promising blessing on peacemakers, who will inherit the Kingdom of God (5:10–12). Peacemaking is a divine activity which God's people are called to emulate. John Stott proposes that Christian peacemakers should pray, set an example as 'a community of peace', promote public debate on issues of peace and war, and maintain a confident stance that peace is a realistic and desirable goal.

Summary

- The primary function of the state is to preserve security, and for the people of the Old Testament this was promised by Yahweh as a reward for fidelity to his covenant. War against pagan nations that violated God's standard of justice was required by God, but it was limited in what it could achieve when rooted in human greed. All legitimate biblical conflict anticipates or participates in the eschatological battle between God and Satan. Jesus exemplifies Kingdom ideals of righteousness and peace, whilst engaging in spiritual warfare.

- **Modern warfare** — poses problems for the believer who attempts to establish whether it can ever be legitimate to engage in war: nuclear weapons, expenditure on arms, and the conflict between duty and glorification of war.
- **Just war theories** — attempt to provide a basis from which a Christian can decide when it is legitimate to take up arms. Conditions govern the declaration of resort to war, and its conduct and outcome all may be criticised for attempting to justify the unjustifiable and as invalid in an age of modern warfare.
- **Pacifism** — modelled on Jesus's teaching on non-retaliation (Matthew 5:38–48) and his own attitude to his opponents. But absolute pacifism may neglect the biblical principle of justice. Relative, selective or nuclear pacifism rejects use of nuclear arms as inevitably indiscriminate and disproportionate.
- The goal of the religious believer should ultimately be to promote peace and reconciliation, and to set an example in non-violent resolution of conflict.

Exam watch

Most questions on war ask about the just war theory, but even if your examination board does not ask specifically about more general issues of war, peace and the implications of war, you should bear in mind that these all underpin approaches to the just war. Show that you have a wider knowledge than the conditions of the just war, which can make for a very boring essay, and make sure that you can critically evaluate the various positions on war which may be adopted by a religious believer.

Review questions

1 (a) Examine the conditions for war laid down by the just war theory.
  (b) Analyse the view that fulfilment of these conditions can never be sufficient justification for war.
2 *'All religious believers should aim for peace above all else.'* Examine this claim and consider why a religious believer might argue that sometimes peace is worth sacrificing in the fight against injustice.
3 Can nuclear war ever be justified?

B The environment and human need

(**Note**: The topics covered in sections B, C and D — 'The environment and human need', 'Justice, law and human rights' and 'Financial and business ethics' — are closely interrelated and it is strongly recommended that you study them all, even if your specification only singles out one or two for examination purposes. Some of the concepts are so closely intertwined that you will learn more about each of the three topics from a study of the others.)

1 Poverty and the allocation of resources

One of the concerns of those who care about the environment is wastefulness. Aware that the earth's resources are limited, environmentalists, religious or not, believe that we should look after them carefully, avoiding waste, encouraging reuse and discouraging excess. However, another reason for doing something about wastefulness is to show solidarity with the poor. Not only are the earth's resources finite, they are inevitably unequally distributed and it is arguably impossible for this inequality to be balanced fairly. Religious believers may feel a special impetus to address this issue as best they can, and Christians may particularly feel that it is part of their calling to discipleship — following Jesus in his own work in caring for the poor and outcast.

There can be no one definition of poverty since it encompasses many situations and variables. Media coverage ensures that we are aware of natural disaster and the effects of war and political corruption in the 'Two-thirds World', but poverty is also an issue in the developed world: unemployment, homelessness and destitution are prevalent in the most sophisticated societies. However, in its simplest form, poverty could be defined as a lack of financial resources rendering an individual, community or nation unable to meet the needs basic for survival. Poverty can be relative, however; if we cannot afford whatever we deem necessary for survival, we may consider ourselves or others to be victims of poverty. Poverty can also be hidden, since it is possible to maintain an outwardly affluent lifestyle whilst having very few readily available resources. The poor are therefore not simply those who fall below a certain level of subsistence. Those whose quality of life falls below that of others can suffer great hardship, such as those in the developed world who may have food and shelter but who suffer from unemployment. In the developing world, poverty may appear to be more brutal, where people are totally excluded from education and welfare and can barely scrape enough of a living to eat.

John Stott (1999) draws attention to the fact that poverty has not been eliminated in the developed Western world, observing that in 1995 9.7 million people in the UK lived below the poverty line, and 13.8% of the US population. Stott also explores the question of who, in religious terms, are the poor? He identifies three categories of poverty: the **indigent poor** — those who are economically deprived; the **powerless poor** — those who suffer social or political oppression; and the **humble poor** — those who are dependent upon God. The first category of poverty, with which we are most concerned in this chapter, may, in some cases, be due to the sin or laziness of the individual, but is usually an involuntary evil within society which religious believers should seek to eliminate. In the Old Testament, the people of Israel were instructed to be compassionate and generous in providing for the indigent poor — employers were to pay wages promptly, and farmers were not to farm to the very edges of their fields but to leave the remnants of their crop for the poor — especially widows and orphans. Every seventh year the field was to remain unharvested so the poor could help themselves to what grew naturally.

The Old Testament writers were certainly interested in freedom from want and hardship. The laws reflect a simple, democratic, agricultural society that confronted real problems when the nation developed politically and economically. Under the reign of Solomon, the gap between rich and poor grew wider and the biblical writers adopted a different view of wealth. It was no longer seen as a reward for righteousness, but carried with it the danger of spiritual and moral corruption. The prophets are harsh in their condemnation of the selfish, idle rich, who ignore the needs of the poor. Though charity was still encouraged, the emphasis of the biblical writers was increasingly on the demand for justice and the establishment of an ideal and equal social order.

The Old Testament writers showed a lively interest in economic and property matters. Laws regarding loans, interest and theft guarded property, and the right to private ownership was defended. Before settlement in Canaan, the main concern of the semi-nomad was for access to water and pasture — an issue which could become distinctly contentious, as the account of the separation of Lot and Abraham indicates (Genesis 13) — but once in the promised land, issues of resources and ownership revolved around the welfare of the whole community and inheritance. Slavery was recognised as customary, although the Hebrew slave, who could be forced to remain in his master's household for only six years, occupied a more favourable position than the foreign slave who had been acquired by capture or purchase. The New Testament also takes slavery for granted, and because Paul was unconcerned whether a disciple was a freeman or a slave, he told slaves to obey their masters and not to seek freedom unless it was offered (Colossians 3:22f). The biblical writers frequently expressed a concern for the rights of labourers and those who are dependent on fair treatment from employers.

Jesus conspicuously adopted the Old Testament principle of care and compassion for the poor and destitute, but he made no effort to improve or revolutionise economic conditions. On the other hand, he did teach that in the Kingdom of God, values would be reversed in a startlingly new way, and those who had been perceived on earth as rich and privileged would find themselves giving way to those who had been poor and powerless. Jesus was prepared to adopt this for himself — the incarnate deity who laid aside his divinity to die for humanity (Philippians 2:6–11) — and his ministry is the embodiment of the principle that *everyone who exalts himself will be humbled, and he who humbles himself will be exalted* (Luke 18:14).

Jesus frequently addresses issues of personal wealth, although his advice to the rich man to sell all his goods and give the proceeds to the poor (Mark 10:17–22&//s) does not seem to be a universal requirement. What *is* required of a disciple is a more general readiness to make whatever sacrifice is required, and none of the New Testament writers champion the poor in the way that the Old Testament writers did. Interestingly, the communal lifestyle of the early church in Jerusalem, whereby its members pooled their resources for the well-being of the whole community, despite winning admiration from observers (Acts 4:32–37) does not seem to have become the norm:

Economic democracy as a pattern of industrial and social organisation is not to be found in the Bible, but its basis is given in the conviction of the worth and rights of every man, from peasant to king... It is based on a clear recognition of the common nature and capacities of man, independent of race or sex or any accident of political, economic or social status.

(Burrows, 1946)

Poverty, prosperity and stewardship

The New Testament presents Jesus as encouraging disciples to adopt simple lifestyles that reflect empathy with the poor. However, the Christian attitude to poverty changed drastically in the nineteenth century, when the view that 'the poor are always with you' was aggressively challenged by the emerging social and political forces of communism and socialism. No longer *'the rich man in castle, the poor man at his gate, God made them high and lowly and ordered their estate'*, poverty was seen as something to be fought and not simply accepted. The evangelical movement was responsible for a surge of social action directed against slavery and slum conditions and towards prison reform and education, and in the twentieth century the Christian church continued to respond positively to the needs of the poor. Mother Teresa was quoted as saying *'Poverty is not made by God. Poverty is made by me and you'*, although her example of active involvement with the poor and destitute is, obviously, not exclusive to Christianity.

John Stott observes that there are three responses that religious believers can make to poverty: become poor, stay rich, or be generous and contented. Although there may be arguments that some believers are called to become poor in solidarity with the poor, this is not a realistic option for all believers to take, for it would remove from society far too many of its economy-boosting workers and entrepreneurs. Although the example of Jesus is often cited as a model of 'becoming poor', Martin Hengel (1975) writes: *'Jesus himself did not come from the proletariat of day-labourers and landless tenants, but from the middle class of Galilee, the skilled workers'*; and Stott comments that the women who followed Jesus were evidently able to provide well for his needs.

The second option — to stay rich — is a characteristic of 'prosperity teaching', the claim that those who truly believe will receive financial blessings as a sign of God's favour. This is a feature of the preaching of some well-known evangelists, who overlook the biblical view that true riches go way beyond material possessions. Keith Tondeur (1996b) writes: *'Nowhere in the Bible are we told to give so that we can gain earthly treasures in return. Giving is to be motivated by an unselfish heart that is willing to share unconditionally, regardless of monetary return'*. Stott claims that there are two primary dangers inherent in religious believers conspicuously 'staying rich' — pride and materialism, attitudes which are contrary to the teaching of both Old and New Testaments. (For more on the topic of materialism or consumerism, see pp. 214–215.)

The third option — be generous and contented — is the option that Stott argues is the most appropriate Christian response to poverty. It is closely associated with 'living simply', a lifestyle which concentrates on need rather than want, and on seeing and responding to the needs of others. Tondeur links this too with stewardship — the careful and responsible use of God-given resources. He analyses three approaches to wealth and resources in a useful table.

	Poverty	Prosperity	Stewardship
Possessions are:	Evil	A right	A responsibility
I work to:	Cover basic need	Get rich	Serve Christ
Godly people are:	Poor	Rich	Faithful
Ungodly people are:	Rich	Poor	Faithless
I give:	Because I must	To gain	Because I love God
My spending is:	Without gratitude	Carefree and careless	Prayerful and responsible

(Adapted from Tondeur, 1996b)

2 Conservation

The notion of stewardship does not belong only to material possessions owned by human beings, but to the care and preservation of the natural order and the use that is made of it. The principle of stewardship is that everything comes from God as a gift — personal resources of time, talents and money, as well as the created order — and is to be administered and managed faithfully and responsibly by humanity. Humans are responsible for the use they make of property which is not their own, and failure to recognise this divine ownership is an act of rebellious disobedience. This concept is firmly rooted in the creation narratives of Genesis:

÷ '"*Be fruitful and multiply, and fill the earth and subdue it; and have dominion over the fish of the sea and over the birds of the air and over every living thing that moves upon the earth". And God said, "Behold, I have given you every plant yielding seed which is upon the face of all the earth, and every tree with seed in its fruit; you shall have them for food"*' (Genesis 1:28–29).

÷ '*And the Lord God took the man and put him in the garden of Eden to till it and keep it.*' (Genesis 2:15).

÷ '*And to Adam he said, "...cursed is the ground because of you; in toil you shall eat of it all the days of your life; thorns and thistles it shall bring forth to you; and you shall eat the plants of the field"*' (Genesis 3:17–18).

÷ '*The fear and dread of you shall be upon every beast of the earth, and upon every bird of the air, upon everything that creeps on the ground and all the fish of the sea; into your hand they are delivered*' (Genesis 9:2).

The early chapters of Genesis set out the nature of the relationship between humans and the rest of the created order, as the biblical writers perceived it. Creation is for the benefit of human beings, graciously given to them by God, and whilst they are given the privilege of 'dominion' over creation, they are given the responsibility of 'tilling and keeping' it. The concept of stewardship is vital in these passages — humans are put in a position of trust and responsibility for creation and as such they are allowed to share in God's creative work. If this is so, then the preservation, care and conservation of the environment must be a matter of ethical and spiritual concern for religious believers.

Green issues are prevalent in politics, economics, the media and industry, and so concern for the environment is certainly not an exclusively religious issue. In fact, for some religious believers concern for the natural environment should be tempered with caution, lest it become worship of the natural world for its own sake. The extremes of environmental issues too can become closely connected with violence and anarchy, which lose sight of the essential concern to preserve the natural order, and may become confused with political agendas. Religious believers will be concerned to find a balance between conveying the important message that the environment is a gift from God to humanity, and the suggestion that the environment has value aside from any religious perspectives.

Environmental issues cover a range of specific concerns:

÷ Population growth — the ever-increasing population makes correspondingly increasing demands on food resources that are invariably unequally distributed.

- ✢ Depletion of resources — fossil fuels cannot be recycled and cannot be produced by humans and are thus finite. The pollution of the air and essential environments upon which other creatures depend, and the consistent depletion of the natural order, along with overfishing and deforestation, are all matters of concern.
- ✢ Technological advancement — which makes increasing demands on resources and energy.
- ✢ The atmosphere — the so-called 'greenhouse effect', caused by the trapping of solar heat, will conceivably lead to the melting of the polar ice caps and to serious flooding.

Although these issues are usually spoken of with concern, it is possible to adopt an ethical perspective of **evolutionary humanism**, which views them as an inevitable and not altogether undesirable consequence of the evolution of the human species. Anthony Flew discusses this problem in *Evolutionary Ethics*, identifying the fundamental dilemma of balancing the development of a complex species such as human beings (a matter of fact) with the dangers and benefits of progress, which is a value judgment. **Technological pragmatism** takes an anthropocentric view, which considers that all human technological advances are of primary value, and are subservient to the management of the natural order.

However, more conservative thinkers focus on the question 'To whom does the earth belong?' and take their answer from the Psalms — '*The earth is the Lord's, and everything in it*' (Psalm 24:1); '*The highest heavens belong to God, but the earth he has given to man*' (Psalm 115:16). In a sense, therefore, God is the landlord, but human beings are the tenants with responsibility to care for the landlord's property during the period of their lease on it.

The dominion humans are called to exercise is, however, one that can only be exercised in co-operation with nature. Humans are still dependent on the climate and atmosphere, and the punishments inflicted on them after the fall indicate that nature will not always support their best endeavours. Humans cultivate what is natural; they do not create it or have ultimate power over it. If humanity were to be wiped out tomorrow, the natural order would continue. Humans are also dependent on God to 'give the increase', and the autumn tradition of harvest festival acknowledges that a fruitful harvest is not down to human input alone. Dominion should not become domination and the earth's resources belong to humans for the common good and not for the good only of those who are able to exercise the greatest control.

Summary

- Ethical concerns about the **allocation of resources** focus on the fact that they are not infinite and are unequally distributed. **Poverty** is wide-ranging and diverse, and is a problem that does not only concern the developing world. Who are the poor? The indigent poor (the economically deprived) are championed by the Old Testament writers and the ideal society is envisaged to be one that seeks to meet their needs. Ownership of land and property are rights of free men, but slavery is taken for granted. Jesus's teaching does not seek to revolutionise earthly economies but anticipates reversal of values in the kingdom of God. Giving up wealth is not a requirement of discipleship, though a preparedness to do so is. There are three options for a religious approach to wealth: prosperity, poverty and stewardship (Tondeur); stay rich, become poor, be generous and content (Stott). The latter in each case is the ideal approach.

■ **Conservation** — stewardship of the earth's resources is central to a theocentric view of creation and humanity's relationship with God. Creation establishes a relationship of creativity, fruitfulness, stewardship and dominion. Environmental issues — especially those concerning the depletion of natural resources — are therefore important for religious ethicists, although arguably they are the natural and inevitable outcome of the evolutionary progress of human beings.

Exam watch

The key warning here is 'No GCSE-level answers'. There is a real danger of low-level preaching when dealing with these issues, and of essays full of vague statements such as 'Jesus told us to help the poor because we should all be kind to one another'. You need to be able to show informed and wide-ranging knowledge of the issues involved, including clearly identifiable biblical evidence, scholarship and an understanding of the broader ethical and social issues arising.

Review questions

1 *'There should be no rich Christians whilst there is poverty in the world.'* Examine and evaluate this claim.

2 What problems are raised for religious believers by the pollution and depletion of the natural environment?

C Justice, law and human rights

1 Justice

The concept of justice is a complex one, as there are a number of ways in which it can be legitimately interpreted. Horner and Westacott (2000) offer a definition of a just society that provides a useful starting point: *'Any society that I would want to live in must prize individual freedom, but not to the exclusion of social responsibility or of justice. Justice is fairness, equal opportunities for all to make something of their lives, and a way back from the deaths for those who fail'.*

This view of justice is often associated with social democracy, which aims to establish a society that promotes and provides for an equality of liberty. However, even if we settle on a definition of justice as rooted in equality, we need then to establish what we mean by equality. Augustine claimed: *'When you don't ask me, I know what it is; when you ask me, I don't know. Equality must be something other than treating everyone in the same way since everyone is different.'* The notion of equality may be divided into different categories:

÷ **Fundamental equality** — all people should be treated as equals by their government and by their legal systems, with no special privileges but an entitlement to respect and consideration as human beings.

- **Social equality** — formal rights such as the right to vote and to stand for public office.
- **Equal treatment for equals** — described in Aristotle's book *Poetics*. He speaks of justice as treating people of the same group in the same way. This is generally assumed to be an elitist principle, with no intention to recognise equality as a fundamental human right.
- **Treat equals equally and unequals unequally** — equals are people in the same situation under the same circumstances. Someone in a different situation is an unequal, who may need special help or punishment depending on the circumstances and their actions in those circumstances. This principle recognises that sometimes we have special needs or we may transgress and deserve special treatment. Equality therefore does not imply sameness.

For religious believers the concept of equality is often supported by reference to the creation narrative. Man and woman are made in the image of God (Genesis 1:28), which remains the key principle on which human life is valued. Interestingly, there is no talk of the subordination of women to men until after the fall, when it appears to be one of the punishments incurred for rebelling against God: '*Your desire shall be for your husband and he shall rule over you*' (Genesis 3:16).

Thomas Nagel (1987) observes that despite our concern for equality as the basis for a just society, the world is full of inequalities. Some of these are a matter of luck — we are not responsible for the social or economic circumstances we are born into, or for the natural talents with which we may have been equipped. Other inequalities are deliberately imposed: racial and sexual discrimination, for example, are evidently unfair and it is reasonable to expect that the government enforce measures to overcome them by instituting legislation or sanctions. But the inequalities which arise as a matter of birth or circumstances are another matter — there will always be people are wealthier, people who are more talented, and people who rise to the top in a competitive system. The social system may advocate **equality of opportunity** but **inequality of result** is inevitable, although these inequalities are the outcome of choices and actions which in themselves are not wrong. These inequalities cannot be overcome without enormous implications for the freedom of individuals in society. If we remove the scope for success and failure, we interfere in human freedom to make the best of the opportunities, and that freedom is inherently valuable even if some people *will* fail.

Objections to this system arise out of a sense that it is unfair that some people will not succeed because they suffer disadvantages which are not their fault. Some people are born into rich families, they inherit vast sums of money, or 'marry well'; some go to good schools and graduate from prestigious universities, and receive the opportunity to develop talents and skills that were identified and cultivated by helpful and supportive teachers and parents. Essentially, these inequalities cannot be removed from the system, but we might reasonably expect governments to operate schemes which attempt to balance them out, without imposing on individual freedom. The system of taxation is such a case. By not letting the wealthy keep all their money, the government can try to attack inequality directly, using tax money to provide some of the basics of welfare and education that the less well-off lack. Taxation diminishes the freedom of the rich to dispose of all their wealth as they choose, without removing that freedom completely. And although some may argue that the system of taxation itself imposes unfair penalties on those who have worked hard for their wealth, the alternative — a centrally controlled economy in which everyone is paid the same for doing a job assigned to him or her by a central authority — is even less desirable. **Redistributive taxation** allows the government to interfere in what people do, within reasonable limits, because it contributes to overall equality.

In his book *Justice that Restores*, Charles Colson (2000) identifies another kind of justice which the religious and moral philosopher needs to understand — criminal justice. He writes:

The primary purpose of criminal justice is to preserve order with the minimum infraction of individual liberty. Accomplishing this requires a system of law that people can agree on and that therefore possesses not just power but authority. It also requires moral standards, commonly accepted, that serve as voluntary restraints and inform conscience; an accepted understanding of what is due to — and required from — each citizen. Finally, criminal justice requires a just means to restore the domestic order when it has broken down, and a system of punishment that is redemptive.

Colson argues that in the last decade of the twentieth century there was such a loss of regard for human life and dignity that the criminal justice system now needs to be radically rethought. The first step in this is to think again about what justice and a just society is. He proposes that at the very least it is characterised by people living together in harmony and security. Justice is essential for unity, and a just system has political structures that ensure that citizens can live together in peace. In *Republic*, Plato dismissed the accepted view that justice was what is in the interest of the stronger party, and instead proposed that it is an objective, knowable reality, on which the concept of law rests. Colson writes: '*A society has a foundation for justice when it observes a rule of law grounded in objective truth*'. When the law loses its authority in society, the notion of justice is also diminished and can be taken over by pressure groups, terrorists and collectives. The law must be recognisably a source of moral authority which, Colson argues, should reflect the moral traditions '*and customs of people infused with the Spirit of Christ*'. It should not be relativist, or human rights will not be protected, and without an objective standard of justice, peace will never be able to prevail and order will not be established. Colson sees only one way of establishing such a system of justice: '*It should become obvious that only a biblical worldview can produce true justice. For justice is impossible without the rule of law; and the rule of law is impossible without transcendent authority*'.

2 Rights

If people are capable of interaction with others, capable of making choices and being responsible for the consequences of their choices, then they are moral agents. Being a person also entails certain duties and privileges — things one ought to do (responsibilities or duties) and ought to receive (rights). Rights can be defined as '*powers or privileges which are so justly claimed that they must not be infringed or suspended*' (Macquarrie and Childress (eds), 1990). They belong to individuals absolutely, and cannot be taken away; they are basic and inviolable and are paramount even if they conflict with the more general welfare of society. Rights and duties are complementary, however, since we have a duty to respect the rights of others, as we expect our own rights to be respected. Hence, our rights are relative in that we, as individuals, can only exercise them in total freedom if we are not causing harm to others or violating their rights in the process. In the modern Western world we tend to assume that every individual has inalienable rights, although we still encounter enormous problems with discrimination and bigotry against those on the fringes of society or in minority groups.

Genesis 1:27–28 asserts that God created humans in his image to *'fill the earth and subdue it'*. John Stott argues that three essential relationships based on rights and duties were established at creation:

+ Humanity's relationship with God — the rights and responsibilities to worship. Humans, created in God's image, share a different relationship with the creator than does the rest of creation, and are placed in such a position as to be able to love and serve God, obey his commands and understand his will. From this comes the right to profess and practise religion, thought and speech.
+ Inter-human relationships — the rights and responsibilities of fellowship. In relationship with one another, humans express their right to marriage and family, peaceful assembly, and to receive respect, irrespective of age, sex, race or rank.
+ Humanity's relationship with the earth — the rights and responsibilities of stewardship.

In relationship to the earth, God has given humans the right to share the world's resources and to be free from poverty, hunger and disease. In all three cases, humans should enjoy the dignity of being human, having been created in God's image and having a unique relationship with each other and the earth.

This is a distinctively Christian perspective on rights and duties, however, and would not be considered by all to be a universal approach. Ethicists are concerned with the moral issues raised by political and civil rights. Political rights concern the relationship between the individual and the government, and are central to a democratic society. Civil rights are the fundamental rights we have to be treated equally in relation to the law, whether it concerns our religious freedom, ownership of property, education or privacy.

There are essentially six theoretical bases on which the concept of rights is established:

+ **Divine rights** — rights given by God and which can only be removed by rebelling against the divinely established order.
+ **Natural rights** — duties that are rooted in human nature and take precedence over those required by the law. If humans hold rights simply by virtue of being human, then they are beyond the control of the government. However, we need to account for the disagreements that exist over exactly what constitute natural rights.
+ **Contract** — society agrees mutually to limit the rights of individuals to ensure an ordered society. Under a **social contract**, rights derive from political decisions or conventions rather than from nature, and universal agreement on what constitutes rights and who should bear them is almost impossible to achieve.

* **Utilitarian** — respecting the rights of others in the interest of having your own similarly respected.
* **Totalitarian** — rights can be exercised as long as the government permits them to be exercised.

A key concern in all this is whether and when our rights and liberties can be or ought to be infringed. The *Universal Declaration on Human Rights* (1948) recognises that human rights:

* must be accepted and acted upon
* are possessed by all human beings
* are fundamental to all human life
* must be enforced by any means possible
* may serve to constrain the actions of others
* in some cases cannot be forfeited

However, Ronald Dworkin suggests that we should distinguish between **basic liberties**, which cannot be infringed except in cases that would cause serious harm to individuals, and **general liberties** which can be forfeited in the interests of society's more general welfare.

The Bible commands humans to love God and to love our neighbours, but says nothing about defending our personal rights. Rather, it emphasises that our responsibility is to secure the rights of others. Philippians 2:6–7 suggests that Jesus renounced his right to divine honour while on earth, whilst Paul is proud to lay aside his rights as an Apostle to marriage and to be supported by the Christian community (1 Corinthians 9). He expects the Corinthian Christians to lay aside their own right to pursue legal action against each other (1 Corinthians 6), whilst Matthew 5:38–42 instructs Christians to renounce the right to retaliation under the law (the principle of *lex talionis*) and Romans 12:19 commands them to leave judgment to God.

3 Authority and law

It is the strongest who rule. Whatever anyone says, it is the ability to use force that compels obedience. Look at history: when power fails the state collapses.

(Horner and Westacott, 2000)

Justice and human rights will have little meaning if the governing body of society, whether it be a country or community, cannot ensure that its laws are respected by its citizens. For this to be the case, the state must be seen to have power that is sufficient to require compliance with its laws. Essentially, this means getting people to do what the state wants, and this can be achieved through sheer brute force. We can see that this has occurred often throughout history, although it is true to say that governments which rely on force and violence are rarely enduring. Society in general requires a more compelling and positive reason to obey the government, and most compelling perhaps is the conviction that it gives them more freedom and greater peace than they would otherwise have. A wise subject consents to accept the authority and power of the government in exchange for a degree of protection and security. The relationship is therefore mutual: society accepts the authority of its rulers who in turn know that this consent may be withdrawn, and it is in the rulers' interest to keep the citizens happy, maintaining the balance of power that they have tacitly agreed to.

People accept authority because they sense that without laws the community would suffer, and citizens enter into a social contract with their governing authority, understanding that they are, in the interests of society, diminishing their otherwise absolute freedom. This relationship is consensual, but it does imply obligation, since the government effectively promises to fulfil the pledges made at the time of their election, while the act of voting is a promise of a kind to accept the authority of the government once in office.

This emphasises the importance of the notion of consent in the relationship between the legitimate government and the society that has consented to its authority. The state accepts a contract to deliver more freedom to its citizens than they previously enjoyed and to ensure that everyone is able to enjoy its benefits. Thus, the government accepts the authority to work for the common good, and society accepts the authority of the government to establish laws that will best enable that common good to be brought about. Society accepts a contract to obey those laws in the interest of the common good, acknowledging that law-breaking undermines the authority of law, social stability and general well-being *unless and except* there are exceptional circumstances in which breaking the law genuinely contributes to the common good more effectively than obeying it.

4 Punishment

Punishment is the intentional infliction of pain by a legal authority on those who have breached its standards of behaviour. It can be inflicted by parents, employers and private organisations, but ethical concerns are most often concerned with the infliction of punishment by the legal representatives of society for criminal activity. Punishment, or sanctions for infringements of the laws established by a legitimate authority, is an essential part of a system that takes seriously the notions of justice, rights, authority and law. However, the purpose of punishment must be clearly defined, and if it is to play a useful part in maintaining a just society, we must be sure that it is not going to lead to further, and perhaps greater, wrongs than those for which the punishment is being meted out. It is incumbent on society to ensure that forms of punishment do not impinge on the human rights of the offender. Punishment should be proportional, humane (an argument against capital punishment) and respectful of the equal dignity of all human beings. Four understandings of punishment are most common:

+ retribution
+ vengeance
+ rehabilitation
+ harm to reputation

Retribution stems from the notion of desert. Those who do wrong should bear the consequences of so doing. Retribution defines community values, asserts individual responsibility in the performance of free acts, satisfies the desire for redress, and vindicates the victims of crime. However, those who claim that education and rehabilitation are more effective ways to reinforce values oppose it. If lawbreakers are incapable of making a free choice to obey the law or to disobey it, then retributive punishment has no valuable purpose, but if they act freely then they must accept the responsibility that comes with that freedom.

Vengeance, like retribution, is a backward-looking theory, but whilst retribution is based on logic, vengeance is a more emotional response. It is usually carried out privately and may exceed the damage done by the criminal, whereas retribution works on the principle of *lex talionis* — a punishment that is in proportion to the crime committed.

Both retribution and vengeance focus on the crime and the criminal in order to punish the guilty. Forms of such punishment may include:

÷ harm to the body — corporal punishment and execution
÷ harm to property — seizing of goods or restriction of ownership, fines or restitution to the victim
÷ restriction of movement — house arrest, imprisonment, electronic tagging
÷ harm to reputation — public shaming in some way

Rehabilitation, the third approach to punishment, aims to change the offender's personality or circumstances so that they will not reoffend. This approach assumes that there will be programmes that encourage prisoners to change their lives and not return to crime on their release. Rehabilitation is usually associated with **incapacitation**, where the prisoner fulfils a social good whilst being kept off the streets. However, incapacitation without rehabilitation, and without hope, may simply serve to harden and demoralise prisoners further, and encourage them to return to crime on their release.

Finally, the **deterrence** theory maintains that sufficiently severe punishment will discourage future crimes and will make others think twice before following the criminal's example.

Rehabilitation and deterrence are forward-looking, aiming to improve the prisoner's circumstances and prospects for the future to discourage further criminal activity or to deter them, and others, from crime. However, many oppose these theories of punishment as well as the backward-looking approaches of retribution and vengeance, arguing that there is no evidence that such methods necessarily work any better than others which are more economically viable and which impose less on the offender. Furthermore, it is implicit when punishment is meted out that an offender has committed a crime as an autonomous moral agent, and limits are placed on the extent to which an individual can be punished if there is doubt as to their moral freedom through mental illness, coercion or other restrictions on their liberty.

Although the death penalty is rare in the West, it is still legal in some states of the USA. Whilst the Old Testament appears to sanction and use capital punishment, the teachings of Jesus (albeit indirectly) do not support it. Opponents of capital punishment stress the failure it represents in rehabilitating or deterring the offender, whilst supporters maintain that it is has a powerful deterrent effect on other would-be criminals. Although both Old and New Testaments cite examples of capital punishment (including the death of Jesus), Christians believe that the blood of Jesus is spilt to make any further bloodshed unnecessary, and in the confrontation with the Jewish leaders over the adulterous woman (John 8) Jesus does not appear to condone the practice.

On the other hand, the Law of Moses orders the death penalty for eighteen different offences, ranging from rape to rebellion against parents. Those who argue that the Bible represents unchanging moral standards would, technically, see no contradiction in continuing to impose the death penalty for these offences.

In *Justice that Restores*, Charles Colson (2000) presents a strong case for **restorative** or **relational justice** in response to the desperate plight of prisoners and prisons in the UK and USA. Restorative justice is based on the Hebrew principle of ***shalom*** — a state in which everything is well, complete and present, and which restores the relationships between God and man. He argues that when justice fails to achieve results it is because a vital element in the healing of relationships — which should be the aim of restorative justice — is missing or out of balance. From his own experience, and from years of working with the Prison Fellowship, Colson argues that the prison system has utterly failed, and that prisons are filled with many people who are not dangerous to society and are '*often hardened in their criminal disposition because of their experience*'. He proposes a radical overhaul of the system of justice which responds to God's love for humanity and community, and with the goal of establishing *shalom*. Colson offers practical suggestions for prison reform and reintegration of the criminal into the community, summing up with the observation: '*Central [to achieving this] is a criminal justice system that not only provides just deserts, but provides redemption as well — that recovers the wholeness of the community shattered by crime, a justice that restores*'.

Summary

- **Justice** — establishing a society in which equality of liberty is promoted and provided. Inequalities are inevitable, even if we aim to eliminate deliberate injustices, because despite equality of opportunity there is inequality of result. Taxation aims to redistribute resources more equally. **Criminal justice** aims to preserve order with the minimum of infraction of liberty. An objective system of justice based on a transcendent authority is the only true justice (Colson).
- **Rights** — privileges which cannot be infringed.
- **Duties** — responsibilities to others which complement our rights. Human rights are usually regarded as inalienable, but their precise nature is uncertain, and it is incumbent upon individuals to respect the rights of others, hence limiting their own rights.
- **Authority** — is accepted by a society under the rule of a government which has the power to require compliance with the law. Society and government enter into a social contract with the goal of bringing about the greatest good for all.
- **Punishment** — for infringing the laws established by legitimate authority. May take the form of retribution, vengeance, rehabilitation or deterrence. Restorative justice (Colson) aims to provide redemption and recover wholeness of the community and the individual.

Exam watch

Make sure that you can link these issues with ethical theories, especially deontology and utilitarianism. These are complex issues and you need to understand them well before you write an essay on them. Remember, too, that for a Religious Studies exam you need to make clear connections with religious and/or biblical views — otherwise it will turn into a politics or sociology essay.

Review questions

1 '*In a religious society, there would be no injustice.*' Do you agree? Examine this claim, exploring different points of view.

2 Examine and evaluate different theories of punishment. Which, if any, do you consider most likely to be effective?

3 Jeremy Bentham spoke of human rights as '*nonsense on stilts*'. What are the implications of adopting this position?

D Financial and business ethics

1 Finance and religious ethics

The relationship between religious belief and finance is one which can be traced back to the Bible, and covers virtually every aspect of humanity's relationship with money and with God. Religious ethicists focus on five key areas of finance:

÷ spending and consumerism
÷ borrowing, debt and gambling
÷ giving and tithing
÷ saving and investment
÷ the ethical use of money

Central to all of these areas is the belief that all human resources belong to God, who lends them out of his beneficence and love. Humans are called to exercise the responsibility of good stewardship over these resources, which they should recognise as still belonging ultimately to God. God may call humanity to surrender them at any time, and if an individual, corporation or nation has lost sight of the stewardship principle, they will be severely challenged by this call. The potential for humans to fail to establish a responsible balance between achieving the resources necessary for living and providing for those dependent upon them, and to become overly concerned with the quantity and quality of those resources, is clearly identified by the biblical writers. Both Old and New Testaments offer considerable warnings about the danger of overestimating the value of material goods and of preserving human life at the expense of spiritual development. The expectation upon traders and consumers is that they will respect the weak, worship God, shun immoral and fraudulent dealings and recognise their ultimate dependence on God.

Keith Tondeur (1996b) identifies four dangers of wealth for the religious believer: it separates people from each other; it makes them arrogant; it encourages them to forget God; and it makes it harder for them to trust in Jesus as saviour. He further proposes six principles that the Christian should observe in the attempt to avoid falling into the money-culture trap:

÷ Never say 'if only'.
÷ Do not compare your lifestyle to others or allow others to be influenced in their spending by your lifestyle.

- ✛ Submit all spending decisions to God.
- ✛ Attempt to live more simply.
- ✛ Recognise that money is a weapon in a spiritual battle.
- ✛ Do not conform to the world — i.e. value worldly standards above spiritual ones.

John Wesley, the great Methodist thinker, offered five reasons why Christians should not be able to afford anything other than the basic necessities:

- ✛ God is the true source of wealth.
- ✛ Christians must account to God for how they have used their money.
- ✛ Christians are stewards of God's money.
- ✛ God gives money to Christians to pass on to those who need it.
- ✛ The purchase of luxuries is the equivalent of throwing money away, and of taking food and clothes from those who need them.

These principles throw light on the reasons why religious ethicists are concerned about money, but they are not just shared by Christians or those with other religious motivations. Money and other resources can be tools for great good or great harm; they can enable societies and individuals to develop and to aid the development of others, or they can diminish human worth; they can liberate or imprison.

2 Spending and consumerism

In economic terms, consumerism refers to the using of goods, resources or services; ethically, it tends to be used to refer to the emergence of a society which is motivated by the ownership of goods and utilisation of resources beyond those required for human survival. The phrase 'conspicuous consumption' was first coined by Thorstein Veblen in the nineteenth century to describe the practice of buying and displaying expensive items to enhance social status, although it is commonly used to describe the emergence of a society whose values are focused on the marketplace. Whilst a free-market economy is desirable in many respects and reflects a respect for individual freedom, it can lead to loss of autonomy in other ways.

In the twenty-first century the rise of consumerism, or materialism, has led to the emergence of a vast range of consumer markets, responding to the increased spending power of society and to new sub-groups within society which in earlier generations had little force in the marketplace. Today, teenagers and even younger children influence the fashion, food and popular music markets more than ever before, and even more universal arenas, such as information technology and communications, are driven increasingly by the youth market as much as by commerce. Increased life spans mean that older generations have a longer consumer life, and better private pension and investment funds leave many with more money to spend on luxuries. The church is not untouched by consumerism, as the hugely profitable market for contemporary Christian literature, music, fashion and accessories illustrates.

For the religious ethicist this has had enormous implications for social, family and spiritual life. Competition between consumers leads to increased spending and, as Keith Tondeur (1996b) writes: *'Consumerism can be a hunger within us. The more we feed it the more it grows and the more hungry we become'*. Shopping has become a leisure pursuit rather than a chore or necessary evil: *'Not only is entertainment now something*

to buy rather than do, but buying itself has become entertainment. Shopping malls are theme parks for family outings. The effortless McDonald's culture of fast foods and false smiles epitomises the world of consumerism' (Atkinson and Field (eds), 1995).

The spiritual and ethical dangers of consumerism are considerable. First, it contributes to generating an increasingly unequal society as those with and those without the means to consume are sharply distinguished. People are encouraged to be integrated into the marketplace without being able to afford it, and the gap between rich and poor widens. Those unable to gain credit to enter the marketplace are marginalised, whilst those who are given credit facilities face the dangers of mounting debt.

Second, consumerism increases waste as the world's resources are depleted to meet consumer need. This goes starkly against the principles of responsible stewardship (see pp. 201–204) and encourages a culture of 'built-in obsolescence' whereby products are designed to have a limited life span, driving the consumer back to the marketplace. To object to waste of resources is not merely expressing a disapproval of how individuals freely spend their money, but is influenced by the view that money, like the world's resources, is to be used wisely, as suggested by the parable of the talents (Luke 19:11–27), and that it is not necessary to extract from creation every ounce of its productivity. The biblical principle of **Jubilee** (Leviticus 25:8–55) protected the land from overuse and exhaustion — every seven years a field was to be left uncultivated so that it might benefit from rest and ultimately be more fruitful.

Furthermore, consumerism centres on the self and rests on a mythical foundation — that it can deliver what it promises. Tondeur argues that rather than providing increased security, materialism generates anxiety, guilt and inadequacy. In essence, consumerism appears to maintain social order and an efficient marketplace, but it does so by dangerously pushing its limits as far as the individual consumer and society can go.

3 Debt and gambling

One of the most dangerous effects deriving from the pressure exerted by consumerism is debt. Economically speaking, debt is the obligation to pay for prior receipt of goods, services or money, but it has important ethical implications. The Bible is primarily concerned with the inequity of prosperous creditors and weak debtors, and exposes the dangers of allowing the potentially threatening relationship between creditor and debtor to be pushed to its limits. The power of the creditor to charge escalating levels of interest is easily abused, and the charging of interest at any rate (***riba***) is forbidden by Islam. The Old Testament expressly forbids adding to the burden of a needy human being when it is in the lender's power to free them from it.

Whilst it would be hard for Christian ethical teaching to reject the incurring of all debt (e.g. mortgages and business loans) as morally questionable, it consistently warns against borrowing funds to enhance standards of living or purchase luxuries. Debt is enslaving and against the spirit of the freedom God seeks for his people, and Tondeur argues that spiritual freedom is impossible to attain until financial debt is eliminated. The Bible reflects a real concern for those who have lost their freedom through debt, and the Jubilee principle is applicable here too. Every seventh year all debts were cancelled, and land was returned to its original owner, in order to prevent accumulation of wealth and ownership of land in the hands of a wealthy few. Money lenders were required to consider the long-term interest of the financially distressed.

One of the major reasons why debt has spiralled in the modern consumer market is the easy availability of credit, an offshoot of materialism, as the market seeks to attract and maintain an increasing number of consumers with an apparently infinite amount of money available to them: *'The practical outcome of this is that many families have reached for a standard of living that is years ahead of their income and savings. They have thereby become, in some real financial and psychological ways, servants of their possessions and slaves to their creditors'* (Atkinson and Field (eds), 1995). This raises the ethical question of to whom we should give money. The Pentateuch taught that money should be loaned to the poor — to those in genuine hardship — but no interest charged, reflecting the love of God and compassion for their distress. Arguably, the loan should be made with the intention that it should be paid back (without interest) but with the expectation that it will not, thereby allowing the debtor to feel some responsibility for, and hope to find, the means for its repayment, but preserving the status of the loan as an act of genuine charity on the part of the creditor.

Gambling has long been recognised as one of the major causes of debt, and religious ethicists are, in principle, opposed to it for many reasons. The Churches' Council on Gambling (1974) defined it as: *'an agreement between two parties whereby the transfer of something of value is made dependent on an uncertain event, in such a way that one party will gain and the other will lose'.* Hence, in gambling there is always a loser, and it is usually the one who can least afford to lose. Gambling is recognised as potentially addictive, and whilst for some the purchase of a lottery ticket or the odd flutter on the slot machines at the seaside is a trivial matter, forgotten again for months, for others it has serious implications. In *What Price the Lottery?* Keith Tondeur (1996a) observes that when the National Lottery was introduced in the UK, important lessons from the USA had not been learned. The emergence in the States of the 'lottery addict' had shown that addiction to lottery gaming led to further forms of gambling which, in turn, led to other social and psychological problems. He quotes Valerie Lorenz of the National Centre for Pathological Gambling in Baltimore:

Ten years ago a female compulsive gambler was a rarity in treatment. Lottery addicts were virtually unheard of. Teenage compulsive gamblers were non-existent and compulsive gamblers among senior citizens wee also a rarity... Yet today all these compulsive gamblers abound in every state.

(Cited in Tondeur, 1996a)

Although Aquinas permitted gambling as long as it was not motivated by greed, and some Christians find it acceptable on the grounds of the good results which it may generate (e.g. funding of community resources), William Temple condemned it on four grounds: it glorifies chance; it disregards the principles of stewardship; it makes profit out of someone else's loss; and it appeals to covetousness. Psychologists and counsellors have identified that a pattern can quickly emerge for the gambler: addiction — unemployment — crime — breakdown in relationships. There are, therefore, clearly many reasons for the religious moral philosopher to object to gambling and to be concerned about the close links that it has with debt and the perils of consumerism.

4 The ethical use of money

The principle of stewardship (outlined on pp. 201–204) should govern the relationship that religious believers have with the earth's resources and with their own finances. However, many do not make an association between their ownership of money and resources and a relationship with God. The biblical writers encouraged a recognition of the prior claim that God has on an individual's wealth before all else with the principle of tithing: '*Bring the whole tithe into the storehouse that there may be food in my house, and thereby put me to the test, says the Lord of hosts, if I will not open the windows of heaven for you and pour down for you an overflowing blessing*' (Malachi 3:10). The biblical principle of tithing is argued by some believers to be the solution to an excessive interest in wealth: 10% of the gross income is given annually to the church, and other offerings to missionary work or other special funds may be given on top of that. However, the basic 10% is considered to be sacred to God and should be set aside before any other financial demands are met. In a similar way, followers of Islam give **zakah** — 2.5% of their income to poor and needy Muslims.

However, there is arguably more that religious believers can do to normalise their relationship with money. Keith Tondeur (1996b) proposes a programme of ethical use of resources for religious believers:

- Follow good examples — e.g. Mother Teresa.
- Live more simply — e.g. use public transport, recycle waste, grow fruit and vegetables, buy only what is absolutely necessary.
- Invest wisely and only with companies which have a reliable record of ethical investment.
- Be aware of current affairs and the economy of the developing world.
- Use your power — e.g. letters to MPs complaining about financial, ethical anomalies.
- Watch what you buy, especially from companies that may have a record of human rights or environmental abuses (child labour, exploitation of workers, poor record of concern for conservation or pollution).

5 Business ethics

So far we have been concerned with the relationship between individuals and their money and the ethical and religious implications that arise from this. However, Tondeur's recommendation that Christians carefully examine the ethical record of companies with whom they spend money broadens the field. Until relatively recently, the business world was not particularly encumbered by ethical restraints, and whilst unwritten codes existed to some extent, it was expected to be something of a dog-eat-dog environment. However, there is now considerable interest in the ethics of business. These ethics are largely concerned with financial dealing, but they can cover a wide range of issues such as the rights and duties of the corporate world — whether businesses should have a responsibility towards public welfare, generating income for the community and jobs in areas of low employment; the relationship between employer and employee: sexual harassment, drug testing, rules about alcohol consumption (some companies attempt to enforce a rule that no employee should have drunk alcohol within a certain time period before attending work), and employee rights to privacy. Other areas of concern include the transferability of skills and ideas to other employment — for example, an advertising executive moving to another company may be forbidden by contract to take any clients from the previous company to the new one.

Another sensitive, but interesting, area is that of 'whistle blowing', which contrasts the right and duty of individuals to speak up when they see wrongdoing with loyalty to the company that employs them. The UK Public Interest Disclosure Act 1999 encourages people to blow the whistle on malpractice in the workplace and is designed to ensure that organisations respond appropriately to the message with action rather than act against the messenger. Employees may identify, in confidence, issues of injustice, health and safety violations, harm to the environment or criminal activity.

Financial concerns do remain paramount, however. Fraud, profit-making, insider dealing and lending are just some areas which are fraught with ethical difficulties, and the implications of some of them have already been raised in relation to individuals and their finances. The corporate world has enormous power in dealing with individuals and with the society which depends on their support, often in ways that are hard to measure, but in the modern business world, financial institutions, as well as the medical and legal professions, for example, are required to monitor the ethics of their practices and to account for them. In recent years insider trading — buying or selling of stocks and shares by those who have favourable access to the relevant information — has been a well-publicised phenomenon, and yet companies which have suffered have been criticised for failing to maintain their 'Chinese walls' by using security measures which limit the opportunity for insider dealing. More individuals and companies are supporting **ethical consumerism** — refusing to buy products or raw materials from companies with a poor record of human rights, or refusing to borrow from investors who invest in unethical concerns. On the other hand, it is possible to argue that it is the responsibility of a company to gain profits for its shareholders and that it should do so by the most commercially efficient measures it can. Hence, a textile firm may justify on financial grounds employing children in the developing world who work at a fraction of the cost and without the obligations that would be imposed by an adult workforce in the UK. This raises another problem too: the employment of foreign workers removes jobs from the home market place.

Business is not just about providing for the needs of society, but doing so in order to create resources so that the needs of the owner and their employees may also be met. Few people can run non-profit-making enterprises, and those that are run on such a basis operate according to legislation and on an ethical basis of their own. The profit motive is essentially self-interested, however, and for this reason ethicists tread carefully. Money is more than just a commodity for simple exchange and barter, and the nineteenth-century economist John Maynard Keynes, whose work has had a significant effect on the modern economy, advocated the view that people could hold money for speculative purposes as an asset and not just as a means of payment or exchange.

Profit-making has a strong ethical connotation, however, and religious thinkers warn against obsession with the pursuit of profit. However, as cautious as biblical teaching may be on the issue of profit-making, it does not condemn it as the result of diligent endeavour, as exemplified by the woman of Proverbs 31: *'She considers a field and buys it; with the fruit of her hands she plants a vineyard. She girds her loins with strength and makes her arms strong. She perceives that her merchandise is profitable. Her lamp does not go out at night'* (16–18). The Proverbs 31 woman, something of a paragon in every respect it must be said, provides a role model for the businessman or woman. She is industrious and entrepreneurial, but she does not work for the exploitation of others, or for selfish gain. She takes the initiative for her own business plans, provides for her family, and maintains a position of respect in the community.

Related to these issues is also that of the nature of work, and the concerns that many employees have about the hours of work they are required to put in at the expense of other aspects of their lives. Although they may well be remunerated for it, it is the employer who is felt to be the ultimate winner, as young graduates in the early twenty-first century work longer hours, and yet find it harder than the previous generation to own property and establish independence.

Summary

- **Finance and religious ethics** — the central theme is that human resources belong to God, and human beings are called to exercise stewardship over them and to establish a relationship of responsibility over their finances.
- **Consumerism** — literally means using resources and money, but more commonly associated now with conspicuous and excessive spending and encouragement within the marketplace to do so. It leads to problems of unlimited credit and debt, waste and overuse of resources and to a 'born to shop', self-centred and easily dissatisfied culture.
- **Debt** — credit encourages an increasingly dangerous relationship between creditors and debtors, and debt diminishes humans' spiritual freedom and reliance on God. Interest-free lending is in the spirit of religious teaching. **Gambling** — has a significant part to play in the escalation of debt, and is addictive.
- Religious believers are encouraged to **use money ethically** and to **give** in accordance with the principles of their religion. This encourages an appreciation of their dependence on God and his first call on their resources.
- **Business ethics** — these extend beyond financial concerns to relationships within the workplace, and to the rights and responsibilities of the employer to the employee and to the environment. Profit-making is, however, the major goal of business enterprise, and religious ethicists are concerned about the morality of how that profit is made.

Exam watch

This is potentially a tricky area and wafflers will soon be exposed. There is inevitably a lot of emphasis on 'lifestyle ethics' in this topic, which is dependent upon an understanding of religious teaching as well as broader ethical considerations. Back up your answer with names and references and give it a clear structure by organising it under specific headings, either those in this chapter or others you are already familiar with.

Review questions

1 Examine the problems that the religious believer may face in a consumer society.
2 How far is the view that a person's money belongs first to God an unrealistic approach to financial dealings in the twenty-first century?
3 Is involvement with corporate business incompatible with religious belief?

Christian Belief
and Practice

Topic 1

Christian beliefs about God

The Christian view of God comes from biblical revelation, in which the holy one, the creator of all things, appears also as humanity's redeemer. He is shown as the unchanging sovereign Lord of creation — the all-powerful, all-knowing, eternal God of love, grace, providence, morality and truth.

1 Creator

The notion of God as creator is found at the very beginning of the Bible, in the Book of Genesis, which outlines the nature of creation at the hands of God himself: *'In the beginning God created the heavens and the earth'* (Genesis 1:1). The theme of God as creator is an important one throughout the Old Testament, not only in the Genesis narratives but also in the words of the prophets and in the books of wisdom such as Job 38:1–42 and the Psalms. The same notion prevails: God is the creator of the universe and the one who sustains it.

The central theme in the Old Testament account of creation is the concept of God ordering the creation. He is depicted as creating order out of formless chaos, like a potter working clay (Genesis 2:7; Isaiah 29:16). In certain places there are references to creation bringing order to a series of chaotic forces, often named after dragons and monsters that have been subdued — Behemoth, Leviathan (Job 3, 12, 40; Isaiah 27, 41). What is clear above all else is that creation concerns God's control over chaos and his ordering of the universe.

The notion of God as creator was not, however, without its problems. The Gnostics tried to distinguish between the redeemer God of the New Testament, and a lesser deity, sometimes called the **demiurge**, who they believed created the universe. This was a kind of dualism — an argument for the existence of two gods: one, a supreme god, who was the source of the spiritual world, and the other, a lesser god, who created the physical world. This in itself led to later arguments concerning the goodness of the spiritual world and the evil of the physical world. ·

The Greek philosophers, such as Plato, in turn, did not regard God as having created the world out of nothing (***ex nihilo***), but instead saw God as an architect, who put the matter of the universe into proper order, giving it a definite shape and structure. The early Christian thinkers Theophilus of Antioch and Justin Martyr supported the view that God gave an ordered structure to pre-existent matter. God constructed the universe from material that was already present — material that was often of poor quality, leading to defects and evil within the created universe. However, the Christian writers of the second and third centuries argued against this, saying that God did indeed create the universe out of nothing since there was no pre-existent matter. Irenaeus maintained that this confirmed the biblical claim that creation was *'good'* (Genesis 1:31) and

Tertullian argued that the creation of the world was due to God's own free choice and not to any necessity arising from the nature of matter — the world depends on God for its existence.

By the end of the fourth century the Christian position was clarified, with the confirmation of the belief that God did, indeed, create the universe ***ex nihilo***. This was made clear in the words of the **Nicene Creed**, which declared in faith that God was the '*maker of heaven and earth*' and subsequently ratified in the Fourth Lateran Council (1215) and the Council of Florence (1442).

Issues arising from the doctrine of creation

There are four important issues that arise from the notion of God as creator of the universe:

+ There is a difference between God as creator, and creation itself. It is important to understand that it is not creation that is divine. In his epistle to the Romans, Paul highlighted the fact that humans have a tendency to reduce God to the level of the world and have '*served created things rather than the creator*' (1:25). Thus, although God creates the moon, stars and sun, these do not become gods themselves and should not be worshipped. It is an important aspect of Christian theology that God is distinguished from creation. At the same time, humanity must affirm that the universe is, indeed, God's creation and it should be honoured and respected as such.

+ As creator, God has authority over his creation. Humans are themselves a part, albeit a special part, of that creation and have special functions within it. The Bible talks of humans having stewardship over creation (Genesis 1:28). Creation is simply for the enjoyment and gratification of humanity; humans do not own the world but are stewards who hold the world in trust for God. This stewardship is a matter of deepest responsibility; humans are required to look after the world in a serious and responsible manner and this has all sorts of implications for ecological and environmental issues.

+ God's creation is good. All through the creation story in Genesis the writers make reference to creation being good. The world is not, as the Gnostics suggested, an inherently evil place. However, creation is not perfect; due to human sin, the world is not as it was intended to be by God. The notion of Christian redemption suggests that there will, at some point, be a restoration and that God's purpose for his creation will eventually be fulfilled.

+ Finally, human beings are made in the image of God. This means that humans are inextricably linked to God and their ultimate destiny rests in God. As Augustine of Hippo remarked in *Confessions*: '*You made us for yourself, and our hearts are restless until they find their rest in you*'.

How did God create the world?

There have been many arguments concerning the way in which God acted as creator and there are a number of different possibilities that have been considered:

+ **Emanation** — this is a notion that was favoured by several early Christian writers and stemmed from the Platonic idea that the creation of the world was an overflowing of God's creative energy, like light coming from the sun — the light reflects the nature of the sun itself. In the same way, creation comes ('emanates') from God and shows his divine nature. However, this view seems to imply that creation was a kind of involuntary act, whereas the Bible teaches that God decides to act for himself in the matter of creation. God is seen in the Christian tradition as a personal God, who expresses his love in the act of creation.

÷ **Construction** — the Bible uses the imagery of God as a builder or craftsman who constructs the world (Psalm 127:1). This highlights the idea of planning and purpose and the deliberate intention to create, whilst also highlighting the skill of the creator and the beauty and intricacy of creation. However, this brings back a problem discussed earlier: the image of the builder suggests that God made the world from pre-existent material, which was already available.

÷ **Artistic expression** — a good deal of Christian writing has spoken of creation as the 'handiwork of God', seeing it as a work of art and beauty which expresses the love and personality of God. Although this could still mean that God used pre-existent material, it does open up the possibility of creation out of nothing, just as artists or writers create their work out of nothing.

When was the world created?

Christian theologians have long debated the issue of time in creation. In *Confessions*, Augustine of Hippo argued that creation did not happen at a particular moment in time, but that time itself was created with the rest of the created order: '*You have made time itself. Time could not elapse before you made time*'. This has been the generally held view amongst theologians ever since — that there was no time before creation. Eternity is timeless, but time is part of the created order. (For further discussions on the notion of God as creator, see pp. 6–8.)

2 Omnipotence

An essential aspect of Christian theology is the belief in an omnipotent (or almighty) God. However, the exact meaning of this term has been the subject of considerable debate down the ages. In the everyday sense, omnipotence means that God can do anything — anything, that is, except something that is a logical contradiction, such as making a square circle. However, there are problems. Can God, for instance, build a fence that he cannot climb over? Can he create a being greater than himself? If the answer to these questions is 'no', then is God really omnipotent?

The problem really centres on the definition of the word 'omnipotent'. If it means 'being able to do anything', then it may not be possible to apply the word to God. The reason is that if God has decided to adopt a particular course of action or behave in a particular way, then this will preclude him from doing certain things. For instance, if he decides always to act in a loving way, then he cannot do evil. In *The Problem of Pain*, C. S. Lewis claimed that God could not do anything that was inconsistent with his divine nature, and in *Proslogion*, Anselm observed that if God was omnipotent, then he could tell lies and act unjustly, although this would be contrary to the teachings of the Bible. In *Summa Theologica*, Thomas Aquinas argued that one of the things that God could not do was sin: '*To sin is to fall short of a perfect action. Hence to be able to sin is to be able to be deficient in relation to an action, which cannot be reconciled with omnipotence. It is because God is omnipotent that he cannot sin'.*

William of Ockham argued that there were '*two powers of God*'. He said that once there was a time when God could do anything — this he called '*the absolute power of God*' — ***potentia absoluta*** (McGrath (ed.), 2001). However, God, through his divine will, chose to establish a certain order of things, and this order will remain until the end of time. This is the '*ordering power of God*' — ***potentia ordinata***. The distinction is important. In the '*absolute power*', God was faced with an infinite range of possibilities — he could do whatever he wanted. However, once he chose to create the world his power was restricted to acting within the order he had ordained. In *Christian Theology: An Introduction*, McGrath notes: '*This leads to what seems, at first sight, to be a paradoxical situation. On account of the divine omnipotence, God is not now able to do everything. By exercising the divine power, God has limited options*'.

However, there is an answer to this dilemma. The notion of **divine self-limitation** suggests that if God is really capable of doing anything, then he must be able to become committed to a course of action — and be able to stay committed to it. The Greek term used was ***kenosis*** (emptying) and theologians have used this concept to argue that the supreme example of divine self-limitation was when God chose to become human as Jesus Christ. Charles Gore, in *Incarnation of the Son of God*, said that in giving Christ full human identity, God had to '*self-empty*' himself of his divinity. Jesus had to be fully human, not simply God in disguise.

In his *Letters and Papers from Prison*, Bonhoeffer commented: '*God lets himself be pushed out of the world on to the cross. He is weak and powerless in the world and that is precisely the way, the only way, in which he is with us and helps us*'.

3 A personal God

The Bible speaks of God in personal terms. He is said to be loving and trustworthy and to have a personal relationship, rather like a parent and a child, with those who love him.

The definition of the word 'person' is crucial. The word derives from the Latin ***persona***, which means 'a mask' and, for early Christians, the word 'person' implied more than just an individual human being. It was an expression of the individuality of a human being, as seen in their words and actions — the role they play and the ways in which they relate to others, hence the idea of a mask. Speaking of God as a personal God suggests a deity with whom humans can have a relationship, reflecting their own relationships with each other.

This does not mean, however, that God is just a big human being and Paul Tillich pointed out that it was important not to reduce God to a human level. Nor does the idea of a personal God detract from the notion of God in three persons in the Trinity. The idea of a personal God is an analogy; to say that God is like a person does not mean that he is human, but instead it affirms that God has the ability and willingness to relate to his people.

There are problems with this view, however. In his work *Ethics*, Spinoza argued that although human beings should love God, God could not reciprocate that love. There could not be a personal two-way relationship between humans and God because a relationship, especially one of love, would require God to change in his being. He cannot do this, since he is perfect and this perfection cannot be altered: '*God, strictly speaking, loves no one nor hates anyone. For God is affected with no emotion of joy or sadness, and consequently loves no one nor hates anyone.*'

However, Christian writers argue that to speak of God as a person is to highlight the very fact that it *is* possible to enter into a personal relationship with God. The Jewish scholar Martin Buber, in his work *I and Thou*, argued that there were two types of relationships. The first, which he called 'I–It' relations, were those between subjects and objects, such as between a human and a chair; the human is active and the chair is passive. The second, which he referred to as 'I–Thou' relations, are those between two active subjects, such as two human beings. Buber suggested that 'I–It' relations were indirect. The object has a specific content and description; you can know its colour, shape and size. You can know 'about' it, but you cannot 'know' it. However, the 'I–Thou' relationship is different; it is direct and you can 'know' and 'be known' in the relationship. Buber argues that God can never be reduced to a concept or an 'It', for he is an active subject. In a relationship with God, as with another human, a person is able to become aware of and to 'know' God, as God knows and is aware of them. For Buber, God is the '*Thou who can, by its nature, never become an It. That is, God is a being who escapes all attempts at objectification and transcends all description*'.

Christian theology pursues the course that God has revealed himself to humanity, not just the facts about himself but his personality as well. In a sense, knowledge is of God both as an 'It' and a 'Thou'. We can know things about God and also come to know God.

4 A suffering God

The biblical teaching of a God who is both personal and loving raises the difficult question of whether or not God can be said to suffer. If God creates and loves the world, then does he not also feel the pain of human suffering?

Early philosophers were doubtful. The Platonic view was that, if God were perfect, then he would be unchanging and self-sufficient; it would be impossible for a perfect being to be affected by anything outside of itself. Philo, in *That God is Unchangeable*, argued that God was perfect and unchangeable and therefore could not suffer. In a similar vein, Anselm in *Proslogion* argued that God is compassionate in terms of our human understanding of him, but in divine terms he is not; we experience God as compassionate, but this does not mean that God is actually compassionate: '*...you are compassionate, in that you save the miserable and spare those who sin against you; you are not compassionate, in that you are not affected by any sympathy for misery*'.

Aquinas, too, believed that love implies being vulnerable, and that God could there-fore never be truly affected by human sorrow. Similarly, Spinoza said that if God was truly perfect, then he could never change or experience suffering. However, there are problems here. The Old Testament shows God sharing in the suffering of the people of Israel and the New Testament teaches that Christ suffered and died on the cross. Since Christian theology teaches that Jesus Christ was God incarnate, this suggests that God suffered in Christ. However, others have argued that Christ only suffered in his

human nature, and not in his divine nature; God did not, therefore, experience human suffering. This view gained support after the First World War. Many theologians argued that God was seemingly not affected by the evil and suffering in the world. Moltmann (1974) described the argument against a seemingly invulnerable God as '*the only serious atheism*'.

In the sixteenth century, Martin Luther had argued that God did indeed suffer in the humiliation of the cross — what he called '*a crucified God*'. This theme was adapted by Moltmann in his work *The Crucified God*. He argued that the cross was the basis of Christian theology, and the passion of Christ and his cry of forsakenness in Mark 15:34 shows that God the Father did indeed suffer the death of the Son in order to redeem sinful humanity. Moltmann said that a truly perfect God must be able to experience suffering. Whilst God could not be forced to suffer, he could choose to experience suffering; he chooses suffering because that is the nature of his love: '*A God who cannot suffer is poorer than any human. For a God who is incapable of suffering is a being who cannot be involved…the one who cannot suffer cannot love either. So he is also a loveless being*'.

Thus, for Moltmann, at the cross the Father and Son suffer, but in different ways. The Son suffers physical pain and death; the Father suffers the loss of the Son. Through the cross, God knows what death is like: '*In the passion of the Son, the Father himself suffers the pain of abandonment. In the death of the Son, death comes upon God himself, and the Father suffers the death of his Son in his love for forsaken man*'.

Summary

- God as **creator** is central to the biblical concept of God, creating order from chaos, and sustaining it. Early Christian thinkers debated whether God created **ex nihilo**, or brought order to existing form. God is distinct from his creation, which itself is not to be worshipped, and he has authority over it, although human beings are given a key role as its steward. Creation is perfect ('good') and humans are, at its climax, made in God's image. The method by which God created is a matter of debate, but all suggest that God expressed his full nature and character in the act of creation. Before creation there was no time, which is itself part of the created order.

- An **omnipotent** God can do anything — but what does this entail? All that is logically possible? All that is within his nature? Does God exercise divine self-limitation? Certainly on the cross, God emptied himself of his divine power so that he might die as man.

- The Bible speaks of a **personal God**. Personhood enables God to have a personal relationship with his creation, although this raises questions of exactly how God can be like a human being without being limited. Martin Buber's concept of the 'I–Thou' relationship between God and humanity makes clear that humanity relates to God as a person, not a thing.

- Can God **suffer**? If he is perfect and unchanging, presumably not. However, modern theologians claim that on the cross, God suffered with men in order to express his love for them. Moltmann argued that God suffered the death of his Son, and the Son suffered the physical pain of crucifixion.

Exam watch

These complex ideas must not be oversimplified and you must resist telling the creation story when dealing with God as creator, or relapsing into an essay on the problem of evil when writing about God's omnipotence. You must be able to refer with accuracy and frequency to the scholars involved — these topics simply cannot be discussed on the basis of your opinion or fragmentary pieces of biblical text.

Review questions

1 Examine and assess the issues raised by a belief in a Creator God.
2 For what reasons has the notion of the omnipotence of God caused problems for the Christian church?
3 What theological issues arise from the notion of a suffering God?
4 Consider what is meant by the concept of a personal God.

Topic 2

Christian beliefs about Jesus

1 Christ and the Trinity

The doctrine of the Trinity is one of the most complex aspects of Christian theology. It refers to the apparent paradox of One God in Three Persons: God the Father, God the Son and God the Holy Spirit. The doctrine of the Trinity is based upon divine action: the Father is revealed in Christ through the Holy Spirit, and the three elements are linked together as God's saving presence and power: *'May the grace of the Lord Jesus Christ, and the love of God, and the fellowship of the Holy Spirit be with you all'* (2 Corinthians 14).

In the Old Testament, God is often depicted as three distinct personalities:

÷ In the first, the **Wisdom of God** is shown as a person who is active in creation — and is usually shown as a female: *'Wisdom has built her house; she has hewn out its seven pillars'* (Proverbs 9:1).

÷ In the second, the **Word of God** confronts humanity with the will and purpose of God, bringing guidance, judgment and salvation: *'Your word, O Lord, is eternal; it stands firm in the heavens'* (Psalm 119:89).

÷ Finally, the **Spirit of God** is the agent of the new creation, and will be present in the expected Messiah: *'I will put my Spirit on him and he will bring justice to the nations'* (Isaiah 42:1).

The Bible does not talk of the Trinity. What it does do is portray God in a Trinitarian way: as three. This is shown particularly well in the baptism of Christ (the Son), where the Father speaks from heaven and the Spirit appears as a dove (Mark 1:10–11 &//s).

Throughout history, the doctrine of the Trinity has been controversial. The arguments stemmed from the fact that if Jesus on earth was God, and if God the Father was in heaven, then were there two Gods? In *Demonstration of the Apostolic Preaching*, Irenaeus used the phrase *'the economy of salvation'*, by which he meant the way in which God has ordered the salvation of humanity. He argued that there was a single economy of salvation and that was one God. However, God introduces salvation by portraying himself in three distinct roles:

God the Father uncreated, who is uncontained, invisible, one God, creator of the universe…the Son of God, our Lord Jesus Christ…became a human being amongst human beings, capable of being seen and touched, to destroy death, bring life and restore fellowship between God and humanity. And the Holy Spirit…who, in the fullness of time, was poured out in a new way on our human nature in order to renew humanity throughout the entire world in the sight of God.

In other words, human redemption is achieved as a result of the three persons of the Godhead performing their distinct tasks yet acting together in one unity. But how is this done? There are two distinct ideas. In Eastern theology the viewpoint has generally been that each of the three persons of God has a distinct individuality (**hypostases**) and their unity is maintained because the Son and Spirit derive from the Father himself. In Western theology, however, the three persons are seen to be in mutual fellowship with each other, working together. This view is commonly associated with Augustine, who said that Father, Son and Spirit were equal within the Godhead. He identified the Son with the wisdom of God (***sapientia***) and the Spirit with the love of God (***caritas***) and it was the Spirit who binds humanity to God and also binds together the persons of the Trinity: '*The Holy Spirit…makes us dwell in God and God in us*'.

Augustine argued that the concept of the Trinity resembled the way humans thought and acted and that we should look to humanity in our search for the image of God. Within human beings, he said, there is the trinity of mind, knowledge and love and the human mind is an image of God himself (a psychological analogy). He suggested that, as humans have three persons in their minds, they can, in a sense, be three persons, yet one person at the same time.

In modern times Karl Barth (2000), in his work *Church Dogmatics*, said that the Trinity was the key to God revealing himself to sinful humanity: '*God reveals himself, he reveals himself through himself…*'. He said that the Trinity was God's way of speaking and being heard. Left on our own, sinful humanity was incapable of hearing the word of God and receiving salvation — God must reveal himself (self-revelation). He does this through the Son and His truth is revealed through the Spirit: '*Therefore go and make disciples of all nations, baptising them in the name of the Father and of the Son and of the Holy Spirit…*' (Matthew 28:19).

2 Christology

Christology is the study of the person of Jesus Christ and his place at the centre of Christian theology. Christology is concerned not so much with the historical facts of the life of Jesus as with his spiritual or theological significance — who exactly was Jesus? Christianity is essentially a historical religion; it came into being as a direct result of a specific series of events that centred upon the life and work of Jesus Christ and is a direct response to the issues raised by the life, death and resurrection of Christ himself. There are many issues arising from this; some of the most important are considered here.

+ **Jesus Christ makes God known** — a central aspect of Christian theology is the notion that God is revealed through Jesus Christ in human form, and in this way God is able to show himself to humanity. As Jesus himself said: '*I am in the Father and the Father is in me*' (John 14:11).
+ **Jesus brings salvation** — salvation is said to come from the life, death and resurrection of Christ. The New Testament message is **Christomorphic** in that it affirms that Christ not only makes life possible but can also redeem humanity and determine a new shape for people's lives. The life of Christ gives flesh and substance to ideas, values and virtues of love, hope and forgiveness.
+ **Jesus is the Messiah** — the Greek term ***Christos*** equates to the Hebrew word ***Mashiah*** (Messiah), which means 'one who has been anointed'. In the Old

Testament, anointing was reserved for kings, who were appointed by God and anointed in his name. Anointing itself was done by the pouring on of olive oil — a public sign of having been chosen by God for kingship. The notion of a Messiah came from the hope that one day in the future a new king of Israel, from the House of David, would come from God and rule over a renewed people of God. Some believed that this person would be a divine figure, whilst others suggested that it would be a man especially chosen by God. For Christians, Christ is the Messiah, and Jesus himself admits this in John 4:25–26: *'The woman said, "I know that Messiah (called Christ) is coming. When he comes, he will explain everything to us." Then Jesus declared, "I who speak to you am he."'* Jesus, however, was not the political or warrior Messiah that many had hoped for. The importance of the term lies in the fact that it suggests that Jesus was the fulfilment of God's redemptive plan and so is properly seen as the foundation of Christian belief.

❖ **Jesus is the Son of God** — in the Bible, the term Son of God was usually used in the sense of someone 'belonging to God'. It was not a term that Jesus used of himself, although at his trial he does admit to the chief priests that he is Son of God (Luke 22:70). Paul uses the term when referring to Jesus by drawing a distinction between what he saw as the sonship of believers, who can become children of God by adoption, and Jesus himself, who is God's own son (Romans 8:31). He tends to suggest that the word children (***tekna***) is best applied to believers, whilst Son (***huious***) should be reserved for Jesus. For Paul, all believers are children of God by adoption — they enjoy all the rights of a child of God. Nevertheless, the relationship between Jesus and God the Father is markedly different from this: *'The Spirit himself testifies with our spirit that we are God's children. Now if we are children, then we are heirs — heirs of God and co-heirs with Christ, if indeed we share in his sufferings in order that we may also share in his glory'* (Romans 8:17).

❖ **Jesus is the Son of Man** — the term Son of Man is used in three different ways in the Old Testament: as a form of address to Ezekiel the prophet; to speak of a future eschatological figure, whose coming will bring divine judgment upon humanity (Daniel 7:13–14); and as a way of contrasting the lowliness of humanity with the divinity of God (Psalm 8:14). It is the second of these that most scholars refer to when thinking of Jesus. Bultmann argued that this eschatological figure was Jesus and he uses such references as Mark 13:26 to confirm this: *'At that time men will see the Son of Man coming in clouds with great power and glory'*. Caird (1990), in his commentary *St Luke*, argued, however, that the term referred to Jesus's suffering on behalf of humanity itself. He said Jesus used the term *'…to indicate his essential unity with mankind, and above all the weak and humble, and also his special function as predestined representative of the new Israel and bearer of God's judgment and kingdom.'*

❖ **Jesus is Lord** — in Hebrew, the **Tetragrammaton** or holy name of God (YHWH) could not be spoken and an alternative word, ***adonai***, was used. When translated into Greek, the term ***kyrios*** (Lord) was used as the name of God. Thus, when Paul in Romans 10:9 uses the notion that 'Jesus is Lord', he uses it to identify clearly Jesus and God.

❖ **Jesus is God** — one of the reasons that Jesus angered the Jewish authorities was, as they saw it, his claim to be God — a claim that they regarded as blasphemous since

God was one. Nevertheless, the New Testament does make this claim. In John 1:1 the evangelist writes '*the Word was God*', and in 20:20 the Apostle Thomas, on seeing the resurrected Jesus, declares: '*My Lord and my God!*' To say that Jesus is God is to make a statement concerning the identity of Jesus — to identify him performing the tasks that God performs. For example, Jesus saves people from their sins (Matthew 1:21) and is the Saviour (Luke 2:11). Moreover, early Christians worshipped him as God. In John 16:23, Jesus instructs the disciples: '*I tell you the truth, my father will give you whatever you ask in my name.*' Finally, Jesus reveals God to humanity. The Father speaks through Jesus and acts through him — to have seen Jesus is to have seen God the Father.

The debate over the person of Christ

Throughout the last 2,000 years, the debate has continued as to the true nature of the person of Christ. It centres on the issue of just how human Christ really was and in what respects he differed from other humans.

In the second century the Greek writers known as the **Docetists** argued that Christ was totally divine and that his humanity was just for the sake of appearance. When he suffered, that suffering was apparent, rather than real, since God cannot truly suffer. This view was criticised at that time by Justin Martyr, who developed what became known as **Logos-Christology**. He said that in John's Gospel, Christ is portrayed as the '*Word*' (John 1:1) or, in Greek, **Logos**. *Logos* was a term understood by Christians and non-Christians. It was thought to mean the ultimate source of human knowledge — to which only Christians have full access because it manifested itself in Christ. The *Logos* has been evident throughout history, but only Christianity has been built fully upon it.

Origen took this notion a stage further, by saying that the human soul of Christ was united with the *Logos* and therefore shares the qualities of the *Logos*. Jesus as the **Logos** coexists with the father, although Origen is at pains to point out that the *Logos* is subordinate to the Father.

However, perhaps the greatest debate on the issue was the so-called **Arian Controversy**. The scholar Arius argued that God is the only source of created things and everything comes from God. Therefore, the Son, like all other aspects of creation, comes from God. However, the Son is superior to the rest of creation because he is '...*a perfect creature, yet not as one among other creatures*...' (McGrath (ed.), 2001). Arius said that God was inaccessible and could not be known by any other creature — even the Son could not know the Father. What Christ did in the incarnation, therefore, was to perform the tasks God had ordained him to do. In other words, for Arius:

÷ Christ was a creature created by God.
÷ He had superior status to other creatures (hence the term 'Son'), but not the same status as God.
÷ He had this status because the Father willed it, not because it is in the actual nature of the Son.

Arius's primary opponent was Athanasius. He said that there were many biblical passages that highlighted the unity of the Father and Son (e.g. John 3:35; 10:30). Moreover, he claimed, only God could bring salvation, forgive sin and offer eternal life.

If Jesus were merely a creature, he could not do this, yet the New Testament emphasises the role of Christ as saviour. Athanasius concluded:

P1: Only God saves.
P2: Jesus Christ saves.
C: Therefore Jesus Christ is God.

He commented that in Jesus, as John 1:14 suggested, *'the Word became flesh'* in order that God could come into the human situation and change it for the better. Moreover, Christians worship and pray to Jesus, responding to him as God incarnate.

The debate had to be settled and it was reduced to two points: either Jesus was *'of like substance'* with the Father (**homoiousios**), or he was *'of the same substance'* (**homoousios**). Finally, the Nicene Creed of 381 CE was formulated, adopting the term *'of the same substance'* as the Father, and this has been the mainstream view ever since. Jesus Christ is God incarnate.

The link between the human and divine in Christ
The Council of Chalcedon in 451 CE declared that Jesus Christ was both truly human and truly divine. In other words, Christ has two natures — God and Man. This has been the main view of Christian theology ever since. However, quite how the two natures relate has been an ongoing subject of debate and there are conflicting viewpoints.

+ **Christ is an example** — this is the view that Jesus acts as a living example of how to live the godly life. Christ is a moral teacher and, in his death, shows self-giving love. Moreover, he has a deep inner or spiritual relationship with God that the believer should seek to emulate. This inner life of Jesus is an important aid to religious faith.
+ **Christ is a symbolic presence** — Paul Tillich said that it was not the historical facts about the life of Jesus that are important for faith; what really matters is the symbolic significance of Christ as the Messiah who brings new being and saves humanity from the old, sinful being. For Tillich, Jesus was a human being who achieved a union with God which is open to every other human being. He is a symbol of how humanity can truly achieve salvation.
+ **Christ as mediator** — a mediator is someone who acts between two parties and Christ is depicted in the New Testament as being the mediator between God the Father and humanity (Hebrews 9:15). 'Mediation through revelation' refers to the notion that the *Logos* bridges the gap between God and humanity and this mediation becomes incarnate in Christ. In *Truth as Encounter*, Emil Brunner argued that faith was a personal encounter with God, who meets his people personally in Christ. He suggested that Christ was a unique channel or focus through which God's redeeming work could be made available to humanity. Calvin said that humans lacked the ability to save themselves, so true knowledge of God and salvation must come to them from outside — from Christ. Moreover, Christ had to become human and then obey God as a human in order to be able to offer himself as a ransom for sin. Through his sacrifice, he broke the power of sin and death over the human race. So, for Calvin, God could become incarnate as the Son, yet also remain, as Father, in heaven. For Calvin, Christ had three ministries (**munus triplex Christi**): he was a

prophet who spoke of God's love and grace; a king who ruled over the spiritual heavenly kingdom; and a priest who offered himself as a ransom for humanity's sin.

3 The quest for the historical Jesus

The original quest for the historical Jesus was centred on the idea that there was a huge difference between the historical figure of Jesus, who was a simple religious teacher, and the 'Christ of Faith' figure that had been developed by the Christian church. It was thought that, by going back to the historical Jesus and stripping away all the unnecessary and inappropriate dogma added by the church (such as the resurrection and the divinity of Christ), a more believable and credible version of Christianity could be achieved.

The quest was inspired by Hermann Samuel Reimarus and his work *An Apology for the Rational Worshipper of God*. Reimarus had raised questions about whether or not the early Christians had tampered with the Gospel accounts of Jesus, and suggested that there was a real difference between the beliefs of Jesus and those of the early church. He argued that the disciples invented the concept of '*spiritual redemption*' in place of Jesus's vision of a liberated Israel, freed from the Romans. Moreover, they invented the idea of the resurrection to cover up the embarrassment caused by Jesus's death. To Reimarus, Jesus was simply a political figure who had expected to lead a popular rising against Rome, and was shattered by his failure.

In the nineteenth century, a number of writers tried to get back to the historical figure of Jesus by writing 'Life of Jesus' books, often in the form of novels. However, such 'lives', historical or otherwise, were very subjective and often simply guesswork. As McGrath (2001) notes: '*They certainly saw him as he had never been seen before; sadly, they believed that they saw him as he actually was*'.

At the beginning of the twentieth century, new ideas arose. In particular, three differing critiques dominated the thinking of scholars. The first was the **apocalyptic critique**, associated with Johannes Weiss in his work *Jesus's Proclamation of the Kingdom of God*, and Albert Schweitzer, who believed that Jesus's ministry was determined by his apocalyptic outlook. This view became known as **thorough-going eschatology**. However, the problem with this approach was that it produced a picture of Christ as a remote and strange figure — an unworldly person, whose hopes and expectations came to nothing. The **sceptical critique**, associated initially with William Wrede, questioned the historical basis of our knowledge of Jesus. Wrede suggested that the Gospel of Mark was a theological picture of Christ disguised as a historical one. He said that the Gospel writer had imposed his theology on to the historical material, making it unreliable. The problem here is that this argument is unverifiable; we simply cannot know if the Gospel writer did this or not.

The **dogmatic critique** was highlighted by Martin Kahler in his work *The So-Called Historical Jesus and the Historical Biblical Christ*. He claimed that the historical Jesus was irrelevant to faith, which was, anyway, based on the Christ of faith. He said that a historical portrait of Jesus could not become an object of faith: '*The Jesus of the "life of Jesus" movement is merely a modern example of a brain-child of the human imagination*'. What Kahler thought was important was not who Christ was, but what he presently does for believers; the 'Jesus of history' lacks the real importance of the Christ of faith.

Rudolf Bultmann regarded the whole quest for a historical reconstruction of Jesus as a futile exercise. For Bultmann, although the cross and resurrection are historical events, they must be understood by faith — they are divine acts of judgment and salvation. He said that nothing more could be known about the historical Jesus apart from the fact that he lived.

In 1953, Ernst Käsemann gave a lecture that opened up what became known as the *'new quest for the historical Jesus'*. He claimed that the Gospel writers did express historical information alongside theological truths about Jesus. He said that the important thing was to see the links between the preaching of Jesus and the later preaching about Jesus. The 'new quest', which was taken up by scholars such as Joachim Jeremias and Gunter Bornkamm, was concerned to stress the continuity between the historical Jesus and the Christ of faith, and the continuities between the preaching of Jesus himself and the preaching about Jesus given in the Christian church.

Finally, and most recently, the 'third quest' focuses on the relation of Jesus to his Jewish context. John Crossan (1991), in *The Historical Jesus*, has argued that Jesus was a poor Jewish peasant who led the way in breaking down social conventions, particularly in his teachings about sinners and outcasts. Along similar lines, E. P. Sanders claimed that Jesus was a prophet who was concerned with the final restoration of Israel. However, this third quest has been criticised for lacking a coherent theological and historical core.

Summary

- The **Trinity** is a complex doctrine that caused great problems for the early church as they grappled with the question of how God could be three and yet one. There is no decisive biblical teaching, although the *work* of God as Father, Son and Spirit is made clear. In three persons, God has exercised 'the economy of salvation' and revealed himself in three distinct individual personalities, working together in mutual harmony.

- **Christology** is concerned with the person of Jesus and his role in salvation and revelation. It often focuses around the titles given for Jesus by Christians and in the New Testament, though recent debate is concerned with the nature of Jesus's humanity and divinity. The **Arian Controversy** was crucial for laying down doctrine on the relationship between Jesus and God, finally resolved at the Council of Chalcedon which declared Jesus to be truly human and truly divine. His humanity can be understood as being an exemplar, a symbolic presence, or a mediator between humanity and God.

- The **quest for the historical Jesus** is a scholarly movement concerned with getting back to the real, historical figure of Jesus as opposed to the Christ of faith, or the portrait painted by the evangelists. The goals of the early church may have led to a picture of Jesus which was removed from the reality of him as a poor Jewish peasant leader, or as a charismatic concerned with the overthrow of enemy power.

Exam watch

You can't guess at these topics — you simply know them or you don't, so it's not worth bluffing or trying to get away with using biblical material only. They are rooted in complex theological debates between scholars over the centuries, so don't sell yourself short by skimping on learning. Practise writing them out over and over till you know them by memory — there are no short cuts in this difficult area.

Review questions

1 Examine and comment on the views of scholars concerning the doctrine of the Trinity.

2 What is the purpose of 'Christology'?

3 Examine and consider the meaning of the definitions 'Jesus the Messiah' and 'Jesus the Son of God'.

4 Outline and comment upon the main features of the debate over the nature of the Person of Christ.

5 *'The quest for the historical Jesus was a failure.'* Examine and comment on this view.

Topic 3

Christian practice

1 Worship

Martin Luther said: '*To know God is to worship him*'. Worship is humanity's response to God. It may be through silence, stillness, wonder, praise or dedication. Manson calls it: '*...the sense of awe in the presence of the magnificent*' (Ferguson and Wright (eds), 1988). God himself is at the heart of Christian worship which requires two elements:

1 revelation, through which God makes himself known
2 humanity's response to God

God makes himself known in a number of ways:
- through creation
- through his written word
- through Jesus Christ and the Holy Spirit

Worship depends on revelation and, from this, knowledge of God. Such knowledge, or theology, helps the worshipper to know how God wants such worship to be expressed.

Liturgy is the corporate worship of the Christian church and **doctrine** is the church's formulated teachings. Liturgical worship takes place in church — a ritual of words, praise and gestures between God and the assembled believers. Its characteristics include the reading of the Scriptures, the preaching of a sermon, the saying of prayers and the confession of faith through the recital of the creeds.

In the Old Testament, the most common Hebrew word for worship was ***ebed***, meaning 'servant', and worship itself was akin to acts of service and dedication towards God. But in the New Testament, two different words were used — ***latreia***, meaning 'service', and ***leitourgia***, meaning 'serving the community or state'. The meaning behind these was the notion that Christian worship and service were very strongly linked: '*This service that you perform is not only supplying the needs of God's people but is also overflowing in many expressions of thanks to God*' (2 Corinthians 9:12).

According to the Bible, God alone is to be worshipped. He is to be worshipped and served with the believer's whole being; emotions, physique and feelings should all come together to praise God: '*Love the Lord with all your heart and with all your soul and with all your strength and with all your mind*' (Luke 10:27). In the Old Testament, rituals were widely used in order to please God and allow for the forgiveness of sins. However, with the death of Jesus as the ultimate atonement for sins, such rituals were no longer needed. Nevertheless, the principles behind them — holiness, sincerity and purity — are still constant requirements, as is the offering of one's best to God. Indeed, Jesus gave indications about the nature of worship. In particular, he highlighted the need for fellowship (John 13:34) and evangelism: '*Therefore go and make disciples of all nations, baptising them in the name of the Father and of the Son and of the Holy Spirit and teaching them to obey everything I have commanded you'* (Matthew 28:19–20).

The Holy Spirit is of crucial importance in Christian worship, for the Spirit fills the hearts and minds of believers. In the Christian church, the emphasis is on corporate worship, with a formal structure, or liturgy, of music, prayer and preaching. Manson notes: '*What is central to Christian worship is not "forms", but the presence of the triune God, who through his word, the Bible, and by his Holy Spirit enlivens and enables all who believe in order that they may worship-serve him in spirit and in truth*' (ibid.).

2 Sacraments

Sacraments play a vital part in Christian worship. Hugh of St. Victor said: '*A sacrament is a physical or material element set before the external senses, representing by likeness, sanctifying by its institution and containing, by sanctification, some invisible and spiritual grace*' (ibid.).

The term comes from the Latin **sacramentum**, which was a military oath. It is used to denote those rites and ceremonies in the Christian church which are outward signs conveying an inner truth. The word does not appear in the Bible — the original definition was found in the Book of Common Prayer: '*An outward and visible sign of an inward and spiritual grace.'* Sacraments express the way believers understand the fundamental relationship between God, Christ, the church, humanity and creation. They are, in a sense, the manifestation of the presence of Christ in the world.

In 1142, Peter Lombard, in *The Four Books of Sentences*, laid out the view that has remained the position of the Roman Catholic church ever since — namely that there were seven sacraments: baptism, confirmation, eucharist, marriage, penance for sins, unction for the sick and dying, and ordination:

If anyone says that the sacraments of the new law are not instituted by our Lord Jesus Christ, or that there are more or less than seven, namely baptism, confirmation, eucharist, penance, extreme unction, ordination and marriage, or that any one of these seven is not truly and intrinsically a sacrament, let them be condemned.

However, during the Reformation it was argued in some quarters that the only sacraments should be those '*ordained of Christ our Lord in the Gospel*' (Article 25 of the 39 Articles). This meant that only baptism and the eucharist were retained in most Protestant churches. The reformers also argued against the doctrine of **ex opere operato** — the view that God works simply through the act of administering the sacrament. Instead, it was claimed, the sacraments received their power from the ministry of the word of God.

In recent times, the liturgical and ecumenical movements have emphasised the importance of the sacraments as an aid to faith. Buchanan outlined the position:

The sacraments incorporate believers into the visible people of God and sustain them in that membership. They thus represent to the recipients their calling to fulfil the loving, peace-making, missionary and other tasks of God in the world... They are understood by being done, and it is in the context of obeying the Lord's commands and celebrating the liturgical acts...that we may expect to be led into a true understanding of the sacraments.

(McGrath (ed.), 2000)

One of the most influential of modern writers has been Odo Casel who, in his work *The Mystery of Christian Worship*, argued that the Christian church ought to regard the sacraments as actions of Christ, rather than simply sacred objects. He said that the sacraments should be seen in their celebrative context — in the liturgy and worship of the church. The liturgy, he suggested, enables the Christian community to understand the unique mystery of Christ — his suffering, death and resurrection. This allows believers to experience the saving presence of Christ.

Schillebeeckx (1960) goes on to say that the relationship between Christ and the church was itself a sacramental one and that Christ was the foremost sacrament from which all the other sacraments derive:

The man Jesus is the personal, visible realization of the divine grace of redemption, is the sacrament, the primordial sacrament, because this man, the Son of God himself, is intended by the Father to be in his humanity, the only way to the actuality of redemption.

In the document *The Constitution on the Sacred Liturgy*, Vatican II reflected the insights of Casel and Schillebeeckx by declaring that the sacraments should be understood not as ritual mechanisms of grace, but in their living relationship to Christ and the church. It stated that the preferable way to celebrate the sacraments was in communal worship, with all believers, rather than, as had often been the case, in a private way. The celebration of the sacraments ought to be more active and dynamic, since the sacraments are an important part of growth in the Christian faith: '*Sacraments not only presuppose faith, but by words and objects they also nourish, strengthen and express it. That is why they are called "sacraments of faith"*' (McGrath (ed.), 2001).

3   Baptism

Baptism is a symbolic washing away of spiritual uncleanliness. In the Old Testament, the Law of Moses required ritual bathing for those who were deemed to be spiritually unclean (Leviticus 14:8–9). In New Testament times, the Qumran community followed a ritual of daily bathing followed by acts of repentance, and John the Baptist may have adapted this practice. During his mission of baptism with water in the River Jordan, he preached '*...a baptism of repentance for the forgiveness of sins*' (Mark 1:4).

This was in preparation for the coming of the Messiah, who would baptise not with water but with the Holy Spirit (Mark 1:7). John's baptism, unlike the Jewish rituals, was a once-and-for-all action, and did not have to be repeated later. Jesus was baptised by John too, as an act of identity with the human sinful condition (Mark 1:9–11), and his baptism marked the start of his mission. Later, Jesus commissioned his disciples to go out and baptise all believers, and the baptism ceremony formed an important part of the initiation of Gentiles into the early church (Acts 10:47–8).

For Christians, baptism is a rite that signifies their union with Christ (Galatians 3:27). The imagery used is the taking off of sinful clothes and the putting on of the fresh clothes of a new life. Paul teaches that baptism brings the believer into union with Christ in his redemptive acts and, hence, participation in the new creation brought about by Christ's resurrection:

Or don't you know that all of us who were baptised into Christ Jesus were baptised into his death? We were therefore buried with him through baptism into death in order that, just as Christ was raised from the dead through the glory of the Father, we too may live a new life.

(Romans 5:3–4)

Baptism also signifies union with Christ through his body, the church. To be 'in Christ' is to be at one with all who are united in him (1 Corinthians 12:12). Moreover, baptism signifies renewal by the Holy Spirit and entry into the kingdom of God (Romans 14:17). Finally, baptism means leading a life of obedience to God. As Beasley-Murray notes: '*Baptism signifies grace and a call for lifelong growth in Christ, with a view to the resurrection at the last day*' (McGrath (ed.), 2000).

In recent times, Vatican II concluded that adult baptism was the definitive rite of initiation. The World Council of Churches Lima Document of 1982, entitled *Baptism, Eucharist and Ministry*, stated that baptism:

…is a participation in the death and resurrection of Christ, a washing away of sin, a new birth, an enlightenment by Christ, a reclothing in Christ, a renewal by the Spirit, the experience of salvation from the flood, an exodus from bondage, and a liberation into a new humanity in which barriers of division are transcended.

(ibid.)

4 Eucharist

Eucharist comes from the Greek ***eucharis,*** meaning 'thanksgiving', and was the term first used in the **Didache** to refer to the Lord's Supper, Holy Communion or Mass. It comes from the thanksgivings that are made in the sacramental action. The eucharist is based on the Last Supper of Christ (Luke 22:14–38), in which Christ told his disciples to eat the bread as his body and drink the wine as his blood to symbolise the making of the new covenant: '*And he took the bread, gave thanks and broke it, and gave it to them, saying, "This is my body given for you, do this in remembrance of me". In the same way, after the supper he took the cup, saying, "This cup is the new covenant in my blood which is poured out for you…"*' (Luke 22:19-20).

In the early church, the eucharist was part of a larger feast called the ***agape*** or 'love feast' (Jude 12), which was provided by wealthy Christians for the benefit of poorer ones. The eucharist consisted of two parts: the action surrounding the bread, which happened during the meal; and the action surrounding the cup, which happened after the meal had ended. Later, the two were joined together in a single act of thanksgiving.

Eucharistic actions are symbolic and enable the believers to be spiritually fed with Christ as the '*bread of life*' (John 6:35). However, this has caused controversy over the centuries as theologians such as Aquinas argued that the bread and wine were actually transformed into the body and blood of Christ (**transubstantiation**), whilst others, such as Luther, said that the body and blood of Christ were present in the bread and wine (the **real presence**) but the substances did not actually become Christ's body and blood (**consubstantiation**). John of Damascus observed: '*And now you ask how the bread becomes the body of Christ, and the wine and the water become the blood of Christ. I shall tell you. The Holy Spirit comes upon them, and achieves things which surpass every word and thought*' (ibid.).

A further controversy raged over whether or not the meal was a eucharistic sacrifice in which Christ's body and blood were symbolically offered to God for the forgiveness of sins or, alternatively, the bread and wine were a feast on the sacrifice that had already been made and received by God. The Council of Trent 1562 concluded: '*Christ is contained and sacrificed in an unbloody manner, who once offered himself in a bloody manner on the altar of the Cross.*' In recent times, scholars such as Dix and Mersch have argued that when Christians offer themselves to God, Christ is offering himself, since the church is Christ's body.

5 Prayer

Prayer is communicating with God in worship. God is personal and seeks a loving relationship with humanity, made possible through the ministry of Jesus Christ. Jesus prayed constantly throughout his life and taught his followers how to pray, through the parables and the Lord's Prayer (Luke 11:2–5). He also told his followers that their prayers would be answered if they were made in his name: '*You may ask me for anything in my name, and I will do it*' (John 14:14). Moreover, Christ as heavenly High Priest makes intercessions to God on behalf of all believers, '*…because Jesus lives forever, he has a permanent priesthood. Therefore he is able to save completely those who come to God through him, because he always lives to intercede for them*' (Hebrews 7:24–5).

The Bible emphasises the importance of the Holy Spirit in prayer and highlights the fact that prayer should be in accordance with God's will (1 John 5:14). Prayers must be performed in faith and are part of God's divine plan. They allow the believer to relate to God and to change things in God's world.

There are different kinds of prayer:

÷ prayers of **praise** and adoration, thanksgiving for God's goodness
÷ prayers of **confession** and repentance for sins
÷ prayers of **petition** for personal needs, for guidance and offering of intercession for the needs of the world as a whole

The Bible teaches that God hears prayers and, by faith, will fulfil the needs of believers: '*If you believe, you will receive whatever you ask for in prayer*' (Matthew 21:22). Prayer may be individual or corporate, by believers together in the church of Christ. Prayer may be offered to avoid temptation, receive healing and to seek to fulfil God's will on earth.

Summary

- **Worship** is at the heart of Christian service and activity, and may involve specific practices and actions, but may also be seen to be the attitude that characterises a Christian's whole life and work. Worship is both corporate and personal, and is expressed most fully through the '*work of the people*' (**liturgy**). Christians follow in the example of Jesus and the early church in worshipping God, and in obedience to the biblical call to '*Love the Lord your God with all your heart…*'. Attitude to worship is essential — it should be '*in spirit and truth*' and with a pure heart. When they are acting in true unity, the Holy Spirit directs the worship of God's people.
- **Sacraments** are outward signs of what the Christian believes has already taken place in the act of salvation brought about by Jesus's death, or which commemorate or

symbolise features of that salvation. There are potentially seven sacraments, though some argue that there should only be those performed by Jesus during his ministry. They enable the believer to understand more of Jesus's ministry, death and resurrection and to experience it more fully.

- **Baptism** in the Christian tradition is modelled on the Old Testament rites of purification. Jesus submitted to baptism at the hands of John the Baptist in an act of identification with God's people. Christians signify their union with Jesus through baptism and the cleansing of their sins. Adult baptism is preferred by churches that stress the notion of personal commitment which it demonstrates, rather than infant baptism, which is effectively performed on behalf of the child.

- **Eucharist** is the central sacrament of the Christian church, and is modelled on the Last Supper shared by Jesus and his disciples. It was a regular practice in the early church as a commemoration of his death and as an expression of the shared fellowship of believers. Debate has centred around whether the bread and wine are symbols of Jesus's body and blood, or whether he is really present in them.

- **Prayer** reinforces the personal and involved relationship between God and believers and takes many forms, individual or corporate. Prayer seeks to bring the will and mind of the believer into harmony with the divine.

Exam watch

 These are accessible and interesting topics which you might find more appealing than the complex issues of doctrine. Don't just describe what goes on, however, but make sure that you can talk in some detail about the different interpretations of the sacraments and purposes of acts of worship. Be aware of denominational differences where appropriate.

Review questions

1 What is the purpose of worship?
2 Examine and comment on the theological meaning and significance of the practices of baptism and the eucharist.
3 Explain the importance of the sacraments in Christianity.
4 Explain the nature and significance of prayer in Christian worship.

Topic 4

Christian doctrine

1 Atonement

Atonement is one of the central doctrines of Christianity. According to the Bible, all humanity is deemed to be sinful and has failed to live up to the standards laid down by God. Sin prevents humanity from receiving God's blessing. The doctrine of atonement is concerned with God's love, justice and mercy. Humanity cannot be freed from sin without divine help. God sent Christ to die as a sacrifice and a ransom to pay the price of sin so that humanity could be forgiven and set free. Christ died in the place of sinners; that is atonement:

÷ *'For even the Son of Man did not come to be served, but to serve, and to give his life as a ransom for many'* (Mark 10:45).
÷ *'God presented him as a sacrifice of atonement, through faith in his blood'* (Romans 3:25).

Atonement is depicted in several different ways in the New Testament — as forgiveness for the sin of Adam (1 Corinthians 15:22), as the freeing of a slave (Galatians 5:1), and as escape from the judgment and condemnation of God: *'Therefore, there is now no condemnation for those who are in Christ Jesus, because through Christ Jesus the law of the spirit of life set me free from the law of sin and death'* (Romans 8:1).

With atonement comes reconciliation and peace between God and humanity, and the beginning of a new covenant: *'But the ministry Jesus has received is as superior to theirs as the covenant of which he is mediator is superior to the old one, and it is founded on better promises'* (Hebrews 8:6).

There has been much theological debate concerning atonement. In particular, there has been the dispute regarding for whom Christ actually died. Some theologians have argued that he died only for the 'elect' — that is, those whom God had predestined for eternal life. This is called **limited atonement** and is based on John 17:9: *'I am not praying for the world, but for those you have given me, for they are yours.'* Others, however, have argued that Christ died for all humanity and that all humans are, therefore, saved. His atoning death makes salvation possible for all people who choose to believe in him — this is called **universal atonement**. This is the view taken by the Roman Catholic and Eastern Orthodox churches: *'For God so loved the world that he gave his one and only Son, that whoever believes in him shall not perish but have eternal life'* (John 3:16).

2 Sin and grace

Sin is the state of being that separates God from humanity. It stems from Genesis 3 and the story of Adam's disobedience towards God — a disobedience, or 'original sin', which then afflicted all humanity: *'Surely I was sinful at birth, sinful from the time my mother conceived me'* (Psalm 51:5). Augustine said it was the going-wrong of something that is inherently good, whilst Calvin called it the total corruption of humanity's being. More recently, Barth defined it as *'nothingness'* and an *'impossible possibility'* — the contradiction of God's will and the breaking of the covenant and a rejection of Christ.

Grace is God's love that is given to undeserving humanity, a love that comes through Jesus Christ: *'...just as sin reigned in death, so also grace might reign through righteousness to bring eternal life through Jesus Christ our Lord'* (Romans 5:21).

3 Justification through faith

The reason why some people do not understand why faith alone justifies is that they do not know what faith is.

(Martin Luther cited in McGrath (ed.), 2001)

'Justification' is a legalistic word; the judge decides in favour of one party against the other — the winner is 'justified' in his argument. In biblical terms, justification by faith is the way in which humanity is freed from the guilt and condemnation of sin. The doctrine was first put forward by Paul, who argued that the death of Jesus meant that sin had been vanquished, and the resurrection was God's judgment that all who accept and believe in Jesus are 'justified' before him: *'...for all have sinned and fall short of the glory of God, and are justified freely by his grace through the redemption that came by Christ Jesus'* (Romans 3:24).

Justification is based on faith in Jesus and is available to all who believe (Galatians 2:21). It has nothing to do with 'being good' or 'doing good works'. It is about believing in Christ and his atoning sacrifice: *'He was delivered over to death for our sins and was raised to life for our justification'* (Romans 4:25). Modern theologians such as Kung and Hooker have argued that, whilst it is possible to be saved by believing in Christ, a believer need not actually ever have heard of justification by faith. Wright (1992) notes:

What the doctrine provides is the assurance that, though Christian doctrine is still imperfect, the believer is already a full member of God's people. It establishes, in consequence, the basis and motive for love towards God. The teaching of present justification is thus a central means whereby the fruits of the spirit — love, joy, peace and the rest — may be produced.

Summary

Atonement describes the effect of the saving death of Jesus, which brings sinful humanity back into a relationship with God — literally making him 'at one' with fallen man. The gap which was opened by the fall is breached by the cross and, most Christians argue, is potentially available to all who choose to believe. Humanity has been separated by **sin** — an act of rebellion against God's plans and purposes, and the rejection of Jesus as the way to salvation. Through **grace**, God takes the initiative and reaches out to restore humanity. It is not through works, but through **faith** that humanity is **justified** — made right with God — through an act of believing in Jesus and his saving death.

Exam watch

As with all these topics, the key is not to be floored by the technicalities of these doctrines. You can only approach them with confidence if you have learned them thoroughly — so unfortunately there are no short cuts.

Review questions

1 Examine and comment upon the doctrine of atonement and its theological importance.
2 Why is 'justification by faith' such a controversial doctrine?
3 What is meant by the terms 'sin' and 'grace'?

Topic 5

Christianity and the wider world

Christianity is constantly faced with the task of adapting to the changing needs, demands and circumstances of the modern world. This involves reviewing attitudes and approaches to the problems of the world and keeping the Gospel of Christ alive and relevant to all people. This has not proved to be easy and the Christian church has faced major dilemmas in recent years, particularly concerning the growth in personal awareness amongst those — whom the Bible calls 'the poor' — who are examining or re-examining the Christian faith in the light of their own lives and circumstances:

'Blessed are the poor in spirit, for theirs is the kingdom of heaven' (Matthew 5:3).

The '*poor*' in the Bible are not just those who are financially lacking. The '*poor*' also means the '*poor in spirit*' — those who know the weakness of the human condition and understand their complete dependence on the love of God. In the modern world there are many differing groups who lay claim to this — in particular, those who feel they have suffered racism, sexism and exploitation. Karl Marx wrote: '*Humans make religion; religion does not make humans. Religion is the self-consciousness and self-esteem of people who either have not found themselves or who have already lost themselves again*' (cited in McGrath (ed.), 2001).

Jesus teaches a great deal about the poor. He himself had a poor background and his ministry was to the outcasts, the sinners and the poor. His message to the poor was that forgiveness and salvation were at hand: '*For everyone who exalts himself will be humbled, and he who humbles himself will be exalted*' (Luke 18:14). Jesus teaches that those who consider themselves as rich in worldly terms — either financially or, as the Pharisees, in righteousness — are those who are really poor. Thus, Jesus is able to condemn the Pharisees: '*For judgment I have come into this world, so that the blind will see and those who see will become blind*' (John 9:39). Similarly, when the rich young ruler is unable to give up his wealth, Jesus says: '*Indeed, it is easier for a camel to go through the eye of a needle than for a rich man to enter the kingdom of God*' (Luke 18:25). The Bible teaches that followers of Christ should give to the poor, but in secret, so that they do not receive praise from others (Matthew 6:2–4). Of greater concern is the need for sharing with one another. In *The Church in Response to Human Needs*, Sugden writes: '*Rather the wealthy need the poor to learn from them the nature and meaning of the deliverance God brings to them both*'.

So, for Christians the issue is not primarily one of economics, although charity is important. It is about what it means to be spiritually poor. Society may give the poor little value or status, but the grace of God turns the poor into God's people: '*Has not*

God chosen those who are poor in the eyes of the world to be rich in faith and inherit the kingdom he has promised to those who love him?' (James 2:5).

1 Liberation theology

The starting point of liberation theology is commitment to the poor, the 'non-person'. Its ideas come from the victim.

(Gutierrez, 2001)

Liberation theology is the name given to a wide-ranging movement that first began in Latin America in the 1960s. It is Roman Catholic in orientation and seeks to interpret the Christian faith from the point of view of the poor and oppressed, searching for hope in a world of poverty and injustice. The notion spread out from Latin America to the black theology of the USA and South Africa and the political struggles in Northern Ireland. According to José Miguez Bonino: *'God is clearly and unequivocally on the side of the poor* (cited in McGrath (ed.), 2000).

The origins of the movement came from the experience of extreme poverty found in Latin America — an area that had been deeply Christian for centuries. The liberation theologians declared that such suffering was against the will of God and contrary to the teaching of Christ. Gutierrez remarked: *'We are on the side of the poor, not because they are good, but because they are poor'*.

Many of its ideas came from European political theology and the work of scholars such as Moltmann and Bonhoeffer, who had called for Christianity to enter the political and social arenas of life. But more than this, liberation theology was rooted in Roman Catholicism. When Vatican II (1962–5) examined the social and economic conditions of the world, it opened up the chance for a re-examination of the situation of the church in Latin America and this was undertaken in the Medellin Conference of Latin American Bishops in 1968. The outcome of this meeting sent shockwaves through the region when it was acknowledged that the Roman Catholic church had often sided with oppressive governments in the region and that, in future, the church would be on the side of the poor.

However, the papacy of John Paul II has been suspicious of the movement and its alleged Marxist connections. In the Puebla Conference of Bishops in 1979, the Pope declared: *'…those who sup with Marxism should use a long spoon'*. In 1984 the church questioned liberation theologian Leonardo Boff and later issued a criticism of the 'excesses' of liberation theology in the *Instructions of the Sacred Congregation for the Doctrine of the Faith*. The position softened a little in 1986, when the Vatican issued the *Instruction on Christian Freedom and Liberation*, which recognised some forms of liberation theology and gave a higher priority to the relief of the poor in Latin America. However, the supposed links between liberation theology and Marxism remained a thorny issue, particularly with the use of notions of 'class struggle' and the economic system as a 'factor of oppression'.

To many observers, there seem to be three different strands of liberation theology:

÷ the pastoral one of Gutierrez
÷ the academic emphasis of Segundo
÷ the populist view, based on old-style Catholicism

Certainly, liberation theology is changing. At the beginning, it was found in the universities and amongst the educated middle classes, but it has since moved into the lives of the common people and there has been a growth in 'Base Ecclesial Communities', which are small groups of ordinary people who meet to pray and address the social and political issues which affect their lives. Writers such as Gutierrez have become less academically orientated and now use the language of ordinary people, whilst in the churches, the priests have striven to restore the faith of the people into mainstream Catholicism.

Liberation theology most powerfully argues that the poor and oppressed are not to be pitied, but are to be seen as the shapers of the new path for humanity. In *Christology at the Crossroads*, Sobrino (1978) observed: *'The poor are the authentic theological source for understanding Christian truth and practice'*. The mission of the church is seen in terms of the historical struggle for liberation, and theology is something to be 'done', not 'learned'. This is the concept of 'praxis' or 'action', whereby Christians are urged to seek actively to change society on behalf of the poor. It is a Marxist term, describing the dialogue and action necessary to understand and change the world.

In *Liberation Theology: From Confrontation to Dialogue*, Leonardo Boff summarised the main themes of liberation theology in relation to Jesus. He said that Jesus came to earth as a poor person and his message was that the kingdom of God was concerned with the liberation of the poor. Jesus's death was due to a plot by the rich and powerful to prevent his mission from succeeding. Liberation theology emphasises the notion of *'structural sin'*; it is society, rather than individuals, that is corrupted and requires redemption.

However, to its critics, liberation theology is too shallow and simplistic and avoids some of the deeper theologies concerned with sin, salvation and atonement. It has reduced salvation to a purely worldly affair and neglected the spiritual dimension. But it has also brought new challenges and raised important questions that cannot be ignored. Conn asks: *'Is there a "hidden agenda" in our theological formulations that has helped to make the world-wide church more comfortable with the middle and upper classes than with the poor?'* (cited in Ferguson and Wright (eds), 1998).

2 Black theology

Black theology comes from North American black Christianity and originated as a response by black church leaders to the civil rights and black power movements of the 1960s. The first advocate was James H. Cone who, in his book *Black Theology and Black Power*, argued that black theology was the religious counterpart to black power:

...the religious explication of the need for black people to define the scope and meaning of black experience in a white racist society. While black power focuses on the political, social and economic condition of black people, black theology puts black identity in a theological context, showing that black power is not only consistent with the Gospel of Jesus Christ, but that it is the Gospel of Jesus Christ.

(Cone, 1997)

This theme was taken to its extreme by Albert Cleage in his work *Black Messiah*, in which he urged black people to liberate themselves from white theological oppression. He claimed that the Bible was written by black Jews but was corrupted and perverted by Paul in order to make it acceptable to white Europeans.

Black theology is linked to black history and racism and it represents a growing feeling among black people that their history is theologically significant. It is not just about skin colour — it is a theology that offers a particular outlook on the world. Bediako writes: '...*it emerges from a black reading of the Scriptures, from a black hearing of Jesus and a black appreciation of him as the liberator of black people, Jesus himself being the black Messiah*' (cited in Ferguson and Wright (eds), 1998).

Cone said that the Gospel of Christ was brought to black people by their 'white oppressors'. However, black people did not reject it, but have accepted it in a unique way. In *black religion and black radicalism*, Gayraud Wilmore observed: '*Blacks have used Christianity not as it was delivered to them by segregated white churches, but as its truth was authenticated to them in the experience of suffering*'.

Thus, it is claimed, to call Jesus 'black' is to speak of the freedom black people can find in the Jesus of the black Gospel — a freedom denied to them by white Christianity. Salvation is for all — black and white — who can enter the black experience of oppression, with Jesus as their liberator.

In South Africa, black theology has taken a different course. It has tended to adapt the non-violent views advocated by Martin Luther King and equates 'blackness' with 'humanness'. In *Farewell to Innocence*, Allan Boesak wrote: '*Black theology in South Africa takes Christian love very seriously, opting for agape, which stands at the very centre of God's liberating actions for his people*'.

3 Feminist theology

The women's liberation movements of the mid-twentieth century helped to create a feminist critical consciousness that challenged many Christian theological traditions. Feminism has come into conflict with Christianity mainly through the perception that, as a faith, Christianity treats women as second-rate humans in terms of their role and in the way in which they are understood in the image of God.

There are three different viewpoints. Those who follow the 'rejectionist' view argue that the Bible promoted an oppressive, male-dominated (patriarchal) structure, with a male view of God at the summit. They question the whole of Christian tradition and call for a radical re-evaluation of the Christian church. Writers such as Mary Daly in *Beyond God the Father* and Daphne Hampson in *Theology and Feminism* have argued that Christianity, with its male symbols for God, its male saviour figure and its long history of male leaders and thinkers, is biased against women and incapable of being salvaged. They urge women to leave the faith. Carol Christ in *Laughter with Aphrodite* and Naomi Goldenberg in *Changing the Gods* have suggested that the alternative for women might be a return to the ancient goddess religions.

Followers of the 'reformist' view agree that there is too much emphasis on male dominance in Christianity but do not advocate a rejection of the Christian tradition and instead call for a greater emphasis on equality. Some feminists have called for a more far-reaching **hermaneutica of suspicia** — namely that the Bible, which has been written and interpreted by men, ought to be re-defined so that women can once again occupy a place of importance, as they did in early Christian history. Rosemary Ruether in *Sexism and God-Talk* and Elizabeth Johnson in *Consider Jesus: Waves of Renewal in Christology* have suggested that Christology itself is the basis of many sexist attitudes within Christianity, and the maleness of Jesus has been used to forward the idea that only males are truly in the image of God — that the norm for humanity is male, whilst the female is seen as a less than ideal human being.

Judith Plaskow in *Sex, Sin and Grace* argues that the notions of sin as pride, ambition and excessive self-esteem are essentially male and that what women have experienced in themselves is lack of pride, ambition and self-esteem. She suggests a feminist appeal to the idea of non-competitive relationships, which avoids the traditionally submissive role of women in a male-dominated society.

Finally, those who follow the 'loyalist' view argue that there is no oppressive sexism in the Bible, and many accept the traditional approach that the woman's place in God's creation is fulfilled in her role of submission and dependence on church and family. Male leadership, they claim, does not diminish the freedom and dignity of women.

The Bible itself offers varying, and contradictory, views of women. Under the Law of Moses, there were some clearly male-orientated rules (Leviticus 12:1–5; Deuteronomy 24:1–4); yet at other times, God is depicted in a very feminine light (Isaiah 49:1–5; Psalm 22:9–10). Yet again, within the Law of Moses, there are many laws that specifically protect the interests of women and promote equality (Exodus 20:12; Exodus 22:16–24). Similarly, in Old Testament times, women held high office in Hebrew society, as prophets, judges and rules. In the New Testament, Mary, the mother of Christ, is held in the highest esteem and it is to women that the risen Christ is first revealed.

Feminist theology attempts to reconcile the biblical contradictions with a *hermaneutic of feminism*, which offers a new interpretation of the Bible. It suggests that the message of the Bible is not about male dominance, but about God's relationship with all of humanity. In the creation story, Eve is Adam's equal partner and she has her own same unique qualities just as he does. In the New Testament, women are described as '*the glory of man*' (1 Corinthians 11:7) and a woman is called on to pray with her head covered, not as a sign of inferiority but as a sign of authority because her worth is so great that it must not distract from the glory of God (1 Corinthians 11:15). Both sexes are created equal (1 Corinthians 12:12). Men and women are created in the '*image of God*' (Genesis 1:27), both called to serve God and fulfil his purpose: '*There is neither Jew nor Greek, slave nor free, male nor female, for you are all one in Christ Jesus*' (Galatians 3:28). Yet there are controversial teachings in the Bible. For example, there are Paul's comments on the dominance of the male (1 Corinthians 11:3) and his prohibition on women in church: '*...women should remain silent in the churches. They are not allowed to speak, but must be in submission, as the Law says*' (1 Corinthians 14:34).

Some have argued that the male role is not one of authoritative control, but responsible care. Nevertheless, things have changed — for instance, the ordination of women priests and the rewriting of many service books to incorporate inclusive language.

4 Christianity and world religions

God has revealed the Way and the Truth and the life in Jesus Christ, and wills that this be known throughout the world.

(Kraemer, 2002)

The Christian faith confesses that Christ is the only mediator between God and humanity. This implies a rejection of the claims made in other religions that they too offer the way to salvation. In short, Christianity is regarded as the one true faith: *'Jesus answered, "I am the way and the truth and the life. No one comes to the Father except through me"'* (John 14:6). This has led to much criticism in recent years, and there has been some softening of the position. Vatican II declared that salvation was, in fact, possible to all those who *'...through no fault of their own do not know the Gospel of Christ or his Church, yet sincerely seek God and, moved by grace, strive by their deeds to do His will as it is known to them through the dictates of conscience.'* Moreover, the Council confirmed that, through the universality of God's saving plan, all that was true and holy in other religions would reflect *'...a ray of that Truth which enlightens all men'.*

In modern times, there have been three different Christian responses to other faiths. **Pluralism** is the view that all the major religions are equal and all are valid paths to God. Christ is one revelation among many equally important revelations. John Hick, in *God and the Universe of Faith*, said that it was un-Christian to suggest that God would have *'...ordained that men must be saved in such a way and that only a small minority can, in fact, receive this salvation'.* He argued that the most important doctrine is one of an all-loving God and that all major religions highlight the need to turn away from self-centredness towards a compassionate and loving attitude to all creatures.

Exclusivism is the view that only those who hear the Gospel and believe in Christ will be saved. Supporters of this view claim that humanity is sinful and the different religions are idolatrous, seeking in a sinful and erroneous way to find God. They are the product of the human mind, not divine revelation. Humans cannot save themselves; God has shown himself through Christ and that is the only way in which people can be saved — the **solus Christos**. The Congress on World Mission 1960 declared: *'In the years since the war, more than one billion souls have passed into eternity and more than half of these went to the torment of hell fire without even hearing of Jesus Christ, who he was, or why he died on the Cross of Calvary.'*

Inclusivism is the view that Christ is the primary revelation of God, although salvation is possible through faiths other than Christianity. Supporters of this view argue that although the full light may be seen in Jesus, there is still a ray of light in the other faiths. Karl Rahner, in *Foundations of Christian Faith*, spoke of the universal grace of God. He said that Christ was the sole cause of salvation, but this saving grace could be spread to members of other faiths through the ministry of Christians — what he called 'anonymous Christianity'.

In *Christian Revelation and World Religions*, Neuner argued that most other religions are pre-Christian rather than non-Christian. Thus, in a sense, a person making a genuine commitment of faith and love in another religion is still acceptable to the church and to God. Other religions can, therefore, be called the 'ordinary' way of salvation, whilst Christianity is the 'extraordinary' way. In *Theological Investigations* Karl Rahner wrote: *'Christianity understands itself as the absolute religion, intended for all people, which cannot recognize any other religion beside itself as of equal right'.*

Certainly, according to Scripture, God reveals himself to all humanity through creation and providence, and human nature by being made in the image of God, has a relationship with him. World religions are, therefore, examples of God's revelation of himself to all humanity — although these religions may also be a way in which humanity clouds the issues and refuses to face the ultimate truth. *In Human Religion in God's Eyes,* Bavinck wrote: '*There is deep in the heart of man, even among those who live and believe in non-Christian religions, a very vague awareness that man plays a game with God and that man is always secretly busy escaping from him*'. However, J. Anderson, in *Christianity and World Religions*, claims that, by God's grace and Christ's mediation, it is possible for salvation to extend to followers of other faiths. He says that such followers, although they may not know Christ, can be saved if they have a '*...God given sense of sin or need, and a self-abandonment to God's mercy*'. He cites Acts 17:27: '*God did this so that men would seek him and find him, though he is not far from any one of us.*'

However, biblical teaching does lean heavily towards the saving presence of Christ alone and there is no biblical support for seeing Christ as somehow 'hidden' in other faiths. Despite the apparent universality of God's presence and love, it seems, for Christianity at least, that there is only one way to know him: '*For there is one God and one mediator before God and men, the man Christ Jesus*' (1 Timothy 2:5). In *God and the Universe of Faith* Hick (1993 edn) poses a crucial question: '*But would it not be more realistic now to make the shift from Christianity at the centre to God at the centre, and to see both our own and the other great world religions as revolving around the same divine reality?*'

Summary

- Christianity is a world-affirming religion, in that it reaches out to the world rather than withdraws from it (although individuals might withdraw for specific purposes). Hence, Christianity faces the challenges of the world, such as poverty, racism and oppression. **Liberation theology** attempted to make Christianity compatible with the problems of poverty in Latin America, but reached out also to political and social struggles elsewhere in the world. Poverty is an issue to be challenged, not accepted, through transformation, not platitudes. Originally an academic theology, it has acquired a very practical outlook and the mission of the church is interpreted as being primarily one of struggling to liberate those who are oppressed by their social conditions, just as Jesus was the victim of a plot instigated by the rich and powerful.

- **Black theology** has its roots in the civil rights movement and the struggle for black power. The concept of Jesus as 'black' speaks of the freedom that black people can find in his salvation, even in the face of oppression from white Christians.
- **Feminist theology** challenges the view that women are inferior to men in theological terms and the prevailing masculine presentation of God. The maleness of Jesus is thought to be the basis for sexist attitudes within Christianity. The Bible offers contradictory views of male and female roles, which feminist theology attempts to reconcile. Some interpretations see the masculine role as positive — i.e. caring rather than oppressive.
- Christianity has traditionally seen **other religions** as failing to offer the true way to salvation and as such has been interpreted as **exclusivist**, with Jesus as the only medium of salvation for humanity. **Inclusivist** interpretations acknowledge that Christ is the primary revelation of God, but salvation is possible through other faiths. God reveals himself through the natural order of creation, through the witness of Christians, and through Christ's mediation.

Exam watch

These are interesting topics to explore, but make sure that you do not fall into the trap of making tedious and non-academic comments such as 'Feminists believe that the Bible treats women as second-class citizens' or 'Christians have always oppressed the black races'. These statements are hopelessly generalised and misguided. Ensure that you recognise that in all these issues there are genuine varieties of approach and a range of interpretations. Back up everything you say with relevant scholarship.

Review questions

1 What does the Bible teach concerning the poor?
2 Examine and comment on the main teachings of liberation theology.
3 '*Black theology is a political rather than a religious movement.*' Discuss.
4 What is feminist theology?
5 Examine and analyse the views of scholars concerning the relationship of Christianity to other world faiths.

Topic 6

The Christian church

1 Ordination

Ordination is a liturgical action of the church whereby some of its members are commissioned and consecrated into public pastoral ministry — they are ordained to, and established in, ministries of service and leadership within the church community. In the most formal sense, ordination means becoming a priest.

In the Old Testament, the priesthood was established with Aaron, the brother of Moses (Exodus 28:3). In the New Testament, Jesus is depicted as prophet, priest and king by the consecrating act of God, and Christ's work is seen as continuing through the ministry of the church. Ordination was one of the original seven sacraments. In the early church, there was no ordination as such, though prominent Christians were often designated as **deacons**. They had a largely practical function and it was not until several centuries later that this developed into a more theological and priestly role. By the fourth century, there emerged the **presbyter-priest**, who presided over the Eucharist and whose ordination was seen in terms of an empowerment and blessing from God. By the time of the Middle Ages, the role of priest had become firmly established.

Today, many Christian churches have a hierarchical structure. The Anglican church, for instance, has an **episcopal** structure of clergy leadership, with the monarch and the archbishop of Canterbury, followed by archbishops, bishops and priests. Other churches have a **presbyterate** system of leadership through lay elders. In the Roman Catholic church, priests may not marry and women cannot be ordained. In the Anglican church, marriage is permitted and women can now be ordained.

Those who are ordained have both a practical and a symbolic function in the church. They are a link to the original Church of Christ (the Apostolic church) and this is symbolically expressed by the laying on of hands that a bishop enacts on the newly ordained in order that they may carry out Christ's work. Peter Fink observes: '*It is in function of this awesome commission of the church to some of its members that the church deems it proper, and indeed essential, to lay on hands and to entrust the minister and the ministry, to the power of God's Spirit*' (cited in Ferguson and Wright (eds), 1988). The symbolic manifestation of Christ is also made present in the priestly ministries of preaching, teaching and leadership in prayer. Moreover, as a sacrament, ordination is seen as the embodiment, within the person, of the church itself — so that the church can see its own nature and destiny in the work of its clergy.

Not all who are ordained become priests, however. In some churches, the ordained are lay people who hold a position of leadership, such as an elder. However, ordination is for the purpose of the church, since it is through the church that Christ's work on earth is said to continue. Fink notes that *'The sacramental ministry of the ordained is to manifest in life and action the ways of Jesus Christ'* (Ferguson and Wright (eds), 1998).

2 Laity

The term 'laity' comes from the Greek *laos*, meaning 'people'. It refers to those people who are members of the church but are not ordained clergy. In the early church there was no distinction between clergy and laity (or lay people) — all believers shared a common vocation to be God's people, although each individual church had people with different spiritual gifts to enable the church to fulfil its role: *'And in the church God has appointed first of all Apostles, second prophets, third teachers, then workers of miracles, also those having gifts of healing, those able to help others, those with gifts of administration, and those speaking in different kinds of tongues'* (1 Corinthians 12:27–8).

However, in the Middle Ages the position of the clergy became established and a sharp divide took place between the special functions of the clergy and the more general ministries of lay people. It became the task of the laity to help the clergy rather than develop their own ministries in their jobs and daily lives. Gibbs notes: '*...they were often considered, and considered themselves, a lower grade of Christian than the ordained ministers*' (ibid.).

The position has changed a little, particularly since 1945. In Germany and in other parts of Europe, large lay assemblies such as the **Kirchentags** have been established, and in Britain the work of William Temple and others has led to a greater emphasis on the role of the laity. These developments have highlighted the different types of ministry lay people can offer: the **Sunday ministry** in which the laity help within the church itself, the **personal ministry** of friendship and family, the **Monday ministry** in the workplace and the **Saturday ministry** in places of sport and entertainment.

However, some churches, including the Roman Catholic and high Anglican, have experienced difficulties in the nature of the relationship between clergy and laity; both priests and lay people have found it difficult to work together as equals. The problem does not lie simply with priests being reluctant to hand over parts of their role. A major issue is the fact that many lay people do not want authority and are happy to accept a lower level of Christian commitment and behaviour than the clergy. Moreover, many churches have found that the laity prefer to be led by the clergy in matters of liturgy and worship, rather than take it upon themselves to lead. Most traditional Roman Catholic and Protestant worship is still, primarily, clergy-led.

3 Saints

Saints are people whose lives are deemed to be so close to the example of Jesus Christ himself that, after their death, they are canonised and venerated by Christians. The holiness of saints is based on the personal example of their lives, which have been lived in the image of God and in the imitation of Christ, such that it is possible to say that they are with Christ in heaven.

From the second century onwards, days have been named after saints in the liturgical calendar and churches have been named after them and often built on the tombs of saintly martyrs to the faith. Throughout the ages, Christians have made pilgrimages to the shrines of saints and have venerated the bodies or other relics of the saints themselves.

In the Roman Catholic church, people become saints after their death when they have been canonised by the Pope in a procedure laid down by Benedict XVI called **De Servorum Dei**. The requirements of canonisation are heroic virtue and the occurrence of miracles. An enquiry is made into the whole life of the proposed saint and tests are carried out to see if miracles have actually been performed, either by the person him- or herself, or in response to the intercession by the saint, usually through answered prayer.

Many Christians believe that the saints are in heaven with Christ and, in some churches, particularly the Roman Catholic church, believers may pray to the saints to ask them to intercede with Christ on behalf of humanity. Such direct requests for intercession are called **invocation of the saints**.

Many Roman Catholics and other Christians venerate the saints for their Christ-like example. This stems from the belief that the church is a family united in heaven and on earth in one body, in which all members have a relationship with God. The **Communion of Saints (*Communio Sanctorum*)** is the fellowship of the saints in heaven. It is not a phrase used in the Bible, although there is a veiled reference in Colossians 1:12: '...*thanks to the Father who has qualified you to share in the inheritance of the saints in the kingdom of light.*'

In recent times, the veneration of the saints has caused problems for the Roman Catholic church, and praying to the communion of saints has been questioned, despite its popularity among ordinary believers. In *The Eucharistic Memorial*, Max Thurian (1960) noted: '*They are a reminder of the mediation of Christ in the universal Church of all time. The Son of God has willed to be present in the incarnation to men by the mediation of his humanity... The saints are therefore signs of the presence and love of Christ*'. Today, the term 'communion of saints' is largely taken to mean the fellowship of all Christians — past, present and future — so that it is the duty of the church to preserve the faith and transfer it intact to the next generation.

4 Orthodoxy

Orthodoxy means a belief in, or assent to, the fundamental truths of the faith. It is a slightly ambiguous term, since it can refer to either 'right worship' or 'right belief'. It is not a matter of an intellectual agreement or acceptance of certain statements, but involves giving glory to God through right belief and action. In Christianity, orthodoxy begins with simple confessional truths such as 'Jesus is Lord', 'Jesus is the Messiah' and 'Jesus is the Son of God'. These confessions are then joined by certain lengthier statements of Christian belief that have been developed into 'creeds' that are accepted by believers. The most well-known of these are the Apostles' Creed, the Nicene Creed and the Athanasian Creed.

Since the Reformation, many churches have developed their own confessional statements, which contain their particularly distinctive beliefs — such as the Anglican Thirty-Nine Articles and the Westminster Confession. In the Roman Catholic church, statements of orthodox belief are also made when the Pope speaks **ex cathedra**. These are expansions and clarifications of the substance of orthodoxy and require the assent of the faithful. The most famous of these have been the Immaculate Conception (1854), Papal Infallibility (1870) and the Assumption of the Blessed Virgin Mary (1950). In the Protestant church the Barmen Declaration (1934) denied the claims of Nazism, and the

World Council of Churches has recently looked into matters of ministry, authority, baptism and the eucharist.

5 Spirituality

Spirituality is that which enables believers to reach out towards God. In Christianity, it involves the relationship between the believer's whole being and a holy God who reveals himself in the person of Jesus Christ. The most famous Christian text on the subject is Thomas à Kempis's *The Imitation of Christ*. The test of Christian spirituality is conformity of the heart and life of the believer to Jesus as Lord, and the sign of spirituality is the presence and power of the Holy Spirit in the life of believers and their obedience to God's will: '*A new commandment I give you: Love one another. As I have loved you, so you must love one another. By this all men will know that you are my disciples, if you love one another*' (John 13:34–5).

Spirituality enables the imagination and understanding of the believer to be lifted beyond itself. Spirituality requires practice, involving thought, prayer and meditation. Music, worship and the sacraments all have a special spiritual impact on the believer. Albin writes: '*…spirituality gives shape and substance to theology*' (cited in Ferguson and Wright (eds), 1988).

Summary

- **Ordination** is the means by which individuals are commissioned and consecrated into public ministry. It is rooted in the establishment of Aaron as a priest, although the New Testament prescribes no specific act of ordination. In the Anglican church, ordination is into a hierarchical structure headed by the Archbishop of Canterbury, although non-ordained ministers may carry out some leadership. Christian churches are divided on the topic of women's ordination. The ordained ministry reflects the work of Jesus and may be seen as the way in which he is made manifest in the church today.
- The **laity** — non-ordained members of the church — are essential to its life and function. All members of God's church can fulfil roles of leadership, although many members of the laity would rather not have the responsibility for leadership and pastoral authority. Some churches place a strong emphasis on everyone being involved in some form of ministry or service in order to justify their place in the church body. The laity can have an active ministry to the world outside the church itself.
- **Saints** are venerated and canonised after their deaths because their lives have been deemed to have been examples of Jesus's own life. Catholicism places high value on the lives of the saints and many undertake pilgrimages to their shrines. Other denominations only recognise the value of key saints such as the Apostles. Saints are characterised by **heroic virtue** and the performance of **miracles**. Prayer to saints and invocations of the saints are still popular amongst many Roman Catholic believers.
- **Orthodoxy** is a belief in the fundamental truths of the faith which have been developed into creeds and statements of faith.
- **Spirituality** enables believers to enter into a living relationship with God and to go beyond themselves and enter the realm of the transcendent God. It is a vital characteristic of mysticism.

Exam watch

These are quite straightforward topics, but make sure that you are clear about the different ways in which individual Christians or denominations may approach them. Refer to some specific examples in your answers, and be sure not to make generalised statements such as 'All Roman Catholics are against women priests' or 'Saints are good people'.

Review questions

1 Explain the religious and theological significance of ordination.
2 Examine and comment on the role of the laity in the Christian church.
3 What is the theological significance of the Communion of Saints in the Christian faith?
4 What is orthodoxy?

Topic 7

Christian ethics

(*Note:* A fuller exposition of Christian ethical issues can be found in Section 2, 'Religious Ethics', pp. 127–219.)

1 Sexual ethics

Human sexuality is concerned not just with what people do but with who people actually are. In the biblical account of creation, the making of man and woman as sexual beings is linked to their creation in God's own image (Genesis 1:27). Sexuality, therefore, is an integral part of what makes a person human.

Sexuality is seen as having a part to play in God's plan. In the creation story, God makes the woman to be the equal partner of the man, fulfilling the human need for relationships: '*Then the Lord God made a woman from the rib she had taken out of the man, and he brought her to the man. The man said, "This is now bone of my bones and flesh of my flesh; she shall be called 'woman', for she was taken out of man"*' (Genesis 2:22–3).

The biblical emphasis is on man and woman being united together, ideally in marriage, in order to fulfil God's purpose: '*For this reason a man will leave his father and mother and be united to his wife, and they will become one flesh*' (Genesis 2:24).

1.1 Sex outside marriage

The Bible makes it clear that sexual relationships belong within the marriage and that adultery and extra-marital relationships are forbidden. In the Ten Commandments it specifically states: '*You shall not commit adultery*' (Exodus 20:14). Any behaviour that breaks the links between sex, personhood and relationship is seen as a symptom of sin and disorder and should be avoided:

÷ '*Flee from sexual immorality… Do you not know that your body is a temple of the Holy Spirit, who is in you, whom you have received from God?*' (1 Corinthians 6:19).
÷ '*But among you there must not even be a hint of sexual immorality, nor any kind of impurity, or of greed, because these are improper for God's holy people*' (Ephesians 5:3).

The nature of human sexuality has always caused problems for the Christian church, largely due to the dualism that pervades its thinking, wherein the mind and spirit are seen as being superior to the physical body. In the Middle Ages, the sensual pleasure of sexual intercourse was seen as sinful and celibacy was depicted as preferable — and was compulsory for the clergy. Linked with this was the often unspoken view that Eve (and therefore women generally) was responsible for humanity's fall into sin.

Today the position is much softer; for instance, priests in the Protestant church are allowed to marry. Generally, modern scholars have taken the view that, as the Bible suggests, sex should ideally be confined to matrimony, but there is a growing view that what may be more important is to see sex in the context of loving, though not necessarily marital, relationships.

1.2 Contraception

Contraception is a choice concerning the matter of whether or not a couple should have sexual intercourse with the view to conceiving a child. The Roman Catholic church has generally taken the position that every act of sexual intercourse must, in principle, be open to the possibility of conception, and that to use contraception is to prevent the transmission of a human life.

However, today many Christian couples argue in favour of contraception and family planning. Whilst at some point the marriage relationship will be open to the possibility of having children, it is a matter of social and economic responsibility to avoid conception at other times. For others, the deliberate refusal to conceive children is seen as a sin against God and a rejection of his gift of life.

However, many Christians, even if they favour contraception, feel that some methods are inappropriate — in particular the IUD and the 'morning-after pill' (drug RU468). These types of contraceptive, which act after sex has taken place rather than before, are deemed by many to be unethical since they end the life of the pre-embryo after fertilisation has occurred.

1.3 Marriage

The Bible says that marriage is ordained by God. It is an exclusive and lifelong binding relationship between a man and a woman that ends only with the death of one of the partners.

The New Testament writers have suggested that each partner has a specific role in the marriage relationship. It is a kind of hierarchy, based on that between God and humanity. The man is the head of his wife, just as Christ is the head of the church. His task is to love his wife — not in domination and power, but by ensuring that her needs are met. Like Christ's relationship with humanity and the church, the husband's relationship to his wife is based on love and sacrifice: '*For the husband is the head of the wife as Christ is the head of the church.... Husbands, love your wives, just as Christ loved the church and gave himself up for her...husbands ought to love their wives as their own bodies. He who loves his wife loves himself*' (Ephesians 5:25, 28).

In turn, the wife is required to submit to her husband and to love and respect him, not because she is inferior to him, but because of the man's characteristic need for respect: '*Now as the church submits to Christ, so also wives should submit to their husbands in everything...and the wife must respect her husband*" (Ephesians 5:24, 33).

For Christians, the purpose of marriage is mutual companionship, bodily union and the raising of children in a family setting: '*Marriage is given, that husband and wife may comfort and help each other, living faithfully together in need and plenty, in sorrow and in joy...it is that they may have children and be blessed in caring for them and bringing them up in accordance with God's will*' (*The Church of England Service Book*).

1.4 Divorce

The Bible teaches that divorce is contrary to God's wishes and that a marriage should be preserved as a holy relationship:

❖ *'Therefore what God has joined together, let man not separate'* (Matthew 19:6).
❖ *'To the married I give this command... A wife must not separate from her husband... And a husband must not divorce his wife'* (1 Corinthians 7:10–11).

However, there is also a recognition that relationships do break down. Jesus spoke against divorce, but in Matthew's Gospel there is the suggestion that divorce may be possible on the grounds of adultery: *'I tell you that anyone who divorces his wife, except for marital unfaithfulness, and marries another woman commits adultery'* (Matthew 19:9).

Paul, in turn, also suggests that divorce may be permissible for a Christian and non-Christian partner: *'But if the unbeliever leaves, let him do so. A believing man or woman is not bound in such circumstances'* (1 Corinthians 7:15).

1.5 Homosexuality

Homosexuality has always been an extremely controversial issue within the Christian church. The Bible teaches that all homosexual acts are prohibited:

❖ *'If a man lies with a man as one lies with a woman, both of them have done what is detestable. They must be put to death, their blood will be on their own hands'* (Leviticus 20:13).
❖ *'Neither the sexually immoral nor idolaters nor adulterers nor male prostitutes nor homosexual offenders...will inherit the kingdom of God'* (1 Corinthians 6:9–10).

However, modern scholars have argued that stable, affectionate relationships should be defended on the grounds that the only way to truly judge sexual behaviour is through love: *'There are circumstances in which individuals may justifiably choose to enter into a homosexual relationship with the hope of enjoying companionship and a physical expression of love similar to that found in marriage'* (Church of England Working Party Paper).

2 Medical ethics

Medical ethics is concerned with the relationship between modern medical technology and issues of ethics and morality as they affect the control of human life. In particular, the Bible teaches that life is a holy gift from God (the 'sanctity of life'). Life is sacred, that is, set apart for God's purposes and created by him. Life is therefore precious to God and once God has created a life, only he can end it: *'Before I formed you in the womb I knew you, before you were born I set you apart'* (Jeremiah 1:5). God is therefore seen as having ultimate control over life. Abortion and euthanasia present difficult challenges to this viewpoint.

2.1 Abortion

An abortion is the termination of a pregnancy. A medical abortion is permissible in law in the UK under the Abortion Act 1967 up to the 24th week of pregnancy. Abortion is permitted if two doctors agree that the woman, her existing children or the child itself will suffer physically or mentally.

The problem revolves around the question of whether or not the unborn foetus is a human being. The Bible implies that it is and that life in the womb is a gift from God: '*For you created my innermost being: you knit me together in my mother's womb*' (Psalm 139:13).

The Roman Catholic church is generally opposed to abortion, as the following catechism outlines: '*Abortion is a horrible crime…the law provides appropriate sanctions for every deliberate violation of the child's rights.*' However, other Christian churches take a different view, and the Church of England states:

We affirm that every human life is unique, born or yet to be born…we therefore believe that abortion is an evil. But we also believe that to withdraw compassion in circumstances of extreme distress or need is a very great evil. In an imperfect world, the 'right' choice is sometimes the lesser of two evils.

(Cited in McGrath (ed.), 2000)

The Methodist church adopts a similar position, stating that: '*Abortion is always an evil to be avoided if at all possible… However, in an imperfect world, there will be circumstances where termination of a pregnancy is the lesser of two evils*' (ibid.).

2.2 Euthanasia

Euthanasia, from the Greek **eu-thanatos**, means 'good death', and refers to the concept of 'mercy killing'. It is used to refer to the termination of the lives of people suffering from great physical or mental handicap or a painful terminal illness. In the UK 'active' euthanasia — that is, where a doctor deliberately ends the life of the person by medical means, for example by a lethal injection — is illegal, save in the case of switching off life-support machines in circumstances where the patient is deemed to be 'brain dead'. 'Passive' euthanasia, where medical treatment is not given (for good reasons) and the patient dies naturally, is permissible.

Those who support euthanasia say that it is an act of compassion and mercy, allowing a gentle and dignified death as a relief for those whose suffering is extreme. It also has economic advantages with regard to the price of medical and hospital care. Those who argue against euthanasia say that the task of the doctor is to save life, not end it. Moreover, if we kill the sick, in the end we will stop looking for cures. On the social side, if we allowed the killing of the elderly and those suffering, rather like putting animals to sleep, such people might feel pressured to agree to die.

Most Christian churches are against euthanasia on the grounds of the sanctity of life: '*An act or omission which causes death in order to eliminate suffering constitutes a murder greatly contrary to the dignity of the human person and to the respect due to the living God, his creator*' (Catechism of the Catholic Church); '*We believe that it is right to use medical treatment to control pain. We deny the right to legalize the termination of life by a doctor*' (Salvation Army).

As an alternative, many Christians support the Hospice Movement, which seeks to allow the terminally ill to live out their remaining days being cared for in a peaceful and dignified way: '*We are now always able to control pain in terminal cancer in the patients sent to us…euthanasia as advocated is wrong…it should be unnecessary and is an admission of defeat*' (Christian Hospice Movement).

3 Work and leisure

In the Bible, work is seen as the basic dimension of human existence — humans are made in God's likeness, with the capacity to participate actively in the wider creation. In Genesis, humanity is commissioned to rule over the earth and to administer God's gifts (Genesis 1:28). However, with the fall of Man, work also took on the nature of a burdensome task: *'Cursed is the ground because of you; through painful toil you will eat of it all the days of your life'* (Genesis 3:17). So, on the one hand, work is part of God's divine ordering of the world and, on the other hand, due to human sinfulness, work is a hardship.

There is, however, a wider biblical view of work. Both God's work of creation and human work are linked — as God rested on the seventh day of creation, so humanity rests on the Sabbath (Exodus 20:10). This is seen not in terms of idleness but as a higher form of activity, involving the worship of God and the enjoyment of his creation.

The Bible encourages people to treat work as a way in which they can serve God, since Christians believe that they are 'co-workers' with God in the furtherance of his divine will. Therefore, the motive for working diligently is not for money but in grateful response to the work of Christ (1 Corinthians 3:9). For many Christians, work is a 'calling' or 'vocation' — something that they feel Christ has asked them to do. Luther, Calvin and others all highlighted the fact that work was an important part of Christian life. This was most evident in what became known as the 'Protestant work ethic' — a view that held sway for several centuries. The ethic stated that work was of value and being industrious was a virtue. All legitimate types of work were acceptable. God was seen as giving every person a general call to the Christian life and a particular call to a specific occupation. Luther said: *'Seemingly secular works are a worship of God and an obedience well pleasing to God'* (cited in McGrath (ed.), 2000).

The primary purposes of work were seen as glorifying God and benefiting society — the worker is a 'steward' in the service of God. However, since the Second World War, unemployment, dissatisfaction, globalisation and feelings of exploitation in the workplace have taken over. People are tending to overwork and work has come to be seen, by many, as simply a means of providing for one's own needs so as not to be a burden on others but to enable society to function smoothly. Davies noted: *'A theological understanding…is called for to express the interdependence of human relationships under God in the world of work, no less than in the family, the church or the state'* (ibid.).

Summary

- Christian views of **sexual ethics** centre on the nature of relationships and their purpose. Sex is usually interpreted as being a gift of God within a monogamous, heterosexual **marriage** relationship, although more modern approaches allow for committed and loving homosexual or other non-marital relationships as a legitimate arena for the expression of sexual love. If sexual relationships are ultimately for the purpose of conception, then **contraception** will cause problems for some religious believers, although others will acknowledge that responsible **family planning** is acceptable in the modern world. High value is placed on marriage as ordained by God and providing the ideal environment for the upbringing of children. **Divorce** is permitted, but not desired, and churches are divided on whether divorcees should be remarried, in or out of church. **Homosexuality** is a controversial issue with many extreme views expressed. Essentially, the Bible condemns it, but an attitude of love towards homosexuals is now seen to be more representative of the love of Jesus.

- Issues arising in **medical ethics** focus on the principle of the **sanctity of life** and on the nature of human life — when it begins and ends. Compassion for those who are suffering is a matter of concern for many Christians who, in principle, may allow for both **abortion** and **euthanasia** where compassion and integrity seem to demand it.
- **Work** is seen as a God-given blessing to humanity, corrupted by the fall, which made work onerous rather than joyful. Christians are encouraged to see their work as the arena in which they can worship God and contribute to his plans and purposes for the wider world. **Leisure** is a legitimate counterpart to work, blessed by God's own Sabbath rest, but the use of leisure time may be an issue for Christians. Leisure activities must glorify God as much as those in the workplace.

Exam watch

These are probably the most popular and accessible areas for students studying issues in Christian belief and practice, but make sure you don't over-simplify your responses to them. Don't fall back on your old GCSE notes or textbooks. They will simply not give you the depth of knowledge and analysis you are expected to show.

Review questions

1 Explain and comment upon biblical teaching concerning sex before marriage.
2 Why are some Christians against the use of contraception?
3 What is the purpose of marriage in the Christian faith?
4 Examine and comment critically upon the biblical teaching concerning divorce.
5 'The teaching of the Bible on homosexuality is offensive and should be ignored.' Discuss.
6 Examine and assess the relative value of the religious and secular arguments concerning abortion and euthanasia.
7 In what ways and why does a Christian view of work differ from a non-Christian one?

The New Testament

Topic 1

Introducing the New Testament

 A Background to the life of Christ

1 The setting

1.1 The historical setting

The land of Israel at the time of the ministry of Jesus was a small country, divided into several tiny provinces. The most important was Judea, in the south, where the capital city, Jerusalem, was located. In the middle lay Samaria, and to the north, Galilee. In the west were the minor provinces of Trachonitis, Iturea, Perea and the Decapolis. During the adult life of Jesus, Judea and Samaria were governed directly by the Romans. The Roman 'client' king, Herod Antipas, ruled Galilee and the Decapolis region. Philip, who was Herod's brother, governed the remaining part of the land.

The people of Israel, the Jews, believed that they were God's 'chosen people'. This belief stemmed from the election of Abraham, the first of the Patriarchs, who lived around 2000 BCE. He had been chosen by God to be the father of a race of people who would be a holy, chosen people, and all Jews saw themselves as being sons of Abraham. God and Abraham had made a **covenant** together. This was an agreement by which Abraham and his descendants would be God's people, and God, in turn, would look after them and be their God. Israel itself was regarded as the Promised Land — the land that God had promised to his people.

Several hundred years later, the Jews were held as slaves in Egypt. Under the leadership of Moses, the people were led to freedom and received from God his Law and a renewal of the covenant made with Abraham. The Law, including the Ten Commandments, or the Decalogue, was to be the people's guide as to how they should lead holy and righteous lives.

The Jews settled in Israel and tried to live their lives in accordance with the Law, though frequently failed to do so and lapsed into sinful ways. Under the reign of King David, Israel enjoyed a golden age of prosperity, but around 950 BCE, internal quarrelling led to the land being split into the Northern Kingdom of Israel and the Southern Kingdom of Judah. The people ignored the covenant and neglected God's laws, although a series of prophets were sent by God to urge the people back into ways of righteousness. In 730 BCE the Northern Kingdom was conquered by Assyria and a century later the Babylonians conquered the Southern Kingdom. Most of the Jews were taken into exile in Babylon. About 630 BCE the Babylonian Empire fell to the Persians and the Jews were allowed to return to the Promised Land and a slow process of rebuilding Jerusalem and the Temple began. The monarchy was never re-established.

In 325 BCE the land was conquered by the Greeks under Alexander the Great. Greek (Hellenistic) culture spread throughout the region. As time passed, this led to a division in Judaism. The more liberal Jews were content to keep the Hellenistic culture, but stricter Jews wanted to keep the Law of Moses without Hellenistic influences. In 198 BCE Antiochus II overran the land and a revolt broke out, led by a strict Jewish leader called Judas Maccabeus. He rid the land of invaders and also destroyed Hellenistic idols and rebuilt the Temple in Jerusalem. Peace followed until his death in 160 BCE when the land was conquered first by the Syrians and then, in 62 BCE, by the Romans.

1.2 The social setting

Jewish life centred in the home; men would work as either farmers or fishermen, whilst the poorest worked as shepherds. Some worked for the Romans as tax collectors and were universally hated. The women kept house and some resorted to prostitution. From the age of 6, boys received an academic education in the synagogue and learned a working trade from their father. At the age of 13 a boy became an adult, or son of the Law. Girls, meanwhile, were taught at home by their mothers; their education was usually concerned with household chores and child rearing. Three important customs affected everyone — birth, marriage and death:

- **Birth** — a couple's happiness was measured by how many children, and particularly how many sons, they had. For a woman to be childless was, for her, the greatest sadness of all, and some saw it as a punishment from God. After the birth of her first son, a woman was known as 'the mother of...'. At birth, a baby's skin was rubbed in salt to make it firm and the child was tightly wrapped in 'swaddling clothes' to ensure that its limbs grew straight. After eight days, a boy would be circumcised.
- **Marriage** — the bride's parents usually arranged marriages. There was little social mixing between the sexes. It was the duty of everyone to be married and, because a bride was seen as a working asset, she had to be paid for with a dowry. About a year before the actual wedding, the couple would become formally betrothed. This was a legally binding arrangement, carried out by a formal ceremony and exchange of gifts. At the wedding itself, the bridegroom and his friends would process to the bride's house; there the couple would be blessed and the groom would lead the procession back.
- **Death** — after a person's death, the family would undertake an elaborate ritual. The body would be washed, wrapped in grave cloths, anointed and buried within 24 hours of death. The poor were buried in graves or caves; the wealthy had tombs cut out of rock and sealed with a boulder.

1.3 The religious setting

Religious life was centred on the synagogue and the Temple and was governed by a huge number of regulations which guided everyday conduct, sacrifice and offering at the great annual festivals.

Festivals

The greatest day of the year was the **Day of Atonement** (10th Tishri), which was the one occasion when the High Priest would enter the innermost shrine of the Temple to atone for his own sins and the sins of the people. The other great festivals were **Passover and Unleavened Bread** (14–21st Abib — the first month), which commemorated the escape from slavery in Egypt. The Festival of **Pentecost** or **Weeks** commemorated the start of the harvest, and **Tabernacles** was Harvest itself. **Purim** commemorated Esther's deliverance of the Jews.

The Law of Moses required all Jews to be present at the Temple for these festivals at least once per year. The great weekly festival was the **Sabbath**, which began at 6pm on Friday evening and lasted until 6pm on Saturday evening. It was a day when no work was done and when the people turned their attention to worshipping God in accordance with the commandment: 'Remember the Sabbath day by keeping it holy' (Exodus 20:8).

The Temple and the synagogue

Regular worship took place in the local synagogue. Only men were permitted to play an active part and women and children were usually confined to the gallery. In charge was the ruler of the synagogue and the service followed a pattern: the creed, prayers, readings from the Law and the Prophets, and a sermon. During the week, the synagogue would also act as a school and community centre.

The order to rebuild the Temple in Jerusalem had been given by King Herod the Great, although it was still not completed during the lifetime of Jesus. It was a large open area, divided into several courtyards by a series of walls. Non-Jews were confined to the outer courtyard (the Court of Gentiles). The Temple was also the place where animal sacrifices would be carried out. At the centre was a building called the Holy Place, inside which, covered by curtains, was the Holy of Holies, the dwelling place of God. This was the sacred place the High Priest entered once a year on the Day of Atonement.

The Temple administration was much criticised; the High Priest was a political appointment, and the ordinary priests were civil servants and open to corruption. The ordinary people had to pay a Temple tax for the upkeep of the Temple, which they greatly resented, and the Temple, with its own guards, often resembled a fortress and a treasury rather than a place of worship.

The Law of Moses

The Law of Moses had been expanded and amplified. Along with the Ten Commandments and the first five books of the Old Testament (**Pentateuch**), there had grown up a large body of traditions that had come to be almost as binding as the Law itself. There were, therefore, precise rules for every occasion — for example, 39 types of action were forbidden on the Sabbath. These rules had become very complex, strict and overbearing, governing the lives of all the Jews. The problem was, as Jesus was to point out, that the spirit of God's Law had become lost in a mass of regulations.

1.4 The authorities

The Pharisees

The Pharisees (from **Parash** — 'the separated ones') were the largest of the religious parties, numbering about 6,000. They were purists who had probably grown out of the second-century BCE group the **Hasidim** ('God's loyal ones'). They controlled religious, rather than political, affairs, and worked mostly in the synagogues. Their main concern was to ensure that the people kept the Law and traditions in every exact detail and they saw themselves as model Jews. To this end, they kept themselves apart from the ordinary people. This made them generally unpopular as they were regarded as arrogant and aloof. Moreover, the evangelists' presentation of their insistence on the precise observation of the letter of the Law made them appear dry and legalistic, rather than loving and just, which may not be an altogether fair picture of them.

Jesus is presented as coming into conflict with the Pharisees over this — he did not dispute their faith, but he did argue against the ways in which they interpreted God's Law. The issues they debated are ones which would have been of particular concern at the time: marriage, divorce, adultery, Sabbath regulations and purity laws.

The Sadducees

Although smaller in number, the Sadducees were a very powerful group within Judaism. They were drawn from rich landowners and their main interest seemed to be in maintaining political power. Despite their small numbers, they held half the seats in the Sanhedrin and most of the chief priests were Sadducees. They opposed armed conflict and did not resist the Roman occupation of Israel, choosing instead to compromise, which made them very unpopular with the ordinary people. They were conservative in outlook, refusing to accept any revelation beyond the Pentateuch, and they rejected ideas such as immortality, resurrection and the existence of angels and demons — all of which were supported by the Pharisees.

The Essenes

The Essenes ('pious ones') were a mysterious religious group, founded by the unknown Teacher of Righteousness. They saw themselves as the true people of God and lived a strict, religious life. They believed themselves to be sons of light awaiting the final battle against the forces of darkness. The largest group of Essenes lived in the desert at Qumran, where the Dead Sea Scrolls were found, and it may be that John the Baptist lived amongst them.

The Zealots

The Zealots were probably founded at around 6 BCE and saw themselves as revolutionaries and freedom fighters. They despised the Pharisees and Sadducees, who they felt had accepted Roman rule, and instead fought to free Israel from the Romans. They led many unsuccessful uprisings, based on their intense patriotism and belief that Roman rule was an offence to God. One of Jesus's disciples, Simon (not Peter), was probably a Zealot.

The Samaritans

These people were Israelites who lived in the region of Samaria. The people of Jerusalem did not accept the Samaritans as true Jews because their ancestors had inter-married with the Babylonian invaders centuries earlier. As a result, the Samaritans had their own Temple and worshipped God in their own way. The Jews of Jerusalem and Galilee despised the Samaritans. Interestingly, the evangelists present Samaritans in a positive light in encounters with Jesus and as the chief protagonist in the parable of the good Samaritan (Luke 10: 20–37) and in Jesus's meeting with the Samaritan woman (John 4: 1–26).

The system of justice

In the villages, the priests and elders, who sat at the gates of the village, resolved the everyday matters of justice. The Sanhedrin decided more important cases. This was the supreme court in Jerusalem, which consisted of 70 priests and elders under the rule of the chief priest at the Temple. The Romans had granted to the Sanhedrin the right to pass any sentence permitted under Jewish law except the death sentence.

The Romans

The Romans were the political authorities in Israel. The land was part of the Roman Empire and was a very important province because it lay on the main eastern frontier of the Empire and its security was essential. It was one of the most difficult parts of the Empire to govern, not only because of the harshness of the landscape and the hot climate but also because the Jewish people refused to submit to their Roman conquerors. The Romans, as Gentiles, found it very difficult to understand the Jewish religion and, in order to maintain peace, made allowances for Jewish scruples. When they appointed Herod the Great to rule in 37 BCE, the Romans hoped that because he was half-Jewish he would be acceptable to the people. To an extent this was true, but when he died in 4 CE the Romans found that his sons were not able to rule as firmly as their father had. In 6 CE Judea, the province that included Jerusalem, was placed under the overall command of the Roman governor of Syria and ruled by a Roman officer of the upper-class equestrian rank — later called *procurators* — the most famous of which was Pontius Pilate, who governed Judea from 26–36 CE.

There were many revolts and uprisings against the Romans. For their part, the Jews were angry at their loss of freedom, although there were some within Jewish society who felt that the Romans offered greater protection and had actually made things better. The Romans, meanwhile, found it almost impossible to understand the special problems of the Jewish people and resorted to harsh oppression to keep the Jewish rebels under control. Things came to a head in 66–70 CE, when the Jewish Revolt led to the Roman army destroying Jerusalem.

2 The titles of Jesus

Throughout the New Testament Jesus is given a variety of titles and descriptions, many with symbolic meaning:

÷ **Jesus** — this is a common first name for a Jewish male. It derives from Joshua and means 'The Lord is my help'.

- **Christ** — this was not part of Jesus's name, but was a title given to him. It comes from the Greek **Christos** and Hebrew **Mashiah** (**Messiah**) which mean 'anointed one'. It was first used to describe anyone entrusted with a divine mission, such as a prophet, priest or king. From this, the notion grew up that an anointed one would one day come from God to save Israel and usher in a new messianic age, the kingdom of God. Many Jews saw the Messiah as the ideal human being who would destroy the enemies of Israel and set up a Jewish kingdom, ruled by the line of David. On the Last Day, the Messiah would gather together God's people for Judgment and life in paradise.
- **Lord** — this was a title given to gods, including God in the Old Testament. It was little used by the Gospel writers, but a great deal by Paul (222 times) to express the idea of Christ's rule over the entire world.
- **Son of Man** — this was a title that Jesus used to describe himself. It came from the Old Testament and is the form of address used by God when talking to the prophet Ezekiel. It also refers to a heavenly figure mentioned in Daniel 7:13 as one who will some day come down from heaven to bring salvation and judgment. Jesus seems to fulfil the roles attributed to this eschatological figure. He uses this term when he speaks of his messianic authority on earth and in the age to come, and also of his suffering, death and resurrection.
- **Son of David** — this was a Messianic title coming from the Old Testament notion that the Messiah would be a descendant of King David. Jesus's adoptive relationship with Joseph grafts him onto the Davidic line.
- **Son of God** — in the Old Testament, this phrase was used to describe the King of Israel (Psalm 2:7). In the Gospels it highlights Jesus's unique relationship with God and for the evangelists it is the pre-eminent title for Jesus. Mark brings his Gospel to a climax with the centurion's confession at the foot of the cross that *'Surely this man was the Son of God'* (15:39).
- **I am (Ego Eimi)** — 'I am' is the name of God, given to Moses in Exodus 3:14. Jesus uses it exclusively in the Fourth Gospel to highlight his own divinity.
- **The Lamb** — at Passover, a lamb would be sacrificed as an atonement for sins. The evangelists see Jesus's death in the same way. This was itself highlighted by the Old Testament prophet Isaiah who said that the Servant of God (possibly meaning the Messiah) would be *'led like a lamb to the slaughter'* (53:7).

3 Why did Jesus have to die?

How could Jesus have been brought to the cross by people who were blessed by his signs and wonders?

(Jeremias, 1964)

Understanding the death of Jesus is a problem that has puzzled both believers and scholars. The New Testament addresses the issue in two different ways — one that is based upon the historical events of the time that led to Jesus's death, and the other which offers religious and theological reasons for his death. The two are inevitably interlinked, as the gospel writers demonstrate how the divine plans and purposes are revealed in the working out of the political manoeuvrings in the last weeks of Jesus's life.

3.1 The historical viewpoint

The Gospels show that Jesus's words and actions created unrest amongst those who encountered him, particularly the Jewish and Roman authorities. Jesus angered the Jewish religious leaders with his teachings, his healings on the Sabbath and his interpretation of the Law of Moses. He condemned the Pharisees and Sadducees as hypocritical and angered them with his claims concerning his relationship to God. In particular, the cleansing of the Temple market and the triumphal entry into Jerusalem led them to see him as a great danger, not only to their own status and position but also to the religious faith of the people — they feared that the people would accept the teachings of a false Messiah.

At the trial before the Sanhedrin, Jesus was found guilty of blasphemy — for claiming to be the Christ — and was sentenced to death for the ultimate religious crime. However, the Jewish authorities did not have the power to carry out such an execution; that power lay with the Romans. Blasphemy was not a crime under Roman law, and the Gospels record that when Jesus was brought before Pilate, the Jewish leaders instead suggested that he was a danger to the Romans because he had committed the treasonable act of calling himself the King of the Jews. Pilate was not convinced, but condemned Jesus to death because he did not want to risk trouble by upsetting the Jewish leaders. In a historical sense, therefore, Jesus died as a matter of religious and political expediency.

3.2 The religious viewpoint

The death of Jesus has great religious and theological significance that believers claim has consequences for the whole of creation. Much of the language used is symbolic, and five particular images of the death of Jesus are offered:

- ⁌ **Defeat of evil** — Jesus's ministry has been depicted as a struggle against evil — sometimes in the form of the Devil and the forces of darkness (as in the exorcism miracles), and at other times in the form of Jesus fighting against the power of sin in people's lives. With his death and resurrection, Jesus is seen as having defeated the power of evil and sin for ever.
- ⁌ **An example** — Jesus's life of humility and love for others culminates in the sacrifice of his own life to save people from the power of evil. His life is an example to believers, to encourage them to lead lives of humility and self-sacrifice: '*Christ suffered for you, leaving you an example, that you should follow in his steps*' (1 Peter 2:21).
- ⁌ **A sacrifice** — in the ancient world, animals (and sometimes humans) were sacrificed in the hope of pleasing the gods, to seek favours or as a guilt offering for wrongful actions. In the Old Testament, sacrificial procedures were laid down specifically: '*If a person sins and does what is forbidden in any of the Lord's commands… He is to bring to the priest as a guilt offering a ram from the flock, one without defect and of the proper value. In this way, the priest will make atonement for him for the wrong he has committed*' (Leviticus 5:17–18). At the time of the first Passover, the people of Israel are saved by the sacrifice of a lamb — the blood from the lamb being put on the doors of their houses to save them from destruction (Exodus 12:13).

The sacrificial rituals of Judaism were very elaborate — the animals were killed as a reminder to the people that they were sinners who deserved to die. The priest would take the blood of the animal to the altar as a symbol representing the sinner's life being given up to God — the animal, in effect, died in the place of the sinful human. This was called an act of **atonement** and meant that the punishment due for the sins had been carried out. God, in accepting the sacrifice, forgave the human sinner. Jesus was the ultimate sacrificial lamb. In the Last Supper he showed how his death would lead to the forgiveness of sins and the reconciliation of God and humanity: '*This cup is the new covenant in my blood, which is poured out for you*' (Luke 22:20), and Paul wrote, '*For Christ, our Passover Lamb, has been sacrificed*' (1 Corinthians 5:7).

÷ **A ransom** — a ransom is an offering made to free someone else, for example a fee paid to a kidnapper. In the Roman world, it was possible to pay a ransom to set a slave free. The New Testament often refers to humanity as being slaves to sin, and Jesus's sacrifice is the payment of the ransom price to secure freedom from this slavery to sin: '*For even the Son of Man did not come to be served, but to serve, and to give his life as a ransom for many*' (Mark 10:45). '*His death was believed to bring perfect forgiveness and was a perfect offering of obedience to the Father*' (O'Donnell, 1999).

÷ **Taking humanity's place** — people are seen as being so weighed down by the burden and power of sin that they cannot be freed from it by their own actions, and so Jesus has to die in place of humanity because that is the only way in which humanity can be helped. The prophet Isaiah foretold this in the Old Testament. He spoke of the Suffering Servant who would take the punishment due to the people of God (Isaiah 53). This was later emphasised in 1 Peter 2:24: '*He himself bore our sins in his body on the tree, so that we might die to sins and live for righteousness; by his wounds we are healed.*'

This concept is not about God being a judgmental figure demanding death as a punishment for sins, but is about the nature of love. God cannot just dismiss sins any more than a doctor examining a patient with a life-threatening illness can just say 'forget it and it will go away'. Sin must be dealt with and this is done through an act of punishment. However, humanity cannot itself take the punishment because it is too great. Humanity needs help and this is what Jesus gives. His death means that he takes the punishment for humanity, thus freeing them from sin: '*If there is anything distinctive about the teaching of Jesus, it has to be the way he redefined God, replacing the harsh, confrontational image of judgment and condemnation, with the language of family love and acceptance*' (Drane, 1999).

B The nature of the Gospels

1 The character of the Synoptic Gospels

Although the three Synoptic Gospels tell the story of the life and ministry of Jesus Christ, they all tell it from a slightly different perspective, depending on the author's own particular interests and purposes. The differences between the gospel accounts were overlooked — or blurred — for centuries, but a full appreciation of them is vital to understand the real concerns of the evangelists.

Mark

Mark's Gospel is probably the earliest. It is the shortest, with only 16 chapters. It is interesting for its omission of the birth story and the fact that the earliest manuscripts make no mention of Jesus's resurrection appearances. Many scholars see it as the basic source for the other two Synoptic Gospels, both of which contain a great deal of information from Mark as well as much of their own. The Gospel places great significance on Jesus as the Messiah, the Son of God and the Son of Man, and of particular importance are the passion narratives, the Messianic Secret, and the failure of the disciples and the people to recognise Jesus's true identity. The Gospel was probably written with the view that the **parousia** or Second Coming of Christ was about to happen. There are references to trials and persecutions and some apocalyptic overtones suggesting that the end was thought to be near.

Matthew

The Gospel of Matthew is much more carefully structured than the other Synoptic Gospels, the principal material being organised into topics. The emphasis of the Gospel seems to be that Christ is the fulfilment of Old Testament prophecy and there are several references to Jesus as the Son of David and to Old Testament scripture (e.g. 2:15). Matthew highlights the fact that Jesus is descended from Abraham and that he fulfils God's ancient promise to the Jews. He is the new Moses who brings a fresh interpretation to the Law (chapters 5–7). Drane (1999) remarks: '...*the message is clear. Everything that was central in the relationship of God with the people of Israel has now found its true and final expression in the life of Jesus*'.

The Gospel is possibly aimed at believers coming from Judaism. It emphasises the universality of Christ's message and highlights the shortcomings of Judaism (e.g. 8:10–12; 21:43; 23:1–36). In its place, the Gospel shows the importance of the missionary work of the early church and the disciples (28:16–20). It is the only Gospel in which the word 'church' (**ekklesia**) actually occurs.

There is less emphasis than in Mark on the immediate Second Coming of Christ and more on being prepared for when that event does happen. Parables of the Second Coming and final judgment are aimed at ensuring that believers are in a constant state of readiness because '*you do not know the day or the hour*' (25:13).

Luke

The Gospel of Luke should be read alongside the Acts of the Apostles, which together form a two-part history of early Christianity. Some scholars have suggested that both volumes were written as an **apologia** to convince the Romans that Jesus was not a criminal and that the early church was not a threat to the Empire. Luke's emphasis in the Gospel is on God's fulfilment of his promises and he makes clear that the events he describes are part of God's much wider plan for the whole of human history (e.g. 1:14–17; 4:16–30). The Gospel may be aimed primarily at Gentile readers who are looking into Christianity. It emphasises that Christ's message was for all people — e.g. 2:32 where the infant Jesus is shown '*as a light for revelation to the Gentiles*'. Luke highlights how Jesus's mission is to '*seek and save the lost*' (chapter 15) and how he is a friend to outcasts and sinners (9:51–6; 17:11–19).

The author seems to see the Second Coming of Christ in the more distant future and he emphasises the kingdom of God as a spiritual dimension that is present now and in the future. The Holy Spirit also plays a more prominent role than in the other Synoptic Gospels, highlighting the importance of the Spirit both in the ministry of Jesus and in the development of the early church (3:15–18; 4:1, 14–18).

2 Biblical criticism and the synoptic problem

Biblical criticism is a scholarly activity that aims to make the biblical text more meaningful to the reader today and to gain an understanding of the circumstances and processes of writing.

One of the first and most influential biblical critics was Griesbach, who, in 1789, published the Synoptic Gospels in parallel columns to highlight the similarities and differences between them. It led to the synoptic problem: *'How can the Gospels have, on the one hand, so many things in common, yet, on the other hand, have so many disagreements?'* Using a synopsis, it became possible to see where, for example, two evangelists agreed in their accounts and the third did not, and where material was used by one evangelist alone. Moreover, there were similarities in the actual wording, which suggested that the Gospel writers shared common sources of information, possibly Greek translations of the Aramaic spoken by Jesus. Interesting patterns emerged: Matthew and Luke seemed to follow Mark's Gospel very closely, yet there are also passages in Matthew and Luke that do not appear in Mark at all and some material that occurs in only one of the Gospels. From this, different branches of biblical criticism emerged, each with their particular tools for analysing the narratives.

2.1 Source criticism

Source criticism was an attempt by scholars to establish a relationship between the Synoptic Gospels and their material — did the Gospel writers get their material from the same sources? The Synoptic Gospels share a great deal of common material — for instance, Mark has 661 verses, of which Matthew includes 606, whilst Luke uses 320. There is, therefore, a relation of dependence between the Gospels. Source criticism is the most useful tool in helping to resolve the synoptic problem. With so many similarities yet so many differences between the Gospels, how can we be sure which version is correct?

Most scholars believe that the first Gospel to be written was Mark (Markan Priority) and that Matthew and Luke used Mark as a framework for their Gospels. Graham Stanton (1989), in *The Gospels and Jesus*, describes Mark's Gospel as: *'...the first Gospel to have been written and therefore the Gospel with the highest claims to be accepted as a reliable historical source'*. Certainly there are good reasons for claiming that Mark's Gospel was first:

÷ It is the shortest and misses out key features, e.g. the Lord's Prayer.
÷ It is in poor Greek and the phrases used are tidied up in Matthew and Luke.
÷ Some of Jesus's words are harsh, e.g. Mark 4:39 — 'Why are you afraid? Have you no faith?' These are gentler in Matthew and Luke.
÷ The disciples are superficially presented.

❖ If Mark were simply a poor adaptation of Luke and Matthew it would not have been preserved in the canon.

The synoptic problem was highlighted by B. H. Streeter in his **four-document hypothesis**, which he said would identify the material from which the Synoptic Gospels were compiled:

❖ Only 31 verses from Mark do not appear in one or other of Matthew or Luke.
❖ Matthew and Luke also used Q, an unknown and undiscovered document. They share nearly 200 verses that are mainly sayings of Jesus and parables, which do not appear in Mark. It is possible that the Q document dates from before Mark.
❖ M — material which is contained only in Matthew, such as the birth narrative, some miracles, the suicide of Judas and the extensive references to the Old Testament. There are 282 verses unique to Matthew. This material gives the Gospel its own characteristic flavour.
❖ L — material that is contained only in Luke. There are 490 such verses, including 14 parables, parts of the passion narrative, and characters such as Mary and Martha and Zaccchaeus. As with Matthew's use of M, this material gives Luke its special characteristics.

Minor agreements are also of interest where Matthew and Luke have made small changes to Mark's text, perhaps a change in tense or a small word, to make the meaning more precise. This has led to some controversy, with scholars suggesting that perhaps Mark was written after, and not before, Matthew and Luke. For example, the phrase '*Who struck you?*' is found in Matthew 26:68 and Luke 22:64, but not in Mark. It may be significant if Luke and Matthew, following Mark, both put this sentence in, when Mark did not. Moreover, Luke stops using Mark between 6:20 and 8:3, and Matthew changes Mark's order in chapters 1–10, but follows the order precisely after chapter 11. This does not suggest that either Matthew or Luke used Mark consistently.

Scholars have also been divided over the nature of the Q document. Some have suggested that there was no Q document at all, and that Luke obtained most of his material from Matthew. However, others have felt that Q is almost a fifth Gospel that can be reconstructed from Matthew and Luke. If this is so, scholars have suggested that it is more likely that Luke follows the original Q pattern, whilst Matthew, with the way that Gospel uses block material, such as the Sermon on the Mount, has adapted the material differently. Others still urge the reader to consider the Gospels as a whole — the themes and the narrative are seen as more important than the rather haphazard procedures of source criticism. Perhaps the fairest thing to say is that the synoptic problem remains unsolved.

2.2 Form criticism

Form criticism developed in the early twentieth century. Form critics looked at the way or form in which the Gospels were written, including the parables, sayings, stories and traditions. The best-known form critics are Bultmann and Debelius, who argued that much of the material used in the Synoptic Gospels came from what is known as the oral tradition, that is, from stories passed down by word of mouth. The form of the writing is important since it shows the importance that a writer would place on a particular teaching or event.

A consequence of this, however, is that the Gospels may not be very reliable objective accounts of the life of Jesus, since they have been written to meet the needs of their writers and the early church communities as they were at that particular time (the *Sitz im Leben* or 'life setting'). The suggestion was that much of the material was adapted by the early church to fit its needs and that, consequently, only a fraction of the words ascribed to Jesus were authentic. For example, the material in Matthew 18:15–22 is concerned with church discipline and could hardly have been spoken by Jesus himself. The form critics therefore argued that the Gospels convey not historical truth but spiritual truth, and the historical Jesus is not relevant to the Christ of faith. They argued that the Gospel writers have merely linked together units of parables, sayings, stories and pronouncements, with the needs of the early church taking precedence over historical accuracy. In order to get closer to the actual truth, form critics claimed that the Gospels had to be stripped of these extra elaborations to find the original, unbiased material.

Form critics said that the Gospel material could be divided into six categories or forms:

÷ Legends and myths — unreliable material mainly dealing with the divinity of Jesus, e.g. birth narratives.
÷ Parables — stories that teach about God and the kingdom.
÷ Miracles — healings, exorcisms and nature miracles.
÷ Teachings and pronouncements — narratives ending with an important teaching.
÷ Speeches — lengthy sayings by Jesus, e.g. Sermon on the Mount (Matthew 5–7).
÷ Shorter sayings — such as prophecies, eschatological warnings and church rules.

These categories show how the writers used their material in particular ways. The importance of form criticism is that it highlights the role played by the Gospels in the early church. It suggests that the Gospels were not biographies of Jesus, but were a reflection and interpretation of his life and teaching, which could be adapted by the early church to meet new needs and challenges.

2.3 Redaction criticism

Redaction criticism developed after the Second World War, although it had originated with William Wrede's study of Mark in 1901. Redaction critics suggested that the Gospel writers were more creative than the form critics had given them credit for. They claimed that the evangelists used the traditions for their own purposes and gave their Gospels a unique identity of their own. Redaction critics looked not just at the possible sources but beyond, at how the writers used their material and what emphasis they put on it — their theological views and insights. For example, Wrede suggested that Mark included the Messianic Secret as a device to give particular christological emphasis to his Gospel. Later, Conzelman used redaction criticism to argue that, contrary to the views of the time, Luke was not a historian, but a theologian writing a salvation history.

Redaction critics looked at the editorial (redaction) work of each evangelist — how they chose and used their material — and examined the changes each writer had made to his sources, as well as what material was unique to his Gospel. These distinctive differences enabled the critics to identify the main interests and characteristics of each Gospel. It appeared that each evangelist had his own characteristic theology. For example, Bornkamm noted that, in the story of the storm of the lake, Mark uses it to focus on christology and the authority of Christ (4:35–41), whilst Matthew uses the same story (8:23–27) to focus on faith and discipleship.

Redaction criticism has been criticised for its dependence on the four-document hypothesis and for the assumptions it makes about very minor differences between the Gospels.

2.4 Narrative or literary criticism

This is a more recent approach, whereby the reader is encouraged to see the Gospel in its entirety, without worrying about questions of reliability, history or use of sources, and instead just trying to understand and appreciate it for what it is. Narrative critics ask the reader to consider the Gospel as a narrative, with a recognisable structure, characters, settings and events, which the writer has used in order to shape his account.

Narrative critics suggest that the Gospels are written in the style of an *implied* author, who acts as a narrator, reporting the words and actions of the characters and, sometimes, making an assessment of his own (e.g. Matthew 13:34–35). He writes for an *implied* reader who is someone whom the *real* reader should seek to become, accepting the implied author's viewpoints and recognising when the characters in the Gospel fail to accept them. There are two levels to the Gospels: the story, which is the plot, characters and events; and the discourse, which is the way the story is told, and the meaning behind it.

Narrative critics argue that certain things are particularly important to certain evangelists. For instance, Mark makes it clear in 1:1–13 that Jesus is the Son of God and this theme carries on throughout his Gospel. Elsewhere, symbolism is important — for example, for Luke Jerusalem is the centre of activity, whereas in Matthew and Mark the area of Galilee is depicted as the place where the post-resurrection community will gather. Similarly, events and characters are given different narrative significance in the way they are expressed. For instance, the feeding miracles are given varying degrees of prominence and Peter and John the Baptist are given greater or lesser roles in the different Gospels.

3 Authorship and date

None of the Gospels contains the name of its author and we must not assume that men called Matthew, Mark and Luke necessarily wrote them. In order to find the identity of the author, scholars have to examine a range of evidence, both inside the Gospel and outside, and their conclusions are far from certain.

3.1 Matthew

Traditionally, credit is given to the Apostle Matthew, the ex-tax collector, someone who would have been an eyewitness to the events of Jesus's life. Scholars supporting this view suggest that Matthew, as a tax collector who worked for the Romans, might have understood Greek and been educated enough to write such a Gospel, or at least to support its content. However, most scholars dispute this claim. Some say that an eyewitness would not have had to rely so heavily on material from Mark's Gospel. Other scholars have suggested that the writer was either a member of the early church or someone steeped in the tradition of the Old Testament. Due to the universalism of its message and some apparent misunderstandings of Jewish practices, some believe the Gospel may have been written by an unknown Gentile.

The date of the Gospel is also uncertain. If material has been taken from Mark's Gospel, then it dates from after that time and the words of 22:7 and 24:3–28 may refer to the fall of Jerusalem in 70 CE. Some scholars have also suggested that the type of church organisation outlined in the Gospel reflects a time towards the end of the first century. The majority of scholars date the Gospel at between 80 and 100 CE.

3.2 Mark

Traditionally, the author is believed to be John Mark, a member of the early church who was a companion of Paul and is mentioned in Acts 12:12. According to Acts, a group of Christians met in his mother's house in Jerusalem, and he collaborated with Paul and Barnabas in the early mission work (12:25; 15:37–41). He is also mentioned favourably in Paul's letters (Colossians 4:10, Philemon 24). It was often the case that in the second century, Christians tended to associate books in the New Testament with key figures in the early church. John Mark was a fairly insignificant person, yet some scholars feel that this actually increases the likelihood that he wrote the Gospel, since there must have been a good reason for attributing it to him.

John Drane supports the views of Irenaeus and Clement of Alexandria, and suggests that it was probably written in Rome for the church there. This would also support the biblical evidence of the time which suggests that John Mark was in Rome. It was probably aimed at a non-Jewish readership, since many Aramaic phrases and Jewish customs are explained for the readers (e.g. 5:41; 7:3–4). There are difficulties in dating the Gospel. The evidence from the early church fathers is not clear: Clement of Alexandria suggested it was written under Peter's dictation and approved by him, whilst Irenaeus claimed it was written after the deaths of Peter and Paul. Arguably, references to trials and persecutions suggest that believers at that time were suffering for their faith (e.g. 8:34–8; 13:8–13) and this implies a date during the persecution by Nero, between 60 and 70 CE. Conceivably too, the apocalyptic reference in 13:1–37 presupposes that Jerusalem had already fallen to the Romans, which would date the Gospel after 70 CE. Most scholars therefore think that it was the first Gospel, dating from around 60–70 CE.

3.3 Luke

Traditional authorities such as Irenaeus and Clement of Alexandria, together with ancient sources including the Muratorian Canon, seem to indicate that the author of the third Gospel was Luke. The Gospel is not complete in itself; it is the first of a two-volume history of the early church, the second volume of which is the Acts of the Apostles. The style and language of both books are so similar that they are seen as the work of the same author and both are addressed to the same person, Theophilus.

In Acts, the so-called 'we passages' indicate the presence of the author alongside Paul on his missionary journeys (e.g. 16:10–17; 20:5–15). The person who best fitted this role was Luke, a doctor and travelling companion of Paul. This is also highlighted in the Gospel itself where, say some scholars, the author shows a particular interest in medical issues, e.g. 8:43.

Luke himself is mentioned three times in the New Testament, as a companion to Paul and also as a Gentile (Colossians 4:14, Philemon 24:2 and Timothy 4:11). Certainly, the Greek style of Luke and Acts suggests that the author was a Greek speaker, which would make him the only Gentile writer of the New Testament.

The dating of Luke is uncertain, although it must post-date Mark if it used part of that Gospel. Drane suggests that Luke 21:5–24 shows knowledge of the fall of Jerusalem in 70 CE and so the Gospel must have been written after that date.

Summary

- A key aspect in the history of the Jews is the **covenant** with God, by which they are required to obey the **Law** and, in return, God makes them his holy, **chosen people**. The **patriarchs** are the fathers of the Jewish race. The Jewish people live their lives according to the Law, with the synagogues, the Temple and the great festivals at the centre.
- The land of Israel is part of the Roman Empire and political authority rests with the Romans. Religious authority, however, rests with the Jews themselves — the chief priests, scribes, Sadducees and Pharisees.
- The Gospels show Jesus as the long-awaited saviour or **Messiah**, who has come from God. He is known by various titles, including **Christ**, **Son of God** and **Son of Man**. He comes to preach the 'good news' of God.
- Jesus angers the religious authorities, who see him as a blasphemer, and his mission ends with his crucifixion and, ultimately, his resurrection. He dies in order that the sins of humanity can be forgiven and that a new covenant of love between God and all people can become a reality.
- A close examination of the Gospels has been made by scholars, called **biblical criticism**. These scholars have attempted to make the text more meaningful for modern readers through an analysis of the source, the form and the redaction of the material itself.

Exam watch

This unit deals with material which will help you to develop your overall understanding of the text itself. It provides essential information on the historical, social, cultural and religious setting of the time. Make sure you understand all the main terms and the importance of Jesus in the light of the settings — his coming in fulfilment of prophecy, his messiahship and the covenant.

Review questions

1 What is the importance of the covenant for Judaism?
2 Examine and comment on the religious meaning of three of the titles of Jesus.
3 What is biblical criticism and how has it helped us to understand the Gospels?
4 What were the main beliefs of the Pharisees and Sadducees?

Topic 2

The Gospels of Matthew and Mark

A The early ministry of Christ

1 Early life

1.1 Matthew's birth narrative

Of the four evangelists, only Matthew and Luke (see pp. 308–312) offer a birth narrative, and in so doing it is clear that they were responding to two needs. One was the early church's need to know something more about Jesus's early life and to establish when he was designated Son of God — the birth narratives indicate clearly that this was from conception. The second was to anticipate themes which are developed throughout the Gospel and in this sense the birth narratives are, in Morna Hooker's phrase, *'keys that open the gospels'.* The narratives should therefore be read with the whole Gospel in mind, and not as appealing stories of a rather naïve character with no relevance to the more gritty stuff that follows.

Matthew's narrative seeks to unlock several significant themes. First, its christological message is clear — Jesus is the divine Son of God from conception, the one who will *'save his people from their sins'* (1:21), whom Gentiles will worship, but, despite the promises that his coming fulfils, the majority of Judaism will reject. The theme of Matthew's birth narratives — that the coming of Jesus Christ fulfils the promises made in the Old Testament — begins with the genealogy (family tree) of Jesus, taking his ancestry right back to Abraham and fulfilling the promise that God made to Abraham in Genesis 12:3: *'All the peoples on earth will be blessed through you.'* Matthew firmly engrafts Jesus onto the Davidic line through this genealogy and it serves to identify the reason for the prominent role that Joseph plays in this narrative (he is virtually written out of the story by Luke). Joseph's sole function is to provide the link with the line of David which ensures that Jesus is fully Davidid, and can be referred to as the Son of David (1:1), fulfilling the Old Testament promise that the throne of King David would be established for ever (2 Samuel 7: 6).

There are other interesting features of the genealogy, not least the inclusion, contrary to Jewish tradition, of five women: Tamar, Rahab, Bathsheba, Ruth and Mary. There has been much scholarly debate over why Matthew took this unusual step, and perhaps the most interesting solution is that all these women had liaisons which were in some way unusual: Tamar, a victim of incestuous rape; Rahab, a prostitute; Bathsheba, the woman with whom David committed adultery; Ruth, a Moabite woman who married an Israelite; and Mary — who Joseph initially believes to have been sexually unfaithful. Matthew makes subtly clear that the Messiah's line is flawed, and yet God has richly blessed this same line. Krister Stendahl writes: *'The common denominator for these four women [Tamar, Rahab, Bathsheba and Ruth] is found in that they all represent an 'irregularity' in the Davidic line, an irregularity which is not only overcome by God's recognition of them as mothers of Davidic descendants; exactly by the irregularity the action of God and his Spirit is made manifest'* (Stanton (ed.), 1983).

Matthew fills his birth narrative with titles for Jesus and with geographical locations which acquire special significance, or which already have meaning for the reader. Joseph, a pious and law-abiding Jew, for whom it would be unthinkable to marry a woman who had been unfaithful to her betrothed, has to be prompted to fulfil his role in the drama by an angel in a dream who assures him that the strange circumstances which are unfolding in his life have been set in motion by God. He reveals the name and purpose of the son whom Mary will bear, using the first of Matthew's ten Old Testament fulfilment clauses (of which five are found in these narratives alone). Matthew uses Isaiah 7:14 with great freedom, in order to establish that Jesus is Immanuel — 'God with us'. He is to be the incarnation of God, physically present among his people for the first time in salvation history, and later in the Gospel Matthew assures his readers that this will be a lasting presence. At 18:20, Jesus promises the future church that whenever they are gathered together he will be with them, and at 28:20 he reassures the disciples that he will be with them *'even to the close of the age'*. Of course, no one actually calls Jesus 'Immanuel'; quite the contrary, since Joseph is instructed to call him Jesus, which means 'Yahweh is salvation'. But in him the promise of God's presence holds firm, even to the end of time.

Interestingly, in its original context Isaiah 7:14 was not intended as a messianic prophecy, but refers rather to an event that will take place in the lifetime of Ahaz, King of Judah, or at least in the foreseeable future. However, Matthew's use of the verse has led Christians to identify Isaiah's words as messianic, and, more crucially, to develop the doctrine of the virgin birth. Matthew's use of the Greek **parthenos**, which is translated as 'virgin', need not technically mean a woman with no sexual experience, since the Hebrew original, **almah**, may simply imply a young woman, whose virginity is merely implicit.

Although Joseph responds obediently to the angel, as did the men of God in the Old Testament who received similar divine visitations, the Messiah is not out of danger. The visit of the magi to Herod, in search of the King of the Jews, raises a new spectre — rejection by his own people. Representative, perhaps, of the nations of the world who will come to worship the Messiah, the magi's visit to Herod troubles him *'and all Jerusalem with him'* (2:3). It provides an opportunity for another fulfilment clause, as Herod's advisors tell him that according to Micah 5:2 the Messiah is to be born in Bethlehem (2:6), the town where King David came from. But despite their knowledge of scripture, Herod's religious advisors do not hurry to Bethlehem to worship; this is left to the Gentile magi. It is interesting that Matthew does not use the opportunity to cite Numbers 24:17 — *'A star shall come forth out of Jacob and a sceptre shall rise out of*

Israel', although it may be implicit in the magi's question: *'Where is he who has been born king of the Jews? For we have seen his star in the east and have come to worship him'* (2:2).

Dreams continue to structure the birth narrative, as the magi are warned not to return from their visit to Jesus by way of Herod. Having seen the baby and offered their symbolic gifts — gold (royalty), myrrh (passion) and frankincense (divinity) — they return by another route, and the Messiah is again preserved by the divine direction of events. Hooker (1997) writes: *'One cannot help but feel that the star, however divine in its origin, made a mistake in leading the wise men first to Jerusalem, for the result was the massacre of the infants'*, but aside from the fact that there is no traceable historical event of this kind having taken place, the massacre serves to anticipate another important theme for Matthew — the rejection of Jesus by the Jewish leaders. He uses it, too, as an opportunity for two more fulfilment clauses. After the birth, Mary and Joseph take the baby to safety in Egypt, giving rise to the Old Testament prophecy of Hosea 11:1: *'Out of Egypt I called my son.'* Even Herod's order to slaughter the baby boys is not forgotten, and Matthew uses the incident to echo the prophecy of Jeremiah 31:15: *'A voice is heard in Ramah, weeping and great mourning, Rachel weeps for her children and refusing to be comforted, because they were no more.'* Again, however, Matthew clearly takes these passages from their original contexts with considerable freedom. The use of the verse from Hosea is understandable, inferring that Jesus has now replaced the nation of Israel as God's first-born son, through whom the true fate of Israel will now pass. The Jeremiah passage is less convincing, although he is a prophet who appears to have special significance for Matthew. However, Hooker (1997) observes: *'What Matthew does with this particular text is the kind of thing that spiritual men and women, Jews and Christians…have always done with the text: they see new meanings in it, and realise its relevance to different situations'*.

Interestingly, however, Matthew seems to go too far in 2:3. Referring to Jesus growing up in Nazareth, he apparently quotes a prophecy: *'He will be called a Nazarene'.* There is, in fact, no such saying in the Old Testament, although an allusion may be being made to Isaiah 11:1: *'There shall come forth a shoot out of the stump of Jesse, and a branch shall grow out of its roots'*, as Matthew plays on the Hebrew word **nazir**, meaning branch. He also clearly wants to place the settlement in Nazareth as within the divine plan of God, just as he later links Jesus's move to Galilee with Isaiah 9:1–2 (Matthew 4:15–16).

Matthew's editorial and narrative activity may well stretch the bounds of credulity, but there can be no doubt that he sees the whole of Jesus's life, from birth to death, as within the revealed will of God. The Gospel as a whole testifies to this, and for a Jewish-Christian church it would have been vital. In Jesus, God has proven that he has not abandoned his people, but is with them *'even to the close of the age'* (28:20).

1.2 Baptism and temptation narratives

Mark

Unlike Matthew, Mark's earlier tradition includes no birth narrative, and for him Jesus's designation as Son of God is made at the baptism. Mark uses the first 13 verses of his

Gospel as a prologue, introducing key narrative themes as Matthew does in his birth narrative. And for Mark there is one key theme — the divine identity of Jesus. In *An Introduction to the Christology of Mark* George Amoss, Jr writes that christology is a very important, if not *the* most important, element in Mark and the evangelist himself indicates this in the way he opens his Gospel: *'The beginning of the gospel about Jesus Christ, the Son of God'* (1:1). Jesus the Christ is himself the Gospel (good news), and by reading Mark's Gospel the reader encounters him and learns, with the disciples, the mystery of who he is. The impact is immediate, with Mark's declaration to the reader in the opening chapter: *'It is written in Isaiah the prophet: "I will send my messenger ahead of you, who will prepare your way"'* (1:2). And it is John the Baptist who is sent to declare the way for Jesus: *'After me will come one more powerful than I, the thongs of whose sandals I am not worthy to stoop down and untie... I baptise you with water, but* he *will baptise you with the Holy Spirit'* (1:7–8). With these words, John the Baptist, whose garb and demeanour clearly evoke that of Elijah, very effectively prepares the way, to point to the one coming after him, who is stronger than himself.

What Mark is setting out to tell the reader is the good news of the story of God's salvation of his people; and this story is about Jesus Christ, or Jesus the Messiah, who is also the Son of God. Although there is some doubt as to whether Mark himself wrote that last phrase 'Son of God', or whether it is a later scribal interpolation, what Mark certainly told the reader is that Jesus is the Messiah. The title 'Son of God' would have been familiar to Jewish readers, as it was a title rooted in the Old Testament and the first thing Mark tells the reader concerning the content of the Gospel is that it took place *'as it is written in Isaiah the prophet'*. Mark was undoubtedly excited by the fact that what the great prophet Isaiah had promised centuries earlier had now happened: a messenger to prepare the way of the Lord, who in turn would bring salvation to Israel. After years of hoping and waiting, the promises were at last being fulfilled.

Mark continues to reveal Jesus's identity to the reader in his description of the baptism when Jesus sees heaven being torn open and the Spirit descending on him like a dove: *'And a voice came from heaven: "You are my son, whom I love; with you I am well pleased"'* (1:11). The voice from heaven is God's and the words are addressed to Jesus with no suggestion that they are heard by anyone else, either John or the crowds. Only the readers of Mark's Gospel are allowed to overhear these words and be let into the secret of Jesus's identity, confirming what Mark has already told us in 1:1. Mark clearly means the reader to see this as the full truth about Jesus, spoken with divine authority. As God's view is the most reliable possible, then the reader must accept it as true. According to Hooker, it is clear Mark believed that knowing the Spirit had come upon Jesus was of vital importance for understanding who Jesus is and what he does. The descent of the Spirit is not a transitory experience but the explanation of the events that are to follow. In 1:10 Mark tells the reader that the heavens have been rent asunder and the Spirit of God has descended on Jesus — an eschatological event; the barrier dividing God and humanity has been torn aside, graphically symbolised again at the end of the Gospel, when the Temple curtain is torn in two at the moment of Jesus's death (15:37).

The details of the baptism have strong links to the Old Testament. It is clearly an anointing for ministry, and the voice from heaven is based on Psalm 2:7 (the coronation psalm of the Davidic kings) and Isaiah 42:1 (the suffering servant of God). Jesus is being anointed for a ministry that will incorporate both roles: he is the servant-king. As the beloved son, Jesus is sacrificed by his Father for the salvation of the world, as Abraham was prepared to sacrifice his 'only son' (Genesis 22:2). The Spirit's descent marks the beginning of the messianic age in which God is once again active among his people, and the opening of heaven sees the fulfilment of Isaiah 64:1: 'O that thou would rend the heavens, and come down.'

Events in the Prologue move rapidly, as they do in the Gospel as a whole. James Still (1985) describes the Gospel as a *'tersely written, fast-paced roller coaster ride that drops into the river Jordan with John the Baptist and doesn't pause for breath until we reach the empty tomb'.* Paula Fredriksen (2000) comments that *'Mark's Jesus is a man in a hurry, dashing through Galilee in rapid, almost random motion, from synagogue to invalid, from shore to grain field to sea, casting out demons and amazing those who witness him.'* And so Mark takes the reader rapidly from the Jordan into the wilderness proper, an environment that had great significance in Jewish thinking. The wilderness was where the great saving events of the Exodus were accomplished, and inevitably the prophets looked for a new experience there when God would again save his people. Jesus now fulfils the role that Israel as a nation once fulfilled as they were tested in the desert.

Mark deals with the temptations with remarkable brevity; he supplies no details of what they constituted and does not even makes clear the outcome. However, the outcome is implicit — Jesus obviously resisted Satan and survived the experience intact. Having faced down Satan in the wilderness, Jesus is clearly equipped to do so when he confronts demons and evil spirits during his ministry.

Thus, Mark has used the Prologue to make clear exactly who Jesus is — the divine Son of God, fulfilling the Old Testament, and the one who will defeat Satan — and he has done this is the space of 13 terse verses. The effect on the reader is powerful, for we are now in a position to read the rest of the Gospel equipped with everything we need to know to understand what follows. Hooker (1997) writes:

Mark has given us the key which will enable us to understand the rest of the Gospel. And from time to time, as he tells his story, he will, as it were, nudge his audience in the ribs and say, 'You see? You realise why this is happening?'... So he will make sure that we, at least, realise that the story he is unfolding is the good news about the Son of God, in whom God's Spirit is at work.

Matthew

Matthew uses the Marcan source for his account of the baptism and temptations as a framework, adding details which make it his own, and drawing on Q for the account of the temptations. Matthew's account of the baptism reveals the problems that the early church had with the narratives as christology developed. Matthew's birth narrative unambiguously declares Jesus to be the Son of God, so the reader could be forgiven for wondering why the baptism was necessary. The role of John the Baptist too was causing problems by this stage, and both Matthew and Luke make various attempts using their own sources to explain what had become a rather complicated relationship between Jesus and John. In Matthew 3:13ff, Jesus comes to the Jordan with the express intention of being baptised by John, but John asks: *'I need to be baptised by you, and do you come to me?'* The question is not really the Baptist's, but the early church's. John acknowledges the pre-eminent superiority of Jesus and his lower status, which he has already done in his earlier witness to Jesus — *'One who is coming after me is more powerful than me; I am not worthy to carry his sandals'* (3:11). Jesus's answer seems to solve the problem at a stroke: it is God's will that it should be so. John and Jesus together are required to perform this act *'to fulfil all righteousness'*. The phrase is a little awkward, but the concept of righteousness is important for Matthew's Gospel. Joseph is a righteous man (1:19); the disciples are to ensure that their righteousness *'exceeds that of the scribes and Pharisees'* (5:20), and to *'seek first the kingdom and his righteousness'* (6:33). Like true disciples, John and Jesus must perform that which satisfies the will and plan of God. Only when assured of the place of the baptism in God's will does John 'consent' (3:15).

From this point, Matthew follows Mark closely, adding more of his characteristic words — *'behold'*, *'lo'* — which give an Old Testament flavour to the passage. The voice from heaven utters the same words, but the impact is less than in Mark's Gospel, since this is information we have already been given in 1:18–23. His account of the temptations is far more detailed, however, as, like Luke, he draws on Q material to explain the precise nature of the temptations that Jesus faced. Both evangelists describe three temptations, although in different orders:

Matthew	**Luke**
Stones to bread	Stones to bread
Pinnacle of the Temple	High mountain
High mountain	Pinnacle of the Temple

Conceivably, the original order is best represented by Matthew's account, whilst Luke, who places great significance on the Temple in the life of Jesus and the early church, makes this the climax of the temptations. Each temptation tests Jesus to see if he will use his divine power for the furtherance of his own needs and glory, or if he will test his relationship with God. Each time he refuses, and offers Satan scriptural justification for so doing. Each passage he cites is from Deuteronomy — 8:3; 6:16; 6:13 — key passages from Israel's 40 years in the wilderness, when God tested their obedience to him. Whereas the people of Israel found obedience difficult, Jesus does not, and the reader is left in no doubt that he is pre-eminently equipped to meet the spiritual challenges of his ministry.

1.3 The call of the disciples

For both evangelists, Jesus's ministry begins with the same message that John the Baptist had brought — the imminence of the kingdom of God, and the need for universal repentance. He will unfold the significance of this mission statement as his ministry unfolds. The kingdom is both present and future, and will be displayed in miraculous works, preaching, teaching and in his own person.

Both Matthew and Mark describe the call of Jesus's first disciples in the style of a charismatic calling, offering no reason why they should follow Jesus but for the sheer force of his personality. In both accounts, two pairs of brothers — Peter and Andrew, and James and John — are at work in their fishing business, and respond without question (*'immediately'*) to Jesus's call to *'Follow me and I will make you fish for men'* (Matthew 3:19; Mark 1:17). They leave behind family and financial security for a nomadic life, dependent on the generosity of others, and with no assurance that they will see their homes again. The model seems to be the calling of Elisha by Elijah

(1 Kings 19), when Elisha is ploughing with 12 oxen and is quite unexpectedly summoned by Elijah to be his successor. Whether Elisha had any prophetic background, or knew of Elijah, is not made clear, but there is little reason to think that Peter and his fellows had known previously of Jesus. Interestingly, Luke alone provides a concrete reason for them to follow Jesus with the miraculous catch of fish (chapter 5), a story which John's Gospel converts to a post-resurrection appearance.

Summary

- Matthew's **birth narrative** serves to highlight the key theme of fulfilment that runs through the Gospel, and it establishes the Messiahship and divine sonship of Jesus from conception. He fills the narrative with personal names, geographical locations and five Old Testament citations which symbolise and express the nature of Jesus and the meaning of his ministry, underlining the peculiar features of Jesus's genealogy and the circumstances of his birth to show how God works through less than perfect backgrounds and situations to bring about the accomplishment of his purposes. Obedient men respond to angelic messages to ensure the safety of the Messiah and prefigure the differing attitudes that the nations will have to Jesus. Herod and his advisors represent the rejection by Israel that will reach its climax on the cross. Matthew uses great freedom in his application of Old Testament proof texts, which may stretch credulity but which fix Jesus and his ministry firmly within the revealed will of God.
- The **baptism narrative** is used differently by each evangelist. For Matthew it confirms what has already been established at birth — Jesus's divine sonship — but the baptism itself is awkward, and John the Baptist avoids it until assured by Jesus that it is within the divine plan. Mark's narrative introduces **christological themes** which run throughout the whole of 1:1–13 and which are the key to the rest of the Gospel. He has no difficulty with John's baptism of Jesus and deals briefly with the temptations, giving no detail of their content, implying that they were successfully negotiated by Jesus. Matthew, like Luke, uses **Q material** to fill in the details of the **temptations**.
- **The call of the disciples** in Matthew and Mark is modelled on charismatic calling stories like that of Elijah and Elisha. The first disciples follow Jesus for no other reason, it would seem, than the sheer force of his charismatic personality.

Exam watch

If you are faced with a question on the birth narratives, make sure that you never fall into the trap of tedious story-telling, which will gain you the barest minimum marks. Comparisons between Matthew's and Mark's accounts of the temptations are important, and make sure that you show an understanding of how these early narratives fit into the Gospel as a whole.

Review questions

1 How does Matthew's birth narrative reflect his interest in fulfilment?
2 Compare and contrast the baptism and temptation narratives in the Synoptic Gospels and show how they reflect the evangelists' peculiar concerns.
3 Examine and comment on the religious symbolism contained in the birth narratives.
4 What can be learned about the nature of Jesus's future mission from the birth narratives?

2 The teaching of Jesus

In their accounts of the ministry of Jesus, Matthew and Mark share a considerable amount of material in common (see pp. 275–276 on the question of sources). Although Matthew, like Luke, had access to Q and to his own material (M), much of Matthew's account of Jesus's teaching is drawn from his Marcan sources, which he occasionally adapts to suit his particular interests. A great deal of Jesus's teaching was in the form of parables — short stories using real-life situations, which Jesus used to teach deep religious truths. The word comes from the Greek *parabole*, in turn from the Hebrew *masal*, meaning proverb or riddle as well as parable, and clearly for the evangelists the parables had a distinctly enigmatic quality. Jesus was not the first to use parables — such teaching was already very popular amongst Jewish teachers, and as such would have been familiar in its style and approach to Jesus's listeners. Jesus's technique was to use his parables to make his listeners think. The meanings are not, therefore, always immediately clear — people had to discover them for themselves. Hooker observes that for Mark, in particular, the parables go some way to explaining why Jesus was rejected by Israel; Israel failed to respond to him because they did not understand his teaching. The disciples were especially blessed in being given the key to understanding the parables, but Jesus makes clear that this is not available to all — for some, their meaning will always be obscure: *'To you has been given the secret of the kingdom of God, but for those outside, everything is in parables'* (Mark 4:11). Hooker also notes that there was inevitably a shift in the meaning and interpretation of the parables between Jesus's time and that of the evangelists. New situations had arisen which gave new meaning to the parables, and in the transitional process their relevance may have become obscured.

2.1 Parables of the kingdom

In the Old Testament, God's kingdom was revealed to his people through his mighty power and deeds and by the time of Jesus the people believed that God would rid the land of the Romans and, under the Messiah's rule, establish his kingdom on earth. Many of Jesus's parables were about the kingdom of God, beginning with the words *'the kingdom of God is like...'* and introducing a simile or metaphor for the kingdom and its character. However, Jesus taught that the kingdom was present on the one hand and, on the other hand, would arrive at some time in the future. This has caused intense debate among scholars.

Schweitzer suggested that Jesus was preparing the people for an imminent coming of the kingdom (**present eschatology**), whilst Dodd preferred the concept of **realised eschatology** — that is, that the kingdom of God was already present in the person and ministry of Jesus. Sanders argued that the kingdom was coming in the distant future, possibly after a Day of Judgment. **Inaugurated eschatology** blends present and realised views — some of the blessings of the coming age are available in the present, but will not be fully realised until the future.

In some of the parables, such as the mustard seed (Mark 4:30–2), the kingdom is directly mentioned, but in others, such as the tenants (Mark 12:1–11), it is implied. In the Gospels there is a feeling of mystery concerning the nature of the kingdom, for example in the parable of the hidden treasure (Matthew 13:44) and in Mark 4:11, where Jesus observes to his disciples that *'The secret of the kingdom of God has been given to*

you' (Mark 4:11). Many parables revolve around the theme of growth — the kingdom starts off small and grows; this is evident in the parable of the mustard seed (Mark 4:30–2). Jesus emphasised that, in one sense, the kingdom had arrived in him, but that there were also future aspects to the kingdom, as in the parable of the ten virgins, where the message is clearly to be ready for the sudden coming of the kingdom: *'Therefore keep watch, because you do not know the day or the hour'* (Matthew 25:13). David Hill (1973) writes: *'If, then, Jesus was telling a story about the preliminaries to an actual wedding feast, its purpose...would be to offer a warning in view of the threatened eschatological crisis'*.

The parable of the sower

The parable of the sower (Matthew 13:1–23; Mark 4:1–20) uses a familiar agricultural image of a sower sowing seeds: some fall on the path and are eaten by birds; some fall on rock and cannot grow properly; some fall among thorns and are choked; but the rest fall on good soil and produce much, far more than the initial sowing may have been expected to yield. This parable deals with the reasons why not everyone who hears the message of the kingdom of God acts upon it, showing that not everyone hears God's word in the same way. It can only grow if the hearer has faith and a responsive heart. The seeds represent the word of God — sometimes it falls on deaf ears, or on people who are too busy to listen. Yet those who do hear it and accept it will benefit greatly: *'But the one who received the seed that fell on the good soil is the man who hears the word and understands it. He produces a crop, yielding a hundred, sixty or thirty times what he has sown'* (Matthew 13:23).

Hooker (1991) writes: *'It is far from easy to determine the original meaning of the parable... the debate centres on whether the harvest is taking place in the ministry of Jesus, or whether it lies in the future, the ministry of Jesus being the time of sowing'*. Fitzmeyer suggested that the disciples were to be encouraged by small beginnings which would lead to a rich harvest, whilst Marshall argued that the important point must be the way in which people react to the message — a right response produces positive results; a wrongful response leads to nothing. Tinsley (1979) claims: *'It is as near as Jesus ever comes to explaining himself and his mission... Jesus sees his mission as a way of speaking and acting which will give men the greatest opportunity to respond to the word of God'*.

The parable of the banquet

The setting for this parable (Matthew 27:1–14) is a wedding feast for the king's son. The invitations have been sent in accordance with Jewish custom, that is, the time of the feast is not specified — the servants will summon the guests when the feast is prepared. When all is ready, the guests fail to come. They make excuses and some even kill the servants. The king punishes them and invites new guests in their place. This parable symbolises God, as the king, inviting first his chosen people (the Jews) and then, when they reject his invitation, others (the Gentiles and those on the fringes of Jewish society). The message is clear — the invitation to the feast is made through God's grace to all, the deserving and the undeserving, and it will be an occasion of great joy, but those who refuse the invitation will miss out. It may be that the reference to the burning of the city (22:7) is a prophecy of the destruction of Jerusalem in 70 CE.

Barclay (1975) writes that the initial invitation '...*came to them from nothing other than the wide-armed, open-hearted generous hospitality of the King. It was grace which offered the invitation and grace which gathered men in'*.

In the final part of the parable a guest appears without a wedding garment and is thrown out. This is a warning that God's gift is not to be taken lightly — if people accept the offer of the kingdom of God they must change their ways accordingly. Moreover, this change is reflected in their spirit and the way they are. They must dress in new clothes — in other words, repent and change their lives: *'For many are invited, but few are chosen'* (22:14).

2.2 Parables of judgment

A small number of parables (in Matthew 25) deal with the nature of God's judgment and teach about the importance of being prepared for the coming of the Messiah and the offer of salvation.

The parable of the ten virgins

This parable (25:1–13) is set in the context of a traditional Jewish wedding at the time of Jesus. A wedding was a joyful occasion that involved the whole village and would last for a week. The very closest friends would be invited to the feast itself but the actual time of the ceremony would be kept secret, and the guests would have to be alert, waiting for it to happen. In the parable, ten virgins are waiting for the bridegroom to arrive; the five wise ones have enough oil in their lamps to last a long time, the five foolish ones do not. When their oil runs out the foolish virgins have to go and get more and while they are away, the bridegroom comes. The wise virgins go to the feast, but the foolish ones, who were not alert, miss out. The meaning of the parable is that the Jews, as God's chosen people, should have been prepared for the coming of the Messiah, but they were not and may therefore be shut out of the messianic banquet: *'Therefore, keep watch, because you do not know the day or the hour'* (25:13).

The parable of the talents

The parable of the talents (25:14–30) is also based on the social customs of the day. A talent was a type of coin, but its value depended on its weight, which in turn depended whether it was made of gold, silver or copper. A gold or silver talent, by the standards of today, would be worth several hundred pounds. In the parable, a master takes three servants and entrusts the first with five talents, the second with two talents, and the third with one talent. The first invests wisely, and gains five more talents, and the second, likewise, gains two more. The third, however, buries his talent, afraid that he might lose it. When the master returns, he praises the first two, but condemns the third for wasting the opportunity he had been given.

Jesus is not talking about making vast financial profits; his teaching is concerned with how people approach their relationship with God. The first two servants represent the people to whom God has given different gifts and who have used them wisely for God's glory. To them, even greater gifts will be given. The third servant represents the Jewish religious authorities. They were entrusted with God's Law and the welfare of his people, but they failed to act wisely — they did not allow God's Law to grow or his people to develop in righteousness. Thus, the gift will be taken away from them: *'For everyone who has will be given more, and he will have an abundance. Whoever does not have, even what he has will be taken from him'* (25:29). R. T. France (1989) observes:

Of the three men who are at the beginning equally servants of the master, two finish up in 'the joy of their master', the other in outer darkness, weeping and gnashing of teeth. The difference lies in how they have made use of what was entrusted to them. Preparedness for the judgment seems then to consist in action appropriate to the privilege the disciple has received, not merely in the receipt of that privilege itself.

The parable of the sheep and the goats

This parable (25:31–46) contains perhaps the clearest teaching on judgment. It is an apocalyptic discourse that seems to suggest that those who help the needy with an open heart and who do not seek reward for themselves will escape judgment, since by helping someone in such a way they are actually loving God himself: *'For I was hungry and you gave me something to eat. I was thirsty and you gave me something to drink...whatever you did for one of the least of these brothers of mine, you did for me'* (25:35, 40). This poses some considerable theological problems, since the implication appears to be that acceptance of Jesus by faith counts for nothing in the end, if judgment is based on social outreach, an understanding of salvation which would clearly be at odds with Paul's, for example. In *A Gospel for a New People*, Graham Stanton (1992) suggests that this passage is the most debated of all in Matthew's Gospel, and that it offers two natural interpretations. One is that it should be seen as *'a dramatic and powerful insistence that in the final judgment men and women of all nations will be separated like sheep and goats on the basis of their concern and care for the poor and needy. Acceptance of those in need is acceptance of Jesus himself'*. This is a universalist interpretation. The other is particularist: *'non-Christian nations (among whom Israel may or may not be included) will be judged on the basis of their acceptance or rejection of Christians (or a particular group within Christian communities, such as missionaries or Apostles)'*. Stanton's preference is for the second interpretation, and he observes: *'Whereas it was originally an exhortation to all to show loving concern for all men and women in need, it became an assurance to Matthew's anxious readers that the nations would ultimately be judged on the basis of their treatment of Christians'*. This is a useful example, therefore, of how the meaning of parables changed between the time of Jesus and that of the evangelist's community.

2.3 The Sermon on the Mount

No other short section of the Bible has been more prominent in theological discussion and in the general life of the church than the Sermon on the Mount. Even in our modern secular societies the Sermon's influence continues. Though they may have given the matter little careful thought, many men and women who have little or no contact with the church believe that the Sermon contains clear ethical teaching for all people of goodwill.

(Stanton (ed.), 1983)

The contents of Matthew chapters 5–7 are famously known as the Sermon on the Mount. In the Gospel, the sermon is presented as a long speech, given by Jesus, covering the bulk of his teaching in one sustained discourse. It is unlikely that it happened in this way in reality, but it is a device commonly used by writers in those times. Matthew has a special purpose in presenting it in this way, and that is to emphasise his portrait of Jesus as the new Moses giving the Law from the mountain. It is the first of five blocks of teaching, identified by B. W. Bacon as the most striking feature of Matthew's Gospel, and may constitute the 'new Pentateuch'. The sermon comes at the start of Jesus's ministry and is followed by two chapters devoted to miracles. Matthew is perhaps trying to highlight Jesus as a teacher rather than a miracle worker, and the sermon shows that Jesus is not abolishing the Law of Moses, but he interprets it in a new and more uplifting way, traditionally described as a way based on love: *'Do not think that I have come to abolish the Law or the Prophets; I have not come to abolish them but to fulfil them'* (5:17). W. D. Davies (1964) observed that Matthew takes the new Moses theme to its furthest extent: *'the strictly Mosaic traits in the figure of the Matthean Christ... have been taken up into a deeper and higher context: he is not Moses come as Messiah...so much as Messiah...who has absorbed the Mosaic function'*.

The sermon can be broken down into six sections:

1 the Beatitudes and the sayings about salt and light (5:1–16)
2 the new Law (5:17–48)
3 true discipleship (6:1–18)
4 true righteousness (6:19–7:12)
5 the narrow gateway (7:13–23)
6 building on secure foundations (7:24–29)

The Beatitudes

The Beatitudes (or Blessings) are a collection of statements and prophecies. They are written in the same style, showing the blessedness that will one day exist for those who are described. They highlight a lifestyle in the kingdom of God that is, in a sense, the reverse of earthly life, where the qualities of meekness, mercy and peace will become paramount: *'Blessed are the meek, for they will inherit the earth'* (5:8). Jesus is teaching about spiritual qualities — those who mourn at the godlessness of the world and who strive to seek the will of God will be blessed. However, there will be a high price, for such people face great persecution: *'Blessed are those who are persecuted because of righteousness, for theirs is the kingdom of heaven'* (5:10). The message for believers is to remain strong and steadfast, because in the end they will make a difference to the world. They are called to remain distinctive and to fulfil a function only they can fulfil — to be salt and light to a flavourless and darkened world, even when to do so means they are rejected and discounted by it.

The new Law

In the sermon, Jesus appears to highlight the fact that the Law of Moses needs to be understood in a new light. Righteousness requires even higher standards, but standards based upon love: *'For I tell you that unless your righteousness surpasses that of the Pharisees and the teachers of the law, you will certainly not enter the kingdom of heaven'* (5:20). Jesus seems to be saying that obedience to God's Law must come from the believer's heart. Indeed, Jesus did not condemn murder, adultery and divorce in the way that the Law of Moses did — he actually addressed his teaching against the emotions, such as anger and lust, which lead to such actions. So, if you cease hating, you will not kill: *'You have heard it said to the people long ago, "Do not murder", and anyone who murders will be subject to judgment. But I tell you that anyone who is angry with his brother will be subject to judgment'* (5:21–2). *'Love your enemies and pray for those who persecute you'* (5:44). These sayings are known as **antitheses** — the standard of the old Law is set directly in contrast with the intensified standards of the new. Jesus's relationship with the Law is at stake here, particularly in a community where conservative Palestinian Christians would have been under pressure to defend their understanding of the relation between Jesus's teaching and the Law against more liberal, and even antinomian, interpretations.

True discipleship

Jesus taught that those who wish to follow him must adopt a new approach to their lives and to worship. They should give to the poor and needy, and worship God as part of a personal, living relationship. Such worship should be done in secret and not as part of a great public display: *'So when you give to the needy, do not announce it with trumpets as the hypocrites do in the synagogues and in the streets to be honoured by men'* (6:2). Worship should be private and with a view to seeking God's will. Jesus may be alluding to common practices such as blowing trumpets at the time of collecting alms in the Temple, or when prayers were led in the synagogue and a member of the congregation stood in front of the Ark. At times of public fasting, prayers could be offered in the streets. However, Jesus's criticisms are levelled not so much at the practices themselves as at the temptation to public play-acting and showiness which devalues the true spirit of worship.

In keeping with other religious teachers of his time, Jesus offers his disciples a distinctive prayer that characterises the priorities of one who seeks after kingdom values, not worldly interests. The priorities of the true disciple are identified in the Lord's Prayer: honouring of God's name; hope for the establishment of his kingdom; a commitment to obedience to his will; supplication for daily necessities; a plea for forgiveness and a commitment to a personal attitude of forgiveness; and prayer for protection against the spiritual enemy.

True righteousness

Jesus said that disciples should be single-minded in their commitment to the kingdom of God and the demands that are made of them. He encouraged his followers not to build up earthly treasure or to worry about earthly needs. They should have faith that God will provide for them: *'But seek first his kingdom and his righteousness, and all these things will be given to you as well'* (6:33).

The narrow gateway

Jesus did not say that the path of discipleship was easy, but warned that there would be troubled times ahead, false prophets and temptations to lead people astray. Discipleship will require deep commitment: *'Not everyone who says to me "Lord, Lord" will enter the kingdom of heaven, but only he who does the will of my Father who is in heaven'* (7:21).

Building on secure foundations

Jesus emphasised that the important qualities his followers should seek are humility, love and righteousness. If followers build their life on these foundations, they will be on safe ground: *'Therefore everyone who hears these words of mine and puts them into practice is like a man who builds his house on the rock'* (7:24). Barclay (1975) suggested that the Sermon on the Mount is best summed up in what he thought were the most universally famous words which Jesus spoke, namely 7:12: *'So in everything, do to others what you would have them do to you'.* He writes: *'With this commandment, the Sermon on the Mount reaches its summit'.*

Summary

- Use of the **parabolic method** of teaching is consistent with Jewish tradition in Jesus's time, but the parables acquire a special significance to the evangelist. They conceal and reveal their meanings and expose those who will never understand as well as those who have been given 'the secret of the kingdom of God'. Parables illustrate themes of judgment, eschatology, the spread of the Gospel message, and the appropriate responses of those who receive it and who are waiting for the return of Jesus.
- **The Sermon on the Mount** offers a continuous block of teaching covering issues of discipleship, particularly in relation to the new Law of the Gospel.

Exam watch

The key to these topics is — as ever — demonstrating your knowledge of the meaning and the significance of the teaching of Jesus, and not just its content. You will be able to show that you know the content of what he taught if you can write intelligently about its meaning.

Review questions

1 What can be learned about the nature of the kingdom of God from the parables of Jesus?
2 With reference to two different parables, examine the nature and importance of Judgment in the teaching of Jesus.
3 What contribution does the Sermon on the Mount make to the teaching of Jesus?
4 *'The parables were the most important part of Jesus's ministry.'* Discuss.

3 The miracles of Jesus

The miracles of Jesus play a vital part in his mission, and they emphasise the fact that he had the authority and power of God over both the natural and the spiritual world. The miracles are shown as acts of power that not only reveal Jesus's authority but also highlight his teachings about God. The miracle stories come under three broad headings: healings, exorcisms and nature miracles.

The evil spirit (Mark 1:21–7)

In the synagogue Jesus was confronted by a man who was possessed by an evil spirit. The spirit appeared to know exactly who Jesus was: *'What do you want with us, Jesus of Nazareth? Have you come to destroy us? I know who you are — the Holy One of God!'* (1:24). Jesus cast the spirit out of the man, to the astonishment of the onlookers. This story illustrates the authority of Jesus over the spiritual world — he simply utters the word of command and, such is his authority, the spirit must leave. Interestingly, the evil spirits universally recognise who Jesus is, even whilst the human characters, who are not spiritually discerning, do not. Even when faced with the power of Jesus over the forces of Satan, his opponents do not recognise its significance: *'The leaders of the Jews witness the miracles of Jesus, but the scribes conclude from his exorcisism that he is in collusion with Satan, and the Pharisees demand of him that he have God perform a sign on his behalf to attest to them that he is God's chosen agent'* (Kingsbury, 1983).

Simon's mother-in-law (Mark 2:29–34)

Jesus healed Simon's mother-in-law of a fever, this time with a simple touch. In gratitude, she served them with a meal. This miracle, straightforward as it is, highlighted the power of Jesus over physical, as well as spiritual, sickness, and perhaps his special compassion for those close to his disciples.

The man with leprosy (Mark 1:40–5)

Jesus healed a leper with the command *'Be clean!'* (1:41). This miracle story contains several symbolic elements. Leprosy, as well as being a fatal disease, also made the sufferer ritually unclean, and lepers were often cast out of the community and the religious life of Israel. Moreover, the Jewish authorities regarded leprosy as a kind of living death, and the Law could do little for the sufferers. Jesus's miraculous words not only healed the man, but restored his ritual cleanliness so that he could rejoin the community and his faith. This miracle highlights how Jesus fulfilled the needs of the people far more than did the Jewish leaders and their interpretation of the Law. The story ends with Jesus instructing the man not to tell anyone, but to go and make the appropriate sacrifices in the Temple (which were outlined in Deuteronomy 24:8). This is a reference to Jewish practices, and, in a sense, allows the man to show his gratitude to God for what has happened.

The healing of the paralytic (Matthew 9:1–8; Mark 2:1–13)

Jesus was preaching at a house in Capernaum when a paralysed man was lowered by his friends through the roof of the house. Jesus healed the man with the words *'Son, your sins are forgiven'* (2:5). In those days it was believed that certain kinds of suffering, such as paralysis, were a punishment from God for one's own sins or for the sins of one's parents. Jesus acts in response to the faith of the man and his friends by forgiving his sins, and hence curing the man. The Jewish leaders are outraged, believing that only God himself can forgive sins — yet Jesus's healing of the man in this way shows he has the power and authority of God himself and is another powerful revelation of his Messiahship: *'Which is easier; to say to the paralytic, "Your sins are forgiven," or to say "Get up, take your mat and walk"? But that you may know that the Son of Man has authority on earth to forgive sins'* (2:9–10).

The demon-possessed man (Matthew 8:28–34; Mark 5:1–20)

Jesus went to a largely Gentile region, called Gerasenes, where he met a man possessed by many powerful spirits who seemed to know exactly who Jesus was. The spirits asked for mercy, aware of the extent of his divine power: *'What do you want with me, Jesus,*

Son of the Most High God? Swear to God that you won't torture me!' (Mark 5:7). Jesus cast the demons from the man and into a flock of swine, which then rushed into the lake and died. The man was healed, and the onlookers were amazed and frightened and wanted Jesus to leave, but the man asked to go with him. Jesus told him to stay where he was and to tell the people *'how much the Lord has done for you and how he had mercy on you'* (Mark 5:19). Nineham (1963) suggests that Jesus was actually commissioning the man to begin preaching to the Gentiles — the first step towards taking Jesus's message worldwide: *'In effect, the land is cleansed by his coming and the way was prepared for its Christianising, a task which, at the end of the story, Jesus emphatically lays upon the man previously possessed by the demons'*.

The woman with a haemorrhage (Matthew 9:18–22; Mark 5:25–34)

Jesus was heading for the house of Jairus, surrounded by a large crowd, when a woman suffering from a haemorrhage that had left her bleeding for 12 years touched his cloak in the hope of being cured. She was healed, and Jesus, feeling the power leaving him as she touched him, asked the crowd who did it. The woman was frightened, but need not have been, for Jesus said to her: *'Daughter, your faith has healed you. Go in peace and be freed from your suffering'* (Mark 5:34). Here Jesus highlights the importance of faith. He requires the woman to declare her action and faith aloud rather than keeping it secret so that she can truly understand and accept what has happened. As R. Alan Cole points out: *'This brought a realisation of the means by which she had entered the experience, an assurance of God's peace and a sense of security for the future'*.

Jairus's daughter (Matthew 9:18–26; Mark 5:21–4, 35–43)

Jairus was a prominent Jew and the ruler of the local synagogue who asked Jesus to come to his house to lay his hands upon his dying daughter — a remarkable act of faith for a Jewish leader. However, by the time they reached the house, the girl was dead. The miracle that followed showed Jesus's ultimate authority over death itself and was a prelude to Christ's own resurrection. Jesus began by telling Jairus: *'Don't be afraid; just believe'* (Mark 5:36) — God requires his people to have faith and to acknowledge the limits of human helplessness and God's grace. He then took the dead girl by the hand (although ouching a corpse was an act of ritual uncleanliness) and restored her to life with the words: *'Talitha koumi'* (5:41).

The centurion's servant (Matthew 8:5–13)

A Roman centurion comes to Jesus and asks him to heal his servant. He does not need Jesus to come to the house to cure the man, but simply says to Jesus: *'Just say the word, and my servant will be healed'* (8:8). Jesus is amazed at the man's faith, and the servant is cured, prompting Jesus to make the observation: *'I have not found anyone in Israel with such great faith'* (8:10). Matthew uses the occasion to open up the message of Jesus to all who have faith, whether they are Jews or Gentiles: *'I say to you that many will come from the east and west and will take their places at the feast with Abraham, Isaac and Jacob in the kingdom of heaven'* (8:11). The Jews believed that when the Messiah came, there would be a great banquet where they would sit down to feast — the Messianic Banquet. However, Jesus was suggesting here that Gentiles would be invited

too and that the Jews themselves might lose their places. Simply being a Jew was not sufficient to be saved — what was required was faith.

The calming of the storm (Matthew 8:23–7; Mark 4:35–41)

This miracle occurs in all the Synoptic Gospels. In it Jesus gives clear evidence to his disciples of his divine power and control over the forces of nature. When Jesus and his disciples were caught in a storm on the lake, Jesus awoke from sleep and calmed the raging storm with stern words, like those used to cast out evil spirits. He questioned the disciples over their lack of faith; they were simply amazed: '*What kind of man is this? Even the winds and the waves obey him!*' (Matthew 8:27). There is a good deal of symbolism here. In the Old Testament, God is depicted as having control over the waters (Isaiah 40:12) and he calms the storm (Psalm 107:29). The image of the storm is also used to show the power of evil forces in the world (Psalm 69) and the righteous person is said to sleep peacefully in the faith that God will keep him or her safe: '*I will lie down and sleep in peace, for you alone, O Lord, make me dwell in safety*' (Psalm 4:8).

Summary

- The miracles of Jesus not only highlight the power and authority of God, but also are used by Jesus in his teachings about God.
- There are **three** broad types of miracle: the exorcism of demons, the healing miracles and the nature miracles.
- The exorcism of demons shows Jesus's authority over the spiritual world.
- The healing miracles, which range from curing a fever to restoring a paralytic, show how Jesus has authority over the physical world and that he can fulfil the needs of God's people far more than the religious authorities can.
- The nature miracles show the divine power of Jesus over the forces of nature. There is a good deal of Old Testament symbolism within them, highlighting God's control over his creation.

Exam watch

The evangelists use the miracles of Jesus as powerful christological tools, emphasising the identity of Jesus and his authority over nature, sickness and the power of Satan, so make sure you can demonstrate your understanding of this coherently. The point made before about not simply 'telling the story' in your answer is a crucial one here too. The examiner is never going to be interested in how many miracle stories you can write out off by heart; you need to show how well you have grasped the significance of them.

Review questions

1. With reference to three different incidents, examine and comment on the significance of miracles in the ministry of Jesus.
2. (a) What did the Gospel writers mean by the term 'miracle'?
   (b) Using two different miracles, explain what can be learned from them about the person of Jesus.
3. '*Jesus's mission would have been more successful if he hadn't performed the miracles.*' Discuss.

B The passion and resurrection narratives

The last days before Jesus's death are known as the passion and the accounts of this time are of great religious significance.

1 The last week

The passion begins with the triumphal entry into Jerusalem, followed by the cleansing of the Temple, conflict with the authorities, the Lord's Supper, the trial and crucifixion.

1.1 The triumphal entry (Matthew 21:1–10; Mark 11:1–11)

Jesus has decided that the time has come for him to go to Jerusalem and face the Jewish authorities. He knows that the authorities are hostile to him but, instead of coming in secret, he chooses to come openly and in triumph. At Bethany, a village about 2 miles from Jerusalem, he instructs two of his disciples to collect a colt for him — one that has never been ridden before. This is perhaps to show that the animal is unspoilt and therefore suitable for this sacred purpose, but there is clearly an element of divine mysteriousness in the incident — the owners hand the colt over as soon as they hear the words *'The Lord needs it'* (Mark 11:3), which suggests they have prior knowledge.

Jesus rides the colt towards Jerusalem and the people spread their cloaks on the road, making a triumphal carpet for Jesus to ride on. In a way that is reminiscent of the Feast of Tabernacles, they wave branches of greenery as he makes his way into the city. At the Mount of Olives there is a large crowd and the scene is apparently happy, with people praising God for all his works.

It is possible that their enthusiasm was based upon the prophecy from Zechariah 9:9:

Shout, Daughter of Jerusalem!
See, your king comes to you,
Righteous and having salvation,
Gentle and riding on a donkey.

Certainly the people were looking for a king or Messiah — they had seen Jesus perform miraculous works and could well have interpreted his entry into the city as fulfilment of the prophecy: *'Blessed is he who comes in the name of the Lord! Blessed is the coming kingdom of our father David'* (Mark 11:9–10). Hooker comments that the crowd's cries of *'Hosanna'* were, in fact, to celebrate the festival and bless the pilgrims visiting Jerusalem, rather than acclaim Jesus as king. This suggestion fits in well with Mark's story, since it accounts for the apparent fickleness of the crowd, who later in the week demand Jesus's death. In any case, the period between Jesus's arrival in Jerusalem and his crucifixion was probably somewhat longer than the five days the evangelists assign to it.

1.2 The cleansing of the Temple (Matthew 21:12–17; Mark 11:15–19)

Jesus enters the Temple area, probably the court of the Gentiles, where he finds market traders selling animals for sacrifice at very high prices and changing money; the Temple will not accept Roman coinage, so all currency has to be changed into Tyrian coinage. This means a profit for the market traders at the expense of the worshippers. They are all part of the Temple system of sacrifice and offering, but Jesus is angry that such a trade is going on within the Temple precincts and he drives them out, quoting from the prophecy of Isaiah 56:7: *'Is it not written: "My house will be called a house of prayer for all nations?" But you have made it a den of robbers'* (Mark 11:17). The incident ends ominously, with the chief priests and leaders of the people preparing to make a final move against Jesus (11:18).

For the synoptic evangelists, this episode is the catalyst for Jesus's arrest and crucifixion, although we have been prepared for it from the beginning of the Gospels. Jesus's action in the Temple would, under any circumstances, have been viewed as challenging, but to act in such a way during the Passover festival, when the Romans were especially on the lookout for potential Jewish uprisings, was political dynamite. The Jewish authorities, acutely aware that if they did not act against an apparently politically dangerous charismatic, the Roman authorities would come down heavily on them, were now obliged to move fast. The possibility that increasing numbers would follow Jesus, inspired by his actions in the Temple, made it essential that the Jewish authorities not be seen to encourage him, even by their silence. Ellis Rivkin (1984) observes:

What mattered were the consequences for the high priest and procurator if the crowds had gone wild, shouting 'The kingdom of God is at hand, and Jesus is our king'. The coming of God's kingdom would, in fact, have been even more frightening to Pontius Pilate and Caiaphas than a mere human kingdom, since God's kingdom could be blocked by no earthly power, however exalted and mighty.

1.3 Conflict with the authorities

In such a world, where violence stalked the countryside, death frequented the streets of Jerusalem, and riots disturbed the precincts of the Temple, where every flutter of dissidence sent chills of fear up the spines of puppet kings, governors, procurators, and procurator-appointed high priests — even the most non-political of charismatics took his life in his hands when he preached the good news of God's coming kingdom.

(ibid.)

Throughout his ministry Jesus came into conflict with the Jewish authorities, and matters came to a climax during the last days. The cause of the conflict between Jesus and the Jewish authorities centred around the fact that he seemed to pose a challenge to the system of Jewish law, worship and ritual. He was also believed by many to be the Son of God — a concept that the Jews could not accept or understand. They saw such a view as blasphemy, as God was seen as being single and undivided. Moreover, the Jewish authorities were under pressure from the Romans. The Romans allowed the Jewish authorities to retain their power on condition that they kept the people peaceful and prevented anti-Roman demonstrations. The Romans demanded that the chief priests quickly dealt with any troublemakers and those who attracted crowds — Jesus was such a person.

The Jewish authorities tried to trick Jesus into condemning himself. In Matthew 21:23–7, they ask Jesus where his authority comes from. He does not answer their question, but instead asks them where they thought John the Baptist's authority to baptise came from. Many people in Jerusalem believed that John was a man sent by

God and therefore believed his authority came from God. However, the authorities had never acknowledged this. So, if they said his authority was from God, then why hadn't they accepted it? Alternatively, if they said his authority was not from God, they risked angering a lot of people. They cannot answer, and so Jesus refuses to answer their question: *'Neither will I tell you by what authority I am doing these things'* (Matthew 21:27).

Jesus then tells the parable of the tenants and the vineyard (Matthew 21:33–45; Mark 12:1–12), which marks a turning point in the conflict. It highlights the fact that just as the tenants reject the vineyard owner's servants, so Israel has continually rejected God's prophets. The tenants' killing of the son will reflect the rejection and crucifixion of Jesus. Jesus gives them the chance to change their ways, but they will refuse the opportunity and will, in turn, be rejected by God. The chief priests are angered, knowing that this parable is spoken against them: *'Therefore I tell you that the kingdom of God will be taken away from you and given to a people who will produce its fruit'* (Matthew 21:43).

The Jewish authorities try to trap Jesus into making a treasonable statement, so that they can arrest him and send him for trial before the Roman governor. They do this by asking whether the Jews should pay Roman taxes. This is a trick question: if he says they should, then the people might think he is on the side of the Romans; if he says they should not, then the Romans could arrest him for sedition. Jesus's reply is the only safe one: *'Give to Caesar what is Caesar's, and to God what is God's'* (Matthew 22:21).

Jesus is further questioned by the Sadducees concerning marriage and the resurrection in Matthew 22:23–33 and Mark 12:18–27. They did not believe in the traditional Jewish teaching concerning the resurrection of the dead on the last day, but made up a story about what was known as a 'levirate' marriage. This was a legal action designed to make sure that a man's family name did not die out — so if a man died childless, his widow married his brother and the children they had carried the dead man's name (cf. Deuteronomy 25:5). The Sadducees want to trick Jesus into saying that there is no resurrection, and so alienate him from the majority of believers. They ask: if there were seven brothers who all, at one time or another, married the same woman, then which one would be her husband at the resurrection? Jesus's reply is straightforward — life is different in the age to come, and there will be no marriage: *'At the resurrection people will neither marry nor be given in marriage; they will be like the angels in heaven'* (Matthew 22:30).

Jesus warns the people against the Jewish authorities, saying that they enjoy the status and luxury that their position gives them, but they do not practise what they preach and make a display of being holy and righteous: *'Woe to you, teachers of the law and Pharisees, you hypocrites! You shut the kingdom of God in men's faces'* (Matthew 23:13). He goes on to give a long eschatological speech, warning of the signs of the end of the age, a time which will arrive unexpectedly, and he urges believers to be always ready (Matthew 24; Mark 13): *'At that time men will see the Son of Man coming in clouds of great power and glory'* (Mark 13:26).

The Jewish authorities then look for a way to arrest and kill Jesus. Passover is an important religious time and they are anxious not to act during the Feast itself in case they cause a riot. Jesus gives the disciples an ominous warning: *'As you know, the Passover is two days away — and the Son of Man will be handed over to be crucified'* (Matthew 26:2).

Jesus is staying in Bethany, a village near Jerusalem, at the house of Simon the Leper. An unknown woman rushes in and pours expensive perfume on Jesus's head — a symbolic anointing, highlighting the crowning of a king in Old Testament times (1 Samuel 16:3). She is acknowledging the Messiahship of Jesus as the King of the Jews. She is also prophetically preparing his body for burial, for it was the custom of the Jews to pour perfume on a body after death. The disciples do not understand, believing that what the woman has done is wasteful and that the money spent on the perfume should have gone to the poor, but Jesus corrects them — she is honouring Jesus whilst she can; she will not have another chance. Jesus suggests that his followers should not just consider the financial cost — the act of love is more important: '*She has done a beautiful thing to me. The poor you will always have with you, and you can help them any time you want. But you will not always have me*' (Mark 14:6–7). Significantly, Judas (who is identified by the Fourth Evangelist as the complainant) then moves to betray Jesus to the Jewish authorities, possibly for financial gain, suggesting that, for one disciple at least, money was more important than anything else. The episode is all the more interesting in that the anointing is performed by a woman and her action ensures her a place wherever the Gospel is told (Mark 14:9).

2 The last day

2.1 The Last Supper

On the day upon which the Passover lamb is sacrificed, Jesus sends two disciples into the city to prepare a room, which Jesus has already selected for them, to eat the Passover meal. They eat the meal and then Jesus prophesies his own betrayal, saying that one of his disciples will betray him, as predicted in Psalm 41:9: '*Even my close friend, whom I trusted, he who shared my bread, has lifted up his heel against me*'. The meal they eat is known today as the Lord's Supper or the Last Supper. Historically, we do not know whether this is the actual Passover meal or not; what is important are the words and symbolic actions surrounding the meal and it is clearly important to Jesus that he has the opportunity to share this final meal with the disciples as his death approaches. It is conceivable that the meal was eaten a day earlier than the synoptic evangelists record (but as the Fourth Gospel maintains) and that Mark, followed by Matthew and Luke, delays its timing to infer that it was a Passover meal. However, a number of common Passover features are clearly incorporated into the meal, and Hooker (1991) observes: '*It is much easier to understand why Mark should have added details consistent with the meal being a Passover, if he had in fact believed that it was.*'

Jesus breaks the bread and shares it with his disciples. The eating of bread without yeast (called **matzoth**) was a requirement of the Law of Moses (Exodus 12:8), but Jesus adds new meaning to it with the words: '*Take it; this is my body*' (14:22). This is highly symbolic — by eating the bread that is Christ's body, the disciples are able to have Jesus within them. In a similar way, he shares a cup of wine, saying: '*This is my blood of the covenant which is poured out for many*' (14:24). This is linked to the Old Testament — the blood of the first Passover lambs was used to protect the people of God from death (Exodus 12:23). Moreover, the blood from young bulls was used to seal the agreement between God and his people at the making of the covenant at Mount Sinai (Exodus

24:8). Jesus's death therefore marks the beginning of a new covenant, sealed in his blood. Drane (1999) notes:

The Passover festival celebrated and recalled the inauguration of God's covenant with their ancestors. They remembered how, long ago, God had delivered Israel from slavery in Egypt and in gratitude for this deliverance Israel had given their obedience and devotion to God... When Jesus compared his own death to the inauguration of a 'new covenant', he was suggesting to his disciples that through him God was performing a new act of deliverance.

Interestingly, in Matthew's account he also describes the cup as being *'for the forgiveness of sins'* (26:28). This recalls his earlier description of the birth of Jesus as being *'to save his people from their sins'* (1:23), a promise which is now fulfilled. Jesus then predicts that the disciples will run away, as prophesied in Zechariah 13:7, but he encourages them that he will rise and return (Mark 14:28). Here, as in previous incidents, the author of the Gospel uses prophecy to show that everything is happening exactly in accordance with God's plan.

Peter, full of misplaced confidence, boasts that he will never desert Jesus, only to be told that he will have betrayed Jesus three times before the cock has crowed. One interesting, but often overlooked, point is that Matthew 26:35 says that not just Peter, but all the disciples, say that they will never disown Jesus. Peter is, in a sense, therefore a representative of them all.

2.2 Gethsemane

After the meal, Jesus and the disciples go to the garden of Gethsemane, a quiet spot just outside Jerusalem. Jesus divides the disciples into two groups — eight who stay near the entrance, and Peter, James and John, who accompany Jesus into the garden itself. He asks them to keep watch whilst he goes to pray. His words of anguish are a reflection of the words of Psalm 42: *'My soul is overwhelmed with sorrow to the point of death'* (Matthew 15:34).

Jesus prays by falling prostrate to the ground — a sign of great spiritual anguish. He addresses God with the Aramaic expression *Abba*, which is a formal use of the word *'Father'* (Mark 14:36). In the prayer that follows, Jesus shows his humanity, highlighting the pain he must suffer. He asks that the cup might be taken from him — the cup is a symbol of suffering, linked with the Old Testament concept of the cup of the anger of God (Psalm 75). Yet Jesus offers words of obedience; he is to fulfil his earthly mission: *'Yet not what I will, but what you will'* (Matthew 15:36). Twice Jesus returns to the disciples to find them sleeping and rebukes them; he wanted them to remain awake and watchful, which was to be an important aspect of future discipleship, and they failed to do so. The challenge that faces them over the coming days will be too much for them, although they will be restored after Jesus's resurrection.

2.3 Arrest and trial

Finally, Judas appears with an armed crowd. Judas greets Jesus with a kiss and the designation *Rabbi* — titles of respect and love, though, ironically, Judas uses them as signs of betrayal. Jesus replies with the impersonal address *'Friend'*. As Jesus is arrested, a man nearby, traditionally thought to be Peter, draws a sword and cuts off the ear of a servant, but Jesus orders the violence to cease and makes the eschatological claim: *'Do you think I cannot call on my Father, and he will at once put at my disposal more than twelve legions of angels? But how then would the Scriptures be fulfilled that say it must happen in this way?'* (Matthew 26:53–4). He rebukes the Jewish authorities, who were, apparently, too frightened to arrest him by the light of day, a further sign of their complete lack of understanding of Jesus and his identity. Nevertheless, it is clear that the responsibility for Jesus's arrest does not lie entirely with the authorities, who are playing their part in the drama of salvation just as Judas has played his. The moment of Jesus's arrest is the moment when he engages in direct confrontation again with Satan. As Jesus is taken away, the disciples flee, and the reader's attention is again focused on the one who is to suffer.

Jesus is taken before the Sanhedrin, the supreme Jewish Council, in what begins, apparently, as a fact-finding hearing, but swiftly turns into a trial. The proceedings are completely irregular: they take place at night, Jesus is not allowed to call witnesses on his own behalf, and proper trial procedures are not observed. The Gospel writers make it clear that justice is not being done: *'The chief priests and the whole Sanhedrin were looking for evidence against Jesus so that they could put him to death'* (Mark 14:55). Finally, the High Priest asks the crucial question, which is slightly different in Matthew and Mark:

÷ *'Tell us if you are the Christ, the Son of God?'* (Matthew 26:63)
÷ *'Are you the Christ, the Son of the Blessed One?'* (Mark 14:61)

In a very real sense, nothing else matters. To claim to be the Son of God was a blasphemy under the Law of Moses, punishable by death. Jesus's answer is enough to condemn him: *'"I am," said Jesus. "And you will see the Son of Man sitting at the right hand of the Mighty One and coming on the clouds of heaven"'* (Mark 14:62). This episode brings to a climax the religious leaders' assault on Jesus's authority that has run through the Gospel. Once they hand him over to Pilate for sentencing (interestingly, for an offence which would not normally warrant the Roman death penalty), their role is finished. However, Kingsbury (1983) observes that the episode is resolved in the resurrection narrative:

In the resurrection, God vindicates Jesus's claim to divine authority and indeed exalts him to universal rule... Although the religious leaders are not privy to this, the reader knows that they will have no alternative but to acknowledge the truth of it when Jesus returns in splendour as Judge at the consummation of the age.

Meanwhile, outside, Peter, as predicted, disowns Jesus and then breaks down and weeps. It has been a hard lesson, but one which will stand him in good stead for the future. Judas is *'seized with remorse'* (Matthew 27:3) at betraying Jesus. He returns the 30 silver coins that the chief priests had given him and hangs himself. Luke also records in Acts that Judas committed suicide, although by a different method, but either way the message is clear — remorse is not enough to restore Judas. Only true repentance could deal with his guilt and enable him to receive God's grace to understand what had really been going on in the divine drama.

2.4 Before Pilate

Under the state of occupation, only the Roman political authorities could pass the death sentence or **ius gladi**. Therefore, the Jewish leaders take Jesus to Pontius Pilate, the Roman Procurator. Before Pilate, the chief priests accuse Jesus of many things (Mark 15:3), but nothing specific. Pilate himself says little beyond asking Jesus if he is the King of the Jews, and is surprised at Jesus's reluctance to reply to his accusers. Finally, Pilate reverts to the custom of releasing a prisoner to the people at Passover, and he offers the crowd the choice of Jesus or Barabbas. The crowd, probably spurred on by the chief priests, shout for Barabbas, despite the fact that Pilate feels that Jesus has done nothing wrong. In Matthew's account, Pilate's wife tells him she has had a strange dream and that Pilate should not condemn Jesus. But the chief priests and the people insist. Reluctantly, Pilate condemns Jesus to death, even though he is apparently innocent of any crime.

Matthew adds two distinctive episodes to his version of the trial. Like Herod before him, Pilate has no real understanding of who Jesus is, and although he is a relatively sympathetic, but weak, character in the Gospel, he has no choice but to submit to the Jews' evaluation of Jesus. Pilate and his wife are caught in the middle of the conflict and in an ironic and symbolic gesture Pilate washes his hands (Matthew 27:24), a Jewish practice recorded in Deuteronomy 21:6–9, to signify his refusal to accept the guilt for the death of Jesus. The crowd, however, will accept the responsibility themselves — just as Jesus predicted in the parable of the tenants (Matthew 21: 33–43): '*Let his blood be on us and on our children!*' (Matthew 27:25). Pilate's wife, a Gentile, ironically pleads for the Jewish Messiah, whilst the chief priests persuade the Jewish people to ask for the release of Barabbas. Her actions recall the homage of the magi to Jesus and their protection of him, whilst her dream recalls the dreams of Joseph and the magi that ensure the safety of the Messiah. But although Pilate is affected by his wife's pleading, Jesus's fate cannot be changed.

3 The crucifixion

Jesus is handed over to the soldiers, where he is mocked and mistreated — this was common practice because it allowed the soldiers to dehumanise the person they were about to execute, making it easier for them to put him to death. In many cases, prisoners would die before they even reached the cross. The place of execution was a hill outside Jerusalem called **Golgotha** (or **Calvary**). Jesus, like all condemned prisoners, is forced to walk through the city to Golgotha, facing the abuse of the citizens *en route*. Usually the prisoner would carry the crossbeam on his shoulders, but the soldiers seize a man called Simon of Cyrene and force him to carry Jesus's cross. On arrival, Jesus is nailed to the cross and offered myrrh to drink as a painkiller (remember the gift of the wise men?). In fulfilment of the prophecy written in Psalm 69:21, the soldiers draw lots to see who will get Jesus's clothes.

Jesus's crucifixion begins '*at the third hour*' (Mark 15:25), that is, 9am. (Notice how quickly things have happened — he was having the Last Supper the evening before.) He is placed between two robbers. We don't know their names, although traditionally they have been called Zoathan and Chammatha, and their role is given considerably more significance in Luke's account. Darkness covers the whole land until the sixth hour (12 noon) and lasts until the ninth hour (3pm). This may be symbolic of the darkness that fell on Egypt in the Old Testament during the time of Moses as a sign of God's displeasure (Exodus 10:22) but certainly it has dramatic eschatological significance.

On the cross Jesus utters a cry which is a direct quotation from Psalm 22, one of the psalms of the righteous sufferer: *'Eloi, Eloi, lama sabachtani?'* (Matthew 27:46; Mark 15:34). Translated, this means *'My God, my God, why have you forsaken me?'* and is deeply significant, for as Jesus dies, taking upon himself the sins of the world, God must forsake or desert him, as those sins separate him from Jesus. However, Jesus's words are not a cry of despair, but a cry of triumph — his mission is successfully accomplished. R. Alan Cole writes: *'So here we have the agony of one suffering the experience of abandonment by God, and yet certain of ultimate vindication and triumph'*. Nevertheless, it is possible that Luke, writing for a Gentile audience, felt that the psalm would be easily misinterpreted as one of defeat, and he eliminates any reference to it.

Jesus dies at the sixth hour and the curtain in the Temple is torn in two. Again, there is profound significance here. The most sacred part of the Temple was called the Holy of Holies and it was protected with a great curtain. It was the place of the presence of God and the curtains were there to prevent God and humanity from meeting each other directly — it was a barrier between God and his people. The tearing of the curtain, on the death of Jesus, meant that the barrier was no longer needed, because salvation was now available. Mark notes that a centurion standing at the cross was moved to declare: *'Surely this man was the Son of God!'* (15:39), echoing Mark's own opening lines (1:1).

Matthew also adds some unique eschatological references: at the moment of Jesus's death an earthquake shakes the earth, and the bodies of many holy people are brought back to life and are seen walking about in the city (27:52). These images are sustained in his account of the resurrection, when he also records a 'great earthquake' that heralds the appearance of an angel (28:2).

None of the male disciples was present when Jesus died, but some of the women followers, who proved to be Jesus's most faithful disciples, were there. Pilate himself is surprised that Jesus is already dead, and agrees to let a prominent Jew, Joseph of Arimathea, a member of the Sanhedrin, bury the body of Jesus in a tomb cut out of rock. The body could not be buried with the proper ritual at this time because the Sabbath was soon to begin and Jews refrained from work (i.e. burying a body) on the Sabbath in obedience to the commandment in Exodus 20:8: *'Remember the Sabbath day by keeping it holy.'* So the body is buried temporarily, until the proper procedures can be carried out when the Sabbath is over. Yet in Matthew's account the chief priests and Pharisees are not satisfied even with the death of Jesus, and ask Pilate for a guard to be put on the tomb: *'Otherwise, his disciples may come and steal the body and tell the people that he has been raised from the dead'* (27:64). In a final ironic twist, this is the very rumour the chief priests themselves put around later to explain the resurrection (Matthew 28:13). Matthew does not do this purely for effect, but to show that in the death of Jesus, God had broken through in a new, dramatic way, and the order of things will never be the same again.

4 The resurrection

There are important variations in the accounts of the resurrection.

Mark's account

Mark's original account is very brief (16:1–8), with the later additions (9–20) probably by the early church. It begins on the Sunday morning, with three women, named as Mary Magdalene, Mary, the mother of James, and Salome, coming to the tomb to anoint the body of Jesus. At the tomb they see that the stone has been rolled away and a man wearing a white robe (presumably an angel) tells them that Jesus has risen, fulfilling his own prophecy that he would rise and go before them to Galilee (14:28). The women run away and the Gospel ends cryptically with the words: *'They said nothing to anyone because they were afraid'* (16:8).

This ending puzzled scholars because there are no resurrection appearances and the reaction of the disciples is not known. It is conceivable even that the women failed to deliver the message they were given, although in reality this is unlikely. Nevertheless, this was possibly why the early church may have added several verses to complete the story, highlighting the resurrection appearances and showing Jesus giving the disciples the great commission to: *'Go into the world and preach the good news to all creation'* (16:15). These additions owe a considerable amount to the other accounts of the resurrection, including the Fourth Gospel, and are not especially satisfactory. It may be a mistake to recoil from Mark's terse ending, assuming that he did not intend to conclude the Gospel so abruptly. Rather, as Hooker suggests, it is a deliberate invitation to the reader to follow Jesus to Galilee, in the full assurance that he will be there, with or without corroborating accounts of his appearances.

Matthew's account

In Matthew's account (28:1–20) only two women go to the tomb. There is an earthquake and an angel opens the tomb and tells the women that Jesus has risen and will meet the disciples in Galilee. The women encounter Jesus personally, and become the first to see the risen Jesus. The women worship Jesus, just as the three wise men worshipped the infant Jesus at his birth (2:11). In a number of ways, Matthew makes deliberate and stylish links between the birth narratives and the resurrection account. In 1:23 he had told the reader that Jesus was to be *'Immanuel — God with us'* and in 28:20 he assures them that Jesus will be with believers *'till the close of the age'*. God's presence will not be withdrawn from among his people now that he has been made known to them in the ministry of Jesus.

In this account the women do deliver their message, and Jesus meets the male disciples and they too worship him, although Matthew attempts to add a note of realism to the narrative with the observation that *'some doubted'*. The place where it all started, Galilee, is the place where it now ends — the Gospel has come full circle. Jesus gives the disciples the great commission: *'Therefore go and make disciples of all nations'* (28:19). Drane (1999) observes: *'So the resurrection of Jesus was crucial, for if Jesus had only died on the cross, he might well have been understood to have set an example, or offered a sacrifice, or paid the price of human freedom — but his suffering would have had no power to affect everyday living'*.

Summary

- Jesus enters Jerusalem openly and in a symbolic manner, welcoming the time of his passion. The crowd's initial acknowledgement of him turns to open hostility as the passion narrative progresses. The **cleansing of the Temple** serves as the catalyst for his arrest, and the hostility with the authorities, which reaches a climax in the passion, is probably an accurate reflection of the prevailing political climate. In a series of provocative teachings, Jesus makes clear that his rejection by the Jewish authorities is the culmination of Israel's history of rejection of God's messengers. Even the disciples fail to appreciate how close is Jesus's death, except the unnamed woman who anoints him at Bethany.

- The **Last Supper** has all the features of a Passover meal, but acquires new signifiance as Jesus reinterprets the elements as his body and blood, symbols of the new exodus which his death will provide.

- He faces his **arrest** with quiet acceptance, making clear that it is in fulfilment of the divine plan. He is tried before the Sanhedrin on spurious counts, and in a clearly illegal trial. **Pilate** is not convinced that Jesus deserves the death penalty, and attempts to release him, but gives way to political pressure from the Jewish authorities.

- The **crucifixion** narrative is full of symbolism and use of the Old Testament to emphasise that Jesus's death is the culmination of the divine plan of salvation, although brought about by Jesus's enemies.

- Both evangelists record the resurrection differently, drawing on their own traditions, and what would appear to be a very fluid resurrection tradition from the early church. Mark and Matthew disagree over whether the women fulfilled their instruction to tell the disciples that Jesus was risen, and Mark's failure to include accounts of resurrection appearances seems to have led to later additions by early scribes.

Exam watch

There is plenty of excellent material here for good, thoughtful essays, examining issues of conflict, fulfilment and symbolism. Make sure that you think in terms of these issues rather of a generic passion narrative — as each evangelist (Luke and John included) has marked his characteristic stamp on the sources. These are not simple narratives, however, so don't fall into the trap of thinking you can write simple answers about them. You must know the material and its significance very thoroughly.

Review questions

1 'It was Jesus's conflict with the Jewish rather than Roman authorities that led to his death.' Discuss and assess this view.

2 Examine and discuss the meaning of the symbolism in the accounts of the crucifixion and resurrection of Jesus.

3 In what ways do the accounts of the passion, death and resurrection of Jesus in Matthew and Mark differ from each other? To what extent are these differences significant?

Topic 3

The Gospel of Luke

A The birth and infancy narratives

It is thought that the birth and infancy narratives, even though they tell of Jesus's early life, are actually late additions to the Gospels of Matthew and Luke. Mark, the earliest Gospel, and Paul's letters, which are even earlier, make no reference to these narratives and some scholars have suggested that the narratives were put in by the early church to provide answers to christological problems concerning the nature of Jesus. Luke's readers were probably only aware of the adult ministry of Jesus, and the question had inevitably arisen as to when Jesus was designated Son of God. Mark 1:1–11 seems to suggest that it was at his baptism, but Luke and Matthew, without dropping the baptism narrative, push Jesus's sonship back to conception. The narratives in Luke and Matthew are quite different, and each uses them to introduce themes that will be important to the rest of the Gospel. In this respect, they are, in Morna Hooker's phrase, '*keys that open the gospels*', providing the reader with the information that will unlock the significance of the Gospel to them. There are common themes that run through both evangelists' narratives: fulfilment of the Old Testament, rejection and acceptance, and a strong christological theme which establishes Jesus's identity from birth. But Luke's presentation of them is as unique to him as Matthew's presentation is to his Gospel.

Continuity between Judaism and Christianity

The main theme in Luke's account is the continuity between Judaism and Christianity. It begins with its roots in Judaism, with the story of John the Baptist. His parents are of Jewish priestly heritage; his father, Zechariah, is a priest, and his mother, Elizabeth, was descended from the first High Priest, Aaron. They are both righteous Jews and the story begins in the Temple, the very heart of Judaism. On the day that Zechariah has the once in a lifetime honour of burning the incense in the Temple, an angel appears to him and tells him that, after years of intercession, his prayers have been answered and he is going to be the father of a son. But not just any son; it will be the one who '...*will go before the Lord in the spirit and power of Elijah*' (1:17). Thus, even without using any direct Old Testament quotations, Luke shows that Christianity is to be born out of Judaism. But the story is remarkable in many other ways too. Elizabeth and Zechariah have evidently longed for a child, but both are now far beyond child-bearing age. In this way they are typical models of the righteous men and women of the Old Testament whom God blessed miraculously with a child in old age or despite barrenness: Abraham and Sarah; Rebecca and Isaac; Rachel and Jacob. Zechariah, Elizabeth and John himself stand on the cusp of the age between old and new covenants.

The link with Judaism is established consistently throughout the first two chapters of the Gospel. John's parents are of priestly lineage (1:5); the announcement of the birth takes place in the Temple (1:9); Jerusalem, the centre of religious life since the time of David, is at the heart of the Gospel, where it begins and ends (1:8; 24:53). The separation between Judaism and Christianity that was painfully forged during the mission of the early church cannot obscure the fact that Christianity is born out of Judaism, and it is those who have waited patiently for the fulfilment of God's promises — represented in the narrative not only by John's parents but by Simeon and Anna — who will see them come to pass in the person of Jesus. These two minor characters appear when Jesus's parents take him to the Temple for his dedication. They are both elderly prophets who have been waiting for the coming of the Messiah, and are immediately inspired by the Spirit to recognise the significance of Jesus. Even whilst Simeon knows that God's promises of old have been fulfilled, he is also sharply aware that Israel's fate is still to be determined through its response to Jesus. The Messiah is to be a *'light for revelation to the Gentiles'* (2:32), fulfilling the words of Isaiah 42:6 and 49:6, and will be *'set for the fall and rising of many in Israel'* (2:34).

Jesus and John the Baptist

It is with this opening narrative too that Luke establishes the link between Jesus and John the Baptist. Both men are born by miraculous means (1:13, 31); their parents are pious and law-abiding Jews (1:6, 2:21, 22–3); their future roles are prophesied by angels (1:14–17, 32–3), and as they both grow up they reveal their mature spirituality (1:80; 2:52). However, Luke is careful not to draw a parallel so close that Jesus's superiority is not clear. Judith Lieu (1997) writes: *'Both stories follow a similar pattern... Yet the parallelism is soon disrupted by Elizabeth's acknowledgement that Mary is "blessed among women" and "mother of my lord"'*. Hooker (1997) also observes: *'It would be difficult to miss the parallelism between these two stories; they move, as it were, in tandem... The parallels between John and Jesus inevitably run out, however, because Luke has a great deal more that he wants to tell us about the birth of Jesus'*. Hence, the differences, despite the similarities, are made clear: John is born of a barren woman — Jesus of a virgin; John will be prophet of the most high — Jesus, Son of the Most High; John's father receives the news in astonished disbelief — Jesus's mother in quiet, pious acceptance. Luke becomes even more cautious once their ministries begin, describing Jesus's baptism as if John were already in prison when it took place (3:18–20).

Soon after the announcement to Zechariah of John's impending birth, the angel Gabriel's visit to Mary opens with an announcement that she is favoured by God: *'You will be with child and give birth to a son, and you are to give him the name Jesus. He will be great and will be called the Son of the Most High'* (1:31–2). The child will be from the line of David and his kingdom will never end (2:33). He will be conceived by the power of the Holy Spirit and therefore he will be holy: *'The Holy Spirit will come upon you and the power of the Most High will overshadow you. So the holy one to be born will be called the Son of God'* (2:35). Unlike Zechariah, whose apparent lack of faith was to be punished by loss of speech until the angel's words were proved true, Mary's response is one of faithful acknowledgement: *'"I am the Lord's servant," Mary answered. "May it be to me as you have said"'* (2:38), despite the confusing fact that she is a virgin. Lieu (1997) writes: *'Mary has no prior qualifications for this destiny; whereas the gift of a child to Elizabeth was in part a response to Zechariah's prayer, for Mary it is the unlooked for act of God'.*

Luke continues to establish the links between the births of the two men when Mary visits Elizabeth, who is filled with the Holy Spirit when she sees her, and Elizabeth's unborn child leaps for joy in the womb. She refers to Mary as *'the mother of my Lord'* (2:43), an Old Testament reference to God (Psalm 110:1), indicating that she knows the nature of the child Mary is carrying. Mary's reply is a song known as the **Magnificat** (1:46–55), which seems to be modelled on Hannah's song in 1 Samuel 2:1–10, her own response to God's wonderful gift of a child after years of disappointment. The Magnificat is full of Old Testament language and imagery and praises God for his power and great mercy: *'For the Mighty One has done great things for me — holy is his name'* (2:49), and for the fulfilment of his promises from Abraham to David. In similar vein, when John the Baptist is born and circumcised on the eighth day of his life, in accordance with Jewish custom (Genesis 17:12), his father, Zechariah, receives his voice back and sings his own hymn of praise, the **Benedictus**, thanking God for the salvation that is to come: *'Praise be to the Lord, the God of Israel, because he has come and has redeemed his people'* (2:68).

The poor and the outcast

Luke's Gospel provides a graphic account of how those who reject Jesus will be cast aside in favour of those who receive him, and the birth narrative also introduces this vital theme. Simeon foresees this painful process as he encounters the child in the Temple, but he is not the first to do so. In Mary's song she foresees the reversal of fortunes that will be brought to pass in the coming of Jesus. Luke's Gospel is conspicuously full of such characters: Zacchaeus no longer an outcast; the widow of Nain saved from childless poverty; the lost son restored into a relationship with his father. This reversal of fortune is also anticipated by the visit of the shepherds, who clearly represent the 'lost' whom Jesus comes to save. Cast out from religious society, the shepherds are privileged with the angelic announcement of Jesus's birth. The angels speak of Jesus as a Saviour, an important role for the Lucan Jesus. Salvation for those who had suffered the strictures of Jewish society is freely offered in the Gospel, and their responses to Jesus are freely made, irrespective of their former lives. The birth narrative clearly sets the scene for encounters with Jesus that will be controversial, as the murmuring of the Pharisees in 15:2 shows: *'This man receives sinners and eats with them.'*

In response to the decree from the Emperor for a census, Joseph and Mary go to Bethlehem to register and Jesus is born there in humble surroundings, visited by the shepherds and subsequently presented in the Temple in Jerusalem to be circumcised. The focus on Bethlehem is no accident. Influenced by Micah 5:2, which prophesied that the Messiah would arise from Bethlehem, the city of David, both Luke and Matthew take steps to ensure that Jesus is born there. For Luke, it is the census which takes Joseph, a Davidic descendant, and his family there. It is difficult to trace the historical background of the census, which may conceivably have been conducted in 6 CE supervised by Quirinius when Judea first came under direct Roman rule. To pursue the matter would be to ignore Luke's primary motivation, however. It is the place where the Messiah is to be born, and that is all there is to it.

The intriguing details that Luke offers about the inn and the manger are told with great simplicity and directness. Lieu (1997) observes that *'although countless interpreters have used (them) to underline the poverty of Jesus's birth, for Luke, (their) unusualness allows (them) to become part of the theme of prophecy, sign, and fulfilment'*.

The Holy Spirit

The birth narrative is notable too for the significant role it gives to the Holy Spirit. Common belief was that the Spirit had left Israel after the last of the great prophets had died out, and would return with the messianic age. Luke makes clear that the new age has dawned. Zechariah, Elizabeth and Mary are all filled with the spirit of prophecy (1:42, 46, 68), John is anointed by the Spirit even in his mother's womb (1:15, 41), and the incident in the Temple when Jesus is a boy of 12 (2:41–51) suggests that already he is filled with the Spirit. The relationship between the birth narratives and the rest of the Gospel, and Acts too, is important here. The influence of the Holy Spirit in the life and mission of the early church is one of the dominating themes in Acts, and Luke lays the foundation from the beginning of his account.

However, in the birth narrative it is clear that the Spirit is available only to those of a particularly pious and receptive nature, whereas by the end of the Gospel, the reader is prepared for its mighty outpouring on all those who choose to receive it in faith. The disciples are instructed to wait for the Spirit before they can begin their ministry (24:49), and when it comes in Acts 2, Peter recognises it as the fulfilment of Joel 2:28–32. Mary, Elizabeth, Zechariah, Simeon and Anna are the *'sons and daughters…young men…old men…menservants and maidservants'* of Joel's prophecy.

Jesus's messianic self-consciousness

Luke's narrative concludes with a short piece concerning an incident in Jesus's later childhood, the only episode of its kind in the New Testament. At the age of 12, in accordance with tradition (Exodus 23:4–17), he was taken to Jerusalem for the Passover. Jesus was at the age when he would become a son of the commandment — in effect, an adult male, able to take on the rights and responsibilities of an adult. He is inadvertently left behind when his family leave Jerusalem and they find him three days later talking with the teachers in the Temple. His words to his parents show that, from this early age, Jesus knew of his unique relationship with God: *'Didn't you know I had to be in my Father's house?'* (2:49). Its preservation in the New Testament record is intriguing, since all other episodes concerning Jesus's youth had been relegated to the apocryphal books. Luke clearly sees it as prefiguring in an important way Jesus's *messianic self-consciousness*, and confirming what it meant for Jesus to be *'called Son of God'* (1:35).

The significance of the birth narratives must therefore not be underestimated and neither must they be viewed as curious additions to the Gospel which are fit only for nativity plays — as Lieu (1997) observes:

For Luke, this, like all the stories of the 'coming of Christ', is not a sentimental tale to delight his readers; it prepared them for what is to come, and for those who know the events yet to be told it is full of premonition, but also of perplexity, for the faithfulness and the harmony with the Law and Temple (shown in these narratives) will not be sustained.

Summary

- The birth narratives are likely to be late additions to the Gospel tradition, answering puzzling questions in the early church about Jesus's Messiahship. For the evangelists, they set the theme of the Gospel, and introduce issues that will be important for understanding the rest of the narrative.

- Luke establishes that Jesus's birth is rooted in **Judaism** and that there is an essential continuity between old and new orders. **John the Baptist** fulfils the role of Elijah, who returns to usher in the messianic age, and the characters in the narratives are pious, law-abiding Jews, waiting for the Messiah.

- Luke establishes a parallelism between John the Baptist and Jesus, whilst retaining Jesus's clear superiority. The births of both children are a revelation of God's faithfulness to his promises and a sign that the values of the world are about to be abruptly reversed.

- Luke ensures that key Old Testament prophecies are fulfilled, although without direct quotation. The spirit of prophecy hovers over both chapters. Jesus's Messiahship is established at conception, and his awareness and maturity in the Temple come as no surprise to the reader.

Exam watch

The worst thing that students can do when answering questions on the birth narrative is to regress into Sunday School nativity play mode — but they do it in droves! Many fail even to get the factual details of these narratives correct. You can reverse the trend by demonstrating an awareness of how these narratives serve as an introduction to the Gospel as a whole and using narrative details only to support your evaluative points.

Review questions

1 Outline the key features of the birth narrative in Luke's Gospel.
2 Analyse the significance of these chapters for understanding the teaching of the Gospel.
3 Examine and comment on the significance of three religious features contained in the birth and infancy narratives.
4 To what extent do the birth narratives reflect:
 (a) the humanity of Jesus?
 (b) the divinity of Jesus?

B The teaching of Jesus

1 The parables

Much of Jesus's teaching was done in parables — a common method of teaching amongst the leaders of Judaism. A parable is a short story based on real-life situations that Jesus used to highlight religious truths. (See p. 288 for more about the general nature of parables and their application.)

1.1 Parables of the kingdom

In all the Synoptic Gospels, the writers state that the teaching of Jesus was mainly concerned with the kingdom of God. In the Old Testament God's kingdom was shown through his mighty works, and by the time of Jesus the people of Israel believed that God would rid the land of their enemies and establish his kingdom on earth. In Luke's Gospel, the first time that Jesus mentions the kingdom of God is 4:43. It is a simple statement, which Luke uses to highlight how important the theme is: *'I must preach the good news of the kingdom of God…because that is why I was sent.'* The term 'kingdom of God' is used in Luke to refer to the way God acts and intervenes in human history to establish his rule — it refers to God's work rather than the kingdom he rules, and the good news in Luke is that Jesus is the Son of God who enables God's rule to be manifested.

In all the Synoptic Gospels, the teaching on the kingdom is complex. Some scholars, such as Schweitzer, claim that Jesus was teaching that there would be an imminent coming of the kingdom. Others, however, such as Dodd, support the view of **realised eschatology** — that is, that the kingdom of God was already present in the person and ministry of Jesus. In turn, Sanders argues that the kingdom is coming in the distant future, possibly after a Day of Judgment. Jesus's teaching on the kingdom in Luke seems to support all these views. Luke himself does suggest that the coming of the kingdom is close — for example, in 10:9: *'The kingdom of God is near.'* Yet the writer tends not to convey quite the immediacy of the other synoptic writers. Luke, instead, stresses the notion of joy at the closeness of salvation, when the End will bring the fulfilment of God's plan.

Thus, in the parable of the pounds (19:12–27) Jesus seems to suggest to the people that there will be a period of waiting before the kingdom comes. Similarly in 9:27, Luke mentions a future coming of the kingdom, linked to the judgment of God: *'I tell you the truth, some who are standing here will not taste death before they see the kingdom of God.'*

However, Luke's greatest emphasis is on the rather paradoxical notion that on the one hand the kingdom is already present, yet on the other that it is coming soon. How is this explained? It is explained by reference to the fact that through the teaching of Jesus, the power of the kingdom of God will be manifested: *'…the kingdom of God is within you'* (17:21). *'But if I drive out demons by the finger of God, then the kingdom of God has come to you'* (11:20).

This fits in with the Old Testament view that God's word brings life and change — and in the same way the word of Jesus will bring in the kingdom of God. As Marshall (1984) points out: *'Luke associates the coming of the kingdom not only with the preaching but also with the mighty works of Jesus which are signs of the activity of God. The coming of the kingdom is firmly tied historically with the ministry of Jesus. From now on, the kingdom is at work…'.*

Luke makes considerable use of sayings in which blessings and woes are associated with the kingdom — for example in 6:20, where Jesus makes it clear that the kingdom will be for the poor. In 13:30 and 14:14 Jesus suggests that those who are least on earth will be great in the kingdom. Moreover, in 7:28 Jesus highlights the point that even the least in the kingdom of God is greater than the greatest person outside it. This is not because of any personal qualities, but because he who is in the kingdom belongs to the time of fulfilment. Similarly, those who are more interested in worldly wealth and fail to follow Jesus cannot enter the kingdom (18:25; 29). The message is clear: the kingdom is relevant for humanity now — it is not something they should assume will come in the distant future (18:8), but is present in the ministry of Jesus.

Two parables of the kingdom merit particular examination: the sower and the banquet.

The parable of the sower

The parable (Luke 8:4–15) tells of a sower sowing seeds; some fall on the path and are eaten by birds, some fall on rock and cannot grow properly, some fall among thorns and are choked, and the rest fall on good soil and produce much. In those days, sowers sowed first, then ploughed afterwards, and the parable reveals what happened to the seed before it had a chance to be ploughed into the ground. The seed that falls on the path is eaten by birds; the seeds that fall on rock cannot find sufficient moisture in the soil; whilst the seeds that fall among thorns are choked, because the thorns grow quicker than the wheat. The seeds falling on the good soil produce a great harvest.

When the disciples ask Jesus to explain the parable he tells them that he is entrusting them with 'the secrets of the kingdom of God' (8:9). Morris (1988) notes: 'Parables both reveal and conceal truth: they reveal it to the genuine seeker who will take the trouble to dig beneath the surface and discover the meaning, but they conceal it from him who is content simply to listen to the story'.

Nevertheless, this parable deals with the reasons why not everyone who hears the message of the kingdom of God acts upon it. It can only grow if the hearer has faith and a responsive heart. The seeds represent the word of God; sometimes people are never bothered to hear it, or people lack the depth in themselves to take it seriously. Others lose faith at testing times. Yet those who do hear it and accept it will benefit greatly: 'But the seed on good soil stands for those with a noble and good heart, who hear the word, retain it, and by persevering produce a crop' (8:15).

The parable of the banquet

In this parable (Luke 14:15–24) a man is holding a great banquet, the invitations are sent but the guests make excuses and do not come. The man then orders his servants to invite new guests, the crippled, the blind and the lame. The search for guests is extensive — not only is the city searched, but also the country lanes — God seeks everywhere for his people who come and celebrate joyfully.

This story highlights the fact that people will be saved and enter the kingdom by responding to God's invitation: 'Blessed is the man who will eat at the feast in the kingdom of God' (14:15). This is an image of the messianic banquet, where the righteous will eat with the Messiah. The parable addresses an issue at the heart of the Gospel: the places at the banquet will not be given first to those who are just important by human standards — it is the humble who will receive the seats of honour. Moreover, those who share the feast will not necessarily be the ones who were first invited (the Jews); if they refuse, then new guests (the Gentiles and others who were outcast from conventional Judaism) will take their place. The parable ends on a sombre note: those who declined the invitation have lost their opportunity and will not get another. Morris notes: 'The *story of the banquet emphasizes the truth that people are saved by responding to God's invitation, not by their own effort, whereas if they are lost it is by their own fault'.*

1.2 Parables of the lost

Of all the Synoptic Gospels, Luke contains the most parables, and in chapter 15 a distinctive group, known as the parables of the lost, emphasise Luke's theme of seeking God and finding salvation. Moreover, they add a fresh dimension: God does not simply wait for people to find him; he actively helps them to find him and then God's joy is highlighted as a lost sinner is found. The chapter begins with Jesus addressing a crowd of *'tax collectors and sinners'* (15:1) — outcasts from respectable Jewish society, either because they worked for the Romans or because they followed immoral occupations, such as prostitution, disapproved of by the Jewish religious authorities. Alongside them in the crowd are the righteous Pharisees and Teachers of the Law who mutter that Jesus *'welcomes sinners'* (15:2).

The first two parables are brief ones, depicting people who actively seek what has been lost, emphasising the point that God does not stand passively by, but seeks out the lost. There is an important point here. In traditional Jewish teaching at that time, it was accepted that God would welcome back a lost sinner. However, what was revolutionary about Jesus's teaching was the notion that God would actually take the initiative and seek the lost sinner himself.

In the parable of the lost sheep (15:3–7), Jesus depicts God as a shepherd with 99 sheep which are safe in pasture and one that is lost. He seeks until he finds it, and rejoices when he has done so. Jesus highlights the joy of God over the return of one sinner who has repented, a joy that is even greater than his joy at the 99 who had remained safe: *'...there will be more rejoicing in heaven over one sinner who repents than over ninety-nine righteous persons who do not need to repent'* (15:7).

In the parable of the lost coin (15:8–10), a woman with ten silver coins loses one. This is a serious loss for her — she may be poor or the coin may come from a traditional wedding bracelet — and she sweeps the whole house until she finds it, just as God will seek out the repentant sinner, and then rejoices at its recovery.

The parable of the lost son (15:11–32) emphasises the nature of God's forgiving love and highlights the contrast between the repentant sinner and those who feel they are righteous. In the parable, the younger of two brothers asks his father for his share of the estate. This was not a common Jewish practice — under the Law the son would not usually get his share until his father had died. In effect, the son was treating his father as if he were dead. His father agrees and the son goes off to another country and spends all the money on riotous living. Faced with a famine, he is forced to feed pigs in order to live — a distasteful job for a Jew, since the pig was regarded as an unclean creature (Leviticus 11:7). He decides to return home and ask his father to give him a job as a servant. Realising that he has sinned against both God and his father (18:15), he believes that he has forfeited his right to be treated as a son.

His father sees him and, although the son is unworthy, the father overwhelms him with his welcome — he throws his arms around him and kisses him, gets him the finest robe, puts a ring on his finger (to convey authority) and shoes on his feet (slaves went barefoot; free men wore shoes), and orders a feast of celebration. The son acknowledges his sin — *'Father, I have sinned against heaven and against you. I am no longer worthy to be called your son'* (15:21) — but the eldest brother is outraged. He refuses to join the celebrations and complains to his father that he has worked hard, yet has never been given a feast. The father declares his right to be joyful at the return of his younger son, saying: *'...this brother of yours was dead and is alive again; he was lost and is found'* (15:30).

In this parable, the father is God; the eldest son represents the outwardly righteous Jewish leaders and the youngest son the repentant sinner. God welcomes the sinner back and does not accept the complaint of the righteous who refuse to share his joy. Showing love to repentant sinners is not a threat to those who are already within the kingdom of God.

2   Theological and moral teaching

The Sermon on the Plain

The Sermon on the Plain (6:17–49) is a lengthy teaching by Jesus that covers a range of important topics. Jesus is speaking to a very large crowd, including his own disciples and people who have travelled from all over the country to hear him. There are also many in the crowd who have come to be healed or freed from evil spirits. He delivers the sermon on a 'level place', indicating perhaps a mountainside, as this was not the term usually given to a plain.

The sermon breaks down into the following four sections:

1 The blessings and woes (6:20–6)
2 Love (6:27–36)
3 Judging others (6:37–42)
4 Firm foundations (6:46–9)

Throughout the sermon Jesus highlights what it means to be a disciple and true follower.

The blessings and woes

The blessings are a series of statements that turn the values of the world upside down, by praising the qualities the world despises and rejecting the qualities the world admires. Thus, Jesus says: *'Blessed are you who are poor, for yours is the kingdom of God'* (6:20). He is referring to his disciples here. He is not saying that poverty is a blessing, but that those who are blessed are those who know they are spiritually poor in the sense that they have no resources and must rely on God. The rich of the world are self-reliant — they feel that they do not need God. The poor in spirit know that they do.

Jesus goes on to offer blessings to those who are *'hungry'* (6:21) and who know that they need God in order to be satisfied, and those who *'weep'* (6:21), that is, those who see the evil in the world and weep at the suffering caused by humanity's rejection of God. He also offers blessings for those who are persecuted *'because of the Son of Man'* (6:22). Those who suffer in this way should *'rejoice'* and *'leap for joy'* (6:23), because they are suffering for the sake of their belief in Christ and *'great is your reward in heaven'* (6:23).

In contrast, the woes (6:24–6) are a series of expressions, almost of regret, aimed at those who enjoy the qualities that the world approves of. Thus he says *'woe to the rich'* (6:24), because those who are wealthy tend to think that they have everything they need — they rely on money rather than God. This kind of prosperity leads to inner emptiness. Jesus also offers *'woe to you who are well fed'* and who *'laugh now'* (6:25) for much the same reason. Like the rich, these people feel that they lack nothing and do not need God; they are unaware of their own spiritual need and poverty. Finally, Jesus says: *'Woe to you when all men speak well of you'* (6:26). He is suggesting here that the message of God to the world is an uncomfortable one — if people speak well of you, then perhaps you are not giving out God's true message. The word of a true believer is often unpopular.

Love

The central theme of the sermon is the need for love. Jesus makes clear that his followers must love all people, not just those who are easy to love, but the unlovable too. He is speaking of **agape** — love that is not earned, but that is freely given because the believer chooses to be a loving person to all.

Jesus begins with a dramatic statement: *'Love your enemies, do good to those who hate you'* (6:27). Here, Jesus is teaching that a believer cannot pick and choose whom to love — he or she must love all people. Moreover, it is not enough just to be nice; Jesus requires that believers do good. He illustrates this in the famous saying: *'If someone strikes you on one cheek, turn to him the other also'* (6:29). He is talking about an attitude of mind: instead of seeking revenge, the believer should accept injury and, instead of reacting in anger, offer love. Thus: *'Give to everyone who asks you, and if anyone takes what belongs to you, do not demand it back. Do to others as you would have them do to you'* (6:30–1).

Jesus requires his followers to give all they have, out of love for others, to act towards others as they hope others would act towards them. In other words, following Christ is not just about thinking but about doing loving actions. Christians are therefore required to have higher standards than everyone else — not just to love their friends, but to love everyone, and their reward will be great in heaven (6:35).

Judging others

Jesus's teaching is direct and simple: *'Do not judge, and you will not be judged'* (6:37). He is not talking about judgment in courts of law, but instead he is referring to the everyday judgments we make of others — through gossip, backstabbing and false witness. If we judge others in this way, we too will be judged and, moreover, those who judge others bring the judgment of God upon themselves: *'Forgive, and you will be forgiven'* (6:37).

Jesus emphasises to his followers that if they lack love, they cannot guide others, for they cannot see where they are going. Lack of love and spiritual blindness will not bring people to God. Disciples must therefore ensure that they can see clearly before looking at others: *'…first take the plank out of your eye, and then you will see clearly to remove the speck from your brother's eye'* (6:42).

Firm foundations

Jesus uses the illustration of a tree and its fruit to show that the good person produces good things through having a good heart (6:45) — in other words, the good we do or speak comes not from our heads, but from our hearts. The sermon concludes by highlighting the importance of believers acting upon the teaching Jesus has given and giving their lives a firm foundation, so that, when judgment comes, they have built their lives on God.

2.2 Wealth and poverty

In the teaching of Jesus the good news of the kingdom of God was for the poor and there were stern warnings to the rich about the danger of being kept outside the kingdom by their possessions.

(Marshall, 1984)

According to Luke, Jesus came to preach the Gospel to the poor and the preaching of the word of God to the poor seems to be of paramount importance: '*The Spirit of the Lord is on me, because he has anointed me to preach good news to the poor*' (4:18).

Jesus himself is described as having been born into humble circumstances and his first visitors, the shepherds, were from the poorest classes. Luke emphasises throughout the Gospel the dangers of wealth. In the Magnificat, Mary sings of the fact that '*He has filled the hungry with good things, but he has sent the rich away empty*' (1:53). In the Sermon on the Plain, Jesus warns '*Woe to you who are rich*' (6:24) because the rich feel that they have everything, and therefore forget their spiritual need for God. This theme is continued in the parable of the rich fool (12:16), in which Jesus warns against the greed and jealousy that wealth can bring. Jesus is talking to a man who is angry about the inheritance his brother has been given. Jesus tells him that people's lives are not measured by the amount of possessions they have (6:15) and in the ensuing parable shows that what is important is not to store up money, but to be rich in spiritual matters before God: being rich does not mean that you can control your own destiny.

The parable of the shrewd manager

This parable (16:1–9) features a steward who has wasted his master's possessions and then dishonestly tries to cover up his negligence. However, Jesus is not praising dishonesty, but is encouraging believers to be as wise with their money as non-believers are. Morris (1988) observes: '*The sons of light are the servants of God. Well-intentioned as they are, they often lack the wisdom to use what they have as wisely as the worldly use of their possessions for their very different ends*'.

Jesus warns the Pharisees, who '*loved money*' (16:14), that the problem with wealth is that money can itself become a god, and that '*No servant can serve two masters. Either he will hate the one and love the other, or he will be devoted to one and despise the other. You cannot serve both God and Money*' (16:13).

The rich man and Lazarus

In this parable (16:19–31), the rich man is shown as living only for himself — he has all he wants. In contrast, the poor man, Lazarus, has nothing and is forced to eat the scraps from the rich man's table. Lazarus appears to be a religious man, and when he dies he goes to Abraham's side, whilst the rich man goes to hell. Yet in death, the rich man does not change his ways — he still holds on to the world's values and believes that poor Lazarus is still only fit to be his servant: '*Father Abraham, have pity on me and send Lazarus to dip the tip of his finger in water and cool my tongue'* (16:24). Abraham points out to the rich man that he could have helped the poor when he was alive, but chose not to do so. Now, worldly values no longer apply and there can be no crossing of the *'great chasm'* (16:26) that is between them. Even then, the rich man remains self-centred, asking Abraham not to help the poor, but to help the man's brothers. Abraham's reply is that the brothers have all the help they need in the scriptures. In other words, the rich man is in the state he is, not because he had money, but because the attitude to life that money had given him prevented him from accepting the truth of the scriptures. This is the real warning to the wealthy.

God's grace

This theme is highlighted clearly in Jesus's conversation with the rich young ruler (18:18–27), where the rich man is convinced of his own goodness through obedience to the Law, yet still wants to possess eternal life. The rich man is too satisfied with himself and has not truly reflected on what God's goodness means and how far short of God's standards he has fallen. So Jesus issues him with a challenge of faith — to give away all his wealth. If the man had truly understood the laws of God, he would have known that he could not have kept and worshipped his money, as he did, for he had not given God first place in his life. The man became *'very sad'* (18:23) and was unable to rise to the challenge, prompting Jesus's famous saying: *'Indeed, it is easier for a camel to go through the eye of a needle than for a rich man to enter the kingdom of God'* (18:25).

Jesus makes it clear that there are no advantages in being rich when it comes to salvation — salvation is God's gift, given through divine grace: *'"I tell you the truth," Jesus said to them, "no one who has left home or wife or brothers or parents or children for the sake of the kingdom of God will fail to receive many times as much in this age and, in the age to come, eternal life"'* (18:29–30).

The grace of God is clearly shown in the incident with Zacchaeus, another rich man, but this time one who has understood that his money will not bring him fulfilment. He realises his foolishness and returns his property to the poor and receives salvation (19:9). This message is reinforced in the incident of the widow's offering (21:1–4), where Jesus praises the poor widow for giving all she has, rather than the rich who, although they gave more money, did not make so great a sacrifice. Marshall (1984) points out, however, that Luke is not just referring to financial wealth: *'The teaching about wealth and poverty must be set in its context. We have already seen that the "poor" to whom the gospel is preached are those who are needy and dependent on God. By the same token, the "rich" are those who are self-satisfied and feel no need of God'.*

2.3 Prayer and praise

Prayer

Luke highlights the importance to believers of having the right attitude towards God and stresses the vital significance of prayer in this relationship. He does this by recording the prayers of Jesus (including seven prayers that are not mentioned anywhere else) and by explicating Jesus's teaching on prayer through the parables. Jesus is first recorded as praying at his baptism (3:21) and Luke later highlights the importance of prayer in Jesus's own life — he prays in *'lonely places'* (5:16), spends the whole night praying to God (6:12) and prays in private (9:18). Jesus also praises God for what has been done and he is said to be *'full of joy'*; *'I praise you, Father, Lord of heaven and earth, because you have hidden these things from the wise and learned, and revealed them to little children'* (10:21).

Luke shows Jesus teaching the disciples to pray and links prayer closely with the notion of praise — that through salvation and forgiveness humanity is reconciled to God, producing joy and praise. In 11:1–13, the teaching on prayer reaches its climax with the giving of the Lord's Prayer. Jesus gives it to his followers after one of them asks for his guidance on how to pray. As a prayer, it has a pattern which is the model for all prayer:

+ It begins with *'Father'* (11:2), encouraging believers to think of God in a personal and loving way.
+ *'Hallowed be your name'* (11:2) means 'holy' and reminds the people that they should have proper reverence for God.
+ *'Your kingdom come'* (11:2) looks forward to the coming of the kingdom of God and the fulfilment of God's will.
+ The prayer then contains a petition that God will provide for everyday needs. *'Give us each day our daily bread'* (11:3) is a request for continual help, for the believer lives in continual dependence on God's love and mercy.
+ *'Forgive us our sins'* (11:4) is followed by the assertion that the believers will, in turn, forgive those who have sinned against them. Just as God will forgive, so believers should also forgive.
+ *'And lead us not into temptation'* (11:3) allows believers to recognise that they are weak and that they need to ask for God's help to be kept free from the temptation to sin.

Having laid out the format, Jesus goes on to highlight the need for meaningful and persistent prayer. In the parable of the friend at midnight (11:5–8), a man continually asks his friend for bread. The friend refuses, but the man keeps on asking until eventually the friend, impressed by the man's sincerity and persistence, grants his request. The meaning of the parable is made clear by Morris (1988):

We must not play at prayer, but must show persistence if we do not receive the answer immediately. It is not that God is unwilling and must be pressed into answering. The whole context makes it clear that he is eager to give. But if we do not want what we are asking for enough to be persistent, we do not want it very much.

Jesus then goes on to tell his followers: *'Ask and it will be given to you; seek and you will find; knock and the door will be opened to you'* (11:9). By this he is saying that, whilst God is very willing to give, it is important that people do their part by asking. He is not saying that all prayer will be granted immediately, or in the way the believer hopes. He is saying that God hears all true prayers and they are always answered in the way God sees best.

This is shown in the parable of the persistent widow (18:1–8) (sometimes called the parable of the unjust judge), which teaches that believers should not be discouraged if they see no answer to their prayers — they should pray on and not lose heart. Similarly, in the parable of the Pharisee and the tax collector (18:9–14) Jesus shows the importance of praying with the right spirit. Here, although the Pharisee appears to lead a righteous life, the spirit of his prayer is wrong. He has no sense of his own sin or dependence on God — his prayer is full of praise for himself, not God. The tax collector, in contrast, has the right spirit. He knows he is unworthy and is full of sorrow. He knows he is utterly dependent on God and asks for God's forgiveness: *'God have mercy on me, a sinner'* (18:13). God accepts his prayer and his sins are forgiven — he has humbled himself and as a result will find God's mercy.

Jesus uses prayer in time of crisis. In 22:31 he says that he has prayed for Peter, that he will have a strong faith and be able to strengthen his comrades. In 22:41, Jesus prays alone on the Mount of Olives after first telling his disciples to pray for themselves that they *'will not fall into temptation'* (22:40). At that time, Jewish custom was to pray standing up, with the eyes looking to heaven. However, at this time of great crisis, Jesus kneels down — his prayer is a reflection of his fear at the death that lies before him. His prayer is unique, for he asks God, if he is willing, to *'take this cup from me'* (22:42). The cup is an Old Testament symbol of suffering and the wrath of God (Psalm 11:6; Ezekiel 23:33). Yet Jesus's focus remains on the Father; he is obedient to his will and he goes on to pray that God's divine plan will be fulfilled: *'…yet not my will, but yours be done'* (22:42). Finally, at the point of death, just as he had taught his followers to do in the Sermon on the Plain, Jesus prays for his enemies: *'Father, forgive them, for they do not know what they are doing'* (23:34).

Praise

Praising God is seen in Luke to come as an automatic response from people experiencing the good news of salvation and forgiveness — for the effect of this is to feel joy towards God and the knowledge that, through God's grace, the person has been saved: *'…rejoice that your names are written in heaven'* (10:20); *'I tell you, there is rejoicing in the presence of the angels of God over one sinner who repents'* (15:10). Elsewhere, Luke uses praise as an expression of joy in the glory of God — for example, in the birth narratives, where the angels fill the skies, praising God (2:13–14). There is also praise as a result of seeing the works of God — for example, at the healing of the paralysed man (5:26) and the raising of the widow's son (7:16). Moreover, the people praise God when Jesus makes his triumphal entry into Jerusalem (19:37) and Luke even shows the centurion praising God as he witnesses the death of Jesus on the cross (23:47).

Perhaps the most well-known examples of praise are the great hymns in the birth narrative. The song of Mary, known as the Magnificat (1:46–55), is a song of praise in Old Testament language, modelled on Hannah's song in 1 Samuel 2:1ff. It is an appreciation of the mercy of God, his holiness, his power and his mercy in forgiveness. It goes on to look forward to what God will do and his fulfilment of the promises made to his people: *'My soul glorifies the Lord and my spirit rejoices in God my saviour'* (1:46–7).

Zechariah's song, or the Benedictus (1:67–79), is a song of thanksgiving for the coming of the Messiah and the deliverance from sin and the hope of salvation. Like the Magnificat, it uses Old Testament imagery and emphasises the fulfilment of God's divine plan for his people and the forgiveness of sins: *'Praise be to the Lord, the God of Israel, because he has come and has redeemed his people'* (1:68).

Finally, Simeon's song, the Nunc Dimittis (2:29–32), is a hymn of praise for the salvation of Israel. Simeon expresses his desire to die contentedly for he has seen, in the infant Jesus, God's salvation for all people — God's plan will be fully realised: *'For my eyes have seen your salvation, which you have prepared in the sight of all people'* (2:30–1).

The word 'rejoice' occurs more times in Luke than in any other book in the New Testament, and the Gospel itself ends on a note of praise, where, following the return of the risen Jesus to heaven, the Apostles are filled with great joy: *'And they stayed continually at the Temple, praising God'* (24:53). As Morris (1988) notes: *'Luke has written with a profoundly theological purpose. He sees God at work bringing salvation and he enjoys bringing out a variety of aspects of this saving work'.*

2.4 Discipleship

A disciple is a pupil — someone who learns from a teacher. Normally, we use the word to refer to the Twelve Disciples (or Apostles) named by Luke in 6:14–16 as Simon (Peter), Andrew, James, John, Philip, Bartholomew, Levi (Matthew), Thomas, James, son of Alphaeus, Simon the Zealot, Judas, son of James, and Judas Iscariot. However, strictly speaking a 'disciple' is anyone who follows Jesus, and in Luke 6:17, there is a reference to a 'great crowd of disciples'. Marshall (1984) offers this definition: *'Disciples are those who believe in Christ and stand in a personal relationship to him as their Lord'.*

For Luke, discipleship is a life of submission and service, but also one of joy and inner peace that comes from knowing God's forgiveness and acceptance. But first, becoming a disciple involves making a real commitment to follow Jesus. This means repentance and being prepared to give up everything to follow God's call. In 5:1–11, the first disciples, Simon, James and John, are persuaded to become disciples after witnessing a miraculous catch of fish. The Twelve were specifically called by Jesus and gave up all they had to follow him: *'"Follow me" …Levi got up, left everything and followed him'* (5:27–8). With repentance comes humility; disciples must be aware of their own sinfulness and dependence on the grace of God. Pride acts as a barrier between God and his people, and until it is removed, God cannot work in their lives. Thus, in the illustration of the wedding feast (14:8–12), it is those who take the humblest spot who will be raised to the highest. It is through the humility that God can 'raise' his followers up to the place he has prepared for them: *'I have not come to call the righteous, but sinners to repentance'* (5:32).

This is clearly shown in the anointing of Jesus by the sinful woman at the house of Simon the Pharisee (7:36–50). The woman knows of her dependence on God; she has repented and seeks to display unconditional love for Jesus as a sign of her grateful response for God's forgiveness. She anoints Jesus with perfume and dries his feet with her hair and Jesus tells the incredulous Simon: *'Therefore, I tell you, her many sins have been forgiven — for she loved much'* (7:47). Moreover, disciples must not be hindered by the cares of the world. In the home of Martha and Mary (10:38–42), Martha is distracted by her worldly cares, but Mary, like the sinful woman earlier, lays her cares aside in order to express her love for Jesus and her need to be in his company.

Those who became disciples faced a demanding lifestyle that carried with it the real possibility of persecution and death. It was a lifelong commitment: *'No-one who puts his hand to the plough and looks back is fit for service in the kingdom of God'* (9:62).

Disciples had to give up their material comforts, because being tied to earthly possessions would restrict effective discipleship: '*In the same way, any of you who does not give up everything he has, cannot be my disciple*' (14:33). But the disciples would have God's help. They faced the hatred of the world, but the Holy Spirit would aid them in times of trouble: '*When you are brought before synagogues, rulers and authorities, do not worry about how you will defend yourselves or what you will say, for the Holy Spirit will teach you at that time what you should say*' (12:11–12). The disciples received authority from Jesus to act in his name and to preach, heal and cast out demons: '*The seventy-two returned with joy and said, "Lord, even the demons submit to us in your name"*' (10:17). Moreover, they were especially blessed by God and were privileged to know things that others could not know: '*Blessed are the eyes that see what you see. For I tell you that many prophets and kings wanted to see what you see, but did not see it*' (10:24).

The disciples had a unique relationship with God, which would endure for ever, and in his name they would achieve great things. Their prayers would be answered: '*Do not be afraid, little flock, for your Father has been pleased to give you the kingdom*' (12:32). Above all, the disciples brought in the new age, as Taylor (1992) points out: '*There is an immediate hundredfold reward for those who walk out on their commitments and dependants and join Jesus on the road; there will be even greater rewards "in the age to come"*'.

2.5 Salvation

The concept of salvation is more prominent in Luke than in the other Synoptic Gospels. The word 'salvation' comes from the Greek verb **sozo**, which means to 'make safe or well'. Luke suggests that humanity needs to be saved from the power of sin, which has separated humanity from God. This is achieved through the saving power of Jesus on the cross. Luke's concept of salvation is based on the Old Testament notion of the action of God, which saves his people. This was understood by the Old Testament writers as the concept of **salvation history** — God acting in the lives of his people and the nations of the world to bring about his purposes and lead his covenanted people into a special relationship with him. Luke sees the events of the Gospel and Acts in this light — they are the next stage in the working out of God's salvific plans and promises. This is clear from the very start of the Gospel. In the Magnificat, Mary refers to '*God my saviour*' (1:47) and highlights the saving power of God through his actions and the fulfilment of his promises. Moreover, even the name Jesus means 'God saves'.

In the Benedictus, Simeon recognises God's saving power and that he has '*…raised up a horn of salvation for us*' (1:69). This salvation will come from the house of David — highlighting the hope of a Davidic Messiah who would save his people from their enemies. Later, the angel tells the shepherds of the birth of Jesus with the words: '*Today in the town of David a Saviour has been born to you; he is Christ the Lord*' (2:11). Luke highlights the fact that salvation is available to all people, not just the Jews. In the Nunc Dimittis, Simeon declares:

For my eyes have seen your salvation,
which you have prepared in the sight of all people,
a light of revelation to the Gentiles,
and for glory to your people Israel.

(2:30–2)

Luke also suggests that God's salvation made manifest through Jesus is for the Samaritans (9:51) and lepers (17:16) — usually sidelined by the righteous Jew — and his 'great commission' to his disciples is to preach to all nations (24:47). However, not all will be saved, for, although the good news is offered to everyone, people must actually choose for themselves whether or not to accept it, as the parable of the sower suggests: *'But the seed on good soil stands for those with a noble and good heart, who hear the word, retain it, and by persevering produce a crop'* (8:15).

Salvation requires repentance — a change of heart and attitude. John the Baptist (3:3) and Jesus both preach that people must repent in preparation for salvation and the coming of the kingdom: *'But unless you repent you too will all perish'* (13:3). For Luke, the world is corrupt and under the control of the forces of evil (11:18). He suggests that salvation will come because Jesus has ultimate authority and power over evil: *'I tell you, whoever acknowledges me before men, the Son of Man will also acknowledge him before the angels of God'* (12:8).

Salvation is the offer of eternal life and freedom from sin — it is the opposite of death. Luke speaks of Jesus coming to *'seek and to save what was lost'* (19:10) and shows Jesus as the culmination of God's history of salvation for his people. As Marshall (1984) suggests *'...the idea of salvation supplies the key to the theology of Luke'.*

2.6 Eschatology

Eschatology is the study of the things of the end and, in particular, the concept of Christ's **Second Coming**, or his **parousia**. He will return bringing with him judgment and the end of things as they presently are. In Luke, the emphasis is on the supremacy of God over the world and of God as the ultimate source of salvation. Throughout the Gospel, Luke paints an eschatological picture — God controls events in accordance with his divine plan. In turn, the life of Christ is seen in the same eschatological way: Jesus is depicted as the fulfilment of the Old Testament scriptures and the centrepiece of God's plan of salvation.

In Luke 4:7–21, Jesus tells the people that the Old Testament scriptures are fulfilled. The prophet Isaiah has already foretold his work. Jesus will fulfil that prophecy when he preaches *'good news to the poor'* (4:18), gives *'recovery of sight for the blind'* (4:18), and releases *'the oppressed'* (4:18). Christ is the summit of God's plan — and the eschatological message is shown in 18:31: *'...everything that is written by the prophets about the Son of Man will be fulfilled.'*

In terms of the Second Coming of Christ, Luke seems to present a somewhat contrary picture, with two differing strands of thought. On the one hand, there are references to the possibility that Jesus will return quickly and unexpectedly and that believers must be prepared at all times: *'You must also be ready, because the Son of Man will come at an hour when you do not expect him'* (12:40) and *'The Kingdom of God is near you'* (10:9). On the other hand, there are references suggesting that the coming of Christ will be in great glory at a future date: *'The Son of Man in his day will be like the lightning, which flashes and lights up the sky'* (17:24); *'There will be signs in the sun, moon and stars...on the earth, nations will be in anguish'* (21:25); *'At that time they will see the Son of Man coming in a cloud with power and great glory'* (21:27).

Ernst Käsemann (1964) suggested that Luke foresaw a future coming because *'You*

do not write the history of the Church if you are expecting the end of the world to come any day'. Luke does emphasise the notion that the coming of the last days will be a time of joy and salvation. Morris (1988) writes: '*...he looks for the coming of the End when the salvation of which he writes will reach its consummation'*. For Luke, the eschatological message was summed up at the very end of the Gospel: '*Then he opened their minds so that they could understand the scriptures. He told them, "This is what is written; the Christ will suffer and rise from the dead on the third day, and repentance and forgiveness of sins will be preached in his name to all nations"'* (24:45–6).

Summary

- The **Sermon on the Plain** represents a continuous block of teaching on the nature of discipleship. It underlines the theme of reversal of values, the essential Christian witness of love for enemies and refraining from judgment, and the need to build on firm foundations.
- **Wealth and poverty** are key themes for Luke, who, like the Old Testament writers, continually underlines the special concern that God has for the poor. The relationship disciples have with money will indicate whether their hearts are truly focused on the things of God or of the world.
- **Prayer and praise** are key elements in the life of a disciple. Jesus sets the example of the prayerful life as he submits every major episode in his life to God in prayer. The Lord's Prayer summarises the concerns of the true disciple. Prayer must be in the right spirit and offered in quiet humility and expectation of God's blessing. The Gospel resounds with songs of praise from the birth narrative onwards and anticipates the life of praise characteristic of the early church.
- **Discipleship** is a life of submission and service, joy and inner peace, through knowledge of God's forgiveness and acceptance. True disciples acknowledge and respond to their need for repentance, and commit themselves to a life of exclusive devotion to Jesus.
- **Salvation** is God's gift, made available to all disciples in the fulfilment of his promises to usher in the age of eschatological blessings. Jesus is the means by which salvation is made possible, and it requires a genuine change of heart in the believer.
- **Eschatology** is both realised and to come — in Jesus the blessings of salvation and the power of the kingdom of God are made known, but a future culmination still awaits, for which the disciple must carefully prepare.

Exam watch

The message is always the same for these Synoptic Gospel topics. Anybody, within reason, can provide the examiners with a basic summary of the Gospel content. It is far more difficult to show an evaluative understanding of the purpose, significance and background of these teachings, and how they relate to the whole Gospel. Use the review questions below to practise these skills.

Review questions

1 (a) With reference to two parables, examine the teaching of Jesus on forgiveness.

   (b) To what extent did the eschatological message of Jesus differ from that of traditional Judaism?

2 (a) Examine the teaching of Jesus on (i) wealth and (ii) outcasts.

(b) Consider the significance of this teaching for the members of the early church.

3 Examine and assess the extent to which Jesus's teaching in the Sermon on the Plain differed from that of traditional Judaism.

4 (a) Describe and comment upon Jesus's teaching concerning discipleship.

(b) Assess the significance of the part played by the 12 disciples in the ministry of Jesus.

5 (a) Consider and analyse the views of scholars concerning the nature of the kingdom of God in Luke's Gospel.

(b) In the light of these views, examine the teaching of Jesus in two contrasting parables concerning the kingdom of God.

C Themes in the ministry of Jesus

1 Miracles

The miracles of Jesus play a vital part in his mission, and they emphasise the fact that he had the authority and power of God over both the natural and the spiritual world. The miracles are shown as acts of power that not only reveal Jesus's authority, but also highlight his teachings about God. The miracle stories come under three broad headings — healings, exorcisms and nature miracles — and they serve one key function: to reveal and confirm the Messiahship of Jesus. Luke shares a number of miracle stories with Matthew and Mark: the healing of Simon's mother-in-law (4:38–39), the healing of the leper (5:12–16), the paralysed man (5:17–26), the Gerasene demoniac (8:22–33), and the healing of the woman with a haemorrhage forming a pair with the raising of Jairus's daughter (8:4–56), which is paralleled by that of the centurion and the widow of Nain, to name but a few. (Discussion of these can be found on pp. 294–297.) Although Luke occasionally redacts his sources to emphasise themes of interest to him, their broad outlines and their messages remain essentially unchanged.

Luke begins his Gospel with birth narratives which include angelic appearances and miraculous interventions and which directly link Jesus's conception by the Holy Spirit with his identity as Son of God. There is no overlap between Luke's and Matthew's accounts of the angelophanies in the birth narratives. In the body of the Gospel, Luke uses almost all of Mark's miracles in the same order, apart from the cursing of the fig tree, which he puts earlier, and the five miracle stories within Mark 6:45–8:26, which Luke omits entirely. He adds seven miracles which are unique to him: the miraculous catch of fish (5:1–11); the raising of the widow of Nain's son (7:11–17); the healing of the infirm woman (13:10–17); the healing of the man with dropsy (14:1–6); and the healing of the ten lepers (17:11–19). The raising of the widow's son (a parallel with Elijah, which we might expect after Jesus's words in the synagogue at Nazareth (4:25–26)) and the healing of the ten lepers seem especially to focus on matters close to Luke's heart — women and Samaritans.

The raising of the widow's son and the healing of the centurion's servant mirror each other. Although Luke shares the latter miracle with Matthew and Mark, he gives it a

distinctive twist. The Jews actually encourage Jesus to help the centurion, who, it appears, was sympathetic towards Judaism and is one of the few representatives of the hated occupying power who was respected by the Jewish community. He anticipates Cornelius of Acts 10, whose conversion marked the beginning of the Gentile mission, and he may also provide an echo of Naaman the Syrian, who was healed from leprosy by Elisha. Jesus has also alluded to this event in the Nazareth sermon (4:27). Jesus praises the centurion for his faith, which enables him to accept Jesus's authority over sickness, drawing an apt analogy with his own military authority. Jesus sums up the event with the prophetic words: *'Not even in Israel have I found such faith'* (7:9).

Jesus demonstrates this same authority in the raising of the widow's son. Unlike Elijah, he employs no physical contact, only the authoritative command *'Be raised'*, but like Elijah he *'restored'* him to his mother (1 Kings 17:23; Luke 7:15). The response of the witnesses is that *'a great prophet has arisen among us'* (7:16). Although miracles were not usually a characteristic of prophecy, the care that Jesus shows to the woman reflects the care God shows to his people, and more than hints at the dawning of a new age in which God once again directly intervenes. Interestingly, some of Luke's readers may be familiar with similar stories in the accounts of other first-century miracle workers, such as Hanina ben Dosa, and by referring to Jesus as *'the Lord'* (7:13) he reminds them that Jesus is not to be mistaken for one of these itinerant charismatics.

The healing of the ten lepers (17:11–19) recalls the parable of the good Samaritan in which a Samaritan, in contrast to a priest and Levite alone, shows the right response to an individual in need. This is the only occasion on which Luke records Jesus healing more than one person at once, and the lepers are not healed at Jesus's word, but only after they have left him. The focus of the story is, however, on the man's response, which he greets with praise (17:15), Luke's favourite reaction to the revelation of divine grace and authority. Only at this point does Luke reveal that he is a Samaritan, and the impact of the event is made clear: *'Were not ten cleansed?'* asks Jesus. *'Was no one found to return and give thanks except this foreigner?'* (17:17). The word 'foreigner' emphasises the man's alien status within the framework of religious authority that Jesus conspicuously ignores. Although the leper is already cured, Luke rounds off the event with one of his favourite phrases: *'Your faith has made you well'* (17:21). We are probably intended to read 'made well' as 'saved' — the Greek verb **sozo**, which conveniently conveys both meanings.

In various ways Luke leaves his mark on other miracle stories he shares with his Marcan source. He tweaks Mark's terminology, using more literary language; he increases the use of the title 'Lord', uniquely employs the title 'Master', and stresses the fact that miracles are the result of **dunamis** — the power over Satan that is at Jesus's disposal. Busse argued that Luke saw all illness as being caused by demonic activity, although Luke never makes this point explicitly. It was tradition at one point to claim that Luke made use of technical medical language, which supported the view that he was a doctor, but scholars have subsequently suggested that it is only language that would have been well-known to educated writers of the time. Theissen observed that on three occasions Jesus prays before a miracle and in several stories the climax is the praise given to God by the witnessing crowd. Theissen also noted that Luke builds the miracle stories into his presentation of salvation history. Just as Jesus's conception marked the beginning of a new age of God's activity, so his miracles are an illustration of the vibrant 'today' of his ministry — *'We have seen strange things **today**'* (5:26).

The sick

The Jews regarded health as a gift from God and lack of it as a sign of divine displeasure. Doctors were regarded with suspicion, and the only cure for sickness was prayer. A strong link between sickness and sin was traditional, and Jesus intermittently confirms and rejects this link. The Old Testament is full of injunctions to help the sick but only Job really challenges the traditional association of sickness and sin. The social consequences of sickness — particularly illnesses such as leprosy, which utterly alienated the sufferer from religious and social life, and psychiatric disorders, assumed to be demonic possession — were severe. The sick easily fell into vagrancy and begging and on the assumption that their sin had made them sick, the rest of society would reject them. To touch, or even get close to, a sick person led to ritual uncleanness, hence the reluctance of the priest and Levite in the parable of the good Samaritan to get involved in the fate of the man beaten up on the roadside. Because few people had money to obtain medical help, there was little hope left for the sick, except to gather around places like the healing pool in Jerusalem (John 5) and wait for an angel to descend and stir up the healing waters. In the light of all this, it is not surprising that Jesus was in demand for his powers as a healer and exorcist, although he avoids the connotation of being a miracle worker, and at times actively separates himself from the public when he needs to refocus on the other, possibly more important, dimensions of his ministry.

2 Social issues

2.1 Women

Soon afterwards he went on through cities and villages proclaiming and bringing the good news of the kingdom of God. The twelve were with him, as well as some women who had been cured of evil spirits and infirmities: Mary, called Magdalene, from whom seven demons had gone out, and Joanna, the wife of Herod's steward Chuza, and Susanna, and many others, who provided for him out of their resources.

(Luke 8:1–3)

Luke's Gospel highlights Jesus's particular concern for women. It seems that in some ways women had an inferior role in Jewish society, playing little part in religious and political life, although they were not, as sometimes erroneously suggested, outcasts. Their status depended largely on their family and religious background. The Law of Moses required them to be obedient and submissive, raising children and keeping house:

÷ *'In both pagan and Jewish society women were considered to be less intelligent than men…in the wider arena of social life, in politics and religious affairs, women had almost no role at all'* (Vardy and Mills, 1995).
÷ *'The status of women was markedly inferior to that of men throughout the ancient world, including Judaism'* (Stanton, 1989).

÷ Josephus claimed that the Law held women to be inferior in all matters, and that therefore they should be submissive.

÷ Philo referred to women and female traits as weak, and claimed that women should stay at home.

÷ Sirach 42:1 wrote: *'Better is the wickedness of a man than a woman who does good; it is woman who brings shame and disgrace.'*

÷ The rabbinc Tosefta (t.ber 7:18) included a benediction prayed by a man, giving thanks that he was not made a woman. However, this is not as derogatory as it may first appear, since only Jewish men were permitted to carry out the majority of religious observances, a privilege which was valued highly — hence a Jewish man was unlikely to wish he were a woman.

However, Jesus constantly emphasised the importance of women and they appear in important roles throughout the Gospel, from the birth narratives through to the resurrection appearances. Jesus's relationship with women is characterised in several ways:

÷ Jesus allowed certain women to accompany his group during his ministry, including Joanna, who had high social standing. Note that Mary Magdalene, contrary to popular view, is not described as a prostitute, nor identified with the 'sinful woman' of chapter 7. These women provided for Jesus and the male disciples, as Lydia provided for Paul, suggesting they were all relatively wealthy.

÷ Jesus encouraged women to listen to his teaching, as a pupil would to a rabbi — a privilege usually given to men. An interesting insight comes in 10:38–42, where Mary listens to Jesus teach, whilst her sister Martha is preoccupied with traditional female household tasks.

÷ Jesus breaks several social conventions concerning women. For example, at the house of Simon the Pharisee (7:36–50) he allows a sinful woman (note that her sin is unspecified) to anoint his feet — an action usually seen as defilement.

÷ Jesus performs miracles for the benefit of women. He heals the woman with the haemorrhage (8:42) and the crippled woman (13:10), and raises the widow of Nain's son (7:11), Jairus's daughter (8:49). He also refers to their great persistence and faith in the parables of the lost coin (15:8) and the unjust judge (18:1).

÷ Women are always shown in a positive light. In the birth narratives the women are faithful and obedient and in the resurrection narratives it is women who are the first to receive the good news of salvation.

In *Mary Magdalene and Many Others*, Carla Ricci (1994) observes that the key passage in Luke's presentation of women in the ministry of Jesus (8:1–3) is especially significant because it highlights a group of women for the first time in the narrative. Up to this point they have appeared as single figures, cured or cared for in some other way by Jesus, or doing him acts of kindness. This passage indicates that, like the male disciples, there were women too who had left everything behind them and followed him to the cross, where they were the last, and only, faithful witnesses to see him die (23:49). Ricci considers this paragraph to be nothing less than revolutionary:

First because it was revolutionary, for that time, that women should follow a master; second because this is a voice breaking through the silence on women's discipleship and appearing in the written text, if only for a moment. It is a trace that surfaces in the narrative, only to disappear again immediately, but even if the voice hardly surfaces before being stifled, it is unmistakably audible and leaves behind the uncontestable certainty that Jesus wanted the restricted and privileged circle that lived with him as he went from village to village to include a group of women.

(Ricci, 1994)

There are two possible reasons why women play a greater part in Luke's Gospel than they do in the other Synoptic Gospels. The first may be that he was more sensitive to women; the second, that he used a source which had many references to women. Ricci suggests that since Luke was a doctor, he may have had an upper-middle-class background which was more sensitive to women than other sections of society at the time. The reference to Joanna, clearly a woman of some status, may support this hypothesis. In support of the second hypothesis, Ricci notes that of the 21 references Luke makes to women in his Gospel, only 6 are paralleled in Mark and none in Matthew, leaving 16 that derived from Luke's own source. Ricci suggests that this provides evidence that the other writers filtered out information which could have threatened their own androcentric view of the Gospel and Jesus's ministry, and that the special attention which Luke pays to women is made all the more remarkable by the absence of such material in the other Synoptic Gospels.

Interestingly, however, J. and K. Court (1990), in *The New Testament World*, observe that the relative social status of women in the ancient world was more complicated than might be assumed. While Roman law stated that all women *'because of their weakness of intellect should be under the power of guardians'*, Proverbs 31:26ff speaks highly of a woman who *'opens her mouth with wisdom... She looks well to the ways of her household'*. There are also literary examples of women who were held in high regard, and the proponents of feminist theology have developed several theories of the role of women in leadership positions in the early church.

2.2 Outcasts and sinners

Perhaps the most scandalous aspect of Jesus's reputation was that he was known to have reached out to those who were outsiders because they lived immoral lives. Jesus went further than charismatics like Hanina ben Dosa, by his willingness simply to spend time in bad company with people who were shunned by God-fearing members of society.

(Tilby, 2001)

In Judaism, a number of people were considered to be outcasts or sinners, including tax collectors, prostitutes, usurers and lepers. Jesus is seen closely associating with such people — for example, he calls Levi, a tax collector, to be one of his disciples (5:27) and freely dines with sinners, causing the Jewish leaders to complain: *'"Why do you eat and drink with tax collectors and sinners?" Jesus answered them, "It is not the healthy that need a doctor, but the sick. I have not come to call the righteous, but sinners to repentance"'* (5:31–2).

Luke has established his interest in people on the fringes of Jewish society from the birth narrative, in which the shepherds are the first to visit Jesus, and he sustains it throughout the Gospel. If Luke had a key text it could well be *'The Son of Man has come to seek and save the lost'* (19:10), since so many of the parables and incidents which are unique to him focus on this theme. Marshall (1984) observes: *'In singling out this feature as the decisive characteristic of the ministry, Luke was doing something novel as compared with the other Evangelists, and yet at the same time he was not imposing a new motif upon the Gospel tradition'*. The reversal of values anticipated in the Magnificat (1:52–3) is to be accomplished not only in an eschatological future but during the ministry of Jesus.

The parable of the good Samaritan (10:29–37) is related by Jesus in response to the question *'Who is my neighbour?'* Jesus's answer is controversial: to a Jew, one's neighbour was a compatriot, not a Gentile or a Samaritan. But the point is sharply made — those who had been considered far from the kingdom of heaven, outcast because of race, religious background, gender or health, were now heroes of the Gospel. The story remarkably dramatises the fact that a representative of the most hated and despised sect could fulfil the meaning of the law — *'Love your neighbour as yourself'* — better than a priest or Levite. The parable of the great banquet (14:15–24) tells the same story: those who share the banquet in the kingdom of heaven are not necessarily those to whom the invitation was first made. When the servants go to call them to the table, excuses come thick and fast and the opportunity is missed, but not for those in the 'highways and hedges' who will be called to take their place.

Throughout the Gospel, Jesus responds astutely to criticism about his unexpectedly liberal attitude to social relations, and each time turns the complainants' attention to themselves and their own reactions to circumstances about which they are so righteously indignant; Simon the Pharisee fails to offer hospitality; those who complain at Jesus's dining arrangements are like the elder son of the parable, too proud to recognise the legitimate claims of the underdog. In this sense, the parable of the lost son is about two lost sons, one as much lost to self-righteous religious and moral observance as the other is to his sinful life. The former is unable to rejoice at his younger brother's return, and believes that his father's behaviour is inappropriate, rather than rejoicing, as do God and the angels, over the restoration of a repentant sinner.

Different despised classes emerge: the sick, women, gentiles, and tax collectors in particular. Lieu (1997) notes that although Jesus's association with tax collectors is deeply rooted in the synoptic tradition, it plays no part in the Fourth Gospel or early church preaching. For this reason, she argues that it must go back to Jesus's ministry, although *'quite how we are to understand it has yet to be satisfactorily answered'*. Tax collectors were despised for making their living out of dependency on the Romans, and could only make their way back into the Jewish community by a strict regime of purification under the supervision of the priest. Jesus makes light of their social exclusion with the parable of the Pharisee and the tax collector (18:9–14) and the very personal story of Zaccheus (19:1–9). Both are shown to be purified not by ritual baths but by their humble response to divine grace, a fact of spiritual life which is shared by all who respond positively to Jesus, whatever their social, racial or religious status.

Rich and poor

In the teaching of Jesus the good news of the kingdom of God was for the poor and there were stern warnings to the rich about the danger of being kept outside the kingdom by their possessions.

(Marshall, 1984)

According to Luke, Jesus came to preach the Gospel to the poor (4:18). Preaching the word of God to the poor seems to have been of paramount importance: 'Blessed are you who are poor, for yours is the kingdom of God' (6:20). Jesus himself was born into humble circumstances and his first visitors, the shepherds, were from the poorest classes. In the Pharisee's house, Jesus spoke of the importance of caring for the poor: '*But when you give a banquet, invite the poor, the crippled, the lame and the blind, and you will be blessed*' (14:13). On the other hand, Luke emphasises throughout the Gospel the dangers of wealth. In the Magnificat, Mary sings of the fact that 'He has filled the hungry with good things, but he has sent the rich away empty' (1:53).

Jesus continually warns of the problems of wealth, both in the parables such as the rich fool (12:16), the shrewd manager (16:1) and the rich man and Lazarus (16:19) and in personal contacts, such as his conversation with the rich young ruler (18:18–27), where the rich man is unable to give up his wealth, prompting Jesus's famous saying: '*Indeed, it is easier for a camel to go through the eye of a needle than for a rich man to enter the kingdom of God*' (18:25). But salvation is possible; the wealthy Zacchaeus realises his foolishness and returns his property to the poor and receives salvation (19:9), whilst in the widow's offering (21:1), Jesus praises the poor widow for giving all she has, rather than the rich who, although they gave more money, did not make so great a sacrifice.

Marshall (1984) points out, however, that Luke's focus is not just on financial wealth: '*The teaching about wealth and poverty must be set in its context. We have already seen that the "poor" to whom the gospel is preached are those who are needy and dependent on God. By the same token, the "rich" are those who are self-satisfied and feel no need of God*'.

Summary

- Jesus's **miracle-working** as proof of his Messiahship is central to all the Gospel accounts, and Luke generally follows the Marcan pattern, but with significant additions and adaptations. His own additions emphasise his own themes, including stories featuring a widow and a grateful Samaritan, and indicate to the reader that a new era in salvation history has not only dawned but is active among the people of Israel and those traditionally rejected from its society.
- **Women** feature prominently in the Gospel, and Jesus seems to have included a group of women amongst his regular followers and supporters. His attitude to, and inclusion of, women is sharply contrasted with the traditional views of his culture, and places them at the centre of his healing and preaching activity, anticipating a key place for them in the early church. **Outcasts** and **sinners** of all types are also shown to be integrated into Jesus's ministry, drawing sharp criticism from his opponents.

Exam watch

These are topics which must be underpinned by a solid awareness of the social and cultural background, and the textual material must be the servant of your critical evaluation, not the master of your essay, which will otherwise turn into a low-grade narrative.

Review questions

1 Examine the importance for Luke's Gospel of the role of (a) women and (b) Samaritans in the ministry and teaching of Jesus.

2 With reference to at least two miracles, assess how miracles contribute to the evangelist's presentation of the person and purpose of Jesus.

3 Comment on the meaning and significance of Jesus's teaching concerning (a) outcasts and sinners and (b) wealth.

4 To what extent were Jesus's teachings on (a) women and (b) money in contrast to the teachings of Judaism at that time?

D Important figures in Jesus's ministry

1 John the Baptist

John the Baptist plays an important role in Luke's Gospel, and appears prominently in the birth narratives, establishing a parallel with Jesus from conception (see pp. 309–310). He was born a few months before Jesus to elderly parents, Zechariah, a priest, and his wife Elizabeth, a relative of Mary, the mother of Jesus. His birth was unique because his parents were old and Elizabeth was barren. An angel informs Zechariah that they have been chosen by God to bear a son who will be a great man of God and will prepare the way for the Messiah: *'And he will go before the Lord in the spirit and power of Elijah, to turn the hearts of the fathers to their children and the disobedient to the wisdom of the righteous — to make ready a people prepared for the Lord'* (1:17).

As a man, John receives the call from God in the desert and he travels around the land baptising and preaching a message of repentance and forgiveness, in fulfilment of the prophecy of Isaiah 40:3: *'A voice of one calling in the desert'*. He baptises with water, but tells the people that one who is coming is much greater than he and will baptise with the Holy Spirit and fire (3:16). The end of John's ministry signalled the beginning of Jesus's own and Jesus himself gave John the highest praise: *'I tell you, among those born of women there is no one greater than John'* (7:28). John was imprisoned by Herod and executed at the fortress of Machaerus.

Luke's account of the preaching of John the Baptist is the most extensive of all the synoptic evangelists. It is with the beginning of John's public ministry that the three accounts correspond, and all three evangelists describe John's ministry of baptism and preaching in the wilderness, although Matthew and Luke clearly draw upon Q, as well as freely editing Mark's account. (For more on Q, see p. 276.) Mark's presentation of John is the least self-conscious. He does not explain why John baptised Jesus, neither does he use other Baptist traditions in his Gospel to justify John's role in relation to Jesus. Mark uses Isaiah 40:3 and Malachi 3:1 to introduce John, establishing the firm link that all the evangelists make between the Baptist and the prophesied forerunner of the Lord. In their original context, the Old Testament passages referred to a forerunner of God himself; in the Gospel narrative the forerunner is one who prepares for the Messiah's ministry through baptism.

Mark's and Matthew's description of John, dressed in camel hair and living on a diet of locusts and wild honey, identifies him with Elijah, who is so described in 2 Kings 1:8. However, John's teaching about his role is always in terms of the one who will follow him. He declares himself unable even to perform the servant's task of untying his sandals, and whilst John's preparatory baptism in water is an essential part of his task, it is a pale copy of the Messiah's baptism in the Holy Spirit (1:7–8).

Matthew and Luke draw on Q to include John's eschatological preaching. Both report that large numbers come out to the Jordan to receive John's baptism, but whilst Matthew's account specifically identifies the Pharisees and Sadducees as the targets of John's address (3:7), Luke describes the same teaching being made to the multitudes (3:10). Since the tone of the speech seems to apply more to those who were opponents of John, Luke may have edited his account to underline the universal nature of his ministry. He adds a further address in 3:10–14 to the crowds, tax collectors and soldiers (Jewish men in the service of Herod) in which he essentially gives the same instruction to them all: give up your sin and live in a loving way towards all men, characteristic of a repentant heart. Lieu (1997) writes: *'Luke has chosen these three groups to reflect his interest in the despised of society and in the practical application of the Gospel in matters of wealth, as well perhaps, as in the possibilities of the exercise of state power in accordance with God's will'*.

John anticipates that the Messiah will bring an eschatological judgment and warns that the time is at hand for the winnowing out of the righteous and insincere — those whom E. Earle Ellis (1980) describes as seeking baptism as an *'admission ticket'* — and he makes clear that lofty claims to Abrahamic descent will not be sufficient to save them from impending eschatological judgment.

In both Luke's and Matthew's accounts, John sends disciples to question Jesus: *'Are you he who is to come, or shall we look for another?'* (Matthew 11:3; Luke 7:19), and it is conceivable that John's sudden lack of confidence arises from the apparent difference between Jesus's ministry and the eschatological judgment he was anticipating. Jesus sends reassurance back to John, but demands that he should interpret Jesus's ministry aright. To be scandalised by the meek and humble ministry of the Messiah (Matthew 11:28–30) is to miss the best that God has for man.

The way in which Matthew and Luke handle the account of Jesus's baptism betrays the very real problems that the early church had in understanding John's role. That the Messiah was baptised by his forerunner had obvious christological implications. Matthew deals with these by John's suggestion that he should be baptised by Jesus, before Jesus gives him permission to go ahead, in order to *'fulfil all righteousness'* (Matthew 3:14–15). Luke implies that John was already in prison before the baptism took place, leaving it open as to who did baptise Jesus (Luke 3:18–22). Luke does not include an account of John's fatal confrontation with Herod over his marriage to Herodias, which is used by the other evangelists to explain Herod's fears about the true identity of Jesus. For Luke, John's story — which firmly belongs in the age of expectation — is over, and Jesus's must begin.

Nevertheless, along with Matthew, he later draws on Q material that includes Jesus's own assessment of John. This material is particularly interesting since it would be easy for the church to have omitted Jesus's testimony to the Baptist in the interest of playing down his role. In both accounts, Jesus declares that *'among those born of women there has arisen no one greater than John the Baptist'* (Matthew 11:11; Luke 7:28). By saying this, he elevates John above the patriarchs and prophets of the Old Testament, since he is the one to usher in the days of the kingdom. However, the qualifying phrase, *'Yet he who is* least in the kingdom of heaven is greater than he' is puzzling. Since Abraham, Isaac and Jacob are to be in the kingdom (Matthew 8:11), it is odd that John should not be also. Perhaps Matthew and Luke intended to make the distinction that must still exist between those who follow Jesus in a life of discipleship, and John, who is still the forerunner and cannot share in the consummation of his mission. Ellis (1981) writes: *'His place in redemptive history belongs to the time of promise, the pre-messianic era. Therefore, the least in the kingdom has a "greater" status because he belongs to the "greater" time of fulfilment. In the preaching and acts of Jesus the time of fulfilment is now being realised'.*

Recognising John as Elijah who is to come is tantamount to recognising Jesus as Messiah, and thus, many failed to do so. However, those who did grasp John's identity were in a position to receive Jesus and his salvation. Luke identifies the tax collectors and *'all the people'* as those who were able to respond to John and who could count themselves justified (7:29), and when challenged by Jesus to identify the source of John's authority, the chief priests and scribes are forced to admit that *'the people... are convinced that John was a prophet'* (Luke 20:6&//s). Not surprisingly, it is the Jewish authorities that are depicted as rejecting John as they reject Jesus. Nevertheless, John the Baptist's role was ultimately too important to be ignored either by the evangelists or by those who received his message.

Scholars are undecided about the true role of John. H. Conzelmann argued that Luke portrays John as the last of the Old Testament prophets, whilst Marshall prefers to see John as a link between the old and new ages. Marshall (1984) claims that Luke links John closely with the prophets, particularly Elijah, who, by tradition, was said to return to announce the Messiah: *'I will send my messenger ahead of you, who will prepare your way before you'* (Malachi 3:1). He suggests that, for Luke, the era of salvation begins with John and Jesus: *'John is the bridge between the old and new eras. He belongs to both, but essentially to the new one since he is the immediate forerunner of the Messiah. He is portrayed both as a prophet and as the first preacher of the gospel'.*

2 The Holy Spirit

If we ask why Luke gives us an introduction that is so very different from those of the other evangelists, then it is perhaps because he wants to stress, above all, that the Holy Spirit is at work in the ministry of Jesus and in the mission of his followers.

(Hooker, 1997)

More than all the synoptic evangelists, Luke stresses that the Holy Spirit is a vital and active participant in the events of Jesus's birth and ministry, and will continue to be so in the life of the early church. The fulfilment of Zechariah's and Elizabeth's hopes for a son was the opportunity for the Holy Spirit to begin to move again in Israel, as Joel had prophesied. John the Baptist will be a Spirit-filled prophet like Elijah before him, though not as a worker of miracles, but rather as a preacher of righteousness, inspired by the same Spirit that Elijah passed to Elisha. More significantly still, of course, the Holy Spirit is the agent in the virginal conception of Jesus. The angel's message to Mary asserts that through the action of the Spirit, the son she will bear shall be *'holy, the Son of God'.* Schneider observes: *'Jesus is not merely filled with the Spirit, like John, rather his very being is attributed to the Spirit'* (cited in Green, McKnight and Marshall (eds), 1992). The outcome of Jesus's conception by the Spirit is portrayed in Luke 2:41–52, when he is found, aged 12, discoursing with the teachers in the Temple, which is perhaps to be understood against the background of messianic hopes for a ruler endowed with wisdom.

Like Mark and Matthew, Luke describes the baptism as the occasion when Jesus is anointed to begin his ministry, although clearly he has possessed this same Spirit throughout his youth and adulthood thus far, and it is the spirit that leads Jesus deeper into the wilderness after the baptism at the Jordan. Although nothing is said of the Spirit's role in the temptations, Luke states that Jesus faced them *'full of the Holy Spirit'* (4:1) and returned from them *'in the power of the Spirit'* (4:14). Whilst Israel *'rebelled and grieved his Holy Spirit'* (Isaiah 63:10) wandering in the wilderness, Jesus, the embodiment of the new Israel, overcomes temptation, and so demonstrates to the reader that he possesses true messianic righteousness. We are certainly intended to understand that Jesus's success at casting out demons and healing those who were under the power of Satan is not least due to the success of his encounter in the wilderness.

It is in the power of the Spirit that Jesus enters the synagogue in Nazareth and, in an episode only found in Luke's Gospel, causes an outcry when he reads the scripture portion for the day and promptly identifies it as having been fulfilled in his own advent and his impending ministry. John Rea (1990) argues that this episode demonstrates that Jesus did not grow into messianic self-consciousness, but was aware of it from the start of his ministry, and deliberately chose the passage from Isaiah 61:1–3 to identify himself clearly to the people of his home town:

The Spirit of the Lord is upon me,
Because he anointed me to preach the Gospel to the poor.
He has sent me to proclaim release to the captives,
And recovery of sight to the blind,
To set free those who are downtrodden,
To proclaim the favourable year of the Lord.

Jesus's claim that this passage, originally expressing the vocation of the prophet, is *'fulfilled in your hearing'* (Luke 4:21) comes as a shock, and the murmurs of approval quickly change to outrage. Nevertheless, although the bold claim may sound like blasphemy to the Nazareth crowd, it is a manifesto for Jesus's ministry as described by Luke, a ministry for which he has been anointed by the Spirit of God.

The same Spirit is made available to Jesus's disciples even before Pentecost, and in Luke 9:1–5 the evangelist relates how Jesus sent out the 12 Apostles, equipped with the Spirit, to preach the kingdom of God, cast out demons and heal the sick. Later, he sends out 70 on the same task, and they return, rejoicing because they had found that the demons were subject to them (10:17–20). Jesus is delighted, but warns them against spiritual pride, for the true reason for rejoicing is that their names are written in heaven. Nevertheless, the Spirit is to be actively sought and desired by the disciple, and in 11:5–13 Luke adapts Q material to specify that the believer must go on asking God for the Holy Spirit, whereas Matthew simply says they should pray for 'good gifts'.

Finally, in Luke's account, the risen Jesus tells the disciples to do nothing after his ascension until they are equipped with *'the promise of my Father'* (24:44–53). Just as

Jesus's anointing with the Spirit fulfilled Isaiah 61:1–3, so will the pouring out of the Spirit on the Apostles fulfil Joel 2:28, and the disciples return to the Temple in Jerusalem to wait with great joy. Rea (1990) observes that Luke offers this as a lesson for all future believers: '*The earnest child of God today seeking baptism in the Spirit may well imitate their attitude of expectancy, joyous praise, and prayerfulness*'.

3 The disciples

A disciple is a pupil — someone who learns from a teacher. Frequently, the word is used to refer to the Twelve Disciples (or Apostles) named by Luke in 6:14–16 as Simon (Peter), Andrew, James, John, Philip, Bartholomew, Levi (Matthew), Thomas, James, son of Alphaeus, Simon the Zealot, Judas, son of James, and Judas Iscariot. However, strictly speaking, a disciple is anyone who follows Jesus, as in Luke 6:17, where the evangelist refers to a '*great crowd of disciples*'. The Twelve, however, are almost certainly an inner circle chosen from the whole company of disciples, and it is they who receive the post-resurrection command to preach '*repentance and forgiveness of sins to all nations, beginning in Jerusalem*' (24:47).

Becoming a disciple involved making a real commitment to follow Jesus. This involved repentance and being prepared to give up everything to follow God's call. The Twelve were specifically called by Jesus and gave up all they had to follow him. For example, Levi has no hesitation in giving up his occupation and comfortable lifestyle to follow Jesus: '"*Follow me*," *Jesus said to him, and Levi got up, left everything and followed him*' (5:27–28). Luke is the only synoptic evangelist, however, to provide the disciples with a concrete reason to follow Jesus — the miraculous catch of fish in chapter 5 — aside from the sheer force of his personality. Once called, the disciple is expected to make a binding commitment: '*No one who puts his hand to the plough and looks back is fit for the kingdom of God*' (Luke 9:62).

Discipleship itself was very difficult and demanding, carrying with it the real possibility of persecution and death. Disciples had to give up their material comforts, because being tied to earthly possessions would restrict effective discipleship: '*In the same way, any of you who does not give up everything he has cannot be my disciple*' (14:33). The disciples would have divine help, and as they faced the hatred of the world the Holy Spirit would aid them in times of trouble: '*When you are brought before synagogues, rulers and authorities, do not worry about how you will defend yourselves or what you will say, for the Holy Spirit will teach you at that time what you should say*' (12:11–12). Luke anticipates the members of the early church, whom he describes in Acts 2:44 as having '*sold their possessions and goods and distributed them to all as any had need*'. It is clear that a rich disciple is something of a contradiction in terms for Luke: '*In the teaching of Jesus the good news of the kingdom of God was for the poor, and there were stern warnings to the rich about the danger of being kept outside the kingdom by their possessions. The corollary of such warnings is the command to use wealth in the right way*' (Marshall, 1984).

Nevertheless, the rewards of discipleship were great. Disciples had the authority of Jesus to act in his name and were filled with joy at their work: '*The seventy-two returned with joy and said, "Lord, even the demons submit to us in your name"*' (10:17). Moreover, they were especially blessed by God and were privileged to know things that others could not know: *'Blessed are the eyes that see what you see. For I tell you that many prophets and kings wanted to see what you see, but did not see it'* (10:24). The disciples had a unique relationship with God, which will endure for ever, and in his name it was said that they would achieve great things. Their prayers would be answered: *'Do not be afraid, little flock, for your father has been pleased to give you the kingdom'* (12:32).

Above all, the disciples brought in the new age, as D. B. Taylor (1992) observes: *'There is an immediate hundredfold reward for those who walk out on their commitments and dependants and join Jesus on the road; there will be even greater rewards "in the age to come."'*

Summary

- **John the Baptist** is the forerunner of Jesus, fulfilling the role of Elijah, and whilst standing himself in the age of expectation, he ushers in the age of fulfilment. His miraculous birth is paralleled, although exceeded, by that of Jesus. He is presented as clearly inferior to Jesus, but with a vital role to play in bringing men and women to acknowledge their need for repentance and make them ready to receive Jesus. There was evidently some anxiety in the early church as regards the precise nature of John's role, but an awareness that it was too important to eliminate altogether.
- The **Holy Spirit** directs events from the birth narratives, and in Acts will become the driving force behind the early church. Jesus is equipped and anointed with the Spirit and will pass it on to his disciples, who cannot function in their post-resurrection roles without it. Jesus's possession of the Spirit is made clear by the success he has over Satan at the temptations and throughout his ministry. It marks him out as the Messiah, as he himself identifies in the synagogue at Nazareth.
- The **disciples** are a wider group than the Twelve, although the inner circle are those who have the primary responsibility for witnessing and preaching after the ascension. Discipleship is presented as demanding, but ultimately bringing rewards that are worth the price of persecution and leaving behind family and occupations.

Exam watch

These are good, manageable topics, although you will have observed a considerable overlap, so ensure that when you write about discipleship, for example, you include material on the Holy Spirit in relation to them. You need a good working knowledge of the Gospel text for all these topics — particularly discipleship — since relevant material is scattered throughout the narrative and you must be able to manipulate it quickly and fluently. Resist the temptation to preach, e.g. 'Disciples must all love Jesus and give to the poor', as this will not gain marks.

Review questions

1 Examine the teaching on the role and function of John the Baptist in Luke's Gospel.
2 Outline Luke's teaching on the Holy Spirit and comment on its importance to discipleship.
3 Examine and analyse the teaching of the Gospel on the nature of discipleship.

E The passion and resurrection narratives

1 The last week

The last days before Jesus's death are known as the passion and the accounts of these times are of great religious significance because they address the question 'Why did Jesus have to die?' (see pp. 271–273 for a discussion of the importance of this question).

The passion begins with the triumphal entry into Jerusalem, followed by the cleansing of the Temple, conflict with the authorities, the Lord's Supper, and the Trial and Crucifixion. Luke has already prepared the readers for what is to come, by showing Jesus as the means of salvation for humanity.

1.1 The triumphal entry (19:28–44)

Jesus has decided that the time has come for him to go to Jerusalem and face the Jewish authorities. He knows that the authorities are hostile to him but, instead of coming in secret, he decides to come openly and in triumph. At Bethany, which was a village about two miles from Jerusalem, he instructs two of his disciples to get a colt for him — one that had never been ridden before. This is perhaps to show that the animal was unspoilt and therefore suitable for this sacred purpose. Apparently, the owners had previously been contacted, because they hand it over as soon as they hear the words '*The Lord needs it*' (19:31), but nevertheless, the episode has overtones of mysterious divine omniscience. Jesus rides the colt towards Jerusalem and the people spread their cloaks on the road, making a triumphal carpet for Jesus to ride on. At the Mount of Olives a large crowd praises God for all his works. It is possible that their enthusiasm was based on the prophecy from Zechariah 9:9:

Shout, Daughter of Jerusalem!
See, your king comes to you,
Righteous and having salvation,
Gentle and riding on a donkey.

Certainly the people were looking for a king or Messiah — they had seen Jesus perform miraculous works and could well have seen his entry as fulfilment of the prophecy: '*Blessed is the king who comes in the name of the Lord!*' (19:38). Of course, the Pharisees in the crowd are not happy about this, and ask Jesus to rebuke his followers, but Jesus refuses: '*…if they keep quiet, the stones will cry out*' (19:40). Then, in stark contrast to the joy of the crowds, Jesus expresses his sadness at the state of Jerusalem, and the fact that the city is unable to grasp this opportunity for peace and will one day be destroyed. Jerusalem has been important for Luke since the introduction of the Gospel, and it is where both the Gospel ends and the new church begins. Nonetheless, it is in Jerusalem that Jesus is finally rejected, an irony that does not pass Luke by.

1.2 The cleansing of the Temple (19:45–8)

Jesus enters the Temple area, probably the court of the Gentiles, where he finds market traders. They are selling animals for sacrifice at very high prices and changing money; the Temple will not accept Roman coinage, so all currency has to be changed into Tyrian coinage. This means a profit for the market traders at the expense of the worshippers. They are all, in a sense, part of the Temple system of sacrifice and offering, but Jesus is angry that such a trade is going on within the Temple precincts and he drives them out, quoting from the prophecy of Isaiah 56:7: '"*It is written,*" *he said to them, "My house will be 'a house of prayer', but you have made it 'a den of robbers'"*' (19:46). The incident ends ominously, with the chief priests and leaders of the people getting ready to kill Jesus (19:47). They are, however, aware of the tremendous support that Jesus has from the crowds, and their hands are tied by their failure to have a legitimate charge to bring against him. Jesus will ultimately die, accused as a political revolutionary, but Luke makes clear that the charges are trumped-up ones. The Jewish authorities, bound by the nature of their relationship with Romans, must be seen to act in the light of Jesus's dramatic action in the Temple. However, they face a problem, as Rivkin (1984) observed:

It was not easy for the authorities to decide what to do about charismatic leaders who preached no violence and built no revolutionary organisations, but rather urged the people to repent and to wait for the coming of God's kingdom. Were these charismatics harmless preachers, or were they troublemakers?

1.3 Conflict with the authorities (chapter 20)

Throughout his ministry, Jesus came into conflict with the Jewish authorities and this conflict comes to a head in chapter 20. Luke shows here how the opposition between Jesus and the Jews is to be the historical means by which his death comes about — although, as Luke makes clear, everything is within the divine plan of God. The cause of the conflict between Jesus and the Jewish authorities centred around the fact that Jesus seemed to pose a challenge to the system of Jewish law, worship and ritual. He was also believed by many to be the Son of God — a concept that the Jews could not accept or understand. Moreover, the Jewish authorities were under pressure from the Romans who allowed them to retain their power on condition that they kept the people peaceful and prevented anti-Roman demonstrations. The Romans demanded that the chief priests quickly dealt with any troublemakers and those who attracted crowds; Jesus was such a person.

The Jewish authorities tried to trick Jesus into condemning himself. In 20:1–8 they ask him where his authority comes from, encouraged in their questioning by the way in which '*the people hung upon his words*' (19:48). He does not answer their question, but instead asks them where they thought John the Baptist's authority to baptise came from. Many people in Jerusalem believed that John was a man sent by God and that his authority came from God. However, the authorities had never acknowledged this, and John died the death of a dangerous charismatic revolutionary, just as Jesus would. However, if they now acknowledge that John's authority was from God, then why hadn't they accepted it at the time? Alternatively, if they say his authority was not from God, they risk angering a lot of people to whom John was important. They cannot answer, so Jesus refuses to answer their question. Morris (1988) points out: '*Throughout the whole of the four Gospels it is clear that he is very conscious of possessing the highest authority. But he will not speak about it to men who will not answer a plain question to which they know the answer*'.

Jesus then tells the parable of the tenants (20:9–19), which marks a turning point in the conflict. Borrowing imagery of an absentee landlord and his estate, the parable highlights the fact that just as the tenants reject the vineyard owner's servants, so Israel has continually rejected God's prophets, and the tenants' killing of the son will reflect the rejection and crucifixion of Jesus. Jesus gives them the chance to change their ways, but they will refuse the opportunity and will, in turn, be rejected by God. The chief priests are angered, knowing that this parable is spoken against them, and the final note is clearly one of threat. Jesus warns them that the stone which has *'become the head of the corner'* will crush those on whom it falls (those who reject Jesus), whilst the authorities make an attempt to arrest Jesus which is immediately frustrated by their fear of the crowd's reaction.

The Jewish authorities try to trap Jesus into making a treasonable statement, so that they can arrest him and send him for trial before the Roman governor. They do this by asking whether he thinks Jews should pay Roman taxes. This is a trick question: if he says they should, he will appear to be supporting the hated Roman occupation. If he says they should not, the Romans could arrest him for sedition. Jesus's reply is the only safe one: *'Then give to Caesar what is Caesar's, and to God what is God's'* (20:25).

Jesus is then questioned by the Sadducees (20:27–39), who did not believe in the traditional Jewish teaching concerning the resurrection of the dead on the last day. They proffer a grossly exaggerated story about what was known as a levirate marriage. This was a legal action designed to make sure that a man's family name did not die out, so if a man died childless, his widow married his brother and the children they had carried the dead man's name (see Deuteronomy 25:5). The Sadducees want to trick Jesus into saying that there is no resurrection (and so alienate him from the majority of believers). They ask: if there were seven brothers who all, at one time or another, had married the same woman, then which one will be her husband at the resurrection? Jesus's reply is straightforward — life is different in the age to come and there will be no marriage: *'But those who are considered worthy of taking part in that age and in the resurrection of the dead will neither marry nor be given in marriage'* (20:35).

The series of conflict episodes concludes with Jesus warning the people against the Jewish authorities, observing that they enjoy the status and luxury that their position gives them but have cheated the poor and make a display of being holy and righteous: *'Beware of the teachers of the law. They like to walk around in flowing robes and love to be greeted in the market places and have the most important seats in the synagogues'* (20:46). There is to be no reconciliation or understanding between them and Jesus and his disciples.

As the Passover approaches, the Jewish authorities finally take the initiative to get rid of Jesus, although they *'were afraid of the people'* (22:2), suggesting that they are worried about possible rebellion at a politically volatile time, which would inevitably lead to Roman action against the Jews. Thus, they need to arrest Jesus secretly, away from the crowds. One of the disciples, Judas, agrees to betray Jesus, though Luke — as with all the evangelists — does not say why, beyond the statement that Satan entered him (22:3). Nevertheless, this may be reason enough for Luke. After the temptations, he noted that Satan had left Jesus *'until an opportune time'* (4:13). That time has now come and Judas makes a financial arrangement to hand Jesus over to the authorities in secret.

2 The last day

2.1 The Last Supper (22:7–38)

On the day on which the Passover lamb is sacrificed, Jesus sends Peter and John into the city to prepare a room that Jesus has already selected for the Passover meal. Jesus seems to have made a secret arrangement with the owner of the house, probably to prevent his enemies knowing where he will be. It is an important and symbolic meal, with meat, unleavened bread and bitter herbs, and is eaten by the group together, seated in the reclining position. The meal begins with Jesus saying how much he has looked forward to this moment, but then adding: '*I will not eat it (again) until it finds fulfilment in the kingdom of God*' (22:16). Scholars are divided as to whether Jesus himself ate the meal, or only presided over it. His words are ambiguous as some manuscripts omit 'again', implying that Jesus did not eat with his disciples. If this is the case it may be, as Jeremias suggests, an act of prayer and fasting for Jesus before dedicating himself to his death.

Luke adds a second cup to the Marcan account of the meal. In fact, at the Passover meal, the participants drank four cups of wine, and the sharing of a cup of wine, by passing it around the guests, was a token of fellowship. As they share the wine, Jesus once again looks towards the future age, saying he will not drink wine again until the coming of the kingdom (22:18). It was the custom at Passover to share together the bread and the wine. Jesus breaks the bread and shares it with his disciples. The eating of bread without yeast (called **matzoth**) was a requirement of the Law of Moses (Exodus 12:8), but Jesus adds new meaning to it with the words: '*This is my body given for you; do this in remembrance of me*' (22:19). This is highly symbolic — by eating the bread that is Christ's body, the disciples are able to have Jesus within them and it symbolises his saving death for his people.

In a similar way, he shares a cup of wine, saying: '*This cup is the new covenant in my blood, which is poured out for you*' (22:20). This is linked to the Old Testament — the blood of the first Passover lambs was used to protect the people of God from death (Exodus 12:23). Moreover, the blood from young bulls was used to seal the agreement between God and his people at the making of the covenant at Mount Sinai (Exodus 24:8). Jesus's death therefore marks the beginning of a new covenant, sealed in his blood. His death brings in a new way for humanity to approach God. In *The Gospel According to St Luke*, Harrington points out: '*Jesus lets it be understood that his imminent death is going to replace the sacrifices of the Old Law*'. Drane (1999) observes:

When Jesus compared his own death to the inauguration of a 'new covenant', he was suggesting to his disciples that through him God was performing a new act of deliverance, and that a similar promise of loyalty and devotion would be required of those who would share in its benefits. God's new kingdom makes demands of those who would be part of it.

Jesus prophesies his own betrayal, saying, to their horror, that one of his disciples will betray him. This was predicted in Psalm 41:9: '*Even my close friend, whom I trusted, he who shared my bread, has lifted up his heel against me*.' Soon after, the disciples begin to argue about which of them is the greatest. Jesus replies by saying that the greatest is not the one who behaves as though he has authority; it is the humblest. Faithful service produces true greatness: '*Instead, the greatest among you should be like the youngest, and the one who rules like the one who serves*' (22:26).

Jesus tells the disciples that there will be trials ahead, and warns Simon Peter in particular that he has prayed for him — not that he will be spared the trials, but that his faith will not fail and that he will be able to give strength to the others. Peter does not realise quite how difficult the situation will be and he brashly declares his willingness to die for Jesus (22:33). But Jesus knows Peter well, and tells him that '*...before the cock crows today, you will deny three times that you know me*' (22:34). Jesus concludes the meal with a warning to the disciples of the strife they will have to face. They will need a purse, a bag and a sword (22:36), as predicted in Isaiah 53:12. Whether Jesus was actually advocating the use of violence is not clear. Stephen Brandon maintained that this was precisely what he was doing, and that the presence of swords at the meal and later in the garden suggests that Jesus's disciples were intent on responding aggressively to any threat to Jesus. However, Jesus's '*It is enough*' (22:38) may not be intended to suggest that two swords are enough for their purpose, but may be a rebuke — 'Enough of that!'

2.2 The Mount of Olives (22:39–46)

After the meal, Jesus and the disciples go to the Mount of Olives, a quiet spot just outside Jerusalem. He asks them to pray that they do not fall into temptation, while he goes to pray alone. Jesus prays by kneeling to the ground — a sign of great spiritual anguish, as Jewish men would normally pray standing — and addresses God directly as Father. In the prayer that follows, Jesus shows his humanity, highlighting the pain he must suffer. He asks that the cup might be taken from him; the cup is a symbol of suffering, linked with the Old Testament concept of the cup of the anger of God (Psalm 11:6; Ezekiel 23:33). But Jesus swiftly offers words of obedience — he is to fulfil his earthly mission: '*Father, if you are willing, take this cup from me; yet not my will, but yours be done*' (22:42). The agony of the moment is emphasised in 22:43–4, which are omitted by some manuscripts. Jesus appears to sweat droplets of blood, allegedly possible under conditions of great stress. However, the omission of these lines from most manuscripts suggests that early scribes found the implication of Jesus's humanity and fear problematic.

Jesus returns to the disciples to find them sleeping and is greatly saddened. He wanted them to remain awake and praying, which was to be an important aspect of future discipleship, and they have failed to do so. They are unprepared for the events that are about to unfold, and it is not surprising that they are not able to stay by Jesus during his passion.

2.3 Arrest and trial (22:47–23:25)

Judas appears with an armed crowd and approaches Jesus to greet him with a kiss — a gesture of respect and love, though, ironically, Judas uses it as a sign of betrayal (22:48). As Jesus is arrested the disciples ask if they should fight with their swords and one, traditionally thought to be Peter, draws a sword and cuts off the ear of the servant of the high priest. Jesus orders violence to cease, heals the man and rebukes the Jewish authorities, who are, apparently, too frightened to arrest Jesus by the light of day: '*But this is your hour — when darkness reigns*' (22:53).

Jesus is taken to the house of the High Priest. Peter has followed at a distance and sits with the people around a fire in the courtyard where a servant girl challenges him, saying that he was with Jesus (22:56). Peter denies it. Then another person claims Peter was also 'one of them' (22:58) and again Peter denies knowing Jesus. An hour later a third identifies Peter as having been with Jesus and a third time Peter denies it, whereupon the cock crows. Luke heightens the drama of the incident as Jesus, passing by to be tried before the High Priest, looks at Peter. Peter remembers Jesus's words and weeps.

Jesus is guarded by soldiers, probably Temple guards, who take the opportunity to mock him. At daybreak he is taken before the Sanhedrin. The proceedings are completely irregular — no accusations are made against him, nor are any witnesses called, and proper trial procedures are not observed. Instead, the Sanhedrin seem to want Jesus, quite illegally, to incriminate himself by telling them he is the Christ. Jesus knows that his view of Messiahship and theirs is different, so he does not answer them directly, for he knows that they will not believe him (22:67). Instead, he warns them that his death and resurrection will change everything: 'But from now on, the Son of Man will be seated at the right hand of the mighty God' (22:69). Morris (1988) observes: 'The right hand was the place of honour and sitting was the posture of rest. Thus the meaning is that, his saving work done, he would have the place of highest honour'.

Finally, the Sanhedrin ask the crucial question: 'Are you then the Son of God?' In a very real sense, nothing else matters. To claim to be the Son of God was a blasphemy under the Law of Moses, punishable by death. Jesus's answer is enough to condemn him: 'You are right in saying I am' (22:70). The Sanhedrin have heard enough. They do not ask Jesus to explain himself or say more — in their eyes, Jesus is guilty. The Jewish leaders condemned Jesus for a number of reasons — the Pharisees saw him as a blasphemer, the high priests probably saw him as a troublemaker and a subversive. Lieu (1997) observes, however, that the trial before the Sanhedrin, and that which will follow, before Pilate, leave unclear exactly what Jesus was condemned for: 'There is no obvious connection with Jesus's ministry, neither with what he has said and done, nor with the controversies with which he was engaged. The issues or titles named in his interrogation reflect Christian faith more than convincing charges that might provoke condemnation.'

2.4 Before Pilate (22:66–23:25)

Had there been no Roman imperial system, Jesus would have faced the buffetings of strong words, the batterings of skilfully aimed proof texts, and the ridicule of both Sadducees and Scribes-Pharisees, but he would have stood no trial, been affixed to no cross.

(Rivkin, 1984)

The Jewish leaders had no authority to condemn a person to death; only the Roman political authorities could pass the death sentence or **ius gladii**. Therefore, they take Jesus before Pontius Pilate, the Roman Procurator. Such was their depth of feeling against Jesus that apparently the whole Sanhedrin brought him before Pilate. However, there was a problem, for blasphemy was not a crime in Roman law. So the Jews instead accused Jesus of matters that the Romans would find serious: 'subverting our nation' (23:2), opposing the payment of taxes to Caesar and claiming to be 'Christ, a king'

(23:2). It is clear to the reader that these charges are false, since they have been comprehensively dealt with in earlier scenes, but Pilate, of course, is not to know that.

Nonetheless, Pilate himself says little beyond asking Jesus if he is the King of the Jews, and declares that he finds there is no charge against Jesus. When Pilate discovers Jesus is a Galilean under King Herod's jurisdiction, he sends Jesus to Herod, who happens to be in Jerusalem at the time. (Herod was a puppet Jewish king with little real power, but sufficiently prominent for Pilate to want to be on good terms with him.) Jesus refuses to answer any of Herod's questions and so Herod and his soldiers mock him and send him back to Pilate. In this way, Luke suggests that the combined weight of Roman and Jewish authority failed to find a crime with which Jesus could legitimately be charged. Jesus may die a criminal's death, but he is no criminal and Luke ensures that his readers know that. Once again, Pilate says to the Jews that he can find nothing wrong with Jesus and wants to release him. However, the crowd, probably spurred on by the chief priests, shout for him to release a murderer called Barabbas and to crucify Jesus. Despite feeling that Jesus has done nothing wrong, Pilate condemns Jesus to death. He will die as an innocent martyr, falsely accused by those who should have known better, and condemned by a weak Gentile ruler who could not trust his instincts. Luke makes it clear that in his view (and that of the early church) Pilate only condemns Jesus because the Jews demanded his death. Morris (1988) writes: '*It was not Pilate or his Romans who called for Jesus's execution: it was the Jewish chief priests and their followers*'.

3 The crucifixion (23:26–56)

The place of execution was a hill outside Jerusalem called Golgotha (or Calvary). Jesus, like all condemned prisoners, was forced to walk through the city to Golgotha, facing the abuse of the citizens *en route*. Usually the prisoner would carry the crossbeam on his shoulders, but the soldiers seize a man called Simon of Cyrene and force him to carry Jesus's cross. As Jesus walks through the streets of Jerusalem, he quotes from the prophet Hosea, prophesying a future of terror (23:30), possibly referring to the destruction of Jerusalem in 70 CE.

Jesus is to be crucified along with two criminals, as prophesied in Isaiah 53:12, although Luke seeks to avoid the implication that he was a criminal himself, referring to them as '*two others also, who were criminals*' (23:32). Jesus utters the famous words of forgiveness against those who have sought his death: '*Father, forgive them, for they do not know what they are doing*' (23:34). He is nailed to the cross and offered wine-vinegar to drink as a painkiller. In fulfilment of the prophecy written in Psalm 22:18, the soldiers draw lots for Jesus's clothes and the crowds mock him and make fun of the fact that he will not save himself. Above him reads a notice, '*This is the King of the Jews*' (23:38), an ironic taunt by Pilate to those who have apparently sought the death of their king. One of the two criminals (traditionally called Zoathan and Chammatha) crucified next to Jesus seems to understand who Jesus really is and asks Jesus to remember him when he comes into his kingdom. Jesus's reply highlights the nature of God's love and forgiveness for all who believe: '*Today you will be with me in paradise*' (23:42). This episode is unique to Luke's Gospel, and significantly highlights his theme of seeking and saving the lost. Even on the cross Jesus continues to reach out to those who come to him in an attitude of true repentance, irrespective of their background. Frank Matera (1986) observes: *'Luke portrays Jesus as the Messiah who refuses to save himself, but continues to save others even at the moment of death'*.

Darkness covers the whole land from the sixth hour (12 noon) and lasts until the ninth hour (3pm). This may be symbolic of the darkness that fell on Egypt in the Old Testament during the time of Moses as a sign of God's displeasure (Exodus 10:22). Jesus dies at the ninth hour and the curtain in the Temple is torn in two. Again, there is profound significance here. The most sacred part of the Temple was called the Holy of Holies and it was protected with a great curtain. It was the place of the presence of God and the curtains were there to prevent God and humanity from meeting each other; they formed a barrier between God and his people. The tearing of the curtain, on the death of Jesus, meant that the barrier was no longer needed, because salvation was now freely available to all.

Luke avoids the ambiguity of the cry from Psalm 22:1 used by Matthew and Mark. Jesus's last words are *'Father, into your hands I commit my spirit'* (23:46), a quotation from Psalm 31:5 and, interestingly, one that Jewish mothers commonly taught their children as a prayer before they went to sleep at night. The centurion watching identifies Jesus not as the Son of God, as in Matthew and Mark, but as an innocent martyr. As Jesus dies, the centurion praises God. Luke continues his theme of Jesus's innocence, showing the dying Jesus as, in Matera's words, *'The suffering righteous one who peacefully entrusts his soul to the Father'*. None of the disciples were present when Jesus died, but some of the women followers, who have been faithful throughout the whole of Jesus's ministry, are there.

Pilate agrees to let a prominent Jew, Joseph of Arimathea, bury the body of Jesus in a tomb cut out of rock. The body could not be buried with the proper ritual at this time because the Sabbath was soon to begin following the Commandment in Exodus 20:8: *'Remember the Sabbath day by keeping it holy'*, and Jews were not allowed to do work (i.e. burying a body) on the Sabbath. The body is buried temporarily; the proper procedures will be carried out when the Sabbath is over and the women, obedient to the Jewish rituals, rest until they can anoint Jesus's body.

4 The resurrection (chapter 24)

The resurrection, as well as the cross, was an indispensable part of the arrival of God's kingdom.
(Drane, 1999)

The Gospel does not describe the resurrection, but instead begins on the Sunday morning, with three women, named as Mary Magdalene, Mary, the mother of James, and Joanna, coming to the tomb to anoint the body of Jesus with spices. At the tomb they see that the stone has been rolled away. Then two men wearing shining white robes (presumably angels) ask them why they are looking for one who is living, among the dead. This is the heart of the matter — Jesus is not dead, therefore cannot be found among the dead. The angels tell them that Jesus has risen and remind the women, who have bowed their heads in fright, of Jesus's own prediction: *'Remember how he told you, while he was still with you in Galilee: The Son of Man must be delivered into the hands of sinful men, be crucified and on the third day be raised again'* (24:7). The women go to the disciples to tell them, but the men do not seem to believe them. However, Peter rushes to the tomb to see for himself. He sees only the strips of linen that Jesus was wrapped in, and goes away, wondering. The disciples seem to forget or not understand what Jesus told them earlier.

Luke alone proceeds to tell a long narrative that confirms the truth of the women's story. On the road to Emmaus, the risen Jesus meets two believers, one of whom is called Cleopas. They do not recognise him at first and he talks to them at some length about the destiny of the Christ: *'Did not the Christ have to suffer these things and then enter his glory?'* (24:26). Finally, as he breaks bread with them, they see who he is, before he *'disappeared from their sight'* (24:31). It is interesting that they do not recognise Jesus for so long, but it is important that their spiritual eyes are kept shut until they are able to grasp the significance of what he has to tell them. Luke records that *'beginning with Moses and all the prophets he interpreted to them in all the scriptures the things concerning himself'* (24:27). Only then are they able to understand that his death has not been a tragic accident, but a carefully crafted part of the divine plan, and they are freed to recognise him in the light of their new understanding.

Jesus later appears to the remaining eleven inner-circle disciples. (How interesting that the first appearance has been to outer-circle disciples.) They are afraid at first, but they touch him and are convinced. They are filled with joy and, at last, Jesus is able to open their minds *'so they could understand the scriptures'* (24:45). He explains how his mission has fulfilled the prophecies: *'This is what is written; the Christ will suffer and rise from the dead on the third day and repentance and forgiveness of sins will be preached in his name to all nations, beginning at Jerusalem. You are my witnesses of these things'* (24:46–8).

Finally, Jesus leads his disciples out into Bethany; he blesses them and is taken up into heaven (the Ascension). The disciples return to Jerusalem with great joy. Drane (1999) observes: *'Without the resurrection, the cross might have been an interesting theological talking point, but would have been powerless to have any lasting effect on the lives of ordinary people'*. The scene is set for the early church to be born, and it will begin where the Gospel started, in Jerusalem, as the Apostles wait for the Holy Spirit to come upon them.

Summary

- Jesus enters Jerusalem openly and in a symbolic manner, welcoming the time of his **passion**. The crowd's initial acknowledgement of him turns to open hostility as the passion narrative progresses. The **cleansing of the Temple** serves as the catalyst for his arrest, and the hostility of the authorities, which reaches a climax in the passion, is probably an accurate reflection of the prevailing political climate. In a series of provocative teachings, Jesus makes clear that his rejection by the Jewish authorities is the culmination of Israel's history of rejection of God's messengers. Even the disciples fail to appreciate how close is Jesus's death, but Luke adds a note of cosmic drama, ascribing Judas's decision to betray Jesus to Satan, who has entered into him.
- The **Last Supper** has all the features of a Passover meal, but acquires new significance as Jesus reinterprets the elements as his body and blood, symbols of the new exodus which his death will provide. Luke does not make clear whether Jesus himself

participates in the supper or only presides. The Lucan account includes an extra cup and extended sayings on the eschatological expectation expressed in the meal. Jesus has already prayed for Peter to stand firm after the shattering experience of denying him, and warns the disciples that with his death they must be ready for opposition. Whether he intended that they should use violence is ambiguous.

- He faces his **arrest** with quiet acceptance, making clear that it is in fulfilment of the divine plan. He is **tried** before the Sanhedrin on spurious counts, in a clearly illegal trial. **Pilate** is not convinced that the false charges Jesus faces deserve the death penalty, and attempts to release him, appealing to Herod Antipas who confirms his judgment. Ultimately Pilate is forced to give way to political pressure from the Jewish authorities.
- The **crucifixion** narrative is full of symbolism and use of the Old Testament to emphasise that Jesus's death is the culmination of the divine plan of salvation, although brought about by Jesus's enemies. Luke sustains key themes throughout: Jesus's **innocence** and his **saving of the lost**.
- Luke's account of the **resurrection** narrative draws on his own traditions, and what would appear to be a very fluid resurrection tradition from the early church. The long Emmaus Road narrative serves to place Jesus's death firmly within the divine plan and culminates in a joyful acceptance of the risen Christ. Luke's Gospel alone records the Ascension, after which the disciples wait in Jerusalem for the Holy Spirit.

Exam watch

Luke's passion and resurrection narratives are full of wonderful detail and fascinating cameos, so make sure you are fully aware of them and can show how they serve to offer the reader a distinctive look at the death of Jesus. Ensure that you are aware too of how the passion narrative grows naturally out of the theology of the Gospel as a whole. As ever, avoid the pitfall of endless storytelling.

Review questions

1 (a) Discuss the teaching of Jesus concerning the nature of salvation.
  (b) Assess the importance of the resurrection for the author of Luke's Gospel.
2 (a) For what reasons did Jesus come into conflict with the Jewish authorities?
  (b) Assess the view that, in Luke's Gospel, it was the Jewish, rather than Roman, authorities which were responsible for the death of Jesus.
3 Examine and comment critically upon the religious symbolism and significance of the accounts of the crucifixion and resurrection narratives.
4 What can be learned about the nature of salvation and eternal life from the death and resurrection of Jesus?

Topic 4

The Fourth Gospel

A The nature of the Gospel

1 Origin

1.1 Authorship

Arguments in favour of apostolic authorship

From the second century, the Fourth Gospel has been said to be 'according to John' and there is, therefore, a long Christian tradition that the Apostle John, the son of Zebedee, was in some way responsible for its writing, either personally or by giving his authority to the writer of it. The Gospel is regarded as John's testimony to the life and teaching of Jesus Christ. This is crucial, for if the Gospel is indeed the testimony of one of the original Twelve Apostles, then it carries great authority, since the Apostles were those who knew Christ in a far deeper way than anyone else, and were presumably eyewitnesses to a significant proportion of his ministry.

Let us therefore begin by looking at the evidence for and against the view that with the Gospel was written by, or under the authority of, **John the Apostle**, brother of James, son of Zebedee. There is no better place to start such an investigation than with the words of Archbishop William Temple, who wrote in *Readings in St John's Gospel*: '*I regard as self-condemned any theory about the origin of the Gospel which fails to find a very close connection between it and John the son of Zebedee. The combination of internal and external evidence is overwhelming on this point.*'

Internal evidence

If John the Apostle were the author, then he would have been an eyewitness to the events of Jesus's life. There are several indications within the text of the Gospel itself that the author was, indeed, such an eyewitness. Three particular examples stand out.

1 In chapter 18 the author records Jesus's questioning by the High Priest; this was a private meeting and Peter had to wait outside (18:16), but 'the other disciple' was allowed in. The passages at 18:19–24 appear to be an eyewitness account of the meeting — presumably written by this 'other disciple'. Was this John?

2 In chapter 19 the writer seems to know a great deal of the detail surrounding the trial before Pilate. His account includes the smallest of details, indicating that he had witnessed them for himself. For instance, he records that Pilate '...*brought Jesus out and*

sat down on the judge's seat at a place known as the Stone Pavement' (19:13).

3 In 21:11, the author not only notes that the disciples had made a large catch of fish, but is even able to give the exact number — 153 (21:11). This is probably something only an eyewitness would have known.

Going a stage further, the Gospel seems to provide evidence that the author was, like John, a Jew. Some scholars have claimed that the Gospel has a Jewish character and contains many Jewish references, such as at 2:6: *'Now six stone jars were standing there, for the Jewish rites of Purification, each holding twenty or thirty gallons.'* Moreover, the author is also, possibly, a native of Jerusalem, for he seems to have a good knowledge of the geography of Jerusalem and the surrounding areas. For example, he describes in detail the setting of the pool at Bethesda *'…which is surrounded by five coloured colonnades'* (5:2).

More importantly, the author seems to know certain facts that only a disciple of Jesus could have known. He describes precisely the setting of Jesus's final supper with his followers — details that could only have been known by one who was there: *'so he got up from the meal, took off his outer clothing, and wrapped a towel round his waist'* (13:4). Similarly: *'One of his disciples, whom Jesus loved, was lying close to the bosom of Jesus; so Simon Peter beckoned to him and said, "Tell us who it is of whom he speaks"'* (13:24). In the resurrection appearances likewise, the writer highlights detail only a disciple would know: *'And he breathed on them and said, "Receive the Holy Spirit"'* (20:22). Finally, and possibly most importantly, the Gospel itself declares that the writer is a disciple — the one following behind Peter and Jesus during their post-resurrection conversation: *'This is the disciple who testifies to these things and who wrote them down'* (21:24).

External evidence

John the Apostle, as we have seen, has been identified as the author of the Fourth Gospel since earliest times. In the late second century, Irenaeus (140–210 CE), the Bishop of Lyons, in his book *Against Heresies*, actually declared that the 'witness' behind the Gospel was *'John, the disciple of the Lord who reclined on His breast and himself issued the Gospel at Ephesus'.* He claimed that his information came from a very reliable source, Polycarp, the Bishop of Smyra, who, in turn, was said to have heard this from John himself. Clement of Alexandria, also writing in the late second century, spoke of John as having written a *'spiritual gospel'* and in the anti-Marcionite prologue Papias, a disciple of John, claimed that he had written the Gospel from John's dictation. Furthermore, Polycrates, the Bishop of Ephesus, said in a letter to Victor, the bishop of Rome, in 190 CE that the Gospel was written by *'John, who reclined on the breast of the Lord, was a witness and teacher'.* However, these claims, though interesting, may not be totally reliable, since John the Apostle had rejected Marcion not only on the grounds of heresy but also because the Gnostics were keen to associate John Zebedee with the Fourth Gospel in order to lend authority to what they regarded as a Gnostic interpretation of Christianity.

In more recent times, scholars and archaeologists have uncovered new evidence concerning the authorship. The **Muratorian Fragment**, dating from 170 CE, gives a list of books regarded as Holy Scriptures and mentions that John approved the writing of the Gospel. The Codex Toletanus, a tenth-century manuscript of the Latin Vulgate at

Madrid, states that the Gospel '...*was given to the churches in Asia by John.*' Finally, Robinson (1993), suggested that John the Apostle wrote a first draft and that the Prologue and final chapter were added by the early church, and Tasker (1960) suggested that John, if not the actual author, may have told his story to another person, who wrote it down.

Arguments against apostolic authorship

There are good reasons for suggesting that John the Apostle may not, in fact, be the author of the Fourth Gospel. There are two main grounds for objection:

1 Irenaeus claimed that John lived in Ephesus until the time of the reign of the Emperor Trajan (98–117 CE). If this were indeed the case, then John the Apostle would have been very old by that time, probably over 90. Would his memory have been reliable?

2 Tradition states that John was martyred, along with his brother James, about four years after the death of Jesus (Acts 12:2), which was well before Trajan's time.

It is also possible that the text itself offers evidence against his authorship. Some of the events depicted are different to the sequence in the Synoptic Gospels (e.g. cleansing of the Temple), suggesting that the author was not, after all, an eyewitness, although this, of course, assumes that the synoptic dating is correct. Moreover, some of the facts recorded in the Gospel are wrong. For instance, in 6:1 the author notes that the Sea of Galilee was also called the Sea of Tiberius and yet this name was not known at the time of Jesus, suggesting much later authorship. Similarly, there is a problem with the name of the High Priest. In 18:13 the author names Caiaphas as the High Priest, yet in 18:19, the author says, when referring to Jesus's questioning by Annas, that he is the High Priest, before correcting this by referring again to Caiaphas in 18:24.

There are other problems. An eyewitness account of Jesus's questioning by the High Priest suggests that there was a disciple who '*was known to the High Priest*' and was able to be with Jesus during the questioning (18:15). However, if John was just a fisherman, was he educated enough to write the Gospel and, moreover, would he have had access to the High Priest himself? Finally, the claim in the Gospel in 21:24 that the author is an Apostle, traditionally interpreted to be John, could be unreliable, since many scholars believe that this chapter is not part of the original text, but is part of an epilogue, added after the compilation of the Gospel.

Arguments in favour of other candidates for authorship

If not John the Apostle, then who else could have written the Gospel? Scholars have suggested a number of possible candidates:

❖ **The Beloved Disciple** — John is the only disciple not specifically named in the Gospel. There are, however, mysterious references to a disciple known only as '*the disciple whom Jesus loved*' (13:23), more commonly referred to as the Beloved Disciple. He is the disciple referred to in 21:24, and he is also present at the Last Supper (13:23), the Cross (19:26 & 35), at the empty tomb (20:2) and at the resurrection appearances (21:20). He is, therefore, a witness to all that has happened. Some scholars have suggested that the Beloved Disciple might be John himself, whilst others think he may be either Nicodemus, or Lazarus, whom Jesus raised from the dead and who was referred to in the cryptic way, '*Lord, the one you love is sick*' (11:3).

B. F. Westcott (2001) argued that the author was a Palestinian Jew, an eyewitness and a disciple, and deduced therefore that the Beloved Disciple was John, since the others are specifically named. Others have suggested that the Beloved Disciple may be a description of an ideal disciple (rather than a real one), although Tasker (1960) rejects this on the grounds that '*...this view is plausible on the wholly unwarranted assumption that the incidents in which he plays such a specific and important part are imaginary*'. Joseph Grassi (1992) observes that the real significance of the Beloved Disciple is the insight he has into Jesus's ministry to which the author owes his inspiration: '*He is a mystic and creative genius who is able to look deeply into externals and find a deep meaning in the miracles of Jesus as well as in the "ordinary" events of his life. He will see in them the fruition of a secret divine plan found especially in the scriptures*'.

+ **John the Elder** — The early historian Eusebius quoted from Papias, the Bishop of Hierapolis, who spoke of a man called John the Elder, who lived in Ephesus from around 70 CE to 146 CE. Papias had suggested that this John was a more likely author since he lived through the reign of Trajan, and the two New Testament Epistles called 2 John and 3 John appear to have been written by 'the Elder'. However, neither of these epistles bears any significant similarity to the Gospel, and it is the First Epistle of John, which is anonymous, which is strikingly like the Gospel in theology and style.

+ **John Mark** — John Mark lived in Jerusalem at the time of Jesus, although he was probably several years younger than Christ and the disciples. He came from a priestly family and had a good knowledge of the Temple and may have had access to the High Priest. He was a wealthy man and accompanied Paul on his first missionary journey (before, it seems, causing a split between Paul and Barnabas) and was, apparently, known to the disciples (Acts 12:12–15). He may have been the mysterious young man who fled naked from Gethsemane when Jesus was arrested (Mark 14:51). However, he would still have been very old, probably 80, at the time of Trajan, and it is a rather tenuous inductive argument which leads to the conclusion that he was the author of the Gospel.

+ **Community authorship** — Recently, scholars such as Raymond Brown and J. L. Martyn have turned away from the idea of trying to establish the identity of an individual author of the Gospel, and have, instead, looked at the role of the community behind it. For instance, in 1:14 and 3:11 the expression 'we' is used, suggesting a writer who is reflecting the life and experience of a community which had been oppressed and rejected by Judaism and the synagogue for their acceptance of Jesus as Messiah. Most significant of all is 21:24, which says '*We know that his testimony is true*', apparently linking the Johannine community with the testimony of the Beloved Disciple. The Gospel might therefore be the work of a community which revered and preserved the witness of the Beloved Disciple, whether he was John or an anonymous figure. Bultmann (1971) goes further and suggests that an ecclesiastical redactor was behind the final editorial work. The Fourth Gospel was produced, it is claimed, from the life and experience of a community which had moved away from Judaism and was recording its beliefs and experiences through a reliable witness and writer.

Ultimately, however, one is perhaps forced to conclude that it is impossible to establish for certain who the author of the Gospel actually was, since the evidence is, at best, inconclusive. As Marsh (1968) notes, '*The identity of the author must remain, like that of the beloved disciple, wrapped in anonymity*'.

1.2 The dating of the Gospel

Just as there is a mystery surrounding the identity of the author of the Fourth Gospel, so too is it a mystery at what date it was written. We cannot date the Gospel with accuracy, since all we have is a range of circumstantial evidence, and yet a knowledge of dating would contribute significantly to an understanding of the Gospel, its background and its readership.

Arguments in favour of a late first-century dating

The majority of ancient manuscripts suggest that the Fourth Gospel was the last of the Gospels and, indeed, Clement of Alexandria wrote in 212 CE that the Fourth Gospel was the final one to be written. If this is so, and the author was John the Apostle, then, given his age, it must date from no later than the end of the first century.

Internal evidence seems to support early dating. In 9:22 and 16:2, the author speaks of Christians being expelled from the synagogues for belief in Jesus as Messiah. From 85 to 90 CE a series of Jewish–Christian talks were held under Rabbi Gamaliel, leading to what was known as the **Synagogue Benediction**, comprising a formal excommunication of those who dissented from Judaism. It seems that the author of the Gospel may have been aware of this as a current issue for the readers at that time, although not necessarily at the time of Jesus. This is an example of the way in which the Gospel is written on two levels: at one level it records the life and ministry of Jesus — what he did and said and how people reacted to him — but on the other it reflects the experiences of a community living and worshipping some 40–50 years after his death.

With regard to the style of writing itself, the Gospel arguably contains ideas similar to first-century Essene writings, and it may have been written in Aramaic and translated much later into Greek, explaining some of the clumsy expressions. This is particularly seen in the Prologue, where there are awkward-sounding expressions such as 1:3: '*...all things were made through him, and without him was not anything made that was made*'.

Arguments in favour of second-century authorship

The evidence for second-century authorship is even more circumstantial, although there is some suggestion that the Fourth Gospel was used by second-century Gnostics, including Ptolemaeus. Equally, it is possible that the writers of the *Gospel of Peter* and the Valentinian *Gospel of Truth* around 150 CE use vague references to aspects of the Fourth Gospel in their works. Finally, there are no references in historical records to the Fourth Gospel before 150 CE, which suggests that it was not in circulation before the beginning of the second century.

However, arguments which favour this late dating tend to rely on theories which predate the discovery of the Dead Sea Scrolls in 1947. This vital discovery led to what is termed the 'new look' on the Fourth Gospel, prior to which it was thought that the Gospel was influenced primarily by Hellenism. The Scrolls revealed that much terminology and philosophy that had been thought to be exclusively Hellenistic had already infiltrated Jewish ways of thinking in the first century. Hence, it was possible that the Gospel could have been written in the first century, and reflected a Jewish culture far more prominently than a Hellenistic one.

Arguments in favour of an early date

Robinson (1993) radically proposed an early date for the Fourth Gospel, suggesting that it was in fact the first, rather than the last, to be written. Proposing a date as early as 50 CE, he claimed that the differences between the Fourth Gospel and the Synoptics might render it more, rather than less, historically reliable, and that no Apostle would draw on other sources for their own account of the life of Jesus. Furthermore, Barrett (1975) observed that the messianic fervour evident in the account of the feeding of the five thousand — *'Perceiving that they were about to come and take him by force to make him king, Jesus withdrew again to the mountain by himself'* (6:15) — would have died out after the destruction of the Temple in 70 CE. However, these interesting suggestions may be countered by the style of the Gospel, which appears to be highly reflective and more in keeping with second-generation Christianity, meeting the needs of a community that felt significantly removed from the time of Jesus and the first disciples.

Where did the Fourth Gospel originate?

There are two main possibilities:

÷ It may have come from **Ephesus**, the capital of the Roman province of Asia, a city used as a central base by Paul for his mission and which had a thriving Christian community. Irenaeus said that it was the town where John the Apostle lived and the language of the Gospel contains phrases common to the area.

÷ The alternative suggestion is the city of **Antioch**, a view supported by the Syrian writer Ephraim Syrus (306–370 CE), who called this city 'the home of the Gospel'. It was the third city of the Roman Empire and was the place where the followers of Christ were first called 'Christians' (Acts 11:26).

Summary

- Most scholars favour the view that the author of the Fourth Gospel is **John the Apostle**, Son of Zebedee. The internal evidence tends to support this. There are several eyewitness references and details of conversations that could only have been known by an Apostle who was actually there, e.g. the Last Supper and resurrection appearances. The Gospel also has a Jewish character and there are local geographical references. And there is a declaration in 21:24 that a disciple is the author. External evidence supporting John the Apostle includes the testimony of early writers and archaeological evidence such as the **Muratorian Fragment**.

- However, evidence against the author being John the Apostle are the extreme age he would have been when the Gospel was written and the fact that, as a fisherman, he may have lacked the education to write such a Gospel.

- Another possible candidate could be the **Beloved Disciple**, an enigmatic character who is not named specifically in the Gospel but who could have been John the Apostle. Some scholars, though, favour either **John the Elder** or **John Mark** as the author. It has also been suggested that the Gospel may have been the work of an early-church community.

- The evidence in favour of a first-century dating for the Gospel comes from the testimony of **Clement of Alexandria** and a number of Essene-type references in the Gospel itself. Evidence for a second-century dating revolves around the considerable number of possible Gnostic references in the text. Arguments for an early date rely on suggesting that the Gospel was written before the Synoptics and reflects a date prior to the destruction of the Temple.

- The Gospel probably came from **Ephesus**, where there was a strong Christian community, although there is some support for the notion that it stemmed from **Antioch**.

Exam watch

Authorship and date form a very popular examination question. As an area of great scholarly debate and controversy, these matters offer very good opportunities to demonstrate skilled argument and critical awareness. But beware — although this is a popular area for examiners, many candidates fail to do themselves justice because they do not address the question set and instead write all they know about authorship and date. This results in answers which are far too general — a regurgitating of notes rather than a properly constructed examination answer. To do well, try to ensure that you build up the right kind of argument to support the authorship credentials or otherwise of the candidates. Use the evidence in the biblical text carefully and make sure you can cite relevant views of scholars. Don't just make sweeping generalisations that you cannot justify later.

Review questions

1 Who is the strongest candidate as the author of the Fourth Gospel? Why?
2 What were the major influences on the Gospel writer?
3 Assess the textual evidence that supports the view that the author was an eyewitness.
4 (a) Examine the evidence for and against the view that the author of the Fourth Gospel was John the Apostle.
 (b) How successful have scholars been in fixing a date for the authorship of the Fourth Gospel?
5 *'The author of the Fourth Gospel was a Jewish eyewitness.'* Examine and consider critically this claim.

2 Influences

2.1 Greek influences on the Gospel

Greek, or Hellenistic, influences played a very important part in the formation of the Fourth Gospel. Although the Middle East was dominated by the Roman Empire, the most important cultural influences were Greek, due to the legacy left by the conquests of Alexander the Great, 300 years earlier. At the time of Jesus, most educated people could speak Greek, allowing the Christian message to reach educated people throughout the known world. There are many strands of Greek thought identifiable in the Gospel:

+ **Platonism** — Platonic philosophy taught that this world of time and space would pass away and that behind it was an eternal and changeless world — the world above. The Hellenistic-Jewish philosopher Philo, for instance, said that the aim of religious people was to bring their life into relationship with reality and thus achieve immortality by bridging the gulf between divine ideas and the physical world. Such teaching was utilised by the author in the Prologue to the Gospel, where he portrays the ***Logos*** as the image of God, also found in humanity, which will enable humankind to see the ultimate truth and reach a relationship with God.

+ **Stoicism** was developed by **Zeno** around 300 BCE. It was a philosophy based on the belief that the world depends on reason (*Logos*) and those who wish to lead a good life must follow their conscience, which is inspired by reason. For the Stoic, reason, or the *Logos*, was God and, in some sense, the universe. The seeds of the divine *Logos* are found in the minds of people, but the individual would have to choose to do something about it. In the Gospel, the author suggests that the special relationship between God and humanity is achieved when humanity lives according to the *Logos*.

+ **Gnostics** believed that there were two worlds: the world of the spirit, where God is, and which is pure and holy; and the world of physical matter, where humanity dwells and which is evil and corrupt. Humanity's only escape is in death, when the soul leaves the physical world behind. However, for Gnostics, only those who have the divine light will reach the spiritual world and this spark comes with knowledge (***gnosis***). The Fourth Gospel uses several of these ideas — light/dark, evil/good, physical/spiritual, flesh/spirit, above/below — that later found expression in Gnostic literature. However, it is not a Gnostic Gospel since, for example, it does not suggest that humanity is saved by knowledge, but only by Jesus.

2.2 Jewish influences on the Gospel

The Essenes believed in a dualism between good and evil, light and dark, and saw themselves as Sons of Light, the true people of God, who would one day fight the final battle against the forces of evil. The Fourth Gospel contains a considerable amount of material reflecting Essene ideas — for example: '*Now is the judgment of this world, now shall the ruler of this world be cast out*' (12:31) and '*While you have the light, believe in the light, that you may become sons of light*' (12:36) — although it does not suggest that only Sons of Light would receive salvation. Salvation is potentially available to all, although not all will choose to avail themselves of it.

The most significant evidence of Jewish influence in the Gospel is the author's use of the Old Testament. It seems that he knew it well, sometimes using his own translation into Greek, and sometimes utilising the Septuagint (the Greek Old Testament). Apart from specific quotations from the Old Testament — for example 12:15, which cites Zechariah 9:9, and 19:36, which quotes Exodus 12:46 — there are many allusions to it. The author makes veiled references that would only be picked up by a reader who had a good knowledge of the Old Testament, but which illuminate the significance of the Gospel as a whole. A classic example of this technique is at 3:14 — *'And as Moses lifted up the serpent in the wilderness, so must the Son of Man be lifted up...'*. This clear allusion to Numbers 21:9 sets the scene for the Fourth Evangelist's whole theology of the cross and fits in with the theme of replacement (Jesus superseding the Old Testament) which runs through the Gospel.

The author also makes use of his knowledge of the Jewish festivals, and structures key events around them. Three Passovers set the scene for important moments in Jesus's ministry — the cleansing of the Temple, the feeding of the five thousand, and Jesus's crucifixion — and at the Feast of Tabernacles, which featured symbols of light and water, Jesus declares himself to be living water (7:37–9) and the light of the world (8:12). Other events echo Old Testament themes and settings: the Samaritan woman meets Jesus at Jacob's well; the paralysed man is healed at the pool with five porticoes (symbolic of the Law?); Nicodemus represents old Israel that must be reborn of the spirit, as prophesied in Ezekiel 37.

Interestingly, however, the Jews themselves are generally presented in a negative light in the Fourth Gospel, at best as ignorant and stumbling, and, at worst, as bitter enemies of Jesus (and the Johannine community). Robert Kysar (1993) writes: *'Any person who refuses to accept the human identity proposed by Christ in the Gospel is for the Evangelist a "Jew"'*. The Jews, therefore, are those in the Gospel who refuse to see that in Jesus is a fulfilment of their heritage, which they must accept if they are to enter into the promises which God will make good to all those who *'are born, not of blood, nor of the will of the flesh, nor of the will of man, but of God'* (1:13).

2.3 The purpose of the Gospel

All the Gospels were written for the purpose of telling the 'good news' of Jesus Christ. Yet there is more, and the author of the Fourth Gospel makes his particular purpose clear in 20:31: *'But these are written that you may believe that Jesus is the Christ, the Son of God, and that by believing you may have life in his name.'* An examination of the textual narrative shows how far this purpose is borne out.

(a) *'Jesus is the Christ...'*

The author frequently uses Old Testament prophecies to show how the work of the promised Messiah will be fulfilled in Jesus. In particular, the author highlights the fact that the salvation that Jesus will bestow will be the climax of the Jewish religion. This is seen in the following incidents:

- Jesus cleansing the Temple (2:13–17) — a promised Messianic action, reflected in Psalm 69:9: *'Zeal for your house will consume me.'*
- The healing at the pool, which takes place on the Sabbath (5:1–16).
- It is as the Messiah that the disciples become aware of him (1:41, 49).
- As the Messiah he shows himself to the Samaritan woman (4:25–6).
- There are Messianic overtones when he feeds the people (6:1–15).
- He makes a triumphal entry into Jerusalem riding a donkey in fulfilment of prophecy (12:12–19), reflecting Zechariah 9:9: *'Do not be afraid, O daughter of Zion; see, your king is coming, seated on a donkey's colt.'*

Moreover, the author reminds us constantly of the Jewish authorities' refusal to accept him as the Messiah (5:18, 7:47, 10:33, 19:7). This is contrasted with the disciples' acknowledgement of him (1:41, 1:49, 6:68–9, 7:41).

(b) 'The Son of God...'

There are several important references to Christ as the Son of God. At the very start, John the Baptist testifies that *'I have seen and have borne witness that this is the Son of God'* (1:34). Throughout the Gospel, Jesus refers to his intimate relationship to God. He was sent by God to accomplish a unique task; he knows the Father's will and he and the Father are one (3:35, 5:19–20, 8:4, 14:10). These claims incur the charge of blasphemy levelled against him by the Jews, leading to his crucifixion: *'We have a law, and according to that law he must die, because he claimed to be the Son of God'* (19:7).

(c) '...that by believing you may have life in his name'

In the Gospel, 'life' means 'eternal life' and the author shows that eternal life comes from believing in Christ. Such belief comes from knowing who Christ is, what he teaches and the work that he has done to accomplish salvation. Thus:

- He lays down his life for the sheep (10:11).
- He is *'the Lamb of God, who takes away the sin of the world'* (1:29).
- He is lifted up and draws all to him (12:32).
- Those who accept him receive the gift of eternal life (3:16).
- He dedicates himself and offers himself as a sacrifice, and, in doing so, makes it possible for others to consecrate their lives to God (17:9).
- He sacrifices himself in order that humanity may have life (12:24, 10:10). Tasker (1960) notes: *'His whole incarnate life is, in fact, meaningless apart from "the hour" to which it is inevitably moving, and that hour is none other than the hour of His passion'*.

However, scholars have concluded that the purpose of the author of the Fourth Gospel may be more than these things. There are other possible purposes too, which merit examination.

Is it a 'spiritual Gospel'?

Last of all, John, perceiving that the external facts had been made plain in the Gospels, being urged by his friends and inspired by the Spirit, composed a spiritual Gospel.

(Clement of Alexandria)

Some scholars have suggested that the author of the Fourth Gospel went beyond writing a historical narrative of the facts of Jesus's life, and instead wrote a spiritual Gospel, where the message lay not in the facts as recorded but in their allegorical interpretation. The purpose of this was not to write an accurate biography of Jesus's life but to express vital christological truths about Jesus in order to lead people into faith. Westcott (2001), comparing the Fourth Gospel with Luke's Gospel, suggested: *'The real difference is that the earliest Gospel contained the fundamental facts and words which experience afterwards interpreted, while the latest Gospel reveals the facts in the light of their interpretation'*.

It is claimed that, for the author of the Fourth Gospel, the important thing was to lead his readers into the belief that Jesus was the Son of God and that, through his name, they might have eternal life. This is highlighted in 10:37–8: *'Do not believe me unless I do what my Father does. But if I do it, even though you do not believe me, believe the miracles, that you might know and understand that the Father is in me, and I in the Father.'*

In order to achieve this purpose, the author makes alterations to the historical sequence of events in Jesus's life. He does this to highlight important theological points. For example, in the Fourth Gospel, the cleansing of the Temple occurs at the start of Jesus's ministry (2:12–25), whereas in the Synoptic Gospels it occurs near the end. The author does this in order to emphasise the theological point that Jesus has come to bring a new era of fulfilment that is characterised by:

÷ an inner worship with the Father and the Son (6:56–7)
÷ worship in spirit and truth (4:24)
÷ Jesus as the place where humanity meets with God (1:51, 2:21)

The author also alters the timing of Jesus's death. In the Synoptic Gospels, Jesus shares the Last Supper with the disciples on the Day of Passover, but in the Fourth Gospel, events are brought forward by 24 hours, and Jesus dies on the Day of Preparation, just as the Passover lambs are slaughtered. The author does this to develop the theme that Jesus is the perfect Passover lamb, which he brings to a conclusion on the cross, when Jesus's legs, like those of the Passover lamb, are not broken (19:33, 36).

In the same way, the author uses Jesus's death on the cross to emphasise the theme of fulfilment of Scripture. Thus, in 19:38 we read: *'Later, knowing that all was now completed, and so that the Scripture would be fulfilled, Jesus said, "I am thirsty".'* It seems unlikely that Jesus, dying on the Cross, would say this simply to fulfil Scripture, but the author uses this incident to highlight his theological point.

The author also seems to have the purpose of making it clear to believers exactly who Jesus really was. From the very start, the author emphasises Jesus's divinity (unlike the Synoptic Gospels, where there are several incidents in which Jesus tells his followers not to say who he is — the so-called Messianic Secret). Throughout the Gospel, the author makes Jesus's identity known, both through Jesus's own words (5:26, 6:54, 10:25–6) and from his actions and authority (5:17–18). He also uses witnesses to support this theme, for example John the Baptist (1:29) and the Samaritan woman (4:25–6). For believers, the author leaves no room for doubt about the divinity of Jesus. This is made particularly clear in the crucifixion narratives, where the author emphasises the relationship between Jesus and the Father and shows how Jesus is in control of all the events leading up to the cross: *'Now my heart is troubled, and what shall I say? "Father, save me from this hour?" No, it was for this very reason I came to this hour. Father, glorify your name!'* (12:27–8).

Are there other possible purposes?

At the time of the writing of the Gospel, Christianity was expanding into the Gentile world and it was being put before educated people. In certain aspects, the Fourth Gospel appeared to correct many of the false teachings about Jesus which had sprung up; that Jesus was just a good or a special man. It also addressed many of the great philosophical arguments of the day, breaking away from primitive and superstitious ideas and offering a new paradigm. In particular, it seemed to counteract the doctrines of **Docetism**. The Docetists (from the Greek *doke*, which means 'it seems') suggested that Jesus was a phantom by which God revealed himself, but not a real person. This prompted Ignatius, in his *Epistle to the Trallians*, to argue against them, saying: '*Jesus Christ was truly born, both ate and drank, was truly persecuted under Pontius Pilate, was truly crucified and died in the sight of those in heaven and on earth and under the earth; who also was truly raised from the dead.*'

Irenaeus suggested that the purpose of the Gospel was to oppose Gnosticism, expressing ideas contrary to Gnostic teaching by suggesting that the word actually became flesh (1:14), and that Christ really died and was raised in bodily form (20:20). Tasker (1960) supports this view, saying that 1:14 makes it clear that Jesus was fully human: '*...it is on the true humanity of the Saviour that this evangelist throughout his Gospel lays great stress*'.

Certainly, the author occasionally emphasises Jesus's human qualities: he is weary and thirsty by the well at Sychar (4:6); he spits on the ground when healing the blind man (9:6); he weeps at the tomb of Lazarus (11:35); and he thirsts on the cross (19:28):

The supreme wonder of the incarnation was that He who had come down from heaven was revealing Himself not as a demigod, but as the Son of man without in any way ceasing to be divine; and that the climax of that revelation would be when this Son of man, despised, humiliated and rejected, would be exalted by being lifted up on a cross.

Modern writers such as Lindars and Brown, however, have argued that the Gospel was actually influenced by Gnostic ideas and question whether Gnosticism was the threat Irenaeus suggested it was. Painter (1979), in *John: Witness and Theologian*, said that the main purpose was to bear witness to Christ as the Son of God and he supports this by citing the references in the Prologue and the meetings with Nicodemus, the Samaritan woman and during the Passion narratives. Barrett thought that the Gospel was written for a Jewish church in a Gentile area, whilst Smalley argued that the Gospel has universal appeal, with the emphasis on salvation for all humanity. Finally, Robinson, in *Re-dating the New Testament*, argued that the Gospel was written for the Jews themselves, to convert them to Christianity, whilst Schnackenburg (1980) claimed that it was to encourage secret followers. Both these views are upheld to an extent by the Jewishness of the writing and the recurring theme that Jesus was fulfilling and superseding Judaism.

In conclusion, it might be said that the author seemed to be writing for all believers at all times and places, rather than addressing himself to one group at one time. His emphasis on the spiritual over the historical allowed him to address the real needs of believers throughout the ages.

Summary

- The **purpose** of the Gospel is laid down in 20:31: '*...that you may believe that Jesus is the Christ, the Son of God, and that by believing you may have life in his name.*' This is highlighted in a number of ways: by reference to the Old Testament message of a promised Messiah, by emphasising Jesus's unique relationship to God as Father and Son, and by Jesus's teaching on salvation through him.

- Some scholars have suggested another purpose: that the author has written a **'spiritual gospel'**, which expresses christological truths about the person and nature of Christ and emphasises the importance of worship and the Spirit. This is particularly highlighted in references to the divinity of Christ and his death on the cross.
- Other possible purposes include the notion of the Gospel being a counter to the claims of both **Docetism** and **Gnosticism** and emphasising that Jesus was both fully human and fully divine.

Exam watch

Questions on the purpose of the author can be deceptive and you need to prepare yourself thoroughly. You will need to know about the early Christian community, the cultural and social influences and debates of the time, and the varying and controversial views of scholars. For the most part, questions will focus on general purposes, such as 'telling theological truths about Jesus, rather than historical ones', or 'bringing the good news to the Gentiles'. Make sure that you can back up all your arguments not only with scholars' views, but also with textual evidence.

Review questions

1 What were the major social and cultural influences on the author of the Fourth Gospel?
2 For what reasons may the Fourth Gospel have been written?
3 'The Gospel was written to tell religious rather than historical truths about the life of Jesus.' Examine and comment critically on this view.
4 'The Gospel was written to bring the good news of salvation to the Gentiles.' Discuss and evaluate this view.

B The Prologue

...the preface to the Fourth Gospel, with its movement from the Word to the Son of God, is both an introduction and a conclusion to the whole work. The relation between creation and salvation, prophets and Apostles, history and that beyond history, time and eternity, law and grace, death and life, faith and unbelief — these are the themes of the Fourth Gospel.

(Hoskyns and Davey, 1947)

1 What is the Prologue?

The introduction to the Fourth Gospel, known as the **Prologue** (1:1–18), is regarded by many as the greatest piece of theological writing in Christian literature. It is a work that was designed to appeal to all readers, not just Jews. It contains elements of both Greek and Stoic philosophy which would make the Gospel story meaningful not only to Jews and Christians, but also to the Hellenistic thinkers and the educated minds of the Greek and Roman worlds.

There are many differing views as to what the Prologue actually is. Robinson claims that it is a **later addition** to the Gospel and was put in to bring things to a conclusion. Burney suggests that it is an **Aramaic hymn**, written in poetic style with simple construction and frequent use of the word 'and', which was a common device in Hebrew poetry. Moreover, he argues, it was translated clumsily into Greek (e.g. 1:5) — a sign that it was originally written in Aramaic. Barrett disagrees and argues that the Prologue is in a style unique to John because of its **thematic approach** and use of language and sentences originally written in Greek, which have no Aramaic version (e.g. 1:10).

Stanton speaks of the Prologue as the '*lens*' through which to view the rest of the Gospel, whilst Morna Hooker describes it as a '*key*' which unlocks the Gospel as a whole. It offers the reader an insight into the way in which the Gospel narrative will unfold and a means to avoid the traps of misunderstanding into which the Gospel's characters invariably fall. Everything the reader needs to understand the Gospel narrative, plot and events is provided by the Prologue, and the reader is placed in a unique position, knowing how the story will begin, develop and end, even before the incarnate Jesus has taken his place.

2 The Word (*Logos*)

In the Prologue, the author declares that Jesus Christ is God himself, who came into the world as a human being. The story of Jesus is the story of the *Logos* or Word.

The Prologue starts with the brief story of the *Logos* — its heavenly origin, work alongside God in creation, its incarnation, rejection, and ultimate victory over the darkness of opposition — which is amplified in the text of the Gospel itself. The term '*Logos*' is a useful one, because it allows the author to link together concepts from the **Old Testament**, the Jewish **Rabbinic tradition**, **Hellenistic and Stoic thought** and early Christian theology. In the Prologue, the reader is introduced to the Fourth Evangelist's important **replacement theology** — the perspective that in Jesus all that was previously revealed and experienced in Israel's relationship with God has been transcended and fulfilled, in the sense that the Word has become tangible, empirical flesh.

John brings from Judaism the idea of God's **creative breath** (*ruah*) — his speech, wisdom and purpose, from which creation comes — for in Hebrew thought, when God speaks, things happen. According to Dodd (1968), the Jews identified the Word of God with the **Torah**; the Word was, in a sense, God's wisdom, embodied in the **Law**. The Word gave meaning to life: '*Then God said "Let there be light"; and there was light*' (Genesis 1:3); '*The Lord God formed the man from the dust of the ground and breathed into his nostrils the breath of life, and the man became a living being*' (Genesis 2:7); '*By the word of the Lord were the heavens made*' (Psalm 33:6).

According to Marsh (1968), the author also incorporates the Hellenistic notions of the ideal world and the ideal human — the Gospel is therefore not just a series of interesting stories and incidents, but: '*...a meeting place, in a historic person, at a specific moment in human history, of time and eternity, of God and man, of all that lies beyond history and what takes place in it*'.

The word is not an 'it', but a living and distinct person within the **Trinity** and the one source of true **light**. Without the Word, life is **dark** and existence is meaningless. For the author of the Gospel, the Word or life which is Christ offers more than just physical existence; it is the light and only true source of intellect, understanding and spiritual truth.

The origins of the Word

The Prologue begins with the same words as Genesis 1:1 — 'In the beginning...' — and therefore places the Word with God from the start of all things, before creation itself. In Hellenistic terms, the **Logos** is 'the satisfying rational principle for understanding the universe' (Marsh, 1968). The Word is the eternal purpose of God — it is that which gives meaning to life — and the author is trying to show to the readers the fact that, in Jesus, the whole purpose of God and creation acquires meaning. The Word is, indeed, the source of life and creation. It is a living person; it is life itself: 'Through him all things were made; without him nothing was made that has been made. In him was life...' (John 1:3–4).

Not only that, the **Logos** is the source of light, or **enlightenment** for humanity. He is the true light, which the darkness of the world (represented in the Gospel by Jesus's Jewish opponents) can never put out. Interestingly, the evangelist uses the verb **katabaino**, which can be translated as either 'understand' or 'overcome'; the darkness of the world is unable to overcome the light of the **Logos** because it does not understand it: '...that life was the light of men. The light shines in the darkness, but the darkness has not understood it' (John 1:4–5).

3 John the Baptist

John the Baptist is an enigmatic character, depicted by the author as the one sent from God to announce the coming of the light into the world. The Baptist bridges the gap between the Old Testament and the New — showing humanity how to recognise the Word made flesh. According to the Gospel of Luke, John the Baptist was a relative of Jesus, born at about the same time to an elderly couple called Zechariah and Elizabeth. He grew to adulthood in the wilderness, possibly with the **Essenes**. He was filled with the spirit of God and began his mission around 26 CE when he became a charismatic preacher, calling the people to repent. He dressed in animal skins and baptised people in the River Jordan and many thought he was the Old Testament prophet **Elijah**, returned to earth.

The key issue for the Fourth Evangelist is that 'He came as a witness to testify to the light, so that through him all men might believe' (1:7). John the Baptist offers **testimony** — this was an important legal concept in those times. He is a witness to the light and the testimony of a witness was crucial in establishing truth. Interestingly, this dominates the Fourth Evangelist's presentation of John the Baptist, who, Stanton (1989) observes, is more accurately described as John the Witness than John the Baptist. The Word of God is known through testimony — either from God himself, or from his divinely inspired messenger. The author uses John the Baptist, as an Old Testament-style figure, to show that the message of the Old Testament is now understood. The 'light' of the Scriptures is fulfilled in Christ, the incarnate Word of God.

However, the role of the Baptist in the Fourth Gospel is not entirely straightforward. It is possible that a **polemic** might be at work in the way the evangelist has used his Baptist material — deliberately presenting the figure as one whose role is not to be overestimated as some may have done. Unlike Matthew, the Fourth Evangelist denies the Elijah role to the Baptist, making clear that he is to be understood as no more than a herald for the Messiah: 'He himself was not the light, but he came to testify to the light'

(1:8); 'He confessed, "I am not the Messiah". And they asked him, "What then, are you Elijah?" He said, "I am not"' (1:20–1).

4   The Word Incarnate

Humanity is encouraged to recognise Christ as the **Word Incarnate** — to realise that God is working among his people, helping them to understand and be in the light. However, this is not easy, and the world, living in darkness, has not recognised him. Even his own people, the people of Israel, have failed to recognise the light that is the Messiah: 'He came into the world, and though the world was made through him, the world did not recognise him. He came to his own, but his own did not receive him' (John 1:10–12).

Some did receive him — rather like the Old Testament notion of **the remnant** who stay loyal to God. To these are given the right to become 'children of God' (1:12). This is an important concept. To become children is described not as an act of human sexuality, but as a gift of God. This is to be the essential difference between the Jews — God's chosen people by birth — and Christians, chosen through God's grace. It is not a physical birth, but a spiritual one, achieved through faith in Jesus Christ, although it is anticipated in the Old Testament, when Ezekiel is told by God to breathe on the dry bones of Israel and give them new spiritual life (Ezekiel 37).

Perhaps the most controversial notion in the Prologue concerns the words 'The Word became flesh and made his dwelling among us' (1:14). Here the author is saying that God became human through the Word. This is more than just human *appearance* (as some early Christian heretics tried to claim); it means God actually becomes fully human — with human flesh, blood, emotions and fears. Such an idea would have been unacceptable to the Stoics, who saw the ***Logos*** as a rational principle, rather than a living being. Similarly, in Judaism, the word was God's creative force, but it could not become incarnate as a human being.

Moreover, the notion of 'dwelling' is probably a reference to the Old Testament, where God is said to have descended as a bright cloud to dwell in the '**Tent of Meeting**', to be among his people (Leviticus 9:6). It may also refer to Israel's hope that God would finally come and be tabernacled among his people: 'Oh that you would tear open the heavens and come down...' (Isaiah 64:1).

5   The Law, grace and truth

The author makes it clear that Jesus Christ is the incarnate word of God, which has existed from the beginning — this is the notion of **pre-existence** that runs throughout the Gospel (8:58, 17:5). Moreover, the word becoming flesh is not just for effect or for humanity to marvel at; it is a gift from God to all who believe, a gift which establishes a new relationship between God and humanity, a gift of God's **grace**, his divine favour, shown to man. 'From the fullness of his grace we have all received one blessing after another...' (1:16).

In the final verses of the Prologue, the Evangelist makes a vital reference to the Law: 'For the law was given through Moses; grace and truth come through Jesus Christ' (1:17). This is the key to understanding the Fourth Evangelist's perspective, and one which Morna Hooker (1997) describes in terms of 'a gigantic takeover bid'. The old firm,

Judaism, is to lose its promises and hopes to the new firm, Christianity (the Law replaced by grace and truth), but the irony is that this had been God's intention all along: the old firm was merely caretaking until it was time for the new firm to claim its rightful inheritance. The first sign, at Cana, demonstrates this perfectly. The steward at the feast marvels to the bridegroom that '*You have kept the good wine till now*' (2:10), which is exactly how the Fourth Evangelist understands what God has done in saving Jesus for this stage in salvation history — he, not the Law, is the '*good wine saved till now*'. In the Old Testament, the Law was a gift from God for the people of Israel, but they were unable to save themselves by it. Now, grace and **truth** through Christ are the way to **salvation**. A new relationship with God comes through faith in Jesus.

The Prologue closes with a verse which sums up the new message: the incarnation of the ***Logos*** as God's Son has made God himself known in terms of human flesh and blood. God has become human, the fullest revelation of God available to humanity. '*God has…in the person of his Son, himself become flesh. God's eternity has been joined to man's temporality in man's history. At last man can truly know God*' (Marsh, 1968).

The Trinity

One important aspect that is touched upon in the Prologue and developed later on in the Gospel is that of the **Trinity**. This is one of the most difficult concepts in the Christian faith, and the term is never mentioned in the Bible. It is the doctrine that there is one God, who is revealed in three Persons — **God the Father**, **God the Son** and **God the Holy Spirit**. However, the Fourth Evangelist has no developed doctrine of the Trinity, which was a mystery to the early church fathers and the cause of many divisions within the early church.

In the Old Testament, the emphasis was on one God, the Father, whose holy name was **Yahweh** and who made himself known to Moses as '**I am**' (Exodus 3:14). References to the Holy Spirit were oblique, but both are present in the act of creation: '*In the beginning God created the heavens and the earth…and the Spirit of God was hovering over the waters…And God said "Let there be light" and there was light*' (Genesis 1:1–3).

In the Fourth Gospel the task of the Son is clearly seen: he is to bring light and truth and thus reveal the Father. In a sense, therefore, the Trinity (a) allows God to be revealed, (b) allows God to be communicated with, and (c) embodies divine fellowship and love between the three persons of the Godhead, which is available to all those who believe.

Summary

- The Prologue (1:1–18) is the story of the ***Logos*** or word.
  1 The *Logos* was with God from the beginning.
  2 The *Logos* is the source of life.
  3 The *Logos* brings truth and light to a world of darkness.
  4 Through the *Logos*, God's grace and truth comes to humanity, superseding all that has previously been revealed to humanity through the Law and the prophets.
  5 John the Baptist testifies to this truth.
  6 The *Logos* is God Incarnate — Jesus Christ, the fullest revelation of God to humanity.

Key terms

Hellenistic — Greek thought and culture.

incarnate — the taking on of flesh.

Logos — Greek term, meaning 'word', with a wide cultural significance in Hellenistic and Jewish thought. Best understood with reference to the Fourth Gospel as the incarnate, living presence of God made known through Jesus.

polemic — material directed against a particular point of view.

pre-existence — existence before creation.

tabernacle — to dwell amongst.

testimony — bearing witness to, or making known, the truth.

Torah — the Old Testament or Jewish Law.

Trinity — the Christian doctrine that God is made known in the three persons of the Godhead: Father, Son and Holy Spirit.

Exam watch

Questions on the Prologue should be more popular and more well done than they are, since you are only being asked to consider 18 verses of material, which should be relatively easy to remember. The key to success, however, is to make sure that you know how these verses relate to the rest of the Gospel. Too often, candidates emphasise a few points to the detriment of the whole. Unless the question asks you specifically about the cultural background to the Prologue, for example, you don't need to go into a blow-by-blow account of all the possible ways the author may have utilised the prevailing philosophies of the time. Similarly, the Prologue amounts to more than its first five verses, so don't only write about *Logos*. Include critical scholarship — some key names have been given to you here — but not at the expense of showing your careful and relevant textual knowledge. Finally, make sure you are crystal clear about how the material in the Prologue relates to the rest of the Gospel, and how its themes are programmatic — they introduce concepts which are essential to an understanding of the whole Gospel structure. Be able, also, to identify where those links are made later on — for example, 17:5 refers again to Jesus's pre-existence, and the confrontation between the light and darkness draws to a head in 18:3.

Review questions

1 'The Prologue introduces the reader to the idea that Jesus Christ is equal to God.' Assess how far this is an accurate summary of the purpose of the Prologue.

2 Discuss and assess the views of scholars concerning the purpose and nature of the Prologue.

3 Consider the importance of (a) the Hellenistic and (b) the Jewish background to the Prologue of the Fourth Gospel.

C The early ministry

1 The first four signs

The author of the Fourth Gospel uses the word ***semeia*** or 'signs' to describe the miracles of Jesus. This is different from the word ***dunameis*** or 'act of power/mighty work', which is the term used in the Synoptic Gospels. It would seem that the author's reason for doing this is to emphasise that it is not so much the actual event that is important but instead the meaning or significance behind it. In this sense, the 'sign' points beyond itself to highlight a spiritual truth. Moreover, when Jesus himself speaks of the miracles, he uses the word *erga* ('works'). This term is used in the Old Testament to mean God's works, particularly creation and God's saving power with his people. Thus, in the Fourth Gospel Jesus links God's work in the past with his own in the present; God's power continues in him. This is highlighted in 5:36: *'For the very work that the Father has given me to finish, and which I am doing, testifies that the Father has sent me.'*

So what is the purpose of the signs? It seems that, first and foremost, the author uses them to show the fundamental and crucial link between Jesus and the Father. Jesus performs signs because he has been **sent** by God and he has a unique relationship with the Father. Barrett (1975) wrote that there are *'…clear indications that he by whom the signs are wrought is the Son of God and equal to God himself'*, and it is this issue which is at the heart of Jesus's conflict with the authorities.

In fact, the author himself states his purpose at the end of the Gospel in 20:30–1: *'Jesus did many other signs in the presence of his disciples, which are not recorded in this book. But these are written that you may believe that Jesus is the Christ, the Son of God, and that by believing you may have life in his name.'* Despite the extensive amount of miracle material that must have been available to the author (assuming at least his knowledge of oral tradition, if not the Synoptic Gospels) the evangelist has selected only seven (conceivably six) signs — those which appear to be best suited to filling his christological purpose. The reality, however, was that the signs did not always lead people to believe. Instead, they often brought controversy, conflict and condemnation. Jesus is blamed for working on the Sabbath and making himself equal to God, and the Jewish authorities seem unable and unwilling to see the meaning of the signs; instead, they seek to kill him: *'Jesus said to them, "My Father is always at his work to this very day, and I, too, am working." For this reason the Jews tried all the harder to kill him: not only was he breaking the Sabbath, but he was even calling God his own father, making himself equal with God'* (5:17–18).

Many did believe, however, and the author makes it clear that belief would lead to eternal life. The 'signs' are not metaphorical depictions of some future event; they are signs of the present, and reveal that the Messianic era has arrived. The signs are an aid to faith. Jesus often seems to imply that he hopes that people will believe without the signs, but that to believe with the signs is better than not believing at all: *'Do not believe me unless I do what my Father does. But if I do it, even though you do not believe me, believe the miracles, that you may know and understand that the Father is in me, and I in the Father'* (10:37–8).

Although believing without the benefit of a helpful sign is certainly advocated by the Fourth Evangelist, Kysar (1993) observes: *'The Gospel of John, along with the biblical tradition in general, affirms that faith arises from contact with a sensually perceptible object'*. However, that *'sensually perceptible object'* — Jesus and his works — needs interpretation, which the evangelist richly provides, most often in the form of an extended discourse between Jesus, disciples and opponents.

Most scholars maintain that there are seven signs in the Fourth Gospel:

- the changing of water into wine (2:1–11)
- the healing of the official's son (4:46–54)
- the healing of the crippled man (5:1–18)
- the feeding of the five thousand (6:1–15)
- the walking on the water (6:16–21)
- the healing of the man born blind (9:1–41)
- the raising of Lazarus (11:1–46)

Although this list represents those events most usually accepted by scholars as signs, it is not without dispute. The walking on the water is arguably not a sign. It does not fulfil quite the same functions as the other signs, and there are problems of translation which might render it a far from miraculous event — although not one without significance for discipleship. Joseph Grassi (1992), in *The Secret Identity of the Beloved Disciple*, identifies the blood and water from Jesus's side as the seventh sign (19:34), omitting the walking on the water from his calculations. He links the first (water to wine), fourth (feeding) and seventh (blood and water) in a special relationship, drawing together sacrificial themes, witnessed by Jesus's mother and the Beloved Disciple. He suggests this kind of relationship between all the signs:

The healings of the lame man and blind man are foils for each other — note the remarkable number of similarities in setting between these two signs, and yet the differences in the way the two characters respond to Jesus and their healing. Furthermore, the official's son is healed at Cana — a place where Jesus is accepted and welcomed — and the raising of Lazarus prefigures Jesus's own death and resurrection. The resurrection of Jesus himself is not a sign in quite the same way as the others; it is more than an event and is not performed by Jesus himself. However, it may be seen, in a sense, as the event to which the other signs actually point, and will be dealt with separately.

There is much debate as to whether or not the miracles of Jesus are genuine historical events or whether they are simply symbolic. Certainly Marsh (1968) suggests that they can be both and that the author understands the actions of Christ to be both real events and possessing symbolic meaning, enabling the readers to see that Jesus is, indeed, the Son of God. However, historically accurate or not, the purpose of the Gospel writer is to convince his readers of those aspects of the person of Christ which will lead them to belief and eternal life. The signs also highlight the most important aspects of faith — life, light, glory and the sacraments — as well as showing how the author believes that Jesus and what he has to offer have transcended all that was offered by Judaism. Thus, rather than a mere description of certain actions and events, the signs in the Fourth Gospel lead to a greater understanding of Christ.

1.1 The wedding at Cana (2:1–11)

The narrative of the wedding at Cana is not in the Synoptic Gospels and is used by the author to show how Jesus has come to replace the old Jewish rituals with the new way, of life through him. In the Old Testament, God was depicted as the bridegroom of Israel — and Israel was the unfaithful bride (Isaiah 54:5; Hosea 2:19). At this wedding, Jesus is symbolically shown to be the bridegroom returning to Israel, the unfaithful bride, restoring her to a relationship with God.

The action takes place 'on the third day', with its inevitable imagery of the resurrection. It has been argued by Russell (1993) that this wedding also reflects the creation of Adam and Eve; Jesus calls his mother '*woman*' (Eve?) and the six stone jars could represent the sixth day of creation, when Adam and Eve were made. This has the additional symbolism that the '*sixth day*' is the equivalent to Friday — the day of Jesus's crucifixion. It may be, therefore, that the symbolism is of Jesus's death rather than his resurrection. This view is supported by Jesus's words to his mother that his time has not arrived yet — pointing to the hour of his death. Thus, the evangelist makes clear that Jesus's death is already in view, even at this early stage in the Gospel, and must influence the way in which the reader approaches the events which follow. Furthermore, the number six may be thought of as a number of incompleteness within Judaism, where the number seven represents perfection. Jesus will bring to perfection that which was lacking within the old order — and significantly, perhaps, he meets the Samaritan woman at the sixth hour. However, Sanders and Mastin (1968) suggest that '*It is a standing temptation to read an allegorical interpretation into all the numbers in the Fourth Gospel; many no doubt have a symbolic significance, but six here does not seem to be one of them. There just were six*'.

Jesus is invited to the wedding with his disciples — the symbolism of the Messiah coming to his people, who will become the renewed Israel. Jesus's mother is there, observing at 2:3: '*They have no more wine*'. These words symbolise the crucial problem the evangelist believes to be facing Judaism: it does not possess the 'wine' of salvation, which can only be provided by Jesus's death. Wine in the Old Testament was the bringer of life and strength (Psalm 104) but the stone jars contained only the water needed for the Jewish purification rites (nobody could enter the feast without being purified). They are made of stone, which can be contrasted with the living body of Jesus and they are not completely full. Jesus changes the inadequate water into excellent wine and the jars are full to the brim. Even more, the best wine, the grace of God, has been saved until last — the feast is complete and the grace of God replaces the legalism of the Jewish purification rites. This reflects perfectly the words of the Prologue (1:17): '*For the law was given through Moses; grace and truth came through Jesus Christ.*'

There are clear Eucharistic overtones in this sign. The wine may be symbolic of the blood of Christ, which is the way of salvation and may be seen as the wine of the eschatological messianic banquet, when the righteous would finally gather with the messiah and share table fellowship. It leads, most importantly of all, to belief in Christ on the part of the disciples (2:11); the embryonic belief that had led them to follow him in 1:19–51 is confirmed by what they see. Jesus, as the bridegroom, is betrothed to his bride, the church, which is the new Israel, represented at this stage by those who have placed their trust in him. The meaning of the first sign is clear: the water of Judaism is inadequate for salvation — the wine/blood of Christ is the path to eternal life. John Aston (1991) writes of this episode: '*This miracle, so different from those that were to come, resembles them in the most important point, for it too suggests…the kind of faith it is designed to inspire: a faith of fulfilment and of transformation, of joy and celebration*'.

The cleansing of the Temple

This incident (2:13–25), which follows the wedding at Cana, occurs at the beginning of Jesus's ministry, although the Synoptic Gospels place it at the end. In the Old Testament, it had been foretold that the Lord would one day come and cleanse his Temple (Malachi 3:1; Isaiah 56:7) and this is why the story is included in the Synoptic Gospels. However, in the Fourth Gospel there is a different emphasis. The Temple market was where faithful Jews could buy animals for sacrifice in the belief that this could lead to the forgiveness of their sins (atonement), but Jesus is angered because the people have not listened to God's message that he wants not animal sacrifices but worship from the heart (Psalm 51:16, Hosea 6:6). The message is clear: salvation will not come through ritual cleansing or through the sacrifice of animals. What is needed is faith from the heart, which comes from salvation through Jesus Christ, who is the new Temple, the place where man meets with God.

1.2 The healing of the official's son (4:46–54)

Jesus performed the second sign in the same place as the first, Cana. The official was probably a Roman administrator working in Herod's court who came from Capernaum — about two days' travel — and asked Jesus to heal his sick son. As with the wedding sign, the focus is on death. This time, the son is '*close to death*' (2:47) and at first Jesus seems reluctant to act, saying: '*Unless you see signs and wonders…you will never believe.*' At the seventh hour (1.00pm), possibly symbolic of the 'perfect' time, and also the time of his later trial before Pilate, Jesus heals the son, saying, '*You may go. Your son will live*' (4:50). The official *believes* Jesus and does not require any further signs or evidence. He has such great faith in Jesus that he is able to accept his word without question and goes home to his healed son. Moreover, as a result of the sign, all his family believes as well.

The message of the sign is clear: by the word of Jesus, life is given. The son symbolises Jesus's work; death is followed by life and the nature of true belief is to show obedience and trust in the word and power of Christ. However, further significance can be drawn from the sign if we are conscious of the place it fills in the narrative. Jesus has already had one unsatisfactory conversation with a Jewish teacher (Nicodemus), which has left us uncertain of what Nicodemus has believed but quite clear that Judaism is about to face a serious challenge from Jesus. He then talks at length with the Samaritan woman, an outcast from a despised quasi-Semitic race, who nevertheless shows far greater perception of Jesus than has Nicodemus. However, it is the official — who conceivably is a Gentile (non-Jew) — who shows the most ready, willing and open faith of them all. Perhaps this is indicative of the way the Gospel will go beyond Judaism to embrace '*other sheep that are not of this fold*' (10:16), which is clearly what the evangelist believes to be the case.

1.3 The healing of the crippled man at the pool (5:1–30)

Jesus went back to Jerusalem and visited a pool known as Bethesda (meaning 'House of Olive'). It was a well-known gathering place for the very sick and there was a legend that, at certain times, an angel would stir the waters and whoever climbed in first would be healed. Jesus met a crippled man who had been there for 38 years (the same length of time that the Israelites had wandered in the desert under Moses (Deuteronomy 2:14)). In this incident, the symbolism is of a sinful man who has awaited cleansing before entering into the Promised Land, but the cleansing waters have been unavailing — the Law has left him unaided, but in Christ he may have new life.

Jesus asks him if he wants to be healed. It is a symbolic question; Jesus is asking whether the man could be satisfied with life under the Law of Moses. The man does not answer directly and simply says that no one has been able to help him into the pool. Jesus then heals him with the words: *'Pick up your mat and walk'* (5:8). The man is healed and goes on his way. However, this causes controversy, because the healing is performed on the Sabbath, which the Jewish authorities see as being contrary to the Law of Moses. The author highlights all these issues in the discourse that follows.

The man who was healed did not know who Jesus was and was unable to give the Jewish authorities any information. Later, he meets Jesus, who tells him: *'See, you are well again. Stop sinning or something worse may happen to you'* (5:14). This seems to suggest that true healing from Christ is more than just a physical thing — you can be physically well but spiritually sick. A person who is truly well must be 'born again' into the life of Christ. Moreover, such a new person must avoid the temptation to return to former ways.

Yet the man seems not to understand and goes to the Jewish authorities to tell them that it was Jesus who cured him. This has the effect of saving the man from persecution by the authorities, but leads itself to the persecution of Jesus. The man was failed by Judaism and is restored by Jesus, but he is spiritually unaware of what has happened and, by going to the authorities, shows that he has immediately returned to his former ways. He rejects what Jesus offered him, which is, of course, far more than the physical healing of his paralysis.

The real purpose of the sign emerges. The evangelist is far less interested in the Sabbath controversy, which he probably simply lifted from his source, than in the christological dispute which follows. When the Jewish authorities question Jesus about healing on the Sabbath, he highlights his unique relationship with God: *'My Father is always at his work to this very day, and I, too, am working'* (5:17). As God's Son, he did only what the Father required him to do, and a vital part of that work is to share in the divine acts of creation and judgment. He works in total unity with the Father: *'…whatever the Father does the Son also does'* (5:19). God gives life and God can judge, but will not do so without the Son, and humanity has been given a chance of eternal life, by freely choosing to follow him: *'I tell you the truth, whoever hears my word and believes him who sent me has eternal life and will not be condemned. He has crossed over from death to life'* (5:24).

All that Jesus testifies to himself is supported, he claims, by the combined witness of God and John the Baptist (5:30ff), and he can therefore legitimately claim to be fulfilling the legal requirement that a person could not testify on his own behalf but must have two witnesses (Deuteronomy 19:15). The theme of witness cannot have escaped us even at this relatively early stage in the Gospel. The claims made by the evangelist and his chief protagonist, Jesus, are not idle claims, but are backed up by a host of witnesses: God himself (the most reliable witness that can surely be presented to the reader), the disciples, the Samaritan woman, John the Witness/Baptist, Jesus's works and words. Later the Holy Spirit, or **Paraclete**, will join these witnesses to provide a testimony to Jesus's divine identity and continuing presence among his people, even after his death.

The lame man is a weak character who shows no insight into Jesus's identity or the significance of what has happened to him. He is sharply contrasted with the blind man (the sixth sign) who, faced with a similar set of circumstances and threatened with excommunication from the synagogue, testifies boldly on Jesus's behalf, and emerges as the ideal Johannine disciple.

1.4 The feeding of the five thousand (6:1–15)

This sign is the only miracle story which appears to have survived almost wholesale from the Synoptic tradition, although the evangelist makes it his own with the explanatory discourse which follows. Jesus was in Galilee, being followed by a large crowd, and along with his disciples, he goes to the mountainside. Marsh (1968) highlights the possible symbolic nature of this; in Matthew 5–7, Jesus delivers his greatest teaching, the Sermon on the Mount, from such a place and is clearly depicted as the new Moses. It is the time of the Passover and, like Moses, Jesus feeds his people, although with bread which is far superior — the bread which leads to eternal life, not the manna which could provide no eternal guarantees (Exodus 16). Thus, this sign takes a central place in the development of the Gospel's replacement theology.

Jesus appears to test his disciples by asking Philip how the people might be fed. Philip does not really understand. Andrew has some small notion of what might happen when he says that there is a boy with five small loaves and two fish. Jesus takes the food, gives thanks to God and feeds them all (5:11). The disciples gather up twelve baskets full of fragments. There is great symbolism here. Jesus apparently does not give the bread to the disciples to distribute — he gives it to the people *himself,* just as he gives his body on the cross. Moreover, there is a Eucharistic link once again with the priest giving the bread to the people, and further hints of the Messianic banquet. The crowd shares bread together, just as the disciples would later at the Last Supper (although the Fourth Gospel has no Synoptic-type account of this final meal) and as all the faithful would at the end of time (Revelation 19:17). Moreover, the twelve baskets of fragments are the same number as the tribes of Israel — an image of the new community of God's people.

However, this symbolism is misunderstood by the crowd. They regard Jesus as a great prophet and miracle-worker and want to crown him as king, thus forcing him to withdraw. They are unable to appreciate that the bread Jesus is truly offering is the bread of life, and are concerned only with their immediate physical needs. Jesus's discourse on the bread of life expounds on the significance they are intended to perceive in the feeding, but even this fails to lead to any real understanding and '*after this many of his disciples drew back and no longer went about with him*' (6:66).

2 Teachings

In the Prologue, the author of the Fourth Gospel highlights the radical new notion of salvation: *'Yet to all who received him, to those who believed in his name, he gave the right to become children of God — children born not of natural descent, nor of human decision or a husband's will, but born of God'* (1:12–13). This was a new concept — that it was not a person's race, deeds or status that would bring them salvation. Salvation comes instead from an act of God's grace, which brings with it new birth and new life. It is in this context only that we can understand the conversation with Nicodemus, and, indeed, Marsh (1968) suggests: *'Not only Christ and Nicodemus, but the church and Judaism, may be held to meet in this story'*.

2.1 Born again — Jesus and Nicodemus (3:1–21)

The conversation between Jesus and Nicodemus highlights the struggle between traditional Judaism and the teaching of Jesus. Nicodemus, in the opinion of Marsh, represents the 'best' of Judaism. Although he only speaks four sentences, his role is very significant — he is a Pharisee and, probably, a member of the Sanhedrin. He is portrayed as a Jew who, in his heart, would like to follow Jesus, but he cannot because he is hampered by his religious situation. He comes to Jesus at night, perhaps symbolising the spiritual 'darkness' he lives in, and he acknowledges Jesus as a teacher who has come from God. However, he flounders badly when Jesus says: *'I tell you the truth, no one can enter the kingdom of God unless he is born again'* (3:3). The word for 'again' in Greek is **anothen** and means both 'again' and 'from above'. It is almost without doubt that the evangelist intends both meanings to be picked up by the reader in that new birth is necessary *and* involves a spiritual or heavenly renewal. Nicodemus's knowledge of the law and the Scriptures is not enough for salvation but Jesus explains that, in the world of the flesh, Nicodemus can see God's power but he cannot truly experience a personal relationship with God. To do this he must be born again.

Not surprisingly, Nicodemus cannot fully understand and sees Jesus's words in physical terms: *'How can a man be born when he is old… Surely he cannot enter a second time into his mother's womb to be born!'* (3:40). This exposes the shortcomings of Judaism. Nicodemus believes that on the 'last day', God will come in judgment and establish his kingdom. But Nicodemus is bound to the physical world and is incapable of accepting what Jesus is telling him, that the future age (or kingdom) is, in fact, already with him in the person of Jesus. Jesus tells Nicodemus: *'I tell you the truth, no one can enter the kingdom of God unless he is born of water and the spirit'* (3:5). What he is saying is that the Jewish rituals and traditions (water purification) will not lead to salvation, and that rebirth in the spirit (**pneuma**) is necessary. The image of new birth stems itself from the Old Testament imagery in Ezekiel 37 in which the valley of dry bones represents the spiritually dead Israel, brought to life by the spirit and breath of God.

It is possible that the evangelist, or a subsequent scribe, intended the reader to identify 'water and spirit' as Christian water baptism followed by (or simultaneous with) baptism in the Holy Spirit. However, given that water is clearly a symbol for the Spirit in subsequent episodes (7:37–9), it seems more likely that we are intended to read the phrase as 'water, which is the Spirit'. The evangelist plays around with the interlinking themes of blood, water, spirit, wind and breath so often in the Gospel that it seems reasonable to assume that where one is used, the other is implicit.

The evangelist uses Old Testament imagery linking the lifting of the serpent by Moses (Numbers 21:9) with the lifting up of the Son of Man (on the cross). Such lifting up not only means the crucifixion, but also Christ's raising in glory (Psalm 27:6). In this way, whoever believes in him will have eternal life: 'For God so loved the world that he gave his one and only Son, that whoever believes in him shall not perish but have eternal life' (3:16). It is fundamental to salvation that humanity sees the need to set aside the old ways and be born again into a new spiritual life. Jesus is saying that God's love is not just for the Jews but for everyone, and those who believe will avoid judgment and condemnation and receive everlasting life.

We know little more of Nicodemus, but what we do know is significant. He appears on two further occasions in the Gospel — at 7:45–52 when he appears tentatively to defend Jesus to his fellow members of the Sanhedrin, and at 19:38–42 when, along with Joseph of Arimathea, 'who was a disciple of Jesus, but secretly, for fear of the Jews', he buries Jesus.

Raymond Brown (1979) designates secret disciples as '**crypto-Christians**', believers for whom the evangelist has little regard (12:42). If Joseph is one such secret disciple, then presumably Nicodemus is too, and whilst he may not be prepared to stand up and be counted and face the fate of the blind man, he is further along the spiritual path than when he first came to Jesus at night.

2.2 Living water — Jesus and the Samaritan woman (4:1–45)

The Jews saw themselves as the chosen people of God; non-Jews (Gentiles) were not. There was, however, an ambiguous third group of people, the Samaritans, who did not fit neatly into either category. Samaria lay to the north and was originally part of the Promised Land. After the death of Solomon, the Northern and Southern Kingdoms split and enjoyed varying fortunes until, in 721 BCE, the area became part of the Assyrian Empire and the Israelites were taken away in slavery. Foreigners moved into the land and when, much later, the Israelites returned, they intermixed with the foreigners and, in a sense, lost their 'pure' Judaism. As a result, for traditional Jews, Samaritans were neither Gentiles nor true Jews and were despised for abandoning true Judaism.

At the beginning of this fascinating narrative, Jesus is going through Samaria (a rather circuitous route) and he stops for a rest at Jacob's Well, a deeply significant spot, where the patriarch Jacob changed his name to Israel. Jesus, having met the 'best' of the Jews in Nicodemus (in that he was at least prepared to attempt to understand Jesus), encounters the 'best' of the Samaritans. As with Judaism, the religious traditions of the Samaritans were insufficient, and the woman's eschatological and doctrinal beliefs alone will not lead her to salvation. Furthermore, she appears to be a character against whom all the odds are stacked: she is unmarried, with a questionable marital history.

Nevertheless, Jesus asks her for a drink. This is unusual; the woman has come at the hottest part of the day, possibly to avoid the company of others, perhaps because she is shunned or despised for leading an immoral life. She is taken aback, for a Jew would not normally speak to a Samaritan, let alone a woman. However, as Brown (1979) points out: 'She serves to modify the thesis that male disciples were the only important

figures in church founding'. She is poised to fulfil the highest calling of a Johannine disciple: to believe and to bear witness to others to that belief.

Jesus says to her: *'If you knew the gift of God and who it is that asks you for a drink, you would have asked him and he would have given you living water'* (4:10). At first, she does not understand and, like Nicodemus, can only see things in physical, and not spiritual, terms. She wonders how he can fetch water when he has nothing to draw it with. Moreover, she questions whether he is greater than their ancestor, Jacob, who used the well and gave it to the Samaritans (rather as the crowd at the feeding asks whether Jesus is greater than Moses who gave the manna). Ironically, of course, she speaks the truth: Jesus is greater than all those who have played a part in Israel's history, however significant they may have appeared at the time. Nevertheless, she takes Jesus's words literally, seeing this as a chance to get water without having to keep on coming to the well. But Jesus is talking about spiritual, rather than physical, truths: *'Whoever drinks the water I give him will never thirst. Indeed, the water I give him will become in him a spring of water welling up to eternal life'* (4:14). He is telling her that it is he alone who can provide satisfaction of the spiritual thirst of humanity, and of the need to be reconciled to God. This reflects the Old Testament teaching in Psalm 42:2: *'My soul thirsts for God, for the living God. When can I go and meet with God?'* As with Nicodemus, Jesus tells her that her religion is inadequate.

The conversation then takes an unexpected turn when Jesus tells the woman to call her husband, knowing (omnisciently) that she has no husband. Here the analogy of 'husband' refers to 'God', just as the reference to 'bridegroom' did at the wedding in Cana. In fact, the woman has had five husbands — a possible reference to 2 Kings 17, when the Assyrians introduced pagan gods into Samaria, leading the people into apostasy. Jesus has thus highlighted again the poverty and inadequacy of the Samaritan religion. However, unlike Nicodemus, the woman is able to respond positively. She realises that Jesus is special; she calls him a 'prophet' (4:19) and seeks his view on the true place where people ought to worship — Jerusalem or the Samaritan Mount Gerizim, where their Temple had stood before it was destroyed by John Hyrcanus. Jesus, however, replies that the issue is not *where* to worship but the true *nature* of worship — based on spirit and truth: *'Yet a time is coming and has now come when true worshippers will worship the Father in spirit and truth...'* (4:23). Jesus replaces the Temple as the meeting place between God and humanity (cp. 1:51, 2:21). There is no longer a geographical limit placed on God's relationship with his people, for worship is centred upon Jesus himself.

The woman finally appreciates that the things of which Jesus speaks are those that she would expect of the Messiah, and Jesus tells her that *he* is the Messiah (4:26). She abandons her water jar — possibly a symbol of abandoning her old life and incomplete water rituals in place of living water — and returns to the town with the good news. On hearing her testimony, the townsfolk, a new harvest of believers, eagerly receive Jesus and accept him: *'We know that this man really is the Saviour of the world'* (4:42).

2.3 The Holy Spirit — *pneuma*

One of the most characteristic features of the Fourth Gospel is the evangelist's presentation of the Holy Spirit. Unlike in the Synoptic Gospels, the Holy Spirit is described as both **pneuma** and **Paraclete**, two Greek terms which express different but related functions of the Spirit. The term *pneuma* is used to speak of the role of the Spirit prior to the Passion, in the life and ministry of Jesus and the functions it performs in salvation.

The Holy Spirit is present from the beginning of Jesus's ministry, setting him aside as the one anointed for God's purpose, fulfilling John's testimony that *'the man on whom you see the Spirit come down and remain is he who will baptise with the Holy Spirit'* (1:33). In the Old Testament, God's Spirit empowers Israel's judges and kings (1 Samuel 11:6), equipping them to fulfil vital roles in times of crisis. However, they possess the Spirit temporarily, whereas it 'remains' on Jesus (1:32). Thus, the coming of the Spirit on Jesus points to the fulfilment of the Old Testament prophecies (Isaiah 42:6–67), and it is Jesus, as the one sent by God, who will baptise with the Holy Spirit, and by implication, the Spirit will be at work in all the activities and ministries of Jesus. In turn, the disciple who responds to the Spirit working in and through Jesus will be led to the gift of eternal life. For the Fourth Evangelist, the *pneuma* spirit is the way in which man's longing for God will be satisfied, quenching his thirst for God (Psalm 42:1). Unlike the Old Testament leaders, Jesus is the central and enabling figure in the fulfilment of God's promise to pour out his Holy Spirit, so God's people may remain his people for ever. As Marsh (1968) suggests, this was only possible because Jesus himself was perpetually indwelt by the Spirit.

The Fourth Evangelist plays distinctively on the term *pneuma*, which can be variously translated from the Greek as 'wind', 'breath' or 'spirit'. The opening verses of the Gospel — *'In the beginning was the Word'* — echo Genesis 1:1–2, where we read that *'In the beginning…the spirit of God moved over the face of the waters'*. Clearly the evangelist expects the reader to make a link between the work of God's spirit in creation and the work of Jesus the *Logos*. The same connection is made in the conversation with Nicodemus, and the Samaritan woman is a better example still of a disciple who drinks from the living spiritual water Jesus offers, making eternal life possible by transforming old into new.

It is the *pneuma* spirit which is itself the 'agent of regeneration' (Smalley, 1978), but it is Jesus, as the one who has come down from heaven, who through the Spirit makes regeneration possible. He is the Lord of the harvest who unites Jews and Samaritans.

The Fourth Evangelist makes explicit the link between water and spirit in 7:37–9, explaining that *'rivers of living water'* flowing from the heart of the believer are the spirit which will be poured out on them after Jesus's death. Water is not something separate from the spirit, but a way of describing its effects and tasks, and will be made accessible to all believers when the blood and water flow from Jesus's side on the cross.

Summary

- The **miracles** of Jesus are seen in the Fourth Gospel as **signs** rather than 'mighty works' — the emphasis is on the meaning behind them rather than the actions themselves.
- They highlight the link between Jesus and the Father, and lead people into belief (20:31), but also show the anger and spiritual blindness of the Jewish authorities that finally leads to Jesus's arrest and execution.
- The signs point to the power of God and the saving message of Christ. They show how Christ's teaching supersedes the rituals and traditions of Judaism, and place

emphasis on Old Testament imagery, highlighting the importance of light, truth, belief and eternal life.

- Finally, the conversations with **Nicodemus** and the **Samaritan woman** show how salvation cannot be achieved through the old ways, but only through **rebirth** and belief in Christ himself.
- The Holy Spirit is introduced by the term ***pneuma*** in these early chapters. It is used to describe the role and function of the Holy Spirit in relation to Jesus's own activity and the life-giving power it makes available to believers.

Exam watch

Questions dealing with the signs tend not to refer to individual signs themselves, but to the meaning and significance of the message behind them — particularly teachings concerning salvation and eternal life. In answering questions, don't spend too long writing about the action surrounding the miracle itself, but instead, concentrate on its meaning and symbolism. Make sure, therefore, that you can see the link between the sign and the meaning surrounding it. It will help if you know something about the background and the social and religious setting.

Review questions

1 Examine the meaning and significance of the incident at the wedding in Cana.
2 What can be learned about the ministry of Jesus from the healing at the pool?
3 (a) Examine the meaning of two signs in the Fourth Gospel.
   (b) '*The purpose of the signs in the Fourth Gospel was to convert Gentiles to Christianity.*' Discuss and comment critically on this view.
4 Examine and consider the extent to which it may be accurate to describe the Fourth Gospel as a 'Book of Signs'.

D The later ministry

1 The first five 'I am' sayings

Jesus uses the phrase '*I am*' (Greek ***ego eimi***) 26 times in the Gospel. It seems to be a phrase used deliberately and possessing great significance. In his book *Christianity According to St John*, Howard (1943) suggests that the phrase may have a Hellenistic origin, since this was the language used by the deity in Hermetic books and in certain '*magical papyri*'. However, other scholars, such as Barrett (1975), believe that the phrase comes from the Old Testament, when it is used as the divine word of self-revelation from God himself: '*God said to Moses, "I am who I am"*' (Exodus 3:14). Similar uses occur in Deuteronomy 32:39 and Isaiah 43:10, and Brown (1979) explains that, in the Old Testament, the phrase is used to show the different perspectives of God — for example, as healer (Exodus 15:26) and the bringer of salvation (Psalm 35:3).

Brown suggests that in the Fourth Gospel there are three types of 'I am' sayings:

÷ Those with no predicates and which seem, in some way, incomplete. For example, in 8:28 Jesus says: '...*then you will know that* ego eimi'. Similar passages are evident in 8:24, 8:58 and 13:19.

❖ Those where there is no predicate, but the meaning is clearly understood — for example 18:5: '"I am he," Jesus said'.

❖ Those where there is an expressed predicate — for example 6:35: 'I am the bread of life.'

There are seven predicated 'I am' sayings in the Gospel — again, the 'perfect number' in Judaism, perhaps suggesting the 'perfection' of Jesus's teaching.

1.1 'I am the bread of life'

This passage follows on from the feeding of the five thousand. The people have seen the sign of the bread, but they still lack faith — they are still 'spiritually hungry'. Jesus reminds them that, under Moses in the desert, God gave the people 'bread from heaven' (Exodus 16:12) and that now he has come from God too. This time, he tells them, the bread will satisfy their spiritual hunger: *'For the bread of God is he who comes down from heaven and gives life to the world'* (6:33). The author highlights the superiority of the bread Jesus is offering to the physical bread which the people received under Moses, trying to lead his readers away from Moses and the past and to look to the 'new age', for it is only with Jesus that spiritual hunger will be satisfied. He is the bread, and, although this will only be really understood after his death and resurrection, this 'true' bread has life-giving qualities: *'I am the bread of life. He who comes to me will never go hungry, and he who believes in me will never thirst'* (6:35).

For the Jews, the Law (Torah) was symbolised by bread, and here again the author is trying to show that the bread which is Christ will supersede both the bread of Moses and the Torah. Moreover, Jesus uses the present tense — it is available now. In other words, eschatologically speaking, the messianic age is in the present and can guarantee life in the present. The people, however, as is characteristic of the Fourth Gospel, cannot understand, and think only in physical, rather than in spiritual, language, asking how they can eat a man's flesh. Jesus replies by talking in sacrificial terms: *'Whoever eats my flesh and drinks my blood has eternal life and I will raise him up at the last day'* (6:54). Brown highlights the possible eucharistic significance of this — the sharing of the bread by the people of God. Indeed, Bultmann (1971) feels that a later redactor, for just such a reason, may have added the material, not least because they may have felt that the Fourth Evangelist had given insufficient consideration to the sacraments in the Gospel.

It is of interest to note that bread was also associated with the Temple. 'Temple bread' was kept in the Temple (1 Samuel 21:1ff) and this may be contrasted with Jesus's body which, as well as being bread, is also a Temple (2:21) which will be given to those who receive it to provide spiritual nourishment and salvation. The important thing is belief in Christ: *'The work of God is this: to believe in the one he has sent'* (6:29). Such belief in Christ is the first step in true discipleship — for those who eat and drink of Christ will have him abiding within them and they in him. It will be a two-way relationship: just as the Father and the Son are united, so too will be the Son and the believer. Indeed, the passage ends with Peter's confession of belief: *'We believe and know that you are the Holy One of God'* (6:69). Significantly, however, it is after this discourse that many disciples withdraw, finding Jesus's teaching too demanding.

1.2 'I am the light of the world'

Jesus first refers to himself as the light of the world (8:12) at the end of the Feast of Tabernacles, and during the preceding evening there would have been a rite of light, when four golden candlesticks were lit in the Temple precincts, symbolising the pillar of flame by which God led the Israelites through the desert (Exodus 13:21). Jesus uses this setting to proclaim his second saying, 'I am the light of the world', throwing out a clear challenge to those in the Temple to see him as the fulfilment of all that is represented by the festival.

In this passage, Jesus is the main speaker and it seems to come over almost as a trial between Jesus and the Pharisees, whose rejection of Jesus has left them in darkness. The Jews accuse Jesus of not telling the truth because he has no witnesses other than himself (Jewish legalism required two witnesses for a testimony to be valid). Jesus, however, replies that God the father is his witness: *'I am the one who testifies for myself; my other witness is the Father, who sent me'* (8:18). Jesus explains his unique relationship with the Father: humanity lives in a world of darkness and sin, but Jesus has come with God's light to reveal truth and lead men to spiritual understanding. Those who follow Jesus will never walk in darkness again: *'Whoever follows me will never walk in darkness, but will have the light of life'* (8:12).

The Pharisees dispute his claims, but, typically, do not understand. All they see is a physical man in a physical setting; they cannot grasp the spiritual significance. Alan Culpepper (1983) describes them thus: *'By not having heard or seen the Father, they are Jesus's opposite; in their response to Jesus they are the opposite of the disciples. The pathos of their unbelief is that they are the religious people, some even the religious authorities, who have had all the advantages of the heritage of Israel'*. Jesus tells them that he has not come to judge or condemn, but the light he will bring will show everyone the truth of their situation. He explains: *'You are from below; I am from above. You are of this world; I am not of this world'* (8:23). For all their religion and piety, the Pharisees do not understand spiritual truths. Jesus tells them that just being Jews or Sons of Abraham is not enough; to be freed from the darkness of sin, they must believe in him: *'He who belongs to God hears what God says. The reason you do not hear is that you do not belong to God'* (8:47). Jesus's divine claims are interpreted as blasphemous and the Jews are ready to kill him. Jesus leaves the Temple grounds, turning away from the centre of Judaism, leaving it in its own darkness: *'"I tell you the truth," Jesus answered, "before Abraham was born, I am!" At this, they picked up stones to stone him'* (8:58–9).

With the Pharisees refusing to see the light of the world and blind to Jesus's teaching, the drama then moves into chapter 9, where they are truly judged on failing to see even when an enlightening sign is performed before them. When Jesus heals a man born blind — bringing light to his darkness — he uses the 'I am' formula again: *'While I am in the world, I am the light of the world'* (9:6). There is much symbolism here. In Greek and Roman mysticism, light was identified with God. Moreover, in the Old Testament, God is seen as light (Psalm 27:1) and God is the creator of light (Genesis 1:3). Interestingly, Jesus heals the man by putting mud on his eyes — reflecting the way in which Adam was given life in Genesis 2:7. Thus he replicates and shares in the creative activity of God (compare 1:3).

The man receives the light when he washes the mud off his eyes in the water of the

Pool of Siloam. The name of the pool means 'sent', perhaps reflecting the point that he has obeyed the one who was 'sent' by God. In this way the blind man provides an interesting comparison to Naaman the Syrian leper who initially refused to obey Elisha's instructions to wash in the River Jordan in order to receive his healing (2 Kings 5). Moreover, the washing could be a kind of baptism, representative of new life in the Spirit. The blind man's willingness to engage with Jesus is quite contrary to the grudging lame man, who even after receiving his healing was more concerned to avoid trouble for himself with the Pharisees than to understand the mysterious nature of the man who has made him well.

Now cured, the blind man is investigated by the Pharisees, who question whether he was truly blind. Even the man's parents are called to testify. Their reluctance to become involved '*because they feared the Jews*' is fascinating. That they are Jews themselves and yet are afraid of their own people is like, in Brown's phrase, '*The Americans being afraid of the Americans*'. This, of course, reflects the circumstances not of Jesus's ministry but of the Johannine community, which by the end of the first century had cut its ties with Judaism. Although still technically Jews, they now identified Jews as the opponents of Johannine Christianity. The man's parents want nothing to do with the dispute: '*Ask him; he is of age, he will speak for himself*' (9:23).

The Pharisees meanwhile, instead of seeing the marvel of God's work, focus on Jesus being a sinner for breaking the Law concerning work on the Sabbath: '*This man is not from God, for he does not keep the Sabbath*' (9:16). Ironically, the Law (Torah) was supposed to be a light (Psalm 119:105), yet they use it to keep themselves in darkness. Even the blind man recognises this and points out to the Pharisees that '*God does not listen to sinners… If this man were not from God, he could do nothing*' (9:31–2). The Pharisees, perhaps knowing their argument is lost, fight back with abuse and throw the man out. He finds Jesus and confesses his belief in him (9:38), reflecting the words of the prophet Isaiah 9:2: '*The people walking in darkness have seen a great light.*' However, those who are blind will see, whilst those who believe themselves to be righteous in the Law will remain blind, for they refuse to see the light of the world. The Pharisees cautiously question whether such a fate awaits them (9:40), but in reality show no sign of wanting to follow the blind man in his confession of faith.

1.3 'I am the gate for the sheep'

The excommunication of the blind man leaves a question for the reader: 'Who was the real leader of God's People, Jesus or the Jewish authorities?' For those who have read the Prologue, of course, the answer is clear, but for the characters within the Gospel it depends on their understanding of the nature of authority. The analogy of a good shepherd attempts to unpack this. A shepherd is the guardian of his sheep — he leads them, they know his voice and he protects them and guards the entrance to the sheepfold. This is what the true leader of God's people must also do. The figure of the shepherd was used in the Old Testament to depict a ruler or king (Ezekiel 34) and this was central to the issue between the religious authorities and Jesus. Jesus is the real shepherd; they are false shepherds, who enter by stealth and use threats and force. They are not the true leaders of the people. On the other hand, Jesus says of himself: '*I am the gate for the sheep…whoever enters through me will be saved*' (10:8–9).

The reference to the gate has great symbolism. The Jews believed that there was a gate of heaven (Genesis 28:17), which was opened by God himself (Psalm 78:23). Jesus, therefore, is depicted as the heavenly gate that leads to salvation and eternal life. In earthly terms, the gate is the place through which the sheep will pass in order to find safe pasture (Psalm 23:2). Traditionally, a shepherd would sleep at the gate, usually lying across it, so that nothing could harm his flock. Jesus is using the same analogy for himself and his people. The sheepfold that Jesus guards probably refers not to heaven itself, but to the church, the community of believers amongst whom followers (the sheep) will gain salvation. The thieves and robbers are not only the chief priests and Pharisees, but also the kings, false prophets and careless religious and political leaders of the old Israel who lead them into religious apostasy and national exile.

However, what is most important to emphasise is the need for the believer to be proactive. Jesus is the means through which salvation is gained, but the believer must act on the choice to enter through it.

1.4 'I am the good shepherd'

There is considerable debate amongst scholars as to the meaning of this saying. Bultmann (1971) noted that it was Jesus's last such speech to the people, and as such is his final appeal to the world as a whole. Certainly, the use of a shepherd as an important image was common. Schnackenburg (1980) points out that *'In the Orient of ancient times, as well as in Greece and the Hellenistic world, the use of "shepherd" as a designation for a divine or human ruler was widespread'*. Bultmann considered that there might be a link to the Gnostic notion of a revealer-shepherd, although Schnackenburg disagreed, saying that Jesus is crucially different from the revealer-shepherd because the latter includes no notion of self-sacrifice.

There are several references in the Old Testament to God being the shepherd, for example Psalm 23 and Isaiah 40:11. A good shepherd was required to sacrifice his own life for his sheep and, in the Old Testament shepherd imagery, the ruler of Israel should do likewise (Isaiah 53:5). David was able to fight Goliath with confidence, not just because God was with him, but because as a shepherd he had killed lions and bears in the defence of his sheep (1 Samuel 17:34). Equally, of course, a bad shepherd would have no real concern for the sheep (Ezekiel 34:2), only for himself. Jesus used this analogy to highlight his own calling: *'I am the good shepherd: I know my sheep and my sheep know me — just as the Father knows me and I know the Father — and I lay down my life for the sheep'* (10:14–15).

The reference to the self-sacrifice of the shepherd, according to Bultmann (1971), is not found in the Old Testament, although Beasley-Murray (1999) suggests that it refers to the crucifixion. Grayston (1990) says that this shows Jesus's goodness and his concern for the good of his sheep, whilst Barrett (1975) says that it highlights the fact that Jesus is not simply executed as a criminal, but that his death was a sacrifice. He notes that this voluntary act of the shepherd is *'…an important part of the Christian apologetic'.*

Moreover, the authority of Jesus himself is highlighted in 10:18, where he shows that he is not only a sacrificial shepherd but is also the risen Lord: *'I have authority to lay it down and authority to take it up again.'* Jesus also makes reference to *'other sheep that are not of this sheep pen'* (10:16), perhaps in reference to the Gentiles, who will also become part of his flock. This shows the universality of Christ's message and may reflect the words in Ezekiel 34:23, where God will raise up a messianic descendant of David as shepherd for all people: *'I will place over them one shepherd, my servant David, and he will tend them; he will tend them and be their shepherd.'*

The Jews, understanding, perhaps, the allusion to them as the *'hired hand who cares nothing for the sheep'* (10:13), demand more proof from Jesus of his identity and authority, but he refuses to give any, on the grounds that the true sheep have already heard his voice and recognised him and he need do no more. He then utters what, to many, was the ultimate blasphemy, by declaring that *'I and the Father are one'* (10:30). Inevitably, they try to stone him and he is forced to leave.

1.5 'I am the resurrection and the life'

The raising of Lazarus is the setting for what is felt to be the greatest 'I am' saying: *'I am the resurrection and the life. He who believes in me will live, even though he dies, and whoever lives and believes in me will never die'* (11:25).

Having received word that Lazarus is sick, Jesus tells the disciples that his illness will not end in death, but is for the glory of God. However, Lazarus does need to truly die in order for Jesus's words to be fulfilled, and Jesus delays going to Lazarus for a further two days. Lazarus dies (11:14) and the author uses this to highlight the very nature of Jesus — he can and will awaken Lazarus to life. When Jesus finally arrives, Martha shows some understanding of Jesus's power when she suggests that if he had been there, he could have saved Lazarus from death. She then goes on: *'But I know that even now God will give you whatever you ask'* (11:22). Jesus tells her that her brother will rise, but she misunderstands him and thinks that he is referring to the teaching of the Pharisees that Lazarus will rise 'at the last day' (11:24). Yet Jesus is actually saying that the real resurrection will not take place on some future date; the resurrection will take place for believers in and through Jesus, in the present, because all who believe will never die. What he means here is not immunity from physical death, but immunity from spiritual death; the expected age has arrived.

Lazarus has been in the tomb for four days — truly dead in Jewish terms, for they believed the soul departed from the body after three days. Jesus calls to Lazarus in spectacular fashion and he is raised from the dead. He hears the voice of Christ and lives, fulfilling a prophecy Jesus had made earlier in 5:25: *'...the dead will hear the voice of the Son of God and those who hear will live.'* Significantly for the Fourth Evangelist there are two real and vital stages to this: eternal life given only by Jesus in the present *and* resurrection on the last day. Jesus shows the onlookers that he has defeated death itself and offers eternal life with the Father. Moreover, the event foreshadows Jesus's own resurrection. Belief is once again paramount; the sign was done so that the disciples 'may believe' (11:15) and Martha is herself challenged to believe (11:26), replying: *'I believe that you are the Christ, the Son of God, who came into the world'* (11:27). Finally, when Jesus prays to the Father, he asks that the act may be done so that those watching will believe (11:42), which many subsequently do (11:45).

Inevitably, the wave of popular support for Jesus generated by the raising of Lazarus angers the Jewish leaders. Pharisees and Sadducees join forces and, at a meeting of the Sanhedrin, condemn Jesus as a danger to Judaism, because, somewhat ironically,

they fear: *'Here is the man performing many miraculous signs. If we let him go on like this, everyone will believe in him...'* (11:47–8), and the High Priest, Caiaphas, utters the ominous words: *'...it is better for you that one man die for the people than that the whole nation perish'* (11:50). Jesus's life was now in grave danger. As Tasker (1960) notes: *'It was his claim to bestow upon believers the gift of eternal life by raising them from spiritual death which led to his crucifixion'.*

2 Further signs

2.1 Walking on the water (6:16–24)

This is a controversial event and its status as a sign has long been questioned by scholars. There is some dispute about the original wording. In 6:19 the Greek phrase **'epi tes thalasses'** is used, translated as 'on the sea'. Yet in 21:1 the same phrase is translated as 'by the sea' and hence there is the possibility that Jesus is not performing a miracle at all, but is simply walking on the seashore. Yet whatever view is taken, there is much symbolism here.

It was the evening after the feeding of the 5,000 and the disciples were on a boat in rough weather on the lake, when Jesus miraculously walked on the water to them. They were terrified, but Jesus calmed their fears and they all returned safely to land. The evangelist uses symbolism of night and darkness again to reflect fear and lack of faith, and the disciples are terrified of what they cannot see. However, they take Jesus on board willingly, in an act of faith; they are saved and reach a safe haven. Barrett (1955) sees this as a reflection of Psalm 107:29–30 — salvation and a safe haven are available to all who welcome Jesus into their lives:

He stilled the storm to a whisper:
The waves of the sea were hushed.
They were glad when it grew calm,
And he guided them to their desired haven.

2.2 The healing of the blind man (9:1–41)

When Jesus and the disciples are in Jerusalem they encounter a man who has been blind since he was born. The blind man probably begged at the gate of the Temple. The disciples, reflecting popular belief at that time that such afflictions were a punishment from God, ask Jesus whether the blindness is due to the sins of the man himself or those of his parents. Jesus says neither: *'...this happened so that the work of God might be displayed in his life'* (9:3). Jesus restores the man's sight by spitting into some clay and anointing the man's eyes with it — the same technique God used in Genesis 2 to create Adam. The symbolism is clear: Jesus is making the blind man into a new person. The man washes his eyes in the Pool of Siloam, and receives his sight. This again is symbolic: Siloam means 'sent' and the man is thus 'sent' by Jesus (as Jesus is sent by the Father) to be cleansed in 'living water'. He receives a new baptism in which his physical disability is removed and he receives spiritual enlightenment and faith in Christ. The 'light of the world' has entered into him.

The man does not know Jesus and, when questioned by the Jewish authorities, identifies him as a prophet (9:17), although this is only the first stage for him in a growing awareness of who Jesus is. The Pharisees say that Jesus is a sinner and cannot be from God because this healing happened on the Sabbath, an action contrary to the Law of Moses: *'This man is not from God, for he does not keep the Sabbath'* (9:16). The Pharisees do not believe that the man was blind in the first place, but his parents are called, and testify that he was born blind. The Pharisees want the man to condemn Jesus, but he refuses to do so and instead he seems almost to mock them by asking if they too want to become Jesus's disciples (9:27). In Johannine terms he correctly observes that Jesus's actions reveal him as a man from God, not a sinner.

The man is threatened with excommunication from the synagogue, and essentially from the whole Jewish community, the most severe of punishments, since it would mean that no other Jew could associate with him and that God would reject him for ever. This is nevertheless what members of the Johannine community have done, and his actions distinguish the blind man as an ideal Johannine disciple. Jesus seeks the man out and asks: *'Do you believe in the Son of Man?'* (9:35). The man understands that Jesus is referring to the Messiah and Jesus is able to tell him: *'You have now seen him; in fact, he is the one speaking with you'* (9:37). The man has no hesitation in worshipping Jesus — he has received both physical sight and spiritual sight. During the incident, his awareness has grown from simply knowing Jesus's name, through seeing Jesus as a prophet, to the realisation that he is, indeed, the Son of God. The Pharisees, however, remain spiritually blind and in darkness, for they saw Jesus, yet chose to reject him. They are the ones who are under God's judgment: *'If you were blind, you would not be guilty of sin, but now that you claim you can see, your guilt remains'* (9:41).

2.3 The raising of Lazarus (11:1–44)

For many, the raising of Lazarus is the crux of the Gospel as it symbolises the end of the old Israel and the birth of the new. Lazarus dies as a member of the old Israel and was raised through belief in Christ. The action points forward to the resurrection of Jesus and the bringing of his people out from death to eternal life. The sign takes place among people who believe in Jesus and love Lazarus (the name means 'God helps'), who was a friend and follower of Christ. Warfield (1950) writes: *'The raising of Lazarus thus becomes a decisive instance and open symbol of Jesus's conquest of death and hell.'*

Lazarus has been dead and buried for four days before Jesus arrives, and although Martha is likely to have believed that Lazarus's soul had departed from the body, she seems still to believe that Jesus can do something — her faith makes her bold enough to ask: *'But I know that even now God will give you whatever you ask'* (11:22). However, she does not really understand the power of Christ. She is probably thinking that Jesus could do something for Lazarus in the life to come, as she mentions the *'resurrection at the last day'* (11:24). Yet this **futuristic eschatology** is about to be overtaken by a **realised eschatology** of the present as Jesus declares that he is 'the resurrection and the life' (11:25). Martha declares her belief that Jesus is *'the Christ, the Son of God'* (11:27).

In contrast, Mary arrives and although she uses the same greeting as Martha, that if Jesus had been there then Lazarus would not have died, she cannot go further, as

Martha did. Nevertheless, Jesus is touched by the emotions of those around him, such that he himself weeps (11:35) — conceivably intended by the Fourth Evangelist to be read as a sign of his humanity. He commands that the stone be taken away and challenges Martha and the others to believe (11:40, 42). He cries out for Lazarus to come out, and Lazarus emerges from the tomb. Jesus orders the people to take away Lazarus's grave clothes; he is physically and spiritually reborn.

Summary

- The **'I am'** (*ego eimi*) **sayings** are linked with the Old Testament name of God and are used by the author to emphasise the origin and divinity of Christ and to highlight his message of salvation.
- All seven sayings use **Old Testament imagery** — as bread Jesus will spiritually feed his people, as light he will bring truth, as the good shepherd he will protect and nurture his people, and as the resurrection he will bring them into eternal life.
- As with the signs, the sayings reinforce Christ's message, but also highlight the blindness of the Jewish authorities and their unwillingness to listen to him.

Exam watch

The 'I am' sayings are a very important part of the Fourth Gospel and must certainly be included in your studies. They form the central part of the christology of the Gospel, along with the signs and discourses. Remember, however, that you must view the Gospel as a whole, as each topic intertwines with the others. In terms of the examination itself, you may be asked about the 'I am' sayings specifically or as part of a question on a particular incident or episode, such as the feeding of the five thousand or the raising of Lazarus. Make sure that you are also aware of the Old Testament background and symbolism and the Gospel's replacement theology — that is, how Jesus transformed the old order of things and replaced it with the new. This is key to understanding the 'I am' sayings.

Review questions

1 How do the 'I am' sayings illustrate the person and purpose of Jesus?
2 Examine the controversy and religious significance of the feeding of the five thousand.
3 Examine and comment critically upon the significance of three of the 'I am' sayings in the Fourth Gospel.

E The road to the cross

1 Discipleship

1.1 The disciples

Certainly the Fourth Gospel is a Gospel for Christian disciples. The Christ of St John invites people not only to live, but also to go on living in him.

(Smalley, 1978)

Raymond Brown (1979) claims that *'Discipleship is the primary Christian category for John...'* and it is clear that the Fourth Evangelist extends this category as far as it will go. He certainly goes beyond the Twelve, a designation he uses only three times (6:70, 71; 20:24), to include women, future believers and the *'other sheep that do not belong to this fold'* (10:16). Discipleship is dealt with in terms of special individuals — the Beloved Disciple, Mary Magdalene and Peter, for example — and in terms of the wider community of believers, some of whom may be the original readers of the Gospel. The designation 'disciple' can legitimately belong to anyone who has responded in faith to Jesus, and so the Gospel is full of disciples and quasi-disciples who struggle to come to terms with his identity and the claim he makes on their lives. Even Nicodemus, who first comes to Jesus at night, seems to be at least a crypto-Christian, or secret disciple, when he appears alongside Joseph to bury Jesus after the crucifixion. Some characters appear to be deliberate foils for each other: the lame man, who refuses Jesus's offer of salvation, and the blind man who responds to it so readily; the crowds who follow Jesus after he has raised Lazarus, and the authorities who use it as an opportunity to consolidate their plot against him. It is clear with whom the reader is intended to identify and to join in their life of discipleship beyond the cross and the resurrection.

But although the Fourth Evangelist has a long-distance view of discipleship, the inner circle who gather around Jesus during his earthly ministry and who will be the primary witnesses to him after the resurrection are not neglected. The private teaching that Jesus shares with them in the Fourth Gospel is of a particularly specific nature. In the Synoptic Gospels, Jesus's teaching to the Twelve is largely concerned with the kingdom of God, the spread of the Gospel, and the nature of the evangelistic task. In the Fourth Gospel, however, his discourses with them deal with the personal relationship between disciple and master, and the implications this has for their relationship with the world. We should not dismiss this lightly. In the Fourth Gospel, discipleship is essentially about **relationships** — with the Father, with Jesus, with fellow disciples, and with those as yet outside the Johannine community. Although the farewell discourses (chapters 13–17) provide the fullest exposition of the life of the disciple, Jesus's other discourses, not just with the inner circle, also reveal its nature.

Jesus explains to Nicodemus that discipleship involves new birth and revival from the dryness of Israel's spiritual death (Ezekiel 37). Each disciple must experience a new spiritual birth from above which is in no way related to their physical birth (3:3–7). The Fourth Evangelist introduces this theme in the Prologue when he speaks of those who accept Jesus as becoming children of God: a spiritual, not fleshly, descent (1:13), which transcends earthly, racial and gender boundaries, to incorporate *whoever* believes (3:16). Once disciples have experienced this new birth they receive eternal life. For John, this gift is the hallmark of discipleship. Freely received as the result of belief in Jesus as the one sent by God (6:29), the disciple passes from death to life, into a quality of relationship with God that cannot be experienced by those who remain 'of the world' (15:19). Disciples pass from judgment to salvation on the basis of their decision to accept Jesus and the one who sent him.

Such is the radical nature of discipleship, belonging to the new order ushered in by Jesus at Cana, that the disciples must be able to lay aside old traditions and prejudices.

The conversation with the Samaritan woman reveals that discipleship involves a new approach to worship. Formerly, Jewish worship revolved around the Temple and its ritual, or, for a Samaritan, Mount Gerazim. Jesus speaks to the woman of worship in 'spirit and truth' (4:23). The disciple's worship must reflect the nature of God and should be based on a personal, spiritual relationship with him. The prophets had long called for such personal devotion to God: Amos and Hosea taught that God despised feasts and sacrifices that were made with cold and unfaithful hearts. The Fourth Evangelist too shares the call for worship that is inner and not merely external.

Above all, the Fourth Evangelist teaches that discipleship involves a relationship with Jesus that reaches an intimacy never before encountered in Judaism. The incarnation brought God among his people in a dramatic and personal way (1:14), opening up the opportunity for a far closer relationship than that expressed in the old covenant. Jesus calls disciples in all ages to abide in him: to dwell in him and he in them, a radical call vividly illustrated by the bread of life discourse. The images of eating Jesus's flesh and drinking his blood express the depth of commitment between Jesus and disciple. Some find the demand too great, and withdraw (6:60ff).

In the farewell discourses the intimacy of the disciple's relationship with Jesus is again expressed in terms of abiding. Jesus is the vine and his disciples the branches (15:1–11). Just as a branch severed from the vine can only wither and die, so too can the disciples only enjoy his spiritual life whilst remaining on the vine. The vine being the source of life and nourishment, the branch draws from it the necessary sustenance for growth. But even healthy branches are pruned so that they might become yet more fruitful. The disciples are warned that they will experience God's pruning, and this is evidence of the life of the vine running through them. Dead leaves can only fall from a living branch, pushed off by the new growth that lies underneath, but unless the dead leaves fall, that new growth cannot reach its potential. The disciple who surrenders his life to the vine will grow beyond human limitations, but Jesus explains that it is only if he goes away that this potential can be truly fulfilled. Thus it is clear that the life of the vine is available through the Holy Spirit to all future believers: '*Very truly I tell you, the one who believes in me will also do the works that I do and, in fact, will do greater works than these, because I am going to my Father*' (14:12). These 'greater works' promised may indeed be signs and wonders, and certainly have been anticipated at 1:50 — '*You will see greater things than these*' — but Marsh suggests that the work will be proclaiming Jesus's death and resurrection as a historical event that has accomplished reconciliation between God and humanity.

But none of this is possible if the disciples do not dwell in unity with Jesus and with one another. The keys to abiding in the vine are love and obedience, and they are the unavoidable tools of discipleship. If disciples truly love Jesus, they will seek to be obedient to his commands and that obedience will ensure that they stay in his love. Jesus tells the Twelve, '*Love one another as I have loved you*' (13:34) and '*If you love me you will keep my commandments*' (14:15). Jesus's commandments can be summed up in the single commandment of love. If the disciple obeys this, all else will follow. Jesus demonstrates the meaning of such love in the foot washing (12:1ff); a message to all disciples, present and future, it symbolises the sacrificial love that distinguishes the real disciple from the false.

Discipleship too will involve opposition and conflict, just as — indeed, because — Jesus experienced it himself (15:18). As representatives of Jesus, the disciples cannot expect to be treated more favourably than Jesus was treated, but he urges them to rejoice that they share his sufferings just as they should rejoice at his death: *'In the world you will have trouble, but be of good cheer; I have overcome the world'* (16:33). Disciples can live in the ultimate victory of the cross and its exaltation. There is nothing that the world can throw at them which Jesus has not vanquished, and this is made clear by the Fourth Evangelist in Jesus's triumphant cry from the cross: *'It is accomplished'* (19:30).

Discipleship involves unity not only with Jesus but also with each other. In his final prayer (chapter 17), Jesus prays for a unity between disciples of all ages that will mirror the unity of the Father and the Son. Unity, rooted in love, is a witness to the world of the disciples' calling and to Jesus himself, and it ensures an unbroken line of discipleship. There is no suggestion in Jesus's prayer of a time when there will be no others who *'believe in me through their word'* (17:20). The key to that unity is love, just as love has bound Father and Son together in mutual dependence.

1.2 Women

A distinctive feature of the Fourth Gospel, and its teaching on discipleship in particular, is its presentation of women. Barrett (1975) argues that *'John intended to bind the church to apostolic witness, but in other respects leave it free'*. Thus, he can give women disciples a position comparable with that of the Twelve, and he chooses five female characters to present this important development:

- ❖ **Jesus's mother** — she is never named, and appears only twice, at the beginning and end of Jesus's ministry, witnessing its commencement and fulfilment. At Cana she bears witness to his authority through her confident appeal to Jesus that *'they have no wine'* (2:3) and, despite his apparently discouraging reply, she orders the servants to *'Do as he tells you'* (2:4). At the foot of the cross she must have seen the spear thrust, the final sign, and she is part of the foundational witness on which the Johannine community is based. Grassi (1992) observes that in the Fourth Gospel the mother of Jesus is thus less important as a mother, but of such importance as a disciple and witness that the author is able to speak of her in conjunction with the Beloved Disciple. However, Grassi may be overstating the case, since there is little textual evidence — eight verses in all — on which to base his thesis.
- ❖ **The Samaritan woman** — arguably a prototype of the ideal woman disciple, appearing briefly, and with none of the obvious advantages that Nicodemus had. Her response to Jesus is initially clumsy, but subtly she is revealed as a true disciple by her desire to know more of Jesus and her witness to her fellow Samaritans. As an individual, she meets Jesus in a state of ignorance and fear, but leaves him having been renewed by living water to bear fruit amongst her people. Brown (1979) suggests that she represents the vital 'Samaritan connection' in the Johannine community, to whom the community's founder had a special mission, but more importantly for the reader, her faith and response to Jesus are matched only by that of the blind man (chapter 9). The response of her fellows to her testimony is significant; they show no inclination to doubt her just because she is a woman. The male disciples are rather more circumspect. Their amazement in 4:27 reveals real

perplexity and offence, and Boer suggests that since this verse could easily have been omitted, its presence must be significant. He suggests that the testimony of the Samaritan woman represents an important modification of the Jesus tradition, which focused on men, and the perplexity of the male disciples may echo that of the Johannine community as they struggled initially to accept both women and Samaritans into the church.

÷ **The woman caught in adultery** — this rather strange incident is thought by many scholars not to be part of the original text of the Fourth Gospel. A woman who was probably guilty of fornication before marriage (an offence punishable by death under the Law of Moses (Deuteronomy 22:23)) was brought before Jesus by the Jewish authorities who hoped to trap him into breaking the Law. Jesus, however, is aware of the trap and neatly avoids it with the words: *'If any one of you is without sin, let him be the first to throw a stone at her'* (8:7). The woman is saved, although Jesus does not excuse her sin — he shows insight; the Law is not wrong, but it should not be imposed in such a strict, uncaring way. Interestingly, we do not know if the woman becomes a disciple, and the episode focuses more on Jesus and his relationship with the authorities and the Law than on her. What he wrote in the ground is a mystery, but it may have been the Ten Commandments. As he wrote a new commandment, gradually more of her accusers withdrew, aware that they could not declare themselves guiltless in keeping the Law.

÷ **Martha** — the closest parallel in the Fourth Gospel to Peter's synoptic confession is Martha's three-fold identification of Jesus at 11:27, as *'Christ, the Son of God, the one who is coming into the world'*. John makes it clear that at a time when the church was developing, Peter was one of a number of characters who had pre-eminence, and Martha is clearly among them. Furthermore, Martha perceives that it is Jesus's relationship with the Father that enables him to act as he does, and for the Fourth Evangelist this is the key to discipleship and eternal life (17:3, 8). Mary comes into her own at the anointing at Bethany (12:1–8). Although she does not speak, her act of extravagant devotion to Jesus receives the highest praise, and she has perceived what none of the male disciples have grasped — that he must die. She serves as a foil to the deceitful Judas and Jesus interprets her action as prophetic (12:7).

÷ **Mary Magdalene** — it is to Mary that Peter loses his pre-eminence as the first to testify to having seen the risen Jesus. Not that she is a flawless witness: despite, or perhaps because of, standing by the cross (19:25), she cannot understand Jesus's death as glorification. She has seen him die, but it is now more important that she understand his new status. She is then free to take to the male disciples the word of the Gospel — that Jesus Christ has been raised from death.

These episodes are individually significant, but as a whole speak even more powerfully of the perspective in which the Fourth Evangelist and his community were prepared to see women. Brown (1979) writes: *'Thus, if other Christian communities thought of Peter as the one who made a supreme confession of Jesus as the Son of God and the one to whom the risen Jesus first appeared, the Johannine community associated such memories with heroines like Martha and Mary Magdalene'.*

2 The farewell discourses

2.1 The Last Supper

The final part of Jesus's ministry begins with a supper. In the Synoptic Gospels, this supper is depicted as the Passover meal. However, there are indications in the Fourth Gospel that this is not so, and the meal is eaten a day before Passover. There seem to be two reasons for this: Peter is later seen carrying a sword, which was not permitted at Passover, and, the following day, the priests refuse to enter the palace of the Roman governor because it would defile them before Passover (18:28). However, the theological significance is more important still, and by moving the final meal forward by a day, the Fourth Evangelist ensures that Jesus dies at the moment that the Passover lambs are being slaughtered. Jesus himself is, of course, the perfect Passover lamb.

The supper begins with Jesus washing the disciples' feet, showing that he has come as a humble servant. Peter protests, showing the false pride of a sinner who resists the need for divine help, but also responding as a disciple who cannot accept that Jesus is going to die. Jesus rebukes him — the believer must accept Christ's offer of service, which is embodied in his sacrificial death, for otherwise there can be no true relationship of salvation. Equally, Christ's followers will themselves have to serve others humbly: *'I have set you an example that you should do as I have done for you. I tell you the truth, no servant is greater than his master, nor is a messenger greater than the one who sent him'* (13:15–16). The Fourth Evangelist appears to have substituted the well-known synoptic institution of the Lord's Supper with the foot-washing, but he does not leave the final meal free of sacramental overtones. The foot-washing is a model of baptism, symbolising the immersion into Jesus's death that the disciples must accept and the washing in his blood that will be accomplished on the cross.

As the supper goes on, Jesus is clearly troubled as the final battle between good and evil draws closer. Though he knows that Judas will be his betrayer, in an act of love and peace he performs the custom whereby the host offers the bread to the most honoured guest, offering it to Judas (13:26). Judas then goes out into the night, leaving the true light. It seems that only the Beloved Disciple, introduced here for the first time, has any notion of what Jesus's words to Judas mean, as ironically, the others believe that Judas is leaving the gathering to buy something for the feast. Indeed, he leaves to ensure that the true Passover lamb will be offered at the fitting time.

With Judas gone, Jesus speaks directly to the disciples, telling them that he is soon to leave them. But he gives them fresh hope: *'A new commandment I give you: Love one another. As I have loved you, so you must love one another. By this all men will know that you are my disciples'* (13:34–5).

In a burst of well-intentioned enthusiasm, Peter vainly offers to lay down his life for Christ (13:37), although he does not really understand what Jesus is saying, or the implications of his own offer. Jesus calmly tells him: *'I tell you the truth, before the cock crows, you will disown me three times!'* (13:38). After the resurrection Jesus echoes Peter's bold claim with his own prediction of Peter's death: *'"When you are old, you will stretch out your hands and another will gird you and carry you where you do not wish to go." This he said to show by what death he was to glorify God'* (21:18–19).

2.2 The Holy Spirit — Paraclete

The concept of the Paraclete is a stroke of genius... It gave the Christians a distinctive way of thinking about the presence of God, answered the nagging question of the delay of the Parousia, and solved the problem of the growing temporal separation from the historical revelation.

(Kysar, 1993)

Although the Fourth Evangelist has already dealt in some depth with the role that the Spirit plays in salvation and the life of the disciple, it is not until the farewell discourses that a new dimension to his teaching on the Holy Spirit is revealed. Kysar observes that for the Johannine community, there was clearly something about the simple title of Spirit that was unsatisfactory, and they needed a distinctive title which would express, especially in situations of conflict and uncertainty, the special reality of the living presence of God in their midst two and three generations after the death of Jesus. The concept adds a crucial dimension to the community's understanding of eschatology. So valuable was the presence of the Spirit in their midst, that they were able to claim that the future blessings had already become a present reality to them.

The central function of the Paraclete is to communicate the revelation of God given by Christ and to lead believers into a radically new life. However, that role is complex and involves the Paraclete in a range of activities in relation to the disciples, the church and the world. Furthermore, there are four primary ways of translating Paraclete:

÷ An **advocate** — one called to the side of another to assist.
÷ A **defence counsel** — one who intercedes for another.
÷ A **comforter** — one who comforts and consoles.
÷ A **proclaimer** — one who exhorts and encourages.

Evidently, the word was rich in meaning for the evangelist and his readers and there is no reason to assume that he did not choose it for this very reason.

Assuring the disciples that he would not leave them alone, Jesus promises that to enable them to carry on his work, the Father will send the Holy Spirit to the disciples. The Spirit will be a Counsellor, who will equip them to bring the good news to all people: *'But the Counsellor, the Holy Spirit, whom the Father will send in my name, will teach you all things and will remind you of everything I have said to you'* (14:25–6). The Counsellor, or Spirit of Truth, will be of equal stature to Christ himself and will enable the disciples to grasp fully the truth. He will live within the disciples (14:17). Moreover, Jesus assures the disciples that anything they ask for in his name will be given to them: *'And I will do whatever you ask in my name, so that the Son may bring glory to the Father. You may ask for anything in my name, and I will do it'* (14:13–14). He tells the disciples to obey his words and trust in God (14:23) and not to be afraid (14:27), despite the fact that the ordeal of the passion is near and he must now obey the Father: *'The prince of this world is coming. He has no hold on me, but the world must learn that I love the Father and that I do exactly what my Father has commanded me'* (14:30–1).

The promise of the Paraclete has run throughout the Gospel since John the Witness saw the Holy Spirit descend on Jesus and remain on him at 1:32–4. The term **pneuma** has served to describe the role and function of the spirit throughout Jesus's ministry, but now the evangelist uses his distinctive term, **paracletos**. The primary characteristic of the Paraclete is that he will be 'another' like Jesus (14:16) and will fulfil the roles and functions that Jesus performed when he was on earth — hence Raymond Brown's famous description of the Paraclete as *'the presence of Jesus when he is absent'.* The Paraclete spirit will be the living presence of Jesus amongst believers, not merely an instrument of power to wield. It will dwell in the disciples just as Jesus himself does, and as such, the world, dependent on the tangible and the rational, will not be able to accept it (14:17). The relationship between the Spirit and the disciples is one that the world will be unable to comprehend, but for the believer it will intercede, guide and teach — leading them into a deeper knowledge of Jesus's own words. Just as the evangelist has made clear throughout the Gospel that Jesus is one with the Father, inseparable from him in every way (10:30), when he introduces the Paraclete he makes clear that he too is sent in God's name and with his authority, as Jesus was sent, and hence his message and his work cannot be understood separately from that of the Father and the Son.

The Paraclete will be part of the process of salvation for believers. Because only those who have believed in Jesus can receive it, it is a characteristic that separates them from the world and singles them out as those who have passed from death to life. Indwelling of the Spirit is a necessary part of the life of discipleship, bearing witness in the disciple's life to the truth of Jesus and his words. Luke depicts the Spirit as the directing force of the Apostles' ministry in Acts; the Fourth Evangelist describes it in terms of the personal relationship that the believer has with the Father and the Son, which will be the means by which they continue to abide in the vine (15:1–11).

In chapter 16 the evangelist presents the Paraclete as being integral in the eschatological judgment of the world: *'And when he comes he will convince (convict?) the world concerning sin and righteousness and judgment'* (16:8). In this role the Paraclete clearly plays the part of the prosecuting counsel, exposing the world's sin and calling it to account. Bultmann (1971) suggests that the lawsuit that the Paraclete will conduct is *'one of cosmic dimensions'* and the essential reason for the Paraclete's judgment of the world and *'the ruler of this world'* (Satan) will be for the sin of rejecting Jesus. Furthermore, the Paraclete will not just prosecute but judge the world, anticipating the last judgment and bringing into the present the eschatological activity which it will ultimately face at the end times.

This brings into focus the other central function of the Paraclete for the Fourth Evangelist: it is the Johannine church's solution to the problem of the delay of the **Parousia**. Rather than look to the future, he urges them to look to the present and see that Jesus is already among them and that the Parousia has occurred already — not a distant event which most will not live to enjoy, but something which can be realised in the here and now.

The second problem for the church that the Paraclete solves is how those who were never able to meet the earthly Jesus face to face can still have a relationship with him. The Paraclete bridges the temporal gap between the Johannine community and the historical Jesus, and thus the evangelist stresses that the Paraclete does not teach new things, but reminds the church of Jesus's own words, consolidating and illuminating them for each new generation of believers. In this way all believers have as direct access to Jesus as the first disciples, and the Paraclete keeps alive the revelation of God in Christ so it is available to all. It is for this reason that Sören Kierkegaard writes:

There is no disciple at second hand. The first and the last are essentially on the same plane, only that a later generation finds its occasion in the testimony of a contemporary generation, while the contemporary generation finds the occasions in its own immediate contemporaneity, and in so far, owes nothing to any other generation.

(Cited in Aston, 1991)

2.3 'I am the way, the truth and the life' (14:1–14)

Jesus reassures his disciples, telling them that soon all will become clear and that they are to trust in God. He highlights his unique role with the Father: '*I am the way and the truth and the life. No one comes to the Father except through me*' (14:6). He tells them plainly that he and the Father are one and that they have to keep their faith in the confidence that '*I am in the Father, and the Father is in me*' (14:10). This 'I am' saying is made in response to Thomas's anxious question: '*Lord, we do not know where you are going, so how can we know the way?*' (14:5). Jesus's reassurance to the disciples that he is going to prepare them a place makes little difference to their fear and ignorance of his destiny and fate. Interestingly, the disciples are as much at a loss as the Jews were earlier in the narrative when they naively asked, '*Where does this man intend to go that we cannot find him?*' (7:35), but Thomas's question suggests that the disciples are keen to know so that they truly might follow and learn from him.

Just as Jesus has described himself earlier as the bread and the one who gives it, and as both door and shepherd who leads the sheep through it, so too he provides the way to the Father by going that way himself. Jesus *is* the way, and the Fourth Evangelist makes no apologies for his exclusivism. Barrett (1975) observes, '*there is no access to God independent of him*', and Jesus makes clear that he is the fullest revelation of God available to humanity (compare 1:18). But once on the road, the disciple needs directions and the means to reach his or her goal, and Jesus provides these too: the truth and the life. Both concepts have been vital in the Gospel from the Prologue, and the evangelist has made crystal clear that only Jesus *is* the truth and offers the true way to know the Father. The discourses with Nicodemus and the Samaritan woman exposed the need to accept that knowing Jesus and the truth of his words is the only way in which humanity can be born anew and receive eternal life, and yet even now the disciples demand: '*Show us the Father and we will be satisfied*' (14:8). The reader has already grasped so much more than the inner circle, who still stumble with misunderstanding.

Truth and life are inextricable, for without following the way of truth the disciples will never reach the goal of life. The quest they are to undertake is the same that the Old Testament writers sought after. The Psalmist wrote, '*Teach me thy way O Lord that I may walk in thy truth*' (Psalm 86:11) and '*Make me know thy way O Lord*' (Psalm 25:4), and, of course, for him it was the Law which was '*a light to my feet and a lamp to my path*' (Psalm 119:105). Jesus replaces the Law as the way to salvation and fellowship with God and although subsequent discourse makes it clear that it will not be an easy way to follow, it is the only way for the disciple who truly wants to know God.

2.4 'I am the true vine' (15:1–11)

When Jesus declares himself to be the true vine, he uses one of the richest symbols in the Old Testament, where the figure of the vine was used to symbolise the nation of

Israel. Chosen, set aside and planted by Yahweh, Israel was given everything necessary to flourish, and yet, *'The more his fruit increased, the more altars he built* (Hosea 10:1b), and God's people became a *'corrupt, wild vine'* (Jeremiah 2:21). Whilst the fruit of the old Israel might initially have been evident in its prosperity and political strength, it soon became valueless, as the people drifted into paganism and apostasy. The most important passage is clearly Isaiah 5:1–7, which condemns Israel for failing to produce the fruit that God had hoped they would, i.e. the taking of his word to all peoples.

In the Fourth Gospel, Jesus depicts himself as the true vine — *'I am the true vine and my Father is the gardener'* (15:1) — that *will* produce fruit and so all nations will know God. Marsh (1968) observes: *'...it was natural that, as the one in whom was embodied the new beginning of the life of God's people, Jesus should use such an Old Testament figure to make plain to his Israelite contemporaries what his nature and functions were'*. Believers in Jesus will be the branches of the vine, receiving life from the vine and bearing fruit. Like all vines, they will need pruning and cutting back, and this highlights the importance of a close relationship with God, for a branch cannot bear fruit on its own, and neither can a believer unless they abide in the love of Jesus: *'No branch can bear fruit by itself; it must remain in the vine. Neither can you bear fruit unless you remain in me'* (9:4).

In this saying, the Fourth Evangelist subtly conveys the depth of his replacement theology. Jesus has already indicated that he replaces and fulfils the Law, the festivals and the rites of Judaism. Now he replaces Israel as a whole. Where they were apostate and faithless, Jesus and his disciples (in the widest sense of all believers in Christ) will be the faithful vine, giving glory to the Father through its faithfulness. Old Israel has passed away and the new community, rooted in an intimate relationship with the Father and the Son, is now the bearer of the promises of Israel. That community does, of course, include some members of the old Israel, but they can only share in it by coming to the light and accepting the witness of Jesus.

Abiding in the vine (15:7) is the heart of fruitfulness, and it brings with it the promise of answered prayer. The intimacy suggested by abiding in the vine is, of course, characteristic of the Gospel as a whole. Jesus invites his disciples to eat his flesh and drink his blood, and the symbolism of the foot-washing conveys the intimate union that Jesus and the believer enter through his death. Only a deep, abiding and ongoing relationship with Jesus can bring the disciple abundant life, rooted in love and obedience (15:9–10). The call to obedience, implicit in all these sayings, marks the beginning of a new relationship between God and his people — which will finally eclipse the failures of previous generations.

2.5 The disciples' future role

The saying of the vine leads directly to some of Jesus's most important teaching concerning the nature of discipleship. To remain in Jesus meant obedience to his words and teachings. The relationship of the believer to Christ should be one of love. So, too, must believers love each other: *'My command is this: Love each other as I have loved you. Greater love has no one than this, that he lay down his life for his friends'* (15:12–13). Jesus tells the disciples that, not only are they his friends, but also they have been especially chosen by him: *'You did not choose me, but I chose you and appointed you to go and bear*

fruit — fruit that will last. Then the Father will give you whatever you ask in my name' (15:16).

Jesus warns the disciples that life will not be easy, for the world will hate them because they will no longer be part of it, but will be part of a new way (15:19). They will suffer persecution, as he has — but it will not really be a hatred of them, rather a hatred of Christ, born out of sin: *'If the world hates you, remember that it hated me first'* (15:18). However, their task is not impossible, for the Holy Spirit will be with them.

Jesus warns the disciples about persecution in order to prepare them properly, so they will not give up and abandon their work. The Holy Spirit will help them in three ways:

÷ He will show people that they are sinners and that Christ died for them (15:8).
÷ He will show the world the love and righteousness of God (15:9–10).
÷ He will show the world that judgment is to come and that the 'prince of this world' has been condemned (15:11).

The Holy Spirit will not bring new truths, but will declare what he was told by God. He will bring the disciples into a greater understanding of Jesus's death and resurrection and the salvation of the world. Moreover, the disciples have been given a high position. Just as God's love was in Christ, so too it was in them. The Father loves them because of their love and belief in the Son. Therefore, after the resurrection, they will be able to ask the Father in their own right (15:23). Finally, Jesus warns them that they will initially be scattered, but Jesus will not be alone, for the Father will be with him. The disciples will not need to despair: *'I have told you these things, so that you may have peace. In this world you will have trouble. But take heart! I have overcome the world'* (15:33).

2.6 The High Priestly Prayer

Chapter 17, which concludes the farewell discourses, is written in the form of a long prayer, divided into three parts. Its origin is uncertain, although Smalley (1978) suggests that despite it clearly being a *'literary composition'* (i.e. freely composed by the evangelist), the origin of its ideas and themes may well lie in the upper room and the last meal between Jesus and his disciples. It is commonly called the High Priestly Prayer or the Prayer of Consecration, which asks for God's blessing on that which is to be offered as a sacrifice. The sacrifice, which, in Judaism, was offered by the High Priest, must be consecrated, that is, made holy and acceptable to God. In this prayer, Jesus is both the priest praying for consecration and the sacrifice to be consecrated. He has prepared the disciples for his death and warned them of what lies ahead once they are without the security of his physical presence. There is still much to learn, but the Paraclete will be their teacher when they are ready to receive it. Now Jesus must leave the disciples to continue his witness, but he is sharply aware of the difficulties they will face. These difficulties have been implicit in the good shepherd discourse; it would not be necessary for the good shepherd to protect the flock if discipleship did not present dangers. These difficulties become all the more apparent after Jesus's physical departure, and the High Priestly Prayer serves therefore not only to dedicate Jesus to his death — the good shepherd's death — but to provide a blanket of protection for the disciples.

In the first part (17:1–5), Jesus prepares and prays for himself. He makes two requests:

❖ That he will be used by the Father for the full and final display of their mutual love in sacrifice.

❖ That the hour of his death will be a time of glory. He speaks to the Father of their relationship and their communion together. God had given Jesus authority over all creation and now Jesus will exercise that authority and then return to the Father's side: *'Glorify your Son, that your Son may glorify you. For you granted him authority over all people that he might give eternal life to all those you have given him'* (17:2).

Although Jesus is praying for himself, the disciples are still firmly in view. His ministry has been for the purpose of giving *'eternal life to all whom you have given him'* (17:2) and the work Jesus has done, soon to be fulfilled on the cross, is for their benefit. We know already that those who have accepted the offer of eternal life have passed from death to life (5:24). Even Jesus's pre-existence — *'the glory that I had in your presence before the world was made'* (17:5) — is relevant to the disciples who, Jesus prays, *'may be with me where I am, to see my glory, which you have given me because you loved me before the foundation of the world'* (17:24, compare 14:2).

In the second part (17:6–19), Jesus prays specifically for the disciples. He asks God to bless them, to keep them strong in faith and to make the new church secure. He asks that they be kept safe and be filled with the truth and made ready for their mission: *'Sanctify them by the truth: your word is truth. As you sent me into the world, I have sent them into the world'* (17:18). Jesus's earthly ministry is a time during which he has led those who believe him into a true knowledge of God (17:6). They have enjoyed his divine protection, having been chosen by the Father and set apart from the world. Jesus must pray for them specifically, not because he does not love the world (3:16), but because at this stage he must focus on those he leaves behind. They are no longer of the world, but must continue to be in it (17:16), as he himself was; this is true of disciples in all ages. It is necessary to be in the world if any witness is to be accomplished, but in order to remain effective, the disciple must be uncorrupted by the world. Judas is already lost (17:12), but Jesus's prayer that none of the others shall be lost is fulfilled in the garden at the moment of his arrest (18:9). The links with the good shepherd discourse are apparent once again: *'I give them eternal life and they will never perish. No one will snatch them out of my hand'* (10:28). Jesus's protection of his sheep is guaranteed, and in the garden he lays down his life for the disciples, even before the salvific act on the cross.

In the third part (17:20–6), the scope of the prayer is widened as Jesus prays for future believers. He asks that all who come to believe will share the same love and fellowship that he shares with the Father. The future believers need protecting as well as the disciples: *'I pray also for those who will believe in me through their message, that all of them may be one, Father, just as you are in me and I am in you'* (17:20–1). Jesus envisions a community united in love and witness, which lies beyond the life and ministry of the inner circle. Separated as they are from the world, unity is not just desirable; it is essential for their survival. It will be the most influential way in which they can show the world something of the love and reflected glory between the Father and the Son (17:21, 23) and the best way they can be effective in their ministry. During his earthly ministry, the source of Jesus's strength was his unity

with the Father, and the work he accomplished was made possible only by his dependence on him — *'My food is to do the will of him who sent me, and to accomplish his work'* (4:34). In the same way, future believers will only be effective in the world whilst they remain united and dependent on the Father and the Son. Disciples who attempt to operate outside this dependent unity will fail and, like the fruitless branches, they will be stripped away.

Through future believers, Jesus will continue to make known the love of the Father and to draw all of humanity into the love he shares with him. Thus the vision of chapter 17 is far-reaching indeed. There are many 'greater works' (14:12) that will be accomplished, and it is clear that discipleship is not a passive relationship between the believer and Jesus. Rather, the unity between them opens it up to limitless possibilities as *'the love with which you have loved me may be in them and I in them'* (17:26).

Summary

- **Discipleship** — *'The primary Christian category for John'*. An open category that goes beyond the Twelve and is essentially concerned with building a relationship between Jesus and the believer. Discipleship involves new birth, spiritual inheritance, eternal life, separation from the world, inner worship, and membership of a new order that is free from the prejudices of the past. It is an intimate relationship, which provides nourishment and equips the disciple to do greater things. The relationship is rooted in unity, love and obedience, and in the perspective of Jesus's triumphant glorification.

- **Women** — are given positions of authority and insight, commissioned to call others to faith in Jesus and given some of the fullest christological declarations in the Gospel. **Jesus's Mother** — paired with the Beloved Disciple as a crucial witness to the beginning and end of the Gospel. **Samaritan woman** — prototype of disciple who understands more than the Jewish teacher and witnesses to her fellow Samaritans. **Adulterous woman** — Jesus demonstrates compassion and wisdom. **Martha** — offers the Fourth Gospel's equivalent of Peter's Confession. **Mary** — prophetic anointing of Jesus for burial. **Mary Magdalene** — Apostle to the Apostles.

- **Last Supper** — sacramental foot-washing rather than Eucharistic meal. Not a Passover meal, but Jesus will die as the perfect Passover lamb. A crisis looms for Peter and Judas.

- **Paraclete** — the Fourth Evangelist's distinctive means of presenting the Holy Spirit as the replacement for Jesus, the continuum of his ministry in the early church: advocate, counsellor, comforter and proclaimer. Resolves problems of the delayed **Parousia** and the possibility of how future generations could know the living Jesus.

- **'I am the way, the truth and the life'** — Jesus as the way to God, transcending the Law and all others who may have pointed that way in the past.

- **'I am the true vine'** — Jesus as the true Israel that will yield good fruit and give to God what is his due.

- **Disciples' future role** — to face persecution; to rejoice in Jesus's death; to bear witness to the world; to be empowered by the Holy Spirit.

- **High Priestly Prayer** — Jesus's consecration to his death for the sanctification of all believers, past, present and future.

Exam watch

There are some very popular examination topics amongst this material, especially the Holy Spirit (see also p. 375 and Women in the Fourth Gospel. As ever, ensure that your answers are not narrative-based, but draw out the distinctiveness of the Fourth Evangelist's presentation of these themes. Use quotations from the text to support the critical points that you make.

Review questions

1 (a) Examine the role of the Holy Spirit in the Fourth Gospel.
  (b) Assess the importance of the Holy Spirit in the ministry of Jesus.
2 (a) With reference to three separate incidents, examine the importance of women in the ministry of Jesus as presented in the Fourth Gospel.
  (b) To what extent do these incidents reflect the social and religious conditions of the time?
3 Examine and evaluate the teaching of the Fourth Gospel on the nature and character of Christian discipleship.
4 Outline and discuss the contribution of the farewell discourses to the teaching of the Fourth Gospel on (i) discipleship and (ii) the person and work of Jesus.

F Passion and resurrection narratives

1 Arrest and trial

The Fourth Evangelist prepares his readers well for the events of the passion. The foot-washing, the prediction of the betrayal and the lengthy farewell discourse have served to delay the action of the passion and to prepare the reader — and the disciples — for an understanding of its meaning and significance. From the moment of Jesus's arrest in the garden it is clear that he is in complete control of the events, and in the approach to the crucifixion the author highlights the fact that the death and resurrection of Jesus will mean the glorification of God, the fulfilment of scripture and the end of the old and the beginning of a new age. As Marsh (1968) says: *'In Jesus Christ, the whole universe is made anew'*. Jesus is not the victim, but the initiator. For the Fourth Evangelist, the responsibility for Christ's death is seen to rest with men: Judas, the chief priests and Pilate. Most of all, he shows the death of Jesus as a great victory over evil and darkness.

After the Supper, Jesus and the disciples spend the evening in an olive grove or garden (possibly Gethsemane) outside Jerusalem. Note the symbolism here: just as Adam was expelled from the Garden of Eden (Genesis 3), so the scene of the final conflict is in a garden. Judas comes at night (symbolic of darkness and evil) with a group of soldiers to arrest Jesus. Jesus does not hide, and as he addresses his accusers with the words 'I am', the soldiers fall to the ground — overwhelmed, if unconsciously, by his divine glory. The use of the 'I am' formula is clearly a divine declaration of his identity, although this is probably a narrative device rather than a historical record. Throughout the Gospel, premature attempts to arrest Jesus have been frustrated (8:20, 59), and even at this final hour it will not be accomplished by force. The Father and the Son remain in control of the timing of this climax in salvation history, so even if Satan will be permitted a temporary victory, it is only with the consent of God: *'I will no longer talk much with you for the ruler of this world is coming. He has no power over me, but I do as the Father has commanded me...'* (14:30). Jesus's death, therefore, is not the result of a miscalculation, but the very reason for which *'the Word became flesh'* (1:14). He can face the arresting party without flinching as he had anticipated in 12:27: *'Now is my soul troubled, and what shall I say? "Father, save me from this hour?" No, for this purpose I have come to this hour.'*

1.1 Before the Sanhedrin

From the garden, Jesus is taken for interrogation to the house of Annas, the father-in-law of the High Priest, Caiaphas. Peter and another disciple follow at a distance and wait in the courtyard, and as Jesus is questioned by Annas, Peter denies three times that he knows Jesus (18:27), just as Jesus had earlier predicted. Annas questions Peter about his teaching, already, it seems, having drawn his own conclusions about Jesus's identity. The Fourth Evangelist has dealt with such christological matters as are the subject of the trial in the Synoptics, particularly through the disputes of chapters 5–8. Jesus answers simply and points out that he taught openly, for everyone to hear (18:20), and refuses to condemn himself. The inevitability of Jesus's death does not require that he should bring it about recklessly, or allow corrupt forces to prevail. He does not avoid his death by refusing to bow to the illegalities of the trial, and the reader is aware that the events which will reach their climax on the cross do so not through the efforts of Jesus's opponents, but rather because the Father has determined that it will be so.

1.2 Before Pilate

The story cannot be read without realising how profoundly the roles of judge and prisoner are really reversed.

(Marsh, 1968)

Annas sends Jesus to Caiaphas, although the author does not tell us what happens in this second priestly trial. Early in the morning Jesus is taken before Pontius Pilate, the Roman governor. As it is Passover, Pilate is in his residence in Jerusalem, but, ironically, the Jews will not enter because they would be defiled, so Pilate has to go to them. Pilate and Jesus both appear to stand as victims of a plot. It is possible that Pilate and the Jewish authorities have already discussed Jesus's case; the Jews, realising that their charges against Jesus are fragile, hope that Pilate can be encouraged to negotiate — hence their vague reply to his question about what charges are being brought against Jesus: *'"If he were not a criminal," they replied, "we would not have handed him over to you"'* (18:30). If this is so, as he stands face to face with Jesus, Pilate comes to a growing awareness that he is faced with no political rival. The Fourth Evangelist is unclear whether the authorities have told Pilate that Jesus has supposedly claimed to be King of the Jews and Jesus himself asks, *'Do you say this of your own accord, or did others say it to you?'* (18:34), to ascertain Pilate's own evaluation of him.

Pilate evidently does not want to get involved, but the Jews insist, because they do not have the power themselves to execute Jesus — power that rested only with the occupying power of the Romans. Pilate's initial reaction is to free Jesus and he clearly sees the whole matter as a Jewish problem. He cannot understand what Jesus is supposed to have done wrong and why he refuses to defend himself: *"Am I a Jew?"* *Pilate replied. "It was your people and your chief priests who handed you over to me. What is it you have done?"* (18:35). He attempts to set Jesus free by applying the custom of releasing one prisoner at Passover (although, technically, Jesus is not a prisoner since he has not been found guilty of any offence). However, the Jews ask Pilate to release another man, Barabbas, instead (18:40). Pilate's failure is to grasp the real meaning of Jesus's words and the true nature of his kingship. Indeed, as a heavenly king Jesus could call upon a legion of angels to protect him, but this would be inconsistent with the nature of his messiahship and God's plan for salvation. Pilate struggles to understand, but demonstrates that he is not *'of the truth'* as Jesus declares: *'You say that I am a king. For this I was born and for this I came into the world, to bear witness to the truth'*. The witness can only be made through the cross, and Jesus's persistent refusal to speak in his own defence grows out of his understanding of the inevitability of his divinely ordained death.

Pilate orders Jesus to be flogged and, after the soldiers have humiliated him, Pilate shows Jesus to the Jews, perhaps in the hope that this will be punishment enough, and presses the accusation of royalty, perhaps to shame the authorities for seeking the execution of their 'king'. The chief priests are not satisfied and Pilate angrily declares: *'You take him and crucify him. As for me, I find no basis for a charge against him'* (19:6). The Jews remain adamant. They tell Pilate that Jesus has to die because he claims to be the Son of God (19:7). This frightens Pilate, a superstitious man, who only now becomes aware that he too is a pawn in a dangerous power game. He questions Jesus further, but to no avail, and Jesus's words, *'You have no power over me, unless it had been given you from above'* (19:11), show where the real balance of power lies. Until the end, Pilate wants to free Jesus, but the Jews threaten him by saying that if he frees Jesus — the King of the Jews — then Caesar will be angered. Understanding only too well the political implications of failure to condemn Jesus, Pilate reluctantly hands Jesus over to be crucified, but not without forcing the Jewish authorities to accept the charge they brought against Jesus, writing over the cross, *'The King of the Jews'*, a strike against the treachery of Jesus's accusers. The trial ends on a further note of irony. When Pilate asks the chief priests, *'Shall I crucify your king?'* (19:15), their reply is *'We have no king but Caesar'* — the ultimate blasphemy.

2 Conflict

The contrast between Jesus as light and his enemies — who are also the enemies of God — as darkness, is sustained throughout the Gospel, particularly in the debates between Jesus and the Jews.

(Smalley, 1978)

The author seems to suggest that the primary responsibility for Jesus's death lay with the Jewish leaders. They acted as they did not because they were evil, but in a real sense, from their limited perceptions, Jesus had committed blasphemy. He had ridden triumphantly into Jerusalem and his presence could have caused civil unrest during the Passover. He could not simply have been imprisoned, since his followers would have rioted. Execution therefore seemed a prudent option. According to Marsh (1968), the crucifixion was the result of the fact that *'...good men are driven to evil sometimes by the*

very soundness of their good intentions'. The Fourth Evangelist makes heavy use of irony in his presentation of the conflict between Jesus and his opponents. They, of all people, should have been able to perceive the truth of Jesus's identity, and yet they conspicuously failed to do so. Alan Culpepper (1983) writes:

Their inability to comprehend Jesus's glory sets up most of the irony, since the reader is able to see both their blindness and Jesus's glory through the eyes of the evangelist... Although they do not recognise who Jesus is, there is willfulness in their blindness. They love darkness rather than light... As a result, they do not recognise the higher plane of their own words.

The passion narrative has brought to a climax the theme of conflict which has run throughout the Gospel from the telling prediction in the Prologue that Jesus would not be received by 'his own' (1:11). In developing a systematic replacement theology, it is inevitable that the evangelist has written polemically of Judaism and in chapters 7–9 we see some of the most anti-Semitic statements in the New Testament. The Jews respond to Jesus in kind with accusations of illegitimacy (8:41), false prophecy and sorcery (7:12, 47), and demonic possession (7:20, 8:48). Jesus's confrontation with the Jews in chapter 8 leads him to say that their true father is Satan (8:44), the harshest accusation he could bring against God's covenant people. The Fourth Gospel includes 70 references to 'the Jews', a general term sometimes without particular significance, but in most cases, strongly negative. It usually refers to the Jewish authorities which oppose Jesus and which were clearly in conflict with the evangelist's community, as the telling incident with the blind man's parents reveals (9:1–41). Most broadly, 'the Jews' are those who belong to the world and who reject Jesus. To a considerable extent they are destined to do so because they fail to understand his teaching, especially about his own person (8:21). Yet some respond more positively, and there is always divided opinion about Jesus (10:19). Nicodemus becomes a representative of the Jews who do not remain overtly hostile, but who are not prepared to make a full commitment to Jesus, *'lest they be put out of the synagogue'* (12:42). It seems likely that he remains ambivalent, despite burying Jesus, though Brown (1979) argues that Nicodemus's actions at the end of chapter 19 are effectively a public testimony of discipleship.

The language of the Gospel emphasises the line that has been firmly drawn between the Johannine community and the synagogue by the end of the first century. Jesus speaks of 'your law' (10:34) when addressing the Jew, and the Fourth Evangelist specifies that feasts are 'of the Jews', as if to stress that they are not festivals observed by his community: *'The Passover of the Jews was at hand'* (2:13). In Jesus's dialogue with Nicodemus, the acrimonious split between church and synagogue is plain. The dialogue shifts from being between two individuals to being between two communities, Johannine and Jewish: *'We speak of what we know and you do not receive our testimony'* (3:11). Jesus addresses Nicodemus as representative of *all* Jews, telling him that *'you* [plural] *must be born again'* (3:7). Although he holds out a promise of new birth, he also conveys a sharp criticism: if Judaism needs to be revived, it is because it is dead.

The Fourth Gospel presents a picture of the Johannine community as being closed and protective. The members of the community are called to love one another, but not to love the world; they must be apart from it. Life as a Johannine Christian cannot include compromise with, or assimilation into, the world. Persecution is inevitable, but is to be welcomed as part of the community's ministry. Those within it have made the right decision, as far as the Fourth Evangelist is concerned, but it is not an easy one to make. The conflicts between Jesus and the Jews show why that separation has become inevitable, as persecution grows to become life threatening. Those who have committed their lives to Jesus are, however, granted divine protection, and the unity of the community will be the basis for their enduring witness, despite continued hostility: *'I have said all this to you to keep you from falling away. They will put you out of the synagogues; indeed the hour is coming when whoever kills you will think he is offering service to God. And they will do this because they have not known the Father, or me. But I have said this that when their hour comes you may remember that I told you of them'* (16:1–4).

3 The crucifixion

Kysar (1993) identifies four themes around which John's understanding of the cross pivots: the cross as the enthronement of Jesus as king; his ascension and glorification; the new Passover; and the ultimate expression of God's love. In conveying these rich themes the Fourth Gospel's account of the crucifixion itself is relatively brief, but contains much symbolism from the Old Testament:

1 Jesus carries his own cross, just as Isaac carried the wood upon which he was to be sacrificed (Genesis 22:6). The Fourth Evangelist eliminates the role of Simon of Cyrene who, according to the synoptists, carried Jesus's cross. He wants to make clear that Jesus needs no human help in the act of salvation that is about to be accomplished.
2 He is crucified between 'two others' (Isaiah 53:12). Interestingly, the Fourth Evangelist does not specify that they were criminals. Rather, they appear to be honouring Jesus on his right and left side, as he dies enthroned on the cross.
3 His clothes are divided among the soldiers (Psalm 22:18).
4 He is offered vinegar to drink (Psalm 69:2).
5 His garment is without seam, like the High Priest's ephod (Exodus 28).
6 On the cross, he speaks words from Psalm 69:21 — *'I thirst'* — apparently fulfilling scripture.
7 Like the Passover sacrificial lamb, Jesus's bones are not broken (Exodus 12:6).
8 Blood and water flow from a spear wound in his side (Zechariah 12:10).

The Fourth Evangelist's free use of Old Testament allusions is an important part of the overall theme of divine control that underlies the passion narrative. In common with the synoptic writers, the evangelist makes use of Psalm 22, a psalm of the righteous sufferer, and gives a characteristic Johannine twist to the casting of lots for Jesus's garment — a priestly ephod, fitting for the sacrifice of the one who prayed the High Priestly Prayer. Jesus's cry *'I thirst'* echoes a number of possible passages: Psalm 22:15, 69:3, as well as 69:21b. Rather than suggesting that Jesus is deliberately fulfilling scripture in the cry, it is more likely that the Fourth Evangelist intended it to be understood as a moment of utter and profound weakness and despair which preceded the glorious uplifting of the righteous sufferer who trusts in God. This too would explain the use of *'None of his bones shall be broken'* at 19:36. Whilst more usually linked with Exodus

12:46, in Psalm 34:29 the righteous sufferer is said to *'keep all his bones, not one of them will be broken'*. However, the Fourth Evangelist avoids the use of Psalm 22:1 — *'My God, my God, why have you forsaken me?'* — used by Mark and Matthew, since this would clearly not correspond with his theology of Jesus's divine control over the events of the passion. Rather, Jesus's final words from the cross in the Johannine narrative are the victorious *'It is accomplished'*. Nevertheless, it seems that these psalms of suffering were not far from his mind. Finally, with the use of Zechariah 12:10 — *'They shall look on him whom they have pierced'* — the evangelist links the death of Jesus with the pouring out of God's spirit on the Davidic house as they mourn the one who has suffered at their hands.

At this point in the narrative, the images of blood and water, which have run through the Gospel, reach a climax with the spear thrust (see p. 368 for a discussion of the spear thrust as the final sign). At the wedding at Cana, the six stone water jars show how the inadequate water of Jewish purification is to be transformed into the rich wine of the Gospel. To Nicodemus, Jesus has spoken of being reborn in water and Spirit, in one act of purification and salvation. Water represents the medium of the Spirit, but water alone as a means of baptism is insufficient. Christianity is Judaism baptised in the Spirit, which enables humanity to live in the knowledge and experience of the kingdom of God. To the Samaritan woman, Jesus spoke of being living water, and at 7:39 it was made clear that this water is none other than the Spirit: *'which believers in him were to receive; for as yet there was no Spirit* [i.e. during his ministry], *because Jesus was not yet glorified'*. Like water on dry land, the Spirit refreshes a barren heart, empowering it for growth and fruitfulness. Now, at the moment of his death, it is poured out on a waiting world.

The combination of water and blood as a means of spiritual renewal was deeply engrained in Jewish thought. Leviticus 14:1ff laid down in the Mosaic Law the ritual cleansing of a leper by means of blood and water. A healed leper was required to appear before the priest, who would testify to the cleansing in the taking of two birds. One of them was killed over a vessel of running water. The other, together with scarlet *stuff and hyssop*, was dipped in the blood of the dead bird and the blood sprinkled seven times onto the leper. Seven days after the rite, the leper was to wash in water and he would be clean. The blood and water from Jesus's side pronounce a cleansing made possible by his death that far exceeds the cleansing of the leper. The analogy is clear, however. Even the use of hyssop, on which the vinegar-soaked sponge is offered to Jesus on the cross, links the two acts of purification. It was also hyssop that was used to mark with blood the doors of the Israelites in Egypt as a sign that the angel of death was not to enter the houses of God's people. Christ's death now brings a new Passover, and with it a release — not from Egypt, but from slavery to sin, as anticipated by John the Baptist at 1:29 — *'Behold the Lamb of God, who takes away the sin of the world'*.

The Fourth Evangelist adds a further unique episode to the crucifixion narrative — the handing over of Jesus's mother to the care of the Beloved Disciple (19:25–7). This account has been variously interpreted, but it fits in well with the Gospel's presentation of both characters. Still nameless, Jesus's mother makes only her second appearance in the Gospel — the first was at Cana when she witnessed the beginning of Jesus's ministry. Now, at the side of the other great unnamed figure in the Gospel, the Beloved

Disciple, she witnesses its fulfilment and climax, and the two characters represent the embryonic Johannine community which must now make its own way in the world without the physical presence of Jesus. Grassi (1992) identifies this passage as central in establishing the future role of the Beloved Disciple as Jesus's successor and the creation of a new family of God — *'Jesus's last will established the blessed disciple as his successor and son by having his own mother continue the relationship by adopting the blessed disciple as her own son'* — whilst Marsh (1968) suggests that it represents the necessary relationship which must now be established between Judaism (represented by Jesus's mother) and the Johannine church (the Beloved Disciple). The latter must not forget its roots, and the former must not reject its fulfilment. Marsh writes: *'It was the deep insight of the Fourth Evangelist to see that these two great religions are incomplete, the one without the other'.*

Joseph of Arimathea and Nicodemus — secret disciples or crypto-Christians — hastily bury the body. They bind it in linen cloths (Psalm 45:8) and bury Jesus before the beginning of the Sabbath (Deuteronomy 21:23). The body will be properly buried on Sunday morning, when the Sabbath is over (Psalm 16:10). The narrative ends on a note of anticipation. The men have taken generous, but temporary, measures to bury Jesus before the Sabbath sets in, and the scene is set for the resurrection, which will render a more permanent resting place unnecessary.

4 The resurrection

This is the heart of the matter…in the whole of the Fourth Gospel; the new age of fulfilment is here, and Judaism has been replaced by Christianity.

(Smalley, 1978)

The resurrection is the final sign. On the Sunday morning, Mary Magdalene goes to the tomb and sees that the stone covering the entrance has been rolled away. She tells Peter and the Beloved Disciple, who go to the tomb, fulfilling the requirement of Jewish Law that two adult male witnesses were required to prove the truth of a testimony. Peter sees the empty tomb, containing just the linen wraps, and is puzzled. The Beloved Disciple, unsurprisingly, however, seems to realise what is going on, as the author tells us: *'He saw and believed'* (20:8).

The empty tomb is important to all the evangelists, who each describe a visit by women to the tomb on the first day of the week. The empty tomb — as the Beloved Disciple realises — is a witness to the reality of the resurrection, but it is only in the Fourth Gospel that it is greeted by immediate belief. The Fourth Evangelist appears to use his own material to describe the men's visit to the empty tomb. They have been subtly contrasted since the final meal (chapter 13), but in the final two chapters the contrast increases and the Beloved Disciple's exemplary faith is made clear. Without the benefit of a resurrection prediction (as in the Synoptic Gospels), he immediately draws the right conclusion, and because the Fourth Evangelist has placed so much emphasis on Jesus's crucifixion as the means of his glorification, the Beloved Disciple's leap of faith and understanding is all the more impressive. It is not entirely clear what Peter believes, but it is evident that despite being faced with the same set of data, he is not able to reach the same conclusion unaided. The evangelist links seeing and believing in 20:8. These two concepts have a curious relationship in the Gospel. Here sight leads to a positive conclusion, but elsewhere the need for sight before belief is negative — as in those who need to see signs before they believe.

Oddly, the men go away again, with no word to Mary, who is left weeping outside the tomb, thinking that Christ's body has been stolen. Unusually for the Fourth Gospel, she sees two angels in the tomb (probably borrowed directly from the Fourth Evangelist's synoptic source), who do no more than ask her why she weeps. More importantly for this Gospel, she also sees a man she thinks to be the gardener, and asks him where he may have laid the body. She only recognises him to be Jesus when he calls her by name (as the good shepherd calls his sheep) and in turn she greets him as *Rabboni* (20:16). This word was unusual, for it meant more than just teacher as John suggests — it was used at that time almost exclusively to address God himself. Jesus tells her to go and assure the disciples that he has risen and thus she is given the apostolic commission to carry the news of the resurrection. Paul had understood that the essential criteria for apostleship were having seen the risen Jesus and being sent to proclaim him, and there is little doubt that Mary Magdalene fulfils this role in the mind of the Fourth Evangelist. Kysar (1993) observes: *'She is cast in the eminent role as the first to discover the empty tomb, the first to witness the risen Christ, and the first to announce the good news of the resurrection. Not even Peter or the Beloved Disciple is so privileged'*. Crucially, she is called to share exactly the same relationship with Jesus as the male disciples enjoy, which is the same as Jesus shares with the Father: *'My Father and your Father...my God and your God.'* The resurrection has broken down the last barriers between God and man, but to enter fully into this new relationship, Mary, and the others, must not hold on to Jesus, but let him return to the Father — to the pre-existent glory from which he came.

That evening, the male disciples, fearing the Jews, lock themselves into a room. Jesus appears to them and they are overjoyed. He greets them with peace and the gift of the Holy Spirit to prepare them for the task ahead of founding his church, and gives them the authority to act in his name to forgive sins: *'Receive the Holy Spirit. If you forgive anyone his sins, they are forgiven'* (20:22–3). One disciple, Thomas, is absent and when he returns he refuses to believe the disciples, demanding proof; he wants to see the wounds of Christ for himself (20:25). A week later, Christ appears to Thomas and shows him the wounds and, presumably without taking up Jesus's offer to place his hand in his side, Thomas believes. Thomas's doubt gives way to the fullest christological confession in the Gospel — *'My Lord and my God'.* The author used Thomas to represent all the future believers who would need to believe without the benefit of physical proof: *'...blessed are those who have not seen and yet believed'* (20:29), and as a character in the Gospel Thomas is, Culpepper (1983) suggests, more a realist than a doubter: *'Thomas is the opposite of Peter, who saw Jesus's glory but could not accept his suffering... Thomas stands in for all those who...embrace the earthly Jesus but have yet to recognise the risen Christ'.* The demands that Thomas made cannot be made by the next generation of believers for whom the witness of the first generation must be sufficient.

The Epilogue

Such a chapter is more than an appendix; it is not less than epilogue and crown.

(Marsh, 1968)

The Epilogue to the Fourth Gospel contains many possible layers of meaning. Its existence itself is a mystery, since it seems to be an addition to the Gospel, and not likely to be the work of the same hand responsible for the preceding 20 chapters. Although only one Syriac manuscript omits chapter 21 from the text, it is easy to argue a case that the Gospel concludes at 20:31. The subsequent chapter includes differences in literary style, and some 28 Greek words not used elsewhere in the Gospel. At the same time, however, there are some classic Johannine traits.

If it is an addition, it was clearly added with the intention that the issues unresolved in chapters 1–20 should be resolved. Its function therefore could be to answer one of the many questions that faced the Johannine community, particularly about the pastoral roles of the individuals associated with it — Peter and the Beloved Disciple. Alternatively, the events of the chapter could satisfy the need for a further post-resurrection appearance like that promised in Mark 14:28. The chapter effectively divides into two major sections: the miraculous catch of fish (21:1–14) and Jesus's conversation with Peter (21:15–25).

The catch of fish (21:1–14)

The narrative of chapter 21 picks up awkwardly from the end of the previous chapter that has drawn the Gospel to a neat conclusion (which the editor attempts to echo at 21:24). At 21:1 we learn that seven of the disciples are once again taking to their nets and resuming their earthly occupations as fishermen — despite having seen the risen Christ. Perhaps we are meant to understand that they have abandoned their life of discipleship, unable to continue without the presence of Jesus. However, the giving of the Spirit in 20:22 would suggest that they had received all they needed to empower them for ministry. Perhaps, therefore, there is nothing untoward in their going out fishing; Paul continued in secular work during his ministry (1 Corinthians 9:15).

A fruitless night's fishing leaves Peter and the others with empty nets when Jesus, unrecognised by the disciples, tells them to throw their nets on the right side of the boat and, having done so, they make a huge catch of fish. It seems likely, therefore, that the passage is intended to provide guidance to disciples living in the post-resurrection age. Jesus had instructed Mary Magdalene not to 'hold on' to him (20:17), but to enjoy the new relationship with Jesus and the Father made possible by his resurrection and his return to pre-existent glory. This chapter too seems to testify to the 'greater things' that Jesus had promised, but they will be possible only if the disciples are able to allow the reality of that new relationship to affect their lives. Jesus's appearance on the shore shocks them back into that reality, which is not a return to secular life but quite the opposite — just as the true bread was not the bread that Moses gave in the desert (6:32) and the water that provides true refreshment is not the water from the well at Sychar (4:13).

Peter, who earlier denied knowing Jesus, following the Beloved Disciple's prompting, jumps into the water to swim to meet him on the beach. Jesus has already lit a fire and when the boat arrives the net contains 153 fish. There is a good deal of symbolism here — Peter, who earlier denied he knew Jesus, is now the first to affirm him, and the 153 fish may serve to represent the 153 nations that will become part of the new faith.

Jesus now shares bread and fish with the disciples, recalling the feeding of the five thousand with its Eucharistic overtones, and one early manuscript (Codex Bezae) includes the words: *'gave thanks and gave it to them'*. The account of the catch itself has remarkable similarities to Luke's account of the calling of Peter in Luke 5, and this episode has all the hallmarks of a re-calling. In a Gospel in which the Beloved Disciple has apparently emerged as the spiritually dominant figure, it is perhaps surprising that the one to be called to do a specific task is Peter. It is possible that the Johannine community was in the process of reconciling the position of the Petrine churches with their own based on the authority of the Beloved Disciple. The evidence of chapter 21 suggests that they were accepting Peter's status as divinely commissioned, whilst at the same time retaining allegiance to the Beloved Disciple.

Jesus's conversation with Peter (21:15–25)

But Peter's post-resurrection conversation with Jesus is also important for him personally. At first (21:15) Jesus calls Peter 'Simon', the name he had before he was a disciple, and asks if he loves him *'more than these'*. Although a cursory reading may lead us to think that Jesus is asking Peter if he loves him more than the other disciples do, it seems clear, on closer examination, that he is asking whether the disciple's love for his master goes beyond his commitment to worldly things — in this case the trappings of his former trade as a fisherman. Peter knows he can no longer boast, for he has earlier denied Jesus, so he is forced to think before giving his answer. Here the English text is not quite accurate. Peter's reply in the original Greek is not that he 'loves' (**agape**) Jesus, but that he 'cares' (**phileo**) for him; Peter is too ashamed to say more. This is important: if Peter is to lead the church, then he has to learn to know himself and to speak the truth. Jesus's reply is a commission to Peter to preach to Christ's people — *'Feed my lambs'*. Jesus asks a second time (21:16), but this time without reference to earthly distractions, challenging Peter to consider in isolation his own relationship with Jesus. Peter, again ashamed, can only reply that he *'cares'* for Jesus. Jesus's own reply is a commission to look after his people — *'Tend my sheep'*. Finally, Jesus asks again (21:17), this time in the original Greek, using Peter's own expression: *'Do you care for me?'* Peter has reached the end of the line. He states the truth in his heart — that he actually *'loves'* Jesus. This is crucial for Peter — his bravado has gone and he is a new man, living by realism and truth. Jesus gives him the greatest commission of all, *'Feed my sheep'* (21:17), which means that he is to be the leader of the new community. Peter has truly demonstrated his fitness to take over pastoral care of the good shepherd's flock.

Inevitably, the Beloved Disciple makes an appearance at the end of the dialogue. Here we may feel confident that the Epilogue is meeting the needs of the community, as it would appear that tradition in the Johannine church was that the Beloved Disciple would remain alive to see the Parousia. His death must have caused much anxiety and the Epilogue sets the record straight. Jesus did not prophesy the immortality of the Beloved Disciple; rather his words were another clue to the nature of discipleship. Peter's own commitment to Jesus must be his concern, and not the fate of others, and Jesus calls Peter to follow him irrespective of whether other disciples are called to apparently higher offices, or to none.

In an echo of 20:31, the Gospel ends with the author telling the readers that the material he has used has been selective and that much of what Jesus did went unrecorded. As Marsh (1968) comments: '...*there is a great deal more that can be known about Jesus, but nothing more needs to be known*'.

Summary

- **Arrest and trial** — the Fourth Evangelist prepares his readers thoroughly for the passion through the **farewell discourses** and establishes the theme that Jesus is in control of all events of the passion and initiates his own arrest.
- **Before the Sanhedrin** — the trial at the High Priest's house focuses on Jesus's public activity, not christological issues as in the Synoptics.
- **Before Pilate** — Pilate's reluctance to condemn Jesus to death is played off against the blasphemy and hypocrisy of the Jewish authorities. Both Jesus and Pilate are victims, but Jesus is still in control: '*You have no power over me unless it had been given you from above.*'
- **Conflict** — the passion brings to a climax the conflict that has run through the Gospel from the beginning. Jewish authorities are the primary opponents of Jesus and the Fourth Evangelist exposes the irony of their failure to recognise their king. Conflict should be seen against a background of the Johannine community's separation from the synagogue.
- **Crucifixion** — rich Old Testament symbolism is sustained through a short narrative emphasising triumphant and deliberate fulfilment of the divine plan. Blood and water from Jesus's side bring the themes based around these images to a climax and echo Old Testament images of purification, which are transcended by Jesus's death. The Beloved Disciple and Jesus's mother stand united as witnesses at the foot of the cross — the embryonic Johannine community awaiting the gift of the Spirit.
- **Resurrection** — Mary Magdalene, Peter and the Beloved Disciple are key figures for the unfolding of the significance of the empty tomb and the revelation of the risen Jesus. Mary emerges as the 'Apostle to the Apostles'. The giving of the Spirit fulfils a long-awaited promise (1:33). Thomas's need for physical proof provides the opportunity for special blessing on those who will believe without the benefit of sight.
- **Epilogue** — an addition to the Gospel, but containing key Johannine concepts and reconciling the roles of the Beloved Disciple and Peter for the community. The catch of fish may serve as an allegory for discipleship and evangelism. Jesus's conversation with Peter recommissions him and calls him to a crucial pastoral role. The death of the Beloved Disciple is put into context — Jesus did not say that he would live to see the Parousia.

Exam watch

As with all essays about the Gospels, the worst trap you can fall into is story-telling, and these chapters could easily lead you down that road. Make sure that everything you say about what happens is supported by a critical and exegetical point concerning the significance, background, implications and interpretation of events. Try to avoid always falling back on the usual scholars — Marsh et al. quoted — but include some of the comments (quoted in this section) from the very interesting schools of American New Testament scholarship.

Review questions

1 (a) Analyse and assess the relationship of the religious and political authorities to Jesus in the Fourth Gospel.
  (b) Evaluate the reasons why, according to the author of the Fourth Gospel, the religious and political authorities put Jesus to death.
2 (a) Explain the meaning of *two* religious features in the crucifixion narrative in the Fourth Gospel.
  (b) Assess the significance of the crucifixion for the author of the Fourth Gospel.
3 Examine and evaluate the contribution of the resurrection narratives to the Fourth Gospel.

G Eschatology

The atmosphere into which Christianity was born was one of lively hope for an imminent salvation. For Judaism this was expressed in the hope of the coming Messiah and the age that he would usher in, and it was inevitable that Jesus's ministry and its immediate effects were to be seen as the arenas in which this would be realised. However, hopes of salvation were complex. Was the hoped-for salvation to be a future possibility alone, or would it be found in the believer's present experience? Or, more interestingly, would it be known in some way in the present, and realised fully at some future date? Clearly, Christians soon came to believe that they could experience divine fulfilment in the present, and that they had been given gifts which could be used in the present but which gave them a foretaste of the even greater blessings that awaited them in the future. The particular view of the Fourth Evangelist on this has been the matter of wide scholarly debate, but, as Kysar (1993) observes: '*all must agree that there is a remarkably strong emphasis in the Gospel upon the presence of salvation in the believer's life'*. He identifies it as being developed through:

÷ eschatological teaching
÷ the Gospel's view of the Spirit
÷ the Gospel's view of the church
÷ the Gospel's treatment of the sacraments

We are specifically concerned with the first of these categories here.

Humanity's need for salvation

Whether salvation lies in the present, future, or both, the Fourth Evangelist is clear why the events of Jesus's ministry and their implications are so crucial. He teaches that God the Father sent Jesus the Son for the salvation of the world so that the world should be given the chance to avoid judgment. He does not provide a comprehensive summary of why the world is in need of salvation, as Paul does, for example, in Romans and Galatians, but he does make clear that the world is under the power of Satan — '*the ruler of this world'* (14:30) — who was a '*murderer from the beginning'* (8:44). Because the Gospel's purpose is evangelistic, the message of salvation is thus at its heart. The evangelist intends that his readers, once they have read the Gospel, should be in a position to make a confession of faith in Jesus as the divine Son of God and, having made that decision, will pass from death to life (5:24), i.e. will enter into salvation.

The evangelist makes it clear that Jesus is the one and only way to salvation, as no other way can lead to God (14:6). This is an uncompromising claim, which, at a stroke, dismisses every other claim made by Judaism and its laws as the way to the Father's heart. Although *'salvation is from the Jews'* (4:22), it is only when Judaism is completed and fulfilled in Christ that humanity can enter into the abundant life that he promises. No other decision and no works are required for humanity to enter into eternal life, the gift that follows from salvation.

However, the evangelist shows that making the decision will not be easy. It is necessary for Jesus's hearers to accept that he is the way to the Father, which requires an acceptance of his own divine identity and that the old ways of Judaism alone cannot bring salvation. This is clearly illustrated in the feeding of the five thousand when the crowds ask: *'What must we do to perform the works of God?'* Jesus answers them: *'This is the work of God, that you believe in him whom he has sent'* (6:28–9).

The Fourth Evangelist is also uncompromising in his teaching on humanity's need for salvation. To be saved is also the opposite of being condemned — humanity is literally 'made safe' through faith in Jesus. His view of humanity is realistic: he knows that people would rather flee from the light than be exposed to its beams, and so they stay in the cover of darkness (3:19–21). In doing so, however, they are unable to find salvation from the power of sin. Jesus's hearers are slow and incredulous, unable to accept that they are slaves to sin (8:34), under the judgment of death (8:21), and subject to the power of the world (8:23). However, for John it is these things that separate humanity from God and condemn humanity to spiritual death. Before people can attain eternal life, they must be saved from these powers, and this necessitates recognising the true source of life and shunning all others. The Fourth Evangelist is aware of the irony inherent in this; Jesus challenges his hearers: *'You search the scriptures because you think in them you have eternal life, and it is they that testify on my behalf. Yet you refuse to come to me to have life'* (5:39–40). However, Jesus's opponents appear not to understand their need for salvation, and until this is grasped they will not be able to recognise the true source of eternal life.

The nature of eternal life

If all that the Fourth Evangelist says in his Gospel about Jesus is ultimately concerned with how humanity can enter into salvation through Christ, he stands apart from the synoptic evangelists in choosing the term 'eternal life' (rather than entering the kingdom of God/heaven) to describe the nature of that salvation. Eternal life is a gift from God, mediated to the believer through Christ. Thus, Jesus's activity is 'life-giving' and in this sense is often linked with light (1:4). Eternal life is only possible in so far as it derives from God through Christ by the Spirit. Humanity can pass from darkness into life and from death to life. A believer who has passed into life and light is then called upon to practise a love and service reflecting that of the earthly Jesus (13:15, 34). The risen Christ sustains the spiritual life of the believer who can confidently expect to share the resurrection of the life of the age to come.

Jesus describes eternal life in 17:3: *'And this is eternal life, that they know you, the only true God, and Jesus Christ, whom you have sent.'* Thus, unless a person can accept that Jesus has come from the Father, equipped with his full authority and acting in obedience to him, he or she cannot gain access to eternal life. This was the problem that faced Jesus's most vociferous opponents in the Gospel, and as we have already seen, the Fourth Evangelist has no doubts that for these people salvation and eternal life are inaccessible, barred as they are from receiving it because of their hard-heartedness. Their refusal to believe the one truth that leads humanity into life ensures that they will forever be left in darkness. The Fourth Evangelist uses the image of darkness to describe unsaved people and their state: *'And this is the judgment, that the light has come into the world, and men loved darkness rather than light, because their deeds were evil'* (3:19). Humanity's natural tendency, until touched by the Spirit, is to remain in darkness, preferring it to the light because it hides sin and ignorance. Few therefore are able to receive salvation and enter into eternal life. Only by admitting our spiritual need can we lay claim to it. The Fourth Evangelist shows how characters, such as the blind man, are able to lay themselves open to receive the blessings of salvation, and in so doing he provides a foil for the Pharisees, whose opposition to him and to Jesus highlights his own willingness to believe: *'Do you believe in the Son of Man?... Who is he, Sir, that I might believe in him?'* (9:35–6).

Because salvation involves a response to Jesus that is made in this life, John teaches that as soon as a person makes that decision they enter into eternal life. The transition from death to life has already taken place, and thus Jesus can say: *'I am the resurrection and the life; he who believes in me, though he die, yet shall he live, and whoever lives and believes in me shall never die'* (11:25–6). At the moment that believers receive Jesus in faith, death no longer has any power over them. Eternal life transcends physical death and nothing can separate people from the communion they have with God: *'I give them eternal life, and they will never perish. No one will snatch them out of my hand. What my Father has given me is greater than all else, and no one can snatch it out of the Father's hand'* (10:28–9).

Jesus describes the purpose of his ministry as being to bring eternal life to those whom God gave him (17:4). Although those who accepted Jesus during his earthly ministry had an especially privileged position, it is those who will enter into eternal life without having seen Jesus who receive the greatest blessing (20:29). They too become part of a flock guided by the good shepherd and receive the guarantee that nothing will remove them from his care. They have been chosen to receive the protection of the Father and the Son so that none may be lost, and they will enter into abundant life, bound in an unbreakable unity with other believers. The source of that unity is the Father and the Son, and if they do not have a relationship with them, the disciples' new life will wither and die (15:4). The Holy Spirit will be the means by which they will continue to grow in their new life, coming to a deeper understanding of its meaning and able to do greater works even than Jesus himself (14:12).

Throughout the Gospel, the evangelist shows how Judaism has failed to bring refreshment, knowledge of God, and freedom from the slavery of sin and death. The 'I am' sayings are a powerful means by which Jesus asserts his supercession of all that has gone before as the way to salvation and life in the presence of God. For the evangelist, the new has come and the old has passed away, as Jesus opens the gate to God in a radical way: *'Truly I say to you, you will see heaven opened and the angels of God ascending and descending upon the Son of Man'* (1:51).

Present or future?

Kysar (1993) argues that there are not just two but three different kinds of eschatology expressed in the Fourth Gospel: present, future and heavenly eschatology.

- **Futuristic eschatology** is the most traditional view. Salvation is in the future, and judgment will come on the last day when the dead will be raised, preceded by tribulations experienced by Christians — persecution most notably among them. This eschatological future will be characterised by the grand conclusion of history, the defeat of Satan and the return of Christ.
- **Present eschatology**, however, expresses the view that the expectations of the future are now realised in the believer's present relationship with Jesus, reversing the traditional forward-looking Christian expectation of salvation. Jesus's reassurance to Martha that *'I am the resurrection and the life'* (11:25) serves as a corrective to her rather impersonal statement to him, *'I know he* [Lazarus] *will rise again in the resurrection on the last day'* (11:23–4). The Fourth Evangelist seems to be saying that a faith relationship with Christ is what leads to resurrection: *'Resurrection is not some vague hope for something that will happen way out there in the shadowy future. It is a present experience when Christ is present'* (Kysar, 1993). Eternal life is therefore something to be enjoyed in the present, a peculiar quality of life which results from belief in Jesus and which, in the future too, will not be destroyed by physical death.
- **Heavenly eschatology** is also futuristic, but anticipates the heavenly home that is waiting for Christians, which Jesus has gone ahead to prepare (14:2–3). In that home the relationship between the believer, Father and Son will be perfected and they will be perfectly one. This seems to be a dualistic notion — there are two realms, earth, where believers must dwell during their physical life, and heaven, which they can look forward to after the death of their physical bodies.

How can these three forms of eschatology be reconciled? The simplest solution is that they are all present in the thought of the evangelist: the future blessings of discipleship are already beginning to be available through the disciples' relationship with Jesus and the fulfilment of them will be enjoyed in the future. However, a more interesting solution is what Kysar calls the **spoiler alternative**. Drawing on the thought of Rudolph Bultmann, he suggests that all references to future eschatology were the work of a later editor of the Gospel who was uncomfortable with the fact that it included no futurist thought. The present eschatology represents the original work of the evangelist who believed only in the fulfilment of the promises in the present. Bultmann maintained that the editor had left traces of his work, evident in the disjointed flow of passages that include futurist references. Alternatively still, the **preserver theory** claims that the evangelist included some futurist references in order to preserve the traditional view alongside his own present perspective, even though they were contradictory and, arguably, the evangelist feels that it is no longer meaningful.

Kysar suggests that the Fourth Evangelist was drawing a line under the thought that had been prevalent in the church for the preceding 50 years — that Jesus's return was imminent — and encouraging his community to stop focusing on the future and turn its attention to the present. It is, Kysar (1993) claims, *'one of the most drastic revisions of traditional Christian thought the Gospel proposes'*. Yet the evangelist does not dismiss all futurist claims, but presents the reader with a **dialectical eschatology**: *'That means that the truth is not found in one or the other position, but only in the dynamic interchange between both of them'* (ibid.).

Summary and key terms

- The key issue is whether salvation and eternal life belong in the present or the future. The evangelist thoroughly addresses the issue of why humanity needs to be saved — to be liberated from Satan, *'the ruler of this world'*. Jesus is the only legitimate way to salvation and he has transcended all other routes. Eternal life — a quality the believer enjoys — is achieved through knowledge of the Father and the Son, and yet few will recognise this. Most will reject the way to eternal life, preferring to stay in the darkness. Jesus protects those who have committed themselves to him and who receive the benefits of eternal life, even if they have not had the privilege of seeing him in the flesh.
- **Futurist eschatology** — most traditional view — expressed in some Johannine passages which anticipate the raising of the dead on the last day and the defeat of Satan.
- **Present eschatology** — expectation of future realised in the believer's present relationship with Jesus.
- **Heavenly eschatology** — Jesus goes to prepare a place for the disciples to which they will follow him.
- Are future references later additions by an editor, or has the evangelist preserved them despite their lack of consistency with his own theology? The Fourth Evangelist's present eschatology is *'one of the most drastic revisions of traditional Christian thought in the Gospel'* (Kysar, 1993).

Exam watch

Candidates tend to jettison questions on this topic in favour of more narrative-based ones, and not necessarily to their credit. A strong grasp of the different perspectives on eschatology, along with good supporting reference to the text and an appreciation of the needs of the early church, will provide the material for an academically sound essay which should single you out from the candidates who fall back on the rather tired, tried-and-tested routes such as authorship. Be brave!

Review questions

1 Examine and assess the teaching of the Fourth Gospel on (a) salvation and (b) eternal life.
2 How far is it true to say that the Fourth Gospel's eschatological teaching is entirely concerned with present, rather than future, realities?
3 *'The message of salvation is at the heart of the Gospel.'* Discuss.
4 Examine and comment upon the link between eschatology and eternal life in the Fourth Gospel.

Topic 5

The early church

A The church in Jerusalem

1 First developments

1.1 The ascension

You shall receive power when the Holy Spirit has come upon you; and you shall be my witnesses in Jerusalem and in all Judea and Samaria, and to the end of the earth.

(Acts 1:8)

Luke's second volume of his composite work, Luke-Acts, begins as the Gospel has ended, with the promise of the Holy Spirit and a slightly elaborated account of the ascension of Jesus. In both volumes Luke explains how the disciples — originally a group of 120 men and women — returned to the city after the ascension and waited for God's promise to be fulfilled. It was a crucial promise, for Luke makes clear that without it, nothing further can be accomplished in the lives of the disciples or in fulfilling the commission Jesus has left with them. They will need empowering by God's Spirit before the great evangelistic ministry can be carried out, but it surely will be carried out, and Luke has a clear vision of the extent and influence of the Gospel in the coming years of the early church.

Jesus's words to disciples in 1:8 describe something of a ripple effect, whereby the Gospel will move across the Mediterranean Sea from Jerusalem to Rome. Although this is generally taken to be a historically accurate account of how the church expanded, it is not, perhaps, likely to be authentic. Nevertheless, for Luke, it marks the historical, geographical and theological progress of the message of salvation. The key element is that it is a mission to the whole world and not just to Israel, as Jesus instructed the disciples in Luke 24:47: '... *repentance and forgiveness of sins should be preached to all nations, beginning from Jerusalem.*'

The ascension makes clear that a new age in salvation history is dawning, although it is not quite what the disciples anticipated. They ask Jesus: '*Lord, will you at this time restore the kingdom to Israel?*' (1:6). It seems quite ironic that even after all they have experienced and witnessed, they still seem to be thinking in terms of a traditional messianic role. Jesus makes clear that this still lies in the future, and its timing is firmly in the hands of God. Marshall (1980) observes: '*Instead of indulging in wishful thinking or apocalyptic speculation, the disciples must accomplish their task of being witnesses to Jesus. The scope of their task is worldwide*'.

The mysterious angelic figures who greeted the women at the tomb on the day of the resurrection reappear to assure the disciples that they can anticipate Jesus's return — but not yet. Their question to the disciples, *'Why do you stand looking into heaven?'* (1:11), is like their question to the women at the tomb, *'Why do you seek the living among the dead?'* (Luke 24:5). Just as the women's behaviour was inappropriate, so too is that of the disciples. They have a command to fulfil and should do so without delay.

They do delay, nevertheless, but only to wait for the Holy Spirit and to deal with internal matters before the ministry can begin. Prior to Pentecost, the life of the 120 seems to prefigure the life of the early church; they devote themselves to prayer, the necessary prerequisite to receiving the Spirit. Luke records that 'the women' were among their number, presumably including the women described in Luke 8:1–3, who provided for Jesus and the male disciples during his ministry. Judas, however, whose suicide is briefly described by Luke, has left a gap. Luke's account is quite different from Matthew's, describing the suicide as fulfilling Psalms 69:25 and 109:8. Neither the evangelist nor Peter shows any sympathy for the departed Judas, who, it seems, existed merely to fulfil scripture. But his place must be filled, and Peter presides over the traditional drawing of lots to determine the divinely ordained replacement. Matthias is chosen — the mysterious Twelfth Apostle of Acts who is never heard of again. The filling of Judas's place is nevertheless important, since twelve is a symbolic and significant number. In Luke 9:1–6 Jesus had told the disciples that they could look forward to sitting on thrones and judging the twelve tribes of Israel. Interestingly too, 120 was designated by Jewish law as the required number to establish a community with its own council, so the election of the new twelfth man is carried out legally. The qualifications for apostleship are outlined in this episode: to have been with Jesus from the time of his baptism by John and to have witnessed his resurrection. It is remarkable how Matthias and the unappointed Barsabbas, who both fulfilled these requirements, immediately disappear from the record, whilst Paul, who fulfilled none in the strictest sense, later establishes himself, although not without controversy, as the pre-eminent Apostle to the Gentiles.

1.2 Pentecost

The long anticipated day had finally come! A new era in God's gracious dealings with humankind was dawning. God the Father would keep his promises; Jesus Christ the Son would pour forth the Spirit. Joel's prophecy was about to be fulfilled, and the messianic age would be inaugurated.

(Rea, 1990)

Acts 2 brings the great event that Luke has anticipated all through his Gospel and records with great ceremony and joy. On the day of the Jewish feast of Pentecost, the Holy Spirit comes to them as Jesus had promised, in a rush of wind and tongues of fire. The event is deeply symbolic. The Greek word for Spirit — **pneuma** — can be translated also as wind or breath, and the image of fire is firmly established in biblical tradition as an agent of purification and judgment and as a sign of God's visible and manifest presence (e.g. Exodus 19:18).

The significance of the Pentecost events passed unnoticed by the huge numbers of pilgrims who would have been in Jerusalem at the time to celebrate the Feast of Weeks; Jeremias postulated as many as 180,000, of which up to 150,000 may have been from non-Greek, Hebrew or Aramaic speaking countries. It begins as a private, charismatic experience for the disciples in their upper room, empowering them to *'speak in other tongues as the Spirit gave them utterance'* (2:4). This is the vital new phenomenon that signals the beginning of a new age. **Glossolalia**, or speaking in tongues, is not experienced in the Old Testament, but will have a vital place in the life of the early church. Essentially, it is the ability to speak in otherwise unknown languages, which were clearly not gibberish, as the effect on the Pentecost pilgrims makes clear. It is a sign for unconverted Jews present for the festival, as they hear the Gospel message spoken in their own tongue. Some certainly scoff, however, attributing the disciples' behaviour to drunkenness, but as John Rea writes: *'It is evident from the experience of the Day of Pentecost that speaking in tongues is not only rational discourse in an unknown language, but on occasion may be accompanied by a holy joy, a kind of divine inebriation'.*

Peter's immediate understanding of the event is that it fulfils the prophecy of Joel 2:28–32 and is undeniably a sign that the last days have arrived. The empowering of the Spirit will radically change the disciples' ministry. Whilst Jesus was on earth he delegated authority with each missionary journey (Luke 9:1, 2) and it is clear that sometimes they were not able to minister in difficult circumstances (Mark 9:14f). But now the Spirit will be a permanent and powerful presence in their lives and the lives of the church, and the sign that Jesus remains with them, although physically departed. Although the Spirit of God was available to men and women in the Old Testament, Pentecost brings to it a new dimension, which transforms the disciples from tentative would-be witnesses into powerful speakers and evangelists.

The Spirit will now direct events, and the disciples become increasingly responsive to its prompting. The geographical path identified — Jerusalem, Judea and Samaria, the ends of the earth — is followed as the Spirit dictates, and even apparently negative events, such as the death of Stephen, are used to maximise the evangelistic task.

Peter's first sermon, delivered to the astonished crowd, singles him out as the leader of the Jerusalem church. Filled with the Spirit, he delivers a powerful message to the assembled pilgrims who respond immediately to the Gospel message. Clearly, the Spirit brings with it the spirit of repentance, as the pilgrims ask Peter and the others: *'What shall we do?'* (2:37). Peter's message is uncompromising; he makes clear that Jesus's death was due to the divine foreknowledge of God, but that those who rejected him and failed to recognise his significance must take responsibility for that rejection — *'The paradox of divine predestination and human freewill in its strongest form'* (Marshall, 1980). The appropriate response therefore is to repent, be baptised, and receive salvation from the one and only Son of God. Peter's hearers take his words personally and seriously. Maybe some of them had tacitly agreed with their leaders in putting Jesus to death, but Peter's revelation of his divine status and authority comes as a shock to them, and they are *'pierced to the heart'* (2:37).

Peter's response to them follows the standard pattern of early preaching, going back even to John the Baptist: disassociate yourselves from the corruption and faithlessness of the present generation, repent, be baptised and become part of a new community of God's people, in whom his promises are being dramatically fulfilled. The effect is miraculous: the 120 disciples grow to more than 3,000 in one day, and the Apostles' ministry has begun.

1.3 The early believers

Luke immediately informs the reader of the establishment of the early Christian community in Jerusalem, the leadership of which lay initially in the hands of the Apostles, and occupied an important place in relation to other churches that were subsequently established. Without delay they appear to adopt a communal lifestyle, focused around the teaching of the Apostles, and dedicating themselves to fellowship, breaking of bread and prayer (2:42). The outpouring of the Spirit has been no temporary phenomenon, for Luke reports that *'many wonders and signs were done through the Apostles'* (2:43), and the community appears to be characterised by a Spirit-inspired unity. Marshall observes, however, that it appears to be a voluntary unity, and that we should not be quick to assume that the members were *required* to sell their goods for the common good. The episode with Ananias and Sapphira in chapter 5 suggests that this was an individual matter and Peter's concern is the fact that they lied, not that they had failed to be suitably generous. He suggests that, in reality, each person in the community offered his property to the disposal of the others as the need arose, with the central concern that none should be genuinely in want.

The early believers were clearly remarkable in other ways, however. Their joy and good fellowship are noted outside the community, and in these early stages, when the community is effectively a Jewish sect, they win universal favour. Luke appears to indicate that they met together in the Temple and in each other's homes, signalling their continuity with their Jewish roots but also their distinctiveness. Presumably something quite different went on in the two venues, and breaking of bread is likely to have been home based, rather like the meal the Corinthians shared in their homes and which Paul was so concerned should reflect the love and unity of the church, not divisions caused by social distinctions (1 Corinthians 11). The Jerusalem church appears to have no such difficulties.

The daily life of the new community appears to have been carried out in the full glare of the public eye, offering them a unique chance to witness and to grow rapidly in number. Luke refers to new believers as those *'who were being saved'* (2:47), underlining the key to what he understands to be involved in becoming a Christian. Those who become part of the church are saved from belonging, even if by default, to the generation who are guilty of rejecting the Messiah.

The initial establishment of the church in Jerusalem consolidates the link already made in the Gospel. Jerusalem has been the setting for Jesus's death, resurrection and ascension, and in the second and third cases the accounts of these are quite different from those in Matthew and Mark. The disciples have waited there for the coming of the Spirit and it will now be the setting for the first seven chapters of Acts. It is not until persecution scatters the believers that they can fulfil the second stage of Jesus's commission — to take the Gospel to Judea and Samaria. Only when that movement begins to take place does Luke show how the church developed from a pious, although not insubstantial, group in Jerusalem, to a potentially worldwide order that will include Jews and Gentiles. He has no rigidly drawn idea of a church, however, although clearly conversion, faith in Jesus, and baptism are considered to be the basic requirements for entry.

The life of the community seems to be quickly established, as already described, but Luke does not tell the reader whether it was the express instructions of Jesus or the

Jerusalem Apostles that influenced its style and character. Issues are dealt with as they arise, and they do so quickly. The healing of the lame man at the Temple gate by Peter and John is a two-edged sword. It offers Peter the chance for another powerful evangelistic sermon, and the church increases to 5,000 members. However, it also brings the church under critical scrutiny, and Peter and John are forced to defend themselves before the Sanhedrin. For the first time, their freedom to preach is challenged, although this serves only to inspire them further. As the Apostles return to their community, they commit themselves all the more to the spread of the Gospel, and *'the place in which they were gathered together was shaken; and they were all filled with the Holy Spirit and spoke the word of God with boldness'* (4:31).

Given the events of the passion only a few weeks before, it is perhaps surprising that it took as long as it did for opposition to arise against the Apostles and the new community of believers. However, the effect seems to serve only to bind the church together more strongly, and as Marshall (1980) observes: *'The activity of God's grace was seen not merely in the preaching, but also in the way in which the members of the church were freed from material need'*. The summary of community life in 4:32–26, which seems to parallel that given in 2:43–7, serves as a prequel to the next major incident in the life of the early believers. The extraordinary voluntary generosity of Barnabas, who sold a field and gave the proceeds to the church, is given special mention, and is highlighted by the incident that follows. The gist of it appears to be that a married couple, Ananias and Sapphira, attempted to gain credit for making a greater personal sacrifice than was actually the case (5:1–11). The story is astonishing in that the couple were clearly not required to give the full value of the property they had sold, and their offence lay in deceitfully attempting to claim that they had done so, not in the *fact* that they had failed to give all the proceeds. When Peter discovers the deceit, in separate incidents the two fall dead at his feet.

Marshall allows that the story is difficult for modern readers to understand. Peter demonstrates extraordinary gifts of supernatural insight; Ananias and Sapphira are offered no chance to repent, and the swift burial of Ananias before his wife even knows of his death is, he suggests, *'heartless, to say nothing of being improbable'*. The story is therefore doubtless a legend that had become considerably exaggerated by the time it reached Luke's narrative. Nevertheless, the episode allows the reader a glimpse into an entirely different world, and one in which it was possible for serious judgments to be passed on sinful acts. It is useful to compare Paul's claim in 1 Corinthians 11:27–32 here, to the effect that several members of the Corinthian church had died as a result of eating the Lord's Supper in an unworthy manner.

Luke is quick to get back into a more positive mood in 5:12–16, however, immediately describing once again the signs and wonders prevalent in the community, the high esteem in which the believers were held, and the astonishing healing power of Peter. Peter now appears to be equipped with the same charismatic power as Jesus himself, as his shadow alone is thought to bring healing to the sick (5:15). It is not clear, however, whether this was actually the case, or a superstition that arose amongst those desperate for ministry.

Just as Jesus had faced inevitable opposition from the Jewish authorities, afraid of the effect that a charismatic leader might have on Jewish–Roman relations, so too does

Peter's activity draw renewed attention from the Sanhedrin. Peter and the Apostles spend their first night in prison, only to be miraculously released, to return to preach in the Temple by daybreak (5:17–21). Hostility reaches boiling point until Gamaliel, a teacher of the Law, who we later learn had educated Paul, advises caution: *'So in the present case, I tell you, keep away from these men and let them alone* [5:38a]*; for if this plan or this undertaking is of men, it will fail* [5:38b]*, but if it is of God, you will not be able to overthrow them'* [5:39a]. Schweizer (1961) notes: *'The change of mood in Acts 5:38f probably indicates that the speaker (as represented by Luke) may well know that the truth lies, not in the possibility of 5:38b, but in the reality of 5:39a'*.

2 The church is established

2.1 Apostles and deacons

The growth of the Jerusalem church began to have repercussions for its administration and Luke reports in 6:1ff that the Greek-speaking Christians took issue with the Aramaic-speaking believers over the fair distribution of aid to their widows. The Apostles decided that domestic matters of this kind were not their responsibility and the way was opened to appoint a new category of leader who would take over this important area, but leave the Apostles free to minister in the way they believed they had been called to serve. It is only here, at 6:2, that Luke refers specifically to the Twelve, probably to distinguish them from the new group of seven who are appointed to fulfil this new area of ministry. The number seven probably relates to the Jewish custom of setting up boards of seven men for particular duties or as local rulers. The reluctance of the Twelve to be involved in serving at tables does not necessarily suggest that it was considered a lower form of service, but may indicate that it was not the task to which they were called. The Twelve need to be free to witness and evangelise. Nevertheless, Schweizer (1961) suggests that Luke makes the seven subordinated to the Apostles, and the co-existence of two groups now makes possible *'the successive existence of two stages of historical development within a single unified church'*.

The Twelve determine that those chosen for this service should be of *'good repute, full of the Spirit and wisdom'* (6:3), and clearly spiritual qualifications were required of all those who were appointed to tasks within the church. Inevitably, perhaps, two — Stephen and Philip — emerge as having the kind of evangelistic and teaching skills associated with the Twelve, and their significance soon outstrips the domestic matter that prompted their appointment. Marshall (1980) suggests that the appointment may indicate something more significant altogether: a growing division between Greek-speaking and Aramaic-speaking Christians, and that the appointment of the seven was, in fact, the appointment of a distinct set of leaders for the Greek-speakers. He observes: *'Although Luke depicts them formally as being in charge of the poor relief, he does not disguise the fact that they were spiritual leaders and evangelists'*.

Despite their obvious, although perhaps subtle, significance, the seven are not given a formal title. Although they are traditionally referred to as 'deacons' (from the Greek verb 'to serve'), this designation is not officially bestowed upon them. Schweizer suggests that this coheres with the almost casual way in which Luke introduces new orders within the church which evolve only when a new situation — such as that which faced the Hellenists — necessitate a new form of service. What is more important to Luke, he argues, is the *way* in which it is done, and in the case of the seven, it is that those appointed be spirit-filled. Schweizer (1961) observes: '*Luke is…writing about what he considers to be a subordinate ministry, and the absence of a title shows, too, that he is thinking of a single case in a special situation, not of the introduction of a general diaconate'*. Nevertheless, the laying-on of hands (6:6) suggests that the community was involved in the commissioning of them, and the act is usually associated with the ordination of an individual to an office or calling in the service of God.

The role of **Apostle** is highly distinctive for Luke and it seems to be distinguished from Paul's idea of apostleship as well as from the role the Twelve played during Jesus's ministry. For Luke, the Apostle is not primarily so-called because he has received a commission from the risen Christ (as per Paul) but because he is the eyewitness to the earthly life and work of Jesus and as such he is called to the role of witness. It is for this reason that Apostles can have no direct successors, and whilst Paul and Barnabas are called Apostles, they are still distinguished from '*the* Apostles'. On 24 out of 26 occasions when Luke uses the title 'Apostle' it refers to the Twelve. Luke also adds that an Apostle must have received a post-resurrection call and it is this that distinguishes them from other eyewitnesses, since doubtless several could claim to have been eyewitnesses to the whole of Jesus's ministry. In the case of the election of Matthias it is clear too that the company did not choose him, but recognised God's choice. We have already noted that he is never mentioned again in Acts, but nor are the others of the Twelve — save Peter, James and John.

2.2 Conflict and its consequences

The growth of the church has other implications too. Stephen, who seems to be the most spiritually gifted of the seven, engages in an apostolic-type ministry of preaching and healing which brings him into conflict with the Greek-speaking synagogue, leading to charges against him on the grounds that he was speaking against Moses, God and the Temple. So far, conflict has been containable, as Peter's escape from prison dramatically highlighted. Now it takes a more sinister form, and Stephen faces the combined wrath of the Greek- and Hebrew-speaking Jewish leaders. Luke records his defence in considerable detail, giving it a significant place in the history of the early church. This is not by accident. It occurs at the first great crisis of Acts and marks the conclusion to the first major section of the book. It is the last event to be confined to Jerusalem and the persecution that follows is specifically pointed out as marking the beginning of the next two stages in salvation history — the taking of the Gospel to Samaria, Judea and Galilee (8:11:18) and then on to southern Asia Minor (11:19–15:35). Furthermore, the event introduces Saul (later Paul) to the history of the early church; in his role as persecutor of the Way, he stands by, 'consenting' to the death of Stephen (8:1).

Stephen's speech is decisive in the life of the Jerusalem church. Caird (1975) observes: '*Stephen, then, seems to have been the first Christian to realise that Christianity meant the end of Jewish privilege, and the first to open the way for a mission to the Gentiles'*. He comments that up to this point, the Jerusalem Christians had emphasised those elements in the teaching of Jesus which united them with Judaism, but Stephen draws attention to those elements which had brought Jesus into controversy with the religious authorities and, not surprisingly, he ends up facing the same charges that had been brought against Jesus. In a long speech he summarises the history of Israel's dealings with God, emphasising their guilt at rejecting God's divinely ordained prophets and leaders, their disobedience to the Law, and their murderous refusal to accept Jesus. The speech is offered in response to specific charges laid against Stephen in 7:13–14: that he had spoken against the Temple and had said that Jesus would destroy the Temple and the Law of Moses. Interestingly, Luke has reserved the charge of speaking against the Temple to be levelled at Stephen, whereas in Mark's and Matthew's accounts of the trial of Jesus, it is one of the key charges against him. Jesus too is accused of attempting to overthrow the Law of Moses, although he always rises to the challenge, illustrating that he is preserving the true essence of the Law rather than observing its minutiae. Stephen, meanwhile, turns both charges back on the Jews, and demonstrates that it is they, not the Christians, who have disobeyed the revelation of God and the teaching of Moses. Loisy (1920) observes: *'The true representatives of the religion of Abraham, Moses and the prophets are not the Jews, ever stubborn and rebellious, but the Christians'*.

Stephen's speech serves three purposes: first, it is a defence against the charges brought against him; second, it is an attack on the Jews for their failure to obey the revelation of the Old Testament and for their rejection of the Messiah; and third, it clears the way for the church to move away from Jerusalem and evangelise further afield.

Inevitably, the speech arouses a hostile reception, fuelled all the more by Stephen's claim to see the *'Son of man standing at the right hand of God'* (7:56). In what we can only assume was an illegal outbreak of violence (the Jews had not had the authority to condemn Jesus to death, but had to seek the death penalty through Pilate), Stephen is taken outside the city (another parallel with Jesus) and stoned (the traditional Jewish method of execution). Like Jesus, too, his last words are words of forgiveness for his attackers (7:59) and the reader is left in no doubt that Stephen is received into the presence of Jesus at the moment of his death. Just as Luke presented the death of Jesus as the death of a true, obedient and righteous martyr, so too does Stephen die innocent and vindicated, a model for all subsequent martyrs of the early church.

Luke refers twice to the presence of Saul at the killing. He appears to be an unmoved and objective witness, holding the coats of the executors, and clearly having agreed to the execution. Whilst we know nothing of Saul's feelings at this point, Luke is laying the groundwork for the reader's response to his later conversion. It would be no simple task to convert such a man as this, and what takes place is nothing less than a miraculous transformation. It is no wonder that the church later greeted the news of his conversion with some scepticism (9:26).

A brief paragraph concludes the story of Stephen in 8:1b–3, and shows that his death has opened the way for the next stage of the mission plan to unfold. The church in Jerusalem is forced to scatter, with the exception of the Apostles, who remain in the city, which may suggest that it was predominantly the Greek-speaking Christians associated with Stephen who were the primary targets for attack. Saul is mentioned again, the only individual specifically identified as a persecutor, and clearly taking a leading role, *'ravaging the church, and entering house after house, he dragged off men and women and committed them to prison'* (8:3). However, in scattering to Judea and Samaria, the church is now in a position to fulfil the second part of Jesus's command and the community continues to grow.

3 The church expands

3.1 The role of Peter

Luke's story of the establishment of the Christian church is structured around the careers of the two primary leaders, Peter and Paul, and if Peter was the leading figure responsible for guiding the church from its infancy to the point where it acknowledged the Gentile mission, Paul is the hero of the second part of its development from Antioch to Rome. Peter's leadership of the Twelve is made clear from the first chapter of Acts in which he is responsible for setting in motion the election of Judas's replacement. No-one questions his authority to do so, and nor does anyone question his right to act as spokesman on the day of Pentecost. Although Luke has not included Matthew's account of Jesus's appointment of Peter as *'the rock on which I will build my church'* (Matthew 16:18), it would appear that it is an accepted part of the tradition with which he is working. Peter's last appearance in the Gospel has not been auspicious. He has denied Jesus three times, and in 24:12 he visited the empty tomb, but left without having come to believe that Jesus had been raised from the dead, yet he appears at the beginning of Acts in a position of unquestioned authority. Readers of the Gospel know that Jesus had assured Peter that he had prayed for him to withstand the traumatic experience of his denial, and that he would later strengthen the others (22:32), but he does not recall what happened to him between the denial and the beginning of Acts. Clearly, something significant had occurred, for even before the coming of the Holy Spirit, Peter appears to be strong and in command.

Peter's role as a preacher and evangelist quickly takes shape. Caird (1975) observes: *'Luke tells us that the church "continued steadfastly in the Apostles' teaching" (2:42), but among the Apostles Peter showed pre-eminently the ability and authority necessary for leadership'*. At Pentecost, and later before the Sanhedrin, he speaks with boldness, and the numbers that respond to his message and join the church are remarkable. Clearly, a great move of God takes place, in which Peter plays an essential role. He emerges too as a charismatic healer and the healing of the crippled man at the Temple gate is decisive, leading both to a tremendous response to Peter's subsequent sermon and to opposition. Only after the healing does the embryonic church face serious challenges, and Peter and John are brought before the Sanhedrin. But in every case of opposition, Peter uses the opportunity to witness and evangelise, and his stature as a leader grows. When Luke informs the reader that people brought the sick into the streets in the hope that Peter's shadow would touch them (5:15), it is clear that Peter has grown into a charismatic leader of enormous influence.

Peter does not deliberately seek conflict, but does not avoid its implications either, and when forced to defend himself before the Sanhedrin he is, as Marshall (1980) observes, *'too good an evangelist to let a valuable opportunity slip'*. He remains committed to the task to which the Apostles have been called, and makes clear that the church cannot obey orders from the Jewish council to give up its distinctive role and purpose

— to preach the Gospel. If he, and the other Apostles, must pay the price for this, he does not flinch from it (4:19–20; 5:29). The characteristic that seems most to impress the Sanhedrin about Peter's defence before them is its 'boldness' (4:13) and it is clear that he is inspired by the Spirit to speak with a confidence that his educational background would not suggest.

One of the most puzzling stories of the New Testament is the incident of Ananias and Sapphira in which Peter is presented as having supernatural insight and the ability to pronounce fatal curses on the sinful (see p. 418). However anachronistic the story may appear to modern readers, it clearly underlines Peter's spiritual and ecclesiastical authority. No one disputes what has taken place, but rather *a great fear seized the whole church and all who heard of these things'* (5:11).

Traditionally Paul is called the Apostle to the Gentiles, and it is true that without the impetus of Paul and Barnabas, the Gentile mission would doubtless have taken much longer. However, Peter's visit to Cornelius is decisive, and makes clear to the Jerusalem church that God intends the Gospel to spread outside Judaism. Peter is forced to confront his own prejudices, to lay aside beliefs which he thought to be sacrosanct, and to realign his thinking with God's. Once he sees the Holy Spirit come upon Cornelius and his household, his perspective changes and he recognises that *'God shows no partiality, but in every nation anyone who fears him and does what is right is acceptable to him'* (10:35) and asks: *'Can anyone withhold the water for baptising these people who have received the Holy Spirit just as we have?'* (11:47). Peter faces opposition from the strong Jewish element of the Jerusalem church, however, and is forced to justify sharing table fellowship with Gentiles. It is clear that others do not come to share Peter's viewpoint without difficulty, and even he finds it hard to maintain consistently, but the turning point in the early church has been reached. From the Council of Jerusalem onwards it is clear that Christianity can no longer be considered a sect within Judaism, and Peter's influence in making that change has not been inconsiderable.

Peter's later career, after the watershed of the Council of Jerusalem, is obscure. After James died under Herod Agrippa's attack on the church, he was forced to flee, and he may have worked in Asia Minor before ultimately settling in Rome, where he was martyred under the Neronian persecutions around 64 CE. Arguably, he was the primary source for Mark's Gospel, and several apocryphal works are associated with him.

2.2 The beginning of the Gentile mission

Luke records the considerable tension that existed in the church over the establishment of the Gentile mission. Although at Pentecost there is no mention of Gentiles being present, within a few years the church was preaching to Samaritans (8:4ff), God-fearers (8:26–40, 10:1ff) and eventually to pagan Gentiles. Once persecution has opened the way for missionary activity outside Jerusalem, the progress of the Gospel is remarkably swift and inclusive. Initially, the invitation to receive the Gospel still goes first to the Jews (14:1), but as it becomes clear that outside Jerusalem they are resistant to it, Paul and Barnabas turn their attention almost exclusively to the Gentiles: *'And Paul and Barnabas spoke out boldly saying, "It was necessary that the word of God should be spoken first to you. Since you thrust it from you, and judge yourselves unworthy of eternal life, behold we turn to the Gentiles"'* (13:46).

The first mission to the Gentiles — which was, in fact, Peter's visit to Cornelius — was essential for fulfilling Jesus's command to preach the Gospel to all nations, and although he is the first to recognise God's call upon the Gentiles as well as the Jews, the focus quickly turns to Paul. It was Peter, however, who brought the news of the outpouring of the Holy Spirit on the Gentiles at Cornelius's house and he faces sharp challenges from the 'circumcision party' — those Jewish Christians who strongly held that even under the new covenant, separation between Jews and Gentiles was required as it was under the Law. His argument in 11:4ff makes clear that he believes that Gentiles are to be admitted as full members of the church, and thus that circumcision and the keeping of the Law are not to be required. It also makes the Jewish distinction between clean and unclean obsolete, whether it referred to people or foods. Although the detractors are convincingly won over by Peter's speech, Marshall (1980) observes that *'We should not take verse 18 to imply that the church at Jerusalem forthwith entered zealously into a mission to the Gentiles; indeed it never seems to have done so, and as a result it lost its importance in course of time'.*

In fact, the impetus immediately passes to the activities taking place in Antioch, where men who had heard the Gospel from Stephen in Cyprus had begun preaching to the Gentiles. Barnabas is sent to investigate, and inspired by what he finds there, he seeks out Paul, who begins his ministry alongside Barnabas in Antioch, where they stay for a year. So begins Paul's first missionary journey, and over the course of a turbulent and colourful mission, the Gospel is preached to Gentiles in Pisidian Antioch, Derbe, Iconium and Lystra. Returning to Antioch, Paul and Barnabas give a full report to the church of the work they have seen God accomplish among the Gentiles (14:27), a report which clearly confirms that God has called the church to wider missionary work.

3.3 The Council of Jerusalem

In general the relationship between Jews and Gentiles in the church in Acts seems to be dominated by questions of cultic observances. The problem of table-fellowship is solved in principle before the first Gentile is converted and the problem of circumcision is met by imposing four requirements relating to food and marriage as the most that should be demanded of Gentile Christians. The Paul of Ephesians seems unhappily excluded from these comfortable situations. He has to fight for the principle of table-fellowship even after the Gentile mission has been fully authorised by the Jerusalem leaders; he was never freed from the necessity of doing theological battle to show that the circumcision of the Gentiles was an abandonment of loyalty to Christ; and he was unable to appeal to regulations which would provide a simple answer to the problem of whether to eat meat which had been offered to idols.

(O'Neill, 1961)

Before the Gentile mission could continue unhindered, however, important issues had to be resolved. After Peter had been forced to leave Jerusalem, the church there came under the leadership of James, the brother of Jesus. Although he had remained aloof during Jesus's public ministry, he is converted after the resurrection and accepted as an Apostle in Jerusalem. However, he believed that the Law of Moses was permanently valid for Jews (understandably, perhaps, for where was the evidence that the Law had been repealed?) and resolved that no Gentile mission should be allowed to frustrate the primary task of preaching the Gospel to Jews. It was unthinkable to him that Jewish and Gentile Christians should mix, fearing that it would have a detrimental effect on the opportunity for evangelism amongst the Jews. Friction between the Jerusalem church and the church of Antioch arose and the issues had to be resolved if church expansion was to continue effectively and with enduring effect, and, crucially, was not to face an irrevocable split.

Paul reports on the matter at some length in Galatians 2:11ff, writing that Peter, and even Barnabas, had become confused and anxious over the grounds of the conflict, and were clearly afraid of alienating James and his party. Their compromise angers Paul, and his dissent ensures that James's suggestion that Jewish and Gentile Christians meet separately for the Lord's Supper is dismissed. The issue is forced when Paul and Barnabas are opposed by visitors from the circumcision party who declare uncompromisingly that *'It is necessary to circumcise them* [Gentiles], *and to charge them to keep the Law of Moses'* (15:5). Ten years after the conversion of Cornelius, Peter stands before the assembly of Apostles and elders in Jerusalem as they debate this vital issue. His argument is incontrovertible: if Jewish Christians are not saved by the Law, but by faith in Jesus, then Gentile Christians certainly cannot be expected to submit themselves to the same futile yoke. His speech is decisive, for James quickly suggests a new compromise: that Gentile Christians should not be required to be circumcised, that they should refrain from sexual immorality (a problem that persists in Corinth), and that the only laws they should observe are those which will make it possible for Jewish Christians to eat with them without violation of the Torah.

Caird (1975) claims that *'this was a good working compromise, but it was not a permanent solution. The two points of view were utterly irreconcilable, and sooner or later the church would have to decide whether it was going to live by the Law or the Gospel'.* Marshall notes that since Paul makes no reference to the decision of the Council in 1 Corinthians 8–10 or Romans 14, where he is discussing these very issues, it is conceivable that he may not know of the Council's final decision. In fact, the reliability of the Lucan record is considered questionable on many counts, although what is clear is that it dealt with a principle that was to be of basic significance for the future of the early church and ever after: *'no national, racial or social requirements can ever be made conditions for salvation and membership of the church alongside the single and sole requirement of faith in Jesus Christ…'* (Marshall, 1980).

Summary

- Luke alone records the **ascension**, an event that makes clear that a new era in salvation history is dawning. The eleven Apostles are commissioned to take the Gospel to Jerusalem, Judea and Samaria, and to the ends of the earth (1:8), which effectively lays out the programme for Acts. The mission is to be worldwide and the Apostles must look forward and not back. They must wait for the Holy Spirit to equip them for ministry, and in the meantime Peter takes the initiative in enrolling **Matthias** to take Judas's place as the Twelfth Apostle.
- The events of **Pentecost** empower the Apostles to begin their evangelistic ministry and set the programme for the rest of Acts, which will truly be the Acts of the Holy Spirit. The gift of tongues (**glossolalia**) is used for the purpose of evangelism and has a powerful effect on the visitors to Jerusalem. Peter's first sermon is equally decisive, and many Jews are called to repent and accept the Gospel. The initial group of 120

disciples grows in a single day to more than 3,000.

- The **early believers** establish a close-knit and supportive community. They are well-favoured in society and are an ever-increasing group. The first stage of Jesus's commission to witness in Jerusalem is clearly fulfilled, but soon leads to opposition after Peter and John heal the lame man at the Temple gate. Nevertheless, the church grows to 5,000 and Peter uses conflict as an opportunity for witness. Peter is also responsible for church order, as the remarkable story of **Ananias and Sapphira** demonstrates. His charismatic authority is held in high regard and even the great Pharisee Gamaliel recognises that if the church is truly of God, nothing will stop its increase.
- As the church is established, the role of the **Apostle** is clearly defined as one who is called to witness and to teach. Domestic matters still need attention, and the Hellenist Christians elect seven Spirit-filled members to serve their widows. **Stephen** and **Philip** emerge as powerfully anointed speakers and evangelists, but Stephen's bold preaching against the Jews for their rejection of Jesus leads to his death.
- The **death of Stephen** leads to **conflict** and the Jerusalem church is scattered until the immediate danger passes. Luke refers to Saul's presence at the killing, preparing the ground for the remarkable nature of his conversion.
- **Peter** remains at the centre of the action until the Council of Jerusalem. He guides the church from its infancy to the point where it is able to welcome Gentiles into the faith. His authority appears to be unquestioned, and only Paul dares to challenge him. He emerges as a powerful, charismatic leader, and his visit to Cornelius plays a decisive role in opening the way for the Gentiles to come to Christ.
- The **Gentile Mission** nevertheless falls into the hands of **Paul** and **Barnabas**, who are set apart by the church for the task in accordance with God's words to Paul at his conversion. Although the evidence seems clear that God has called the Gentiles to receive the Gospel, the Jerusalem church are slow to acknowledge that it is inappropriate to ask them to keep the Law and to submit to circumcision. It is not until the **Council of Jerusalem** that the issue of **fellowship** between Gentile and Jewish Christians is resolved, and the way is clearly open for Christianity to spread worldwide.

Exam watch

Good answers on the early church are, for some obscure reason, rarer than those on the Gospels. Perhaps this is because the issues are not so lively as those in the Gospels, less well-known, and more theologically complex. First, make sure you know the sequence of events extremely well. A lot happens in a short space of time. Once that is secure, eliminate the trivia and concentrate on the central and crucial issues described in this chapter. Make sure that you are completely *au fait* with the theological significance of what takes place and not just with its chronology, and that you can write critically and evaluatively.

Review questions

1 Examine the role of Peter in Acts. Was he more, or less, important than Paul?

2 'The Acts of the Holy Spirit.' How far is this an adequate description of the Acts of the Apostles?

3 What is the significance of (a) Stephen and (b) the Council of Jerusalem in the development of the early church?

B The ministry of Paul

1 The beginning

The ministry of Paul was not bounded by the limits of a life. It influenced decisively all European history, and through European history the history of the whole modern world. Paul's was the most significant human life ever lived.

(Blaiklock, 1959)

We know very little about the early life of Paul, or Saul, as he was originally known. He was probably born around 6 BCE in Tarsus in the Roman province of Cilicia. He was a Jew, a Roman citizen and a Pharisee of the tribe of Benjamin. He was educated in Jerusalem under Rabbi Gamaliel the elder. As a young man he had some kind of official position within Judaism, with the authority to vote against Christians who were being tried for their faith at a synagogue council and, possibly, in the Sanhedrin itself. As a learned Pharisee, he probably shared the view that God would intervene in history to rescue the Jewish people from their enemies. In particular, he would have believed in his youth that the Messiah would arrive from God in dramatic fashion, drive out the Romans, and establish God's kingdom on earth. He would therefore have felt contempt for the followers of Jesus, the crucified Messiah, who were claiming that after his crucifixion this Jesus had risen from the dead and was the true Messiah (Acts 2:22–4).

Paul does not appear ever to have met Jesus Christ in person, but he was present at the martyrdom of Stephen, a follower of Christ who had dared to say in public that the days of the Temple and traditional Jewish practices were over. Stephen was stoned to death by a Jerusalem mob, whilst Paul guarded their coats (Acts 7:54–8:1): *'And Saul was there, giving approval to his death'* (8:1).

However, this event was to have a profound effect on Paul. At first he realised that Christians were moving out of Jerusalem into other parts of the Roman Empire, and needed to be stopped from spreading their message. Many were in Damascus, an independent city in the Nabatean kingdom. Paul knew that the Romans had given the High Priest in Jerusalem the right to have Jewish criminals brought back from other areas of the empire, so he gained permission from the High Priest to go to Damascus and bring the Christians back to Jerusalem for trial and sentence (Acts 9:1–2).

1.1 Conversion

If Paul was 'converted' 'from' something 'to' something else, it was certainly not 'from' Judaism 'to' 'Christianity'. Paul continued to be a Jew to his dying day…

(Wilson, 1998)

Paul and his companions have set off on the road to Damascus when, suddenly, a bright light from heaven shines down and the risen Christ challenges Paul, saying, *'Saul, Saul, why do you persecute me?'* (9:4). Paul is blinded and his life is changed for ever. He is taken to Damascus, unable to see and overwhelmed by his experience. He cannot eat or drink until Ananias, a Christian living in Damascus, comes to him and restores his sight through the power of God. Paul is converted to Christianity by his experience and goes to meet the Christians in the city. He is made very welcome and witnesses for himself their love and affection for him and for each other. He develops a burning inspiration to carry the Christian message to the furthest corners of the known world. In *Acts*, Marshall (1980) notes: '*Paul was no sooner converted and called to be a witness to Jesus Christ than he began to fulfil his commission.*'

This experience is recorded in three different places in Acts — 9:3–19, 22:6–16 and 23:9–23 — highlighting just how important this moment was, not only for Paul but for the history of the early church. It was key not only to Paul's conversion but also to his view of Christ and to the manner in which he saw his mission to the Gentiles. In *Introducing the New Testament*, Drane (1999) observes that Paul '*...emphasised his conviction that people of different social and religious backgrounds could come together only through living a shared commitment to Jesus Christ.*'

1.2 Relationship with the early church

However, Paul was not able to stay in Damascus, for the Jews denounced him for changing his views and he was forced to leave secretly by being let down over the city wall in a basket (Acts 9:23–5). He went to Jerusalem, but his arrival struck terror into the members of the church, who feared him from his earlier days of persecution. After preaching in Jerusalem, he was forced by the Apostles to leave for his own safety and he returned home to Tarsus. There he remained for several years until he was remembered by a Christian called Barnabas, who asked Paul to come to work with the Gentile mission in Antioch (Acts 11:19–26). This was the place where the designation 'Christians' was first used. About a year later, a prophet called Agabus said that a famine was coming to Jerusalem and the members of the church at Antioch delegated Paul and Barnabas to take famine relief to Jerusalem. This was probably in 43 CE, during the height of the persecution of the early church. It was at this time that Paul again met the leaders of the Jerusalem church — a meeting which was crucial to the emergence of his own ministry, for it marked the time when the Apostles themselves recognised the need for the message of Jesus Christ to be taken to the Gentiles. Paul was willing to undertake that ministry.

The early church had been faced with a serious problem. The members of the Church were Jews, **proselytes** (non-Jews who had become members of the Jewish faith by circumcision and obedience to the Law) or God-fearers (people who were permitted to join in Jewish worship without taking upon themselves the whole burden of Jewish Law). The leaders in Jerusalem, who were all Jews, did not see themselves as leading a new faith, but more likely regarded themselves as leading a reforming movement within Judaism. It seemed clear to them, therefore, that any Gentiles who wished to become Christians should first become Jews, by being circumcised.

Peter, in his meeting with Cornelius (Acts 10:1–11, 18), had understood that Gentiles could be converted and receive the Holy Spirit, but Cornelius was a God-fearer and Paul would be converting people who had had no contact with Judaism at all, and that presented different kinds of problems. The Jerusalem leadership, therefore, whilst recognising what the value of this work would be, nevertheless refused to accept any responsibility for it. It was inevitable that this would lead to serious problems for the early church.

2 Paul's work

2.1 The first missionary journey (Acts 13–14)

The Holy Spirit said, 'Set apart for me Barnabas and Saul for the work which I have called them.'
(Acts 13:2)

Paul and Barnabas returned to Antioch and, soon afterwards, the church there commissioned them to embark upon an evangelistic tour. They went first to Cyprus. There, the Roman Proconsul, Sergius Paulus, warmly welcomed them. Paul had now abandoned his Jewish name, Saul, and it was here that he faced his first spiritual challenge, in the shape of Elymas, or 'Bar-Jesus', a magician who tried to turn Sergius Paulus away from Paul's message. Paul's response was swift: *'Now the hand of the Lord is against you. You are going to be blind…'* (13:11).

From Cyprus Paul and Barnabas sailed to Asia Minor, across the mountains to Pisidia and another town called Antioch (Pisidian Antioch). From there, they went east to Lycaonia and through several towns in Galatia, before returning to Antioch. In every town they followed the same pattern, which became the model for all the missionary journeys. First they would preach in the local synagogue, where they might meet sympathetic Jews and Gentile God-fearers who would accept their message and become the centre of the new community. Later, on the return journey, they would revisit the new congregations of Christians that had been formed, and encourage them in their new faith and help their leaders (Acts 14:21–3). Many Jews rejected Paul's message, some acting with violence, and in Perga Paul's companion, John Mark, left them. However, the mission succeeded in establishing a Christian witness in Pisidian Antioch, Derbe, Iconium and Lystra.

Many Gentiles were converted to Christianity, along with Jewish proselytes and 'God-fearers'. Paul began to realise that the Gentile believers should be admitted to the Christian community purely on the basis of their faith in Christ, and ought not to have to be circumcised and observe the conditions of the Jewish Law that were totally alien to them. Marshall (1980) notes: *'There was the problem of the entry of the Gentiles into the church. This not only intensified the opposition against the church from Judaism. It also raised acute questions within the church regarding its character and its way of life'.*

When Paul and Barnabas returned to Antioch, they were warmly welcomed back. However, problems soon began to arise. Emissaries from the Jerusalem church arrived. These Jewish Christians became known as Judaisers because they visited some of the new churches Paul had established and caused great confusion and anger by telling the new Christians that to be part of the community of God's people, a person must be circumcised and agree to follow many other regulations linked to Judaism. The new Christians, under the guidance of the Judaisers, found they were faced with a mass of rules and regulations that seemed distant and irrelevant — and they had no inclination to comply with them.

When Paul heard about this he was furious, seeing it as a threat to the very mission to the Gentiles and to the truth of the Gospel itself. He expressed his opposition very firmly, even rebuking Peter (Gal. 2:14), and wrote his famous letter to the Galatians in which he outlined his belief in salvation by grace through faith.

These events caused the first great theological crisis in the early church. To resolve the problems that were raised, the church in Antioch sent Paul and Barnabas to Jerusalem to confer with the Apostles and leaders of the Jerusalem church. The Council of Jerusalem (Acts 15) met and finally established that Gentile Christians should have *'no greater burden'* than abstaining from food offered to idols, blood-meat, meat from strangled animals and immoral sexual practices. The decision meant that Gentiles were not put under an obligation to obey the Law of Moses and did not have to undergo circumcision. It was a compromise agreement. Drane (1999) observes:

Paul was, at heart, a conciliatory and pragmatic sort of person... he was content to accept that, regardless of theological difficulties, Jews and Gentiles had to live together within the local church, and the acceptance of these guidelines was a straightforward means of achieving this.

2.2 The second missionary journey (Acts 15:40–18:22)

The death of Jesus at the hands of the Roman authorities...was a political event which Paul transformed in his imagination into a moment of cosmic religious significance.

(Wilson, 1998)

For his second missionary journey, Paul was to travel to the great population centres of Asia Minor. Paul and Barnabas disagreed over whether or not to take John Mark with them (Paul thought John Mark had deserted them the first time) and, as a result, Paul took a new companion, Silas, on the second missionary journey. They set off first to revisit the churches of south Galatia that had been founded earlier, and were joined by Timothy in Lystra. Paul had planned to go to the Roman province of Asia but was forbidden by the Holy Spirit to travel west, so instead he journeyed into Troas, where he met Luke, the physician.

Paul received a vision from God of a 'man of Macedonia' (16:9), beckoning him to come to Macedonia (16:9–10). So, Paul travelled to Greece. The first town he visited was Philippi, a town largely populated by retired soldiers from the Roman army. There was no synagogue there, so Paul began by going to the Jewish 'place of prayer', which was by the riverside. Here, his message was well received and one of the most significant converts was a woman of some importance, called Lydia. She opened her own home to Paul and soon it became the centre of their activity and a place of unity and fellowship for believers. It was also in Philippi that Paul healed a slave girl who was possessed by a spirit of clairvoyance. This was much to the annoyance of her owners, who had used her abilities to make money. Paul was accused of creating a public disturbance, by commending customs that were unlawful for Roman citizens (16:16–21). Paul and Silas were thrown into prison, where they spent the night singing praises to God. During the night an earthquake opened all the prison doors, but Paul and the other prisoners stayed where they were and did not run away. The local jailer was ready to kill himself, thinking his prisoners would have escaped, but when he saw that they were there, praising God, he too became a Christian, in response to Paul's encouragement: *'Believe in the Lord Jesus, and you will be saved — you and your household'* (16:31).

Soon afterwards Paul claimed his rights as a Roman citizen not to be imprisoned and received an apology from the authorities before leaving the city. Luke stayed behind to help the established Christian communities in Philippi, whilst Paul, Silas and Timothy

moved on to Thessalonica and Beroea. Paul then went on to visit Athens. Here he had to adopt a different approach because the city was a place of learning and there were many young Romans and Greeks who were studying philosophy and the mystery religions. They had no Jewish or biblical background and to talk of Jesus as the Messiah would have meant nothing to them. So Paul began first by observing what was going on and listening to the debates. When at last he did speak, he began from the Greek view of God as creator and invisible presence in the universe and then spoke of humanity's search for God. He referred to the many shrines and altars that there were in the city, including the altar 'to the unknown god', which he identified with Jesus. His message received a mixed reception and Paul was not able to establish a Christian community.

Around 51 CE, Paul moved on to Corinth, a thriving commercial city located at the narrowest point in the Greek mainland and with easy access to the Aegean and Adriatic seas. It was a place of many diverse cultures and a perfect place to establish a Christian ministry. Paul stayed there for nearly two years with a married couple of believers called Priscilla and Aquila. During the day Paul worked as a tentmaker and on the Sabbath he preached at the synagogue, soon establishing a major Christian fellowship. At one point the Jewish authorities tried to force him out by telling the proconsul Gallio that Paul was '....*persuading people to worship God in ways that are contrary to the Law*' (18:13). But the charge came to nothing because Gallio would not judge Paul under Jewish Law, and under Roman Law he had done nothing wrong.

From Corinth, the Holy Spirit led Paul, along with Priscilla and Aquila, to Ephesus, the Roman capital and commercial heart of Asia. He stayed a short while and left Priscilla and Aquila there to help the local community of believers before returning to Antioch.

2.3 The third missionary journey (Acts 18:23–20:38)

The third missionary journey centred on two main places, Ephesus and Corinth. Paul travelled back to Corinth first, where he met a devoted follower of Christ called Apollos. He then went on to Ephesus and baptised many believers who had only received baptism from John: '*Paul said, "John's baptism was a baptism of repentance. He told the people to believe in the one coming after him, that is, in Jesus." On hearing this, they were baptised into the name of the Lord Jesus*' (19:4–5).

Paul was able to perform many miracles there, including healing the sick and casting out demons. He was so successful that some Jewish exorcists began to use the name of Jesus in their work, but in vain. However, Paul did encounter problems. Ephesus was a centre of spiritual traditions, at the middle of which was the Temple of the city's patron goddess, Artemis (Diana). It was also home to a large number of magicians and astrologers, and one rich idol-maker called Demetrius incited the people to riot against the Christians in the city: '*Paul has convinced and led astray large numbers of people here in Ephesus... He says that man-made gods are no gods at all*' (19:26).

Paul left Ephesus and made final visits to the communities he had helped to establish in the area. In Troas, Paul was able to restore Eutychus to life after he fell from an upstairs window (20:12) before returning to Jerusalem. He brought with him a gift from the Gentile congregations for the church in Jerusalem as a sign of fellowship and solidarity between Gentile and Jewish believers. He was in the company of Christians from Beroea, Thessalonica, Derbe and Ephesus. However, he knew he faced difficulties with the Jewish believers in Jerusalem.

Paul met the leaders of the Jerusalem church and reported on the success of God's work amongst the Gentiles. At first there was great rejoicing, but soon some Jews from Asia saw Paul at the Temple and convinced themselves that he had defiled the sacred site by taking Gentiles into the inner court (21:27–37). A riot followed. Paul was taken captive by the Romans because the crowd wanted to kill him. The Roman commander was going to have Paul flogged, but he claimed immunity from such treatment because he was a Roman citizen and was sent instead before the Sanhedrin. The Jewish authorities could not agree about Paul, and that night he had a message from God: '*Take courage! As you have testified about me in Jerusalem, so you must also testify in Rome*' (23:11).

On hearing of a Jewish plot against Paul's life, the Romans took Paul under armed guard to Caesarea.

2.4 On to Rome

Paul...still believed that, as the 'Apostle to the Gentiles', he had something to contribute to the church in the most strategic position of all: Rome, the capital of the empire.

(Drane, 1999).

At Caesarea, Paul was tried before the Roman procurator, Felix, under the charge of provoking civil disorder. Felix did not believe he was guilty and delayed his decision for two years. His successor, Porcius Festus, wanted Paul to return for trial in Jerusalem, but Paul chose to exercise his right as a Roman citizen to appeal to the supreme court of the empire — the emperor himself (25:12). Festus then consulted with King Herod Agrippa, who heard what Paul had to say. He also thought Paul was innocent, but as Paul had already appealed to the emperor, he had to go to Rome. Paul set sail for Rome on a prison ship.

He was treated as something of a special case, being accompanied by Luke and Aristarchus and enjoying reasonable conditions on ship. The ship was wrecked in Malta during a storm and it was several months before Paul finally landed in southern Italy. There, he was warmly welcomed by the Christian community (28:14). He remained in Rome for two years under house arrest in a property he rented for himself and was protected by Roman guards, whom he also had to pay. He preached for two years and then his story ends. Blaiklock (1959) observes: '*...when he came to Rome, the purpose for which he had toiled and striven was virtually achieved*'.

We do not know exactly what happened, but the traditions of the early church say that Paul met a martyr's death, probably by beheading, during the persecution of Rome's Christians by the Emperor Nero in 64 CE. A. N. Wilson (1998) concludes:

The religion of Paul...contains all the makings of a religion with universal appeal even though he himself, like Jesus, would perhaps have been astonished by the turns and developments which the Christian religion was to take after his death... The essential things — the certainty of human unworthiness before the perfection of God, the atoning sacrifice of Christ on the Cross, the glorious promise of the Resurrection and everlasting life — these are the core of Paul's religion. And above all, the knowledge that Christ, the drama of his passion, death and resurrection, but also the continuing presence in the world are in us. That is the winning formula…

Summary

- **Paul** came to Christianity from a strong Jewish background, trained in the Law as a Pharisee, and a powerful opponent of 'the Way' in its early years. He remained firmly Jewish in his thinking, although at the same time fought vigorously against those who continued to maintain that the Law was the way to salvation. His conversion experience set him apart as Apostle to the Gentiles and transformed the life of the early church. His relationship with them was, at first, difficult, until he emerged as the obvious candidate (with Barnabas) to take responsibility for the Gentile mission. Peter had already met with Cornelius and witnessed the first conversion of a non-Jew, but the Jerusalem church did not want overall responsibility for a Gentile mission.
- Paul's mission took the form of **missionary journeys** that followed a clear pattern. On the first, he began by preaching in the synagogue, giving Jews the opportunity to hear the Gospel, but he was furious to learn that Jewish Christians were continuing to advocate obedience to the Law, including circumcision. He expressed his view strongly to Peter and following the decision of the Council of Jerusalem that Gentile Christians were not required to follow the Law of circumcision, he and Barnabas were clearly distinguished in their ministry.
- On the second missionary journey Paul travelled into the heart of Gentile territories and confronted Greek magic and philosophy, reaching a climax in Corinth before moving on to establish the church in Ephesus.
- The third missionary journey focused on Corinth and Ephesus, once again confronting established pagan beliefs. Paul was forced to return to Jerusalem to deal with problems that had arisen in his relationship with the leaders there. He was arrested for causing a riot in the Temple, but his Roman citizenship ensured him protection.
- On the way to Rome, Paul faced trial before the Roman governor, and was clearly given preferential treatment, and although he lived under house arrest in Rome for two years he was able to preach freely there.

Exam watch

This is all heavily narrative material, so you must make sure that writing an essay on the activities and movements of Paul does not become an exercise in story-telling. Ensure that you can comment critically on every aspect of his life and ministry and see it against the background of the establishment of the early church and the problems it faced. Keep in mind the questions, 'How important was Paul?', 'Why was he important?', 'What would have happened to the church if Paul had not been converted?'

Review questions

1 Examine and assess the relationship between Paul and the early church in Jerusalem.
2 *'Paul's missionary journeys were crucial to the development of the early church'.* Discuss.
3 To what extent is it accurate to describe Paul as the *'Apostle to the Gentiles'*?

C The teaching of Paul

1 The Pauline epistles

For Paul, the whole world — indeed, the whole universe — was the stage on which the drama of redemption was to be played out. Personal and individual salvation was important, but could never be separated from social and cosmic salvation. The life, death and resurrection of Jesus was the hinge on which the whole of world history turned; it was the beginning of God's 'new creation'.

(Drane, 1999)

The **Pauline epistles** are a series of letters written to the churches that Paul had helped to establish during his missionary journeys. They contained encouragement and instruction to the Christians whom Paul saw as being under his care. These letters account for almost one-third of the whole of the New Testament. They were real letters written to real people, dealing with real-life situations. They are not a comprehensive account of the Christian faith, but guidance for the followers of Jesus Christ.

The letters followed a style common in that day. They would begin with the name of the writer and the name of the person to whom the letter was addressed. Then there would be a greeting. Following this, there was an expression of thanks for the good health of the person addressed, followed by a thanksgiving to God. After this came the main body of the letter, usually divided into two parts — doctrinal teaching and advice on aspects of Christian lifestyle. The letter concluded with personal news and greetings, a blessing and a word of farewell.

Throughout the epistles, it is clear that Paul believed that what he taught came from Jesus Christ, the Son of God, through whom God is revealed to humanity: '*...the gospel I preach is not of human origin. I did not receive it from a human source, nor was I taught it, but I received it through a revelation of Jesus Christ*' (Galatians 1:11–12). Paul gives to Jesus the Old Testament title 'Lord', which was reserved exclusively for God, and belief that Christ is 'Lord' is crucial to Paul's teaching: '*That if you confess with your mouth, "Jesus is Lord", and believe in your heart that God raised him from the dead, you will be saved*' (Romans 10:9).

Paul makes clear in the epistles that salvation is through God's love — an act of God's grace to his undeserving people. In turn, the believer needs to make a response to God's love — to believe in God's love and have faith in him. Drane (1999) observes:

These then were the key features of Paul's gospel: God's undeserved love ('grace') shown to humankind through Jesus, to which the appropriate response was 'faith', which included a commitment to God that was based not on wishful thinking, but on the absolute facts of Jesus's life, death and resurrection, and the arrival of God's kingdom.

For Paul, belief was based on personal experience and had to have some connection with social and cultural realities. For example, it meant that Christians could not remain in an enclosed group; if God accepted them without conditions, so they should accept other people without conditions. This openness in relationships to others was a key part of Paul's teaching: '*...there is no longer Jew nor Greek, slave nor free, male or female; for you are all one in Christ Jesus*' (Galatians 3:28).

As a Jew, Paul had believed that observing the Law of Moses was an important part of a person's faithful response to God's love. However, his view changed when he realised that such strict observance of the Law hindered his belief that Jesus was the promised Messiah, because the Law had decreed: *'Cursed is anyone who is hung on a tree'* (Deuteronomy 21:23; Galatians 3:13). Paul therefore realised that the life of a Christian should be based not on strict observance of the Law, but on trusting Jesus and allowing God to change their hearts. Paul knew that the presence of the living Jesus in his life would give him victory over sin and, with Christ leading him, he could end his life of sin and receive new life in Christ: *'For through the law I died to the law so that I might live for God. I have been crucified with Christ and I no longer live, but Christ lives in me. The life I live in the body, I live by faith in the Son of God, who loved me and gave himself for me'* (Galatians 2:20).

Paul believed that Christians were intended to become children of God. Jesus had fulfilled God's will perfectly and believers could now do the same, thanks to the presence of the risen Christ living within them, through the work of the Holy Spirit: *'The Spirit himself testifies with our spirit that we are God's children. Now if we are children, then we are heirs — heirs of God and co-heirs with Christ, if indeed we share in his sufferings in order that we may also share in his glory'* (Romans 8:16–17).

1.1 Ephesians 1–4

Paul's letter to the Ephesians is different to his other letters in that it does not deal with specific or doctrinal problems, nor does it contain messages for individual believers. It reads more like a sermon or prayer than a letter written to address a particular need or issue. It is a message for all the *'saints in Ephesus, the faithful in Christ Jesus'* (1:1). In *Ephesians*, Foulkes (1989) observes: *'It is like a sermon on the greatest and widest theme possible for a Christian sermon — the eternal purpose of God which he is fulfilling through his son Jesus Christ, and working out in and through the church'*. In his epistle, Paul emphasises the central place of Christ in God's divine plan. He begins by showing the believers that they are part of God's new creation in which God's plan is *'...to bring all things in heaven and on earth together under one head, even Christ'* (1:10).

Paul reminds the believers that they have been granted great privileges — they have been chosen, forgiven and saved from their sinful nature: *'But because of his great love for us, God, who is rich in mercy, made us alive with Christ even when we were dead in transgressions — it is by grace you have been saved'* (2:4–5). Paul tells them that they will only find true satisfaction if they are willing to be filled with the love of God, which they could find only through Jesus Christ: *'And I pray that you, being rooted and established in love, may have power, together with all the saints, to grasp how wide and long and high and deep is the love of Christ and to know this love that surpasses knowledge — that you may be filled to the measure of all the fullness of God'* (3:18–19).

Paul goes on to describe Jesus in terms of the cosmic saviour of the world and the source of all physical, mental and spiritual knowledge and activity. This is important for the believers in their everyday lives too — for, as members of Christ's body and children of God, they must show by their actions who they really are: *'I urge you to live a life worthy of the calling you have received. Be completely humble and gentle; be patient, bearing with one another in love...'* (4:1–2). He tells the believers to expect the unity of the Spirit to be displayed in the giving of gifts of grace to the members of the church to enable the body to develop and grow. Some are prophets, others evangelists or teachers. Christ is the head of the church, and the believers are the body: '...*we will in all things grow up into him who is the Head, that is, Christ. From him the whole body, joined and held together by every supporting ligament, grows and builds itself up in love, as each part does its work*' (4:15–16). Foulkes (1989) makes an important observation:

It means more than saying the church is the company of the disciples of Christ, the people of God; it expresses the essential union of his people with him — the same life of God flows through all; and it speaks of the whole as functioning in obedience to him, carrying out his work in the world.

Paul encourages the believers to develop close relationships with each other, and warns that any wrong done by one member affects all the others. People must put away sinful habits and avoid anger, lies and deceit. '*Be kind and compassionate to one another, forgiving each other, just as in Christ God forgave you*' (4:32).

1.2 Galatians 2, 5

The letter to the Galatians was probably written hurriedly at a time of controversy within the early church. In it Paul deals with the problems relating to the false ideas being spread by the Judaising teachers who believed that Gentile members of the church should first adopt the traditions and practices of Judaism. The Judaisers claimed that Paul had no right to teach new Christians because he was not a proper Apostle or one of the original twelve, nor had he been accredited by the Apostles in Jerusalem. In reply, Paul said that he needed no authorisation from the Apostles because he had met the risen Christ on the road to Damascus (1:15–17). Paul proved his point by indicating that the Apostles did approve of what he was doing:

For God, who was at work in the ministry of Peter as an Apostle to the Jews, was also at work in my ministry as an Apostle to the Gentiles. James, Peter and John, those reputed to be pillars, gave me and Barnabas the right hand of fellowship when they recognised the grace given to me. They agreed that we should go to the Gentiles, and they to the Jews. (2:8–9)

Paul then goes on to recount how he fell into a dispute with Peter, who he claimed had broken off eating with Gentile Christians simply because some Jewish believers had arrived from Jerusalem (2:11). It is implied that Peter accepted Paul's rebuke, which highlights Paul's apostolic authority. As Drane (1999) observes: '*Subsequent events at Antioch had proved conclusively that Paul was in no way inferior to Peter, who was commonly reckoned to be the greatest of the Apostles*'.

Paul was deeply concerned that the new Gentile believers should not be unnecessarily burdened with obedience to the Law of Moses. The Galatians had attempted to place themselves under the Law and Paul made the point in his epistle that it was of no value either way whether a Christian was circumcised or not. Their standing before God depended not on external signs but on their faith: '*For in Christ Jesus neither circumcision nor uncircumcision has any value. The only thing that counts is faith expressing itself through love*' (5:6). In fact, he went so far as to suggest that circumcision would be a denial of what Christ had done for them (5:2) and, moreover, to be circumcised brought with it an obligation to observe all the Law (5:3) — the very thing Paul had rejected as impossible. Paul saw the Law as a 'yoke of slavery' (5:1), which was incompatible with the freedom given by Christ.

Paul knew that Judaism required high moral standards and he urged Christians to behave with equally high standards. He made four important points:

❖ 'Freedom in Christ' is not a freedom to do whatever you like, but to serve one another in love.
❖ A Christian's life is marked out by the fruit of the Spirit, and the demands of Christ are far greater than any ethical rules.
❖ Christians should not judge others, for they too would have no moral strength to do what is right without the power of the Holy Spirit.
❖ Believers should not look to their own selfish pleasures, but to the Spirit and their new life in Christ: *'He told them that if they trusted Christ, then the Holy Spirit would enable them to live as Jesus lived: "Since we live by the Spirit, let us keep in step with the Spirit. Let us not become conceited, provoking and envying each other"'* (5:25).

1.3 Romans 1–8, 13

Paul's letter to the Romans, probably written in 57 CE, is a reflective and carefully thought-out account of the major themes in Paul's teachings, especially those found in Galatians and Corinthians. It was written for two different audiences:

❖ Christians in Rome. It contains a summary of his beliefs in preparation for his long-expected visit there.
❖ Those members of the Jewish establishment in Jerusalem and elsewhere who violently disagreed with his views concerning the place of Gentiles within the Christian community.

Romans 1–8 is a theological argument in defence of the Gentile Christians. Paul argues, using the prophet Habakkuk's words, that *'The righteous will live by faith'* (Romans 1:17; Habakkuk 2:4). Paul's principal claim is that everyone, whether a Jew or a Gentile, is under the power of sin and, without Christ, will face God's judgment: *'But because of your stubbornness and your unrepentant heart, you are storing up wrath against yourself for the day of God's wrath, when his righteous judgment will be revealed'* (2:5). Paul argues that being born a Jew is not sufficient to escape judgment. The true Jew is the person of God who obeys with their heart, not with outward physical signs such as circumcision: *'No, a man is a Jew if he is one inwardly; and circumcision is circumcision of the heart, by the Spirit, not by the written code'* (2:29).

In *Romans*, Bruce says: *'When men and women have been justified by faith, right is still right and wrong is still wrong, and the will of God is still the rule of life. But for them the will of God is not simply enshrined in an external code of regulations; it is implanted within their hearts as a new principle of life'.* Paul uses Old Testament imagery to reinforce his message that everyone, Jew and Gentile, is under the power of sin and that obedience to the Law is not enough: *'Therefore no one will be declared righteous in his own sight by observing the law; rather, through the law we become conscious of sin'* (3:20).

Paul teaches that there is only one way to escape the judgment of God, which is through faith in Jesus Christ:

This righteousness from God comes through faith in Jesus Christ to all who believe. There is no difference, for all have sinned and fall short of the glory of God and are justified freely by his grace through the redemption that came by Christ Jesus. God presented him as a sacrifice of atonement, through faith in his blood.

(3:22–5)

Bruce (1995) observes: *'The gospel of justification by faith sets human beings by themselves before God. If it humbles them to the dust before God, it is that God may raise them up and set them on their feet'.*

Paul illustrates his theme by reference to the life of Abraham, who followed God by an act of faith. He then goes on to highlight the consequences that this new relationship with God can produce — freedom from God's judgment (5:9), freedom from slavery to sin (6:18) and freedom from death: *'For the wages of sin is death, but the gift of God is eternal life in Christ Jesus our Lord'* (6:23). Paul uses imagery in which he compares the baptism of Christians to the death and resurrection of Jesus. In baptism, Christians were covered with water as an outward physical symbol of something that would happen inwardly and spiritually. Being soaked with water was like Jesus being buried, and coming out of the water was like being raised from the dead: *'...all of us who were baptised into Christ Jesus were baptised into his death'* (5:3). As Drane (1999) observes: *'The essence of Paul's understanding of these events was that becoming a Christian involved a willingness to "die", in the sense of shedding a self-centred existence, in order to be "raised" again and receive a new existence, the life of Jesus Christ himself living within'.*

Paul makes it clear that, although Christians are set free from the need to observe formal rules, this does not mean that they have no responsibility for their actions. They have entered into a new kind of life where, instead of being slaves to sin, they are *'slaves to God'* (6:22). Christ has set them free, not in order to do as they please but so that they might become like Christ himself. In this, they are aided by the work of the Holy Spirit: *'Therefore, there is now no condemnation for those who are in Christ Jesus, because through Christ Jesus the Law of the Spirit of life set me free from the law of sin and death'* (8:1–2).

Romans 13 is concerned with the relationship between Christians and the State authorities. The Jews, even though they were members of a subject nation, nevertheless enjoyed exceptional privileges under the Romans. They had the status of '***collegia licita***' ('permitted associations') and many Jewish Laws, including those relating to the Sabbath, food laws and graven images, were safeguarded by Roman imperial law.

However, the position of Christians was more problematic. The Roman authorities tended to see Christians as a variety of Jews, but sometimes there were difficulties. These stemmed from the fact that Christianity was founded by a 'criminal' whom the Romans had crucified. The position was further complicated by the fact that there were often problems when Jews and Christians met — for example the riots that occurred during Paul's missionary journeys. As Bruce (1995) observes: *'It was all the more necessary, therefore, that Christians should be specially careful of their public behaviour'.*

In chapter 13, Paul addresses this matter at the highest level. For Paul, God is the source of all authority, and those who exercise authority on earth do so by delegation from God. Those who disobey the authorities are disobeying God: *'...he who rebels against the authority is rebelling against what God has instituted'* (13:2). Christians, therefore, should obey the laws of the state, pay their taxes and respect the authorities, not out of the fear of punishment but because it is a way of serving God: *'This is also why you pay taxes, for the authorities are God's servants...'* (13:6). Paul realises that the times are dangerous and he urges all believers to behave correctly at all times and to be ever ready and vigilant: *'So let us put aside the deeds of darkness and put on the armour of light'* (14:12).

1.4 1 Corinthians

Corinth was a cosmopolitan seaport city, filled with people from a wide range of social, cultural and intellectual backgrounds. Those who had joined the church at Corinth had brought with them many different ideas and concepts and this had caused problems. Essentially, the church at Corinth had divided into four different groups. The *libertines* claimed to follow Paul and encouraged the members of the church not to worry about moral norms. The *legalists* claimed to follow Cephas (Peter) and were raising the old questions concerning what kind of food Christians should eat. The *philosophers* followed Apollos, and insisted that they had a form of wisdom that was superior to anything Paul had taught. Finally, the *mystics*, who claimed to follow Christ alone, argued that the sacraments of the church acted in a magical way, and therefore they did not need to worry about the consequences of their own lifestyles. In 1 Corinthians, Leon Morris (1988) observes: *'Paul's purpose then is principally to set right disorders which the Corinthians took lightly, but which he saw as grave sins'*.

Paul saw that one of his largest churches was in a state of great confusion. He knew that the answer must be found in Christ; following anyone else would not be sufficient. So, in his letter, Paul repeated this message: *'For no one can lay any foundation other than the one already laid, which is Jesus Christ'* (3:11). Paul then went on to address the specific problems of the church at Corinth. He turned his attention first to the problems of Christian behaviour. Many of the members of the church felt that they need not follow accepted standards of behaviour, particularly over **sexual relations**. Paul addressed their permissiveness by condemning outright any such immorality: *'It is actually reported that there is sexual immorality among you, and of a kind that does not even occur among pagans; a man has his father's wife'* (5:1). Paul instructed the church members not to associate with the individual concerned until he changed his ways. If he failed to do so, that person should be expelled from the Christian community. Paul went on to emphasise the fact that freedom in Christ does not mean the freedom to be immoral. Christians are not free to do as they please; they are free to serve God: *'Do you not know that your body is a Temple of the Holy Spirit, who is in you, whom you have received from God? You are not your own, you were bought at a price. Therefore honour God with your body'* (6:19–20).

Paul then addressed the question of **marriage**. He said that Christians could marry (7:1–9), but he was not married himself and suggested that others should remain single too. He said that divorce was not permitted, except in the case of a non-Christian deserting a Christian partner (7:12–16). His overall recommendation was that the Christians at Corinth should remain in their present condition, either married or single, though he recommends celibacy as the most preferable state. Drane (1999) makes an interesting observation:

This was clearly advice given for a specific situation that had arisen in Corinth, and it is interesting to note the way Paul separates his own advice and opinion from what he believed to be the teaching of Christ. He felt that he had Jesus's authority for saying there should be no divorce among Christians, but of the other issues with which he deals, in one case he makes it plain that it is 'not the Lord' who is speaking (7:12).

Paul then turns his attention to matters of **worship**. Paul had earlier taught that, in Christ, there was no distinction of race, sex or class (Galatians 3:28). With particular reference to women, Paul had said that women could play a full part in the Christian ministry. However, some of the women in the Corinth church who were taking a leading part in the church services were appearing with their heads uncovered, which was contrary to the norms and culture of the day. Paul took the unusual step of advising the women that they should veil their heads in accordance with social custom, even though this seemed like a limitation of their Christian freedom: '*A man ought not to cover his head, since he is the image and glory of God; but the woman is the glory of man...*' (12:7). Paul offered advice on the importance of orderly worship (14:26–39), with quietness as the key, although one of his suggestions appears to be particularly controversial: '*...women should remain silent in the churches...*' (14:34).

The way the church was observing the **Lord's Supper** or **Eucharist** was also giving cause for concern (11:17–34). The church was not following the instructions given first by Jesus and later by Paul (11:23–6). Some members were bringing their own food and making the service into a time of feasting and drunkenness. Moreover, different groups were eating different foods and there was discrimination between rich and poor. This was dishonouring both to the Christians themselves and to the purpose of the service. Paul ordered such practices to stop: '*Therefore, whoever eats the bread or drinks the cup of the Lord in an unworthy manner will be guilty of sinning against the body and blood of the Lord*' (11:27).

A very important feature of the church in Corinth was the use of **spiritual gifts**. Christians in the early church believed that they were empowered by the Holy Spirit — they were **charismatics**. These spiritual gifts included speaking in tongues, prophecy, and the working of miracles. The problem was that the Corinthians, who possessed these gifts in abundance, allowed them to dominate and override their worship, causing much confusion. Paul was forced to remind them that it was important to use spiritual gifts properly, under the inspiration of God and for the benefit and growth of the whole church: '*There are different kinds of gifts, but the same Spirit. There are different kinds of service, but the same Lord*' (12:5). Paul told the church members that all spiritual gifts come from God and that every gift had its rightful place and function. Just as the human body has many parts, each of which contributes to the overall operation of the body, so also is the church a body. Each member possesses a different gift, but they are all of value in the smooth running of the church: '*...there should be no division in the body, but that its parts should have equal concern for each other...you are the body of Christ, and each one of you is a part of it*' (12:25–6). This was quite a revolutionary teaching, as Morris (1988) observes: '*Paul's discussion of this subject is epoch-making. In contrast*

to the usual idea, he was clear that the Holy Spirit comes not only on a few outstanding people, but on all believers'.

Finally, Paul turned to what he regarded as the core of Christian belief, the **resurrection** of Jesus. He instructed them that Jesus was indeed resurrected and that this, in turn, guaranteed that Christians would also be raised to life on the last day, just as Jesus was: *'For as in Adam all die, so in Christ all will be made alive'* (15:22). Resurrection would be physical, though the 'new' body would be imperishable: *'So it will be with the resurrection of the dead. The body that is sown is perishable, it is raised imperishable; it is sown in dishonour, it is raised in glory; it is sown in weakness, it is raised in power; it is sown a natural body, it is raised a spiritual body'* (15:42–4).

Summary

- **Paul's epistles** form a substantial part of the New Testament and offer an insight into the real problems that the early churches faced internally, and in relation to the development of the church and the spread of the Gospel in general. Paul was clear that his authority to preach and to convey the Gospel message was given to him by the risen Jesus and he could claim the title of Apostle with as much integrity as the Jerusalem church leaders, with whom he did not always have an easy relationship.

- The key to Paul's preaching is **God's grace** — God's favour bestowed on individuals, irrespective of obedience to the Law or religious background. He argued that the Law had had its day, and although it was an essential means of staying in relationship with God before the coming of Christ, it had now been replaced by the saving death of Jesus as the means to salvation.

- His teaching was set against the background of real-life situations and the life of the church within the world. He did not advocate that Christians withdraw from the world, because they were called to make a difference to it.

- **Ephesians 1–4** — a general epistle addressing the theme of how God has fulfilled his purposes through Jesus and in the church. The life of the church must reflect its special calling.

- **Galatians 2, 5** — Paul wrote in his defence as he faced continuing attack from the Judaising members of the church for his attitude towards the Law. He felt called to defend his right to claim apostleship. Paul maintained that forcing Gentile believers to follow the constraints of the Law was placing them under the very burden from which Jesus's death freed them. Christian freedom involves responsibility, however.

- **Romans 1–8, 13** — a powerful theological argument which ranges widely over the themes of Law, grace, justification by faith, a comparison between the Old Testament and the Gospel, and the relationship between the Christian believer and the secular authorities which have been established in the world by God.

- **1 Corinthians** — Paul addressed a community which was still deeply influenced by its Greék philosophical and moral background and was seeking to establish how its acceptance of the Gospel should impact on its daily life. Sexual relations, marriage, worship, the eucharist, law suits, eating of meat offered to idols, the use of spiritual gifts, and the question of resurrection are all covered in the longest of Paul's letters.

Exam watch

Paul's theology is often complicated and sophisticated, so you will need to have a very thorough working knowledge of the texts and their meaning. Make sure that you don't fall back on narrative when you are being asked about the significance of aspects of Paul's theology, and that you are able to back up your arguments with scholarship.

Review questions

1 Consider and assess the contribution of Paul to the development of the early church.

2 (a) Outline and explain Paul's teaching on authority in Romans 13.

  (b) To what extent did the relationship between Paul and the authorities reflect this teaching?

3 (a) Identify the problems which faced the early church at Corinth.

  (b) To what extent were these problems caused by the social and cultural background of the members of the church?

4 Explain and assess the significance for the members of the early church of Paul's teaching in 1 Corinthians concerning (i) marriage and (ii) the resurrected body.

5 In what ways does a study of Paul's teachings contribute to an understanding of the beliefs and practices of the early church concerning (i) baptism and (ii) the eucharist?

Bibliography

Ahluwalia, L. (2001) *Foundation for the Study of Religion*, Hodder and Stoughton.

Aston, J. (1991) *Understanding the Fourth Gospel*, Clarendon.

Atkinson, D. and Field, D. (eds.) (1995) *New Dictionary of Christian Ethics and Pastoral Theology*, IVP.

Augustine of Hippo (1998 edn) *Confessions*, Oxford Paperbacks.

Ayer, A. J. (1936) *Language, Truth and Logic*, Penguin.

Bailey, D. S. (1986) *Homosexuality and the Western Tradition*, The Shoe String Press.

Banner, M. (1990) *The Justification of Science and the Rationality of Religious Belief*, Oxford University Press.

Barclay, W. (1975) *The Gospel of Matthew*, Westminster John Knox Press.

Barrett, C. K. (1955) *The Gospel According to St John*, SPCK.

Barrett, C. K. (1975) *The Gospel of John and Judaism*, Fortress Press.

Barrow, J. and Tipler, F. J. (1986) *The Anthropic Cosmological Principle*, Oxford University Press.

Barth, K. (2000 edn) *Church Dogmatics*, T&T Clark.

Beasley-Murray, G. (1999) *John*, W. Publishing Group.

Blaiklock, E. M. (1959) *Acts*, Tyndale.

Bonnington, M. and Fyall, B. (1996) *Homosexuality and the Bible*, Grove Books.

Brown, R. (1979) *The Community of the Beloved Disciple*, Chapman.

Bruce, F. F. (1995) *Romans*, IVP.

Bultmann, R. (1971) *The Gospel of St John*, Basil Blackwell.

Burrows, M. (1946) *An Outline of Biblical Theology*, The Westminster Press.

Caird, G. B. (1975) *The Apostolic Age*, Duckworth.

Caird, G. B. (1990) *Luke*, Penguin.

Coggins, R. J. and Houlden, J. L. (eds) (1990) *A Dictionary of Biblical Interpretation*, SCM.

Cole, P. (1999) *Philosophy of Religion*, Hodder and Stoughton.

Colson, C. (2000) *Justice that Restores*, IVP.

Cone, J. H. (1997) *Black Theology and Black Power*, Orbis.

Copleston, F. C. (1961) *Aquinas*, Penguin.

Court, J. and Court, K. (1990) *The New Testament World*, Prentice Hall.

Crossan, J. (1991) *The Historical Jesus*, T&T Clark.

Cruz, N. (1968) *Run Baby Run*, Hodder and Stoughton.

Culpepper, A. (1983) *Anatomy of the Fourth Gospel*, Fortress Press.

Daly, M. (1986) *Beyond God the Father*, The Women's Press.

Davies, B. (1982) *Introduction to the Philosophy of Religion*, Oxford University Press.

Davies, B. (ed.) (2000) *The Philosophy of Religion*, Oxford University Press.

Davies, W. D. (1964) *The Setting of the Sermon on the Mount*, Cambridge University Press.

Dawkins, R. (1986) *The Blind Watchmaker*, Longman, Scientific and Technical.

Descartes, R. (1970 edn) *Discourse on the Method*, Penguin.

Dodd, C. H. (1968) *The Interpretations of the Fourth Gospel*, Cambridge University Press.

Drane, J. (1999) *Introducing the New Testament*, Lion.

Durkheim, E. (1954) *The Elementary Forms of Religious Life*, The Free Press.

Durkheim, E. (1961) *Moral Education*, The Free Press.

Earle Ellis, E. (1981) *The Gospel of Luke*, Marshall, Morgan and Scott.

Edwards, D. (ed.) (1969) *The Honest to God Debate*, SCM.

Ereckson Tada, J. (1992) *When is it Right to Die?*, Marshall Pickering.

Ferguson, S. and Wright, D. (eds) (1988) *The New Dictionary of Theology*, IVP.

Feuerbach, L. (ed.) (1957) *The Essence of Christianity*, Prometheus Books.

Fletcher, J. (1966) *Situation Ethics*, SCM.

Flew, A. (1955) *Theology and Falsification*, SCM.

Flew, A. (1984) *God, Freedom and Immortality: A Critical Analysis*, Prometheus Books.

Foulkes, F. (1989) *Ephesians*, Send the Light.

France, R. T. (1989) *Matthew: Evangelist and Teacher*, Paternoster Press.

Frankena, W. K. (1973) *Ethics*, Prentice Hall.

Fredriksen, P. (2000) *From Jesus to Christ*, Yale University Press.

Gaebelein Hull, G. (1987) *Equal to Serve*, Scripture Union.

Goldberg, N. (1979) *Changing the Gods*, Beacon.

Grassi, J. (1992) *The Secret Identity of the Beloved Disciple*, Paulist Press.

Gray, J. (1986) *Joshua*, Marshall, Morgan and Scott.

Grayston, K. (1990) *The Gospel of John*, Epworth Press.

Green, J, McKnight, D, and Marshall, I. M. (eds) (1992) *A Dictionary of Jesus and the Gospels*, IVP.

Griffin, D. (1976) *God, Power and Evil: A Process Theodicy*, The Westminster Press.

Gutierrez, G. (2001 edn) *A Theology of Liberation*, SCM.

Halverson, M. and Cohen, A. (eds) (1960) *A Handbook of Christian Theology*, Fontana.

Hampson, D. (1990) *Theology and Feminism*, Basil Blackwell.

Harris, J. (1984) *The Value of Life*, Routledge.

Hart, H. L. A. (1986) *Law, Liberty and Morality*, Oxford University Press.

Hawking, S. (1987) *A Brief History of Time*, Bantam Books.

Hay, D. (1990) *Religious Experience Today*, Mowbray.

Hengel, M. (1975) *Property and Riches in the Early Church*, SCM.

Hick, J. (ed.) (1964) *The Existence of God*, Macmillan.

Hick, J. (1966) *Faith and Knowledge*, Fount.

Hick, J. (1968) *Evil and the God of Love*, Fontana.

Hick, J. (1973) *Philosophy of Religion*, Prentice Hall.

Hick, J. (1985) *Death and Eternal Life*, Palgrave.

Hick, J. (1993) *God and the Universe of Faith*, Oneworld Publications.

Hill, D. (1973) *The Gospel of Matthew*, Marshall, Morgan and Scott.

Hooker, M. (1991) *The Gospel According to Mark*, A&C Black.

Hooker, M. (1997) *Beginnings*, SCM.

Horner, C. and Westacott, E. (2000) *Thinking Through Philosophy*, Cambridge University Press.

Hoskyns, E. and Davey, F. (1947) *The Fourth Gospel*, Faber.

Howard, W. F. (1943) *Christianity According to St John*, Duckworth.

Howatch, S. (1990) *Scandalous Risks*, HarperCollins.

Hughes, S. (1983) *Marriage as God Intended*, Kingsway.

Hume, D. (1975 edn) *An Enquiry Concerning Human Understanding*, Oxford University Press.

Hume, D. (1998 edn) *Dialogues Concerning Natural Religion*, Oxford Paperbacks.

Hunt, D. (1996) *In Defense of the Faith,* Harvest House.

Jeremias, J. (1964) *Unknown Sayings of Jesus*, SCM.

Johnson, E. (1992) *Consider Jesus*, Crossroad.

Jones, D. Gareth (1999) *Valuing People*, Paternoster Press.

Kant, I. (1977 edn) *Prolegomena to Any Future Metaphysics*, Hackett.

Kant, I. (1999 edn) *Critique of Pure Reason*, Cambridge University Press.

Kasemann, E. (1964) *Essays on New Testament Themes*, SCM.

Kingsbury, J. D. (1983) *The Christology of Mark*, Fortress Press.

Kitto, D. F. (1951) *The Greeks*, Pelican.

Kuhn, T. S. (1970) *The Structure of Scientific Revolutions*, University of Chicago Press.

Kysar, R. (1993) *John, the Maverick Gospel,* The Westminster Press.

Leibniz, G. (1988) *Theodicy*, Open Court Publications.

Lieu, J. (1997) *The Gospel of Luke*, Epworth Press.

McCabe, H. (1980) 'A modern Cosmological Argument', *New Blackfriars*, Vol. 61.

McDowall, J. (1999) *New Evidence That Demands a Verdict*, Thomas Nelson.

McGrath, A. (ed.) (2000) *The Blackwell Encyclopedia of Modern Christian Thought*, Basil Blackwell.

McGrath, A. (ed.) (2001) *Christian Theology: An Introduction*, Basil Blackwell.

Mackie, J. L. (1955) *Evil and Omnipotence*, Mind.

Mackie, J. L. (1982) *The Miracle of Theism*, Oxford University Press.

Macquarrie, J. and Childress, J. (eds) (1990) *A New Dictionary of Christian Ethics*, SCM.

Magee, B. (1997) *Confessions of a Philosopher*, Phoenix.

Marsh, J. (1968) *St John,* Penguin.

Marshall, I. H. (1980) *Acts*, IVP.

Marshall, I. H. (1984) *Luke – Historian and Theologian*, Paternoster Press.

Matera, F. (1986) *Passion Narratives and Gospel Theologies*, Paulist Press.

Mitchell, B. (ed.) (1971) *The Philosophy of Religion*, Oxford University Press.

Moberly, E. (1983) *Homosexuality: A New Christian Ethic*, James Clarke.
Moltmann, J. (1974) *The Crucified God*, SCM.
Moody, R. (1988) *The Light Beyond*, Bantam Doubleday.
Moore, G. E. (1993) *Principia Ethica*, Cambridge University Press.
Morris, L. (1987) *I Corinthians*, W. Erdmans.
Morris, L. (1988) *Luke*, W. Erdmans.

Nagel, T. (1987) *What Does it all Mean?*, Oxford University Press.
Nineham, D. (1963) *St Mark*, Pelican.

O'Donnell, K. (1999) *Introduction to the New Testament*, Hodder and Stoughton.
O'Neill, J. C. (1961) *The Theology of Acts*, SPCK.

Painter, J. (1979) *John: Witness and Theologian*, SPCK.
Pepper, M. (ed.) (1991) *The Pan Dictionary of Religious Quotations*, Pan.
Phillips, D. Z. (1976) *The Concept of Prayer*, Routledge.
Plaskow, J. (1980) *Sex, Sin and Grace*, University Press of America.
Plowman, K. (2001) *Madison's Song*, Camelot Press.
Porter, J. (1995) *Moral Action and Christian Ethics*, Cambridge University Press.

Rea, J. (1990) *The Holy Spirit in the Bible*, Marshall Pickering.
Ricci, C. (1994) *Mary Magdalene and Many Others*, Burns and Oates.
Richardson, A. and Bowden, J. (eds) (1989) *A New Dictionary of Christian Theology*, SCM.
Rivkin, E. (1984) *What Crucified Jesus?*, SCM.
Roberts, D. (1994) *The 'Toronto' Blessing*, Kingsway.
Robinson, J. A. T. (1963) *Honest to God*, SCM.
Robinson, J. A. T. (1993) *Re-dating the New Testament*, XPRESS Reprints.
Rosenstand, N. (2000) *The Moral of the Story*, Mayfield.
Ruether, R. (1983) *Sexism and God-Talk*, SCM.
Russell, J. (1993) *Signs*, Abacus.
Ryle, G. (1949) *The Concept of Mind*, Penguin.

Sanders, J. N. and Mastin, B. A. (1968) *The Gospel According to John*, A&C Black.
Schillebeeckx, E. (1960) *The Sacramental Economy of Salvation*, Sheed and Ward.
Schnackenburg, R. (1980) *The Gospel According to St John*, Seabury Press.
Schweizer, E. (1961) *Church Order in the New Testament*, SCM.
Sire, J. (1994) *Why Should Anyone Believe Anything at All?*, IVP.
Smalley, S. (1978) *John: Evangelist and Interpreter*, Paternoster Press.
Sobrino, J. (1978) *Christology at the Crossroads*, Orbis.
Spinoza, B. (2001 edn) *Ethics,* Wordsworth Editions.
Stanton, G. (ed.) (1983) *The Interpretation of Matthew*, SPCK.
Stanton, G. (1989) *The Gospels and Jesus*, Oxford University Press.
Stanton, G. (1992) *A Gospel for a New People*, T&T Clark.
Still, J. (1985) *What is a Gospel?,* Mercer University Press.

Storr, A. (1964) *Sexual Deviation*, Penguin.

Stott, J. (1999) *Issues Facing Christians Today*, Marshall Pickering.

Strauss, D. F. (1972 edn) *The Life of Jesus Critically Examined*, Fortress Press.

Swinburne, R. (1971) *The Concept of Miracle*, Macmillan.

Swinburne, R. (1979) *The Existence of God*, Oxford University Press.

Swinburne, R. (ed.) (1989) *Miracles*, Macmillan.

Swinburne, R. (1996) *Is There a God?*, Oxford University Press.

Tasker, R. V. G. (1960) *John*, IVP.

Taylor, D. B. (1992) *Mark's Gospel as Literature and Story*, SCM.

Temple, W. (1998) *Readings in St John's Gospel*, Paternoster Press.

Thompson, M. (1996) *Philosophy of Religion*, Hodder and Stoughton.

Thomson, J. (1971) 'A defence of abortion', in *Philosophy and Current Affairs*, Vol. 1, No. 1.

Thurion, M. (1960) *The Eucharistic Memorial*, Lutterworth.

Tilby, A. (2001) *Son of God*, Hodder and Stoughton.

Tinsley, E. J. (ed.) (1979) *Modern Theology*, Epworth.

Tondeur. K. (1996a) *What Price the Lottery?*, Monarch.

Tondeur, K. (1996b) *Your Money and Your Life*, Triangle.

Vardy, P. (1998) *And If It's True?*, Marshall Pickering.

Vardy, P. (1999a edn) *The Puzzle of God,* Fount.

Vardy, P. (1999b) *What is Truth?*, UNSW Press.

Vardy, P. and Grosch, P. (1994) *The Puzzle of Ethics*, Fount.

Vardy, P. and Mills, M. (1995) *The Puzzle of the Gospels*, Fount.

Warfield, B. B. (1950) *The Person and Work of Christ*, Presbyterian and Reformed Publishing Company.

Weiss, J. (1971) *Jesus's Proclamation of the Kingdom of God*, Fortress Press.

Westcott, B. F. (2001 edn) *The Gospel According to St John*, Wipf and Stock.

Westermann, C. (1987) *Genesis*, T&T Clark.

Wiles, M. (1986) *God's Action in the World*, SCM.

Wilkerson, D. (1978) *The Cross and the Switchblade,* Zondervan.

Wilson, A. N. (1998) *Paul — The Mind of the Apostle*, Pimlico.

Wilson-Thomas, C. and Williams, N. (1996) *Laid Bare: A Path Through the Pornography Maze*, Hodder and Stoughton.

Wright, J. (1999) *The New Testament and the People of God*, Fortress Press.

Wyatt, J. (1998) *Matters of Life and Death*, IVP.

Yancey, P. (1997) *What's So Amazing About Grace?*, HarperCollins.

Zacharias, R. (1999) *Can Man Live Without God?*, Word Publishing.

Specification summary

Board	OCR	AQA	Edexcel
Specification code for AS	AS 3877	AS 5061	AS 8562
Specification code for A2	A2 7877	A2 6061	A2 9562

Philosophy of Religion

Topic 1 Influences and philosophical principles

	OCR	AQA	Edexcel
A The Ancient Greeks			
1 Plato	AS		
2 Aristotle	AS		
B Judaeo–Christian influences			
1 God as Creator	AS		
2 God's goodness	AS		
3 God at work in the world	AS		
C The principles of proof			
1 Types of proof		A2	A2
2 Proving God's existence		A2	A2
D Faith and reason			
1 What is faith?		A2	
2 Bliks		A2	
3 Anti-realism		A2	
4 Non-foundationalism		A2	
5 The will to believe		A2	

Topic 2 Arguments for the existence of God

	OCR	AQA	Edexcel
A The Cosmological Argument			
1 The need for an explanation	AS	AS	AS
2 Aquinas and the Five Ways	AS	AS	AS
3 Other approaches to the argument	AS	AS	AS
4 Criticisms of the argument	AS	AS	AS
5 The perennial value of the argument	AS	AS	AS
B The Teleological Argument			
1 Explaining order and purpose	AS	AS	AS
2 Classic approaches to the argument	AS	AS	AS
3 Other applications of the argument	AS	AS	AS
4 Criticisms of the argument	AS	AS	AS
C The Ontological Argument			
1 Anselm's *Proslogion*	AS/A2	A2	A2
2 Descartes and the perfect being	AS/A2	A2	A2
3 Gaunilo and Kant	AS/A2	A2	A2
4 Evaluating the argument	AS/A2	A2	A2
D The Argument from Religious Experience			
1 The value of the argument	AS/A2		A2
2 Religious experience as proof of the existence of God	AS/A2		A2
3 Arguments against the case for religious experience	AS/A2		A2
E The Moral Argument			
1 Aquinas and the Fourth Way	AS/A2		A2
2 Kant: morality alone proves the existence of God	AS/A2		A2
3 Objective moral laws	AS/A2		AS/A2

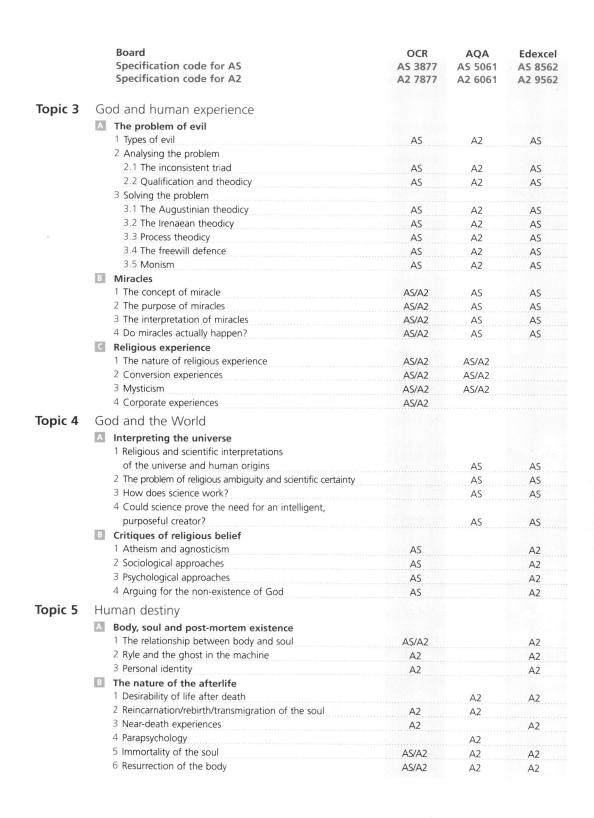

Board	OCR	AQA	Edexcel
Specification code for AS	AS 3877	AS 5061	AS 8562
Specification code for A2	A2 7877	A2 6061	A2 9562

Topic 3 God and human experience

	OCR	AQA	Edexcel
A The problem of evil			
1 Types of evil	AS	A2	AS
2 Analysing the problem			
2.1 The inconsistent triad	AS	A2	AS
2.2 Qualification and theodicy	AS	A2	AS
3 Solving the problem			
3.1 The Augustinian theodicy	AS	A2	AS
3.2 The Irenaean theodicy	AS	A2	AS
3.3 Process theodicy	AS	A2	AS
3.4 The freewill defence	AS	A2	AS
3.5 Monism	AS	A2	AS
B Miracles			
1 The concept of miracle	AS/A2	AS	AS
2 The purpose of miracles	AS/A2	AS	AS
3 The interpretation of miracles	AS/A2	AS	AS
4 Do miracles actually happen?	AS/A2	AS	AS
C Religious experience			
1 The nature of religious experience	AS/A2	AS/A2	
2 Conversion experiences	AS/A2	AS/A2	
3 Mysticism	AS/A2	AS/A2	
4 Corporate experiences	AS/A2		

Topic 4 God and the World

	OCR	AQA	Edexcel
A Interpreting the universe			
1 Religious and scientific interpretations of the universe and human origins		AS	AS
2 The problem of religious ambiguity and scientific certainty		AS	AS
3 How does science work?		AS	AS
4 Could science prove the need for an intelligent, purposeful creator?		AS	AS
B Critiques of religious belief			
1 Atheism and agnosticism	AS		A2
2 Sociological approaches	AS		A2
3 Psychological approaches	AS		A2
4 Arguing for the non-existence of God	AS		A2

Topic 5 Human destiny

	OCR	AQA	Edexcel
A Body, soul and post-mortem existence			
1 The relationship between body and soul	AS/A2		A2
2 Ryle and the ghost in the machine	A2		A2
3 Personal identity	A2		A2
B The nature of the afterlife			
1 Desirability of life after death		A2	A2
2 Reincarnation/rebirth/transmigration of the soul	A2	A2	
3 Near-death experiences	A2		A2
4 Parapsychology		A2	
5 Immortality of the soul	AS/A2	A2	A2
6 Resurrection of the body	AS/A2	A2	A2

Religious Ethics

Board	OCR	AQA	Edexcel
Specification code for AS	AS 3877	AS 5061	AS 8562
Specification code for A2	A2 7877	A2 6061	A2 9562

Topic 4 Practical ethics and society

A **War and peace**

	OCR	AQA	Edexcel
1 The biblical view of war	AS/A2		AS
2 The implications of modern warfare	AS/A2		AS
3 Just war theories	AS/A2		AS
4 Pacifism	AS/A2		AS

B **The environment and human need**

	OCR	AQA	Edexcel
1 Poverty and the allocation of resources	AS/A2	AS	
2 Conservation	AS/A2	AS	

C **Justice, law and human rights**

	OCR	AQA	Edexcel
1 Justice	AS/A2		A2
2 Rights			A2
3 Authority and law			A2
4 Punishment			A2

D **Financial and business ethics**

	OCR	AQA	Edexcel
1 Finance and religious ethics		A2	
2 Spending and consumerism		A2	
3 Debt and gambling		A2	
4 The ethical use of money		A2	
5 Business ethics		A2	

Christian Belief and Practice

Topic 1 Christian beliefs about God

	OCR	AQA	Edexcel
1 Creator			AS
2 Omnipotence			AS
3 A personal God			AS
4 A suffering God			AS

Topic 2 Christian beliefs about Jesus

	OCR	AQA	Edexcel
1 Christ and the Trinity		A2	A2
2 Christology			A2
3 The quest for the historical Jesus			A2

Topic 3 Christian practice

	OCR	AQA	Edexcel
1 Worship		AS	AS
2 Sacraments		AS	AS
3 Baptism			AS
4 Eucharist			AS
5 Prayer			AS

Topic 4 Christian doctrine

	OCR	AQA	Edexcel
1 Atonement		A2	A2
2 Sin and grace		A2	A2
3 Justification through faith		A2	A2

Topic 5 Christianity and the wider world

	OCR	AQA	Edexcel
1 Liberation theology	AS		
2 Black theology	AS/A2		
3 Feminist theology	AS/A2		
4 Christianity and world religions	AS/A2		

The New Testament

Board	OCR	AQA	Edexcel
Specification code for AS	AS 3877	AS 5061	AS 8562
Specification code for A2	A2 7877	A2 6061	A2 9562

	OCR	AQA	Edexcel
2 The teaching of Jesus			
2.1 Parables of the kingdom	A2		
2.2 Parables of judgement	A2	AS	
2.3 The Sermon on the Mount	A2		
3 The miracles of Jesus	A2	AS	
B The passion and resurrection narratives			
1 The last week	AS	AS	
1.1 The triumphal entry	AS	AS	
1.2 The cleansing of the Temple	AS	AS	
1.3 Conflict with the authorities	AS	AS	
2 The last day			
2.1 The Last Supper	AS	AS	
2.2 Gethsemane	AS	AS	
2.3 Arrest and trial	AS	AS	
2.4 Before Pilate	AS	AS	
3 The crucifixion	AS	AS	
4 The resurrection	AS	AS	
Topic 3 The Gospel of Luke			
A The birth and infancy narratives		AS	AS
B The teaching of Jesus			
1 The parables			
1.1 Parables of the kingdom		AS	AS
1.2 Parables of the lost	AS		AS
2 Theological and moral teaching			
2.1 The Sermon on the Plain			AS
2.2 Wealth and poverty			AS
2.3 Prayer and praise			AS
2.4 Discipleship			AS
2.5 Salvation			A2
2.6 Eschatology			A2
C Themes in the ministry of Jesus			
1 Miracles		AS	AS
2 Social issues			
2.1 Women			AS
2.2 Outcasts and sinners			AS
D Important figures in Jesus's ministry			
1 John the Baptist			AS
2 The Holy Spirit			AS
3 The disciples			AS
E The passion and resurrection narratives			
1 The last week		AS	A2
1.1 The triumphal entry		AS	A2
1.2 The cleansing of the Temple		AS	A2
1.3 Conflict with the authorities		AS	A2
2 The last day			
2.1 The Last Supper		AS	A2
2.2 The Mount of Olives		AS	AS
2.3 Arrest and trial		A2	A2
2.4 Before Pilate		A2	A2
3 The crucifixion		A2	A2
4 The resurrection		A2	A2

Advanced Religious Studies

Board	OCR	AQA	Edexcel
Specification code for AS	AS 3877	AS 5061	AS 8562
Specification code for A2	A2 7877	A2 6061	A2 9562

Topic 4 The Fourth Gospel

	OCR	AQA	Edexcel
A The nature of the Gospel			
1 Origin			
1.1 Authorship			AS
1.2 The dating of the Gospel			AS
2 Influences			
2.1 Greek influences on the Gospel			AS
2.2 Jewish influences on the Gospel			AS
2.3 The purpose of the Gospel			A2
B The Prologue			
1 What is the Prologue?		AS	A2
2 The Word (*Logos*)		AS	A2
3 John the Baptist		AS	AS/A2
4 The Word Incarnate			A2
5 The Law, grace and truth			A2
C The early ministry			
1 The first four signs			
1.1 The wedding at Cana		A2	AS
1.2 The healing of the official's son		A2	AS
1.3 The healing of the crippled man at the pool		A2	AS
1.4 The feeding of the five thousand		A2	AS
2 Teachings			
2.1 Born again – Jesus and Nicodemus		A2	AS/A2
2.2 Living water – Jesus and the Samaritan woman		A2	AS/A2
2.3 The Holy Spirit – *pnuema*			AS
D The later ministry			
1 The first five '*I am*' sayings			
1.1 'I am the bread of life'		A2	AS
1.2 'I am the light of the world'		A2	AS
1.3 'I am the gate for the sheep'		A2	AS
1.4 'I am the good shepherd'		A2	AS
1.5 'I am the resurrection and the life'		A2	AS
2 Further signs			
2.1 Walking on the water			AS
2.2 The healing of the blind man			AS
2.3 The raising of Lazarus			AS
E The road to the cross			
1 Discipleship			
1.1 The disciples			AS
1.2 Women			AS
2 The farewell discourses			
2.1 The Last Supper			AS
2.2 The Holy Spirit — *Paraclete*			AS
2.3 'I am the way, the truth and the life'		A2	AS/A2
2.4 'I am the true vine'		A2	AS/A2
2.5 The disciples' future roles		A2	AS
2.6 The High Priestly Prayer			AS/A2

Index

A

B

C

D